European Administrative Governance

Series Editors
Thomas Christiansen
Maastricht University
Maastricht, The Netherlands

Sophie Vanhoonacker
Maastricht University
Maastricht, The Netherlands

The series maps the range of disciplines addressing the study of European public administration. In particular, contributions to the series will engage with the role and nature of the evolving bureaucratic processes of the European Union, including the study of the EU's civil service, of organization aspects of individual institutions such as the European Commission, the Council of Ministers, the External Action Service, the European Parliament, the European Court and the European Central Bank and of inter-institutional relations among these and other actors. The series also welcomes contributions on the growing role of EU agencies, networks of technical experts and national officials, and of the administrative dimension of multilevel governance including international organizations. Of particular interest in this respect will be the emergence of a European diplomatic service and the management of the EU's expanding commercial, foreign, development, security and defence policies, as well as the role of institutions in a range of other policy areas of the Union. Beyond this strong focus of EU administrative governance, the series will also include texts on the development and practice of administrative governance within European states. This may include contributions to the administrative history of Europe, which is not just about rules and regulations governing bureaucracies, or about formal criteria for measuring the growth of bureaucracies, but rather about the concrete workings of public administration, both in its executive functions as in its involvement in policymaking. Furthermore the series will include studies on the interaction between the national and European level, with particular attention for the impact of the EU on domestic administrative systems. The series editors welcome approaches from prospective contributors and are available to contact at t.christiansen@maastrichtuniversity.nl and s.vanhoonacker@ maastrichtuniversity.nl for proposals and feedback.

More information about this series at
http://www.palgrave.com/gp/series/14977

Olivier Costa
Editor

The European Parliament in Times of EU Crisis

Dynamics and Transformations

Editor
Olivier Costa
Sciences Po Bordeaux
Centre Emile Durkheim
Pessac Cedex, France

European Administrative Governance
ISBN 978-3-319-97390-6   ISBN 978-3-319-97391-3   (eBook)
https://doi.org/10.1007/978-3-319-97391-3

Library of Congress Control Number: 2018961743

Cover illustration: STOCKFOLIO® / Alamy Stock Photo

This Palgrave Macmillan imprint is published by the registered company Springer Nature Switzerland AG
The registered company address is: Gewerbestrasse 11, 6330 Cham, Switzerland

Foreword: The European Parliament— Understanding a Unique Institution for Europe's Citizens

Since the first direct elections to the European Parliament in 1979, the world's only transnational, democratically elected parliament has emerged as an increasingly powerful player in the European political system. From the start, the European Parliament sought to exercise a decisive influence on the development of the policies and the institutions of the European Communities (now European Union), and over the last 40 years it has been extremely successful in doing so. As a result, over time, political scientists have become increasingly interested in the dynamics, impact and evolution of the European Parliament as a political institution—one which is quite unlike any other parliament in Europe or the wider democratic world.

As both an individual Member of the European Parliament, and as its President, I am therefore delighted that a group of distinguished academics from the College of Europe have come together to write a book that traces and analyses recent developments in the Parliament as a political institution. The successive sections of their work address various aspects of the Parliament's place in the EU system, the contribution of the Parliament to EU law-making, the internal politics of the Parliament and the impact of the Parliament on specific EU policies. The book covers much new ground and fills several gaps in the current academic literature, not least in sketching how the Parliament has responded to the various crises that have characterised European, and indeed global, politics and economics over the last decade. Coming as we prepare for the 2019 European elections, when the Parliament will feature prominently in general political reporting and discussion, the timing of this initiative could not be better.

Moreover, since the Parliament has been, and remains, a constantly changing institution in a very fast-paced scenario, it is especially valuable that the College of Europe invited several current or former members of the Parliament's staff to contribute to the project. This has brought a strong 'practitioner' perspective to the exercise, in a way that usefully complements the academic analysis which forms the backbone of the book.

The European Parliament has a special place in the design of today's EU. It is the forum for the direct representation of European citizens in the common governance of our continent. It provides a real and direct democratic dimension to EU politics and policy-making, at a time when common European action is more necessary than ever to address many of the challenges and choices we face together. As such, I strongly welcome the process of academic study of the Parliament, welcome this book as an important contribution to such study and hope that it will contribute to a better and deeper understanding of the unique institution which I have the privilege to lead.

Brussels, Belgium   Antonio Tajani

Acknowledgements

The writing and preparation of an edited volume of this kind always involves many debts of gratitude. In particular, this project would not have been possible without the financial support of the College of Europe, as well as the intellectual and practical support of many in the European Parliament.

Among those who have greatly contributed to the development of this book, notably by commenting on and reviewing its chapters, are Ariane Aumaître-Balado, Dimitra Chrysomallis, Frederik Mesdag, Ernestas Oldyrevas, Thijs Vanderbussche, Sam Verschraegen—all academic assistants of the Department of European Political and Governance Studies in the College of Europe—and Ioanna Anagnostopoulou, Alessandro D'Alfonso, Etienne Bassot, Sarah Blau, Jesús Carmona Nuñez, Ralf Drachenberg, Kajus Hagelstam, Rafał Manko, Monika Nogaj, Philippe Perchoc, Alessandro Piccioli, Stéphane Reynolds, Christian Scheinert, Gianluca Sgueo, Sara Sheil, Laura Tilindyte-Humburg and Alex Benjamin Wilson—all staffers of the European Parliament.

Special thanks go to Gaby Umbach (European Parliament) and Frederik Mesdag (College of Europe) for their constant help in putting this manuscript together, and to Anthony Teasdale, Director General of the European Parliamentary Research Service (EPRS), for his enthusiasm in developing cooperation between the Parliament and the College of Europe in this and other fields.

Olivier Costa

CONTENTS

NOTES ON CONTRIBUTORS

Naja Bentzen is Policy Analyst External Policies, Directorate A, European Parliamentary Research Service (EPRS), Brussels. Naja covers issues related to foreign influence and disinformation, as well as Ukraine, Belarus, Moldova and the Arctic in EPRS. She studied linguistics and political science at the University of Copenhagen (Denmark), the University of Vienna (Austria) and the University of Jyväskylä (Finland). She also holds an MAS in interdisciplinary Balkan studies from the Austrian Institute for the Danube Region and Central Europe (IDM). Prior to her current position as a policy analyst at the EPRS, she worked as a media analyst at the US Embassy in Vienna and as a journalist, covering central and southeastern Europe for the Danish weekly *Weekendavisen*. She received the Milena Jesenská Fellowship from the Institute for Human Sciences, Vienna, in 2005.

Frédérique Berrod is Professor of Public Law at Sciences Po at the University of Strasbourg, and teaching EU law from an institutional and material perspective. She is also teaching EU energy law and EU health policy. She is an invited professor at the College of Europe in Bruges and is invited by the ENA for vocational training sessions.

She is responsible for a Master 2 degree on EU health products at the Law Faculty of Strasbourg. She is an elected member at the Conseil d'administration of the University of Strasbourg.

Her fields of research are EU energy law and health policy. She is developing research on borders within the internal market and cross-border cooperation in the context of EU integration.

Nathalie Brack is a visiting professor, Department of European Political and Governance Studies, College of Europe; academic coordinator, European Studies Programme, College of Europe; assistant professor at the Department of Political Science of the Université libre de Bruxelles, alumnus of the College of Europe (Beethoven Promotion, 2005–2006) and receiver of the grant "European Spirit" from the Bernheim Foundation (Belgium). Between 2007 and 2013, she worked as a teaching assistant at the Université libre de Bruxelles, where she received her PhD (L'euroscepticisme au Parlement européen. Stratégies d'une opposition anti-système au cœur des institutions, Larcier, 2014). Brack conducted postdoctoral studies on the linkage between parliamentarians and citizens in Europe at Oxford University (European Studies Center, St Antony's College). She was a visiting professor at the Université catholique de Louvain (2013–2014), at Sciences Po Bordeaux (2015–2016) and at the University of Lausanne (2017–2018).

Michele Chang is a permanent professor, Department of European Political and Governance Studies, College of Europe. Her previous professional affiliations entail Boston University; Centre for European Policy Studies; Cornell University; and Colgate University. She holds a PhD from the University of California San Diego and a BA from Smith College. Michele is also executive board officer of the European Union Studies Association and board member of the TEPSA.

Olivier Costa is Director of the Department of European Political and Administrative Studies at the College of Europe (Bruges, Belgium) and CNRS Research Professor at Sciences Po Bordeaux (Bordeaux, France). He is also co-director of the Jean Monnet European Centre of Excellence of Aquitaine (Bordeaux, France). Costa holds a PhD in political science from the University of Paris 8 (1998) and an "Habilitation à diriger les recherches" from Sciences Po Bordeaux (2013). He previously worked at Sciences Po Paris, Sciences Po Strasbourg, the Université Libre de Bruxelles and the University of Geneva. He has been visiting professor at Ritsumeikan University (Kyoto), Washington State University (Pullmann, WA), University of Colorado (Boulder, CO), University of Cologne (Germany) and University Luiss-Guido Carli (Rome). He is Associate Editor of the *Journal of European Integration* and member of the editorial board of the *Journal of Legislative Studies* and the *RISP: Italian Political Science Review*. His research and teaching deal with the European Parliament comprises European integration (institutions, actors, policies), legislative studies and French politics.

Amandine Crespy is a visiting professor, Department of European Political and Governance Studies, College of Europe; and Associate Professor at the Department of Political Science of the Université libre de Bruxelles. Over the past few years she was invited as a visiting fellow at Sciences Po in Paris, Harvard University, the London School of Economics, Queen Mary University of London and the Universiteit van Amsterdam. Her research deals with the politicization of EU integration and socio-economic policies (welfare services marketization, post-crisis socio-economic governance). She has a special interest in the role of ideas, discourse and conflict in relation with democracy in Europe. Besides publications in numerous highly profiled international journals, she co-edited *Social Policy and the Eurocrisis* (Palgrave, 2015) and authored *Welfare Markets in Europe: The Democratic Challenge of European Integration* (Palgrave, 2016).

Brice Cristoforetti is Manager for Lifelong Training and Job Placement, Lyon Institute of Political Studies. He is a graduate from Lyon Institute of Political Studies (2004–2009), has an MA in European affairs (2008–2009), and spent an academic year at the Copenhagen University, Denmark, Department of Political Sciences (2006–2007). His professional background entails Academic Assistant, Department of European Political and Administrative Studies, College of Europe (2015–2017); and Parliamentary Assistant, European Parliament, Brussels (2010–2014).

François Decoster is Mayor of Saint-Omer, France, as well as President of the Communauté d'agglomération de Saint-Omer; Vice-President of the Conseil régional des Hauts-de-France (Culture); President of the CIVEX commission, European Committee of the Regions, Brussels, Belgium. He has been a diplomatic adviser and political strategist with extensive knowledge of public policy. He served as a technical advisor to Noëlle Lenoir, Minister Delegate for European Affairs. While serving as Diplomatic Advisor to Gilles de Robien, French Minister for Infrastructure, Transport, Housing, Tourism and the Sea, François published a book on EU transport policy. He was also Diplomatic Advisor to the cabinet of Valérie Pécresse, Minister of Higher Education and Research, during which his work included overseeing the French presidency of the European Union. François is a French national and a graduate of the Institut d'Etudes Politiques, Paris Descartes University (Master of Law) and the College of Europe (European Political and Governance Studies Department). He has lectured at the College of Europe Executive Education Programmes in Bruges.

Vincent Delhomme is Academic Assistant at the Department of European Legal Studies, at College of Europe, and a PhD candidate at Université Catholique de Louvain. Vincent holds an LLM in EU law from the College of Europe and a master's degree in economic law from Sciences Po Paris. His research interests include EU internal market law, EU lifestyle risks regulation, the behavioural analysis of law and the constitutional aspects of EU law.

Justin Greenwood is a visiting professor, Department of European Political and Governance Studies, College of Europe; and Professor of European Public Policy at the Robert Gordon University, Aberdeen, UK. His career-long research specialism is EU interest representation (see publications section). He is currently the principal investigator on an ESRC (UK Economic & Social Research Council) grant on 'Democratic Legitimacy in the EU: Inside the 'Black Box' of Informal Trilogues', to which his co-author Professor Roederer-Rynning is the International Collaborator. He is a member of the Editorial Advisory Boards of the journals *Interest Groups and Advocacy* (Palgrave Macmillan), the *Journal of Public Affairs* (Wiley), and previously *Business & Politics* as well as Editor-in-Chief of *Current Politics and Economics of Europe* from 1997 to 2002. He has delivered training for organisations, including the International Labour Organisation, the European Commission (then DG RELEX, external relations), the EU engineering association Orgalime, the government of Catalonia, and at the Moscow State University (MGIMO) via a European Commission programme.

Roderick Harte is Policy Analyst International Trade, External Policies, Directorate A, European Parliamentary Research Service (EPRS), Brussels. Roderick holds degrees in EU international relations and diplomacy studies from the College of Europe (2010–2011) and in European law, law and economics, and political sciences from Leiden University in the Netherlands (2004–2010). Before joining the EPRS in 2017, he worked as a lawyer in the EU Competition Law and Administrative Law departments of the law firm Stibbe in Amsterdam (2012–2015). As a policy analyst, he focusses on the EU's international trade policy, including EU-US trade relations, CETA, modernization of the EU-Mexico Global Agreement, WTO and multilateralism, globalization, services, investment, procurement and agriculture.

Dermot Hodson is Reader in Political Economy at Birkbeck College, University of London, and Visiting Professor at the College of Europe,

Bruges. His works on European integration and governance have been published extensively and his books include *Governing the Euro Area in Good Times and Bad* (2011), *The New Intergovernmentalism: States and Supranational Actors in the Post-Maastricht Era* (with Christopher Bickerton and Uwe Puetter, 2015), *The Institutions of the European Union*, fourth edition (with John Peterson, 2017) and *The Transformation of EU Treaty Making: The Rise of Parliaments, Referendums and Courts since 1950* (with Imelda Maher, 2017).

Rudolf Hrbek is a visiting professor, Department of European Political and Governance Studies, College of Europe; and Professor Emeritus of Political Science at the University of Tübingen – Chair for Political Science (1976–2006). His major fields in teaching and research are political systems in Europe (focus on political parties/party systems, territorial structure, governmental system); political system of the EU (focus on multi-level governance, with special attention to the role of political parties, interest organisations, the civil society and regions/municipalities); and study of federalism (since 1993 chairing the European Centre for Research on Federalism – EZFF/ECRF – at the University of Tübingen). He is also a visiting professor in prestigious universities in the USA, Switzerland, Italy and Thailand. His works have been published widely in edited volumes and leading journals (publication list with approx. 300 titles). He is co-editor of three book series, has been engaged in academic associations and networks, and is involved in several research projects.

Beatrix Immenkamp is Policy Analyst Foreign Affairs & Security, Directorate A, European Parliamentary Research Service (EPRS), Brussels. Beatrix covers the Middle East, Central Asia, the Gulf states, and Egypt for the EPRS. She has worked for the Western Asia Regional Office of UNDP, the Euro-Mediterranean Regional and Local Assembly (ARLEM), and as a commercial lawyer in private practice. She holds a PhD in Arabic and Middle Eastern Studies from Cambridge University. She was a lecturer in Arabic and Middle Eastern studies at Cambridge University in 1998–1999.

Michael Kaeding is a visiting professor, Department of European Political and Governance Studies, College of Europe; Professor for European Integration and European Union Politics, University of Duisburg-Essen; Jean Monnet Professor ad personam; Chairman of TEPSA, and H2020-SEnECA project leader. His previous professional affiliations are Leiden University, Centre for European Policy Studies

(CEPS), Delegation of the European Commission to the United States in Washington, DC, Secretariat General of the Council of the European Union, European Institute of Public Administration (EIPA), University of Wisconsin–Madison (Political Science/La Follette School of Public Affairs). Michael holds an MA from the University of Konstanz and a PhD from the Leiden University. His other professional activities are Visiting Fellow of EIPA and the Turkish-German University (TAU/TDU) in Istanbul, and Advisor to the government of North Rhine Westphalia on EU affairs (NEW:NRW).

Elena Lazarou is a policy analyst at the European Parliamentary Research Service, where her research focuses on EU foreign and security policy, global governance and transatlantic relations. She is also Assistant Professor of International Relations at the Getulio Vargas Foundation (FGV) (currently on leave) and was formerly Head of FGV's Center for International Relations (2013–2014) and Head of the Euro-Mediterranean Observatory of the Hellenic Center for European Studies (EKEM), Athens, Greece (2009–2010). Dr. Lazarou received a PhD in international relations from the University of Cambridge in 2008. She has held post-doctoral research positions at the University of Cambridge and the London School of Economics and Political Science (LSE) and various visiting affiliations in think tanks and universities in Europe and the USA. Several of her articles, edited volumes and book chapters have been published in English, Greek and Portuguese and in the Brazilian and Greek press. She is a non-resident research associate at ELIAMEP, Athens.

Vicky Marissen is Partner at EPPA. She has a legal background (Master of European Law, Institut d'Etudes Européennes (Université Libre de Bruxelles); law degree, the University of Antwerp) and has been active in EU Public Affairs for 18 years. Over this period, she has built up expertise and experience with regard to comitology and delegated acts and EU decision-making procedures in general. Besides her expertise on the subject, Vicky is recognized as a good pedagogue and trainer, able to communicate clearly and transfer know-how on complex topics. She is also Visiting Professor at the College of Europe, Bruges, of secondary legislation. She co-authored two books: *The New Practical Guide to the EU Labyrinth* and *The Handbook on EU Secondary Legislation*.

Frederik Mesdag is Academic Assistant at the Department of European Political and Governance Studies, College of Europe. He holds an MA in

European political and administrative studies from the College of Europe, Bruges (2014–2015), an MA in European studies from the Université catholique de Louvain (Louvain-la-Neuve) (2012–2014) and a BA in classical Oriental languages from the Université catholique de Louvain (Louvain-la-Neuve) 2009–2012. His former experiences include Bernheim scholarship at the Belgian Ministry of Foreign Affairs (EU Trade Policy Unit) and at the Permanent Representation of Belgium to the EU (COREPER II), 2015–2016; European Health Parliament (2014–2015); Network Manager of Transnational Giving Europe (King Baudouin Foundation), 2016.

Johannes Müller Gómez is a doctoral researcher at the Ludwig-Maximilians-Universität München and the Université de Montréal (cotutelle). He further works as a research assistant at the Jean Monnet Centre Montréal and the Montréal Centre for International Studies (CÉRIUM). From 2014 to 2017, he was a research associate and lecturer at the Jean Monnet chair and the CETEUS at the University of Cologne. He is programme director and board member of the Cologne Monnet Association for EU Studies (COMOS), co-president of the Young Researchers Network within the European Community Studies Association Canada (ECSA-C) and director of the Jean Monnet project DAFEUS. In his research, he focusses on multilevel systems and federalism, European and Canadian politics, EU institutions, matters of democracy and legitimacy as well as climate action.

Louis Navé is a PhD candidate at the University of Strasbourg, Centre d'Études Internationales et Européennes. He holds degrees from the Institut d'Études Politiques de Strasbourg (2011–2015); a master's degree in European law from the Université de Strasbourg (2015); and an MA in European political and administrative studies from the College of Europe, Bruges (Chopin promotion, 2015–2016). He has been a teaching assistant at the Institut d'Études Politiques de Strasbourg since 2016, and has research interests and publications in EU energy law.

Louisa Parks is Associate Professor of Sociology at the University of Trento, Italy. She has long studied different forms of citizen activism, publishing 'Social Movement Campaigns on EU Policy: in the corridors and in the streets' in 2015, along with numerous articles on social movements and the EU and the EP in particular. Her recent work in the ERC-funded project 'Benelex, benefit sharing for an equitable transition to the green economy' focuses on local and indigenous community activism for the environment, in particular with regard to the Convention on Biological Diversity. She has worked previously as a senior lecturer at the University of Lincoln, UK; for the Subterranean Politics in Europe Project coordinated by Mary Kaldor; and as a member's assistant in the EP. She holds a PhD from the European University Institute, Florence, completed under the supervision of Donatella della Porta.

Eva-Maria Poptcheva holds a PhD in European constitutional law from the Autonomous University of Barcelona (Spain) and a degree in law from the Albert Ludwig University in Freiburg (Germany). She started her professional career as a lawyer in Germany and Spain. Before joining the European Parliament in 2012, she was a lecturer and a research fellow in EU and constitutional law at the Autonomous University of Barcelona, as well as a member of the Expert Group on Spain of the EU Fundamental Rights Agency. She has authored several book chapters and journal articles on the constitutional set-up of the EU and EU citizenship, as well as the book *Multilevel Citizenship: The Right to Consular Protection of EU Citizens Abroad.*

Laura Puccio is Policy Analyst, Directorate A, European Parliamentary Research Service, Brussels, and also collaborateur scientifique at the Institute for European Studies (IEE) of the Université Libre de Bruxelles (ULB), where she teaches European Union trade law. Since Fall 2018, she teaches European external relations law at the Brussels School of International Studies of Kent University. Prior to joining the European Parliament, she was a DISSETTLE- ITN Marie Curie Fellow and a post-doctoral fellow at the ULB (ECARES), working on law and economics trade research projects. During her doctoral studies at the European University Institute (EUI), she was a visiting scholar at the Columbia University Law School in New York (2010), a visiting lecturer at the University of Passau and the Euro-College of Tartu, and collaborated with the RSCAS. She holds a PhD in law, an LLM from the EUI, an MA from Sciences Po Paris, and a BSc in international economics from Bocconi University.

Lara Querton is a PhD student and teaching assistant, Department of Political Science and Centre for the Study of Politics, Université libre de Bruxelles. She holds a master's degree in European studies from the Institute for European Studies (ULB). Her previous experiences entail Doctoral Research Assistant at the Centre for the Study of Politics (ULB),

Brussels, 2014–2016; and Academic Assistant, Department of European Political and Administrative Studies, College of Europe, 2016–2017.

Christilla Roederer-Rynning is Professor with Special Responsibilities at the Department of Political Science and Public Management, the University of Southern Denmark. Her research examines the role of parliamentary actors and the development of legislative institutions in the EU (Economic and Social Research Council [ESRC] grant ES/N018761/1). Her work has appeared in journals such as the *Journal of European Public Policy*, the *Journal of Common Market Studies*, *West European Politics*, and the *Journal of European Integration*. She co-edits and contributes to the forthcoming eighth edition of *Policy-Making in the European Union* (Oxford University Press), with Helen Wallace, Mark A. Pollack, and Alasdair R. Young.

Jennifer Rousselle is Director of Cabinet at the Mairie de Saint-Omer and Committee of the Regions. After having obtained her degree from Sciences Po Lille and a master's degree in European politics at the Institut d'Etudes Européennes in Bruxelles, she started her professional career as an intern at the cabinet of the European Commissioner in charge of transports, Jacques Barrot. She then pursued her career in consultancy and worked for the Bureau Européen de l'Agriculture Française. After having taken part in the campaign for the 2014 European elections, she decided to reorient herself as an advisor to elected representatives. At the end of 2014, she became Head of Cabinet of François Decoster, at Saint-Omer. She also works with him at the European Committee of the Regions. She is furthermore engaged in several humanitarian and European associations, and attended, in 2017, the Cycle des Hautes Etudes Européennes of the Ecole Nationale d'Administration.

Sabine Saurugger is Professor of Political Science and Research Dean at Sciences Po Grenoble. From 2016, she holds a visiting professorship at the College de Bruges.

Her research focuses on interest groups, theories of European integration, European public policies and the politics of law. Most recently she analysed the impact of economic and financial crises on public polices and legal frameworks. Results of her research have been published in journals such as the *European Journal of Political Research*, the *Journal of Common Market Studies*, *West European Politics*, *Political Studies*, the *Journal of European Public Policy* and *Revue française de science politique*. More recently, her co-authored book *The Court of Justice and the Politics of Law* (with Fabien Terpan) has been published in the European Union Series with Palgrave (2017).

Fabien Terpan is Senior Lecturer in Public Law and European Studies at Sciences Po Grenoble, Deputy Director of the CESICE (Center for the study of international security and European cooperation) and the holder of a Jean Monnet Chair. His works on EU law, European external action, and law and politics in the EU have been published widely and in journals such as *Policy Sciences*, the *European Law Journal, Comparative European Politics, European Security*. Among his recent publications are *Droit et politique de l'Union européenne, The Court of Justice of the European Union and the Politics of Law* (with S. Saurugger, Palgrave Macmillan, 2017), *Crisis and Institutional Change in Regional Integration* (with S. Saurugger, eds. 2016).

Samuel Verschraegen is an associate in energy law at Janson Baugniet law firm (Belgium). He holds a master's degree in European political and administrative studies from the College of Europe (Bruges) and another master's in law (specialisation in public and European law) from the Université Libre de Bruxelles. Following his studies, he was for three years an academic assistant at the Department of Political and Administrative Studies at the College of Europe before becoming a lawyer in 2018.

Anne Vitrey de Gardebosc is Visiting Professor at the Department of European Political and Administrative Studies, College of Europe; and Coordinator for European Issues, Ecole Nationale d'Administration (ENA). She was Director for Budgetary Affairs, European Parliament (until February 2017).

She graduated from the Institut Politique de Paris: civil service section; Université de Paris IV Panthéon-Sorbonne: PhD in Hispanic civilisation; University of Pennsylvania: bachelor of philology.

Birte Wassenberg is Professor of Contemporary History at the Institute for Political Studies (IEP) of the University of Strasbourg and a member of the Research Institute for History Raymond Poidevin at the UMR Dynamiques européennes. Her research fields are border regions, Euroscepticism and the history of European organizations, especially the Council of Europe. She holds a Jean Monnet Chair and is director of the Master in International Relations. She teaches international relations, border studies, regionalism, the history of European integration and

Franco-German relations. She is also a former student from the College of Europe, promotion Charles IV (1992–1993).

Wolfgang Wessels held a Jean Monnet Chair at the University of Cologne from 1994 to 2016. Since 2016, he has been Director of the Centre for Turkey and European Union Studies (CETEUS) at the University of Cologne. He has been Visiting Professor at the College of Europe, Bruges and Natolin, since 1981 and Part-Time Professor at the European University Institute since 2018.

He was Director of the Institut für Europäische Politik in Bonn (1973–1993) and Head of the Department of Political and Administrative Studies at the College of Europe in Bruges (1980–1996). He is Chairperson of the Executive Board of the Institut für Europäische Politik (IEP, Berlin) and was Chairperson of the Executive Board of the Trans European Policy Studies Association (TEPSA, Brussels) until 2016. Since 2010, he has been Vice-President of the German consortium for the foundation of the Turkish-German University, Istanbul.

Martin Westlake is a visiting professor, Department of European Political and Governance Studies, College of Europe; and senior visiting fellow, European Institute, and David Davies of Landinam Fellow, Department of International Relations, both London School of Economics and Political Science, London. Martin has spent over four decades studying European integration and working in EU government and politics. Having completed a first degree in philosophy, politics and economics at University College, Oxford, he went on to take a master's degree at the Johns Hopkins University School of Advanced International Studies (Bologna Center) and a PhD at the European University Institute in Florence. Since beginning his professional life as a clerk to the Parliamentary Assembly of the Council of Europe in Strasbourg, he has worked in the Council of Ministers and the European Commission, with the European Parliament and, since 2003, in the European Economic and Social Committee, where he served as Secretary General, 2008–2013. Martin's works on the European institutions and European and British politics have been published widely. He is also the author of a major political biography (*Kinnock: The Biography*). He has occupied a number of visiting positions and, from 2000 to 2005, was a visiting professor at the College of Europe, Bruges, teaching a seminar on the European Parliament. He is a visiting professor at the College, running a research seminar on constitutional, institutional and political reform in the EU.

Johannes Wolters is a research fellow at the CETEUS at the University of Cologne. He also works for the European Commission's Service for Foreign Policy Instruments (FPI) in communications. Wolters was a researcher at CETEUS from October 2015 until September 2017. His research interests are differentiated integration, economic policy coordination in the European Union as well as the Union's Common Foreign and Security Policy. Wolters has a background in political science and economics and has studied at the Universities of Bonn and Cologne as well as at Sciences Po Bordeaux.

LIST OF FIGURES

LIST OF TABLES

LIST OF BOXES

CHAPTER 1

Introduction: The Need for Further Research on the European Parliament

Olivier Costa

'Highly organized research is guaranteed to produce nothing new.'
Frank Herbert, Dune

1 A VERY BROAD LITERATURE

In the last two decades, around a hundred books and a thousand papers have been devoted to the study and analysis of the European Parliament (EP)—mainly in English, but also in French, German, Italian, and Spanish. On top of that, numerous PhD students have also proposed their own vision of the most diverse aspects of the assembly. This literature is very rich but, with the exception of a few textbooks, quite fragmented and increasingly specialised. It is organised around two key dimensions—disciplines and methods—but also by topics.

First, there are diverse approaches depending on the *discipline*. Public lawyers were first to study the EP—which was the case for all European institutions. They soon proposed institutional analyses, describing the

O. Costa (✉)
College of Europe, Bruges, Belgium

CNRS, Bordeaux, France
e-mail: olivier.costa@coleurope.eu; o.costa@sciencespobordeaux.fr

© The Author(s) 2019
O. Costa (ed.), *The European Parliament in Times of EU Crisis,*
European Administrative Governance,
https://doi.org/10.1007/978-3-319-97391-3_1

1

assembly's organisation, powers, and activities. Political scientists started to complement those views by the end of the 1980, with a major contribution by authors working within EU institutions. The EP became a mainstream subject for political science in the 2000s, when a growing number of scholars, specialised in legislative and electoral studies, started to apply their methods, concepts, and hypotheses to the European assembly and European elections. Since then, most social sciences have started to pay attention to the assembly. Sociologists have studied in detail the identity, values, and careers of members of the EP (MEPs), but also of their assistants and other staff members. Historians have assessed the developments of the institution and its role in European integration. Anthropologists and ethnologists have analysed the actors and 'tribes' of the EP. Specialists of quantitative methods and economists have mobilised their skills to make a sophisticated use of data, in order to analyse the behaviour of members and voting patterns. Philosophers and political theorists have included the EP in their reflexions on the possibility of democracy or deliberation at supranational level. The EP's contribution to main EU policies has also been studied, sector by sector, by specialists of each field. Finally, international relations scholars have explored the role of the EP in external affairs and its relations with other international parliamentary organs.

The literature on the EP is also structured around the use of different *methods and approaches.* Obviously, each discipline and sub-discipline is grounded on specific epistemological and methodological choices. But there is more: there are continuous scientific discussions on the kind of data and analyses that should be chosen in order to better understand the EP. Today, academics use a very vast array of sources: databases on EP or EU activities; data sets on MEPs' socio-biographical profiles and roll-call votes; the results of closed questionnaires with MEPs and staff members; open or semi-structured interviews with them; observations conducted in plenary sessions or within various EP organs; quantitative and qualitative analyses of all kinds of official documents; public opinion surveys; media databases, and so on. There are also many scientific discussions around the suitability of the use of comparison in order to study the EP: Can it be compared to national parliaments? Or better, to the US Congress? To which extent is it possible to apply classic tools, theories, and hypotheses of legislative studies to the EP? Can we consider the EP and the Council as the two chambers of a bicameral European legislature?

It is worth mentioning that not all central debates around EU studies make sense in the EP's case. The various approaches of neo-institutionalism are obviously prominent in the research field, and scholars are endlessly discussing the compared merits of its various declinations (historical, rational-choice, sociological, discursive…), including deep controversies between partisans of the rational-choice approach and supporters of a constructivist/cognitivist one, or between proponents of quantitative and qualitative approaches. Compared to neo-institutionalism, the classic controversies between neo-functionalists and intergovernmentalists do not make much sense in the case of the EP, because both are quite unable to account for its historical developments and empowerment, and do not propose an institutional model in which it plays a central role. In contrast, part of the research devoted to the EP is better linked to the general debates in social sciences than the studies focusing on the other EU institutions which are more specific. At least in the field of political sciences, the EP has indeed attracted the attention of 'mainstream' scholars, especially in legislative studies, and elections specialists, which is still not the case of the Commission or of the Court.

2   THE SIX MAIN TOPICS UNDER STUDY

The literature on the EP is also structured around *topics*. There are several textbooks that propose a more or less exhaustive approach of the EP, but most of the work focuses on a specific aspect of the institution. We can distinguish six main areas of research that have all generated a significant amount of publications.

First, there is the *institutional approach*. Since the 1950s, the EP has been obviously addressed by all EU institutional law textbooks, but the main books that are specifically focused on the institution itself have always included considerations about the political dynamics or the sociological dimensions of the assembly (Corbett et al. 2016; Costa 2001; Judge and Earnshaw 2008; Palmer 2015; Ripoll Servent 2018; Steunenberg and Thomassen 2002; Westlake 1994). They all deal with the main features of the EP: its role, competences, process of empowerment, interaction with other institutions, and so on. The question of the history (Corbett 1998; Priestley 2008; European Parliament 2009) and empowerment of the EP (Christiansen 2002; Farrell and Héritier 2005; Hix 2002b; Hix and Høyland 2013; Judge and Earnshaw 1994; Rittberger and Schimmelfennig 2006; Rittberger 2005 and 2014; Tsebelis 1994) has attracted many publications. As previously stated, a growing number of researchers, trained in comparative politics, tend to consider that the EP is a 'normal' parliament, which should be compared to national legislatures (Hooghe and Marks 2008; Hix and Høyland 2013; Kreppel 2012; Young 2016; Yordanova 2011). However, most international relations scholars refuse this idea of 'normalisation' or, better, propose an alternative approach of it: they consider the EP as an international parliamentary organisation among others, to be compared to its peers (Costa et al. 2013; Malamud and Stavridis 2011; Šabič 2008).

A second set of researches discuss the *organisation* of the EP. They focus on MEPs (see below), political groups (Brack 2018; Kreppel 2002; Raunio 1997), various organs (committees, delegations, intergroups, leadership structures) (Coman 2009; Whitaker 2011; Costa 2013), staff (Egeberg et al. 2013; Winzen 2011) and assistants (Pegan 2017), procedures (Bressanelli et al. 2016; Kreppel 2000; Brack and Costa 2018b), or specific issues such as the seats or languages (Priestley and Clark 2012).

The first direct elections of the EP in 1979 have led to a vast literature analysing *European elections* and discussing their specificities (Déloye and Bruter 2007; Gabel and Hix 2002; Hix and Hagemann 2009; Hobolt 2015; Lodge 2016; Reif and Schmitt 1980; Viola 2015), or developments such as the 'Spitzenkandidaten' procedure (Schmitt et al. 2015; Priestley and Peñalver García 2015). They have led to researches dealing with the question of electoral support, attitudes of the public opinion towards the EP and its members (Blondel et al. 1998), and the public image (Lord 2018) and communication strategy of the assembly (Anderson and McLeod 2004).[1]

The interactions between the EP and *external actors* are a fourth stream of studies. It includes national and European parties (Gallagher et al. 2011; Hix 2002b), national parliaments (Auel and Benz 2005; Hefftler et al. 2015; Maurer and Wessels 2001), interest groups (Marshall 2010; Kluger Dionigi 2016), and civil society organisations (Warleigh 2000; Foret 2017). It also comprises organisations and actors outside the EU, with researches analysing the relations of the EP with other parliamentary bodies, at the national level and within international organisations, as well

[1] The creation by the EP of the 'Parlemeter', a biannual survey similar to the Eurobarometer, conducted twice a year in all EU member states, has provided researchers with a huge amount of data on a wide range of issues, such as citizens' knowledge of the EP, their perceptions of the EU, and their expectations in view of the European elections, the EP, and the EU in general.

as with the representatives of states outside of the EU (Diedrichs 2004; Thym 2006). The analysis of the EP, thanks to the various tools of *legislative studies*, has given birth to a very vast body of literature. These studies focus on MEPs' socio-biographic profiles (Kauppi 2005; Scarrow 1997; Whitaker et al. 2017), professionalisation (Beauvallet and Michon 2010), views and beliefs (Whitaker et al. 2017), and allegiances and representational roles (Hix 2002a; Noury 2002; Wessels 2005). A central question has always been the one of socialisation: do MEPs go native, that is, do they become more favourable to European integration during their time in the EP (Franklin and Scarrow 1999; Scully 1998, 2006)? MEPs' voting behaviour has also attracted a lot of interest (Hobolt and de Vries 2016; McElroy and Benoit 2012; Ringe 2010), especially since the introduction of roll-call votes for the final vote on each text (Carrubba et al. 2006; Hix et al. 2007). Other activities of MEPs, in the plenary meetings and committees (Hurka and Kaeding 2012; Judge and Earnshaw 1994; Bowler and Farrell 1995), or in the constituency (Poyet 2018), have also generated much research.

Finally, the *activities* of the EP are quite well-studied nowadays. The objective of this vast array of work is to understand how the assembly implements its competences. Authors deal with the question of coalition building (Kreppel and Tsebelis 1999; Kreppel 2000), interinstitutional relations and negotiations (Rasmussen and Toshkov 2011), and influence within the EP (Burns 2005; Tsebelis et al. 2001) and of the EP (Héritier 2017; Maurer 2003; Shackleton 2000; Tsebelis 1994; Yordanova 2013). They analyse the EP's impact on internal (Ripoll Servent 2013) and external policies (Herranz-Surrallés 2014; Stavridis and Irrera 2016), its capacity to control other organs (Raunio 1996), as well as its role in constitutional matters (Fossum and Menéndez 2005) and as a public forum (Crespy 2014).

In recent years, this typology of topics has, however, partially lost its relevance. Some interesting pieces of work have bridged various approaches, linking, for instance, the literature on institutional change with the one on MEPs' individual behaviour or social profiles. Authors have shown that the institutional changes undergone by the EP have impacted MEPs' identity (Daniel 2015), their behaviour (Ringe 2010), the sorts of careers they choose (Daniel and Metzger 2018), their links to their respective constituencies (Poyet 2018), or the way groups select their rapporteurs (Hermansen 2018).

3   THE RECENT DECLINE OF RESEARCH ON THE EP

Over the past ten years, the EP has somehow lost part of its attractiveness in the eyes of scholars. This is the result of several factors.

The primary one is directly linked to the type of research devoted to the EP, which has experienced a continuous process of routinisation and specialisation. First, there is a form of routinisation, since the scholars involved in the field of EP studies tend to endlessly reproduce the same research on the same subjects: MEPs' voting behaviour or role perception, coalition-building, evolutions of the legislative procedure, EP electoral rules, turn-out in EU elections, influence of national delegations within the house, and so on. It is obviously necessary to update the existing work, since the EP constantly evolves, through elections, enlargements, new treaties, and internal reforms. However, the added value of each new piece of work tends to regress. Also, many publications or PhD theses do not emanate from an interesting or original research question, or from the will to study or understand a new phenomenon. They are quite often rather data-driven; that is, they result from the availability of certain types of data: roll-call votes, MEPs' surveys, data on EP or EU activities, and so on. Thus, most contributions merely update existing information, and are affected by a phenomenon of declining scientific added value.

A second difficulty derives from the overspecialisation of research. In the field of EP studies, more and more detailed and sophisticated approaches—that do not necessarily allow for a better understanding of the dynamics of the EP as a whole—have appeared. These works are often very self-referential, with a limited number of authors quoting each other's studies or discussing tiny details in their respective researches. There are constantly new papers considering new evidence or proposing specific improvements to a given empirical or theoretical design. We are thus losing the capacity to assess the general evolution of the EP. While several textbooks do propose an exhaustive approach of the institution, of its role, history, activities, and organisation, they yet tend to overlook the dynamics of the institution, especially in the case of new editions of existing volumes.

Research on the EP has also slowed down since the beginning of the 2000s as a result of a conjunction of political events. The fiasco of the constitutional process, citizens' and elites' enduring lack of interest for European elections, the institutionalisation of the European Council by the Lisbon Treaty, the growing role of the Commission, the European

Central Bank, and the European Council in the context of the Eurozone crisis, and the overall rise of Euroscepticism—in member states and within EU institutions—have challenged the developments of politics at the supranational level, as well as the idea of the EP's centrality in the EU regime. As a result, EU studies specialists have paid less attention to the EP—even if the Eurocrisis has led to interesting publications. This turn has also led to the reviving of theoretical debates on the nature of European integration and on its dynamics. This controversy, mainly articulated between revised approaches of intergovernmentalism and neo-functionalism (Bickerton et al. 2015; Fabbrini 2015; Monar and Chang 2013; Puetter 2012), does not pay much attention to the EP, which is only central to some federalist theories—keeping in mind that neo-institutionalism is not a theory per se.

4   THE NEED FOR NEW RESEARCH

Regardless of this decline in academic interest, the EP has continued to evolve, as a result of the transformation of the EU's institutional context, which has created new constraints on the assembly, but also new opportunities and challenges (Brack and Costa 2018a). In 2009, the Lisbon Treaty recognised the EP as a central institution of the EU regime and a key player of democracy and legitimacy (articles 10 and 14 TEU). It also induced a different balance of powers between the main institutions (Fabbrini 2015; Héritier 2017; Shackleton 2017). It has created new prospects for the EP that have notably led to the generalisation of legislative trilogues and early agreements (Bressanelli et al. 2016; Roederer-Rynning and Greenwood 2017; Rasmussen and Reh 2013; Reh 2014) as well as the implementation of the 'Spitzenkandidaten' procedure. The later has modified the institutional arrangements, creating a new political situation within the EP (with a formal coalition between the groups EPP, S&D, and ALDE, called the 'block') (Hobolt 2014; Schmitt et al. 2015), a new kind of relationship between the EP and the Commission, and a more political role for the EP President. The crisis of European integration and the rise of Euroscepticism have also increased the presence of European issues in national political debates, induced a better connection between domestic and EU politics, and given more relevance to European elections (Taggart 1998; Brack 2018). Furthermore, the 2008 financial crisis has also led to significant reflections on the best way to democratise—with or without the EP—the governance of the Eurozone (Cooper and Smith 2017; Rittberger 2014).

In this changing context, we have witnessed the emergence of some original research based on new questions or methods. Scholars have studied EP deliberations (Roger 2016), the place of religion within the house (Foret 2017), the way EP staff members make choices (Kuehnhanss et al. 2017), and the establishment of the EP policy agenda (Greene and Cross 2017), and analysed online contestation during the 2014 campaign (Wilde et al. 2014). However, plenty of other aspects and evolutions of the EP remain unstudied, because of the routinisation of research and of the focus of EU scholars on other institutions and processes.

This book is based on the idea that things do change at a rapid pace within the EP, in many respects. There has been a real shift in the partisan landscape, with the emergence of the 'block' and the empowerment of Eurosceptic groups. The EP is still adapting to its new competences granted by the Lisbon Treaty (legislation, budget, appointment, approval of international agreements, delegated legislation, etc.). Moreover, interinstitutional negotiations play a growing role in the functioning of the EU political system. The EP is also developing strategies to increase its control capacity on the Commission, the Council and even the European Council, and its influence on areas such as external relations, defence, and macroeconomic governance. The relations between the assembly and its environment—civil society, interest groups, national parliaments, EU agencies—are also carefully considered by MEPs.

The objective of this book is thus to go beyond the existing literature so as to fill some of its gaps. To do so, the aim was to focus on unstudied topics, innovating approaches, and novel methods or data. This project results from research conducted at the Department of European Political and Governance Studies of the College of Europe. Individual research of several policy analysts of the European Parliamentary Research Service (EPRS) has contributed to this endeavour. The overall book project was launched during a workshop organised in Bruges in October 2016, and the first drafts were presented and discussed during a two-day workshop at the EP in May 2017.

The 34 authors of the book have been encouraged to focus on the recent evolutions, changes, and developments within the EP, and to underline emerging trends. They all have been studying the EP for many years, which allows them to appreciate its evolutions and to contextualise them. This volume, without purporting to do so exhaustively, covers—with its 20 chapters—the main points of interest concerning the EP today. It addresses a vast range of topics, questions, and issues, and relies on various methods and approaches. Some have benefited from original data gathered by the EPRS.

5 THE VOLUME

The book is laid out in four parts, dealing respectively with the place of the EP within the EU political system, its role in the EU policy-making, its election and internal politics, as well as its impact on EU policies. The first part deals with the **changing role of the EP within the EU regime**. It has evolved considerably in recent years, thanks to the Treaty of Lisbon and to the formal and informal changes it has induced. In this part, attention is paid to the changing relations between the EP and four key actors: the Commission, the European Council, the Court of Justice of the EU (CJEU), and the Committee of the Regions (CoR).

In her chapter, **Eva Poptcheva** examines the different types of parliamentary oversight at the EP's disposal, grouping them into classical control instruments of ex-post, negative, oversight and ex-ante, steering, oversight. She seeks to establish whether the EU political system has transformed from a system which has a separation of powers to one with a fusion of powers, since scrutiny instruments become more relevant. Her hypothesis is that the more the EP is asserting positive scrutiny, the more this stimulates a shift towards a parliamentarian system of fusion of powers.

Wolfgang Wessels, Johannes Müller Gomez, and **Johannes Wolters** focus on the evolution of the balance of power between the EP and the European Council. They argue that it is a key dimension of the EU regime, yet under-researched and under-theorised. On the basis of three theoretical models, they conduct three case studies on the management of the euro crisis, the investiture of the Commission President, and the adoption of the multiannual financial framework. The authors explore the communalities and differences that exist among the various kinds of interinstitutional relations between the EP and the European Council.

Sabine Saurugger and **Fabien Terpan** address the relations between the EP and the CJEU, another under-researched issue, at least in the recent period of time. They aim to analyse whether and, if so, why the jurisdiction of the CJEU supports the EP's decision-making powers in the European governance system since the entry into force of the Lisbon Treaty. While, according to many authors, the Court has historically played a role in empowering the Parliament, some arguments support the idea that this support has declined since Maastricht, and even more since the post-Lisbon period. Through the case study of the Court's case law on the external powers of the Parliament, Saurugger and Terpan argue that there is no systematic bias in favour of it in the Court's case law, but that the Court may still be supportive of the Parliament, in particular when it also develops its own jurisdiction over European law and helps strengthening the European legal order.

François Decoster, Jennifer Rousselle, and **Vincent Delhomme** explore a neglected dimension of the EU political system: the relationship between the CoR and the EP. They argue that a strong relationship is profitable for both institutions and for European democracy as a whole. Indeed, the CoR, as a purely consultative body, needs the EP to carry its voice, while the EP relies on the CoR to increase consideration for regional and local interests. Despite the improvement that has been made since the Lisbon reforms, the CoR's positions benefit still from very little consideration by the EP. This chapter provides an assessment of the current situation, and sketches out some avenues for progress.

The second part of this volume deals with the **role of the EP in the EU policy-making**. The Treaty of Lisbon has provided many changes in this respect, and the situation is in constant evolution.

Justin Greenwood and **Christilla Roederer-Rynning** deal with the generalisation of legislative trilogues. The topic is not a new one, but the way institutions organise their legislative negotiations is constantly evolving, especially in the case of the EP. As the people's tribune, a core question is whether it has come to a stable set of arrangements in order to be able to assert itself in co-decision with other EU institutions. The secluded nature of trilogues and the lack of record has made them targets for public anxiety, and as the directly elected institution, the EP has been most aware of its role in this process of negotiation. The authors examine the internal mechanisms of the EP when preparing for trilogues, as a critical moment of the institutionalisation of the assembly as a legislature. They also discuss the political implications of these developments using a comparative perspective in light of recent developments in US legislative politics.

Vicky Marissen examines another aspect of EU policy-making that has been deeply reformed by the Treaty of Lisbon, namely the adoption of secondary legislation. Scholars have paid much attention to the increase of EP powers in legislative, budgetary, and trade matters, but far less to the—long battled for—strengthening of its prerogatives in the area of EU secondary legislation, which is delegated and implements acts. To do so, the author first describes the formal prerogatives of the EP in this matter. She then moves on to an in-depth analysis of the practical arrangements it has put in place to deal with its powers over secondary legislation, the challenges it faces, and the points on which further progress could be made.

Michael Kaeding further explores delegated legislation. He examines the EP's and Council's use of post-Lisbon legislative vetoes to override the Commission's rule-making. Using an original data set of legislative vetoes by both European legislators from 2006 to 2017, he shows that the frequency of use of the formal veto to overrule regulatory policies is very low. What is particularly interesting is that they have not increased significantly since the Lisbon Treaty came into effect, suggesting that the ways in which the treaty formally expanded the powers of legislative scrutiny have not resulted in an appreciably greater formal exercise of these powers. Moreover, significant differences have not appeared between the two EU legislative bodies.

Anne Vitrey and **Frederik Mesdag** propose a reflection on another key competence of the EP, namely its contribution to the EU budget. They first show that MEPs have always been eager to use their budgetary competences to promote particular policies and to extend their other powers. The authors show that dialogue and soft law have allowed for institutional progress and maturity, in a spirit of loyal cooperation. They then explore how, over four decades, the EP has battled to maintain the original balance of powers and to increase its legislative and budgetary powers, sometimes at the institutional level, and sometimes within the institution itself. The article argues that the strive for balance is ongoing and faces new challenges in the aftermath of Lisbon, to ensure that the EP remains a fully-fledged part of the budgetary authority.

The third part of the book deals with **the EP politics**, that is the way it represents citizens and the civil society, and the way it is politically structured.

Amandine Crespy and **Louisa Parks** propose a reflection on the array of relationships between the EP and organised civil society (OCS). The EP has been an active agent in securing its growing power over time but, as a co-legislator with relatively few resources, it became a key target for OCS. Also, unlike the Commission, the EP is a representative democratic institution. This forms a central dilemma regarding OCS: as the 'voice of the people' the EP is open to civil society, yet at the same time, retains a suspicion of groups that may not represent the 'people'. The chapter discusses this dilemma through a focus on the EP's role in the regulation of interest groups' involvement in EU politics, the formal events it hosts for OCS (intergroups, public hearings, and the European Citizens' Initiative), and the relations between individual MEPs and OCS, including the right-wing nationalist groups.

Nathalie Brack and **Olivier Costa** explore the territorial dimension of the European mandate and its recent evolutions. This dimension is generally considered as central to the process of representation at the national level, but has been relatively neglected so far in the EP. Rather than assuming an electoral disconnection between MEPs and EU territories, Brack and Costa take an inductive approach to empirically examine to what extent territorial representation is reflected in members' practices. To do so, they do not use questionnaires, but rely on an analysis of MEPs' written questions, which constitutes another understudied topic. The content of those questions is used as an indicator of members' priorities as well as their centres of interest, conception of their mandate, and of their evolution over recent years. The point of the chapter is notably to determine whether one can witness an evolution of MEPs' approach to territories as a result of the confidence crisis in the EU, that is, a process of re-nationalisation.

Rudolf Hrbek comes back to the old question, that originated in the 1960s, of the adoption of a single electoral system for the EP. His chapter deals more specifically with the most recent attempt—initiated in the EP—to introduce a uniform electoral system. He first identifies the challenge which is the major weaknesses of previous EP elections and existing rules. On the basis of this analysis, he examines the response and the major innovations of the EP's new proposal. Finally, the author explains why this new initiative will not be successful nor implemented for the 2019 EP elections.

Birte Wassenberg questions both theoretically and historically the link between Euroscepticism and European elections. She first proceeds with a country-specific, differentiated analysis of the 2014 EP elections which identifies different logics working behind the general banner of anti-Europeanism. Her chapter continues to investigate, more in detail, the relationship between Euroscepticism and European elections, taking into account the 'historical' development of Eurosceptical political forces in the EP. Finally, she studies the current results of the EP elections, and embeds them into the general framework of European integration, by demonstrating that we are confronted with a deeply rooted phenomenon of Euroscepticism that has accompanied this process from the start.

Brice Cristoforetti and **Lara Querton** explore the internal politics of the EP. Focusing on migration policies, the main objective of their chapter is to explore a potential discursive contagion effect from the periphery to the mainstream of the assembly over an eight-year period (2009–2017). More precisely, their study examines the narratives stated in plenary speeches by the mainstream right MEPs, by comparing them to the speeches of three peripheral right groups (ECR, EFDD, and ENF), which have gained political weight following the 2014 European elections. With regard to this extremely topical and controversial policy, the expected result is a sharpening of the discourses of the mainstream right political group reflecting a more restrictive, culturally conservative and nationalist position after the 2014 elections.

Martin Westlake concludes the third part of the book with a chapter examining the possible future for the EU party political system. He first reviews post-war steps to a parliamentary and a party political EU, concluding that they are irreversible. He considers the 'Spitzenkandidaten' procedure, and assumes, more debatably, that this also is irreversible. He acknowledges six 'known unknowns' that could have consequences for the evolution of the EU's party political system. He also considers several basic questions about the model the EU has cumulatively chosen, before examining some of the 'discontents' towards party political systems and their potential relevance to the EU's emerging system. Westlake concludes that the existence of a parliamentary party political system, with electoral linkage between the executive and the legislature, is a necessary but far from sufficient condition for viable governance—and opposition.

The fourth and last part of the book deals with the **role of the EP in internal and external EU policies**.

Dermot Hodson and **Michele Chang** explore the involvement of the EP in the governance of the Eurozone. There is a debate in the literature about how much influence it had in its reforms after the euro crisis. Most scholars accept that the EP punched above its weight when it comes to the powers allocated to it in the treaties, but less has been written about what the EP used its influence for. This chapter shows that the Economic Dialogue is less effective than the Monetary Dialogue, although there is room to enhance the former. The authors first examine the origins of the Economic Dialogue, looking at how the idea emerged in negotiations over the so-called Six-Pack. They then review the early experiences of the Economic Dialogue, noting its diffuse configurations, and asking whether it has had any early wins. The final section puts forward some tentative ideas for how it could be strengthened.

Frédérique Berrod, Louis Navé, and **Samuel Verschraegen** address the question of the EP's influence in the European energy policy, as this policy is largely driven by member states' interests. The purpose of their contribution is to determine to what extent the EP can exploit the social objectives of the energy policy with the aim of influencing and shaping the current debate on the Energy Union. To that effect, they explore the fight against energy poverty that the EP is actively promoting, via a set of means and instruments. They especially analyse the various initiatives undertaken by the EP in the attempt to lay the basis of a social policy in the field of energy, despite a highly constrained environment.

Beatrix Immenkamp and **Naja Bentzen** explore the role of the EP in EU external relations, dealing more specifically with European parliamentary diplomacy. They focus, mainly, on the EP's recent activities in the area of democracy support. These activities focus on a number of priority countries: Ukraine, Moldova, and Georgia in the Eastern Neighbourhood, Tunisia and Morocco in the Southern Neighbourhood, Tanzania and more recently Nigeria in Africa, Myanmar in Asia, and Peru in South America. The authors first define the concepts of 'parliamentary diplomacy' in general, and 'democracy support' in particular. They then present the EP's activities in the areas of 'democracy and election action' and 'mediation' in the context of specific countries. Finally, they analyse the EP's activities in Ukraine, arguably the country in which the diplomatic activities have been the most successful and have produced tangible results.

Elena Lazarou addresses the EP's involvement in the field of security and defence. The chapter outlines the main changes in the EP's role in the area of Common Security and Defence Policy (CSDP) and, more generally, in the Common Foreign and Security Policy (CFSP) since the entry into force of the Lisbon Treaty. It then assesses how the EP has since used its general powers (elective, budgetary, and legislative) in order to increase its role in the policy-making process in this area. The author focuses particularly on developments related and subsequent to the conception and release of the EU's Global Strategy (2015–2017), as a reaction to new geopolitical realities in the EU's security environment.

Finally, **Laura Puccio** and **Roderick Harte** analyse the role of the EP in monitoring the implementation of EU international trade policy. The Lisbon Treaty substantially increased the Parliament's powers in the field, by extending the ordinary legislative procedure to it and applying the consent procedure to trade agreements. The chapter focuses on analysing how the EP monitors implementation of EU trade policies after they have been adopted. With the increase in decision-making powers, the control function of the EP has become key in verifying that its legislative contributions are actually implemented. A survey is used to examine the EP's monitoring process, including its instruments, triggers, and frequency, to better understand its control function in the area of EU trade policy.

REFERENCES

Anderson, P. J., & McLeod, A. (2004). The Great Non-Communicator? The Mass Communication Deficit of the European Parliament and Its Press Directorate'. *JCMS: Journal of Common Market Studies, 42*(5), 897–917.

Auel, K., & Benz, A. (Eds.). (2005). The Europeanisation of Parliamentary Democracy. *Journal of Legislative Studies, 11*(3–4, Special Issue), 372–393.

Beauvallet, W., & Michon, S. (2010). Professionalization and Socialization of the Members of the European Parliament. *French Politics, 8*(2), 145–165.

Bickerton, C., Hodson, D., & Puetter, U. (2015). *The New Intergovernmentalism. States and Supranational Actors in the Post-Maastricht Era.* Oxford: Oxford University Press.

Blondel, J., Sinnott, R., & Svensson, P. (1998). *People and Parliament in the European Union: Participation, Democracy, and Legitimacy.* Oxford: Clarendon Press.

Bowler, S., & Farrell, D. M. (1995). The Organizing of the European Parliament: Committees, Specialization and Co-Ordination. *British Journal of Political Science, 25*(2), 219–243.

Brack, N. (2018). *Opposing Europe in the European Parliament. Rebels and Radicals in the Chamber.* London: Palgrave.

Brack, N., & Costa, O. (Eds.) (2018a). The EP Through the Lens of Legislative Studies: Recent Debates and New Perspectives. *The Journal of Legislative Studies, 24*(1, Special Issue), 1–178.

Brack, N., & Costa, O. (2018b). Democracy in Parliament vs. Democracy Through Parliament? Defining the Rules of the Game in the European Parliament. *The Journal of Legislative Studies, 24*(1), 51–71.

Bressanelli, E., Koop, C., & Reh, C. (2016). The Impact of Informalisation: Early Agreements and Voting Cohesion in the European Parliament. *European Union Politics, 17*(1), 91–113.

Burns, C. (2005). Who Pays? Who Gains? How Do Costs and Benefits Shape the Policy Influence in the EP? *Journal of Common Market Studies, 43*(3), 485–505.

Carrubba, C. J., Gabel, M., Murrah, L., Clough, R., Montgomery, E., & Schambach, R. (2006). Off the Record: Unrecorded Legislative Votes, Selection Bias and Roll-Call Vote Analysis. *British Journal of Political Science, 36*(4), 691–704.

Christiansen, T. (2002). The Role of Supranational Actors in EU Treaty Reform. *Journal of European Public Policy, 9*(1), 33–53.

Coman, E. (2009). Reassessing the Influence of Party Groups on Individual MEPs. *West European Politics, 32*(6), 1099–1117.

Cooper, I., & Smith, J. (2017). Governance Without Democracy? Analysing the Role of Parliaments in European Economic Governance After the Crisis: Conclusions. *Parliamentary Affairs, 70*(4), 728–739.

Corbett, R. (1998). *The European Parliament's Role in Closer European Integration*. London: Macmillan.

Corbett, R., Jacobs, F. B., & Neville, D. (2016). *The European Parliament* (9th ed.). London: John Harper.

Costa, O. (2001). *Le Parlement européen, assemblée délibérante*. Brussels: Editions de l'Université de Bruxelles.

Costa, O. (2013). The President of the European Parliament. *Il Filangieri*, vol. 2012–2013. In Jovene (Ed.), *Le trasformazioni del ruolo dei Presidenti delle Camere* (pp. 143–160). Naples.

Costa, O., Dri, C., & Stavridis, S. (Eds.). (2013). *Parliamentary Dimensions of Regionalization and Globalization: The Role of International Parliamentary Institutions*. Basingstoke: Springer.

Crespy, A. (2014). Deliberative Democracy and the Legitimacy of the European Union: A Reappraisal of Conflict. *Political Studies, 62*, 81–98.

Daniel, W. T. (2015). *Career Behaviour and the European Parliament: All Roads Lead Through Brussels?* Oxford: Oxford University Press.

Daniel, W. T., & Metzger, S. (2018). Within or Between Jobs? Determinants of Membership Volatility in the European Parliament, 1979–2014. *The Journal of Legislative Studies, 24*, 90–108.

Déloye, Y., & Bruter, M. (2007). *Encyclopaedia of European Elections*. Basingstoke: Palgrave Macmillan.

Diedrichs, U. (2004). The European Parliament in CFSP: More than a Marginal Player? *The International Spectator, 39*(2), 31–46.

Egeberg, M., Gornitzka, A., Trondal, J., & Johannessen, M. (2013). Parliament Staff: Unpacking the Behaviour of Officials in the European Parliament. *Journal of European Public Policy, 20*(4), 495–514.

European Parliament. (2009). *Building Parliament: 50 Years of European Parliament History – 1958–2008*. Luxembourg: OPEC.

Fabbrini, S. (2015). *Which European Union? Europe After the Euro Crisis*. Cambridge: Cambridge University Press.

Farrell, H., & Héritier, A. (2005). A Rationalist-Institutionalist Explanation of Endogenous Regional Integration. *Journal of European Public Policy, 12*(2), 273–290.

Foret, F. (2017). *Religion at the European Parliament and in European Multi-Level Governance*. London: Taylor & Francis Group.

Fossum, J. E., & Menéndez, A. J. (2005). The Constitution's Gift? A Deliberative Democratic Analysis of Constitution Making in the European Union. *European Law Journal, 11*(4), 380–440.

Franklin, M., & Scarrow, S. (1999). Making Europeans? The Socializing Power of the European Parliament. In R. Katz & B. Wessels (Eds.), *The European Parliament, the National Parliaments, and European Integration*. Oxford: Oxford University Press.

Gabel, M., & Hix, S. (2002). Defining the EU Political Space: An Empirical Study of the European Elections Manifestos, 1979–1999. *Comparative Political Studies, 35*(8), 934–964.

Gallagher, M., Laver, M., & Mair, P. (2011). *Representative Government in Modern Europe*. London: McGraw-Hill.

Greene, D., & Cross, J. P. (2017). Exploring the Political Agenda of the European Parliament Using a Dynamic Topic Modelling Approach. *Political Analysis, 25*(1), 77–94.

Hefftler, C., Neuhold, C., Rozenberg, O., & Smith, J. (Eds.). (2015). *The Palgrave Handbook of National Parliaments and the European Union*. Basingstoke: Palgrave Macmillan.

Héritier, A. (2017). *The Increasing Institutional Power of the European Parliament and EU Policy Making*. EIF Working Paper, 2017-1.

Hermansen, S. S. L. (2018). (Self-)Selection and Expertise Among Decision-Makers in the European Parliament. *The Journal of Legislative Studies, 24*(1), 148–172.

Herranz-Surrallés, A. (2014). The EU's Multilevel Parliamentary (Battle)Field: Inter-Parliamentary Cooperation and Conflict in Foreign and Security Policy. *West European Politics, 37*(5), 957–975.

Hix, S. (2002a). Constitutional Agenda Setting Through Discretion in Rule Interpretation: Why the European Parliament Won at Amsterdam. *British Journal of Political Science, 32*(2), 259–280.

Hix, S. (2002b). Parliamentary Behavior with Two Principals: Preferences, Parties, and Voting in the European Parliament. *American Journal of Political Science, 46*, 688–698.

Hix, S., & Hagemann, S. (2009). Could Changing the Electoral Rules Fix European Parliament Elections. *Politique européenne, 28*(2), 37–52.

Hix, S., & Høyland, B. (2013). Empowerment of the European Parliament. *Annual Review of Political Science, 16*, 171–189.

Hix, S., Noury, A., & Roland, G. (2007). *Democratic Politics in the European Parliament*. Cambridge: Cambridge University Press.

Hobolt, S. B. (2014). A Vote for the President? The Role of Spitzenkandidaten in the 2014 European Parliament Elections. *Journal of European Public Policy, 21*(10), 1528–1540.

Hobolt, S. (2015). The 2014 European Elections: Divided in Unity? *Journal of Common Market Studies, 53*(S1), 6–21.

Hobolt, S. B., & de Vries, C. (2016). Turning Against the Union? The Impact of the Crisis on the Eurosceptic Vote in the 2014 European Parliament Elections. *Electoral Studies, 44,* 504–514.

Hooghe, L., & Marks, G. (2008). European Union? *West European Politics, 31*(1/2), 108–129.

Hurka, S., & Kaeding, M. (2012). Report Allocation in the European Parliament After Eastern Enlargement. *Journal of European Public Policy, 19*(4), 512–529.

Judge, D., & Earnshaw, D. (1994). Weak European Parliament Influence? A Study of the Environment Committee in the European Parliament. *Government and Opposition, 29*(2), 262–276.

Judge, D., & Earnshaw, D. (2008). *The European Parliament* (2nd ed.). Basingstoke: Palgrave Macmillan.

Kauppi, N. (2005). *Democracy, Social Resources and Political Power in the European Union.* Manchester: Manchester University Press.

Kluger Dionigi, M. (2016). *Lobbying in the European Parliament: The Battle for Influence.* Cham: Springer.

Kreppel, A. (2000). Rules, Ideology and Coalition Formation in the European Parliament: Past, Present and Future. *European Union Politics, 1,* 340–362.

Kreppel, A. (2002). *The European Parliament and the Supranational Party System.* Cambridge: Cambridge University Press.

Kreppel, A. (2012). The Normalization of the European Union. *Journal of European Public Policy, 19*(5), 635–645.

Kreppel, A., & Tsebelis, G. (1999). Coalition Formation in the European Parliament. *Comparative Political Studies, 32,* 933–966.

Kuehnhanss, C. R., Murdoch, Z., Geys, B., & Heyndels, B. (2017). Identity, Threat Aversion, and Civil Servants' Policy Preferences: Evidence from the European Parliament. *Public Administration, 95*(4), 1009–1025.

Lodge, J. (2016). *The 2014 Elections to the European Parliament.* Berlin: Springer.

Lord, C. (2018). The European Parliament: A Working Parliament Without a Public? *The Journal of Legislative Studies, 24,* 34–50.

Malamud, A., & Stavridis, S. (2011). Parliaments and Parliamentarians as International actors. In B. Reinalda (Ed.), *The Ashgate Research Companion to Non-State Actors* (pp. 101–115). Surrey: Ashgate.

Marshall, D. (2010). Who to Lobby and When: Institutional Determinants of Interest Group Strategies in European Parliament Committees. *European Union Politics, 11*(4), 553–575.

Maurer, A. (2003). The Legislative Powers and Impact of the European Parliament. *JCMS: Journal of Common Market Studies, 41*(2), 227–247.

Maurer, A., & Wessels, W. (2001). *National Parliaments on Their Ways to Europe. Losers or Latecomers?* (p. 521). Baden-Baden: Nomos Verlag.

McElroy, G., & Benoit, K. (2012). Policy Positioning in the European Parliament. *European Union Politics, 13*(1), 150–167.

Monar, J., & Chang, M. (2013). *The European Commission in the Post-Lisbon Era of Crises: Between Political Leadership and Policy Management.* Brussels: Peter Lang.

Noury, A. (2002). Ideology, Nationality and Euro-Parliamentarians. *European Union Politics, 3,* 33–58.

Palmer, M. (2015). *The European Parliament: What It Is, What It Does, How It Works.* Burlington: Elsevier.

Pegan, A. (2017). The Role of Personal Parliamentary Assistants in the European Parliament. *West European Politics, 40*(2), 295–315.

Poyet, C. (2018). Working at Home: French MEPs' Day-to-Day Practice of Political Representation in Their District. *The Journal of Legislative Studies, 24,* 1–18.

Priestley, J. (2008). *Six Battles that Shaped Europe's Parliament.* London: John Harper.

Priestley, J., & Clark, S. (2012). *The European Parliament. People, Places and Politics.* London: John Harper.

Priestley, J., & Peñalver García, N. (2015). *The Making of a European President.* Berlin: Springer.

Puetter, U. (2012). Europe's Deliberative Intergovernmentalism: The Role of the Council and European Council in EU Economic Governance. *Journal of European Public Policy, 19*(2), 161–178.

Rasmussen, A., & Reh, C. (2013). The Consequences of Concluding Codecision Early: Trilogues and Intra-Institutional Bargaining Success. *Journal of European Public Policy, 20*(7), 1006–1024.

Rasmussen, A., & Toshkov, D. (2011). The Inter-Institutional Division of Power and Time Allocation in the EP. *West European Politics, 34*(1), 71–96.

Raunio, T. (1996). Parliamentary Questions in the European Parliament: Representation, Information and Control. *The Journal of Legislative Studies, 2*(4), 356–382.

Raunio, T. (1997). *The European Perspective: Transnational Party Groups in the 1989–1994 European Parliament.* London: Ashgate.

Reh, C. (2014). Is Informal Politics Undemocratic? Trilogues, Early Agreements and the Selection Model of Representation. *Journal of European Public Policy, 21*(6), 822–841.

Reif, K., & Schmitt, H. (1980). Nine Second-Order Elections: A Conceptual Framework for the Analysis of the European Election Results. *European Journal of Political Research, 8*(1), 3–45.

Ringe, N. (2010). *Who Decides, and How? Preferences, Uncertainty, and Policy Choice in the European Parliament*. New York: Oxford University Press.

Ripoll Servent, A. (2013). Holding the European Parliament Responsible: Policy Shift in the Data Retention Directive from Consultation to Codecision. *Journal of European Public Policy, 20*(7), 972–987.

Ripoll Servent, A. (2018). *The European Parliament*. London: Palgrave.

Rittberger, B. (2005). *Building Europe's Parliament. Democratic Representation Beyond the Nation State*. Oxford: Oxford University Press.

Rittberger, B. (2014). Integration Without Representation? The European Parliament and the Reform of Economic Governance in the EU. *Journal of Common Market Studies, 52*(6), 1174–1183.

Rittberger, B., & Schimmelfennig, F. (2006). Explaining the Constitutionalization of the European Union. *Journal of European Public Policy, 13*(8), 1148–1167.

Roederer-Rynning, C., & Greenwood, J. (2017). The European Parliament as a Developing Legislature: Coming of Age in Trilogues? *Journal of European Public Policy, 24*(5), 735–754.

Roger, L. (2016). *Voice(s) in the European Parliament: Deliberation and Negotiation in EP Committees*. Nomos Verlagsgesellschaft.

Šabič, Z. (2008). Building Democratic and Responsible Global Governance: The Role of International Parliamentary Institutions. *Parliamentary Affairs, 61*(2), 255–271.

Scarrow, S. (1997). Political Career Paths and the European Parliament. *Legislative Studies Quarterly, 22*(2), 253–263.

Schmitt, H., Hobolt, S., & Popa, S. A. (2015). Does Personalization Increase Turnout? Spitzenkandidaten in the 2014 European Parliament Elections. *European Union Politics, 16*(3), 347–368.

Scully, R. (1998). MEPs and the Building of a Parliamentary Europe. *Journal of Legislative Studies, 4*(1), 92–108.

Scully, R. (2006). *Becoming Europeans? Attitudes, Roles and Socialization in the EP*. Basingstoke: Palgrave.

Shackleton, M. (2000). The Politics of Codecision. *Journal of Common Market Studies, 36*(1), 15–130.

Shackleton, M. (2017). Transforming Representative Democracy in the EU? The Role of the European Parliament. *Journal of European Integration, 39*(2), 191–205.

Stavridis, S., & Irrera, D. (2016). *The European Parliament and Its International Relations*. London: Routledge.

Steunenberg, B., & Thomassen, J. (2002). *The European Parliament: Moving Toward Democracy in the EU*. Lanham and Oxford: Rowman & Littlefield.

Taggart, P. (1998). A Touchstone of Dissent: Euroscepticism in Contemporary Western European Party Systems. *European Journal of Political Research, 33*, 363–388.

Thym, D. (2006). Beyond Parliament's Reach-The Role of the European Parliament in the CFSP. *The European Foreign Affairs Review, 11,* 109.

Tsebelis, G. (1994). The Power of the European Parliament as a Conditional Agenda Setters. *American Political Science Review, 88,* 128–142.

Tsebelis, G., Jensen, C. B., Kalandrakis, A., & Kreppel, A. (2001). Legislative Procedures in the EU: An Empirical Analysis. *British Journal of Political Science, 31*(3), 573–599.

Viola, D. M. (Ed.). (2015). *Routledge Handbook of European Elections.* London: Routledge.

Warleigh, A. (2000). The Hustle: Citizenship Practice, NGOs and 'Policy Coalitions' in the European Union. The Cases of Auto Oil, Drinking Water and Unit Pricing. *Journal of European Public Policy, 7*(2), 229–243.

Wessels, B. (2005). Roles and Orientations of Members of Parliament in the EU Context: Congruence or Difference? Europeanisation or Not? *Journal of Legislative Studies, 11*(3–4), 446–465.

Westlake, M. (1994). *A Modern Guide to the European Parliament.* London: Pinter Publishers.

Whitaker, R. (2011). *The European Parliament's Committees: National Party Influence and Legislative Empowerment.* London: Routledge.

Whitaker, R., Hix, S., & Zapryanova, G. (2017). Understanding Members of the European Parliament: Four Waves of the European Parliament Research Group MEP Survey. *European Union Politics, 18*(3), 491–506.

Wilde, P., Michailidou, A., & Trenz, H.-J. (2014). Converging on Euroscepticism: Online Polity Contestation during European Parliament Elections. *European Journal of Political Research, 53*(4), 766–783.

Winzen, T. (2011). Technical or Political? An Exploration of the Work of Officials in the Committees of the European Parliament. *The Journal of Legislative Studies, 17*(1), 27–44.

Yordanova, N. (2013). *Organizing the European Parliament: The Role of Committees and Their Legislative Influence.* Colchecter: ECPR Press.

Young, A. (2016). An Inflection Point in European Union Studies? *Journal of European Public Policy, 23*(8), 1109–1117.

PART I

The EP and the EU Political System

Parliamentary Oversight: Challenges Facing Classic Scrutiny Instruments and the Emergence of New Forms of 'Steering' Scrutiny

Eva-Maria Poptcheva

Dr Eva-Maria Poptcheva is Chief Policy Analyst in Constitutional Affairs at the Members' Research Service of the European Parliamentary Research Services (EPRS). All opinions expressed in this chapter are her own and do not represent the view either of EPRS or of the European Parliament. She thanks Anthony Teasdale and Martin Westlake for their highly valuable comments on an earlier version of this chapter.

E.-M. Poptcheva (✉)
European Parliamentary Research Service, European Parliament,
Brussels, Belgium
e-mail: evamaria.poptcheva@europarl.europa.eu

© The Author(s) 2019
O. Costa (ed.), *The European Parliament in Times of EU Crisis*,
European Administrative Governance,
https://doi.org/10.1007/978-3-319-97391-3_2

25

1   THE CONSTITUTIONAL SIGNIFICANCE
OF PARLIAMENTARY OVERSIGHT AT EU LEVEL

Parliamentary oversight of the executive branch of state power has long been established as one of the cornerstones of parliamentary democracy.[1] The shift in recent decades from legislation by the legislature to (quasi-) legislation by the executive, partially due to the highly specialised law-making context (Isensee and Kirchhof 2005, 718), has put parliamentary scrutiny under the spotlight of constitutional and political studies. Alongside this evolution, a paradigm shift occurred: parliaments are seen as powerful not (only) when the constitutional order has equipped them with fully fledged legislative functions but also when they are enabled to effectively oversee the executive.

In the European Union (EU) context, parliamentary oversight has also gained prominence as the attention of political actors has shifted from legislation towards effective enforcement. The EU has a long history of building its legal architecture through sophisticated and, in some areas, comprehensive law. However, some recent experiences, for instance, the migration crisis, have shown that the EU is often lacking not legislation addressing the issues at stake but rather executive competence or capacity complementing that of the member states, enabling effective enforcement of EU law also where member states are unable or unwilling to do so. A case in point here could be the successor of Frontex, the European Border and Coast Guard Agency, which has been empowered to assist member states experiencing high migratory pressure on the EU's external borders, so that they can comply with their obligations under EU migration and asylum law.[2] The newly conferred executive competences for an EU

---

[1] Already since John Stuart Mill for whom "Instead of the function of governing, for which it is radically unfit, the proper office of a representative assembly is to watch and control the government; to throw the light of publicity on its acts; to compel a full exposition and justification of all of them which any one considers questionable; to censure them if found condemnable, and, if the men who compose the government abuse their trust, or fulfil it in a manner which conflicts with the deliberate sense of the nation, to expel them from office, and either expressly or virtually appoint their successors. The proper office of a representative assembly is to watch and control the government", in *Considerations on Representative Government* (London: Parker, Son, and Bourn, 1861), p. 104.

[2] Regulation (EU) 2016/1624 of 14 September 2016 on the European Border and Coast Guard (OJ L 251, 16.9.2016, p. 1).

agency require of course a sufficient degree of accountability and oversight.[3]

From a constitutional law point of view, parliamentary oversight is an abstract structural condition for democratic legitimacy. It follows from this concept of parliamentary control as legitimising the exercise of executive power that there is a need for an uninterrupted chain of responsibility, where decisions can be attributed and decision-making processes can be influenced (Schmidt 2007, 18). This is equally true for EU decision-making, where the parliamentary system has been evolving not only by giving the European Parliament (EP) far-reaching legislative powers, but also through strengthening its scrutiny powers.

Lately, the EU parliamentary system has often found itself subjected to, at least at first sight, contradictory criticism. Functionalists measure the success of EU decision-making by its capacity to efficiently deliver solutions to citizens' problems. Majone (1994, 94; 2000, 276) refers in this sense to the credibility of EU regulation through its effectiveness, emphasising its output legitimacy. Whilst, in this context, the legislature is urged to ensure a high quality of the legislation it adopts, the output legitimacy of decision-making is closely related to the implementation of that legislation. There the role of the legislature is to effectively and meaningfully scrutinise such implementation, both in order to hold to account the executive and to feed the implementation results into the new legislation process, completing this way the legislative cycle (Welle 2016, 17). The increasing awareness of the importance of parliamentary scrutiny over the implementation of adopted legislation has been translated at EU level into increasing efforts at 'better regulation' and the need to feed evaluation results into the new law-making process.

From an institutionalist theoretical approach, on the other hand, shortcomings in the input legitimacy of EU decision-making have been denounced, bemoaning the source of legitimacy of EU institutions in a multilevel political system (Follesdal and Hix 2006, 535). Parliamentarisation is often seen as the response to criticism of insufficient politicisation of decision-making at EU level (Hix 2006, 15) and as a compensation for the general shift towards executive power at EU level at the expense of national parliamentary control (Lodge 1994; Andersen

---

[3] See EP resolution on improving the functioning of the EU building on the potential of the Lisbon Treaty (2014/2249(INI)).

and Burns 1996; Raunio 1999). The long-demanded political link between the Parliament and the Commission seemed to have been established with the 2014 *Spitzenkandidaten* process that has already been translated into a further parliamentarisation of EU decision-making, not only within the legislative process itself but also in the rest of the EU policy cycle, including agenda-setting and evaluation. Some have warned, however, that this newly formalised political link could adversely affect the institutional balance as foreseen in the EU treaties, by preventing the Parliament from exercising a meaningful scrutiny over the executive (Grabbe and Lehne 2013, 5), which, on the other hand, would have a negative impact on the input legitimacy of EU decision-making.

It seems indeed that the EU is transitioning from a system of 'separation of power', where the executive was formed in a process detached from the elections to the EP, towards a system of 'fusion of power' (Fabbrini 2017, 13–14), as found in most EU member states, with the outcome of the parliamentary elections determining also the political orientation of the executive branch. This change in the constitutional relationship between the Parliament and the Commission is already reflected in the way the Parliament exercises its power of oversight over the Commission.

Accordingly, the democratic legitimacy dilemma surrounding parliamentary control refers to the question of how to achieve a better legislative and policy output, not least through an improved parliamentary oversight over the executive, whilst further parliamentarisation and politicisation of the decision-making process are also called for, which is paradoxically seen as problematic for meaningful parliamentary oversight over the executive. The debate between Hix and Bartolini on the need for, or the risks of, politicising the EU decision-making process (Hix 2006; Bartolini 2006) is herewith reproduced within the discussion on how to ensure an effective parliamentary control over executive action.

The institutional balance resulting from emerging accountability chains and political links between the EU institutions affects not only the question of 'how' parliamentary scrutiny can be exercised most effectively, but also 'who' and 'what' should be scrutinised. Classic punitive scrutiny instruments at EU level mirror the design of national parliamentary means to control the executive. However, not only do they often remain short of the control powers at the disposal of national parliaments in their substance (Poptcheva 2016, 3), but they also fail to take into account the fragmentation of executive power (Verhey 2009, 67) and the co-existence of several executive actors at EU, national, and sometimes regional and local, levels that only together complete certain executive actions. In this context, whilst classic EU scrutiny instruments are generally directed towards the European Commission, it is, however, far from being the only institution implementing EU law, with many other actors formally or informally assuming executive functions. This has made an adaptation of scrutiny necessary, developing further its ex-ante steering aspects, along with the classical punitive scrutiny mechanisms. Furthermore, classic parliamentary scrutiny's effectiveness relies strongly on an antagonistic relationship between a government and a parliamentary opposition that does not sustain the government politically. This traditional understanding of effective parliamentary scrutiny has indeed changed over time, with the increasing overlapping of the functions of legislature and executive leading to a cooperative process of political decision-making, often blurring the lines between strictly legislative and strictly executive business (Isensee et al. 2005, 716).

In this chapter we will examine the different types of parliamentary oversight at the EP's disposal, grouping them into classical control instruments of punitive oversight and steering oversight tools. The chapter will seek to establish whether the latter could be a partial answer to the emergence of many formal and informal actors within the executive branch on the one side, and help address the particularities of a consensual democracy such as the Union one, at EU level on the other.

2   CLASSIC INSTRUMENTS OF PUNITIVE SCRUTINY

The EP is equipped with substantial control instruments, which resemble in many aspects those at the disposal of national parliaments. It exercises its functions of political control (article 14(1) Treaty on the Functioning of the European Union (TFEU)) by means of instruments such as the motion of censure of the Commission (article 234 TFEU), the power of inquiry (article 226 TFEU), oral and written questions (article 230 TFEU), budgetary control (article 319 TFEU) and, indirectly, through the possibility to lodge complaints with the Court of Justice of the EU. Most of these instruments have a rather ex-post and punitive character, except for oral and written questions, whose punitive nature lags far behind their contributive and information character (see below). Due to space constraints and their rather specific character, budgetary control and the recourse to the Court of Justice will not be dealt with here.

2.1   Motion of Censure

Article 234 TFEU contains a specific notion of responsibility of the Commission to the EP, by conferring on the latter the right to censure the Commission by a two-thirds majority of the votes cast, representing an absolute majority of the members of Parliament. The submission of such a motion requires the support of one-tenth of the members of the European Parliament (MEPs) (Rule 119 EP Rules of Procedure).

Although, formally, individual Commissioners cannot be censured, the Parliament can, according to the 2010 Framework Agreement on relations between the EP and the European Commission, ask the Commission President to withdraw confidence in an individual member of the Commission. The Commission President will 'seriously consider' whether to request that member to resign according to article 17 (6) TEU and would need to explain his/her refusal to do so before Parliament in the following part-session.

The motion of censure concerns the 'activities of the Commission', a rather broad notion. According to the Court of Justice of the EU, the Commission can act as an EU body also outside the framework of the Treaties, when entrusted by the member states with the task of coordinating a collective action undertaken by them on the basis of an act of their representatives meeting in the Council.[4] This would mean that the Commission cannot escape Parliament's political control when acting outside the EU framework, notably with regard to measures of economic governance (Fasone 2014, 168–171).

In this regard it should be noted that the sanction instrument of the motion of censure does not adopt a functional, but rather an institutional approach. This means it does not establish political control over all executive action, but only over the Commission, regardless of whether the action concerned is (strictly) executive in nature or not. This becomes evident from article 234 (2) TFEU according to which the High Representative of the Union for Foreign Affairs and Security Policy will resign from duties that he or she carries out in the Commission, not, however, from his/her position in the Council if a motion of censure succeeds.[5]

---

[4] Court of Justice of the EU, C-181/91, European Parliament v Council, para. 20.
[5] See also Article 17 (8) TEU.

Thirteen motions of censure have been tabled in the Parliament so far, four of them before direct elections to Parliament were introduced in 1979 (Corbett et al. 2016, 362–363). None of them passed. The motion of censure remains, however, an important instrument of political leverage vis-à-vis the Commission, as the resignation of the Santer Commission in 1999, in the shadow of the imminent prospect that such a motion would pass, showed.

The success of a motion of censure has, however, become even more improbable for the future, because of the 'election', and not mere 'approval', of the President of the European Commission by the Parliament, as well as the Spitzenkandidaten 'process' involving a stronger political link between Parliament and Commission. This decreasing probability is due to the fact that the Commission President who had to secure a parliamentary majority to be elected—and whose working programme is designed in close cooperation with Parliament—would be expected to be responsive to criticism from Parliament and to accepting adjustments of his/her position to respond to the concerns of the parliamentary majority that elected him/her in office. Furthermore, the political links of the different Commissioners with the political groups in Parliament would make it difficult for a censuring two-third majority to materialise (Teasdale and Bainbridge 2012).

2.2   Power of Inquiry

The power of inquiry is an important instrument for the exercise of Parliament's control functions. Whilst there is still no regulation governing the right of inquiry, as foreseen in article 226 TFEU, it is exercised according to a 1995 inter-institutional agreement (Annex VIII to the EP's Rules of Procedure),[6] and Parliament's Rules of Procedure.

Under article 226 TFEU, committees of inquiry are established to examine alleged contraventions and maladministration in the implementation of EU law. 'Contraventions' mean violations of EU law, whilst 'maladministration' includes, inter alia, 'administrative irregularities, omissions, abuses of power, unfairness, malfunction or incompetence,

---

[6] Decision of the European Parliament, the Council and the Commission of 19 April 1995 on the detailed provisions governing the exercise of the European Parliament's right of inquiry.

discrimination, avoidable delays, refusal to provide information, and negligence'.[7] As a consequence of the fact that EU law is primarily implemented by national authorities, the Parliament has the right to investigate alleged maladministration also by national authorities, as well as by natural and legal persons involved in EU law implementation.

Unlike committees of inquiry, 'special committees' can be set up for any parliamentary inquiry, also involving actions by third countries, and have therefore been used more often (Poptcheva 2016), not least because they often examine a more general policy issue instead of focusing on a particular contravention (Syrier 2013, 189–190).

The EP's investigative powers fall short of those of national parliaments, particularly as regards the power of its committees of inquiry and special committees to summon individual witnesses, request access to documents, and notably to sanction in order to be able to assert its investigative powers (Poptcheva 2016, 16–17). Committees of inquiry can indeed gather evidence by inviting witnesses, requesting documents, or holding hearings with experts, but no sanctions instruments are at the disposal against authorities and persons refusing to appear before the committee or refusing to give access to relevant documents. More recently, the EP has been working on a legislative initiative for a regulation governing its right to inquiry seeking to make it more effective and adapt it to its political weight in a multilevel governance space, which has, however, met strong opposition in the Council (ibid., 8–10).

Committees of inquiry and special committees conclude their work by submitting a report to the plenary. The resolution adopted by the Parliament on the basis of the committee report can contain recommendations to EU institutions as well as bodies and to member states. The recommendations are, however, not binding, and their addressees 'shall draw therefrom the conclusions which they deem appropriate' (article 4(3) Inter-institutional Agreement).

The power of inquiry in its current form has proven to be an effective tool of political control over the Commission, both in terms of compliance with investigative requests and with the final recommendations adopted, as can be seen from the work, for instance, of the Committee of Inquiry into Emmission Measurements in the Automotive Sector (EMIS) .[8] This again can be seen as a consequence of the strong political

---

[7] European Ombudsman, Annual report 1997, p. 22.
[8] European Parliament decision of 17 December 2015 on setting up a Committee of Inquiry into emission measurements in the automotive sector, its powers, numerical strength,

link between Parliament and Commission. Conversely, member states' cooperation with the Parliament's committees of inquiry and special committees remains generally unsatisfactory. This has partially been justified with national parliaments' inquiry prerogatives over national administrations, but disregards the fact that cross-border issues can only be addressed effectively at EU level (Poptcheva 2016).

2.3   Control Over Implementing Acts

The Lisbon Treaty created a new framework for the old 'comitology' procedures. For the first time, it now differentiates in articles 290 and 291 TFEU between conferring law-making and executive powers to the Commission. In the first case, the legislator delegates the power to adopt norms of general application, yet no legislative acts under a legislative procedure, to the executive. Such delegated acts are not only not unusual. They are even increasingly used also in the national context, in order to react rapidly to events and to profit from the executive's technical expertise. Delegated acts are non-legislative acts of general application foreseen to amend or supplement certain non-essential elements of the basic legislative act.[9]

Conversely, implementing acts are executive and not law-making in nature, so that their adoption by the executive does not represent an exceptional conferral of (law-making) powers. What is rather exceptional with the Commission's implementing acts is the fact that, as a general rule, member states' administrations are in charge of implementing EU law, so that under article 291 TFEU the Commission (or under certain circumstances, the Council) is conferred the power to adopt implementing acts only when this is necessary in order to secure the uniform implementation of the law.

The different nature of delegated and implementing acts as law-making in the first case and executive in the second, also determines the extent to which Parliament can exercise scrutiny over the executive in this context. Whilst Parliament can veto delegated acts and revoke the delega-

and term of office (2015/3037(RSO)).

[9] See Article 290 TFEU and EP Handbook on delegated and implementing acts, 2014, p. 10. Available at: http://www.ipolnet.ep.parl.union.eu/ipoladm/webdav/site/ipoladm/shared/dire/code/docs/dia/Key%20documents/Handbook%20on%20Delegated%20and%20Implementing%20Acts.pdf (12.10.2017).

tion to the Commission and, in this way, take back its law-making powers, implementing acts cannot be blocked by the Parliament. Instead, the latter's scrutiny power is limited to the mere possibility of indicating to the Commission the *ultra vires* character of the draft implementing act, namely that it exceeded the implementing powers provided in the basic act (article 11 of Regulation 182/2011 laying down the rules and general principles concerning mechanisms for control by member states of the Commission's exercise of implementing powers). The Commission is yet not obliged to amend or withdraw the draft implementing act as a result.

These limited scrutiny powers of the EP concerning the executive functions of the Commission with regard to implementing acts, which according to Brandsma account for between 45 and 60 per cent of all EU executive acts (Brandsma 2013, 150), are at odds with the need for the body that confers powers to hold the empowered institution accountable. The Parliament's limited control powers seem, however, to be compensated by scrutiny rights conferred to member states, the reasoning behind being that they are in the first place the ones in charge of implementing Union acts. Member states' representatives have a crucial role in the adoption of implementing acts by the Commission through the so-called advisory and examination procedures (articles 4 and 5 of Regulation 182/2011).

It should yet be noted that although member states' involvement in the adoption of implementing acts at EU level is largely called 'control', it is not a parliamentary one, since member states' are represented within the advisory and examination committees by governmental officials. It is therefore a matter of national executive control over EU executive action. From a multilevel constitutional perspective (Freixes 2013; Pernice 2009, 2015), national parliaments should be scrutinising the members states' representatives' actions within the adoption of implementing acts by the Commission (Brandsma 2013, 161). This is, however, highly problematic in practice due to the nature of the multi-actor decision-making process underlying the adoption of implementing acts, with national parliaments being able to exercise control only over the individual input of their national government representative, but not over the result of a collaborative decision-making (ibid., 146–147). This is why a parliamentary control by the EP at EU level seems more appropriate and the only feasible option (Bradley 1997, 2008), at least as regards the final decision taken at EU level (ibid., 161).[10]

---

[10] See also Kaeding and Hardacre (2013).

2.4   Oral and Written Questions

Questions for oral and written answer are an important tool of parliamentary scrutiny. Under article 230 (2) TFEU, the Commission shall reply orally or in writing to questions put to it by the EP or by its members. Any member may put questions for written answer to the Commission, whereby each member may submit a maximum of twenty questions over a rolling period of three months (Rule 130 EP Rules of Procedure).[11] Questions and replies are published in the *Official Journal of the EU*.

It should be noted that the treaties confer no similar (general) question right to members of Parliament as regarding the Council. Article 36 TEU merely establishes a right of the Parliament to address questions only in the field of Common Foreign and Security Policy to the Council and the High Representative. The Council agreed, however, already in 1973 to answer to oral and written questions by members of Parliament and its Rules of Procedure refer to this practice (Rule 12 (2) a) Council Rules of Procedure).

Furthermore, the treaties do not provide for a right of Parliament to ask questions to the European Council. However, in 2010, the then President of the European Council, Herman Van Rompuy, voluntarily agreed to answer members' questions for written answer, in so far as they deal with his own political activities rather than those of the European Council as an institution (Vanden Broucke et al. 2015, 6), and the Parliament's Rules of Procedure in the meantime provide for this possibility too (Rule 130 EP RoP and Annex III RoP).

Questions for oral answers may be put by a parliamentary committee, a political group, or one-twentieth of Parliament's component members (Rule 128 and Rule 168a (1) a). Moreover, any member is entitled to participate in Question Time in plenary (Rule 129).

Questions for written or oral answers are very useful as scrutiny tools due to their *ad hoc* character, not requiring specific previous steps, which allows members to quickly react to events. Their importance derives particularly from the fact that they represent a scrutiny tool at the disposal not only of the political groups, but also and foremost of individual members.

[11] See also Annex II to the EP Rules of Procedure on criteria for questions and interpellations for written answer, http://www.europarl.europa.eu/sides/getDoc.do?pubRef=-//EP//TEXT+RULES-EP+20170116+ANN-02+DOC+XML+V0//EN&language=EN&navigationBar=YES (accessed 12.10.2017).

This can be of relevance where the political links between the Commissioners and the different political groups in Parliament would prevent the building of majorities necessary to trigger some of the other scrutiny instruments, such as motion of censure or the creation of special or inquiry committees. As in national parliaments, oral and written questions are therefore particularly important for the parliamentary minority to be able to exercise scrutiny over the executive sustained by a parliamentary majority (Raunio 1996, 377), in a system of fusion of powers.

The limitations of the parliamentary questions can be seen especially with regard to their addressees, with the European Council not being subjected to this type of parliamentary scrutiny and the Council being subjected to such questions mainly voluntarily, on a non-Treaty basis, which is only scarcely used by members of Parliament. Between 2009 and 2014, MEPs submitted only 2469 questions for written answer to the Council compared to 53262 questions to the Commission (Corbett et al. 2016, 370). It should be noted that oral and written questions by members addressing the Council are answered by the rotating Presidency, which faces considerable challenges in doing so on behalf of the Council, that is on behalf of all member states (ibid., 372). In order to reply to MEPs questions on behalf of the Council, the rotating Presidency undertakes a process of consultation with the Permanent representations of the member states before the EU, which leads to the replies provided to MEPs being considerably watered down.

Also because of their 'soft sanction' character, questions for oral and written answer hold the potential to serve as effective steering scrutiny instruments. Members of Parliament use them not only to obtain information to better scrutinise executive action, but also to highlight problems to the Council and Commission (Proksch and Slapin 2011), which is *a posteriori* used by the Parliament as a base to hold both institutions accountable if they have not addressed the Parliament's concerns.

3   Shortcomings of Classic Scrutiny Instruments: Whom and What to Scrutinise at EU Level?

3.1   The Contest to Exercise Executive Power

3.1.1   The Challenges of Executive Federalism
Punitive scrutiny instruments at the Parliament's disposal resemble to a great extent those in national constitutional systems. Two particularities of

the EU's multilevel constitutional system, however, need to be taken into account when assessing their efficacy in controlling executive action.

First, from a functional point of view, EU law, notably in the area of competition and trade, is implemented only partially at EU level by the European Commission through a so-called direct execution. The general rule established in article 291 (1) TFEU is that member states are in charge of the implementation of EU law (indirect execution).[12] This vertical structure of EU executive competences (Dann 2006, 237) operates therefore in a multilevel system and diffuses executive functions across the different administrative levels: European, national, and sometimes regional and local, constituting one of the aspects of executive federalism (*Vollzugsföderalismus*).

Also in the horizontal executive structure at EU level, several actors are in charge of implementation and competing to a certain extent in the area of enforcement. The European Commission is the main body at EU level in charge of implementation, when implementation is not undertaken by national administrations, and particularly when uniform conditions for the implementation of legally binding Union acts are needed so that the Commission is conferred implementing powers (article 291 (2) TFEU). However, the Treaties reserve implementing powers to the Council, the High Representative of the Union for Foreign Affairs and Security Policy and the European Council in certain specific areas, notably the Common Foreign and Security Policy (articles 24 and 26 TEU).

Moreover, the Council can be entrusted with implementing powers in specific cases too, in which uniform conditions for implementing EU law are needed and, due to its specific knowledge, the Council is better placed than the Commission to adopt implementing acts (article 291 (2) TFEU). The hybrid character of the Council as a co-legislator that is composed of members of the national executives and has retained some executive powers at EU level, adds to the complex intertwining of executive competences (Dann 2006, 239) at the different levels of decision-making and implementation, posing a challenge to an effective political scrutiny. In this context, the Council is, for instance, in charge of macro-economic coordination of the member states' economic policies.

Whilst the Commission is scrutinised by the member states when adopting implementing acts—since according to article 291 (1) TFEU the

---

[12] Article 290 (1) TFEU: Member states shall adopt all measures of national law necessary to implement legally binding Union acts.

primary implementing responsibility lies with them, the Parliament and Council retain only a limited scrutiny right on whether an implementing act exceeds the implementing powers provided for in the basic act or not.[13]

From a procedural point of view, it should be noted that the treaties foresee no uniform executive process, nor do they identify 'the executive'. Each legislative act organises the executive process in the concrete policy area concerned and serves as its legal basis, whilst the Treaties set only a very general legal framework. Calls from the early nineties for an 'uniformisation' of the executive process, including a treaty-based list of the policy areas which the European Commission has executive power over (Lenaerts 1991, 32), have remained unanswered in ensuing Treaty reforms.

3.1.2   Agenda-Setting and Implementation: The Role of the European Council

The increasing leadership role of the European Council within the legislative process has further added to the complexity of the 'executive federalism' within the EU decision-making process, including both legislation and implementation. During the financial crisis, European Council leadership proved crucial in order for the EU, be it in- or outside of the EU framework, to forge compromises and to operate in a resolute manner. Overcoming stalemates in the Council on complex and politically sensitive issues, such as migration, became more and more often *Chefsache*, modifying substantially the European Council's role to give impetus and to define the general political directions and priorities of the Union. This effectively turned it into an active agenda-setter and sometimes even a 'super-legislator', the latter often as a result of the Council referring legislative matters to the European Council instead of taking decisions itself by qualified majority voting.[14]

According to Wessels, the European Council has been de facto acting as an ultimate decision-maker when agreeing on concrete actions, adopting a comprehensive package of measures, and endorsing an EU strategy

[13] Article 11 Regulation (EU) no 182/2011 of the European Parliament and of the Council of 16 February 2011 laying down the rules and general principles concerning mechanisms for control by member states of the Commission's exercise of implementing powers.

[14] See in this sense European Parliament resolution of 16 February 2017 on improving the functioning of the European Union building on the potential of the Lisbon Treaty (2014/2249(INI)).

(Wessels 2016, 72). He explains the practice of a more concrete decision-making power for the European Council with the need to deal with technical details in order to achieve consensus (ibid.). The boundaries between strategic decision-making and legislating (substantively, not procedurally speaking), to which the European Council is not empowered according to article 15 (1) TEU, are blurred, not least because of the combination in some European Council decisions of pre- or para-law-setting of general application (Peters 2011, 37) and executive decisions that are implemented ad hoc. This has particularly been the case in the field of economic governance where the European Council 'has taken over executive powers in the economic policies that formerly belonged to national decision making' (De Schoutheete and Micossi 2013, 4) to become a 'gouvernment économique' (Van Rompuy 2010; Wessels 2016, 207).

Many of these executive competences have been created outside of the framework of the EU treaties (such as the European Stability Mechanism or the Fiscal Compact Treaty, officially the Treaty on Stability, Coordination and Governance in the Economic and Monetary Union). Whilst such intergovernmental instruments have created surveillance and other executive powers for the European Commission,[15] which can address far-reaching policy recommendations to individual member states, the Parliament has, at least at first sight, no power to control politically the Commission's action in this area.

Besides its increasing role as decision-maker, the European Council has defined the action of other political actors at EU level, notably the Council and the Commission. Particularly with regard to the latter and although the Commission retains a monopoly over formal EU legislative initiative (article 17(2) TEU), in recent years this key role has been diluted by the de facto involvement of other actors, such as the European Council (Ponzano et al. 2012, 7). Notably, the European Council has included a growing number of specific requests to the Commission in its conclusions, 'inviting' it to undertake specific actions (Alexandrova 2015, 3; Eggermont 2012).

The role of the European Council in agenda-setting has further increased the need for negotiation and cooperation in all phases of the policy cycle—agenda-setting, legislation, implementation and evalua-

---

[15] See on the spill-over effect of such intergovernmental instruments towards supranational surveillance, Fabbrini (2013, 1024).

tion—in a system of interwoven competences. This is due to the need for all actors involved in the different phases of policy-making to be also involved in the other phases of the policy cycle, so as to guarantee an efficient decision-making and foster ownership and engagement with the different initiatives (Dann 2006, 238).

The recent letter of European Council President Donald Tusk points to a newly discovered appetite of the European Council to become a quasi-legislator, not only when its leadership is being demanded to resolve crisis situations, but also for ordinary EU business to offer efficient and effective solutions to citizens' problems. In his letter of 17 October 2017 to the Heads of State and Government he stated:

> *As you know, there are two main reasons why some issues are stuck. The first is that instead of dealing with the issues at stake, leaders allow them to get lost somewhere between their collaborators or in the decision-making system. I am really pleased that you agreed in Tallinn that it is high time to take things into our own hands.*

The fact that this newly claimed role of the European Council as a 'super legislator' would be ad hoc and would not be brought about through Treaty changes becomes clear when he states: '*Institutional innovation can in some cases be a means to an end, but we should be careful not to get bogged down in unnecessary institutional or theoretical debates*' (Tusk 2017).

Despite its crucial role, neither the European Council nor its President is formally accountable to the EP, which has no Treaty powers to sanction their actions. Whilst some place in this context the emphasis on the importance of stronger control by national parliaments (Tans et al. 2007), rather than by the EP, it remains unclear how such a scrutiny by individual national parliaments would effectively hold to account a collective body such as the European Council, and not merely its individual members, which operate at a different political level than the national parliaments.

The President of the European Council presents an oral report to Parliament after each of the formal meetings of the European Council, either at a plenary session or at a meeting of the Parliament's Conference of Presidents 'open to all Members'. However, the Treaties do not provide for a right for Parliament to ask questions to the European Council.

3.1.3   Interim Conclusions: Challenges for Scrutiny Over a Diffused Executive

The structural competition between different institutional actors at all levels of EU decision-making in a multilevel system of interwoven competences poses significant challenges for the exercise of parliamentary scrutiny powers. First, the system of executive federalism is per se characterised by a low degree of parliamentarisation (Dann 2006, 249),[16] at least in those areas where executive competences are created without the corresponding parliamentary control (Fasone 2014, 173–174). In this context, the EP has repeatedly called for national parliaments to scrutinise national governments in EU affairs, whilst the EP exercises political control over the European executive. It has also recognised, however, that it is 'necessary for the European Parliament to reform its working methods in order to cope with the challenges ahead, by strengthening the exercise of its functions of political control over the Commission, including in relation to the implementation and application of the acquis in the Member States'.[17]

Furthermore, the lack of clear-cut executive competences, with executive powers distributed instead among several actors at several decision-making levels, makes it difficult for parliamentary control powers to be designed to exercise efficient scrutiny in the first place. In this sense, the EP has bemoaned, in its resolution from 16 February 2017 on possible evolutions of and adjustments to the current institutional set-up of the EU (2014/2248(INI)), 'the lack of a credible single executive authority enjoying full democratic legitimacy and competence to take effective action across a wide spectrum of policies'. It therefore proposed 'transforming the Commission into the principle executive authority or government of the Union with the aim of strengthening the "Union method", increasing transparency and improving the efficiency and effectiveness of action taken at the level of the European Union'. Parliament is in this sense aware that any further executive powers would need to be personified in the Commission to ensure parliamentary oversight at EU level. It therefore called in the same resolution 'for the executive authority to be

---

[16] Fabbrini in contrast sees the problem with executive federalism not so much in the lack of parliamentary control, but rather in the asymmetry of the member states in the decision-making of the European Council. Fabbrini (2016, 234).

[17] European Parliament resolution of 16 February 2017 on possible evolutions of and adjustments to the current institutional set-up of the European Union (2014/2248(INI)).

concentrated in the Commission in the role of an EU Finance Minister, by endowing the Commission with the capacity to formulate and give effect to a common EU economic policy combining macro-economic, fiscal and monetary instruments, backed up by a Eurozone budgetary capacity'.

A further challenge derives from a global trend of the interlocking between the functions of agenda-setting, legislating and implementation, not least due to the numerous checks and balances between the different powers. As a result, the separation between the different branches of power, particularly the Legislature and the Executive, whose functions complement each other and sometimes overlap, is not perfect, but rather characterised by reciprocal control, bargaining and mitigation (Klein 2005, 716). These characteristics prevent an uncontrolled concentration of power in a single authority (Tribe 1988, 18). This is all the more true at the EU level, with its different institutions and the organic overlapping of executive and legislative functions in the case of the Commission and the Council (Lenaerts 1991, 13–15).

Classic control instruments at the disposal of the EP, whilst being very important to effectively holding executive action politically accountable, fall short of addressing the particularities of a decision-making system characterised by a large number of executive actors at different levels. Furthermore, if executive action is already significantly predetermined at the stage of agenda-setting, for instance, the ex-post control needs to be complemented by an ex-ante control, as well as by other 'steering' oversight tools, so as to be able to pre-empt the effects of agenda-setting and legislation on their implementation.

3.2   Separation Versus Fusion of Power

Different forms of 'positive scrutiny' are not atypical in political systems of 'fusion of power', where parliaments do not exercise their control function only through a critique of the alleged misbehaviour of the executive. Rather, the executive shall not only be held responsible ex-post, but should also be influenced through a parliamentary political will formation (*contributive or steering parliamentary oversight*). This follows in systems of 'fusion of power' directly from the dependency of government on a parliamentary majority. Political power of governance is awarded in such constitutional orders, both to parliament and government in a form of collective ownership. Parliamentary oversight here is the other side of the coin of accountability of the government to the parliament (Maunz and Dürig 2017, Art. 38, Para. 52). In contrast to this, in systems of 'separation of power', whilst depending on many external factors (such as strong political party control from outside the legislature), parliaments have a bigger interest in developing a strong, punitive, ex-post parliamentary oversight over the executive, since the government is not sustained in parliament and the fates of the legislature and the executive are not intertwined as they are in parliamentary systems of fusion of powers.

Whilst the EU's political structure started off as one of separation of power, and formally still is in many aspects, several recent developments have pushed it more on the way towards a parliamentary system of fusion of power. The increasing parliamentarisation of the EU decision-making process has first heralded these changes. But most prominently, the process through which the Juncker Commission was put in place established an unprecedented political link between the Parliament and the Commission, shifting the EU political accountability system to a 'parliament-oriented' one, where a parliamentary majority is seen as the source of legitimacy for the government (Verhey 2009, 59–60). The Spitzenkandidaten process contributed to creating a stronger link and a greater mutual dependency between the Parliament and the Commission, to enhancing the political role of the Commission and to generating greater self-confidence in its legislative programme.[18] Besides the constituing process of the Commission, including the Spitzenkandidaten process, but also the process of the Commissioners-designate hearings before parliamentary committees, the belonging of the Commissioners to the different political families in the EP as well as the consensual way of

---

[18] See on the Spitzenkandidaten-process and its consequences for the institutional balance particularly M. Westlake, Cronicle of an Election Foretold: the longer-term trends leading to the 'Spitzenkandidaten'procedure and the election of Jean-Claude Juncker as European Commission President, LSE Europe in Question Discussion Paper Series, N 102, January 2016; T. Christiansen, EU-Spitzenkandidaten-neue Impulse und ihre Folgen für das politische System der EU, in *Integration 1/2015*, pp. 25 et seq.; S. Hobolt, "A vote for the President? The role of Spitzenkandidaten in the 2014 European Parliament elections", *Journal of European Public Policy*, 2014, Vol. 20, Issue 10, pp. 1528–1540; H. Schmitt, S.B. Hobolt, S. A. Popa, "Spitzenkandidaten" in the 2014 European Parliament Election: Does Campaign Personalization Increase the Propensity to Turn Out?, *ECPR General Conference*, September 2014; J. A. Emmanouilidis, The beginning of a new political cycle: the results and consequences of a nomination summit, European Policy Centre, June 2014.

decision finding at EU level (Lindberg and Scheingold 1970; Lijphart 2012, 40–45) have also led to the emergence of forms of steering scrutiny to complement classic control instruments vis-à-vis the Commission, as well as vis-à-vis other executive actors.

3.3   Quality of Accountability

Accountability mechanisms often focus on sanctions. In this context, Verhey rightly distinguishes 'being accountable, calling to account and holding to account' and concludes that most parliamentary oversight focuses on the latter (Verhey 2009, 68). Indeed, even if without effective sanctions there is no real accountability, the punitive aspects of parliamentary oversight need to be complemented with a constructive learning process analysing what went wrong and why, as well as how such mistakes could be avoided in future, strengthening the quality of the account in this way (ibid.).

4   Emergence of 'Steering' Oversight

As the previous paragraphs have shown, the EU governance system has undergone gradual change. Whilst calls for a shift in attention towards instruments of 'steering' oversight have long been voiced to compensate the limited powers of the Parliament to make legislative proposals, the new institutional dynamics between the Parliament and 'its' Commission have intensified the use of 'steering' scrutiny instruments, allowing the Parliament to more effectively shape the EU political and legislative agenda.

4.1   Monitoring the Implementation of Political Priorities and Legislative Programming

Whilst the Commission holds the monopoly to formally propose legislation, it 'shall initiate the Union's annual and multiannual programming with a view to achieving inter-institutional agreement' (article 17(1)5 TEU). Under the 2010 Framework Agreement on relations between the EP and the European Commission (EP-EC Framework Agreement), the Commission must take into account the priorities expressed by Parliament and justify any departure from the proposals set out in the Commission Work Programme (CWP). In this way, the Parliament's contribution to shaping the CWP results in a greater political influence on the legislative initiatives to be submitted by the Commission.

The adoption of the annual CWP is embedded in a structured dialogue between the Commission and the corresponding parliamentary committees during the first semester of any given year. This ensures the effective monitoring of the implementation of the current CWP and the feeding in of the implementation results into the preparation of the next CWP. Parallel to the dialogue at committee level, the Parliament's Conference of Committee Chairs holds a regular exchange of views with the Vice-President of the Commission responsible for inter-institutional relations. Based on this exchange, the Conference of Presidents (of the political groups) prepares a summary report on the implementation of the CWP. Thereafter, Parliament adopts a resolution at its July part-session (Rule 37 EP Rules of Procedure), outlining its position, including particular requests based on legislative initiative reports under article 225 TFEU.

Also the delivery of the Commission President's State of the Union speech to the EP is part of the accountability exercise surrounding the adoption of the CWP. Each year in the first EP part-session of September, the Commission President uses the State of the Union debate in Parliament to take stock of the current year and to look ahead to priorities for the next year, the latter inspiring the new CWP. The Commission President's State of the Union address does not only serve transparency and communication goals. It also constitutes an important instrument of ex-ante accountability to the EP (Poptcheva 2015, 3). The debates on the State of the Union are an important venue for Parliament to shape, together with the Commission and the Council, the Union's political and legislative agenda, providing it with the possibility to actively participate in political programming. In this sense, the State of the Union debate in Parliament seeks to render the process of forming political priorities for the EU more transparent and indeed more political by making them subject to parliamentary debate and inter-institutional negotiations—as prescribed in article 17(1)5 TEU—instead of mere technocratic, or even political, but non-transparent bargaining. The 2010 EP-EC Framework Agreement reformed the adoption process of the Commission's Work Programme to ensure it being preceded by discussions on the Union's political priorities. This new deliberation process, therefore, adds to the quality of executive political accountability, in an attempt to remedy perceived flaws in the democratic legitimacy of the EU decision-making process (ibid., 4). After the State of the Union debate, the Parliament continues dialogue with Commissioners responsible for relevant policy areas, to ensure that Parliament's priorities are duly respected within the Work Programme.

Another step was recently added to this process to reflect the commitment of the three institutions to agree on major political priorities that, without prejudice to the powers conferred on the co-legislators by the Treaties, should receive priority treatment in the legislative process. For the first time in 2016, a Joint Declaration on annual inter-institutional programming was therefore adopted by the three institutions as foreseen in the 2016 Better Law-Making Agreement (article 7). Another one followed in December 2017 for the rest of the parliamentary term. This lists legislative proposals from the European Commission on which the three institutions commit to make progress in the coming year.

4.2   Review of Commission Impact Assessments and Ex-Post Evaluations

A further steering accountability instrument takes the form of ex-ante, mid-term, and ex-post evaluations of legislation and of the impact of its implementation. Evaluations contribute to learning effects and transparency (Stern 2009, 71). They constitute an important element of the legislative cycle, ensuring efficient and analysis-based legislation, implementation and scrutiny. Whilst evaluations are traditionally undertaken by the executives, experts have called for parliaments, and the EP in particular, to increase their ability to conduct evaluations to gain an own perspective on legislative and implementing measures under consideration (ibid., 82). This seems all the more true since impact assessments and ex-post evaluations are a tool for political actors to make well-informed choices, which should not substitute political decision-taking itself as is recognised in the 2016 Better Law-Making Agreement (article 12 (2)).

The European Commission has committed to carry out impact assessments of its legislative and non-legislative initiatives as well as delegated and implementing acts, which are expected to have significant economic, environmental or social impact, and for all initiatives included into the CWP or the Joint Declaration on annual programming (article 13 Better Law-Making Agreement). The lack of user-friendliness of the Commission's impact assessments in the past and the criticism that these often merely focused on justifying the Commission's preferred option (Court of

Auditors 2010)[19] led Parliament to improve its own systematic review capabilities to scrutinise the Commission's impact assessments. Within the Parliament, the Ex-ante Impact Assessment Unit of Directorate-General European Parliamentary Research Services (DG EPRS) provides critical appraisals of those impact assessments to Parliament's committees since 2012, to inform and facilitate deliberations.

Impact assessment work should ideally take into account any existing ex-post or mid-term evaluations before new legislative proposals are made. This is in principle guaranteed by the inclusion of 'review clauses' in legislation, which ensure that legislation is correctly implemented and that implementation is properly monitored in order for the evaluation results to inform the revision of the legislation and its implementation, which in turn improves the legislative planning and agenda-setting.

Furthermore, whenever a new proposal to update existing EU legislation is foreseen in the CWP, 'Implementation Appraisals' of the legislation in question are prepared within the Parliament's administration by the Ex-post Evaluation Unit of DG EPRS, mainly on the basis of publicly available material. These appraisals are delivered to the relevant parliamentary committee in advance of their consideration of the proposal in question. They include outcome of the Commission consultation, European Court of Auditors' performance appraisals, as well as policy papers or studies by National Parliaments, regional executives, the Committee of the Regions and the Economic and Social Committee.

4.3 Implementation Reports

Implementation reports constitute an important instrument of steering scrutiny. They aim at informing Parliament about the transposition of EU legislation into national law as well as the state of implementation and enforcement of the Treaties and other Union legislation, soft law instruments, and international agreements in force or subject to provisional application.[20] Implementation reports reveal deficiencies in member states

---

[19] Court of Auditors (2010), Impact assessments in the EU institutions: Do they support decision-making?, Special Report No. 3; European Parliament resolution of 8 June 2011 on guaranteeing independent impact assessments (2010/2016(INI)).

[20] Decision of the Conference of Presidents of 12 December 2002, last amendment July 2016, Procedure for granting authorisation to draw up own-initiative reports.

concerning the enforcement of EU law as well as the failure of European institutions to provide remedies for correct implementation. This type of report was first introduced in 2008 as a subcategory of Parliament's own-initiative reports. Due to their relevance for Parliament's scrutiny, they are now exempt from the ceiling for own-initiative reports, so that committees can decide to draft implementation reports at any time.

Implementation reports consist of an explanatory statement, in which the rapporteur describes the case analysed and sets out their findings on the state of implementation. They moreover include a motion for resolution indicating the main conclusions and concrete recommendations for actions to be taken. Parliamentary committees also benefit from a substantive analysis of the implementation issues and experience, in the form of a 'European Implementation Assessment' produced automatically by the Ex-post Evaluation Union of DG EPRS.

During the seventh parliamentary term (2009–2014), 23 implementation reports were adopted on a large spectrum of EU legislation and policy, such as on the implementation of the Professional Qualifications Directive. In the current (eighth) parliamentary term, 35 implementation reports (some of which being annual implementation and monitoring reports) had been adopted by February 2018, amongst others on the EU Youth Guarantee Scheme's cost-effectiveness and on the Energy Efficiency Directive. This type of reports considerably outnumbered those adopted during the same period of the previous mandate. The number has been rising because of the greater interest of committees in undertaking such work and the greater administrative support available for it.

5   Conclusions and Outlook

Steering scrutiny can certainly not replace meaningful punitive parliamentary control. It can, however, strengthen classic scrutiny instruments by creating an information base for their effective deployment. In this way, the boundaries between steering oversight and agenda-setting become blurred, as is increasingly the case for the different phases of the legislative cycle. Their formal distinction has hence become less relevant, given that parliamentary control in the meantime forms an intrinsic part of each and every parliamentary decision-making (Krebs 1984, 122).

The competition between several actors at both the agenda-setting and implementation stages of EU legislation makes it necessary for the different political actors involved, and hence also for the EP, to use their say on legislative and policy programming to insert the insights of their respective scrutiny exercises. The increasingly stronger political link between the Parliament and the Commission also justifies an increased effort on Parliament's side to constructively shape future policy and legislative action based on implementation results. This trend can be also observed within classic scrutiny instruments such as special and inquiry committees, whose reports focus not on blame allocation, but rather on identifying policy and legislative recommendations to address the shortcomings in question (Poptcheva 2016, 13–16).

A persisting challenge facing any type of scrutiny remains the co-existence of numerous executive actors at the different levels of EU multi-level decision-making, which often seek to deliberately escape parliamentary control. Whether steering oversight instruments could become a useful tool to compensate for such a diffusion of executive actors in the near future remains to be seen.

REFERENCES

Alexandrova, P. (2015). *Analysis of Agenda Setting in the European Council, 2009–2014.* Study for the European Parliamentary Research Service, European Council Oversight Unit, Brussels.

Andersen, S., & Burns, T. (1996). The European Union and the Erosion of Parliamentary Democracy: A Study of Post-Parliamentary Governance. In S. Andersen & K. Eliassen (Eds.), *The European Union: How Democratic Is It?* (pp. 227–251). London: Sage.

Bartolini, S. (2006). Should the Union be 'Politicised'? Prospects and Risks. In Simon Hix and Stefano Bartolini, (Eds.), *Politics: The Right or the Wrong Sort of Medicine for the EU?* (pp. 28–50). Notre Europe Policy Papers, No. 19.

Bradley, K. (1997). The European Parliament and Comitology: On the Road to Nowhere? *European Law Journal, 3*(3), 230–254.

Bradley, K. (2008). Halfway House: The 2006 Comitology Reforms and the European Parliament. *West European Politics, 31*(3), 837–854.

Brandsma, G. J. (2013). *Controlling Comitology Accountability in a Multi-Level System.* Basingstoke: Palgrave Macmillan.

Corbett, R., Jacobs, F., & Neville, D. (2016). *The European Parliament* (9th ed.). John Harper Publishing.

Dann, P. (2006). The Political Institutions. In A. von Bogdandy & J. Bast (Eds.), *Principles of European Constitutional Law* (1st ed., pp. 229–279). Hart.

De Schoutheete, Ph., & Micossi, S. (2013). On Political Union in Europe: The Changing Landscape of Decision-Making and Political Accountability. CEPS Essay No. 4/21, February.

Eggermont, F. (2012). *The Changing Role of the European Council in the Institutional Framework of the European Union*. Cambridge: Intersentia METRO.

Fabbrini, F. (2016). *Economic Governance in Europe. Comparative Paradoxes and Constitutional Challenges*. Oxford: Oxford University Press.

Fabbrini, S. (2013). Intergovernmentalism and Its Limits: Assessing the European Union's Answer to the Euro Crisis. *Comparative Political Studies, 46*(9), 1003–1029.

Fabbrini, S. (2017, May 4). *The Dual Executive of the European Union: A Comparative Federalism's Approach*. EUSA Biennal Conference, Miami.

Fasone, C. (2014). European Economic Governance and Parliamentary Representation. What Place for the European Parliament? *European Law Journal, 20*(2), 164–185.

Follesdal, A., & Hix, S. (2006). Why There Is a Democratic Deficit in the EU: A Response to Majone and Moravcsik. *Journal for Common Market Studies (JCMS), 44*(3), 533–562.

Freixes, T. (2013). Multilevel Constitutionalism and Federalism Reflections Upon the Congress on "The Path to Federalism in the State of Autonomies". In *The Ways of Federalism in Western Countries and the Horizons of Territorial Autonomy in Spain* (pp. 61–72) Volume I/coord. por Alberto López Basaguren, Leire Escajedo San Epifani.

Grabbe, H., & Lehne, S. (2013). The 2014 European Elections: Why a Partisan Commission President Would be Bad for the EU. Centre for European Reform.

Hix, S. (2006). Why the EU Needs (Left-Right) Politics? Policy Reform and Accountability Are Impossible Without It, in Politics: The Right or the Wrong Sort of Medicine for the EU? Notre Europe, Policy paper no. 19. Two papers by Simon Hix and Stefano Bartolini.

Isensee, J., & Kirchhof, P. (2005). *Handbuch des Staatsrechts der Bundesrepublik Deutschland, Band III Demokratie-Bundesorgane*. Heidelberg: C.F. Mueller Verlag.

Kaeding, M., & Hardacre, A. (2013). The European Parliament and the Future of Comitology After Lisbon. *European Law Journal: Review of European Law in Context, 19*(3), 382–403.

Klein, H. H. (2005). Stellung und Aufgaben des Bundestags. In J. Isensee & P. Kirchhof (Eds.), *Handbuch des Staatsrechts*, Band III Demokratie-Bundesorgane. Heidelberg: Müller Jur. Ver.

Krebs, W. (1984). Kontrolle in staatlichen Entscheidungsprozessen, Ein Beitrag zur rechtlichen Analyse von gerichtlichen, parlamentarischen und Rechnungshof-Kontrollen. Münsterer Beiträge zum Öffentlichen Recht, Bd. 3.

Lijphart, A. (2012). *Patterns of Democracy, Government Forms and Performance in Thirty-Six Countries* (2nd ed.). London: Yale University Press.

Lindberg, L. N., & Scheingold, S. A. (1970). *Europe's Would-be Polity: Patterns of Change in the European Community*. Englewood Cliffs, NJ: Prentice-Hall.

Lodge, J. (1994). The European Parliament and the Authority-Democracy Crisis. *Annals of the American Academy of Political and Social Science, 531,* 69–83.

Majone, G. (1994). The Rise of the Regulatory State in Europe. *West European Politics, 17*(3), 77–101; The Credibility Crisis of Community Regulation. *Journal of Common Market Studies, 38*(2) (2000, June), 273–302.

Majone, G. (2000). The Credibility Crisis of Community Regulation. *Journal for Common Market Studies, 38*(2), 273–302.

Maunz, T., & Dürig, G. (2017). *Grundgesetz-Kommentar,* 81. EL September 2017.

Pernice, I. (2009). The Treaty of Lisbon: Multilevel Constitutionalism in Action. *Columbia Journal of European Law, 15*(3), 349–407.

Pernice, I. (2015). Multilevel Constitutionalism and the Crisis of Democracy in Europe. *European Constitutional Law Review, 11*(3), 541–562.

Peters, A. (2011). Soft Law as a New Model of Governance. In U. Diedrichs, W. Reiners, & W. Wessels (Eds.), *The Dynamics of Change in EU Governance* (pp. 21–51). Cheltenham: Edward Elgar.

Ponzano, P., Hermanin, C., & Corona, D. (2012). *The Power of Initiative of the European Commission: A Progressive Erosion?* Paris: Notre Europe.

Poptcheva, E.-M. (2015). *The State of the Union Debate in the European Parliament.* Brussels: European Parliamentary Research Service.

Poptcheva, E.-M. (2016). *Parliament's Committees of Inquiry and Special Committees.* Brussels: European Parliamentary Research Service.

Proksch, S. O., & Slapin, J. B. (2011). Parliamentary Questions and Oversight in the European Union. *European Journal of Political Research, 50,* 53–79.

Raunio, T. (1996). Parliamentary Questions in the European Parliament: Representation, Information and Control. *Journal of Legislative Studies, 2*(4), 356–382.

Raunio, T. (1999). Always One Step Behind? National Legislatures and the European Union. *Government and Opposition, 34,* 180–202.

Schmidt, J. (2007). *Die demokratische Legitimationsfunktion der parlamentarischen Kontrolle: eine verfassungsrechtliche Untersuchung über Grundlage, Gegenstand und Grenzen der parlamentarischen Kontrolle unter besonderer Berücksichtigung der ministerialfreien Räume und der Privatisierung, in Schriften zum Öffentlichen Recht,* Band 1064. Berlin: Duncker & Humblot.

Stern, E. (2009). Evaluation Policy in the European Union and its Institutions. Evaluation Policy and Evaluation Practice. *New Directions for Evaluation, 123,* 71.

Syrier, C. (2013). *The Investigative Function of the European Parliament: Holding the EU Executive to Account by Conducting Investigations.* Oisterwijk: Wolf Legal Publishers.

Tans, O., Carla Zoethout, C., & Peters, J. (2007). *National Parliaments and European Democracy. A Bottom-Up Approach to European Constitutionalism.* Groningen: Europa Law Publishing.

Teasdale, A., & Bainbridge, T. (2012). *The Penguin Companion to European Union, Additional Web Entry on Censure Motion.* London: Penguin Books.

Tribe, L. (1988). *American Constitutional Law*, University Treatise Series.

Tusk, D. (2017, October 17). *Letter to the Heads of State and Government.* Press Release 593/17.

Van Rompuy, H. (2010). Communiqué de Herman Van Rompuy, président du Conseil européen, à la suite de la réunion du groupe de travail sur la gouvernance économique, PCE 161/10, Brussels, July 12.

Vanden Broucke, J., De Finance, S., & Poptcheva, E.-M. (2015). *The European Council and Its President.* Brussels: European Parliamentary Research Service.

Verhey, L. (2009). Political Accountability: A Useful Concept. In L. Verhey, P. Kiiver, & S. Loeffen (Eds.), *EU Inter-Institutional Relations? Political Accountability and European Integration.* Groningen: Europa Law Publishing.

Welle, K. (2016). Strategic Planning for the Secretariat–General of the European Parliament. Brussels.

Wessels, W. (2016). *The European Council.* New York: Palgrave.

CHAPTER 3

The European Parliament and the European Council: A Shift in the Balance of Power?

Johannes Müller Gómez, Wolfgang Wessels,
and Johannes Wolters

1   INTRODUCTION: RIVALRY AND PARTNERSHIP BETWEEN 'THE PRIMARY POLES OF POWER'

In the evolution of the institutional architecture of the European Union (EU), the relationship between the European Parliament (EP) and the European Council (EUCO) is of specific importance—for political actors as well as for academic observers. Both institutions represent opposing poles in the constitutional system, with each institution claiming its own specific democratic legitimacy. While the EP is the sole institution whose members are directly elected by European citizens, members of the EUCO

J. Müller Gómez (✉)
Université de Montréal, Montreal, QC, Canada

Ludwig-Maximilians-Universität München, Munich, Germany
e-mail: johannes.muller.gomez@umontreal.ca

W. Wessels • J. Wolters
Universität zu Köln, Cologne, Germany
e-mail: wessels@uni-koeln.de; j.wolters@uni-koeln.de

© The Author(s) 2019   53
O. Costa (ed.), *The European Parliament in Times of EU Crisis*,
European Administrative Governance,
https://doi.org/10.1007/978-3-319-97391-3_3

draw upon the highest democratic legitimacy from the national level as heads of the respective states or governments (Van Middelaar 2013, 285; see Document 1).

Document 1 Democratic representation in the EU's system
Citizens are directly represented at Union level in the European Parliament.
Member States are represented in the European Council by their Heads of State or Government and in the Council by their governments, themselves democratically accountable either to their national Parliaments, or to their citizens. (article 10 (2) TEU)

From a theoretical perspective, the two institutions are often considered the ideal types of an intergovernmental and a supranational-federal institution, respectively. Their relationship may thus be interpreted as a tension of the theoretical dichotomy of supranationalism and intergovernmentalism. Hence, a main point of departure of this chapter is an inbuilt rivalry in the balance of power between the EUCO and the EP, which, yet, has remained an under-theorized aspect of the EU's political system. The entry into force of the Lisbon Treaty in December 2009 changed the legal basis of both the EUCO and the EP. The treaty revision reinforced both institutions, which are now perceived as 'the primary poles of power in the post-Lisbon institutional system' (Monar 2011, 86).

A de jure and de facto need for cooperation among these institutions in relevant treaty provisions serves as a second point of departure.

On the one hand, the treaties stipulate only a few instances at which the EUCO and the EP have to cooperate. The most relevant examples are the investiture procedure of the Commission President (article 17 (7) TEU) and the application of the so-called passarelle clause (article 48 (7) TEU).

On the other hand, the EUCO often acts beyond or besides legal treaty provisions. As a consequence, tensions between the two institutions have manifested themselves in various situations of indirect and direct confrontation. The relationship between the institutions is often characterized by a lack of mutual trust. The members of both institutions appear to lack a spirit of co-operation. Members of the EUCO do not—in most cases— seem to consider the EP as a serious player to be reckoned with, despite its formal legislative powers (de Schoutheete 2017). In addition, exercising its pre-constitutional as well as pre-legislative functions, the EUCO finds itself frequently in a kind of indirect competition with the EP in framing dominant positions and doctrines when it comes to system- and policy-making. The EP is concerned that its treaty powers are eroded every time the EUCO's de facto decisions pre-empt the formal decision-making within the institutional triangle of the ordinary legislative procedure. Hence, members of the EP have regularly and openly criticized the heads of states or governments when they felt that political leaders of the member states have circumvented the Parliament or gone beyond the actual treaty wording. The EP has repeatedly voiced opposition to the increase in intergovernmental agreements of the EUCO, in particular in the course of the Euro crisis. Former EP President Schulz (2012) argued that '[t]he plethora of summits is severely diminishing the part played by the only directly elected Community institution, the European Parliament. The publics are responding to this lack of parliamentary legitimacy by viewing political decisions taken by their leaders as nothing more than a series of dictates from Brussels.'

Overall, interinstitutional relations between the EP and the EUCO are increasingly characterized both by the need for partnership and cooperation in some instances and at the same time by some strong and significant inbuilt rivalries and tensions. Against this background, this chapter analyses the balance of power between the EP and the EUCO, which represents a key conflict in the EU's institutional architecture. The objective of this chapter is threefold. First, we intend to provide a theoretical approach to both the academic analysis and the political discussion of EP-EUCO relations. How can we depict the interinstitutional balance of power from a theoretical perspective? Second, we seek to grasp the actual positions of the EUCO and the EP within the EU's institutional architecture as well as vis-à-vis each other. To what extent has a shift taken place in the institutional balance with the entry into force of the Lisbon Treaty? Third, this chapter aims to identify recurrent patterns regarding the institutional balance between the Parliament and the EUCO. Which conditions may lead to the predominance of one or the other institution?

To answer these questions, we will start by developing three ideal types of interinstitutional relations: the 'Union of Sovereign States model', the 'Federal model' and the 'Cooperation model'. We will then examine systematic trends and patterns by looking into the EU's treaty architecture and by studying three case studies which are representative of different legal constellations: the management of the Euro crisis, the introduction of *Spitzenkandidaten* for the post of the Commission President and the adoption of the EU's own resources and the multiannual financial framework (MFF). Our empirical evidence shows a large variance of interinstitutional power relations. Based on our analysis, we identify three core determinants of concrete EP-EUCO power relations: the internal political coherence of each institution, the treaty provisions and the degree of urgency. These preliminary findings shall serve as a guide for future research.

2   THREE MODELS OF INTERINSTITUTIONAL BALANCE

In this section, we develop three models of interinterinstitutional relations between the EP and the EUCO, which we base on three competing theories of European integration, namely, (neo-)intergovernmentalism, (neo-)federalism and the Fusion thesis.[1]

2.1   The 'Union of Sovereign States' Model: The EUCO as the (Dominant) Key Institution

From an intergovernmentalist perspective (Puetter 2014; Schimmelfennig 2004; Moravcsik 1993; Hoffmann 1966) the national chief executives of the EU member states are the key players in the EU's institutional architecture—in accordance with de Gaulle's credo of 'l'Europe des patries' (de Gaulle 1962, in: de Gaulle 1970). The heads of state or government can be regarded as rational actors who are eager to pursue and impose their respective national interests.

Following the German Federal Constitutional Court's description of the EU as a 'Staatenverbund' (Bundesverfassungsgericht 1993), we dub our first ideal type the 'Union of Sovereign States model'. Here, the EUCO represents the central institution which takes all major decisions. As the body of national leaders, the EUCO should not be subject to any legal constraints and the EU's system of checks and balances. From this perspective, 'Montesquieu did not make it to Brussels' (von Donat 1987, 161). Notwithstanding the primary law's legal language of the Lisbon Treaty, the EUCO is held to be the key locus of power in the EU, exercising the prerogatives of leadership. As the institution is set at the top of the

---

[1] For a similar approach, see Reiners and Wessels (2011).

institutional hierarchy of the EU's architecture, the EUCO can be regarded in this model as the 'principal' (see: Kassim and Menon 2003; Pollack 2003; Moravcsik 1993) vis-à-vis other institutions, which in turn serve as 'agents' of the political leaders, thus disposing merely of a derived form of legitimacy.

Even though the EP can hardly be regarded as a simple agent of the EU's member states, from this perspective it has only a very limited room for manoeuvre. First, it acts within the strict and specific guidelines determined by the heads of state or government and codified in the treaties. Second, the EUCO directly interferes in EU policy-making and eludes the EP and the Council if necessary. Besides, this model implies that the EP does not possess full parliamentary legitimacy despite its label (Bundesverfassungsgericht 1993). Therefore, according to this model, the assembly of parliamentarians is no rival to the EUCO, but merely serves as a forum for exchanging positions, being eventually irrelevant when it comes to making vital decisions in, for and on the EU.

2.2   The Federal Model: The EP as the (Dominant) Key Institution

On the opposite side to the intergovernmental model, we find the federalist perception of EU politics (see Burgess 2004; Pinder 1986). From what we dub the 'Federal model', the EU has been evolving towards a state-like federal system, with the *United States of Europe* being the *finalité* of the integration process (Grimmel and Jakobeit 2009, 23).

This approach considers the EP as the key EU institution. It acts as the direct representation of the Union's citizens and provides the EU's principal basis of legitimacy. Consequently, from such a perspective, the EP must possess extensive competencies and can be understood as the dominant decision-making body. Besides its legal empowerment, the EP applies the 'creeping competences' strategy (for the term: Pollack 1994). It generously interprets the often vaguely formulated treaty provisions to further strengthen its position among the EU institutions. As a result, the EP decisively shapes the EU's political agenda and has a strong or even the final saying in EU policy-making and in the appointment of the EU's relevant office-holders.

Based on this model, the EUCO would function as a forum in which the national governments deliberate and coordinate their interests, and as a kind of collective presidency which is left with some formal and ceremonial tasks. It acts in the background and does not interfere in policy-making procedures, which follow the logic of a bi-cameral system, with the EP being the primary chamber. The community method and the ordinary legislative procedure represent the 'centre of the institutional interplay' (Reiners and Wessels 2011, 45), which implies that the Parliament can formally shape the Union's politics on an equal footing with the Council, and de facto successfully get its position through.

2.3   The Cooperation Model: A Fusion of Powers

The Fusion thesis (Wessels 2016, 18–20; Wessels 1992) regards the EUCO as the centrally located and pivotal player in both a vertical multi-level constellation and a horizontal multi-institutional architecture of the EU system. The main impact of the EUCO can be described and analysed as a process of 'vertical' and 'horizontal fusion' (for the terms, see Tanil 2012; Miles 2011; Mittag 2011; Wessels 2010).

Within the multilevel game, each head of state or government wears 'two hats', as the members of the EUCO act both within the national and the European arena. In this vertical direction, the heads of state or government merge domestic and European agendas and pool national and EU instruments. As a consequence, the EUCO sets a state-like agenda for the Union that covers a broad range of public policies. In a horizontal direction, the EUCO is increasingly forced to co-act with other EU institutions which cannot be simply circumvented.

Thus, in contrast to the intergovernmental and the federal perspectives, the 'Cooperation model' sees a direct interaction between the EUCO and the EP and considers cooperation of both institutions necessary and of increasing relevance. Decisions can only be taken through collaboration and by mutual consent. Both institutions depend on each other and cannot act single-handedly. Office-holders, such as the Commission President, are selected jointly and policy-making outcomes represent compromises of the EP's and the EUCO's positions.

2.4   Summary

The three models of interinstitutional balance between the EUCO and the EP grasp three different perspectives on the interaction of the two institutions, their respective role in the institutional architecture and the main mode of decision-making (see Table 3.1).

Table 3.1 Models of interinstitutional balance

	Union of Sovereign States model	*Federal model*	*Cooperation model*
Key institution/ principal	European Council	European Parliament	Interaction between European Parliament and European Council
Central logic	Intergovernmental method	Federalism/ Parliamentarism	Joint decision-making/ horizontal fusion
Institution serving as a forum	European Parliament	European Council	n/a

Source: Authors' illustration

We underline that we do not expect one model to generally dominate the interplay between the EP and the EUCO. These three perspectives are not mutually exclusive and vary depending on the policy field and the issue at stake.

3   ANALYTICAL APPROACH AND CASE SELECTION

Research on the EUCO suffers from the relatively scarce data disclosed on the internal workings of this key institution: Scholars must build far and foremost on EUCO Conclusions, leaving room for interpretation on the positions of heads of state or government within the EUCO. To grasp the institutional balance between the EUCO and the EP and to uncover the complex and ambiguous workings of the key institutions of the EU in a post-Lisbon perspective, this analysis needs to build on a qualitative case study approach. Despite its limitations (Gerring 2007), this method fits the inductive and explorative purpose of this chapter.

Since the aim is to grasp the diversity in EP-EUCO relations after the entry into force of the Lisbon Treaty, the observation period is limited. Moreover, cases of direct interaction between the EP and the EUCO are rare. We identified three cases of interinstitutional conflict or interaction based on ambiguous treaty provisions. These three distinctly different cases—the Euro crisis management, the (s)election of the Commission President and the negotiations of the MFF—represent particularities of the EU system.

First, the case of the Euro crisis as an 'existential challenge' (Fabbrini 2013) is of particular importance due to the central role of the crisis in EU policy-making throughout almost the entire period after the entry into force of the Lisbon Treaty. Crisis management can be expected to have had a direct effect on EP-EUCO relations, as it favours exceptional, hence extra-treaty measures which by nature fall outside of the EP's treaty competences. Besides the strong crisis momentum, the concerned policy area has seen the largest constitutional evolution and transfer of competences.

Second, in contrast to the crisis momentum, with respect to the (s)election of the Commission President, the treaties clearly stipulate a close interaction of the Parliament and the EUCO: Taking into consideration the outcome of the European elections, the heads of state or government propose a candidate who then has to be elected by the Parliament (article 17 (7) TEU). The wording of the Lisbon Treaty left sufficient room for interpretation, opening the door for serious contestations between the two institutions in the wake of the 2014 EP elections, the first ones after the entry into force of the Lisbon Treaty.

Third, the negotiations of the MFF, determining the main categories of the expenditures of the EU budget, represent a double-edged example. On the one hand, the EUCO comes to bargain directly with the EP although the treaty provisions formally allocate this function to the Council (article 312 (2) TFEU). The current MFF covering the period from 2014 to 2020 was the first adopted under the new Lisbon provisions, which allocated the strong legal power of consent to the EP. On the other hand, the MFF is only adopted based on the decision regarding the EU's own resources, that is, the income side of the EU's budget, which is taken by the member states (article 311 TFEU) while granting the EP only a weak power of consultation.

4   CONSTITUTIONAL TRENDS: THE DEVELOPMENT OF THE LEGAL INTERINSTITUTIONAL POWER RELATIONS

One relevant element for understanding the relationship between the EUCO and the EP is a look at the evolution of the treaty articles which frame the EU's institutional architecture. Following the introduction of universal suffrage in 1979, the 'masters of the Treaties' (Bundesverfassungsgericht 2009), as the German Constitutional Courts dubbed the highest national leaders, have increased the EP's competences with each treaty revision. The ordinary legislative procedure and the procedure for the annual budget put the EP on an equal footing with the Council (article 14 (1) TEU). The Parliament's legislative powers have thus been reinforced and extended to more areas of competences since the 1990s (see Fig. 3.1).[2] Furthermore, the

---

[2] The columns represent the amount of treaty articles which stipulate the application of the respective decision-making procedure.

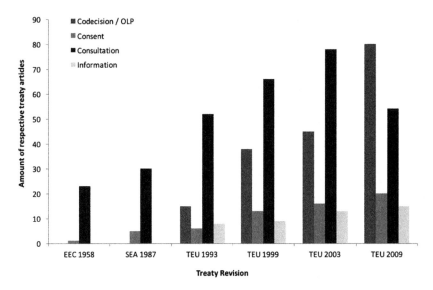

Fig. 3.1   Trends in the European Parliament's competences. Source: Authors' illustration, based on calculations by the Centre for Turkey and European Union Studies of the University of Cologne, 2018

Lisbon Treaty strengthened the EP's role regarding the appointment of the European Commission and its president (article 17 (7) TEU). Some scholars go as far as arguing that this remarkable growth in power and status has made the EP not only the 'winner' of all treaty reforms since Maastricht, but also 'one of the most powerful parliaments in the world' (Pollak and Slominski 2015, 245).

The EUCO, on the other hand, is relatively a newcomer to the original institutional architecture of the European polity. After a step-by-step evolution since its creation at the Paris Summit in 1974, the Lisbon Treaty introduced considerable legal changes and innovations in comparison to previous treaty formulations. In contrast to the EP, the EUCO 'shall not exercise legislative functions' (article 15 (1) TEU). Besides the EUCO's task to 'define general political directions and political priorities thereof' (article 15 (1) TEU), the EU treaties allocate concrete functions to the EUCO in specific policy fields, such as the Common Foreign and Security Policy (article 26 TEU), and in economic and employment affairs (article 121 TFEU). Furthermore, the heads of state or government select, nominate or appoint the personnel for relevant positions in the EU's architecture, such as the President of the European Commission (article 17 (6) TEU), the High Representative of the Union for Foreign Affairs and Security Policy (article 18 (1) TFEU) and the Executive Board of the European Central Bank (ECB) (article 283 (2) TFEU). Furthermore, articles 48, 49 and 50 TEU confirm the former de facto role of the EUCO as the key institution for system-making and system change, thus as the 'constitutional architect' (Wessels 2016, 161).

In sum, through legal innovations, member states have agreed via the Lisbon Treaty to share prerogatives with the EP more than ever before. A look into the trends of the EU's institutional architecture supports the impression that more than one model is needed for explaining the relationship between the EP and the EUCO.

5   EMPIRICAL PATTERNS: TOWARDS A NEW INSTITUTIONAL BALANCE?

In the following empirical analysis, we will attempt to assign each case to one of the three theoretical models. Furthermore, the case studies will help us infer general patterns and detect determinants of the interinstitutional relations between the EP and the EUCO.

5.1   Euro Crisis Management: The Moment of the Heads of State or Government

The Euro crisis has had a significant influence on the economic governance in the EU and, more specifically, in the Euro area. The institutions of the Economic and Monetary Union (EMU) conceived throughout the 1990s and the early 2000s, most notably the ECB, have—in the dichotomy of intergovernmentalism and federalism—fallen under the latter. However, the traditional supranational institutions, namely the European Commission and the EP, and the community method have played only a marginal role: major political decision-making was installed at the so-called Euro group of Euro area finance ministers as well as in the supranational, but politically independent, ECB.

5.1.1   System-Making in the Euro Crisis
When pressure from financial markets on European state bonds' interest rates peaked and the spread between Euro area countries' sovereign bond rates drastically widened, the heads of state or government faced tough decisions on how to proceed (Van Rompuy 2014, 16–38). While a financial

collapse of the most fragile members of the Euro area was widely seen as detrimental for the EMU, some leaders went as far as linking the future of the EMU to the future of the EU as a whole. To remedy some of the shortcomings of the legal framework of the EMU, EU leaders used the EUCO and the newly created Euro Summit. Here, leaders of Euro area member states on several occasions—usually in the early hours of the morning just before the opening of stock markets—acted as constitutional architects and changed treaty provisions on several occasions. In 2011, the EUCO adopted the *Decision amending the TFEU with regard to the setting up of the European Stability Mechanism (ESM)*. In March 2011, it laid down concrete formulations for the amendment of article 136 (3) TFEU. The leaders of the participating member states agreed on the text of the intergovernmental *Treaty establishing the European Stability Mechanism* in February 2012. Furthermore, rules to tighten fiscal discipline were introduced by the EUCO by means of the intergovernmental *Treaty on Stability, Coordination and Governance in the Economic and Monetary Union* (TSCG) in March 2012. The heads of state or government had to create the ESM and the TSCG outside the EU's primary law given the opposition by some member states. Consequently, the EP was only indirectly involved.

Why did the EUCO play such a major role during the *hottest* phases of the Euro crisis, particularly in comparison to the EP? First, executives and governments are generally the dominant actors in 'emergency and crisis politics': Member state governments, acting collectively in the EUCO, are the one actor that can declare the 'state of emergency' and thus shape the agenda (for a discussion of this argument see: White 2015). Second, the EP lacks the powers to mobilize a considerable amount of resources which would have been appropriate to stabilize the financial situation—the so-called *power of the purse*. Only national governments were able to rally sufficient financial leverage to enact both stimulus packages (Howell 2015) and bailout funds to counterweight the pressure from financial markets on crisis economies. In turn, national governments—headed by a very reluctant German government—were able to shape the TSCG and the bailout funds EFSF (European Financial Stability Facility) and ESM, the institutions that would enclose these financial commitments (Epstein and Rhodes 2016, 425; Chang 2013).

5.1.2   Rules for Policy-Making in and after the Euro Crisis

Notwithstanding the leading role of the EUCO and the Euro Summit for the management of the Euro crisis, the EU treaties enable the Parliament and the Council to legislate economic and fiscal surveillance mechanisms (article 121 (6) TFEU). From 2011, the EU enacted a series of legislative acts through ordinary or special legislative procedures, tightening the Stability and Growth Pact and the European Semester through the so-called Six-Pack and the Two-Pack legislative packages (Fasone 2014). Particularly, the Six-Pack legislative package reforms the Stability and Growth Pact by strengthening oversight over national budgets und introducing an early warning mechanism on fiscal imbalances: the Macroeconomic Imbalance Procedure. During the legislative process, the EP showed little internal coherence, allowing heads of state or government to pressure their respective party groups in the EP to accept Council and Commission positions (Bressanelli and Chelotti 2016, 519). EP amendments to the Commission's proposal to prevent strict mechanisms harming economic growth in member states impacted most by the crisis were eventually watered down. Both legislative packages foresee only a weak position for the EP, limited to a consultative role in the tightened national budgetary oversight procedures. Oversight now takes place within the European Semester as well as a socalled economic dialogue in the EP, allowing the Parliament's ECON committee to invite 'the President of the Council, the Commission and, where appropriate, the President of the European Council or the President of the Eurogroup' and the weak power to 'offer' member state officials 'the opportunity' to appear before the EP (article 3 of Regulation 1173/2011).

5.2   The Spitzenkandidaten Procedure: A Preliminary or a Sustainable Victory for the EP?

In 2014, European political parties nominated pan-European lead candidates for the post of the President of the European Commission. The basic idea shared by the majority of the members of the EP was that the candidate of the European party winning most seats in the Parliament would become Commission President. After the European People's Party received most votes in the 2014 European elections, the EP successfully imposed Jean-Claude Juncker as its candidate for the Presidency of the Commission upon the EUCO.

5.2.1   Legal Basis and First Application of the Spitzenkandidaten
Legally, the EP's involvement in the appointment of the Commission President and the Commission as a collegiate body had been constantly increased since the Treaties of Rome: 'The intention has thereby always

been to strike a balance between ensuring control of the Member States on the process and a democratization of the procedure via a stronger involvement of the European Parliament' (Nasshoven 2011, 83). The current provisions (see Document 2) are relevant in two respects: First, they clearly link the (s)election of the Commission President to the EP elections. Second, they underline that the power to elect the Commission President is assigned to the EP.

Document 2 The (s)election of the Commission President
Taking into account the elections to the European Parliament and after having held the appropriate consultations, the European Council, acting by a qualified majority, shall propose to the European Parliament a candidate for President of the Commission. This candidate shall be elected by the European Parliament by a majority of its component members. If he does not obtain the required majority, the European Council, acting by a qualified majority, shall within one month propose a new candidate who shall be elected by the European Parliament following the same procedure. (article 17 (7) TEU)

With the EUCO still having the formal prerogative for the nomination of a candidate for the Commission presidency, one reading of the article 17 (7) TEU is that the Lisbon provisions did not necessarily imply practical renovations or a loss of power of the EUCO. Yet, the new treaty wording induced the nomination of European lead candidates. By intensively supporting this new procedure, the EP aimed at strengthening its role vis-à-vis the heads of state or government and at de facto revoking the right to nominate a Commission President candidate from the member states.

The introduction of *Spitzenkandidaten* was highly controversial among the heads of state or government. Concretely, the German chancellor together with the Swedish and Dutch prime ministers only after some hesitation decided to vote in favour of the new Commission President Juncker. The Hungarian and British heads of government were eventually outvoted, which represented the first application of qualified majority voting (QMV) in the EUCO for the nomination of a candidate for a high-level position at the EU level. On the other hand, the EP's major political groups supported the *Spitzenkandidaten* system and managed to join forces to impose the winner of the European elections as the new Commission President.

By nominating and electing Jean-Claude Juncker, the EP interpreted the treaty provisions in an extensive way and asserted itself cleverly and successfully against the EUCO. At first sight, it might have set a decisive precedent (Hobolt 2014, 1537). Following the previous tradition of a generous interpretation of treaty provisions and playing the role of a 'creeping constitutional architect' (Nasshoven 2011, 94; see also Maurer and Wessels 2003), the EP again vigorously enhanced its position within the EU architecture (Müller Gómez and Wessels 2015).

5.2.2   A Sustainable Shift in the Institutional Balance?

In order to prevent the EUCO from taking steps back and in order to secure the *Spitzenkandidaten* system for future elections, the EP demanded the constitutionalizing of the procedure by amending the European Electoral Act (European Parliament 2015). However, the EP remains internally divided over this question. A relevant part of the political groups did not support the introduction of pan-European lead candidates in 2014 and do not back the parliamentary majority's claim to constitutionalize the *Spitzenkandidaten* procedure. This considerably weakens the EP's negotiation position vis-à-vis the member states. On the other hand, the EUCO has always considered the investiture of the European Commission and particularly of its president as highly relevant (Nasshoven 2011, 75–80). Consequently, despite the apparent victory of the EP in 2014, the heads of state or government have been reluctant to accept a definitive loss of power. In February 2018, the President of the EUCO, Donald Tusk, underlined on behalf of the heads of state or government of the EU-27 'the autonomous competence of the European Council to nominate the candidate' (Tusk 2018). Accordingly, the EUCO will most likely block the legal consolidation, an amendment of the European Electoral Act, which would require a unanimous vote in the Council.

5.3   Own Resources and the Multiannual Financial Framework: The Battle for the Power of the Purse

The power to determine the volume, revenue and the distribution of public financial resources is at the heart of every political system. The so-called *power of the purse* is generally regarded as the most important privilege of parliaments.

5.3.1   The Legal Basis: A Strong Role for the Council?

The adoption of the revenue and the MFF is divided into two steps. First, member states determine the overall size of the budget (see Document 3). In granting so-called own resources, that is the revenue side of the EU's budget, member states determine to what degree they choose to empower the Union 'to provide itself with the means necessary to attain its objectives and carry through its policies' (article 311 TFEU). The EP is only consulted at this stage and still lacks one of the core prerogatives of a parliament, that is to raise taxes.

Document 3 The EU's own resources

The Council, acting in accordance with a special legislative procedure, shall unanimously and after consulting the European Parliament adopt a decision laying down the provisions relating to the system of own resources of the Union. [...] That decision shall not enter into force until it is approved by the Member States in accordance with their respective constitutional requirements. (article 311 TFEU)

In a second step, national governments take decisions about the main categories of expenditure and their respective amounts on a multiannual basis through the MFF (article 312 TFEU). According to this article, the Council of the EU, 'acting in accordance with a special legislative procedure, shall adopt a regulation laying down the multiannual financial framework. The Council shall act unanimously after obtaining the consent of the European Parliament', which shall be given by 'a majority of its component members' (article 312 (2) TFEU). The Lisbon Treaty thus granted the EP a veto right over the MFF.

Despite the political significance of the own resources and the MFF, the EUCO is not mentioned in the relevant treaty articles. The financial provisions of the Lisbon TFEU (article 310–319 TFEU) do not include the EUCO in these formal procedures, except for one unlikely and exceptional case of 'authorising the Council to act by a qualified majority when adopting the regulation' of laying down the MFF (article 312 (2) TFEU).

5.3.2   The Real-World Practice: Sharing Responsibilities?

Since its creation, the EUCO has taken the main decisions on the EU's budget (Wessels 2016, 200–204). Despite the dominant role for the

Council of the EU vis-à-vis the EP foreseen by primary law and confirmed by the Lisbon Treaty, the EUCO has de facto taken up the *power of the purse* and forged consensus on the side of the member states. Once having secured an internal consensus, the EUCO tried to impose its line of negotiation upon the EP. In 2013, in spite of lengthy preparations, it took the EUCO a 'decisive 24 hour non-stop summit' to agree on the MFF 2014–2020 (Van Rompuy 2014, 77). The EUCO agreed upon a reduction of the size of the next MFF, strict categories of expenditures with only very limited room to manoeuvre for the annual budgets and a budget based primarily on national contributions following from the respective gross national income (see European Council 2013). However, the EP rejected the EUCO's pretence to be the decision-maker in the MFF negotiations and negotiated with the Council and the Commission. An interinstitutional agreement was reached in late June 2013 and eventually approved in December 2013 alongside the MFF regulation for the period 2014–2020 (European Parliament, Council of the European Union and European Commission 2013). Dialer et al. (2015, 251) note that the EP has 'successfully resisted the European Council's approach to take the European Council's political, legally non-binding conclusions as given'. In fact, by developing a tough and (internally) coherent negotiation mandate for the consent procedure in the second phase of the negotiations, the EP was able to push through a number of demands, most notably the right to shift resources unused in one year to the following years, the creation of a task force discussing the possibility of a system of genuine own resources (Monti et al. 2016) and a guaranteed mid-term review of the MFF at the end of 2016 (for a discussion of the mid-term review, see Becker 2016). Nonetheless, apart from the above-mentioned rights, the concessions made by the EUCO to the Parliament are rather of symbolic nature than a real victory of the EP.

6   DISCUSSION AND CONCLUSION: PATTERNS OF INSTITUTIONAL BALANCE

In looking at the formal provisions and three concrete situations of inter-institutional competition which serve as cases in point for the evolution of the institutional balance between the EUCO and the EP, this chapter aimed at shedding light on a complex, yet under-theorized aspect of the political system of the EU.

6.1 Variety of Interinstitutional Relations

Building on a set of three models grasping the roles of the EP and the EUCO within the EU system, the Union of Sovereign State model, the Federal model and the Cooperation model, it has been shown that the interinstitutional balance between the EUCO and the EP differs largely from one case to the other, with no balance of power model being predominant. Instead, the interinstitutional balance depends on the concrete circumstances (see Table 3.2).

First, the post-Lisbon trajectory of interinstitutional relations of the EP and the EUCO in EMU affairs has been dominated by the Euro crisis and subsequent institutional realignments. Following the conventional wisdom of an upgrading of the EP by the Lisbon Treaty and a downgrading by the reforms throughout the Euro crisis, the EP was very much sidelined in the immediate decision-making procedures. Generally, the Euro crisis has led to an affirmation of the Union of Sovereign States model and, thus, to a strengthening of the EUCO within the EU system. European leaders in the EUCO were faced with immediate pressure from financial markets and, after an initial period of inertia, took up the leadership in the form of a *gouvernement économique*. Furthermore, the EP only marginally contributed to further legislative acts which were enacted to prevent the emergence of new crises, in particular the Two-Pack and the Six-Pack legislation.

Second, even though a short-term observation of the 2014 parliamentary election indicated an evolution towards the Federal model in which the EP asserts itself against the member states, a mid-term perspective rather suggests a situation in which the EUCO and the EP are forced to

Table 3.2   Patterns of EP-EUCO relations

Case	EP with veto power	QMV possible	Cohesion of EUCO	Cohesion of EP	Urgency	Theoretical model
Euro crisis	No	No	No	Yes	Yes	Union of Sovereign States model
Spitzen-kandidaten	Yes	Yes	No	Yes	No	Federal model/ Cooperation model
MFF	Yes	No	Yes	Yes	No	Cooperation model/ Union of Sovereign States model

Source: Authors' illustration

act together with respect to the appointment procedure of the Commission President. After all, the EUCO still holds the formal right to propose the President of the Commission. Such a development would be in line with the Cooperation model. Hence, we see a mixed picture: Although the EP was able to push through its candidate in the wake of the 2014 elections, the EUCO has not backed its claim to codify the *Spitzenkandidaten* procedure for future cases. What is more, it remains unclear whether the EP itself will be able to develop a coherent approach after the 2019 parliamentary elections.

Third, the MFF is an area where political agreement between the member states and the EP is required by the Lisbon Treaty. Given the legal power of consent which the TFEU now allocates to the EP through the special legislative procedure and in view of the power of the purse which the governmental heads have de facto taken up, increased conflicts between both institutions with respect to the distribution of the Union's budget in the MFF are unavoidably built in to the process. At first sight, the finding that the EUCO and the EP had to collaborate at eye level supports the Cooperation model, that is a fusion of responsibilities. Nevertheless, one has to take the broader picture into consideration in order to understand the effective institutional balance at play: As long as the system of own resources follows almost entirely an intergovernmental logic—and is thus shaped by the EUCO (Becker 2014)—negotiations to the MFF will be of mere secondary importance. In this light, the recent proposals launched by the EP to create an own fiscal capacity for the Euro area as well as a shift to a system of genuine own resources (European Parliament 2017) have to be interpreted as the EP's call to overcome the persisting governments' dominance in this area.

What broader implications can be drawn from these findings? First, the EP has indeed evolved into a strong body with comprehensive competencies. Besides its legal rights as co-legislator, it has always been a strategic actor that deliberately exploits treaty provisions. It has fostered its de facto role in the EU's institutional architecture by extensively interpreting its primary law-based functions; the *Spitzenkandidaten* innovation is only one concrete post-Lisbon example of this recurring method. Second, the role of the EUCO can nevertheless not be regarded high enough: The role assumed by the EUCO in the Euro crisis management and in the EU's economic governance in general confirms the willingness and capacity of the heads of state or government to take the lead when necessary. Third, the legal provisions of the Lisbon Treaty as well as real-world practice confirm a considerable, but still limited, move towards an uneasy sharing of powers. This can be interpreted as a horizontal fusion of respon-sibilities. To sum up, there has been a net power gain for both institutions with the entry into force of the Lisbon Treaty. However, when looking at the interinstitutional balance of power between the two institutions, the EP seems to have experienced a relative loss compared to the EUCO.

6.2 Determinants of Interinstitutional Relations

The case studies helped us identify three core factors which can help explain the concrete balance of power between the EP and the EUCO: the internal coherence of each institution, the treaty provisions and the degree of urgency.

First, internal coherence has been proven to be of major relevance for each institution to secure a strong position vis-à-vis the other institutions. The EP could only impose Jean-Claude Juncker as Commission President because the major parliamentary groups were acting together. Similarly, the concessions achieved in the course of the MFF negotiations were only possible because the main political groups could agree on a clear mandate. Whenever the EP is internally divided, the Federal model will not prevail, as it was the case in Euro crisis legislations. Whereas the members of the EP agreed on a joint position after the 2014 elections, there was no con-sensus among the heads of state or government, which weakened their position vis-à-vis the EP. In the case of the EUCO, internal disagreement has a particular impact on its position vis-à-vis the EP in cases where QMV is possible.

Second, treaty provisions on the role of each institution and on the internal decision-making procedure seem to be of major importance. The EUCO can be expected to predominate in cases of a lack of legal provisions for direct interaction with the EP. The EP may only legislate and get active when treaty provisions unambiguously stipulate its involvement in the respective procedure or its position as a formal veto-player which cannot be circumvented. As the *Spitzenkandidaten* example illustrated, the EP hav-ing a strong say is not automatically accompanied by the predominance of the Federal model or the Cooperation model. However, we expect strong parliamentary competences in legal terms to be a necessary condition for the Federal model. This argument also applies to cases of treaty-making where the EP has no formal right to co-decide. The Euro crisis and the negotiation of treaties outside the EU's framework underlined the EUCO's role as the Union's 'constitutional architect' (Wessels 2016, 161).

As for the decision-making procedure, the possibility of a QMV can affect the EUCO's position vis-à-vis the EP, particularly in cases in which the EUCO is internally divided. The disagreement within the EUCO regarding the *Spitzenkandidaten* procedure could only have an effect since the treaties allowed QMV. Whenever the EUCO has to decide unanimously, it is difficult for the EP to benefit from disagreements among the member states. Such a pattern can be observed in the context of the Euro crisis management. Because of the need for deciding unanimously, the EUCO had to overcome the division between debtor and donor countries.

Third, any situation of urgency, that is a crisis or an emergency calling for an immediate reaction, disturbs the institutional balance by pushing the EUCO to the front. In other words, the Union of Sovereign States model prevails. The role assumed by the EUCO in the Euro crisis management and in the EU's economic governance in general confirms the willingness and capacity of the heads of state or government to take the lead when necessary. Similar observations can be made in other crisis situations, such the Russian annexation of the Crimea and the British decision to leave the Union, at which the EUCO immediately took over the lead (Müller Gómez et al. 2017).

6.3   Academic Tasks for the Future

In a next step, these preliminary results will have to be tested in a more comprehensive study. None of our cases has fully matched the Federal model. In which areas can we expect the Federal model? And which other factors that we could not deduce from our case studies can explain the predominance of one model or another? Additional aspects to look at might be the political relevance of certain issues and the role played by individual personalities.

Other interesting cases to look at would be trade policy, in which the EP has gained decisive competences, the Area of Freedom, Security and Justice, which is now part of the shared competences but has also been in crisis since 2015, and climate and energy issues, which are communitarized but have been a core item on the EUCO's agenda. With regard to institutional and constitutional matters, we suggest examining the interinstitutional balance in recent accession procedures and the Brexit negotiations, in the framework of which the EP holds the right to veto, as well as the current reform debate, including the future composition of the

Parliament. Lastly, the decision on the EU's own resources and the adoption of the MMF in 2019/2020 will represent a major opportunity for research. The pattern of both institutions striving for a strong position in the EU's institutional architecture will persist in the future. The EP might be weakened by growing internal divisions following the 2019 election and a larger share of Eurosceptic MEPs. The EUCO might be the beneficiary of this situation, as long as it manages to maintain a relatively unified position in view of the dividing effects caused by the presence of Euro sceptic governments.

REFERENCES

Becker, P. (2014). *Das Finanz- und Haushaltssystem der Europäischen Union. Grundlagen und Reformen aus deutscher Perspektive.* Wiesbaden: Springer VS.

Becker, P. (2016). The EU Budget's Mid-Term Review: With Its Promising Reform Proposals, the Commission Lays the Groundwork for the Next, Post-2020 Budget. SWP Comments, 48.

Bressanelli, E., & Chelotti, N. (2016). The Shadow of the European Council. Understanding Legislation on Economic Governance. *Journal of European Integration, 38*(5), 511–525.

Bundesverfassungsgericht. (1993). *Urteil zum Maastricht-Vertrag,* BVerfGE 89, 155.

Bundesverfassungsgericht. (2009). *Urteil zum Lissabon-Vertrag,* BVerfGE 2 BvE 2/08.

Burgess, M. (2004). Federalism. In T. Diez & A. Wiener (Eds.), *European Integration Theory* (pp. 25–44). Oxford: Oxford University Press.

Chang, M. (2013). Fiscal Policy Coordination and the Future of the Community Method. *Journal of European Integration, 35*(3), 255–269.

de Gaulle, C. (1970). *Discours et Messages. Avec le Renouvea. 1958–1962.* Paris: Plon.

de Schoutheete, P. (2017). The European Council: A Formidable Locus of Power. In D. Hodson & J. Peterson (Eds.), *The Institutions of the European Union* (pp. 55–79). Oxford: Oxford University Press.

Dialer, D., Maurer, A., & Richter, M. (2015). *Handbuch zum Europäischen Parlament.* Baden-Baden: Nomos.

Epstein, R. A., & Rhodes, M. (2016). The Political Dynamics Behind Europe's New Banking Union. *West European Politics, 39*(3), 415–437.

European Council. (2013). *Conclusion of the European Council,* 8 February 2013 (EUCO 37/13).

European Parliament. (2015, November 11). *Resolution on the reform of the electoral law of the European Union* (Procedure 2015/2035(INL)).

European Parliament. (2017, February 16). *European Parliament resolution on improving the functioning of the European Union building on the potential of the Lisbon Treaty* (2014/2249(INI)).

European Parliament, Council of the European Union and European Commission. (2013, December 2). *Interinstitutional Agreement Between the European Parliament, the Council and the Commission on Budgetary Discipline, on Cooperation in Budgetary Matters and on Sound Financial Management* (2013/C 373/01).

Fabbrini, S. (2013). Intergovernmentalism and Its Limits: Assessing the European Union's Answer to the Euro Crisis. *Comparative Political Studies, 46*(9), 1003–1029.

Fasone, C. (2014). European Economic Governance and Parliamentary Representation. What Place for the European Parliament? *European Law Journal, 20*(2), 164–185.

Gerring, J. (2007). Is There a (Viable) Crucial-Case Method? *Comparative Political Studies, 40*(3), 231–253.

Grimmel, A., & Jakobeit, C. (2009). *Politische Theorien der Europäischen Integration*. Wiesbaden: VS Verlag für Sozialwissenschaften.

Hobolt, S. B. (2014). A Vote for the President? The Role of Spitzenkandidaten in the 2014 European Parliament Elections. *Journal of European Public Policy, 21*(10), 1528–1540.

Hoffmann, S. (1966). Obstinate or Obsolete? The Fate of the Nation-State and the Case of Western Europe. *Daedalus, 95*(3), 862–915.

Howell, P. (2015). Coordination in a Crisis: Domestic Constraints and EU Efforts to Address the 2008 Financial Crisis. *Foreign Policy Analysis, 11*(2), 131–149.

Kassim, H., & Menon, A. (2003). The Principal-Agent Approach and the Study of the EU: Promise Unfulfilled? *Journal of European Public Policy, 10*(1), 121–139.

Maurer, A., & Wessels, W. (2003). *Das Europäische Parlament nach Amsterdam und Nizza: Akteur, Arena oder Alibi?* Baden-Baden: Nomos.

Miles, L. (2011). Thinking Bigger: Fusion Concepts, Strengths and Scenarios. In U. Diedrichs, A. Faber, F. Tekin, & G. Umbach (Eds.), *Europe Reloaded. Differentiation or Fusion?* (pp. 187–210). Baden-Baden: Nomos.

Mittag, J. (2011). Towards Disciplinary Transfers? Benefits and Restraints of European Integration and Fusion Theory for Historical Science. In U. Diedrichs, A. Faber, F. Tekin, & G. Umbach (Eds.), *Europe Reloaded. Differentiation or Fusion?* (pp. 111–140). Baden-Baden: Nomos.

Monar, J. (2011). The European Union's Institutional Balance of Power After the Treaty of Lisbon. In European Commission (Ed.), *The European Union After the Treaty of Lisbon: Visions of Leading Policy-Makers, Academics and Journalists* (pp. 60–89). Luxemburg: Publications Office of the European Union.

Monti, M., Dăianu, D., Fuest, C., Georgieva, K., Kalfin, I., Lamassoure, A., Moscovici, P., Šimonytė, I., Timmermans, F., & Verhofstadt, G. (2016, December). *Future Financing of the EU. Final Report and Recommendations of the High Level Group on Own Resources*, Brussels.

Moravcsik, A. (1993). Preferences and Power in the European Community: A Liberal Intergovernmentalist Approach. *Journal of Common Market Studies, 31*(4), 473–524.

Müller Gómez, J., & Wessels, W. (2015). The EP Elections 2014 and Their Consequences. A Further Step Towards EU Parliamentarism? *Cuadernos Europeos de Deusto, 52,* 39–66.

Müller Gómez, J., Reiners, W., & Wessels, W. (2017). EU-Politik in Krisenzeiten: Krisenmanagement und Integrationsdynamik der Europäischen Union. *Aus Politik und Zeitgeschichte, 37,* 11–17.

Nasshoven, Y. M. (2011). *The Appointment of the President of the European Commission: Patterns in Choosing the Head of Europe's Executive*. Baden-Baden: Nomos.

Pinder, J. (1986). European Community and Nation-State: A Case for a Neo-Federalism. *International Affairs, 62*(1), 41–54.

Pollack, M. A. (1994). Creeping Competence: The Expanding Agenda of the European Community. *Journal of Public Policy, 14*(2), 95–145.

Pollack, M. A. (2003). *The Engines of European Integration. Delegation, Agency, and Agenda Setting in the EU*. Oxford: Oxford University Press.

Pollak, J., & Slominski, P. (2015). The European Parliament: Adversary or Accomplice of the New Intergovernmentalism? In C. J. Bickerton, D. Hodson, & U. Puetter (Eds.), *The New Intergovernmentalism: States and Supranational Actors in the Post-Maastricht Era* (pp. 245–262). Oxford: Oxford University Press.

Puetter, U. (2014). *The European Council and the Council. New Intergovernmentalism and Institutional Change*. Oxford: Oxford University Press.

Reiners, W., & Wessels, W. (2011). Nach Lissabon: Auf der Suche nach einem neuen Gleichgewicht in der institutionellen Architektur der EU. In W. Weidenfeld & W. Wessels (Eds.), *Jahrbuch der Europäischen Integration 2011* (pp. 41–46). Baden-Baden: Nomos.

Schimmelfennig, F. (2004). Liberal Intergovernmentalism. In T. Diez & A. Wiener (Eds.), *European Integration Theory* (pp. 75–94). Oxford: Oxford University Press.

Schulz, M. (2012, January 14). *Inaugural Speech by Martin Schulz Following His Election as President of the European Parliament.*

Tanil, G. (2012). *Europeanization, Integration and Identity: A Social Constructivist Fusion Perspective on Norway*. Abingdon: Routledge.

Tusk, D. (2018, February 23). *Remarks by President Donald Tusk Following the Informal Meeting of the 27 Heads of State or Government* (82/2018).

Van Middelaar, L. (2013). *Passage to Europe. How a Continent Became a Union.* New Haven and London: Yale University Press.

Van Rompuy, H. (2014). *Europe in the Storm. Promise and Prejudice.* Leuven: Davidsfonds Uitgeverij.

von Donat, M. (1987). *Das ist der Gipfel! Die EG-Regierungschefs unter sich.* Baden-Baden: Nomos.

Wessels, W. (1992). Staat *und* (west)-europäische Integration. Die Fusionsthese. In M. Kreile (Ed.), *Die Integration Europas* (pp. 36–61). Opladen: Westdeutscher Verlag.

Wessels, W. (2010). The European Council. Beyond the Traditional View Towards a Fusion. In G. Cohen-Jonathan (Ed.), *Chemins d'Europe. Mélanges en l'honneur de Jean Paul Jacqué* (pp. 751–764). Paris: Dalloz.

Wessels, W. (2016). *The European Council.* Basingstoke: Palgrave Macmillan.

White, J. (2015). Emergency Europe. *Political Studies, 63*(2), 300–318.

CHAPTER 4

The CJEU and the Parliament's External Powers Since Lisbon: Judicial Support to Representative Democracy?

Fabien Terpan and Sabine Saurugger

1 INTRODUCTION

Both the Court of Justice of the European Union (CJEU) and the European Parliament (EP) have gained power since the origin of European integration. The Court was created in 1952 by the Treaty of Paris in order to control the High Authority of the European Coal and Steel Community (ECSC) and to protect the sovereignty of the member states. After a little more than a decade, two new treaties, adopted in 1957 in Rome—the Treaty of the European Community and the Euratom Treaty—began to change it into a supranational jurisdiction, independent of the member states (Rasmussen 2008). Its inherent authority has strengthened over

F. Terpan (✉)
Sciences po Grenoble, CESICE, University Grenoble Alpes, Grenoble, France
e-mail: fabien.terpan@sciencespo-grenoble.fr

S. Saurugger
Sciences po Grenoble, PACTE, IUF, University Grenoble Alpes,
Grenoble, France
e-mail: sabine.saurugger@sciencespo-grenoble.fr

© The Author(s) 2019   77
O. Costa (ed.), *The European Parliament in Times of EU Crisis*,
European Administrative Governance,
https://doi.org/10.1007/978-3-319-97391-3_4

time, thanks to the Court's own rulings, which have helped bolster its institutional legitimacy (Saurugger and Terpan 2017a).

Contrary to the Court's powers, the European treaties in the 1950s have created a quite powerless Parliament. Since the 1970s, however, treaty changes have allowed it to enlarge its legal, budgetary and external competences. The CJEU has equally played a part in this empowerment of the legislative body, by using the principle of institutional balance in order to defend the position of the Parliament towards the Council of ministers (Council). The Parliament has been very pro-active in using litigation strategies, among others (O'Keeffe et al. 2015), with a view to enlarging its own powers (Cullen and Charlesworth 1999; McCown 2003).

This chapter aims to analyse whether and, if so, why the jurisdiction of the CJEU supported the EP's decision-making powers in the European governance system since the entry into force of the Lisbon Treaty. Indeed, there are reasons to question what has been called the Court's pro-parliamentary attitude due to recent institutional and contextual evolutions. First, while the Parliament might not be a full-fledged one (Fasone 2014), it has gained considerable decision-making powers in legislative as well as budgetary and external matters (Carrera et al. 2013; Craig 2008; De Witte et al. 2010; Ripoll Servent 2010, 2014). This may reduce the Court's propensity to compensate for a lack of parliamentary control in the European Union (EU). What is the point of backing the Parliament's position if this position is already forceful? Second, the CJEU itself is said to act in a more constraining context (Dehousse 1998; Kelemen 2012; Martinsen 2015; Pollack 2017; Schmidt 2018), and thus may be less inclined to issue bold pro-integration jurisprudence. While many scholars have long presented the Court as a political power and even a judicial activist (Pescatore 1978; Weiler 1981, 1982, 1991; Burley and Mattli 1993; Alter 1996, Alter 2009; De Witte et al. 2014; Schmidt and Kelemen 2014), some of them argue that there are limits to its power (Wind 2010; Martinsen 2011; Larsson and Naurin 2016; Mayoral et al. 2016), especially since the 1990s. Facing more and more resistance from national governments and the citizens, due to the rise of euroscepticism and claims of sovereignty, the Court would now be more careful, and thus less inclined to support the Parliament.

An abundant law and politics literature on the CJEU (Kelemen 2012; Kelemen and Schmidt 2012; Schmidt 2018; Alter 2001) has analysed the relation between the Court and other European institutions. Embedded in this approach, this chapter aims to answer the question whether the Court is indeed still supportive of the Parliament's quest for more competencies or whether the Court's rulings have become less so. In order to do so, this chapter will concentrate on a case in which we should most likely see Court support: the Parliament's external powers. Both the Common Foreign and Security Policy (CFSP) and the Common Defence and Security Policy (CSDP) remain intergovernmental areas in which the Parliament has little competencies. Hence if the Court supports the Parliament in quest for more competencies, the rulings should be in favour of the Parliament's preferences. Our data is based on a systematic and in-depth small case study (cf. Blatter and Haverland 2012) of three Court cases referring to the Parliament's external powers since the entry into force of the Lisbon Treaty in 2009.

From a conceptual point of view, we start from the basic assumption that both the Court and the Parliament are strategic actors that can advance their positions as well as their legitimacy provided that the EU political system and their interaction within the EU political system allow it. At the same time, they are embedded in the legal framework of the Union and hence act according to their interpretation of treaties. In this chapter, we rely on a strategic constructivist approach (McNamara 1998; Parsons 2002; Blyth 2002; Hay and Rosamond 2002; Jabko 2006; Gofas and Hay 2010; Saurugger 2013) to analyse the way the Parliament uses the Court to reinforce its institutional position in external affairs and the way the Court answers to the Parliament's solicitations.

We assume that legal arguments put forward during judicial proceedings are cognitive usages of European norms, but may also be considered as strategic usages when institutions seek to achieve a precise goal. However, contrary to Jacquot's and Woll's understanding of the concept of usages (Jacquot and Woll 2003, 2004; Woll and Jacquot 2010), which distinguished among strategic, cognitive and legitimation usages attributed to different actors (strategic usages to institutions, cognitive usages to policy entrepreneurs and legitimation usages to political representatives), we consider that cognitive and strategic usages of legal norms can occur *at the same time* and be used *by the same actors.* By bringing a case before the CJEU, the Parliament makes a strategic usage of legal arguments in which it is embedded, to which the Court responds through its own—strategic—use of EU rules.

Two main logics can explain the strategic use of legal arguments in cases brought before the Court: a logic of influence and a positioning logic (Woll and Jacquot 2010). These logics are intertwined. We assume that the Parliament, when bringing a case dealing with its own powers before the CJEU, tries to influence the interpretation of EU treaties in order to strengthen its position in the EU political system. Yet, the reasons why the Court answers positively to the Parliament's demands are less clear. Four reasons will be envisaged in this chapter; all of them put the Court in the wider perspective of the EU political system (Saurugger and Terpan 2014). Following a logic of influence, the Court would choose to give interpretations of the EU treaties leading to (1) more supranational integration and (2) more democratic legitimacy. Following a positioning logic, the Court would choose to interpret the treaties in a way that (1) strengthens its own position in the EU system and (2) legitimizes its own position in the EU system.

We will try to determine which of these four rationales leads to the Court being actively supportive of the Parliament in cases related to external action.

After having recalled, in a second section, the historical role of the Court in empowering the Parliament, we will present in a third section some arguments supporting the idea that this role has stopped in the post-Lisbon period. The last and fourth section is dedicated to the study of our specific case—the Court's case law on the external powers of the Parliament—will partially refute these arguments by using a strategic constructivist approach situating both institutions in the EU system of governance. The four possible logics explaining the Court's strategic action will be tested in this last section.

2   The Historical Impact of the Court: Empowering the European Parliament

Contrary to the European Commission, the Parliament had to seek to empower itself, as it had only few powers in the original treaty of Rome, and no litigation prerogatives from the outset. The European Court's rulings have helped the Parliament enhance its position in the institutional system. This reflected the fact that both institutions had a common interest in strengthening themselves in the face of the Council and the member states (McCown 2003).

2.1   Parliament Empowerment Through Enlargement of Litigation Powers

The Court has increased the number of possible litigants to include the EP. Contrary to the Commission, the Treaty of Rome did not grant the

Parliament legal standing before the European Court, meaning that it could neither refer cases to the Court nor have them brought before the Court by other applicants. However, its legal status has improved significantly, and the Court's rulings have taken a great part in this evolution.

In the early 1980s, the European Court argued in the case '*Les Verts*' (294/83) that the EP could be taken to the Court by a party seeking to annul a legal act or asking the Court to sanction a failure to act. This meant the Parliament could hypothetically find itself a defendant before the Court, but with no right itself to bring actions before the Court. As only the Council and Commission were specified as potential litigants in the Treaty of Rome, the Court considered that this excluded the EP ('*Isoglucose*' 138–179; '*Les Verts*' 294/83; '*Comitology*' 302/87). It was conceivable that the Parliament would need to defend its 'legislative right'. However, one could also argue that the Commission, which enjoyed an unlimited right to bring actions for annulment, could defend the Parliament's rights. The Court chose to follow the letter of the treaty and excluded the Parliament from the category of litigants. In '*Isoglucose*' (138–179), for example, a private litigant, the firm Roquette Frères SA, filed a lawsuit against the Council for annulment of the contested legislation on the grounds of a lack of consultation with the Parliament. However, the Parliament did not have the legal capacity to defend itself before the Court. The Court merely established that the Parliament might act as intervener in legal proceedings, instead of accepting it as litigant.

The Court eventually granted the EP a limited standing to bring actions for annulment if it could show that its prerogatives were affected ('*Chernobyl*' 70–88). In '*Chernobyl*', the Parliament's conflict was with the Commission, which did not respect Parliament's right to be consulted. This led the Court to conclude that the Commission could not always be considered an effective safeguard of Parliament's rights.

The admissibility of legal action from the EP has remained quite controversial—it was not until 1992 that the EP brought its first action, the admissibility of which was not challenged by a member state or the Council (McCown 2003, 977). At the same time, the Maastricht Treaty codified the CJEU's case law, even repeating the language of the rulings, stating that the Court shall review 'actions brought by the European Parliament ... for the purpose of protecting its prerogatives' (now art. 173–3 TEU). Finally, the Treaty of Nice extended the legal standing of the EP. The Parliament now enjoys unlimited powers to challenge the acts of other EU institutions, as well as their failures to act when required to do so (see below Sect. 2.2).

2.2   Pro-Parliament Rulings Accepted by the Member States

Litigation powers are not the only example of a jurisprudence favouring the Parliament. Other rulings testify that the Court has been supportive of the Parliament's position in the institutional setting of the EU: This is more particularly the case in legal basis disputes, where the Parliament's right to participate in the legislative process was involved ('Titanium Dioxide', 300/89; 'Waste Directive', 155/91; Parliament v. Council 187/93; See McCown 2003). The CJEU has used the principle of institutional balance to defend the Parliament in cases where the Council sought to be the only decision-maker (Bradley 1987). This helped the Parliament to acquire legislative as well as budgetary and external powers.

This is not to say that the Court has systematically favoured the Parliament over the Council. Indeed, other rulings would show that, on the contrary, the Court has sometimes put limits to the claims of the Parliament and ruled in favour of the Council. However, the general trend is that the Court has highly contributed to foster the EP and make it a central component of the EU constitutional legal order.

The Court was able to do so because the member states did not oppose these rulings after they were issued. In any legal system, political powers may use 'court curbing' mechanisms to counter jurisdictions that have overstepped the boundaries (Vanberg 2004). It is often argued that in the EU a number of institutional features actually 'insulate (the CJEU) from threats of legislative override and other forms of reprisal by member state governments' (Kelemen 2012). Legislating and revising treaties require large majorities or even unanimous decisions, which enhance the independence of the Court. Decision-making is made more difficult by the need to reach consensus among the 28 member states, which have very different preferences (Stone Sweet 2000; Alter 2001; Pollack 2003; Stacey and Rittberger 2003, 876).

3   Constitutionalization Completed?
A Constrained Court and an Already Powerful Parliament in the Post-Lisbon Period

Some scholars argue that there is less room for judicial activism at the Court of Justice because the constitutionalization process has been completed (Schmidt 2018). 'Constitutionalisation completed' means two different and interconnected things: First, European treaties have been deeply revised in a way that favours supranational integration. After the entry into force of the Lisbon Treaty, the Parliament has increased its decision-making powers as well as its standing before the Court. We would therefore expect that the Court would be less inclined to foster the Parliament's powers even further. Second, the Court is more constrained than before (and more inclined towards self-restraint) due to the end of the permissive consensus.

3.1 The Parliament's Powers Have Been Increased by Successive Treaty Revisions

As we have seen in the first section, the Court issued rulings allowing the Parliament to gain litigation powers in order to defend its own preroga-tives in the EU system. These powers have been codified by the member states—first in the Treaty of Maastricht, then in the Treaty of Nice, which no longer restricts the Parliament's litigation rights to situations where its prerogatives are at stake. Consequently, as shown by McCown (2003), parliamentary litigation increasingly challenges acts that cannot be vetoed in the legislative process, instead of searching for more extended institu-tional competencies.

As pointed out above, litigation is not the only power that has been attributed to the EP though treaty revisions. The Lisbon Treaty is said to have considerably strengthened the powers of the Parliament, with several changes such as the extension of co-decision as the ordinary legislative procedure, the introduction of the assent procedure for international agreements, and even the reform of comitology (art. 291) and the intro-duction of the new instrument of delegated acts (art. 290).

The Lisbon Treaty has not changed the co-decision procedure as such, apart from a change of name (co-decision is now called ordinary legislative procedure); yet, it has widely extended the number of areas where the ordinary legislature procedure applies. With the entry into force of the new treaty, approximately 90% of European legislative acts are adopted through the ordinary legislative procedure (De Witte et al. 2010, 47).

With regard to external action, the EP now has to approve a large majority of international agreements. In particular, article 218 specifies that the Parliament must give its consent to external agreements covering fields in which internal measures are adopted through the ordinary legisla-tive procedure. Given the extension of this procedure, this implies a similar enlargement of the consent with regard to international agreements. Agreements related to the area of freedom, security and justice (AFSJ), in particular, are now subject to the consent of the Parliament.

3.2   The CJEU as a More Constrained Court? Self-Restraint and the End of the Permissive Consensus

While the Parliament has gained powers through treaty revision, the Court is sometimes said to have lost influence in a context of increasing scepticism coming from national governments and administrations as well as the citizens.

Until the 1990s, the Court was described by a majority of scholars as having exercised judicial activism. It means that it has issued audacious rulings and delivered interpretations going beyond the letter of the treaties, in order to foster European integration and limit national sovereignties (Saurugger and Terpan 2017b).

Since the late 1990s, however, a number of scholars have pointed to the fact that the Court does not continuously qualify as a central actor of integration through law. The Court is also constrained by political, administrative and constitutional counteractions (Larsson and Naurin 2016; Carrubba et al. 2008; Nowak 2010; Martinsen 2015). A series of factors have been identified in this respect.

First, the increase of Euroscepticism led to the end of the permissive consensus that prevailed until the 1980s. EU institutions, and supranational ones like the CJEU in particular, seem to be constraint by resistances occurring at the national level, coming from both political authorities and public opinion (Martinsen 2015; Naurin et al. 2013). Second, with the emergence of a new intergovernmentalist decision-making of the EU (Bickerton et al. 2015), by which deliberation and consensus have become the guiding norm of day-to-day decision-making at all levels, the CJEU's judges, increasingly aware of the difficult bargaining between the member states, are now subject to greater stress (Granger 2015). Third, since the Maastricht Treaty, new areas of competence have emerged, which escape the Court's jurisdiction. This is the case for both the CFSP (with a few limited exceptions) and those policy areas covered by so-called new modes of governance, including parts of social policy, economic coordination, education policy, and so on (Abbott and Snidal 2000; Shaffer and Pollack 2009; Pauwelyn et al. 2012; Terpan 2015). The aim was to reduce national resistances through so-called new modes of governance that would use, instead of coercive tools and hard law, coordination mechanisms and soft law. While hard law regularly triggers non-compliance attitudes, soft law is thought to push actors to reach the goal through a learning process leading to the transformation of actors' preferences (Jacobsson 2004; Sabel and Zeitlin 2006). Soft law would allow governments in international arenas to choose their own policy instruments to reach commonly defined goals, thus making the system more efficient. In a context where the introduction of soft law is supposed to decrease compliance problems, the European Court and judicial control more generally would no longer be the cornerstone of compliance attitudes and hence the Court and the legal system would lose their position as central actors in the process of integration through law.

In other words, political and legal developments in the EU since the 1990s have challenged the Court's role, a trend that is in contradiction with the development of other international tribunals, such as those of the World Trade Organization or the International Criminal Court, whose rulings became more salient. Confronted with these challenges, the Court may have responded through greater self-restraint, as if the growing opposition to supranationalism had led the Court to cautiousness and a greater awareness of its political environment.

4   THE CJEU: STILL SUPPORTIVE OF THE PARLIAMENT'S POWERS? THE CASE OF EXTERNAL ACTION

Despite the new context presented in the previous section, the CJEU is still supportive of the Parliament's powers. This section describes and explains this continuous support.

4.1   Imperfect Implementation/Imperfect Contracts

Two basic arguments explain why the Court still has to rule on cases linked with the powers of the Parliament, even in the post-Lisbon period.

First, it has often been said that treaties are incomplete contracts in need of interpretation and specification. Even though new powers have been given to the Parliament, the extent of these powers and the way the EP can use them is still a matter for discussion. As Christiansen and Döbbels argue in the case of the comitology procedure, treaty reform is not complete with the signing of a new treaty, nor even with the ratification and its coming into force. It is a continuous process that 'only reveals (its) ultimate meaning when the new treaty provisions are put into prac-tice' (Christiansen and Dobbels 2012, 18). Hence, the CJEU still has its say on the implementation of the new system.

Second, the implementation of European law is not an easy process and, on the contrary, often creates disputes among actors. Now that the Parliament is endowed with a number of important powers, it relies on the Court to defend it against Council's (and Commission's) attempt at bypassing it. As Carrera, Hernanz and Parkin argue, 'the Council and the European Commission may still have not fully internalised the full reach and implications of the EP's new position as a powerful co-legislat-ing actor in the post-Lisbon EU institutional landscape'. The 'formal recognition of the EP's powers post-Lisbon has not been accompanied by a full transition in "mindset" among the Commission, Council and member states' (Carrera et al. 2013, 15). The Court may have to com-pensate for this weak recognition by reminding of the Parliament's new powers in its jurisprudence. On the other hand, the Parliament may still try to extend its powers through litigation strategies, and it is up to the CJEU to decide whether these demands coming from the Parliament are legally valid.

Thus, despite parliamentary empowerment through treaty revisions, there is still room for further judicial improvement of the Parliament's prerogatives, beyond the stipulations of the treaties. The line between protecting existing powers and enlarging powers is a very thin one, and the CJEU can always improve the Parliament's position by making bold interpretations of primary law. Some powers, although being common in parliamentary regimes, have not been granted to the Parliament. The right of legislative initiative is one of those and can be taken as an example. The Commission, still the only holder of this right in most policy areas, has committed itself to making a proposal on behalf of the Parliament, should the latter ask for it. This commitment is included in an interinstitutional agreement that could be used by the Court to foster the implication of the Parliament at the early stage of the decision-making process.

The fact that the EP has been empowered by treaty revisions, and more recently by the Lisbon Treaty, has not made the CJEU's interventions less likely. It may have inclined the Court towards more cautiousness. As argued above, the following subsection will address this question in evalu-ating whether the jurisprudence of the CJEU with regard to the external powers of the Parliament has been supportive of the Parliament or has become less so in this field.

4.2 Case Study: The CJEU and the External Powers of the Parliament Since Lisbon

In some sensitive policy areas, the member states are still reluctant to let the Parliament have a say. And yet, over time, they accept to share some of their decision-making powers with the EP while retaining others. External action is a crucial case study, as it combines areas where the EP is closely involved (in particular the signing of a large number of international agreements) with areas where the EP is essentially kept aside (the CFSP and the CSDP). There are different possibilities for the Court to give interpretations favouring the EP in this field. In particular, the Court could support an extension of the Parliament's powers in areas where the Community method applies. And as CFSP/CSDP remains largely inter-governmental and excludes the Parliament, the Court could interpret narrowly the scope of CFSP/CSDP, each time it is difficult to determine whether an EU decision falls into CFSP or non-CFSP matters.

Thus, the external powers make it a most likely case for our study. If the Court wants to fully support the Parliament's quest of enlarging its powers in this—intergovernmentally protected—field of external action, it has to provide an interpretation in favour of the Parliament. As CFSP remains a public policy where the Parliament has very limited powers, the CJEU's strong support to the Parliament in this field would require a high degree of judicial activism. However, this is not because the Court exerts activism in this field that it exerts activism in every field of European integration. The chapter is careful not to draw general conclusions from the study of one case. The external powers of the Parliament are an area where the probability of the Court in favour of the Parliament indicates that the Court is in favour of enlarging the Parliaments decision-making competencies, compared to rulings taken in other policy fields where the Parliament already enjoys stronger powers. This allows us to see whether the Court can still be favouring the extension of competencies in one policy area and in a post-Lisbon period where judicial activism is supposed to be less likely. It does not allow us to conclude that the Court has remained a general activist in every field of European integration and at any time.

Since the Lisbon Treaty was adopted and ratified, the Parliament litigated to protect its existing powers and strengthen its participation. However, the decision to bring a case before the Court results from an internal debate, and therefore is not systematic. Sometimes, the Parliament favours a legislative struggle over a judicial one. This has been the case with regard to the 2010 Swift Agreement between the EU and the United States (the so-called TFTP agreement), which gave a legal basis to US requests for European data on financial transactions (within the scope of the US Terrorist Finance Tracking Program). It was the first time the Parliament used its new power under the Lisbon Treaty to veto specific international agreements. The EP was concerned that the agreement did not correctly ensure the independent oversight of EU/US exchanges. In this context, Sophie In't Veld, a member of the EP, decided to bring a case before the General Court of the CJEU against a decision of the Council's legal service denying her access to a document related to the negotiation of the EU/US international agreement (T-529/09 Sophie In't Veld v Council, and then C-350/12 P Council v Sophie In't Veld). Although the case was not brought by the EP as such, it can be seen as a decision protecting the new Parliament's powers.

In general, as pointed out above, it is Parliament as an institution that chooses to trigger litigation. With regard to external action, the EP has been judicially active and has asked the Court to delimit the distinction between CFSP and non-CFSP matters more rigorously (Garbagnati Ketvel 2006; Griller 2013; Hillion 2014; Hinarejos 2009; Terpan 2017; Van Ooik 2008), and consequently to define the extent of the Parliament's powers (much weaker in CFSP than in non-CFSP issues).

We will look more in depth into the three rulings since the entry into force of the Lisbon Treaty where the Court had to determine which legal basis should have been used by the Council, between one favourable to the EP and another one less favourable to the EP. These rulings have not been selected randomly. They are the only rulings where (1) the Court had to rule on the external powers of the Parliament; (2) in the post-Lisbon period; (3) on the basis of a demand made by the Parliament itself, using the annulment procedure.

In Case C-130/10 (sanctions against terrorism), about Council Regulation 1286/2009 amending Regulation 881/2002 'imposing certain specific restrictive measures directed against certain persons and entities associated with Usama bin Laden, the Al Qaeda network and the Taliban', the Court chose to link the fight against terrorism with CFSP (Art. 215 TFEU on restrictive measures based on CFSP decisions) instead of opting for a non-CFSP basis (Art. 75 TFEU dedicated to the fight against terrorism). While Article 215 TFEU transforms the Parliament into a passive actor, only informed by decision-makers (the Council and the Commission), Article 75 TFEU foresees a much greater involvement of the assembly. In order to achieve the objectives of preventing and combating terrorism, 'the European Parliament and the Council, acting by means of regulations in accordance with the ordinary legislative procedure, shall define a framework for administrative measures with regard to capital movements and payments, such as the freezing of funds, financial assets or economic gains belonging to, or owned or held by, natural or legal persons, groups or non-State entities'. Contrary to the argument put forward by the Parliament, yet in line with the opinion of the advocate general, the Court refused to annul Regulation 1286/2009 and ruled in favour of the Council. It considered that nothing in Article 215 TFEU indicates that restrictive measures taken against natural or legal persons, groups or non-state entities, associated with al-Qaeda and the Taliban, should not be included in the category of restrictive measures that are envisaged in this article. Furthermore, Article 215 TFEU, contrary to Article 75 TFEU, was considered as a means to fulfil the objectives of the EU's external action (including CFSP). In other words, the Court refused to give right to the Parliament's claim that a CFSP legal basis was not sufficient. By refusing to do so, the judges in Kirchberg gave precedence to a literal interpretation of the treaties over a more dynamic interpretation, leading to a stronger involvement of the Parliament.

In the Mauritius case (C-658/11), the Parliament sought annulment of Council Decision 2011/640/CFSP (on the signing and conclusion of an agreement between the EU and the Republic of Mauritius). This agreement defined the conditions of transfer of suspected pirates from the EU-led naval force to the Republic of Mauritius, as well as the conditions of suspected pirates after transfer. One of the pleas was about the involvement of the Parliament during the negotiations of the agreement. The Parliament submitted that, by failing to inform it 'immediately and fully' at all stages of the negotiations and of the conclusion of the EU-Mauritius Agreement, the Council infringed Article 218(10) TFEU, which applies to all agreements concluded by the EU, including those falling within the CFSP. The Council argued that this plea was inadmissible: With the contested decision falling exclusively within the CFSP, the Court did not have jurisdiction to rule on its legality (Article 24(1) TEU and Article 275 TFEU). The Court decided that the plea was admissible, arguing that the limitation to its jurisdiction does not extend to Article 218 TFEU, as the latter does not fall within the CFSP, even though it lays down the adoption procedure of an act falling within the CFSP. This enabled the Court to annul the Council

Decision on the grounds that the EP had not been properly informed, which constitutes a violation of an essential procedural requirement.

In the Tanzanian case (C-263/14), the Court examined the aim of the EU-Tanzania Agreement and confirmed that the procedure of transferring persons arrested or detained by the EU military staff (EUNAVFOR), established by the agreement, constitutes an instrument whereby the EU pursues the objectives of Operation Atalanta, in particular by making it possible to ensure that the perpetrators of acts of piracy do not go unpunished. Accordingly, since the agreement falls predominantly within the scope of the CFSP, and not within the scope of judicial cooperation in criminal matters or police cooperation, the contested decision could legitimately be based on Article 37 TEU alone (i.e. the legal basis specific to CFSP agreements). However, the Court ruled that the Council failed to keep the EP immediately and fully informed at all stages in the negotiation and conclusion of the EU-Tanzania Agreement. According to the Court, the Council has infringed the right of the Parliament to be informed in accordance with Article 218(10) TFEU.

4.3   The Strategic Positioning of the CJEU: The Logic behind the Court's Rulings

Why does the Court sometimes choose to support the Parliament's competences in the EU system and sometimes not? To answer this question, we will use the analytical framework sketched out in the introduction, according to which four rationales may explain the jurisprudence of the Court dealing with the external powers of the Parliament (Table 4.2). This chapter does not argue that the judges had the clear 'intention' to follow (some of) these logics, but we can show, at least, and through case law analysis, that the rulings do (or do not) reflect these logics.

The first two rationales follow a logic of influence. The Court would seek to influence European law in a way that would lead to (1) more supranational integration in the EU (= more decision-making powers to supranational institutions, including the EP); (2) more democratic legitimacy (= a strong involvement of the Parliament exercising democratic control). These rationales reflect an existing literature explaining that the Court has always had a pro-integration agenda, since *Van Gend en Loos* (1963) and *Costa v. Enel* (1964). They also expand the idea that the Court has played a great role in the democratization of the European integration progress (Mancini and Keeling 1994).

Some of the Court's rulings seem to follow these logics, in particular those defending its right to be involved in the process of adopting CFSP agreements. Indeed, in the cases of Mauritius and Tanzania, the Court has decided to control CFSP agreements, which had the effect of ensuring the EP's participation in the negotiation of the agreements. But as the CJEU does not systematically rule in favour of the Parliament, we cannot conclude that the CJEU is consistently motivated by a pro-EU integration and a pro-EU legitimacy objective. The Court has not issued interpretations that would have benefited to the Parliament in the cases of Mauritania and the sanctions against terrorism. There is no systematic use of legal activism—defined as a tendency to 'make law' through audacious and innovative interpretations (Saurugger and Terpan 2017a, b)—in support of the Parliament. The Court could have interpreted the treaty in a way that would place every action related to terrorism under the control of the Parliament (sanctions against terrorism).

Table 4.1 Logics of the strategic use of legal arguments

Logic of positioning	Logic of influence
1. More supranational integration 2. More democratic legitimacy	1. Strengthening of Court's own position 2. Legitimizing Court's own position

Table 4.2 Rationales behind the Court's decisions based on a typology of four criteria

	Logic of influence		Positioning logic	
	EU Integration: more competencies to supranational institutions	EU Legitimacy: democratic control of the EP	CJEU Powers: extension of the Court's jurisdiction	CJEU legitimacy: Acceptance of the Court's ruling by the MS
C-130/10 sanctions against terrorism	Weak	Weak	Weak	Strong
C-658/11 Mauritius case	Strong	Strong	Strong	Weak
C-263/14 Tanzanian case	Strong	Strong	Strong	Weak

The other two rationales follow a positioning logic. The Court's motivation would be to strengthen (1) its own position in the EU system (CJEU powers) and (2) its own legitimacy in the EU system (CJEU legitimacy) (see Table 4.1). Case law sometimes gives the CJEU the opportunity to affirm itself as an EU institution. In a way, the first landmark rulings *Van Gend en Loos* (1963) and *Costa v. Enel* (1964), where the Court developed the principles of direct effect and supremacy, were instrumental in bolstering its position as the supreme/constitutional court of the EU. In the three rulings studied in this chapter, when the Court gave an interpretation of law in favour of the Parliament (Mauritius and Tanzania), it was in a situation where such a decision had the effect of strengthening its own position (by enlarging its jurisdiction to CFSP agreements). On the contrary, when the Court issued more cautious rulings at the expense of the Parliament (Sanctions against terrorism), it had very little effect on its own powers. In Mauritius and Tanzania, this was not only about ensuring that the EP is properly involved in the process of adopting CFSP agreements, it was also about enlarging the CJEU's control over CFSP. Thus, one important reason why a decision in favour of the Parliament occurs is when both institutions (and not only the Parliament) seek to strengthen their positions.

The other positioning logic is linked with the legitimacy issue. The CJEU, as any other court, aims to be perceived as legitimate, even more so in a situation where it has 'no Marshalls at its disposal to enforce the law' (Kelemen 2011). It cannot issue rulings that would be so strongly criticized (by the member states in particular) that it would jeopardize compliance with European law and the existence of the EU legal order more generally. Thus, if the Court does not want to put its own legitimacy in danger (Gibson and Caldeira 1995), it should make use of self-restraint instead of activism. This may explain why the Court does not systematically defend the Parliament—even if it wanted to do so—but is more likely to support the Parliament when the Court's powers are also at stake. In the case of sanctions against terrorism, a pro-integration interpretation would have been strongly opposed by the member states, for which fighting terrorism is a sensible issue and an area still placed under national control. Such a reaction has certainly occurred, in the two other cases (Mauritius and Tanzania), but here the powers of the CJEU were at stake, leading to a decision strengthening the Parliament.

5 Conclusion

Historically, the Court has been supportive of the Parliament's powers and has indeed reinforced and enlarged them through successive rulings. More recently, and particularly after the Lisbon Treaty, there were reasons to think that this historical influence would come to an end. The Court was facing a new context leading to cautiousness and self-restraint, and the powers of the Parliament had been enlarged by treaty revisions in many different fields. What could a more constrained Court of Justice add to the largely completed process of constitutionalization and Parliament's empowerment?

This chapter has provided empirical evidence in favour of the opposite argument according to which the CJEU may still play a part in the parliamentarization of the EU, although cautiously and incidentally. From the case study of external action, we can conclude that, although the Court does not *systematically* rule in favour of the Parliament or seek to enlarge the powers of the Parliament, this remains a possibility and occurs in specific situations. When ruling on the Parliament's powers, the Court can defend existing powers of the Parliament, but may also go beyond the letter of the treaties and enlarge these competencies. In the three rulings studied in this chapter, the Court has not always ruled in a way that was supportive of an extension of the Parliament's competencies; some of the rulings, however, have indirectly benefited the Parliament. When the Court chose to get a grip on CFSP agreements, despite the provision of the treaty saying that CFSP is placed outside of the judicial control of the CJEU, it has the consequence of protecting the (small) powers of the Parliament in the field of CFSP.

Hence, the Court is not supportive of the Parliament with the only purpose of increasing the powers of the legislature. The analysis of the rulings seems to indicate that the Court is supportive of the Parliament's powers in CFSP when this develops its own jurisdiction over European law and strengthens the European legal order. This is consistent with the idea that, historically, when the Court has given litigation powers to the Parliament, it was not only to ensure the balance between institutions and reinforce the Parliament's position in the EU system but also to strengthen the Court itself: the Court empowered the Parliament (through the attribution of litigation powers) in order for the Court to be empowered by the Parliament (through the use of litigation strategies).

From this, it can be inferred that, first, there is no systematic bias in favour of the Parliament in the Court's case law; second, even in the post-Lisbon period and despite the high level of constitutionalization that has been achieved, the Court continues to make use of judicial activism and this activism may still benefit the Parliament.

REFERENCES

Abbott, K. W., & Snidal, D. (2000). Hard and Soft Law in International Governance. *International Organization, 54*(3), 421–456.

Alter, K. (1996). The European Court's Political Power. *West European Politics, 19*(3), 458–487.

Alter, K. (2001). *Establishing the Supremacy of European Law: The Making of an International Rule of Law in Europe*. Oxford: Oxford University Press.

Alter, K. (2009). *The European Court's Political Power: Selected Essays*. Oxford: Oxford University Press.

Bickerton, C. J., Hodson, D., & Puetter, U. (Eds.). (2015). *The New Intergovernmentalism: States and Supranational Actors in the Post-Maastricht Era*. Oxford: Oxford University Press.

Blatter, J., & Haverland, M. (2012). *Designing Case Studies: Explanatory Approaches in Small-N Research*. New York: Palgrave Macmillan.

Blyth, M. (2002). *Great Transformations: Economic Ideas and Institutional Change in the Twentieth Century*. Cambridge: Cambridge University Press.

Burley, A. M., & Mattli, W. (1993). Europe Before the Court: A Political Theory of Legal Integration. International Organization, 47(1), 41–76.

Carrera, S., Hernanz, N., & J. Parkin. (2013, September). The 'Lisbonisation' of the European Parliament. Assessing Progress, Shortcomings and Challenges for Democratic Accountability in the Area of Freedom, Security and Justice. *CEPS Paper in Liberty and Security in European No. 58*.

Carrubba, C. J., Gabel, M., & Hankla, C. (2008). Judicial Behavior Under Political Constraints: Evidence from the European Court of Justice. *American Political Science Review, 102*(4), 435–452.

Christiansen, T., & Dobbels, M. (2012). Comitology and Delegated Acts After Lisbon: How the European Parliament Lost the Implementation Game. *European Integration Online Papers (EIoP), 16*(13). http://eiop.or.at/eiop/texte/2012-013a.htm.

Craig, P. (2008). The Role of the European Parliament Under the Lisbon Treaty. *The Lisbon Treaty, 11*, 109–134.

Cullen, H., & Charlesworth, A. (1999). Diplomacy by Other Means: The Use of Legal Basis Litigation as a Political Strategy by the European Parliament and Member States. *Common Market Law Review, 36*, 1243.

De Witte, B., Trechsel, A. H., Damjanovic, D., Hellquist, E., Hien, J., & Ponzano, P. (2010). Legislating After Lisbon. *New Opportunities for the European Parliament. A Study Prepared in the Framework of the European Union Democracy Observatory (EUDO)*. https://www.eui.eu/Projects/EUDO-LegislatingafterLisbon(SD).pdf.

De Witte, B., Muir, E., & Dawson, M. (2014). *Judicial Activism at the European Court of Justice*. Cheltenham: Edward Elgar Publishing.

Dehousse, R. (1998). *The European Court of Justice: The Politics of Judicial Integration*. Basingstoke: Palgrave Macmillan.

Fasone, C. (2014). European Economic Governance and Parliamentary Representation. What Place for the European Parliament? *European Law Journal, 20*(2), 164–185.

Garbagnati Ketvel, M.-J. (2006). The Jurisdiction of the European Court of Justice in Respect of the Common Foreign and Security Policy. *International & Comparative Law Quarterly, 55*, 77–120.

Gibson, J. L., & Caldeira, G. A. (1995). The Legitimacy of Transnational Legal Institutions: Compliance, Support, and the European Court of Justice. *American Journal of Political Science, 39*, 459–489.

Gofas, A., & Hay, C. (Eds.). (2010). *The Role of Ideas in Political Analysis: A Portrait of Contemporary Debates*. London: Routledge.

Granger, M.-P. (2015). The Court of Justice's Dilemma—Between More Europe and Constitutional Mediation. In C. J. Bickerton, D. Hodson, & U. Puetter (Eds.), *The New Intergovernmentalism: States and Supranational Actors in the Post-Maastricht Era* (pp. 208–226). Oxford: Oxford University Press.

Griller, S. (2013). The Court of Justice and the Common Foreign and Security Policy. In A. Rosas, E. Levits, & Y. Bot (Eds.), *Court of Justice of the European Union – Cour de Justice de l'Union Européenne, The Court of Justice and the Construction of Europe: Analyses and Perspectives in Sixty Years of Case-law – La Cour de Justice et la Construction de l'Europe: Analyses et Perspectives de Soixante Ans de Jurisprudence* (pp. 675–692). The Hague: T.M.C. Asser Press.

Hay, C., & Rosamond, B. (2002). Globalization, European Integration and the Discursive Construction of Economic Imperatives. *Journal of European Public Policy, 9*(2), 147–167.

Hillion, C. (2014). A Powerless Court? The European Court of Justice and the Common Foreign and Security Policy. In M. Cremona & A. Thies (Eds.), *The European Court of Justice and External Relations Law* (pp. 47–70). Oxford: Hart Publishing.

Hinarejos, A. (2009). *Judicial Control in the European Union—Reforming Jurisdiction in the Intergovernmental Pillars*. Oxford: Oxford University Press.

Jabko, N. (2006). *Playing the Market: A Political Strategy for Uniting EUROPE, 1985–2005*. Ithaca, NY: Cornell University Press.

Jacobsson, K. (2004). Soft Regulation and the Subtle Transformation of States: The Case of EU Employment Policy. *Journal of European Social Policy, 14*, 355–370.

Jacquot, S., & Woll, C. (2003). Usage of European Integration—Europeanisation from a Sociological Perspective. *European Integration Online Papers (EIoP)*, 7(12). http://eiop.or.at/eiop/texte/2003-012a.htm.

Jacquot, S., & Woll, C. (Eds.). (2004). *Usages de l'Europe: acteurs et transformations européennes*. Paris: L'Harmattan.

Kelemen, D. R. (2011). *Eurolegalism. The Transformation of Law and Regulation in the European Union*. Cambridge, MA: Harvard University Press.

Kelemen, D. R. (2012). The Political Foundations of Judicial Independence in the European Union. *Journal of European Public Policy, 19*(1), 43–58.

Kelemen, D. R., & Schmidt, S. K. (2012). Introduction – The European Court of Justice and Legal Integration: Perpetual Momentum? *Journal of European Public Policy, 19*(1), 1–7.

Larsson, O., & Naurin, D. (2016). Legislative Override of Constitutional Courts: The Case of the European Union. *International Organizations, 70*(2), 377–408.

Mancini, G. F., & Keeling, D. T. (1994). Democracy and the European Court of Justice. *The Modern Law Review, 57*(2), 175–190.

Martinsen, D. S. (2011). Judicial Policy-Making and Europeanization: The Proportionality of National Control and Administrative Discretion. *Journal of European Public Policy, 18*(7), 944–961.

Martinsen, D. S. (2015). *An Ever More Powerful Court? The Political Constraints of Legal Integration in the European Union*. Oxford: Oxford University Press.

Mayoral, J. A., Wind, M., de Witte, B., Jaremba, U., & Podstawa, K. (2016). *National Courts and EU Law: New Issues, Theories and Methods*. Northampton, MA: Edward Elgar Publishing.

McCown, M. (2003). The European Parliament Before the Bench: ECJ Precedent and EP Litigation Strategies. *Journal of European Public Policy, 10*(6), 974–995.

McNamara, K. R. (1998). *The Currency of Ideas: Monetary Politics in the European Union*. Ithaca, NY: Cornell University Press.

Nowak, T. (2010). Of Garbage Cans and Rulings: Judgments of the European Court of Justice in the EU Legislative Process. *West European Politics, 33*(4), 753–769.

O'Keeffe, M., Salines, M., & Wieczorek, M. (2015). The European Parliament's Strategy in EU Economic and Financial Reform. *Journal of European Public Policy, 23*(2), 217–235.

Parsons, C. (2002). Showing Ideas as Causes: The Origins of the European Union. *International Organization, 56*(1), 47–84.

Pauwelyn, J., Wessel, R. A., & Wouters, J. (2012). *Informal International Lawmaking*. Oxford: Oxford University Press.

Pescatore, P. (1978). L'exécutif communautaire: justification du quadripartisme institué par les Traités de Paris et de Rome. *Cahiers de droit européen, 14*, 387.

Pollack, M. A. (2003). *The Engines of European Integration: Delegation, Agency, and Agenda Setting in the EU*. Oxford: Oxford University Press.

Pollack, M. A. (2017). Learning from EU Law Stories: The European Court and Its Interlocutors Revisited. In B. Davies & F. Nicola (Eds.), *EU Law Stories: Contextual and Critical Histories of European Jurisprudence* (pp. 577–602). Cambridge: Cambridge University Press.

Rasmussen, M. (2008). The Origins of a Legal Revolution: The Early History of the European Court of Justice. *Journal of European Integration History, 14*(2), 77–98.

Ripoll Servent, A. (2010). Point of No Return? The European Parliament After Lisbon and Stockholm. *European Security, 19*(2), 191–207.

Ripoll Servent, A. (2014). The Role of the European Parliament in International Negotiations After Lisbon. *Journal of European Public Policy, 21*(4), 568–586.

Sabel, C., & Zeitlin, J. (2006). Learning from Difference: The New Architecture of Experimentalist Governance in the European Union. Unpublished draft.

Saurugger, S. (2013). Constructivism and Public Policy Approaches in the EU: From Ideas to Power Games. *Journal of European Public Policy, 20*(6), 888–906.

Saurugger, S., & Terpan, F. (2014). La Cour de Justice au cœur de la gouvernance européenne. *Pouvoirs, 149*, 59–75.

Saurugger, S., & Terpan, F. (2017a). *The Court of Justice of the European Union and the Politics of Law.* London: Palgrave Macmillan, European Union Series.

Saurugger, S., & Terpan, F. (2017b). *Measuring Judicial Activism: Is the Court of Justice of the European Union an activist court?* Paper presented at the Fifteenth Biennial Conference of the European Union Studies Association, Miami, 4–6 May.

Schmidt, S. K. (2018). *The European Court of Justice and the Policy Process.* Oxford: Oxford University Press.

Schmidt, S. K., & Kelemen, R. D. (2014). *The Power of the ECJ.* London: Routledge.

Shaffer, G. C., & Pollack, M. A. (2009). Hard vs. Soft Law: Alternatives, Complements, and Antagonists in International Governance. *Minnesota Law Review, 94*, 706.

Stacey, J., & Rittberger, B. (2003). Dynamics and Formal and Informal Institutional Change in the EU. *Journal of European Public Policy, 10*(6), 858–883.

Stone Sweet, A. (2000). *Governing with Judges: Constitutional Politics in Europe.* Oxford: Oxford University Press.

Terpan, F. (2015). Soft Law in the European Union—The Changing Nature of EU Law. *European Law Journal, 21*(1), 68–96.

Terpan, F. (2017). The CJEU and the External Powers of the Parliament, New Activism or Self Restraint? In J. S. Vara (Ed.), *The Democratisation of EU International Relations Through EU Law.* London: Routledge, 39–59.

Van Ooik, R. (2008). Cross-Pillar Litigation Before the ECJ: Demarcation of Community and Union Competences. *European Constitutional Law Review, 4*, 399–419.

Vanberg, G. (2004). *The Politics of Constitutional Review in Germany*. Cambridge: Cambridge University Press.

Weiler, J. H. H. (1981). The Community System: The Dual Character of Supranationalism. *Yearbook of European Law, 1*, 257–306.

Weiler, J. H. H. (1982). Community, Member States and European Integration: Is the Law Relevant? *Journal of Common Market Studies, 21*(1), 39–56.

Weiler, J. H. H. (1991). The Transformation of Europe. *Yale Law Journal, 100*(8), 2403–2483.

Wind, M. (2010). The Nordics, the EU and the Reluctance Towards Supranational Judicial Review. *JCMS: Journal of Common Market Studies, 48*(4), 1039–1063.

Woll, C., & Jacquot, S. (2010). Using Europe: Strategic Action in Multi-Level Politics. *Comparative European Politics, 8*(1), 110–126.

CHAPTER 5

The Committee of the Regions and the European Parliament: An Evolving Relationship?

François Decoster, Vincent Delhomme, and Jennifer Rousselle

1 INTRODUCTION

The European Committee of the Regions (CoR), together with the European Economic and Social Committee (EESC), is one of the two advisory bodies of the European Union (EU). It represents European subnational authorities and gives advice to other EU institutions, particu-

F. Decoster (✉)
European Committee of the Regions, Brussels, Belgium

College of Europe, Bruges, Belgium

V. Delhomme
College of Europe, Bruges, Belgium
e-mail: vincent.delhomme@coleurope.eu

J. Rousselle
European Committee of the Regions, Brussels, Belgium

City Hall of Saint-Omer, Saint-Omer, France
e-mail: jennifer-rousselle@villesaintomer62500.onmicrosoft.com

© The Author(s) 2019   99
O. Costa (ed.), *The European Parliament in Times of EU Crisis,*
European Administrative Governance,
https://doi.org/10.1007/978-3-319-97391-3_5

larly during the legislative process. The CoR has asserted its role since its creation in 1994 and is now widely recognized as an important actor on the European arena. However, it remains a consultative body that lacks the binding powers of the two European co-legislators, the European Parliament (EP) and the Council of the European Union (Council), which have no obligation to follow its recommendations. Its influence is therefore only a function of its proximity to other European institutions and the relationship it maintains with them.

Because the CoR and the EP share many similarities, both chambers represent the European citizens and are thought to bridge the European 'democratic deficit', one would think that cooperation between them would naturally run smoothly. However, that has not always been the case. The two institutions have nonetheless managed throughout the years to build a strong relationship, especially since the entry into force of the Treaty of Lisbon. Many points of contact, both formal and informal, render possible a smooth and successful cooperation, ensuring that the opinion and expertise of the CoR is duly considered by the EP. Yet, beyond the observable links existing between the two institutions, the key question is to assess the *real* influence of the CoR on the EP's legislative input and thus its value for European decision-making.

After briefly recalling the history and the functions of the CoR, the nature of its relationship with the EP will be described before critically assessing the CoR's influence on the EP. Some ideas to strengthen this relationship and hence reinforce the CoR's position on the European stage are then outlined.

2   THE COMMITTEE OF THE REGIONS: BASIC FEATURES

2.1   The CoR's Role

The CoR is a rather recent actor within the EU institutional framework, even if its origins can be traced back to the early days of European integration.[1] It was formally created by the Maastricht Treaty and established in

---

[1] Already on 9 May 1960, the European Parliamentary Assembly, which would later become the European Parliament, made a proposal to set up a consultative committee on regional economies. This reflection would take shape after the Single European Act with the creation in 1988 of the Consultative Council of Regional and Local Authorities.

March 1994. The birth of the CoR has been variously construed, but it is possible to distinguish three—complementary rather than competing—reasons behind its creation (for a thorough overview, see Piattoni and Schönlau 2015, 32–56). The CoR can firstly be seen as the embodiment of the 'Europe of the Regions', the idea that European integration would lead to the assertion of regions and regional identities (for a recent and critical assessment of this idea, see Pasquier 2015). Subnational entities were thought to provide a stronger basis for a European sense of belonging and were seen as key allies in the integration process, because they were naturally less reluctant than Member States to see power transferred to Brussels. Secondly, the creation of the CoR answered the need for European institutions to gain expert knowledge and advice from subnational authorities, as the EU was gaining powers in regional and cohesion policies. This proves particularly true after the entry into force of the Single European Act. Lastly, and perhaps most importantly, the CoR fulfilled a democratic purpose, bringing the citizens closer to the European decision-making process. Indeed, its members hold regional/local mandates and enjoy a much more direct relationship with the citizens. Furthermore, with the expansion of the Union's powers, subnational authorities of federal states were also starting to lose vast chunks of their competences to the Union's benefit, and subnational authorities in general had to implement an increasing part of European legislation. It was thus crucial for them to have a say on this legislation.

Today, the CoR is said to assume a double mission that reflects these different logics (Piattoni and Schönlau 2015, 32; Domorenok 2009). It has a representative role, as it defends in Brussels the interests and positions of subnational actors and their citizens, and lobbies for their influence. It also has a consultative role in providing expert knowledge to other European institutions and enhancing European legislation. This latter mission is enshrined in the Treaty on the Functioning of the European Union (TFEU): 'The European Parliament, the Council and the Commission shall be assisted by an Economic and Social Committee and a Committee of the Regions, exercising advisory functions' (art. 300.1 TFEU).

These two missions could be seen as conflicting since they do not presuppose the same investment nor the same influence strategies; however, they seem to mutually reinforce each other (Domorenok 2009). The duality of the CoR's role is clearly expressed by its *Mission Statement*: 'We are a political assembly of holders of a regional or local electoral mandate serving the cause of European integration. Through our political legitimacy, we provide institutional representation for all the European Union's territorial areas, regions, cities and municipalities. Our mission is to involve regional and local authorities in the European decision-making process and thus to encourage greater participation from our fellow citizen' (CoR 2009a).

The CoR's position within the European institutional framework has been constantly reinforced since the Maastricht Treaty, even if it is still formally denied the status of institution by the Treaty on European Union (TEU).[2] It gained administrative and budgetary autonomy with the Treaty of Amsterdam, which suppressed the requirement for the CoR to submit its Rules of Procedure to the Council for approval. But it has especially been reinforced by the Treaty of Lisbon. It gained consultative powers in new areas, greater involvement in the legislative process, and most importantly, the right to bring actions before the Court of Justice of the European Union (CJEU) if it has been bypassed in the legislative process or for breach of the principle of subsidiarity.[3]

2.2   Internal Organization of the CoR

Quite interestingly, the CoR has sought to emulate the EP's internal organization, which is defined by the TFEU and the CoR's Rules of Procedure (CoR 2014a; for a detailed analysis, see Piattoni and Schönlau 2015, 59–67). It is not only a practical matter, but shows that the CoR considers that it is entitled to the same legitimacy as the EP.

The CoR's basic structure is defined in Articles 300, 305, and 306 TFEU. The CoR counts a maximum of 350 members and a number of alternates, appointed for a five-year term in office, raised from four years prior to the Lisbon Treaty. These members must be 'representatives of regional and local bodies either hold a regional or local authority electoral mandate or are politically accountable to an elected assembly'. The CoR's composition is decided by the Council following the proposition of each

---

[2] Pursuant to Article 13 TEU, only the seven following bodies enjoy the status of the Union's institutions: the European Parliament, the European Council, the Council, the European Commission, the Court of Justice of the European Union, the European Central Bank, and the Court of Auditors.

[3] It is to be noted that the EESC does not enjoy a similar right of action.

Member State.[4] Like in the EP, the president of the CoR is elected for a two and a half year mandate. So far, the presidency has rotated between the two main political groups of the assembly, the Group of the European People's Party and the Group of the European Socialist Party. The CoR organizes its work in commissions that significantly resemble the EP's committees in their operations. There are six commissions[5]; each of them appoints a rapporteur to prepare the proposals which are then voted in commissions and plenary sessions that are held five or six times a year. Another illustration of the influence of the EP on the CoR lies in the latter's political organization. The CoR counts five political groups[6] that broadly mirror the ones of the EP and has also set up a Conference of Presidents which '[...] debates any question submitted to it by the President with a view to preparing and facilitating the search for a political consensus on decisions to be taken by the other Committee's constituent bodies' (CoR 2014a, Rule 48).

2.3   The CoR's Position in the Legislative Process

The legal basis establishing the role of the CoR in the European legislative procedure is Article 307 TFEU: 'The Committee of the Regions shall be consulted by the EP, by the Council or by the Commission where the Treaties so provide and in all other cases, in particular those which concern cross-border cooperation, in which one of these institutions considers

---

[4] The composition varies from Member State to Member State. There are two main models: 'On the one hand, in the federal states with strong regional systems, such as Germany, Austria, Belgium, Spain and Italy, the representative role of regions is expressly set out in legal acts. In these countries, the national delegations at the CoR are essentially made up of regional representatives and local authorities are only marginally represented. On the other hand, in countries that do not have regional systems, or where these systems are weaker, representatives are mostly or entirely from the local authorities (for example, Portugal, Greece, Estonia, Latvia, Cyprus, Sweden and Luxembourg)' (CoR 2009b, 1).

[5] The six commissions are Citizenship, Governance, Institutional and External Affairs (CIVEX); Cohesion Policy and EU Budget (COTER); Economic Policy (ECON); Environment, Climate Change and Energy (ENVE); Natural Resources (NAT); and Social Policy, Education, Employment, Research and Culture (SEDEC).

[6] The five groups are the European People's Party, the Party of European Socialists, the Alliance of Liberals and Democrats for Europe, the European Alliance, and the European Conservatives and Reformists.

it appropriate'.[7] Consultation of the committee where the treaties so provide is an essential procedural requirement which, if omitted, may lead to the annulment of an EU act under Article 263 TFEU. Under this article, the CoR can therefore only bring an action for annulment of an act 'for the purpose of protecting [its] prerogatives' and is deemed a semi-privileged applicant. It cannot, for instance, seek to annul an act on the grounds of breach of the treaties, unlike Member States, the Commission, the Council, and the EP, privileged applicants.

During the pre-legislative phase, the CoR is associated with the preparation of the legislative proposal by the Commission. The CoR organizes consultations with local and regional authorities and participates in the elaboration of impact assessments. During the legislative process *stricto sensu*, the CoR adopts opinions on the legislative proposals for which it is consulted. These opinions can also be issued by the CoR on its own initiative. If the legislative proposal is significantly altered during the legislative discussions, the CoR can adopt a revised opinion (CoR 2014a, Rule 57).

Finally, after the act has been adopted, the CoR can bring an action before the CJEU if it finds it in breach of the principle of subsidiarity (art. 8 Protocol 2 TFEU). The CoR has made clear that it 'is determined to use the right to bring actions before the CJEU as a last resort and only when all other means of exerting influence have been exhausted' (CoR 2006, 3.22). It has therefore not yet exercised this right, though it was seriously considering to do so in the case of the Common Provision Regulation[8] a few years ago, but abandoned the idea after a negative opinion of the CoR's legal service.

---

[7] Consultation is mandatory for all EU laws in the following areas: economic, social, and territorial cohesion; trans-European networks; transport, telecommunications, and energy; public health; education and youth; culture; employment; social policy; environment; vocational training; and climate change.

[8] Regulation (EU) No. 1303/2013 of the European Parliament and of the Council of 17 December 2013 laying down common provisions on the European Regional Development Fund, the European Social Fund, the Cohesion Fund, the European Agricultural Fund for Rural Development, and the European Maritime and Fisheries Fund and laying down general provisions on the European Regional Development Fund, the European Social Fund, the Cohesion Fund, and the European Maritime and Fisheries Fund and repealing Council Regulation (EC) No. 1083/2006, OJ L 347, 20.12.2013, pp. 320–469.

3 THE COMMITTEE OF THE REGIONS AND THE EUROPEAN PARLIAMENT: THE STATE OF COOPERATION[9]

The CoR has become a relevant actor of the European decision-making process, both through the progressive expansion of its powers and the establishment of an efficient internal structure. However, its purely consultative nature means that its influence rests on the goodwill of the three actors of the 'Institutional Triangle'. Beyond the formal legislative work, the CoR must convince other institutions that its opinion is worth taking into account. Hence, the links established with the Commission, the EP, and the Council become crucial.

The relationship between the EP and the CoR is particular because of the many similarities between the two institutions: both symbolize democracy in the EU and the voice of its citizens. For this reason, this relationship is characterized at the same time by proximity and rivalry. This relationship, if compared to the one the CoR maintains with the two other main institutions, lies somewhere in the middle. The CoR and the Commission are long-standing allies (Christiansen and Lintner 2005, 8) and the latter was the CoR's strongest advocate. On the contrary, the Council has never viewed very enthusiastically the emergence of a local power at the European level (Piattoni and Schönlau 2015, 82).

3.1 The Evolution of the CoR - EP Relationship

As pointed out by various authors (Christiansen and Lintner 2005, 9; Warleigh 1999, 25), the relationship between the CoR and the EP had an ambivalent start. Warleigh wrote in 1999 that 'Relations between these two bodies have not always been cordial despite the fact that the EP was broadly supportive of the CoR's creation. This tension is largely caused by two factors: the concern that the Committee might be a rival to the Parliament, and the dim view taken by some MEPs of the actual workings of CoR to date' (Warleigh 1999, 25). He added that 'the realisation of a strong partnership between the two bodies is thought by MEPs to be unlikely in the next few years' (Warleigh 1999, 27). This position of the

---

[9] Some of the information presented in this section comes from a meeting with the Secretary General of the CoR Mr. Jiri Burianek, held on 10 May 2017.

EP can be explained by various factors. When the CoR was created, the EP had just obtained its co-decision power with the Maastricht Treaty and some parliamentarians were probably not very satisfied having to share power with what was thought by some to become the EU's 'second chamber', even though this was never really credible (Domorenok 2009, 5; Warleigh 1999, 26). Some CoR members even shared the view that the regional/local mandate they held gave them superior legitimacy over their counterparts within the EP (Piattoni and Schönlau 2015, 75).

The EP, however, did not have a cohesive conception of the CoR at the time, and probably still doesn't: the CoR was seen as a waste of money in the EP's budgetary committee, while the regional committee had a much more positive appraisal of its role (McCarthy 1997, 448). Moreover, the EP's dispositions towards the CoR have improved, mostly because the CoR has acquired far less power and influence than the EP, which no longer feels threatened by the voice of local actors.

Apart from this tension related to power, difficulties also arose from real political divergences. The EP has always been keen to defend the prerogatives of subnational entities that enjoy legislative power within their own national system, regions of federal or highly decentralized states, whereas the CoR defends all subnational authorities including the local ones, such as municipalities, enjoying fewer powers (Domorenok 2009, 157–158). The Parliament has therefore often advocated for the efficiency and centralization of legislative implementation at the regional level, while the CoR wanted to devolve power to the local level (Piattoni and Schönlau 2015, 77).

The relationship between the two bodies took off at the beginning of the millennial thanks to institutional reforms. The Treaty of Amsterdam equipped the EP with the possibility of directly consulting the CoR, a possibility that was used for the first time in March 2002 (Christiansen and Lintner 2005, 9). The Lisbon Treaty reinforced this dynamic by introducing the obligation for the EP to consult the CoR on legislative proposals in the relevant areas. The CoR adapted its procedures subsequently, with the possibility for the CoR to revise its opinions after amendments made by other institutions, thereby developing the cooperation between the two chambers during the legislative procedure.

With the signature of a cooperation agreement in 2014, the working relationship between the EP and the CoR has been taken to another level: 'The European Parliament and the Committee of the Regions will cooperate in order to reinforce the democratic legitimacy of the EU and contribute to the Treaty objective of pursuing territorial, social and economic cohesion in the Union' (CoR 2014b, 1). This agreement puts forth the outline for a sustainable working relationship based on mutual cooperation. It exposes a framework for cooperation both in political and practical matters (administrative, staff, and budgetary issue) whose details are discussed in the next section.

3.2 Current Cooperation Between the Two Institutions

Institutionally, the political cooperation principally takes places at three levels: between the CoR Bureau and the EP Conference of Committee Chairs (CCC), between EP committees and CoR commissions, and finally between rapporteurs in the two institutions (CoR 2017b, 5).

The president of the CoR and the EP CCC (this conference gathers the chairs of all EP committees and takes decisions on the legislative agenda and on the workload of the institution) meet twice a year to define political priorities and reinforce cooperation between both institutions. This allows the EP to define 'priority subjects where deepened input from the CoR would be especially valuable' (CoR 2014b, 1). This process was successfully launched in 2015 and has continued ever since. The CoR's input is also required on the Parliament's Legislative Train Schedule that tracks the progress of the legislative cases following the framework of priorities laid out by the Commission.

The relevant committees of the EP and CoR commissions are also cooperating more closely through bilateral contacts between their chairs and the organization of joint meetings and activities, as well as external activities made in Member States. CoR representatives have a seat in all EP committee meetings, and EP rapporteurs and committee chairs are regularly invited to speak at CoR commission meetings. During the drafting of their opinions, CoR rapporteurs also increasingly meet with EP rapporteurs in order to exchange their views and to provide EP rapporteurs with an initial CoR position.

The EP's Regional and Urban Development (REGI) committee is officially in charge of relations with the CoR according to the EP Rules of Procedure (European Parliament 2014, Annex VI, section XII (7)). This situation is quite surprising since the CoR is not only consulted on regional issues but seeks to provide an added value in all fields of legislation; yet the EP's Rules of Procedure have not been changed in order to reflect this broader focus (Piattoni and Schönlau 2015, 78). Nevertheless, over time more and more CoR commissions have established better contacts with EP committees. Each year during the European Week of Regions and Cities, the CoR's Commission for Territorial Cohesion Policy and EU Budget (COTER) has a joint meeting with the REGI committee. In 2016, the COTER commission had for the first time a joint meeting with the Transport and Tourism (TRAN) committee of the EP, focusing on missing transport links in border regions. This is a practice adopted by a growing number of EP committees and CoR commissions (CoR 2017a, 3). The EP committees can also request a consultation of the CoR (European Parliament 2014, Rule 138), but the exchanges between COTER and REGI remain more intense than those between other CoR commissions/EP committees.

Beyond its efforts to influence the EP's legislative work strictly speaking, the CoR also pushes forward its political agenda and the interests of its members through frequent meetings between members of both institutions, individually or through their political groups. This proximity is reinforced by the fact that an increasing amount of members of one institution have been previously a member of the other (Piattoni and Schönlau 2015, 78).[10] These members who have been part of both institutions naturally act as ambassadors and facilitators of the bilateral relationship.

Moreover, the five political groups of the CoR have close links with their counterparts and increasingly organize joint events and actions: conferences, communications, and so on (Piattoni and Schönlau 2015, 80). This proximity is reinforced by the fact that political groups of both institutions are linked to the same European parties and are therefore involved in these parties' work. In this regard, the Cooperation Agreement between the two institutions provides that 'The Committee of the Regions will be an active partner in the run up to the European Elections' (CoR 2014b, 2).

The general administrations of both institutions are also in contact and maintain ties for smoother cooperation. The CoR secretary general meets regularly with its counterpart at the EP, and the different units and services of the institutions are also in close contact to make sure that the contribution of the CoR is made in good time and effectively channelled, which is a challenge since its time and means are limited (Piattoni and

---

[10] In June 2017, 10 of the current MEPs had previously been COR members and 8 of the current CoR members had been MEPs.

Schönlau 2015, 79). The CoR administration attends the EP Conference of Presidents that prepares the EP plenary sessions in which the CoR is an observer. The European Parliament Research Service (EPRS), as provided by the cooperation agreement, also provides the CoR with expertise and materials. Strong ties have been created between some CoR commission secretariats and units of the EPRS (CoR 2017b, 8).

Finally, the EP and the CoR cooperate on more practical matters. The CoR is of course financially dependent on the EP, with which it negotiates its annual budget, but also relies on it to organize its work. Since the building that it shares with the EESC does not have a meeting room big enough to hold the CoR's plenary session, the EP allows the CoR to use it premises in Brussels for its plenary sessions, in general during the EP's own plenary weeks in Strasbourg. The EP and the CoR also cooperate on staff, interpretation, and security issues (CoR 2014b).

Both institutions seem more willing than ever to strengthen the bonds between them. The CoR wrote in its Annual Impact Report for 2016 that: 'The cooperation with the EP has been systematically upgraded since the signing of the Cooperation Agreement in 2014. The CoR and the EP pursue effective bilateral cooperation on a set of selected priority files which are reviewed and updated every year. As the quality of the relationship with the EP continues to improve at all levels, it has paved the way towards more structured forms of cooperation between the rapporteurs of both institutions and the CoR commissions and EP commit tees' (CoR 2017a, 3). This is something that the first report on the implementation of the Cooperation Agreement conducted in 2017 by the CoR Secretariat has confirmed (CoR 2017b). In the same vein, the EP in 2017 adopted a resolution introducing new ideas to improve the functioning of the EU (European Parliament 2017). It explicitly addressed inter-institutional relations, including relations with consultative committees. It stated that 'the European institutions should take account of the role played by the CoR and EESC in the legislative framework and the importance of taking their opinions into consideration' (European Parliament 2017, 4) and called 'on the European Parliament, the Council and the Commission to improve cooperation modalities with the CoR and the EESC, including at the pre-legislative stage during the conduct of impact assessments, in order to ensure that their opinions and assessments can be taken into account throughout the legislative process' (European Parliament 2017, 13).

4   ASSESSING THE INFLUENCE OF THE COMMITTEE OF THE REGIONS ON THE EUROPEAN PARLIAMENT

As we have seen, the CoR has undeniably become a respected actor in the EU decision-making process and has managed to build a strong and successful relationship with the EP. Its legitimacy is no longer in doubt. However, the question of the influence of the CoR remains unanswered: how much of an impact do its opinions/positions have on the EP's subsequent stances? More than the actual involvement of the CoR in the EP's activities, the answer to this question defines the effectiveness of the CoR and of advisory bodies in general. Hence, it is a crucial and controversial question.

Assessing this influence is unfortunately a complicated exercise which would require, for complete trustworthiness, the monitoring of the MEP's motivation when drafting and amending a piece of legislation or when adopting a political stance. Unlike the Commission, the EP does not produce reports explaining the extent to which it takes the suggestions of the CoR into account. To make such an assessment, three sources can be used: the annual impact report established by the CoR, impact assessments carried out by the political groups' secretariats in the CoR, and studies made by independent scholars. The most reliable way to conduct this assessment would be to trace the content of the CoR's input in the EP's output. However, this would be difficult to study unless done in a systematic manner. Another way is to interview MEPs to discover their own appraisal of the CoR's influence.

4.1   Evidence of Legislative Influence

Available data, to assess the influence of the CoR's opinions on the EP's final position, is scant.

Pursuant to Rule 60 of the Rules of Procedure of the CoR: '[a]t least once a year the Secretariat-General shall submit to the Plenary Assembly a report on the impact of Committee opinions on the basis, inter alia, of contributions sent to it to this effect by each competent commission and information collected from the institutions concerned' (CoR 2014a, Rule 60). If one takes the report for the year 2016, '45 opinions adopted in previous years which had an impact on the EU's legislative activity in 2016 are included' (CoR 2017a, 1). These reports do not offer an exhaustive overview of the CoR's output and its impact during a given year. It is not 'scientific' in that sense, and one should keep in mind that it also functions as a promotion tool for the CoR's activity. It does, however, offer an overview of the areas in which the CoR's contributions have been deemed useful.

To determine whether the impact of its opinions was deemed 'significant', the CoR used the following criteria: 'Specific CoR proposals adopted in final legislation; CoR policy recommendations considered in proposed legislation or in legislative procedures; CoR positions which have made a major contribution to ongoing political debates; References made to CoR positions in other EU documents, e.g. resolutions of the European Parliament (EP)' (CoR 2017a, 1).

For instance, in the area of tourism, following the delivery of an own-initiative opinion of the CoR,[11] the report notes that 'Due to its opinion the CoR is perceived as a driving force for European tourism policy and was for the first time invited to deliver a keynote speech at the European Tourism Day 2016 and European Tourism Forum 2016 alongside Commissioner Bieńkowska and leading Members of the European Parliament' (CoR 2017a, 8). This illustrates the type of qualitative assessment that can be found in this report.

Consulting one of the political group's secretariats,[12] it appears that one area where the CoR recently has had some impact is in the field of space policy, through the CoR rapporteur Andres Jaadla.[13] This has been made possible through a lot of 'lobbying work' by the CoR rapporteur in assistance with the relevant political group secretariat and CoR commission secretariat. The final EP report reflects, in many sections, the CoR's opinion, which has been made possible through meetings with the relevant MEPs and by submitting amendments to them. One example of such a section can be found in the final EP report: '[the EP] highlights the fact that the regional dimension is essential in bringing the benefits of space to citizens, and that the involvement of local and regional authorities can create synergies with smart specialisation strategies and the EU Urban Agenda'.[14] Through his work, the CoR rapporteur also had the possibility

---

[11] 'Tourism as a driving force for regional cooperation across the EU', CDR 6648/2015.

[12] ALDE group Secretariat.

[13] 'Space Strategy for Europe', CDR 6726/2016.

[14] European Parliament resolution of 12 September 2017 on a Space Strategy for Europe, 2016/2325(INI).

to address several important conferences, including the European Interparliamentary Space Conference.

To date, and to the knowledge of the authors, no systematic review of the impact of CoR opinions on the EP legislative work has been conducted. In a paper, Milena Neshkova studied the changes made by the Commission to 60 legislative proposals after it had received mandatory opinions from the CoR (Neshkova 2010). She found that the CoR does have an influence on the Commission, with over a third of the latter's proposals substantially amended in order to take into consideration the CoR's position, but this influence varies across policy areas: 'The Commission appears to value the policy-relevant expertise of the CoR on regional issues, as indicated by the higher number of acceptances in this area. This result empirically substantiates the findings of earlier qualitative inquires about the influence of this body' (Neshkova 2010, 1208). While these results cannot be automatically transposed to the EP, where the legislative process adheres to a partisan logic, they offer an idea of the legislative influence of the CoR.

4.2   Impact on MEPs

The bulk of available studies on the influence of the CoR on the EP focuses on the MEPs' dispositions towards the opinions of the CoR. Christoph Hönnige and Diana Panke have studied extensively this issue through interviews and questionnaires, though it should be noted that their work deals with the influence of both the CoR and the EESC on the EP and the Council.

In a first study, they found the CoR to have a limited influence on European policy-making (Hönnige and Panke 2013). Forty per cent of their respondents, MEPs and Permanent Representations' staff members, fully ignore the opinions of the CoR and the EESC. The impact of the two committees' advice depends on a number of variables: the timing of the recommendation, which should be delivered relatively early and especially before other actors formulate their own position; the expertise of the committee and quality of its recommendations; the distance between the position of the committee and the one of the addressee (Hönnige and Panke 2013, 467). Furthermore, '[w]hile there is variation across policy fields and addressees, neither the core policy fields of the EESC (industry and social policies) nor the CoR (regional policy) have an impact on actual influence' (Hönnige and Panke 2013, 467).

In their book *Consultative Committees in the European Union: No Vote—No Influence?* (Hönnige et al. 2015), the authors report similar findings: '[a]lthough the influence of both consultative committees on final policy outcomes is considerably more limited than the influence of veto players (EP, Council), it is not the case that the EESC and the CoR are irrelevant. [...] Rather than merely inducing grammatical changes to EU policies, the case studies exemplify that the consultative committees can also effectively push for substantial alterations in EU policies (see Chap. 7)' (Hönnige et al. 2015, 162). They also found the EP to be more receptive to consultative committees' opinions. According to the authors, this situation is explained by the higher degree of flexibility of MEPs compared to the rigid positions of diplomats in the Council, the latter getting clear instructions from their national ministries.

In their last paper (Hönnige and Panke 2016), the two scholars found that around 60 per cent of their respondents, EP or Council representatives, never or very seldom read the CoR's opinions (Hönnige and Panke 2016, 629), which confirms the content of the interviews they conducted with recipients from these opinions: 'In the extreme, this leads to not being aware of the committee positions at all: "I really do not read it at all and my staff does not either"' (Hönnige and Panke 2016, 628). Hence, '[t]he results of the survey show that both Committees are confronted with the challenge to get noticed by the MEPs and the member states at all. It is by no means guaranteed that the formal involvement in legislative decision-making guarantees awareness' (Hönnige and Panke 2016, 628).

Despite its widely acknowledged formal role and the increased means of cooperation existing with the EP, it appears that the CoR is still struggling to catch the attention of the EP. If some of its opinions manage to be reflected in the EP's own positions, a majority of MEPs do not seem to take into consideration the work of the CoR. It is a real problem, not only for the CoR's legitimacy but also, more broadly, for the legitimacy of European decision-making process, in which subnational interests are supposed to be reflected.

5   Increasing the Committee of the Regions' Influence on the European Parliament

In order to improve the impact of the work of the CoR concerning the EP, it is necessary to increase the EP's awareness of this work. Indeed, it does not seem to be the quality of the CoR's opinions or advice that is being questioned, even if this undoubtedly plays a role, but rather the EP's lack of interest or awareness. The CoR should therefore adopt strategies in order to provide solutions to this problem, while the EP should give more consideration to the work of the CoR.

5.1   Improving the Impact of the CoR's Opinions

The CoR produces quite a considerable amount of opinions every year. If some of them do have an influence on their addressee's final position, be it the EP or the Council, as well as the legislative outcome, some of them are probably totally ignored.

The fact that the quality and innovative potential of the CoR's opinions play a crucial role in the way they are dealt with by the EP is probably a statement of the obvious, but it must be stressed as a fundamental condition for the CoR to be taken seriously. If the CoR's opinions do not provide any added value, not only will their content be neglected, but they will simply be ignored in the future. Studies also show that an important point for the CoR and consultative bodies in general is the speed with which they produce their recommendations (Hönnige and Panke 2013; Hönnige et al. 2015). The CoR's opinions must reach the EP early enough, before its internal position is finalized. The problem is that the CoR is an organization with limited means but constantly expanding responsibilities. It is an opportunity, of course, but also a challenge. Furthermore, the CoR usually receives legislative proposals at the same time as the EP and the Council, which renders the quick delivery of an opinion even more challenging.

For Hönnige and Panke: 'against this background it is important that consultative institutions facing capacity shortages systematically engage in prioritization. Only if they concentrate their limited staff, expertise and financial resources on a few selected items can they swiftly develop high-quality recommendations, which is crucial for their prospects of success' (Hönnige and Panke 2013, 468). This is not to say that the CoR should only focus on some areas and neglect the others. This would go against its mandate and the mission it is entrusted with to promote subnational positions and interests. But defining political priorities per mandate or half-mandate is crucial.

This is something the CoR has already been committed to and something that should be pursued: '[t]he legal remit of advisory body has recently been better exploited by the Committee, while its consultative function has noticeably been reinforced as a result of several changes in the CoR's political strategy, which is now better focused on the issues covered by mandatory consultation procedure' (Domorenok 2009, 160). Submitting own-initiative opinions is a useful tool when a particular issue is deemed to be of highly relevant interest by the CoR, but it should be used with parsimony.

More broadly speaking, the EP and the CoR must reinforce their coordination. The frequent relations that are being maintained should evolve into a constant cooperation along the legislative cycle: agenda-setting, consultation, legislation, and scrutiny. This requires an operational system facilitating the exchange of information and agenda coordination, something that is being considered by the CoR Secretariat.

5.2   Raising the EP's Awareness of the CoR's Work

As we saw in the previous section, the problem is not only that the EP does not take the CoR's opinions into consideration, after all, the CoR remains a purely consultative body. Rather, the problem is that the EP often completely ignores the CoR's opinions. They are frequently not read by MEPs or their staff, which is highly problematic. Of course, it pertains to each MEP's responsibility to take the advice of the CoR into consideration, but the CoR itself should adopt strategies that aim to raise the EP's awareness of its work.

The most recent study by Hönnige and Panke provides interesting insights into this question (Hönnige and Panke 2016). Their starting point is to consider the CoR, and the EESC, as part of a highly competitive environment in which other organized interests, lobbyists, or NGOs are also seeking to catch the attention of the EP. Even if it is difficult to put the representatives of private interests, however legitimate, on an equal footing with the CoR, it is undeniable that their opinions do not bear much more legal relevance than their advocacy documents. This can be criticized and/or deplored, but reflects the reality.

Moreover, as the two scholars point out: 'consultative committees [...] are disadvantaged compared to the typically considerably more specialized organized interests, which are able to concentrate resources on few issues to develop recommendations and quickly act upon them' (Hönnige and Panke 2016, 629). Therefore, they suggest for the CoR to engage in proactive strategies to better showcase its opinions and interests, through seminars, workshops, conferences, or publications. Evidence also suggests that contacts with MEPs and meetings between rapporteurs, which already take place, are very helpful in securing the EP's attention (Domorenok 2009, 158). Experience shows that, during this meeting, it is important to provide EP rapporteurs or shadow rapporteurs with ready-made amendments that they can propose in committees. The work the CoR has been committed to since the entry into force of the Cooperation Agreement is heading in the right direction.

An example of an effective influence strategy can be found in the recent work of Mr. Bart Somers.[15] In the framework of his work concerning the opinion of the CoR on the prevention of radicalization,[16] a field visit to the Belgian city of Mechelen was organized, to which members of the CoR and of the EP Committee on Civil Liberties, Justice and Home Affairs (LIBE) were invited. It is, of course, a very effective way to raise awareness in parliamentarians about the solutions offered at the local level and to increase awareness of the CoR's work. Such an event can obviously not be repeated for every single opinion of the CoR, but should be considered whenever possible.

In addition, in order to pursue an effective communication strategy, the CoR should probably have recourse to professionals devoted to this task and whose major aim is to influence EP officials. Otherwise, as MEPs are flooded daily with questions, requests, or recommendations, the CoR's message would have difficulty gaining a decisive influence.

Finally, even if the CoR could surely do a lot to better communicate and promote its opinions, one should not downplay the EP's responsibility in the way the CoR's work is perceived and applied. In the areas where the CoR's opinions are mandatory under the treaties, EP rapporteurs and committee chairs should be informed of the role of the CoR and of their obligation, political if not legal, to read the opinions that are sent to them. The CoR is established by the founding treaties of the EU. It is not only a stakeholder or a lobby, it defends public interest and democracy. Hence, its opinions cannot be disregarded to the point of not being read nor treated in the same way as content originating from private interests. Furthermore, MEPs have everything to win from relying extensively on the CoR's work, for it provides them with the additional information and expertise that they sometimes lack.

---

[15] Mayor of the Belgian city of Mechelen and President of the 'Alliance of Liberals and Democrats for Europe' group in the Committee of the Regions.

[16] 'Combatting Radicalisation and Violent Extremism: Prevention mechanisms at local and regional level', CDR 6329/2015.

6 CONCLUSION

From disregard and distrust, the relationship between the EP and the CoR has moved to a successful cooperation, through an enhanced legislative coordination and an increase in relations between members and staff of the two bodies. The CoR has made huge improvements and can be said today to be one of the privileged partners of the EP. This evolution is good for both institutions, good for European democracy and the quality of its legislation.

This positive trend, however, does not hide the many challenges that still remain. From a body only punctually consulted, the CoR must become a real partner of the EP, present throughout the legislative cycle. Improvements must be made on both sides. The CoR must strengthen its message, better advocate for its positions, while the EP must recognize the added value of the CoR. This is currently what the secretariats of both institutions are working on; an improvement of the CoR's impact on the EP can therefore be expected in the coming years. Crucially, the CoR must realize that its influence will depend as much on its informal capacities than on its formal powers.

Of course, there is only so much that can be done by the CoR without a reinforcement of its institutional position. Political will can never overcome legal and financial constraints. The future of the CoR will hence primarily be decided by the evolution of these constraints: increase in staff and budget, binding powers on particular issues, and so on. This, however, remains far less likely to happen.

REFERENCES

Christiansen, T., & Lintner, P. (2005). The Committee of the Regions After 10 Years, Lessons from the Past and Challenges for the Future. *EIPASCOPE, 1*, 7–13.

Committee of the Regions. (2006). *Opinion of the Committee of the Regions on Guidelines for the Application and Monitoring of the Subsidiarity and Proportionality Principles*, 2006/C 115/08.

Committee of the Regions. (2009a). *Mission Statement*, CdR 56/2009.

Committee of the Regions. (2009b). *The selection process for Committee of the Regions members – Procedures in the Member States*, CdR 104/2009.

Committee of the Regions. (2014a). *Rules of Procedure*, OJ L 65/41.

Committee of the Regions. (2014b). *Cooperation Agreement between the European Parliament and the Committee of the Region.*

Committee of the Regions. (2017a). *Annual Impact Report 2016*, COR-2017-02424-00-00-ANN-REF.

Committee of the Regions. (2017b). *Report on the Implementation of the Cooperation Agreement Between the European Parliament and the European Committee of the Regions.*

Domorenok, E. (2009). The Committee of the Regions: In Search of Identity. *Regional & Federal Studies, 19*(1), 143–163.

European Parliament. (2014). *Rules of Procedure of the European Parliament.*

European Parliament. (2017). *Resolution of 16 February 2017 on Improving the Functioning of the European Union Building on the Potential of the Lisbon Treaty.*

Hönnige, C., & Panke, D. (2013). The Committee of the Regions and the European Economic and Social Committee: How Influential are Consultative Committees in the European Union. *Journal of Common Market Studies, 51*(3), 452–471.

Hönnige, C., & Panke, D. (2016). Is Anybody Listening? The Committee of the Regions and the European Economic and Social Committee and Their Quest for Awareness. *Journal of European Public Policy, 23*(4), 624–642.

Hönnige, C., et al. (2015). *Consultative Committees in the European Union. No Vote – No Influence?* Colchester: ECPR Press.

McCarthy, R. E. (1997). The Committee of the Regions: An advisory Body's Tortuous Path to Influence. *Journal of European Public Policy, 4*(3), 439–454.

Neshkova, M. I. (2010). The Impact of Subnational Interests on Supranational Regulation. *Journal of European Public Policy, 17*(8), 1193–1211.

Pasquier, R. (2015). La fin de "l'Europe des régions"? *Politique européenne, 4*(50), 150–159.

Piattoni, S., & Schönlau, J. (2015). *Shaping EU Policy from Below: EU Democracy and the Committee of the Regions.* Cheltenham: Edward Elgar.

Warleigh, A. (1999). *The Committee of the Regions Institutionalising Multi-Level Governance?* London: Kogan Page.

PART II

The EP in EU Law-Making

CHAPTER 6

Taming Trilogues: The EU's Law-Making Process in a Comparative Perspective

Justin Greenwood and Christilla Roederer-Rynning

1 INTRODUCTION

As the directly elected institution of representative democracy, the European Parliament (EP) is at the centre of debates about the nature of the European Union (EU) polity.[1] The dramatic increase in its legislative powers since becoming a directly elected institution in 1979 makes it the central object of analysis about the development of the EU. At the core of the EP's powers is its role as a co-legislator with the Council of the

[1] The authors acknowledge financial support from the Economic and Social Research Council (ESRC), grant ES/N018761/1 received as part of the Open Research Area (ORA) grant 187/2015. Part of the material used in this chapter comes from the field research and interviews conducted by Christilla Roederer-Rynning in Washington, DC from April to July 2017.

J. Greenwood (✉)
Robert Gordon University, Aberdeen, Scotland
e-mail: j.greenwood@rgu.ac.uk

C. Roederer-Rynning
University of Southern Denmark, Odense, Denmark
e-mail: crr@sam.sdu.dk

© The Author(s) 2019
O. Costa (ed.), *The European Parliament in Times of EU Crisis*,
European Administrative Governance,
https://doi.org/10.1007/978-3-319-97391-3_6

121

European Union[2] for the overwhelming majority of legislative files since the 2009 Treaty of Lisbon, making the mechanics of co-decision a key unit of analysis. The core question we address in this chapter is whether the EP, the people's tribune in EU politics, has arrived at a stable set of arrangements in order to assert itself in co-decision vis-à-vis other EU institutions. Trilogues present two potential risks for the EP as an organ of parliamentary representation: (1) depoliticising conflict by delegating decision-making to technical experts; and (2) reducing the accountability and transparency of the decision-making process by making it more informal and ad hoc. The key for the EP to counter these risks is to develop institutional autonomy and a sense of common purpose as a parliamentary institution to prevent it from being drawn into the Council's world of diplomacy.

We approach this question from a comparative institutionalist perspective. As institutionalists, we consider the institutionalisation of political procedures and organisations as a fundamental steppingstone for democratic development (Huntington 1965). Institutionalisation is not a mere process of designing rules. It is about infusing technical organisations with value and meaning, as classic institutionalist accounts remind us (Selznick 1949; Scott 2001). Elsewhere, we have argued that the embrace of trilogues is a 'critical moment of the institutionalisation of the EP-as-a-legislature' (Roederer-Rynning and Greenwood 2017). On these premises, we explore how the EP has responded to trilogues and what this response tells us about its development as an institutionalised organ of representative democracy. Furthermore, we analyse this question in the context of a comparative exploration of the EU and US institutions for bicameral conflict resolution. The politics of private deals within and between chambers of Congress has been at the core of recent political controversies in US politics, too. These controversies have crystallised with the repeated efforts by President Trump and his Republican majority in the US Congress to pass flagship legislation on health care reform and tax reform. Seasoned observers of Congress and law-makers alike have voiced their concerns about what they see as the de facto transformation of the Senate into a majoritarian institution and an opaque process taking place outside the formal institutional arenas of deliberation a well as law-making,

---

[2]Commonly referred to as the Council of Ministers. We use the term 'Council' in the remainder of the text.

concentrating power in the hands of a few congressional law-makers. These developments are interesting because the US Congress and congressional politics have been a prime point of reference in the comparative literature on the EP (e.g., Kreppel 2002; Crombez and Hix 2015).

Our analysis proceeds in four steps. First, we describe the development of trilogues in EU decision-making from the early 2000s, after innovations in the Treaty of Amsterdam gave critical momentum to the phenomenon, to the recent strategic inquiry of the European Ombudsman. Second, we zoom in on the response of the EP and show how the normalisation of trilogues triggered a process of institutional scrutiny and normative assessment, which progressively led to the institutionalisation of trilogues. Third, we zoom out to explore these findings in a comparative perspective, focusing on contemporary developments in US legislative politics. Finally, we wrap up by assessing the institutionalisation of trilogues from a democratic perspective, highlighting both the democratic conquests and the remaining challenges. In conclusion, we discuss the value of these findings for the ongoing reflection on the EP as a normal parliament and the role of informal institutions in EU law-making.

2 TRILOGUES AND EU DECISION-MAKING

The term *trilogues* denotes an informal but institutionalised mechanism providing for *in camera* discussions of legislative texts between the three main EU decision-making institutions,[3] with a view to securing legislative compromises. Although co-decision defines up to three readings between the Council and the EP, trilogues offer the means to achieve early legislative agreements. Their use has mushroomed since the 1999 Amsterdam Treaty made it possible for co-decision to be concluded at any stage in the legislative process, resulting in a search for informal ways of coming to inter-institutional agreements at an earlier stage than might otherwise be the case. Thus, trilogues were born of expediency, in recognition of the logistical challenges raised by the enlargement to 11 countries in 2004–2007 and the legislative empowerment of the Parliament (Shackleton and Raunio 2003; Kreppel 2002; Héritier and Reh 2012, in Broniecki 2017). The results have been startling. Half of all legislative files were concluded at first reading during the course of the 6th EP term

[3] The EP, the Council, and the European Commission.

(2004–2009) (Héritier and Reh 2012). This figure had risen to 97% of legislative files[4] by the middle of the 8th EP term (2014–2019) (European Parliament 2017). Among them, about two-thirds are so-called 'negotiated' legislative files, that is, files that require trilogues. Trilogues have thus become the *modus operandi* of EU law-making.

Until 2007, trilogues went largely unregulated, typically involving *in camera* bargaining between a limited number of 'relais actors' (Farrell and Héritier 2004), that is, the EP Rapporteur, the Presidency and the respective institutional secretariats in a supporting role. Since then, there has been a growing regulation of trilogues, both at the inter-institutional level in 2007[5] and at the EP level in 2012 and 2017.[6] The latter have specified the conditions for authorising the negotiations, the mandate to negotiate with, the composition of the EP negotiating team as well as oversight and reporting back mechanisms. We will examine the EP's response to the trilogues in greater detail in a later section.

Today, a negotiated legislative file will typically involve three to four trilogue summits (European Parliament 2017; European Parliament n.d.), but files with a high political content can involve considerably more (Brandsma 2015).[7] The negotiations become more difficult as the trilogue process advances, given that the most contentious points are often kept for the end game. In today's practice, a trilogue will involve a relatively large number of participants from each of the three EU institutions, which can extend to as many as 100 as in the case of the European Fund for Strategic Investments (European Parliament 2017). Most attendees come from the Parliament, comprising the Committee Chair leading the delegation, sometimes replaced by a Vice-President (Ripoll Servent and Panning 2017), the Rapporteur and Shadow Rapporteurs from the different parties, their assistants, political party functionaries and Committee secretariat

---

[4] This figure includes files concluded at first or early second reading. Early second reading files typically reflect the inheritance of first reading positions adopted at the end of the preceding legislative term (European Parliament 2017). Early second reading is where 'the agreement between the Council and Parliament is reflected in the Council''s Common Position rather than the Parliament''s first reading report. This may be because a compromise was reached between the two only after Parliament had adopted its first reading report' (House of Lords n.d.)

[5] 2007 inter-institutional agreement on codecision, concluded between the European Parliament, the Council, and the Commission.

[6] 2012 and 2017 reforms of the EP rules of procedure.

[7] In EP8, the largest in the first half term involved 14, for the General Data Protection Regulation.

staff. From the Commission, Heads of Unit or Directors attend, supported by the Legal Service and the Co-Decision Unit, although sometimes Director-Generals or their Deputies attend from the outset. A Commissioner often attends the concluding trilogues. The Council is represented by the rotating Presidency, initially in the form of the civil servant who chaired the Council Working Party supported by the Council Secretariat, and at later stages by the Chair of the Committee of Permanent Representatives (COREPER) (Ripoll Servent and Panning 2017). As legislative files are long, negotiations can be exhaustive, some involving all-night sessions. The negotiators work on a four-column document, where the first three columns identify the position of each of the three institutions, and a blank fourth column is filled out during the process to reflect the inter-institutional agreement reached in the trilogue meetings (Fig. 6.1).

A number of 'technical' preparatory meetings precede full 'political' trilogues as a means of coping with the legislative detail, which typically accompanies regulatory policy-making, as well as of making logistical arrangements for trilogues, with different compositions of actors attending the different types of meetings. In the main meeting, attendees of

Fig. 6.1   A full trilogue meeting

technical preparatory meetings come from the secretariats of the respective institutions, rather than the political level. At the more logistical level, there are also bilateral meetings between the secretariat of the EP and the Council (Ripoll Servent and Panning 2017). Heads of Units of the EP Committee Secretariat can be particularly influential players throughout the layers of meetings (Roederer-Rynning and Greenwood 2017). The layers beneath political trilogues contribute to the potential for the depoliticisation of inter-institutional decision-making.

Scholars have noted that, whilst expeditious in facilitating early agreements between EU decision-makers, trilogues have been an opaque and unaccountable form of decision-making (Farrell and Héritier 2004; Héritier and Reh 2012; Rasmussen and Reh 2013; Reh 2014; Roederer-Rynning and Greenwood 2015, 2017; Stie 2013). There is a risk that trilogues depoliticise the decision-making process by delegating undue decisional power to technical experts (Stie 2013). We know that 'when a policy decision point approaches, but clashes between rival advocacy coalitions cause impasse, the EU's natural propensity is to depoliticise issues and "push" them back to the sub-systemic level for quiet resolution' (Peterson 2001, 309). There is also a risk that trilogues give a small set of actors undue influence, leading to a personalisation or privatisation of the decision-making process (Farrell and Héritier 2004). The risk of privatisation is *not* inherent in closed decision-making processes, but lack of transparency compounds this risk by making it more difficult to exercise scrutiny and oversight. 'Trilogues are where deals are done', located somewhere in between 'the [institutional] space to negotiate' and norms of transparency (European Ombudsman 2015). Institutions like these are a means of expediting business, but their secluded nature and lack of record has made them targets for public anxiety (EU Observer 2014; International New York Times 2014). A coalition of 18 NGOs in a 2015 letter to the President of the Parliament and the Commission, and Secretary General of the Council of Ministers, spelt out the dangers of policy-making in a secluded setting, stressing how the secluded nature of trilogues privileges those with the resources and connections to be able to acquire information (Access Info Europe 2015; European Digital Rights Initiative 2015; Transparency International 2015).

Both legislators are vulnerable to these risks, because EU law-making is premised on the idea of a rules-based process. However, the EP is arguably more vulnerable to accusations of democratic deficit of the trilogue process since its legitimacy is bound with ideals of (supranational) democracy, while the Council's has been bound with ideals of (intergovernmental) diplomacy. Democracy gives pride of place to public debate and political deliberation as a means of reaching political compromises. As a result, trilogues have long been the subject of contention in the EP; and EP contention, in turn, was a contributing factor in the decision of the European Ombudsman to open a strategic inquiry on the transparency of trilogues (European Ombudsman 2015).

In her 2016 decision, the European Ombudsman pinpointed the democratic consequences of the trilogue process, drawing on both the EU's representative and participatory strands of democracy:

> A representative democracy…implies that citizens are effectively empowered to hold their elected representatives **accountable** for the specific choices made by their representatives on their behalf. Second, citizens have the right to **participate** in the democratic life of the Union. (European Ombudsman 2016)

> If citizens are to scrutinise how their representatives performed, they need to be able to compare the outcome of the process with their representatives' initial position, so that, if necessary, they can ask why positions changed and be reassured that the process took all interests and considerations into account. (European Ombudsman 2016)

The Ombudsman stressed that Articles 1 and 10(3) of the Treaty on European Union (TEU) ensure that 'decisions are taken as openly and as closely as possible to the citizen', and recalled requirements for the Parliament and the Council to meet in public when considering and voting on a draft legislative act as set out in Articles 15(2) and (3) in the Treaty on the Functioning of the European Union (TFEU). Nonetheless, in an overture to the need for inter-institutional space to negotiate, including elected representatives as participants, the Ombudsman recommended the publication of trilogue documents at the conclusion of the trilogue process. In the following section, we examine the response of the EP to the growing criticism of trilogues.

3   Zooming In: The European Parliament and Trilogues

When the Ombudsman opened her own-initiative enquiry into the transparency of trilogues in 2015, the institutions collectively sought to place on record their concern that she was exceeding her powers, but nonetheless responded. These responses demonstrate a deep commitment to current trilogue practice. The Council's response identified specific concerns about how disclosure of trilogue documents 'may seriously undermine the ongoing decision-making process' (EDRi 2015, 7). On a less defensive but nonetheless devoted tone, the EP's 8th Parliamentary Term Activity Report commits to further reflection on how trilogues can

> *adequately deliver on citizens' legitimate information needs, without undermining the fruitful working environment and conditions that have enabled Parliament, the Council and the Commission to respectfully and responsibly legislate over the years.* (European Parliament 2017, 37)

President Schulz sounded a similar line to the Council in warning the Ombudsman that

> *undue formalisation of the trilogue process could lead to negotiations taking place outside the established process (without, for example, all political groups being present or the orderly exchange of text proposals) and could therefore lead to less transparency rather than more.* (European Parliament 2017, 25)

However, while advocating the trilogue system, the EP has also tried to grapple actively with the issues raised in the public and internal debate, showing its higher sensitivity and vulnerability to criticisms of democratic deficit. These efforts were not purely reactive. In fact, a process of reform had started well before the Ombudsman's own report. Over the last decade, the EP has developed the most extensive internal rules of procedure of the three institutions, notably in 2009 (Annex XX, Code of Conduct for negotiating in the context of the ordinary legislative procedure), in 2012 (Rules 73 and 74, abolished and replaced with Rules 69c, d and f) and in 2017. These changes have introduced comprehensive arrangements for pluralisation of actors in the trilogue process, authorisation, oversight and reporting back; the provision of a mandate; some degree of transparency of the process; and a limited degree of ability to amend trilogue agreements. In 2009, at the end of the 6th EP term, the 'Code of Conduct for Negotiating in the Context of Codecision Procedures' was introduced as an Annex to the Rules of Procedure (Héritier and Reh 2012), carrying, *inter alia*, a proviso that (1) all political groups shall be represented, (2) that the negotiating mandate be provided by the committee or plenary, (3) that the negotiating team report back after each trilogue on the outcomes of the negotiations and update its mandate when negotiations changed the committee position and (4) that all texts be made available to the committee. The 2012 revisions made Annex XX binding and introduced the requirement for the Committee Chair or nominated Vice-Chair to lead the EP's official delegation (and chair the trilogue when the latter is held on EP premises), collectively referred to as part of the 'team'. Rule 73 comprised a comprehensive set of arrangements parallel to the provisions of the Code of Conduct, covering the composition of the negotiating team, the decision to open negotiations, the mandate on which to negotiate (for later consideration in plenary), a vote to approve the result of negotiations and a report back after each trilogue.

The most recent revisions to EP procedures for handling trilogues entered into force in January 2017. These changes extend the powers of the plenary relative to committees to authorise the commencement of inter-institutional negotiations. Thus, Rule 69c(2) gives MEPs or political groups a brief time window to seek a plenary vote on a Committee's decision to enter into negotiations with the Council. A further innovation of the rules was to introduce the publication of documents reflecting the outcome of the concluding trilogue. A little noticed introduction of a new rule, Rule 59(3), gives the plenary the opportunity to decide not to have a single vote on the provisional agreement, but to vote on amendments. This latter change addresses a long-standing criticism made by transparency NGOs of the EP's position being weakened by its continued de facto constraint in being unable to unpick agreements concluded in inter-institutional trilogue negotiations and presented as a *fait accompli*. The extent of use of Rule 59(3) will help address whether this criticism remains valid, but could imply further trilogue negotiations and use of the second reading procedure.

These changes have come about through a process of institutional scrutiny and normative assessment in the EP. The Constitutional Affairs Committee (AFCO) has had a pivotal position in this process as it is the committee in charge of the Rules of Procedure, with support for operational scrutiny provided by two horizontal units, the Conciliations and Co-decision Unit (CODE) and the Co-ordination of Legislation Unit (CORDLEG). The development of procedures in AFCO has been assisted by key Committee Chairs in different parliamentary terms, as well as from the leadership of the political groups. The Economic and Monetary Affairs Committee (ECON) was at the centre of co-decision during the 7th EP term, accounting for over one-fifth of all early legislative agreements in that term. Its Chair in the 6th EP term, Pervenche Berès, was a norm leader in driving for Committee Chairs to be regular members of the EP trilogue delegation, a practice diffused through the Conference of Committee Chairs and continued via her position as Chair of the Employment and Social Affairs Committee in the 7th EP term. Her successor as Chair of ECON, Sharon Bowles, also took up the cause, dynamically placing herself at the centre of each trilogue negotiation with the Council as a means of oversight and enforcement of committee positions. At the other extreme, in the 7th EP term was the Chair of the Committee on Transport and Tourism (TRAN), Brian Simpson, who spared his appearances on the grounds of the psychology of negotiations, intending to give a signal of gravitas by his attendance at the final meetings (Roederer-Rynning and Greenwood 2015). To a certain extent, these approaches will vary between parliamentary terms as Committee Chairs change, but the changes introduced have also become institutionalised (Roederer-Rynning and Greenwood 2017). The permanent secretariat of committees, project teams for different legislative files, the EP Legal Service and horizontal coordination units which service co-decision committees have played a part in this process. All of these have experienced substantial growth during the seventh term of the EP, as part of a wider process of upgrading the capacity of the secretariat which also extends to the European Parliament Research Service (EPRS) (European Parliament 2014). The number of assistants which Members can have has, moreover, been increased to four. Few national parliaments, with the exception of US Congress, enjoy access to knowledge and expertise on the scale displayed by the EP (Roederer-Rynning and Greenwood 2017). Thus, rules of pluralisation, delegation and oversight have been institutionalised in the EP, ensuring that trilogues today are an essentially multilateralised exercise in the Parliament. This means that trilogues in the EP have come a long way from the private deals occasionally stigmatised in the national and global media titles.

4   Zooming Out: The Importance of *Institutions*

Current US discussions on private deal-making give us a good opportunity to probe the importance of institutions and institutionalisation in a broader, comparative perspective. Given the idiosyncratic nature of the trilogue discussions, it is easy to forget that the controversy over trilogues is not unique to the EU. It is found in different forms in all bicameral systems where law-making requires the joint adoption of bills by two parliamentary chambers. The controversy over trilogues therefore allows us to see how similar political systems have dealt with bicameral conflict resolution. In this final section, we share contextual insights into the trilogue controversy by examining the state of current institutions of bicameral conflict resolution in the United States. The US case is interesting for several reasons.

First, comparativists have long highlighted similarities between the US and European polities (see, e.g., Sbragia 1992 and more recently Egan 2015). Both polities display a fragmented, multi-level political system, where the executive, legislative and judiciary powers are separated rather than fused, as in many European political systems. Within this overarching construction, the US Congress and the EU's legislative authority provide examples of some of the world's most powerful legislative assemblies. Article 1 of the US Constitution stipulates that 'all legislative Powers herein shall be vested in a Congress of the United States, which shall consist of a Senate and a House of Representatives'. Though the EP cannot take such pride of place in the Maastricht Treaty establishing the EU or even in the Lisbon Treaty (which, while elevating the EP to the status of co-legislator, still keeps a number of areas outside of its legislative purview), it is widely recognised as a powerful, federal-like legislature, bringing a powerful system of specialised standing committees and its impressive analytical capabilities to bear on EU legislation. Not only are both the US Congress and the EP influential actors in domestic politics, they have also established themselves as leading international diplomatic actors (Jancic 2015).

Second, with regard to the law-making process, both systems are characterised by the need for inter-chamber cooperation since the passage of legislative acts can only happen if the two chambers agree on the same legislative text (Rasmussen, 2011). In the United States, as in the EU, the heterogeneity of the two chambers roots in this constitutional requirement. The US 'Congress' is in reality composed of two chambers with very different traditions, rules, political outlook, operating mode and self-understanding. Moreover, 'each chamber is jealous of its powers and prerogatives and generally suspicious of the other body' (Oleszek 1974, 75). It has been said that the 'natural disinclination of the two bodies to work in tandem has limited joint committees to such housekeeping issues as government printing and overseeing the Library of Congress' (Ritchie 2016, 48). Likewise, the relationships between the two arms of the EU's 'legislative authority'—

epitomised in the pivotal legislative trilogues—can aptly be described as one of 'comity and conflict', to use a phrase applied to Congress (Oleszek 1974). Bearing these similarities in mind, it is interesting to understand the background against which the recent US controversies take place and discuss what kind of insights can be learned from these developments in the context of the EU's own trilogue system.

The controversy over private deal-making is not new in the United States. It has been part and parcel of a broader discussion on the gridlocking of US institutions going back to the 1990s (see recently Fukuyama 2001; Zakaria 2003; Connelly et al. 2017). It has re-emerged periodically, as successive US administrations have tried to push ambitious reform bills through the Congress on tax, health care or immigration reform. Under the Trump administration, the controversy has focused on the reform of Obama's Affordable Health Care Act and the 2017 Tax Cuts and Jobs Act of 2017, widely seen as 'the most drastic changes to US tax code in 30 years' (The Guardian, 20 December 2017). Both reforms have been propelled through informal talks among a small set of Congress insiders. In the health care reforms, the top Republican in the Senate Mitch McConnell first kept the legislative process insulated in a small group of law-makers (New York Times, 8 May 2017)[8] and, when he failed to garner the required number of votes, used an arcane budgetary procedure (Reconciliation Procedure) to force a repeal bill of Obama's Affordable Health Care Act through Congress. Meanwhile, on the equally pivotal tax reform file, the Republicans have pushed through legislation from a core group of six officials from the House, Senate and the White House—the so-called Big Six (*The Wall Street Journal*, 8–9 July 2017). In both cases, informal politics was allowed to circumvent the core institutional features of the Senate, which, as an institution designed to take care of minorities, 'provides extraordinary leverage to individual Senators' (Heitshusen 2014, 2).

These problems have drawn attention to a more long-standing erosion of the institutional foundations of the US law-making process. The institutional erosion of the US bicameral process has several dimensions.

It is thus widely recognised that the contemporary US legislative process is rather unpredictable. As a Congressional expert puts it, 'the process by which a bill can become law is rarely predictable and can vary significantly from bill to bill. In fact, for many bills, the process will not follow

---

[8] https://www.nytimes.com/2017/05/08/us/politics/women-health-care-senate.html?mcubz=3.

the sequence of congressional stages that are often understood to make up the legislative process' (Heitshusen 2014, 1). The life of bills is erratic. 'Many will never be brought up on the floor' while 'it is also possible, although less common, for a bill to come directly to the floor without being reported' (Heitshusen 2014, 7). For Members of Congress, this unpredictability can be a source of problem, as they do not always understand the process very well (interview 1, Congressional Research Service, 4 April 2017). Furthermore, it is interesting that compared with the EU where at least two-thirds of the legislative files are 'negotiated' (i.e., between the three EU institutions, in trilogues), 'negotiated' bills are a minority in the US Congress today. It is indeed estimated that 70% of all the legislative activity in Congress is consensual—there is no need for bicameral bargaining. There can be benign reasons for this. But it is striking that bills often materialise in the Congress in a coordinated way. The two chambers are 'not throwing bills at each other'; they are coordinating in advance. They try to 'iron things out in advance by Members and staff of both chambers talking with one another' (interview 2, Congressional Research Service, 23 June 2017).

Critically, where bills are negotiated between the chambers, the two chambers now tend to settle their differences through other ways than the formal conference committee designed for this purpose (Olezsek et al. 2016). Over the past two decades, the number of reports adopted in conference committees has significantly decreased from 53 under the 104th Congress (1994–1995) to 7 in the 114th Congress (2014–2015) (Bipartisan Policy Center 2017). Over the same period of time, the number of bills reported by committee in both chambers rose from 978 to 1271 (Bipartisan Policy Center 2017). A more informal method of 'exchange of amendments' between the chambers, known as the *ping pong* procedure, has become the favourite mode of reconciling differences (Oleszek 2008; Karadasheva 2012). While this informal method was limited to technical bills, or bills to be adopted under time pressure, the ping pong procedure is now used in a broad range of situations. The conference committee has become the 'dodo bird' while informal conflict resolution has taken over.

In the United States, the rise of informal politics seems to have reflected the polarisation of politics, both outside of Congress and inside the chambers (interview 3, Congressional Research Service, 11 July 2017). Polarisation means that the formal arenas for compromise-making have become gridlocked. This has affected the *standing committees* in both chambers of the Congress: 'the tradition of the committee as a safe place for negotiation has dwindled toward extinction since the 1990s' (Ronald Brownstein, *National Journal*, 11 May 2013). This has also affected the *conference committees* in charge of bicameral bargaining, which have generated their own informal and secretive deal-making outside the formal conference venue. Over time, the very act of convening a conference committee to negotiate compromises between the two chambers has become very difficult because it requires overcoming several challenging procedural hurdles in the Senate, which minorities have blocked. Thus, it is now not exceptional to see important legislation develop across the chambers in ad hoc fashion and under the impulsion of insulated groups of legislators. Informal alliances are now increasingly used to stave off the destructive effects of polarisation.

In sum, these developments bring into relief the importance of informal politics in both the EU and the US polities, but also key differences between the two. In both polities, informal politics has developed to bridge the tensions between fragmentation and integration in these federal legislatures, and eventually deliver policy. However, the sources of informal politics seem to differ greatly. In the United States, partisan polarisation has been driving informal politics, because institutional fragmentation becomes a source of gridlock in the absence of political glue. In the EU, inter-institutional conflict drives informal politics. Political parties are still too weak at the supranational level. Trilogues originated in the competition between the EP and the Council and from the realisation that the Council needed to bring the EP into the negotiations as closely and early as possible in order to avoid 'bad surprises'. Not only the sources of informal politics are different—the thrust of informal politics differs, too. While the trilogue process illustrates a process of institutionalisation of informal politics, the 'gangmen style' of legislative politics, as Brownstein has captured it (Brownstein 2013), can arguably best be understood as a step towards de-institutionalisation: we are in the realm of informal alliances rather than informal institutions. This is an inhospitable realm for democracy.

5   TAMING TRILOGUES: UNFINISHED BUSINESS

In all likelihood, bicameral compromises in the EU and in the United States will continue to involve negotiations in insulated forums. Insulation is not necessarily bad for democracy. It can promote deliberation and persuasion—or the ability to convince others on the basis of reasoned arguments (Checkel 2005). By the same token, open arenas are not necessarily good for democracy. They may foster ideological messaging or 'strategic disagreement', when 'part[ies] to a potential deal "avoid the best agreement that can be gotten given the circumstances in order to seek political gain"' (Gilmour, cited in Binder and Lee 2016, 96). Within this spectrum, we see the institutionalisation of trilogues as a positive but unfinished development.

On the positive side, the EP's participation in trilogues now satisfies core democratic criteria. The mandate to negotiate with the Council is public and endorsed by plenary; all of the political groups are represented in the trilogues; the negotiating team from the EP has the responsibility to stay within the mandate given by the Committee and ensure that a majority in the Committee supports the provisional agreement, that the Chair and Rapporteur report back to Committee, that the provisional agreement is voted on by the Committee (in a single vote) and that plenary can now decide to vote on amendments to the provisional agreement. It is interesting to note that, compared with the situation in the EP, there is nothing but established practice to guide the behaviour of the Council in trilogue negotiations (European Economic and Social Committee 2017). Working procedures are passed over from one Presidency to the next by training provided by the Council Secretariat. When a majority is evident on a given file at COREPER or ministerial level, that is taken to be the signal for the Presidency to open trilogue negotiations, and its initial mandate is public when the ministerial level gives it a 'General Approach'. There are significant differences within the Council as to the need for further transparency in trilogues, with a predictable cleavage between the Nordic countries, the Netherlands and Slovenia on the one hand and other countries on the other hand which raise the traditional objection that further transparency would simply result in more rigid positions and a less flexible approach. Across the Council, nonetheless, there is support for a 'diplomatic tradition' (European Economic and Social Committee, 76) of flexibility. While the diplomatic method gives the Council leverage by ambiguity, it also deprives it from influencing the negotiations by going public, as the EP has done. The Council's position is only known at a late stage, and then in the form of a General Approach (Roederer-Rynning and Greenwood 2015). The EP's mandate, by contrast, is public from an early stage, and the EP has been dexterous in political communication.

However, problems persist that must be tackled to bring trilogues in line with democratic norms of decision-making. Institutionalisation is a fragile process, which is very uneven across policy areas (Roederer-Rynning and Greenwood 2017) and can be reversed especially in its early stages. While the ECON approach strengthened the autonomy of the EP in the midst of the financial crisis, the diminishing grip of the crisis might erode the ECON etiquette (Roederer-Rynning, forthcoming). Furthermore, trilogues have led some EP committees to abandon their most progressive 'green' or 'liberal' standards, for instead to adopt more 'responsible' positions in practice (Burns 2013; Ripoll Servent 2015). Finally, while these changes have improved the EP's internal accountability in trilogues, they continue to suffer from a lack of transparency. The preparatory work in the EP, as in the Council, is opaque, as much of it revolves around the compromises struck by the Rapporteurs and Shadow Rapporteurs in the so-called shadows' meetings (Berthier 2016; Curtin and Leino 2017). The technical character of much EU legislation means that public scrutiny of co-decision files remains effectively performed by elite stakeholders and guardians of the public interest. Specialised EU press outlets, such as *Politico, EurActiv* and *EUObserver*, join with national and global titles to contribute to such monitoring. Another part of the EU ecosystem of monitoring involves a teeming population of interest groups, with an extensive system of funding supporting the presence of EU NGOs, taking their place alongside producer organisations. The main NGOs active in the field of transparency advocacy are *Transparency International* (EU liaison office) and smaller EU-specific NGOs including *Access Info Europe* and the *European Digital Rights Initiative* (*EDRi*). The UK-based NGO *Statewatch* has also historically been an active commentator in the field. These NGOs point to an enduring challenge for the democratisation of trilogues: their lack of transparency. The 2016 Inter-institutional Agreement (IIA) on Better Regulation promised no more than a joint legislative database and 'appropriate handling' of trilogue negotiations in the context of transparency of the legislative process (EDRi 2015). In more general terms, the IIA promised better communication to the public, and 'to facilitate traceability of the various steps in the legislative process' (EDRi, 6), as a means of guarding against the possibility of corruption and potential negative externalities arising from lobbying. These promises have yet to be implemented. Until they are, the lack of traceability tools ensures that public scrutiny of trilogues will continue to be difficult to perform in the foreseeable future.

6 Conclusion

The study of the institutionalisation of trilogues contributes new insights into the discussion of the EP as a 'normal parliament' (Hix et al. 2007; Busby 2013; Ripoll Servent 2015). It also enables us to pinpoint critical differences between informal *institutions* and informal *politics.* Our main argument is that the shift to trilogues has imparted the EP with a heightened consciousness of its role and identity as a normal parliament, and the dilemmas attached to this. The EP has therefore played a pivotal role in seeking to bring trilogues in line with standards of democratic law-making. Institutionalising trilogues has been a key step in this direction.

Trilogues have become the *modus operandi* of EU decision-making. The EP being a directly elected institution, trilogues carry more risk for the legitimacy of the EP than for the Council. Over time, the EP has developed a series of rules to tackle the range of issues around removing decision-making from the public gaze whilst at the same time defending the need for an institutional space to negotiate with the Council of Ministers *in camera.* In the most recent revision of rules, there is a mechanism for the political groups to bring a plenary vote on a Committee's decision to enter into negotiations with the Council on the basis of a particular mandate, meaning that the EP's position is both public and carries the endorsement of elected representatives from across the political spectrum. All of the political groups are represented in trilogues, and the Committee oversees changes to the mandate. At the end of the process, there is an opportunity for plenary to vote on amendments, rather than simply the entire package negotiated with the Council of Ministers. The EP has developed a system, which is much more formalised than the Council, where custom and practice of diplomatic tradition prevail.

Taming trilogues is unfinished business, however. Besides highlighting the value of institutionalisation, we have sounded several cautionary notes. The institutionalisation of trilogues is uneven across the co-legislators and across policy areas. It is also reversible in the EP where it still lacks formal means of enforcement. Furthermore, trilogues are now taking place in a political environment characterised by the increasing diffidence of European publics regarding European integration. This European form of radical polarisation may put EU institutions of bicameral conflict resolution under the same strain as the United States. For in the end, while ideological pluralism is the hallmark of democracy, democracy is inherently difficult to institutionalise in divided societies. The trilogue system is, with all its flaws and weaknesses, an easy target for Eurosceptical narratives based on idealised versions of democracy. Whilst there is still work to be done, and while we can learn from other political systems, trilogues have come a long way from the early day caricature of private deal-making. This gradual process of institutionalising informal politics stands in stark contrast to contemporary developments in the United States, where the story is more one of de-institutionalisation.

REFERENCES

Access Info Europe. (2015). Contribution to European Ombudsman Public Consultation on the Transparency of Trilogues. Retrieved April 26, 2017, from https://www.ombudsman.europa.eu/en/cases/correspondence.faces/en/67629/html.bookmark.

Berthier, A. (2016). Transparency in EU Law Making. *ERA Forum, 17*, 423–436.

Binder, S., & Lee, F. (2016). Making Deals in Congress. In J. Mansbridge & C. J. Martin (Eds.), *Political Negotiation: A Handbook*. Washington, DC: The Brookings Institution.

Bipartisan Policy Center. (2017, March 28). *Proposals to Strengthen and Protect Congress' Legislative Capacities*. Bipartisan Policy Center Seminar, Washington, DC.

Brandsma, G. J. (2015). Co-Decision After Lisbon: The Politics of Informal Trilogues in European Union Lawmaking. *European Union Politics, 16*(2), 300–319.

Broniecki, P. (2017). *Is Informal Decision Making in Bicameral Legislatures Unrepresentative?* Paper prepared for presentation to the 15th Biennial Conference of the European Union Studies Association, Miami, May 4–6, 2017.

Brownstein, R. (2013, May 11). Gangmen Style. *National Journal*, p. 9.

Busby, A. (2013). Normal Parliament': Exploring the Organisation of Everyday Political Life in an MEPs Office. *Journal of Contemporary European Research, 9*(1), 94–115.

Burns, C. (2013). Consensus and Compromise Become Ordinary – But At What Cost? A Critical Analysis of the Impact of the Changing Norms of Codecision Upon European Parliament Committees. *Journal of European Public Policy, 20*(7), 988–1005.

Checkel, J. (2005). International Institutions and Socialization in Europe: Introduction and Framework. *International Organization, 59*(4), 801–826.

Connelly Jr., W. F., Pitney, J., & Smith, G. J. (2017). *Is Congress Broken? The Virtues and Defects of Partisanship and Gridlock*. Washington, DC: Brookings Institution Press.

Crombez, C., & Hix, S. (2015). Legislative Activity and Gridlock in the European Union. *British Journal of Political Science, 45*(3), 477–499.

Curtin, D., & Leino, P. (2017). In Search of Transparency for EU Law-Making: Trilogues on the CUSP of Dawn. *Common Market Law Review, 54,* 1673–1712.

Egan, M. (2015). *Single Markets: Economic Integration in Europe and the United States.* Oxford: Oxford University Press.

EU Observer. (2014). Secret EU Lawmaking: The Triumph of the Trilogue. Retrieved April 28, 2017, from http://euobserver.com/investigations/123555.

European Digital Rights Initiative (EDRi). (2015). Response to the European Ombudsman's Public Consultation on the Transparency of Trilogues. Retrieved April 26, 2017, from https://www.ombudsman.europa.eu/en/cases/correspondence.faces/en/67665/html.bookmark.

European Economic and Social Committee. (2017). Investigation of Informal Trilogue Negotiations Since the Lisbon Treaty – Added Value, Lack of Transparency and Possible Democratic Deficit, Contract No. CES/CSS/13/2016 23284.

European Ombudsman. (2015). Trilogues and Transparent Law Making. Retrieved April 26, 2017, from https://www.ombudsman.europa.eu/en/activities/calendarevent.faces/en/1001/html.bookmark.

European Ombudsman. (2016). Decision of the European Ombudsman Setting Out Proposals Following Her Strategic Enquiry OI/8/2015/JAS Concerning the Transparency of Trilogues. Retrieved April 26, 2017, from https://www.ombudsman.europa.eu/cases/decision.faces/en/69206/html.bookmark.

European Parliament. (2014). Committee Statistical Report: 7th Legislature 2009 2014, DGIPOL – Unit for Legislative Coordination.

European Parliament. (2017). Activity Report on the Ordinary Legislative Procedure, 4 July 2016–31 December 2016 (8th Parliamentary Term). Retrieved May 9, 2017, from http://www.epgencms.europarl.europa.eu/cmsdata/upload/7c368f56-983b-431e-a9fa-643d609f86b8/Activity-report-ordinary-legislative-procedure-2014-2016-en.pdf.

European Parliament. (n.d.). Completing the Legislative Cycle: Legislation: Trilogue Negotiations. Retrieved April 26, 2017, from http://www.europarl.europa.eu/the-secretary-general/resource/static/files/Documents%20section/SPforEP/Trilogue_negotiations.pdf.

Farrell, H., & Héritier, A. (2004). Interorganizational Negotiation and Intraorganizational Power in Shared Decision-Making: Early Agreements Under Codecision and Their Impact on the European Parliament and Council. *Comparative Political Studies, 37*(10), 1184–1212.

Fukuyama, F. (2001). *The Origins of Political Order.* New York: Farrar, Straus, and Giroux.

Greenwood, J., & Roederer-Rynning, C. (2015). The "Europeanization" of the Basel Process: Financial Harmonization Between Globalization and Parliamentarization. *Regulation and Governance, 9*(4), 325–338.

Heitshusen, V. (2014). Introduction to the Legislative Process in the US Congress. *Congresional Research Service, 7–5700*. Retrieved September 7, 2018, from https://fas.org/sgp/crs/misc/R42843.pdf.

Héritier, A., & Reh, C. (2012). Codecision and Its Discontents: Intra-Organisational Politics and Institutional Reform in the European Parliament. *West European Politics, 35*(5), 1134–1157.

Hix, S., Noury, A., & Roland, G. (2007). *Democratic Politics in the European Parliament*. Cambridge: Cambridge University Press.

House of Lords. (n.d.). Codecision and National Parliamentary Scrutiny – European Union Committee. Retrieved May 9, 2017, from https://www.publications.parliament.uk/pa/ld200809/ldselect/ldeucom/125/12504.htm.

Huntington, S. (1965). Political Development and Political Decay. *World Politics, 17*(3), 386, 430.

International New York Times. (2014, April 24). E.U. Chided for Lack of Openness. Retrieved June 16, 2014, from http://news-business.vlex.com/vid/chided-corruption-growing-distrust-507432674.

Jancic, D. (2015). Transatlantic Regulatory Interdependence, Law and Governance: The Evolving Roles of the EU and US Legislatures. *Cambridge Yearbook of European Legal Studies, 17*, 334–359.

Kardasheva, R. (2012). Trilogues in the EU Legislature. http://raya.eu/wpcontent/uploads/2012/08/Trilogues_in_the_EU_Legislature.pdf. Accessed 6 September 2018.

Kreppel, A. (2002). *The European Parliament and Supranational Party System: A Study in Institutional Development*. Cambridge: Cambridge University Press.

Oleszek, W. (1974). House-Senate Relationships: Comity and Conflict. *Annals of the American Academy of Political and Social Science, 411*(1), 75–86.

Oleszek, W. (2008). Whither the Role of Conference Committees: An Analysis. *Congressional Research Service*, CRS Report RL34611.

Olezsek, W., Olezsek, M., Rybicky, E., & Heniff, B. (2016). *Congressional Procedures and the Policy Process* (10th ed.). Los Angeles: SAGE.

Peterson, J. (2001). The Choice for EU Theorists: Establishing a Common Framework for Analysis. *European Journal of Political Research, 39*(3), 289–318.

Rasmussen, A. (2011). Procedural Dis(Obedience) in Bicameral Bargaining in the United States and the European Union. *Journal of European Integration, 33*(3), 267–283.

Rasmussen, A., & Reh, C. (2013). The Consequences of Concluding Codecision Early: Trilogues and Intra Institutional Bargaining Success. *Journal of European Public Policy, 20*(7), 1006–1024.

Reh, C. (2014). Is Informal Politics Undemocratic? Trilogues, Early Agreements and the Selection Model of Representation. *Journal of European Public Policy, 21*(6), 822–841.

Ripoll Servent, A. (2015). *Institutional and Policy Change in the European Parliament: Deciding on Freedom, Security and Justice.* Basingstoke: Palgrave Macmillan.

Ripoll Servent, A., & Panning, L. (2017). *Eurosceptics in Trilogue Settings: Intra-Institutional Interest Formation and Contestation.* Paper prepared for presentation to the 15th Biennial Conference of the European Union Studies Association, May 4–6, 2017.

Ritchie, D. A. (2016). *The U.S. Congress: A Very Short Introduction.* Oxford: Oxford University Press.

Roederer-Rynning, C. (forthcoming). Passage to Bicameralism: Lisbon's Ordinary Legislative Procedure at Ten. *Comparative European Politics.*

Roederer-Rynning, C., & Greenwood, J. (2015). The Culture of Trilogues. *Journal of European Public Policy, 22*(8), 1148–1165.

Roederer-Rynning, C., & Greenwood, J. (2017). The European Parliament as a Developing Legislature: Coming of Age in Trilogues. *Journal of European Public Policy, 24*(5), 735–754.

Sbragia, A. (Ed.). (1992). *Euro-Politics: Institutions and Policymaking in the 'New' European Community.* Washington, DC: The Brookings Institution.

Scott, W. R. (2001). *Institutions and Organizations.* Thousand Oaks, CA: Sage Publications.

Selznick, P. (1949). *TVA and the Grassroots: A Study in the Sociology of Formal Organizations.* Berkeley: University of California Press.

Shackleton, M., & Raunio, T. (2003). Codecision Since Amsterdam: A Laboratory for Institutional Innovation and Change. *Journal of European Public Policy, 10*(2), 171–187.

Stie, A. E. (2013). *Democratic Decision-Making in the EU: Technocracy in Disguise?* Abingdon: Routledge.

Transparency International. (2015). Transparency International's Reply to the European Ombudsman. Retrieved April 26, 2017, from https://www.ombudsman.europa.eu/en/cases/correspondence.faces/en/67617/html.bookmark.

Zakaria, F. (2003). *The Future of Freedom: Illiberal Democracy at Home and Abroad.* New York: Norton and Company.

CHAPTER 7

The European Parliament and EU Secondary Legislation: Improved Scrutiny Practices and Upstream Involvement for Delegated Acts and Implementing Acts

Vicky Marissen

1 Introduction

The Treaty of Lisbon has provided the European Parliament (EP) with increased powers. In legislative terms, the EP has been promoted to co-legislator in a number of additional policy areas (both existing EU competences and new ones). With agriculture in particular, the EP—after many years of struggle—finally obtained codecision power. Regarding the EU budget, the EP is now on an equal footing with the Council of the European Union (Council), at least when it comes to the adoption of the annual budget; with regard to the Multiannual Financial Framework

Visiting Professor on Secondary Legislation at the College of Europe (Bruges and Natolin). Special thanks to Steven Corcoran and Daniel Guéguen for their invaluable assistance with research and drafting.

V. Marissen (✉)
College of Europe, Bruges, Belgium
e-mail: vicky.marissen@eppa.com

© The Author(s) 2019
O. Costa (ed.), *The European Parliament in Times of EU Crisis*,
European Administrative Governance,
https://doi.org/10.1007/978-3-319-97391-3_7

143

(MFF), the Council still has the final say, although politically, the Members of the European Parliament (MEPs) can still flex their muscles quite considerably. On a political level, Parliament has shown strong strategic vision, extensively interpreting its role in the process of nominating the President of the European Commission,[1] thereby bringing about the introduction of the *Spitzenkandidaten* system.

All these changes have been commented on by others in detail.[2] However, one aspect of reinforced EP competences under the Treaty of Lisbon that in our view has been much less discussed to date concerns the institution's powers regarding secondary legislation, that is, delegated and implementing acts.

The Treaty of Lisbon provides for dedicated articles setting out the relevant instruments of secondary legislation (delegated acts and implementing acts). Building on the 2006 reform of the system known as 'comitology' and based on provisions envisaged in the draft Constitutional Treaty—the predecessor of the Treaty of Lisbon which never entered into force—article 290 of the Treaty on the Functioning of the European Union (TFEU) provides a definition of delegated acts and article 291 provides an explanation of when implementing acts should be used in EU legislation.

From a legal perspective, this insertion in the Treaty was a very positive development and a sign of a maturing legal system. Most national jurisdictions envisage an operational process for implementing or complementing the legislative framework set down by primary legislation. The fact that such a process has also developed at EU level symbolises a natural evolution, with features inherent to the specific character of the EU.

2   THE EUROPEAN PARLIAMENT AND DELEGATED ACTS

2.1   *New Powers for the European Parliament Under Article 290 TFEU*

With the entry into force of the Treaty of Lisbon, the EP saw one of its key demands on secondary legislation met: to be placed on an equal footing

---

[1] Article 17, paragraph 7, sub-paragraph 1 of the Treaty on the European Union (TEU).

[2] See, for example, Costa, O. (2014), 'Que peut le Parlement européen', *Pouvoirs, revue française d'études constitutionnelles et politiques*, 149, 77–89; Devuyst, Y. (2013), 'The European Parliament and International Trade Agreements: Practice after the Lisbon Treaty', *The European Union in the World*, pp. 171-189; Crombez, C., Høyland, B. (2015), 'The budgetary procedure in the European Union and the implications of the Treaty of Lisbon, *European Union Politics*, Volume 16, Issue 1, 67–89.

with the Council when it comes to amending or complementing legislative acts adopted by the EU. Whether determining the Commission's mandate to amend or complement non-essential elements of legislative acts, exercising its right to object to (i.e. veto) delegated acts, revoking the delegation from the Commission, or most importantly—although not explicitly mentioned in article 290—its involvement in the preparatory stage of the adoption of delegated acts,[3] the EP gained equality in this area.

Although back in July 2006, the EP was granted a right of objection with the introduction of the Regulatory Procedure with Scrutiny (the RPS),[4] Parliament remained an unequal partner to the Council. The latter enjoyed a privileged role first and foremost because, under the RPS, Member States have the right to send their representatives to the regulatory committees where they discuss and vote on draft measures and, second, due to the Council's call-back right envisaged under previous treaties,[5] which allowed the Council to take back its implementing power if the Member States' representatives were unable to generate a sufficient majority in favour of an implementing measure at committee level.

Article 290 TFEU fundamentally reformed this system. Unlike draft measures under the RPS, delegated acts are not voted in 'comitology' committees. The Commission—once mandated through a legislative act to adopt delegated acts—is essentially autonomous in the adoption of delegated acts. In a Communication published barely eight days after the entry into force of the Treaty of Lisbon, the Commission confirmed that it would be drafting and adopting delegated acts without the involvement of comitology committees[6] and that Member States' experts would only be consulted. This was a rude awakening for many EU Member States, but a victory for the EP in terms of gaining power.

2.2 Providing the Mandate for Delegation

Before addressing how the EP handles its scrutiny power in practice, we must first look at the role of the EP as set out under article 290 TFEU.

---

[3] Inter-institutional Agreement on Better Law-Making of 13 April 2016, OJ L 123/1 to 123/14 of 12.05.2016; notably L 123/6.

[4] Council Decision 2006/512/EC of 17 July 2006, OJ L 200, 22.07.2006, 11.

[5] See article 202 of the Treaty establishing the European Community (Nice consolidated version), OJ C 325, 24.12.2002, 117.

[6] Communication from the Commission to the European Parliament and the Council on the Implementation of Article 290 of the Treaty on the Functioning of the European Union, 9 December 2009, COM(2009) 673 final, 6–7.

In its first paragraph, the article explicitly envisages that: '*A legislative act may delegate to the Commission the power to adopt non-legislative acts of general application to supplement or amend certain non-essential elements of the legislative act.*'

This means that, in areas subject to the Ordinary Legislative Procedure (OLP), it is up to the EP and the Council to decide whether they want to provide the Commission with a delegated power. Likewise, this can be decided by the Council in the context of the special legislative procedure (formerly consultation procedure). The paragraph continues by saying: '*The objectives, content, scope and duration of the delegation of power shall be explicitly defined in the legislative acts.*' In other words, the co-legislators must also define what type of mandate is envisaged and its precise terms.

Within the legal conditions set out in the treaty and the relevant case law,[7] the EP and the Council enjoy broad political discretion during the OLP, whether choosing between a delegated act or implementing act, determining the nature and extent of the power delegated to the Commission, or determining the nature and extent of the implementing power conferred on the Commission.

However, this discretion also means that secondary legislation has often been a flashpoint between the EP and the Council during the OLP. Despite the framework on delegated and implementing acts as set out in articles 290 and 291 TFEU respectively, the EP and the Council—often for political reasons—might disagree on which instrument should be envisaged in the legislative act:

- The EP wants to make sure that its role is taken into account when the conditions for article 290 TFEU are met, notably its right of objection and revocation and its involvement in the preparatory phase of delegated acts; the EP's role for implementing acts is marginal (concerning implementing acts, see Sect. 2 of this chapter);
- The Council on a number of occasions tends to prefer implementing acts since it allows Member States to preserve the role of their national representatives in comitology committees (including voting capacity); although they do discuss and get consulted on delegated

---

[7] See, for example, the judgments of the Court of Justice of the European Union in cases C-427/12 and C-88/14.

acts, Member States' experts have no voting capacity with regard to the latter.

This conflict has regularly played out during trilogue talks on legislative files, including, for example, on novel foods[8] and energy labelling.[9] Efforts have been made, nonetheless, to defuse tensions. In the Inter-institutional Agreement on Better Law-Making of 13 April 2016, the institutions commit themselves to negotiate '*non-binding criteria*' for delineating articles 290 and 291 TFEU.[10] The EP in particular—which has developed its own criteria on this topic[11]—underlines the importance of negotiating and agreeing on such general criteria in order to serve as guidance during the OLP and thereby reduce the potential for disagreement. Inter-institutional talks on these delineation criteria have been ongoing since 2017. The commitment with regard to these criteria comes on top of other commitments in the Inter-institutional Agreement regarding experts' consultation, as mentioned above, and on the setting up of a joint register for delegated acts (see page 13 of this chapter).

In addition, in some cases the co-legislators have opted to insert more details in the text of the legislative act itself, instead of providing for a delegated act or an implementing act. Whilst this means that potentially sensitive issues are regulated in the legislative act rather than inserted into secondary legislation, there is a risk that this can lead to overly detailed legal provisions which can run contrary to the principles of simplification and better regulation.

[8] Regulation (EU) 2015/2283 of the European Parliament and of the Council of 25 November 2015 on novel foods, amending Regulation (EU) No 1169/2011 of the European Parliament and of the Council and repealing Regulation (EC) No 258/97 of the European Parliament and of the Council and Commission Regulation (EC) No 1852/2001, OJ L 327, 11.12.2015, 1–22.

[9] Regulation (EU) 2017/1369 of the European Parliament and of the Council of 4 July 2017 setting a framework for energy labelling and repealing Directive 2010/30/EU, OJ L 198, 28.7.2017, 1–23.

[10] Inter-institutional Agreement of 13 April 2016 between the European Parliament, the Council of the European Union and the European Commission on Better Law-Making, OJ L 123, 12.5.2016, paragraph 28.

[11] See Report of 4 December 2013 on follow-up on the delegation of legislative powers and control by Member States of the Commission's exercise of implementing powers, 2012/2323(INI), paragraph 1 (Rapporteur: József Szájer).

2.3   The Right to Object to Delegated Acts and Right to Revoke the Delegation

Under article 290 TFEU, the EP and the Council obtained a right of objection[12] similar to that which applies under the RPS, albeit with some differences: the standard deadline for objecting to a delegated act is two months as opposed to three months under the RPS, while the grounds that may be invoked to object to a delegated act are not limited.

The majority threshold required for the right of objection (or revocation) to be invoked remains the same: in the EP, a majority of its component members (i.e. 376 out of 751 MEPs); in the Council, a qualified majority of Member States.

In practice, the EP has not frequently made use of its veto. At the time of writing, the institution has issued a very limited number of objections against delegated acts. The author will refrain from elaborating in great detail on this point, as it is the subject of an in-depth contribution to this book by Michael Kaeding (cross-reference to pages of this contribution).

Nonetheless, it is worth noting that in the author's interviews with EP officials, technical nature, workload and the high majority threshold were quoted as factors complicating any motion to veto a delegated act. More importantly, as the next section will show, the upstream reception of information and overall increased involvement of the EP in the preparation phase of delegated acts also go a long way in explaining the low number of vetoes. Limited use of formal powers therefore does not necessarily signify an unwillingness to use those powers or an inability to deal with delegated acts.

As for the right of revocation introduced by the Treaty of Lisbon,[13] to date it has never been used. This power involves the possibility for the EP or the Council to revoke the entire delegated power from the Commission under a given legislative act, thereby terminating its power to adopt any future delegated acts under that legislative act.

From the EP's perspective, the fact that this power has not been used so far is not necessarily a cause for concern. Revocation may be regarded as a kind of nuclear option, to be contemplated only in very exceptional cases.

---

[12] Article 290, paragraph 2, point (b) TFEU.
[13] Article 290, paragraph 2, point (a) TFEU.

Like the right of objection, although different in nature,[14] it may be considered a tool that ensures the Commission respects the role of the EP with regard to delegated acts and is therefore continuously motivated to provide sufficient information and to take the EP's input into account.

2.4 The Informal Role of the EP in the Drafting and Adoption of Delegated Acts

Although the rights of objection and revocation are certainly central components of the EP's power in respect of secondary legislation, it would be misguided to evaluate the EP's practical use of its powers under article 290 TFEU purely on the basis of its exercise of these formal rights to date.

In reality, the EP—similarly to the Member States—increasingly plays a role in the preparation phase of delegated acts—that is, before the Commission formally adopts the delegated act and sends it to the EP and the Council for scrutiny (and potential objection). Essentially, this is a role that is not explicitly envisaged in article 290 TFEU, as the latter does not address the preparatory phase of delegated acts at all. In principle, once the legislators decide to delegate a measure for adoption by the Commission, the latter is autonomous in the drafting and adoption process of that delegated act. In the early days of the Lisbon Treaty system, the Commission had a tendency to interpret this in a very strict way, in effect eliminating the role of Member State experts in the comitology committees.[15]

During these initial years, the EP had to deal with secondary legislation in areas like agriculture and fisheries where it did not previously have codecision power and needed to ensure that its new rights in these areas were respected by the other institutions.[16] A notable example concerned the delegated acts drafted to complement the reform of the Common Agricultural Policy (CAP), where it was necessary for the EP to organise high-level meetings with the Commission.[17]

---

[14] The right of objection involves the rejection of one specific delegated act, whilst the revocation takes away the delegated power altogether.

[15] See note 3 above.

[16] Interview with the Conciliations and Codecision Unit of the EP Secretariat, 4 May 2017.

[17] See Europolitics No. 4761, Thursday 28 November 2013 'Commission to hold high-level talks with MEPs on delegated acts', 12.

From 2012 onwards, the EP further responded to this situation by adopting a variety of measures to reinforce its internal methods for scrutinising and keeping track of delegated acts from the early stages of their preparation by the Commission. These measures relate primarily to the functioning of EP Committees, which are responsible in practice for dealing with delegated acts received from the Commission.

The most important of these internal EP reforms include the following:

- The **EP Conference of Presidents** has taken a keen interest in overseeing scrutiny activities in Committees for some time now.[18] This political oversight was further strengthened by the revised EP Rules of Procedure which now allow political groups to table a motion objecting to an RPS measure directly to the plenary (in other words, bypassing the Committee stage in certain circumstances)[19];
- The holding of regular **scrutiny slots** in EP Committees, whereby the relevant Committee invites representatives of the Commission and/or competent EU agencies to provide an update on planned secondary legislation and answer questions from MEPs.[20] As the latest EP Activity Report states,[21] these scrutiny slots have proven valuable in that they allow the EP to obtain clarifications—and, on occasion, even concrete amendments—regarding the draft delegated act, thereby making it unnecessary to exercise their formal right of objection when the measure is subsequently adopted;
- The appointment of MEPs as **permanent rapporteurs** responsible for following delegated and implementing acts on an ongoing basis within a Committee.[22] Under typical practice, this involves the MEP presenting the measure at a meeting of the relevant Committee and,

---

[18] Horizontal guidance adopted by the Conference of Presidents (CoP) on 19 April 2012 on the screening of pending proposals, confirmed on 27 November 2014.

[19] See Rule 106(4) of the European Parliament Rules of Procedure (January 2017).

[20] For example, see the agenda of the meeting of the Committee on Economic and Monetary Affairs (ECON) on 3 May 2017, item 10 (ECON(2017)0503_1). This practice is recognised in the Inter-institutional Agreement of 13 April 2016 on Better Law-Making, supra, paragraph 28.

[21] Activity Report on the Ordinary Legislative Procedure, 4 July 2014–31 December 2016 (8th parliamentary term), 30.

[22] Report of 4 December 2013, supra, paragraph 16.

if necessary, recommending further action. In some cases, the MEP appointed to this position also acted as rapporteur for the relevant legislative act on behalf of the EP, although this practice tends to vary across different EP Committees[23];

- The circulation within certain EP Committees of **newsletters** providing an overview of all delegated acts, implementing acts and RPS measures recently received. Such newsletters normally indicate the deadline for the potential of raising an objection against a given act[24];
- The **recruitment of extra Committee administrators** in 2016.[25] These administrators are specifically responsible for following secondary legislation within EP Committees and managing the flow of measures to better facilitate scrutiny by MEPs. They also serve as a contact point in the event that an MEP has a query about a given measure;
- The holding of **regular meetings of an informal network** composed of, among others, the Committee administrators mentioned directly above, members of the EP Legal Service and the cabinet of the EP's Secretary General (in total, 30–40 officials). These network meetings, co-ordinated by the EP Secretariat's Unit for Conciliations and Codecision, allow for the identification of horizontal problems relating to secondary legislation and development of solutions[26];
- The development of an **internal handbook** by the Unit for Conciliations and Codecision, intended as a guide for MEPs and officials when dealing with secondary legislation.[27]

In addition, it is essential to highlight the impact of inter-institutional agreements on the EP's upstream scrutiny activities, particularly with regard to expert groups.

By way of background, the Commission has gradually evolved away from the strict interpretation of its autonomy in the drafting and adoption of delegated acts and moved towards an understanding that the involve-

---

[23] Working Document of the Legal Affairs Committee of 17 April 2013, PE506.179v02-00, 7.
[24] Interview with the EP Committee on Environment, Public Health and Food Safety, 11 May 2017.
[25] Activity Report, supra, 30.
[26] Interview with the Conciliations and Codecision Unit of the EP Secretariat, 4 May 2017.
[27] Ibid.

ment of Member State experts is useful and, in certain circumstances, even required from an operational perspective. This has led to the systematic involvement of expert groups for the preparation of delegated acts; such groups are composed of Member State representatives and chaired by a Commission civil servant.

Legally speaking, Member State representatives in expert groups have no voting rights with respect to draft delegated acts. Nonetheless, the Commission requests their input and has discretion on whether to take their comments into account. Thus, Member States acquired a new privileged role regarding delegated acts and the setting up of expert groups became an increasingly common practice over time. This is one of the elements that is expected to make the Council more willing to accept delegated acts.

How does the EP fit into this picture? As indicated above, the Lisbon Treaty put the EP on an equal footing with the Member States in the Council as regards delegated acts, by effectively abolishing Member States' role in the comitology committees. With the rise of the expert groups, a new imbalance was therefore created.

To remedy this imbalance, two important inter-institutional agreements were instrumental:

- The **2010 Framework Agreement** between the Commission and the EP recognised the option for '*EP experts*' to attend expert group meetings at the Commission's invitation, along with a general right to receive information with regard to these meetings[28];
- The **2016 Inter-institutional Agreement on Better Law-Making** further strengthened these rights, in particular by allowing EP experts systematically to have access to expert group meetings without the need for an invitation, whilst continuing to benefit from the reception, in line with the arrangement that exists for the Council, of all relevant documents (e.g. agendas and draft delegated acts) at the same time as they are sent to the members of the expert group, as well as calendars of future expert group meetings.[29]

---

[28] Framework Agreement on relations between the European Parliament and the European Commission, OJ L 304 20.10.2010, paragraph 15.

[29] Inter-institutional Agreement on Better Law-Making, supra, paragraph 28.

In practice, the EP tends to send administrators of the EP Secretariat who are in charge of delegated and implementing acts in the relevant EP Committees to these expert groups. They attend the meetings in an observer capacity and receive first-hand information. This is seen as an important and useful step in understanding the evolution of delegated acts, allowing the EP to be informed at an earlier stage. In the event that issues arise during this preparatory phase, the Commission can be invited to Parliament to discuss the matter with the MEPs. This upstream right of information also provides one reason why the EP has vetoed only a small number of delegated acts to date.

3   THE EUROPEAN PARLIAMENT AND IMPLEMENTING ACTS

Like for delegated acts, the EP, together with the Council, has the power to determine, via the legislative act, the nature and limits of the Commission's power to adopt implementing acts. However, when it comes to scrutiny of individual implementing acts adopted by the Commission, the role of the EP is limited.

3.1   *What the Treaty Says*

This more limited power results from the wording of article 291 TFEU.

Paragraph 1 recognises that Member States are responsible for the implementation of EU legislation.[30] However, paragraph 2 provides that '[w]*here uniform conditions for implementing legally binding Union acts are needed*', the Commission (and in more limited cases, the Council) may exercise implementing powers under EU legislation.

In other words, the power to implement EU legislation resides primarily with the Member States, or alternatively with the Commission or Council on a subsidiary basis.

Article 291 TFEU, paragraph 3, limits the role of the EP to adopting (with the Council) a Regulation laying down in advance the rules and general principles concerning mechanisms for control by Member States

---

[30] Article 291 TFEU, paragraph 1: '*Member States shall adopt all measures of national law necessary to implement legally binding Union acts.*'

of the Commission's exercise of implementing powers. This Regulation—known as Regulation 182/2011[31]—was adopted via the OLP on 16 February 2011 and entered into force on 1 March 2011.

3.2   The European Parliament's Power Under Regulation 182/2011

Under Regulation 182/2011, the Commission adopts implementing acts subject to the supervision of committees of Member State representatives who have the right to vote by qualified majority on the drafts of those implementing acts. Scrutiny is carried out by an Examination or an Advisory Committee and, if necessary, an Appeal Committee.

Besides its right to information, the only power the EP possesses in respect of implementing acts is a right of scrutiny, that is, the right to indicate to the Commission that a given draft 'exceeds the implementing powers provided for in the [legislative] act'.[32] Such opinions are non-binding however; the Commission is not obliged to amend the draft in line with the EP's views, but must only review the measure and then state how it intends to proceed (maintain, amend or withdraw the act in question). Therefore, the right of scrutiny is a far cry from the right of objection envisaged for delegated acts under article 290 TFEU.

Despite the weak character of the right of scrutiny over implementing acts, the EP has nevertheless adopted an increasing number of non-binding resolutions in recent years, in particular with regard to implementing acts granting authorisations of genetically modified food and feed.[33]

---

[31] Regulation (EU) No 182/2011 of the European Parliament and of the Council of 16 February 2011 laying down the rules and general principles concerning mechanisms for control by Member States of the Commission's exercise of implementing powers, OJ L 55, 28.02.2011, 13–18.

[32] Ibid., article 11.

[33] See, for example, European Parliament resolution of 5 April 2017 on the draft Commission implementing decision authorising the placing on the market of products containing, consisting of, or produced from genetically modified maize Bt11 × 59122 × MIR6 04 × 1507 × GA21, and genetically modified maizes combining two, three or four of the events Bt11, 59122, MIR604, 1507 and GA21, pursuant to Regulation (EC) No 1829/2003 of the European parliament and of the Council on genetically modified food and feed (D049280—2017/2624 (RSP)).

3.3 Proposed Reform of Regulation 182/2011: An Opportunity to Increase EP Power?

On 14 February 2017, the Commission put forward an amendment to Regulation 182/2011 aiming to increase Member States' responsibility for sensitive draft implementing acts at the level of the Appeal Committee, especially in the area of genetically modified organisms and plant protection products.[34] Among the suggested reforms are the exclusion of abstentions from voting calculations and the publication of individual Member State voting positions.

While the proposal has no direct impact on the EP's prerogatives regarding implementing acts, it is interesting to note that the Commission has also proposed giving the Council a privileged role in the process via a non-binding opinion in the event of disagreement in the Appeal Committee—without granting a similar role to the EP.

At the time of writing, the draft is making its way through the OLP and amendments are being tabled and voted in the EP Committees. It remains to be seen to what extent the EP can get its amendments, for example, on increased transparency through trilogue negotiations with the Council of Ministers and the Commission.

In any case, certain MEPs may want to expand the scope of the proposal. For example, in a draft Opinion[35] published in May 2017 on behalf of the EP Committee on Constitutional Affairs (AFCO), Rapporteur Pascal Durand tabled a number of amendments to the Commission proposal, including the insertion of a new provision stating that where the EP or Council considers that the conferral of implementing powers in a given legislative act should be reviewed (for instance, as a result of consistent failure to deliver positive opinions in the Appeal Committee on product authorisations), either institution may call upon the Commission to submit a proposal amending that legislative act.[36] However, it must be emphasised that discussions on this proposal are still at quite a preliminary stage.

---

[34] Proposal for a Regulation of the European Parliament and of the Council amending Regulation (EU) No 182/2011 laying down the rules and general principles concerning mechanisms for control by Member States of the Commission's exercise of implementing powers, 14.02.2017, COM/2017/085 final.

[35] Draft Opinion of the Committee on Constitutional Affairs for the Committee on Legal Affairs on the proposal for a regulation of the European Parliament and of the Council amending Regulation (EU) No 182/2011, 12.05.2017, 2017/0035(COD), PE604.673v01-00.

[36] Ibid. p. 11 (Amendment 14).

4   CONCLUSION: MORE EFFECTIVE EP SCRUTINY, AND REFLECTIONS ON CHALLENGES AND REQUIRED IMPROVEMENTS

It is evident from the interviews conducted for this chapter that the initiatives outlined above have brought genuine improvements, compared to the early days of the post-Lisbon era, in the way the EP exercises its scrutiny prerogatives over delegated acts and secondary legislation more generally. That being said, a number of challenges remain:

First of all, the flow of information from the Commission is still very variable and often too ad hoc. EP Committees dealing with certain Commission Directorates-General ('DGs') feel well informed, while other Committees dealing with other DGs feel much less informed.[37] Cases have been noted in which, on certain occasions, an EP Committee did not receive the agenda of an expert group meeting until the very day that the meeting was scheduled to take place.[38] As another example, in late 2016 the EP Committee on Fisheries (PECH) expressed its dissatisfaction with the Commission's '*late submission*' of a Delegated Regulation on discard plans in the Mediterranean[39];

Secondly, the volume of secondary legislation has also been raised as an issue. There are certain EP Committees that receive a significant number of delegated acts, implementing acts and RPS measures from the Commission, which does not necessarily facilitate the scrutiny process since a political determination is required as to which acts require closer examination.[40] The volume of secondary legislation is of course directly linked to the numerous—perhaps overly numerous—references to delegated and implementing acts in legislation.

In an increasingly complex decision-making process, the EP has considerably strengthened its capacity to track delegated and implementing acts, particularly at the level of the European Parliamentary Committees and their Secretariats. This capacity has been further bolstered by interinstitutional agreements. Taken together, the reforms introduced allow

---

[37] Interview with the EP Committee on Transport and Tourism, 8 May 2017.

[38] Ibid.

[39] Minutes of the meeting of the PECH Committee of 5 December 2016, PECH_PV(2016)1205_1, 6.

[40] Interview with the EP Committee on Environment, Public Health and Food Safety, 11 May 2017.

for better access to information and greater involvement in the preparatory phase of delegated acts, which in many cases make the exercise by the EP of its formal prerogatives under article 290 TFEU unnecessary. In order to address remaining challenges, further improvements to EP scrutiny have more recently seen the light of day, that is, the set-up of a joint functional register of delegated acts, operational since the end of 2017. Aiming to '*enhance transparency, facilitate planning and enable traceability of all the different stages in the lifecycle of a delegated act*',[41] the register should further enhance not only the EP's supervisory capacity but equally the participation of EU citizens and stakeholders in the decision-making process. In addition, it might also help to ensure more consistency on the Commission's side as regards the volume and timing of information received by the Parliament.

REFERENCES

Agenda of the meeting of the Committee on Economic and Monetary Affairs (ECON) on 3 May 2017.

C-427/12 *European Commission v European Parliament and Council of the European Union*, Judgment of 18 March 2014.

C-88/14 *European Commission v European Parliament and Council of the European Union*, Judgment of 16 July 2015.

Communication from the Commission to the European Parliament and the Council on the Implementation of Article 290 of the Treaty on the Functioning of the European Union, 9 December 2009, COM(2009) 673 final.

Costa, O. (2014). *Que peut le Parlement européen. Pouvoirs*, revue française d'études constitutionnelles et politiques. *La gouvernance européenne, 149*, 77–89.

Council Decision of 17 July 2006 amending Decision 1999/468/EC laying down the procedures for the exercise of implementing powers conferred on the Commission, 17.07.2006, OJ L 200, 22.07.2006, p. 11.

Crombez, C., & Høyland, B. (2015). The Budgetary Procedure in the European Union and the Implications of the Treaty of Lisbon. *European Union Politics, 16*(1), 67–89.

Devuyst, Y. (2013). The European Parliament and International Trade Agreements: Practice after the Lisbon Treaty. *The European Union in the World*, 171–189.

---

[41] Inter-institutional Agreement on Better Law-Making, supra, paragraph 29.

Draft Opinion of the Committee on Constitutional Affairs for the Committee on Legal Affairs on the proposal for a regulation of the European Parliament and of the Council amending Regulation (EU) No 182/2011, 12 May 2017.

European Parliament. (2017). Resolution of 5 April 2017 on the draft Commission Implementing Decision Authorising the Placing on the Market of Products Containing, Consisting Of, or Produced from Genetically Modified Maize Bt11 × 59122 × MIR604 × 1507 × GA21, and Genetically Modified Maizes Combining Two, Three or Four of the Events Bt11, 59122, MIR604, 1507 and GA21, Pursuant to Regulation (EC) No 1829/2003 of the European parliament and of the Council on Genetically Modified Food and Feed.

European Parliament, Activity Report on the Ordinary Legislative Procedure, 4 July 2014 – 31 December 2016 (8th Parliamentary Term).

European Parliament, Horizontal Guidance Adopted by the Conference of Presidents (CoP) on 19 April 2012 on the Screening of Pending Proposals.

European Parliament, Report of 4 December 2013 on follow-up on the delegation of legislative powers and control by Member States of the Commission's Exercise of Implementing Powers.

Europolitics No. 4761, Thursday 28 November 2013.

Framework Agreement on Relations Between the European Parliament and the European Commission, OJ L 304, 20.11.2010, p. 47.

Inter-institutional Agreement Between the European Parliament, the Council of the European Union and the European Commission on Better Law-Making, OJ L 123, 12.5.2016, p. 1.

Minutes of the Meeting of the PECH Committee of 5 December 2016.

Proposal for a Regulation of the European Parliament and of the Council Amending Regulation (EU) No 182/2011 Laying Down the Rules and General Principles Concerning Mechanisms for Control by Member States of the Commission's Exercise of implementing Powers, 14.02.2017, COM/2017/085 final.

Regulation (EU) 2015/2283 of the European Parliament and of the Council of 25 November 2015 on Novel Foods, Amending Regulation (EU) No 1169/2011 of the European Parliament and of the Council and Repealing Regulation (EC) No 258/97 of the European Parliament and of the Council and Commission Regulation (EC) No 1852/2001, OJ L 327, 11.12.2015, p. 1.

Regulation (EU) 2017/1369 of the European Parliament and of the Council of 4 July 2017 Setting a Framework for Energy Labelling and Repealing Directive 2010/30/EU, OJ L 198, 28.7.2017, p. 1.

Regulation (EU) No 182/2011 of the European Parliament and of the Council of 16 February 2011 Laying Down the Rules and General Principles Concerning Mechanisms for Control by Member States of the Commission's Exercise of Implementing Powers, OJ L 55, 28.02.2011, p. 13.

Working Document of the Legal Affairs Committee of 17 April 2013.

INTERVIEWS

Interview with the Conciliations and Codecision Unit of the EP Secretariat, 4 May 2017.
Interview with the EP Committee on Transport and Tourism, 8 May 2017.
Interview with the EP Committee on Environment, Public Health and Food Safety, 11 May 2017.

CHAPTER 8

Out of Balance? Practical Experience in the European Union with Quasi-Legislative Acts

Michael Kaeding

1 INTRODUCTION

Many contemporary governments couple broad delegation of rule-making powers to administrative bodies with a scheme allowing the legislature to veto or disapprove of administrative rules (Wade and Forsyth 2004; Mullan 2001; Pearce and Argument 2005). From the legislature's perspective, this pairing has some logic. On the one hand,

I thank Laura Tilindyte and Christian Scheinert—both from the European Parliamentary Research Service—for their constructive comments. I gratefully acknowledge the Jean Monnet funding awarded under grant number 542458-LLP-1-2013-1-DE-JM-CL and extend my thanks for the research support to Timo Hülsdünker. An earlier version of this contribution was co-authored with Kevin Stack and published in 2015: 'Legislative Scrutiny? The Political Economy and Practice of Legislative Vetoes in the European Union', *Journal of Common Market Studies* 53(6): 1268–1284.

M. Kaeding (✉)
University of Duisburg-Essen, Duisburg, Germany
e-mail: michael.kaeding@uni-due.de

© The Author(s) 2019
O. Costa (ed.), *The European Parliament in Times of EU Crisis*,
European Administrative Governance,
https://doi.org/10.1007/978-3-319-97391-3_8

legislatures have well-documented incentives to delegate broad powers to administrative agencies in part because of the greater time, flexibility and expertise of dedicated administrators, and in part because it allows the legislature to avoid direct accountability for hard choices (Epstein and O'Halloran 1999). On the other hand, a scheme for legislative scrutiny allows the legislature an institutional means to assert control over the vast law-making activities that their delegations have set in motion.

Until 2006, the European Union (EU) had one of these elements, but not the other (Pollack 2003). The EU legislative bodies—the European Parliament (EP) and Council of the EU (Council)—had an established practice of delegating broad powers to the European Commission (Bergström 2005). The European Commission (Commission), in turn, has been a prodigious maker of delegated legislation.[1] It was not until 2006, in response to growing concerns about comitology's democratic accountability, that both EU legislators obtained a legislative veto, for example, the power to nullify Commission's actions. This creation of the so-called regulatory procedure with scrutiny (RPS) was symbolically important because it granted the EP powers over the formulation of Commission's administrative acts that more accurately reflected its powers in co-decision (Vaccari and Lintner 2009). It also brought the EP's formal role of oversight closer to an equal footing with the Council (Blom-Hansen 2011).

The EP, however, continued to bridle at not standing on perfect equal footing with the Council in oversight of the Commission's delegated legislation (Brandsma 2013). In explicit response to these parliamentary concerns, the Lisbon Treaty eventually provided a new legal basis for delegated legislation in Article 290 of the Treaty on the functioning of the European Union (TFEU), creating so-called delegated acts (DAs), and also established new procedures for the EP and the Council to exercise legislative scrutiny over the Commission's DAs (Hardacre and Kaeding 2011), including elimination of a requirement that the veto be based on one of a designated number of grounds. It is Article 290 TFEU that puts the EP

---

[1] The terminology used throughout the chapter referring to 'delegated legislation', 'delegated acts', 'administrative acts', quasi-legislative acts', 'secondary legislation' and 'Commission's regulatory policies' are the exact same thing.

and Council on a virtually equal footing with regard to the legislative scrutiny of Commission's quasi-legislative acts.

How have these legislative veto rights over quasi-legislative acts operated in practice and why? Have the reforms introduced in the Lisbon Treaty which were heralded as increasing the powers of the EP had concrete effects?

Based on the costs of collective action within the EP, the Commission's institutional interest in avoiding conflict with the EP, and the relatively low costs for individual Members of Parliament (MEPs) to bargain informally with the Commission in response to interest group monitoring and pressure, this chapter hypothesizes that the EP will infrequently invoke its newly granted power to veto DAs. The slightly lower costs of collective action in the Council suggest that it might make more use of its veto powers than the EP.

This chapter tests these hypotheses with regard to the EP's and Council's actual exercise of veto rights between December 2009 and December 2017. Data illustrate an extremely modest formal use of legislative vetoes under the post-Lisbon DAs. In addition, it reveals little difference in the EP's and the Council's formal use of legislative vetoes. By providing a political economy analysis as well as data on recent experience, I am able to explain this practice. Further, by isolating the importance of informal negotiating for amendments to the Commission's draft measures, I expose that a critical aspect of understanding the relationship between the Commission and the EU legislative bodies is understanding the efficacy of individual legislators, committees or representatives in the EP and the Council in obtaining adjustments in secondary legislation from the Commission outside of formal legislative vetoes—aspects which will be critical for future scholarly work on the effective control the European legislators exercise over the Commission.

The chapter is organized as follows. I first briefly describe the DA procedure for exercising legislative vetoes. I then develop hypotheses about how legislators are likely to use formal veto powers over administrative law-making or quasi-legislative actions, for example, how Parliament and Council are likely to use their veto powers over the Commission and then present the empirical analysis for legislative vetoes by Parliament and the Council from December 2009 to December 2017. I conclude by assessing the ways in which legislative scrutiny provisions in the field of delegated legislation affect formal EU policy-making.

2   THE MECHANICS OF SECONDARY LEGISLATION AND LEGISLATIVE VETOES IN THE EU

2.1   Delegated Acts: Variable Time Period for Veto/Objection

The DA process is a sharp departure from the RPS two-tier procedure practice. Overall, the process has been simplified because now the Commission presents its DA directly and simultaneously to both legislators treating Council and EP equally in this respect. The legislators then both have the same time determined by the basic act to object to the act on any grounds, as opposed to only on the three legal grounds for objection specified by the RPS. The new one-tier DA procedure is simpler, but each basic act can set out different conditions for DAs on a case-by-case basis.

While we know a lot about comitology, its various phases of reform since the 1960s (Héritier et al. 2013), its committee workings (Dehousse 2003; Pollack 2003; Christiansen et al. 2009; Brandsma and Blom-Hansen 2010; Brandsma 2013; Dehousse et al. 2014; Brandsma and Blom-Hansen 2017), as well as about how the post-Lisbon comitology regime is helping to reduce the democratic deficit of the EU (Georgiev 2013) and affecting the inter-institutional balance (Hofmann 2009; Moury and Héritier 2012; Héritier 2012; Christiansen and Dobbels 2013), we know very little about the practices of the RPS procedure and DAs (Hardacre and Damen 2009; Kaeding and Hardacre 2013; Voermans et al. 2014). Several years after the entry into force of Article 290 TFEU, one lacks the empirical evidence of the practices of delegated quasi-legislative powers in the EU, which has become a major 'battlefield in EU governance' (Hardacre and Kaeding 2010, 4; Kaeding and Stack 2015a, b).

3   THE POLITICAL ECONOMY OF LEGISLATIVE VETOES

Political economy literature provides a useful reference point to generate some expectations about how these processes might work in practice. I draw on the literature on legislative scrutiny and bargaining in the US context because this literature is well developed (Volden and Wiseman 2011) and because the US has also had a long experience with legislative veto provisions. Even though party dynamics and committee structures are different in the EP and the US Congress, the political economy literature and US experience under the legislative veto are useful because, like the EU, the US is a system of separated powers with a dual legislature and executive, with each body representing a different constituency (Bignami 1999, 466–469).

Two sets of dynamics which operate together—the relative lack of incentives of members of legislatures in systems of separated powers to invest resources to engage in oversight, and the bargaining dynamics between the legislature and a risk-avoiding bureaucracy—suggest that legislative vetoes will be enacted very infrequently. First, consider the incentives of members of the legislature in exercising a legislative veto. As a general matter, legislatures face notoriously high transaction costs to engage in collective action (Moe and Wilson 1994).

Legislative action, particularly in the EP, faces multiple veto points. It can be thwarted at the EP's committee level, in disputes over jurisdiction among multiple EP committees, or by those who set the agenda for floor consideration. Even if a veto measure were able to make it onto the legislative agenda, it would have to obtain an absolute majority (AM) of MEPs and a qualified majority (QMV) of member states in the Council in order to pass either legislative body. Just as important, RPS measures and DAs tend to be technical and thus require significant investment to understand. This suggests that the costs of oversight for members of the legislature, educating others about the Commission's action in question and assembling a coalition are likely to be very high relative to their rewards.

The timing requirements for legislative action to override Commission's act exacerbate these issues. To veto any Commission's regulatory policy, the EP or the Council must normally act within a maximum of four months. That reduces the time for legislators to master the files once they have attracted interest and imposes a very short time line for assembling a coalition.

Furthermore, the Commission—perhaps because of its more attenuated political accountability—is notoriously averse to prompting public conflict with the EP (Gornitzka and Sverdrup 2008; van Gestel 2014). As a result, the MEPs and the Council will have an especially strong capacity to extract concessions from the Commission, and, over time, to create a climate in which the Commission will anticipate legislative policy. Effectively, because the Commission places a high value on avoiding confrontation and sanctions, the EP and the Council will exercise 'latent control' over the Commission without having to exercise the veto (Calvert et al. 1989, 605). In sum, the burdens and obstacles to collective action will frequently outweigh the benefits that members of the EU legislatures will receive from formal exercise of the veto, and the Commission's right of initiative will strengthen the hand of individual bargaining with the Commission to obtain concessions.

While the Lisbon Treaty sought to enhance the oversight powers of the EP through adjusting the grounds and timing for vetoing a Commission's DA (van Gestel 2014), these political dynamics remain fundamentally unchanged, and would appear to matter more than the precise structure of the legislative veto mechanism. Accordingly, I hypothesize:

H1 Neither EP nor the Council veto Commission's quasi-legislative acts more frequently than before.

More specifically, the obstacles to the EP exercising a formal legislative veto are even higher than for the Council. The transaction costs for collective action are obviously higher in Parliament. The existence of multiple parties in Parliament further raises the cost of reaching agreement. Moreover, individual MEPs must mediate between allegiance to their parties and national delegations which also increase the difficulty of finding issues that will gain coalition support. At a practical level, the maximum deadline of four-month deadline for exercising the veto makes external research very difficult to assemble, especially given the small number of secretariat and MEP support staff (Egeberg et al. 2016). As a result, initiating collective action is likely to be led by MEPs with particularly strong stakes in specific Commission acts or policies and with the support by interest groups which enhances their capacity to have timely, ready-made solutions to issues they have followed and monitored for years (Hardacre and Damen 2009).

Council's incentive structure is simpler than the EP's. Instead of political constituencies or independent parties, member state representatives are beholden to their own national governments, and represent their national government's interest in the Union's policy-making process (Beyers and Dierickx 1998). This particular focus on the effects of Union laws on their own member states, however, diminishes the extent to which they are likely to have an incentive to investigate, or invest energies in overriding a Commission's regulatory policy. As long as the Commission strategically avoids directly harming the interests of a particular member state or tight coalition of states, its measures are unlikely to provoke much attention at the Council level, despite lower transaction costs for collective action in the Council.

H2 The Council will more frequently enact vetoes of Commission acts than the EP.

4 RESEARCH DESIGN

To assess the experience and impact of legislative vetoes in EU policy-making, the dependent variable is a count variable representing the frequency of successful and unsuccessful legislative vetoes. I differentiate between EP vetoes and objections by the Council to control for differences in their execution of legislative oversight rights. Considering the different dates of the entry into force of DA provisions (2009), I decided to investigate the complete period from December 2009 until December 2017.

To test the hypotheses, I extracted data from the websites of the EP's and Council's co-decision units and complemented it with information from the EP's Unit for Reception and Referral of Official Documents. For cross-checking purposes and the procurement of additional data, I conducted interviews with civil servants from the secretariats of the EP and Council.

Table 8.1 summarizes the total number of concluded legislative files including provisions for DAs (so-called basic legislative acts). It took about a year after the entry into force of Article 290 TFEU before EP and Council started adopting the first legislative files including provisions for DAs.[2] In the meantime, in 2016, 51 per cent of the total number of concluded legislative files provided for DA empowerments.

Table 8.1 Number of concluded legislative files including provisions for DA (2009–2017)

Year	Number of concluded legislative files including provisions for DA	Number of paragraphs empowering DA	Total number of legislative acts	Per cent—Share between number of concluded legislative acts and those including provisions for DA (%)
2010	22	62	66	33
2011	26	91	64	41
2012	22	207	87	25
2013	62	383	79	78
2014	76	350	192	40
2015	22	79	57	39
2016	34	273	67	51
2017	5	42	(−)	(−)
Total	**270**	**1487**	**612**	**44**

Source: Based on the information from the European Parliament's Unit for Reception and Referral of Official Documents

[2] The first basic acts including DA provision were Regulation 438/2010 on pet animals, Directive 2010/45 on human organs transplantation, Directive 2010/30 on energy labelling, Regulation 973/2010 on customs tariff Azores & Madeira, and Regulations 1092 to 1095/2010 and Directive 2010/78 on financial supervision package.

Table 8.2 DAs submitted to the parliament and the council (2009–2017)

Year	Delegated acts submitted
2009	–
2010	4
2011	7
2012	38
2013	57
2014	177
2015	106
2016	137
2017	137
Total	**614**

Source: Based on the information from the EP's Unit for Reception and Referral of Official Documents

Legislative files with DA provisions most frequently cover environmental policies (20 per cent), financial services (15 per cent), transport (10 per cent), internal market and consumer protection (9 per cent) and agriculture and international trade (8 per cent each), for example, only six policy areas represent 70 per cent of the total number of DA provisions.

Since the number of basic acts does not necessarily correspond to the absolute number of DA and RPS measures eventually adopted by the Commission, as the Commission can issue multiple DAs under a single basic act, Table 8.2 reports on the full list of DAs submitted to Parliament and the Council between 2009 and 2017.

These figures show that the number of DAs submitted to the EU legislators grew steadily with its introduction in 2009, with an all-time peak in 2014 (177), 2016 and 2017 (137 each), and totaling at 614 in December 2017. Most DAs cover only a few policy areas, notably monetary affairs (31 per cent), agriculture (17 per cent) and environment (14 per cent).

5   INFREQUENT USE OF LEGISLATIVE VETOES BY THE EP

The results are presented in Tables 8.3 and 8.4 displaying the frequency of (un-)successful vetoes in the framework of DAs.

For DAs, the figures are revealing. Out of a total of 614 DAs submitted to the EU legislator, EP considered objections in 35 cases (6 per cent) out of which eight files were eventually vetoed successfully.

Table 8.3 Number of (un-)successful vetoes over DAs by the EP (2009–2017)

Result	Number of cases	Details of cases (in chronological order)
Successful veto in plenary (absolute majority)	8	Definition of 'engineered nanomaterials' (ENVI), exemption for cadmium in illumination and display lighting applications (pursuant to rule 105(4)), license for imports of ethyl alcohol of agricultural origin (105(3), AGRI), specific compositional and information requirements for processed cereal-based food and baby food (105(3), ENVI), PRIIPs (105(3), ECON), 3x high risk 3rd countries (105(3), ECON, LIBE)
Unsuccessful veto in plenary	11	Scheme of generalized tariff preferences (INTA); PPP (ECON); OTC derivatives (ECON, withdrawn); ACP group of states (INTA); solvency II (ECON); 2x schemes of generalized tariff preferences (INTA); EU guarantee to the EIB Belarus (BUDG); minimum requirement for own funds and eligible liabilities (ECON); position limits to commodity derivatives (ECON); model financial regulation for PPP (BUDG); union customs code (IMCO)
Unsuccessful motion for veto in parliamentary committee (simple majority)	16	GMES (ITRE); direct payments to farmers (AGRI); integrated administration and control system and conditions for refusal or withdrawal of payments (AGRI); paying agencies and other bodies, financial management (AGRI); public intervention expenditure (AGRI); the European Agricultural Fund for Rural Development (EAFRD) (AGRI); fruit and vegetables and processed fruit and vegetables sectors (AGRI); school fruit and vegetables scheme (AGRI); support programs for the olive-oil and table-olives sector (AGRI); agricultural products benefiting from private storage aid (AGRI); national support programs in the wine sector (AGRI); generalized tariff preferences Philippines (INTA); information relating to infant and young child feeding (ENVI); food for special medical purposes (ENVI); food information of gluten (ENVI); guidelines in the field of officially supported export credits (INTA)
Total	35 (out of 614) (6%)	

Source: Based on the information from the EP's Unit for Reception and Referral of Official Documents

Table 8.4 Number of successful vetoes of DAs by the Council of the EU (2009–2017)

Result	Number of cases	Details of cases (in chronological order)
Successful veto (qualified majority)	2	Galileo (2013), format for research and development expenditure data (2014)
Total	**2 (out of 614) (0.3%)**	

Source: Based on the reports from the Commission on the working of committees, http://ec.europa.eu/transparency/regcomitology/index.cfm?do=Report.Report, updated in February 2018

From the EP's perspective, the two previous tables lead to two central conclusions: firstly, Parliament rarely exercised its veto power to overrule quasi-legislative regulatory decision during 2009 to 2017. In 1 per cent of all cases it opposed successfully to quasi-legislative instruments. Secondly, the EP appears to be more active in using its oversight powers related to DAs than RPS measures (2 per cent) (cp. Kaeding and Stack 2015a, b). In the following, I consider the results for the Council.

6   Isolated Use of Legislative Vetoes by the Council of the EU

Out of the 614 DAs submitted to the Council during a period of eight years, the Council successfully objected in only two cases, which occurred in 2013 and 2014. The first case, for example, concerned common minimum standards on the rules for access to the public regulated service provided by the global navigation satellite system. Member states' concerns focused on three aspects: the scope of the act (e.g. its applicability to the Commission and agencies, not only to member states); some of the definitions; and the question of the attribution of the role of competent public regulated service authority (with a view to giving member states greater freedom in determining their internal organization).

From the Council's perspective, the two tables lead to two central conclusions: firstly, the Council rarely exercised its veto power to overrule quasi-legislative regulatory decision during the period 2009 to 2017. In 0.3 per cent of all cases it successfully opposed to quasi-legislative instruments. Secondly, the Council appears to be more active in using its oversight powers related to RPS measures in comparison to DAs (cp. Kaeding and Stack 2015a, b). In the following, I compare the results for the two EU legislators.

7   Summary of Results

Eight years after the introduction of the EU legislative veto over quasi-legislative acts, both EU legislators have rarely used their formal veto powers. Thus far, both legislators objected to only two (Council) and eight (EP) Das respectively (out of a total of 614 Das adopted between 2009 and 2017). Consequently, I see not only low levels of formal exercise of the legislative veto overruling Commission's regulatory policies by both legislators, but also no significant overall difference between RPS measures and Das (cp. Kaeding and Stack 2015a, b).

8   Discussion

The delegation of rule-making powers has become a nearly universal feature of many modern legal systems. As broad discretionary power is vested in administrative actors, such as the Commission within the EU governance structure, there is a strong legitimacy demand for legislative oversight of administrative action to ensure that it achieves commonly agreed upon objectives of the member states and ultimately the people. One of the most touted EU mechanisms for oversight and respective accountability for collective decisions (Brandsma 2013) of the Commission is the legislative veto, whether in the context of the RPS or post-Lisbon DA.

As it turns out, the EP and the Council have rarely invested in taking formal measures to override Commission's regulatory policies. Over an eight-year period, from 2009 to 2017, the EP and the Council considered legislative vetoes in a meager 6 per cent (DA), and eventually successfully opposed to only 1 per cent and less from all possible cases. These figures may not match the EP's and the Council's energy for including legislative veto provisions in legislation in the first place, and the initial 'fear that Parliament would be tempted to (ab)use the new power too often, thus frustrating the smooth implementation of legislation' (Hardacre and Damen 2009, 3), but follow the expectations of principles of political economy.

The relatively minimal difference between the RPS vetoes and Das (cp. Kaeding and Stack 2015a, b) also suggests that the easing of the formal requirements for exercising a veto under Article 290 TFEU has had only a very modest impact on the patterns of their exercise.

However, these results do not imply that Parliament and the Council have been sitting on their hands. Parliament's ECON (economic and financial affairs) Committee, for example, set up so-called corrective scrutiny and preventive scrutiny slots. About once a month, one or two delegated acts dossiers, selected by the political groups' coordinators, are publicly discussed in the ECON Committee. In addition, the creation of three European Supervisory Authorities (ESAs), which conduct public consultations and make text proposals for DAs, which are then endorsed by the Commission, has been used in an intelligent way. If the Commission wants to introduce non-substantial changes to the text proposals, it is free to do so and then adopt the DA. But if the Commission wants to introduce substantial changes to the agencies' drafts, they need to re-consult the agencies.[3] That is when the EP can intervene as a go-between. The EP would work with the information gleaned during the time-consuming public consultations. In practice, it is the stakeholders who inform the interested ME. Using the preventive scrutiny, the EP (or more precisely the selected MEPs) can intervene in a more subtle way than the 'nuclear weapon' of an accept/reject situation. In fact, the weight of the EP in these negotiations is strengthened by the possibility to use the 'nuclear weapon'. In essence, the EP acts as a transmission mechanism for stakeholders' views.[4]

Consequently, despite the reported low levels of formal exercise of the legislative scrutiny of Commission's quasi-legislative acts, the legislative veto has been a significant tool of oversight with an impact on Commission's actions. Because members of the Commission can anticipate legislative opposition and accommodate it when raised, these new EU legislative veto mechanisms may still have a significant influence on the content of Commission's action. In view of its own attenuated political legitimacy, the Commission has a strong institutional interest in avoiding a direct, open confrontation with either European legislator. Moreover, as a repeat player in drafting quasi-legislation, whether in the form of the RPS procedure or DAs, the Commission has a strong incentive to avoid establishing

---

[3] For more details on the EU agencies' role in drafting quasi-legislative acts see Costa, M. and Kaeding, M. 'The conferral of powers to EU agencies: the case of delegated and implementing acts', Paper presented at the Workshop 'Legislative Choice between Delegated and Implementing Acts' at the Deutsche Universität für Verwaltungswissenschaften in Speyer on 20 March 2017.

[4] For more examples of the practical arrangements the European Parliament has put in place to deal with its powers over secondary legislation, the challenges it faces and the points on which further progress could be made see this volume's chapter by V. Marissen.

a practice of frequent legislative override of its actions (Stack 2014, 84). As a result, there are especially strong reasons to expect that the Commission will frequently be willing to compromise on specific substantive policy to avoid a political confrontation with either European legislator (Calvert et al. 1989), or negotiate to make concessions to the EP and Council (Stack 2014, 84).

Such 'latent oversight' is notoriously difficult to observe, even if its 'role in implementing political control over the [bureaucracy] is in principle just as important as that of active control' (Calvert et al. 1989, 605). While it is beyond the scope of this chapter to theorize or document the practice of negotiations between the Commission and the EP, there is some evidence that a 'de facto legislative right of amendment' (Ponzano 2008) through individual negotiations rather than the formal exercise of the veto have taken hold (Kaeding and Hardacre 2013). These negotiations are not always public and therefore difficult to uncover, but in two cases, parliamentary committees for environmental affairs (on the use of animal testing) and for transport and tourism (on the use of seatbelts for children in air-planes) drafted objecting resolutions which were withdrawn even before the committee vote (see Hardacre and Damen 2009, for a more detailed discussion) after the Commission indicated that the modifications required by the EP would be taken into account in a subsequent revision of the implementing measures.

This chapter reveals the grounds for and documents the infrequent use of the formal exercise of the legislative veto in the EU, even under the reforms of Lisbon. This conclusion provides a critical perspective on the achievements of the Lisbon Treaty's restructuring of legislative oversight.

REFERENCES

Bergström, C. F. (2005). *Comitology – Delegation of Powers in the European Union and the Committee System.* Oxford: Oxford University Press.

Beyers, J., & Dierickx, G. (1998). The Working Groups of the Council of the European Union: Supranational or Intergovernmental Negotiations? *Journal of Common Market Studies, 36*(6), 289–317.

Bignami, F. E. (1999). The Democratic Deficit in European Community Rulemaking: A Call for Notice and Comment in Comitology. *Harvard International Law Journal, 40*(2), 451–515.

Blom-Hansen, J. (2011). The EU Comitology System: Taking Stock Before the New Lisbon Regime. *Journal of European Public Policy, 18*(4), 607–617.

Brandsma, G. J. (2013). *Controlling Comitology: Accountability in a Multi-level System*. Houndmills: Palgrave Macmillan.

Brandsma, G. J., & Blom-Hansen, J. (2010). The EU Comitology System: What Role for the Commission? *Public Administration, 88*(2), 496–512.

Brandsma, G. J., & Blom-Hansen, J. (2017). *Controlling the EU Executive? The Politics of Delegation in the European Union*. Oxford: Oxford University Press.

Calvert, R. L., McCubbins, M. D., & Weingast, B. (1989). A Theory of Political Control and Agency Discretion. *American Journal of Political Science, 33*(3), 588–611.

Christiansen, T., Oettel, J. M., & Vaccari, B. (2009). *21st Century Comitology: Implementing Committees in the Enlarged European Union*. Maastricht: European Institute of Public Administration.

Christiansen, T., & Dobbels, M. (2013). Delegated Powers and Inter-Institutional Relations in the EU after Lisbon: A Normative Assessment. *West European Politics, 36*(6), 1159–1177.

Dehousse, R. (2003). Comitology: Who Watches the Watchmen? *Journal of European Public Policy, 10*(5), 798–813.

Dehousse, R., Fernández Pasarín, A., & Plaza, J. (2014). How Consensual Is Comitology? *Journal of European Public Policy, 21*(6), 842–859.

Egeberg, M., Gornitzka, A., Trondal, J., & Johannessen, M. (2016). Parliament Staff: Unpacking the Behaviour of Officials in the European Parliament. *Journal of European Public Policy, 20*(4), 495–514.

Epstein, D., & O'Halloran, S. (1999). *Delegating Powers: A Transaction Cost Politics Approach to Policy Making under Separate Powers*. Cambridge: Cambridge University Press.

Georgiev, V. (2013). Too Much Executive Power? Delegated Law-Making and Comitology in Perspective. *Journal of European Public Policy, 20*(4), 535–551.

Gornitzka, A., & Sverdrup, U. (2008). Who Consults? The Configuration of Expert Groups in the European Union. *West European Politics, 31*(4), 725–750.

Hardacre, A., & Damen, M. (2009). The European Parliament and Comitology: PRAC in Practice. *Eipascope, 2009*(1), 13–18.

Hardacre, A., & Kaeding, M. (2010). *Delegated & Implementing Acts – The New Comitology. The EIPA Practical Guide*. Maastricht: European Institute of Public Administration EIPA.

Hardacre, A., & Kaeding, M. (2011). Delegated and Implementing Acts: New Comitology. In A. Hardacre (Ed.), *How the EU Institutions Work & How to Work with the EU Institutions* (pp. 185–215). London: John Harper.

Héritier, A. (2012). Institutional Change in Europe: Co-decision and Comitology Transformed. *Journal of Common Market Studies, 50*(1), 38–54.

Héritier, A., Moury, C., Bisschoff, C., & Bergström, F. (2013). *Changing Rules of Delegation*. Oxford: Oxford University Press.

Hofmann, H. C. H. (2009). Legislation, Delegation and Implementation under Treaty of Lisbon: Typology Meets Reality. *European Law Journal, 15*(4), 482–505.

Kaeding, M., & Hardacre, A. (2013). The European Parliament and the Future of Comitology after Lisbon. *European Law Journal, 19*(3), 382–403.

Kaeding, M., & Stack, K. (2015a). Legislative Scrutiny? The Political Economy and Practice of Legislative Vetoes in the European Union. *Journal of Common Market Studies, 53*(6), 1268–1284.

Kaeding, M., & Stack, K. (2015b) A Dearth of Legislative Vetoes: Why the Council and Parliament Have Been Reluctant to Veto Commission legislation. *EUROPP blog*. Retrieved August 29, 2017, from http://bit.ly/2eBuDNo.

Moe, T. M., & Wilson, S. A. (1994). Presidents and the Politics of Structure. *Law & Contemporary Problems, 57*(2), 1–44.

Moury, C., & Héritier, A. (2012). Shifting Competences and Changing Preferences: The Case of Delegation to Comitology. *Journal of European Public Policy, 19*(9), 1316–1335.

Mullan, D. (2001). *Essentials of Canadian Administrative Law*. Toronto: Irwin Law.

Pearce, D., & Argument, S. (2005). Delegated Legislation in Australia. In *Butterworths* (3rd ed.). Chatswood.

Pollack, M. A. (2003). Control Mechanism or Deliberative Democracy? Two Images of Comitology. *Comparative Political Studies, 36*(1–2), 125–155.

Ponzano, P. (2008). 'Executive' and 'Delegated' Acts: The Situation After the Lisbon Treaty'. In S. Griller & J. Ziller (Eds.), *The Lisbon Treaty. EU Constitutionalism Without a Constitutional Treaty?* Vienna and New York: Springer.

Stack, K. M. (2014). The Irony of Oversight: Delegated Acts and the Political Economy of the European Union's Legislative Veto under the Lisbon Treaty. *The Theory and Practice of Legislation, 2*(1), 61–84.

Vaccari, B., & Lintner, P. (2009). The European Parliament's Right of Scrutiny under Comitology: A Legal "David" but a Political "Goliath". In T. Christiansen, J. M. Oettel, & B. Vaccari (Eds.), *21st Century Comitology. Implementing Committees in the Enlarged European Union*. Maastricht: EIPA.

van Gestel, R. (2014). Primacy of the European Legislature? Delegated Rule-Making and the Decline of the "Transmission Belt" Theory. *The Theory and Practice of Legislation, 2*(1), 33–59.

Voermans, W., Hartmann, J., & Kaeding, M. (2014). The Quest for Legitimacy in EU Secondary Legislation. *The Theory and Practice of Legislation, 2*(1), 5–32.

Wade, W., & Forsyth, C. (2004). *Administrative Law* (9th ed.). Oxford: Oxford University Press.

Volden, C., & Wiseman, A. (2011). Formal Approaches to the Student of Congress. In E. Schickler & F. Lee (Eds.), *The Oxford Handbook of the American Congress*. Oxford: Oxford University Press.

CHAPTER 9

The European Parliament's Contribution to the EU Budget: A Power Game

Anne Vitrey de Gardebosc and Frederik Mesdag

1 Introduction

In most democracies, the budget is a power game between the executive and the legislative branches. The *sui generis* institutional construction of the European Union (EU) based on a dual budgetary and legislative authority embodied by the European Parliament (EP) and by the Council, each defending different interests, has generated conflicts over time. However, the search for interinstitutional cooperation to serve common objectives has generally guided the budgetary agreements. The Treaty of Lisbon has brought significant changes to the budgetary procedures, involving new challenges to maintain the institutional balance and a democratic decision-making process in the budgetary domain.

The chapter primarily draws on an insider view of the EU budget practices and only to a lesser extent on existing literature. It describes how the

Anne Vitrey de Gardebosc, Former Director for Budgetary Affairs, European Parliament.

A. Vitrey de Gardebosc (✉) • F. Mesdag
College of Europe, Bruges, Belgium
e-mail: frederik.mesdag@coleurope.eu

© The Author(s) 2019   177
O. Costa (ed.), *The European Parliament in Times of EU Crisis*,
European Administrative Governance,
https://doi.org/10.1007/978-3-319-97391-3_9

EP has battled to maintain the initial balance of power but also to increase its competences, using soft law in parallel to Treaty provisions.

Part one describes the role of the EP over the successive treaty changes and Inter-institutional Agreements (IIAs). Part two shows, through a few examples, how the EP gained or maintained budgetary prerogatives. And part three identifies, in a reflective and prospective manner, some domains in which the EP could gain or lose powers in the coming periods.

2   The Role of the EP in the Budgetary Process: From the Treaty of Rome to the Treaty of Lisbon

This first part focuses on the successive treaty changes and provisions laying out the budgetary principles. It, furthermore, gives an insight into the different IIAs adopted since 1988. This overview is not exhaustive but highlights the main trends throughout the evolution of the EP's budgetary powers since 1957.[1]

2.1   The Genesis of the EP's Budgetary Powers

Under the 1957 Treaty of Rome, the Council was the sole budgetary authority, having the exclusive prerogative to decide on the European Economic Community and Euratom budgets. The Assembly—forefather of the EP—was only provided with a consultation role on the draft budget and the possibility to submit proposals for modifications to the Council before the final vote. The Audit Board, an autonomous body, exercised the control over the budget.

Following these initial elements, two budgetary treaties were adopted, in 1970 and 1975, amending the Treaty of Rome in respect to budgetary powers. As of this point, the budgetary procedure remained almost unchanged until the Treaty of Lisbon, at least from a treaty perspective. It should however be mentioned that, despite the narrow scope of its powers, the Assembly, and later on the EP, has continuously strived to widen its margin of manoeuvre as regards budgetary powers. Throughout the

---

[1] For a more detailed account, see De Feo (2017a)

years, this steady evolution demonstrates a strong willingness to transform itself into a key player.

The 1970 Luxembourg Treaty introduced the distinction between 'compulsory' (CE) and 'non-compulsory' expenditures (NCE) and gave the Assembly the last word on the NCE[2] in the annual procedure. The extent to which this prerogative could allow to increase the budget was however limited by the maximum rate of increase (MRI). The budgetary discharge had to be given through a joint decision from the Council and the Parliament.

The second amending treaty, the Brussels Treaty of 1975, changed the budgetary procedure mainly by giving the Parliament the power to reject the budget as a whole. From this point, the Council and the Parliament became the two arms of the budgetary authority, sharing the decision-making powers. Next to the creation of the European Court of Auditors, the Parliament also gained the budgetary control power by having to discharge the implementation of previous budgets.

From there, a step-by-step strengthening of the EP's budgetary powers can be observed, with the emergence of a *sui generis* financial system. The institutional power-sharing arrangements between both budgetary authorities resulted in a difficult relation, leading to the emergence of a climate of conflict. Budgetary imbalances, the inadequacy of the resources and the increased legitimacy of the Parliament following the 1979 direct elections also had a substantial impact on this phenomenon (De Feo 2017b).

2.2   The Path Towards a New Interinstitutional Balance in the Budgetary Domain

From the mid-1970s onwards, making use of its nascent budgetary powers, the Parliament seized the creation of budgetary policies to support the development of new policies as an opportunity to propose new budget lines. The diverging points of view between the two arms of the budgetary authority however increased the mistrust between the institutions. One of the main divergences between the EP and the Council concerned the role of the budget as a legal act. The Parliament considered the existence of the

---

[2] Initially, the NCE amounted to approximately 3% of the budget, including staff salaries and rents.

budget as a legal basis sufficient to implement appropriations, whereas the Council imposed a separate legal basis. These conflicts led to the budgets of 1980, 1985, 1986 and 1988 not being adopted in time (European Commission 2014). Progressively, the Council nonetheless came to realise that the EP had to be considered as an institution with concrete influence, and not as a mere 'procedural step' (De Feo 2017b).

The Council took the 1980 budget to the Court of Justice in 1982 while facilitating the conclusion of a political agreement with the EP (Joint Declaration 1982), without waiting for the Court's decision. In 1986, the Court ruled the first 'budgetary case' (ECJ Case 34/86), declaring the budget void but preconising an interinstitutional solution. As such, the Court did not rule on the substance and did not determine whether the budget could be considered a sufficient legal basis in order to initiate new policies. The introduction of soft law to resolve conflicts launched the beginning of a new interinstitutional balance, giving the EP an important negotiating tool (Zangl 1989).

2.3   Times of Interinstitutional Cooperation

While the 1978–1988 decade had been characterised by a number of conflicts, the adoption of a first IIA in 1988 led to the progressive establishment of a new base for the EU public finances.

This new era of interinstitutional cooperation has also been marked by the changes made to the EC budget by the Single European Act in 1987. From a budgetary point of view, changes included the new structure of the Own Resources (OR—new system based on direct contributions by member states—MS), the introduction of the principle of budgetary discipline (primarily in the agriculture policy) and in parallel, an increase of the share of NCE. The EP had the last say over the latter and progressively expanded its role over it. For the financial years 1988 to 1992, both arms of the budgetary authority respected the MRI included within the ceilings set by the financial perspective for the NCE.

The progressive introduction of planning method and the adoption of multiannual Financial Perspectives (codified in the Treaty of Lisbon as multiannual financial framework—MFF) reduced the occurrence of conflicts between the institutions. With these IIAs, the institutions committed to consider the financial amounts set as binding expenditure ceilings for the annual budget. During the 1988–1992 period, the annual budget was adopted in due time, free of major institutional conflicts.

Given the positive assessment of the Commission on the innovations introduced in 1988, a second IIA was concluded on 29 October 1993, in light of the new financial perspective for 1993–1999. The major innovations were to be found in the agreement that all expenditures concerning structural action (heading 2) and internal policies (heading 3) were NCE; the introduction of an exchange of views on priorities for the budget and a conciliation on the CE (even though the Council kept the last word); as well as the 'negative co-decision' procedure to mobilise the reserves. This leads the EP to gain a certain insight into CE.

The direct budgetary implications of the Maastricht Treaty were limited. In March 1995, for the sake of improving the 1982 Declaration, the institutions signed a joint declaration on the entry of financial provisions in legislative instruments (Joint Declaration, 1995) (see Part 2.1).

In May 1999, a new IIA containing the financial framework for 2000–2006 was concluded, confirming its importance as a tool to improve the annual budgetary procedure. This new IIA, which provided the necessary flexibility for adjustments to cope with the expenditures resulting from the enlargement, facilitated the 2000–2006 budget procedures.

In the meanwhile, the Treaty of Nice (article 272) continued to limit the prerogatives of the EP to the sole annual budgetary procedure and to the last word on NCE (with the limitation imposed by the respect of the MRI).

In the context of the 2007–2013 financial framework, a new IIA on budgetary discipline and sound financial management was concluded on 17 May 2006. Essential to complement financial discipline, flexibility was key to this new IIA, in an attempt to alleviate the lack of flexibility of the MFF in times of unparalleled budgetary challenges. A number of useful changes were therefore introduced, based on the criteria of simplification, consolidation and flexibility (amongst which the introduction of new flexibility instruments).

2.4 The Treaty of Lisbon: Towards a New Balance of Powers

The Treaty of Lisbon, which entered into force on 1 December 2009, was the first significant modification of the budgetary procedure since the budgetary Treaty of 1975. The MFF—previously agreed upon within the IIA—is now enshrined in the Union's primary law, and codified in a Council Regulation. This regulation is adopted by special legislative procedure, pursuant to article 312 TFEU. Based on a Commission's proposal, the Council decides on the MFF in unanimity, after having obtained the EP's consent.

The Treaty of Lisbon also abolished the distinction between CE and NCE, as well as the MRI. The budget as a whole is now jointly decided by both institutions. Regarding the annual budgetary procedure, laid out in article 314 TFEU, the proposed budget is adopted or amended by the Council by qualified majority and the EP by absolute majority in a single reading.

In view of its entry into force, the provisions of the 2006 IIA had to be aligned with the new Treaty. Consequently, a new IIA was concluded, including and adjusting the provisions on interinstitutional cooperation in budgetary matters (special annex in the 2013 IIA). End 2009, the report on the functioning of the IIA made a positive assessment of the cooperation between the institutions and sound financial management (COM/2010/0185 final).

3   THE SHIFT OF POWERS AND THE EMERGENCE OF THE EP OVER THE LAST DECADES

As seen in part one, soft law and IIAs have filled the vacuum of primary law and imposed new working methods and a more balanced negotiating process between the institutions. This evolution was guided by a number of elements:

- Avoiding budgetary conflicts and blockades as observed in the 1980s decade;
- Ensuring an orderly and continuous development of EU policies;
- Bringing more flexibility to cope with legislation developing beyond the time frame of annual budgets;
- Favouring consensus and results in the context of a regular increase of legislation.

The authors of the Treaty of Lisbon integrated some of these best practices of cooperation into primary law, mainly into articles 312–314 TFEU. These changes were also integrated in the successive revisions of the Financial Regulation (2000; 2006; 2012) which became an ordinary legislation with Lisbon.

3.1 The Build-Up of Interinstitutional Cooperation Over Time Through Soft Law

This part intends to demonstrate, through a few examples, how the EP has managed to maintain or increase its budgetary prerogatives through soft law.

3.1.1 CE Versus NCE: A Long-Lasting Power Game

The legislator of the 1970 and 1975 Treaties had established the division of powers between the two arms of the budgetary authority on the distinction between CE and NCE. The Council had the last word on CE (97% of the budget) arising directly from Treaty competences such as European Globalisation Adjustment Fund (EGAF) direct aids, Common Fisheries Policy and refunds to MS, while the EP had the last word on other expenditures (initially 3% of the budget).

In addition, the right of the EP to increase NCE was limited by the MRI fixed annually by the Commission. This mechanism foresaw that the EP could amend the Council Draft Budget up to half of the annual fixed rate. This limit was binding on the EP. From 1988 to 1999, the slow decrease of CE and the rapid increase of NCE linked to the development of new policies resulted in a mismatch with the existing provisions of primary law.

The 'Agenda 2000' (COM(97) 2000) contained a number of arrangements, amongst which two interesting procedural aspects with an institutional dimension can be recalled: (1) the conciliation procedure laid down initially to facilitate solutions on the agriculture and later fisheries budget was extended to cover all expenditure. This was later formalised by the Treaty of Lisbon as the most appropriate procedure to facilitate the agreement on the annual budget; and (2) guidelines were laid down by broad categories for the future classification of expenditure.

As a matter of fact, after 1988, although the distinction between CE and NCE remained the legal reference, the joint agreement laid down in soft law (declarations, IIA) became politically binding. IIAs could only be amended with the agreement of all institutions. However little by little, the ceilings negotiated in the Financial Perspective annexed to the IIAs (soft law) became more favourable (generous) than the MRI calculation imposed by the Treaty (primary law) as a result of new needs taken on board and as an effect of the negotiating method. From then onwards, the MRI were regularly exceeded, by consensus between the two arms of the budgetary authority. The three institutions were indeed bound by the IIA, in a spirit of loyal cooperation, even if the Parliament sometimes used the threat of the supremacy of the Treaty over the IIA during the negotiations of the annual budget.

3.1.2   *The Need to Accommodate Legislation and Budget*

Each legal act laying down a multiannual programme with a budgetary incidence always includes financial provisions reflecting the decision of the legislative authority. These financial envelopes are a compulsory reference for the budgetary authority.

It is interesting—in the context of this chapter—to recall the origin of the inclusion of provisions for the financing of multiannual programmes in the IIA on budgetary discipline, which goes back to the 1980s.

The treaties of 1970 and 1975 contained the seeds of dispute between the EP and the Council which developed from 1975 to 1982. Prior to this period, while legislative power was exercised exclusively in the Council, budgetary power was shared between the EP and the Council. With the acquisition of its budgetary power, the Parliament considered the budget as a legal basis sufficient to use the appropriations. From 1975 onwards, it therefore inserted numerous budget lines and entered appropriations for new actions, with gradually increasing amounts. The Council, however, responded by setting maximum amounts in the legislative instruments it adopted with the view to ring-fence (limit) the development of multiannual programmes and avoid that the Commission and the Parliament would increase successful programmes over time. A provocative case occurred around the education programme 'Socrates' (2000–2006) which represented the reference in the domain of education, after the Maastricht Treaty gave a new competence to the EU (article 126). For this programme, the Council imposed an 'amount deemed necessary'[3] which was the first compulsory envelope. The Parliament, as part of the budgetary authority, argued that this encroached on its budgetary power over NCE. After a tough negotiation, a joint declaration was agreed upon (Joint Declaration, 1982). The declaration makes a distinction between legislative acts adopted under the co-decision procedure, where the amount constitutes the principal reference for the budgetary authority, and legislative acts not subject to the co-decision procedure, which do not

---

[3] French acronym 'Montant Estimé Nécessaire' (MEN).

contain an 'amount deemed necessary' but constitute an illustrative will of the legislator. Not only has this provision been included in all IIAs since then, but it also reflects a search for balance between both arms of the budgetary authority, as well as a search for supremacy of legislation over the budget.

3.1.3 The Growing Influence of Mid-Term Programming Over Annual Budgets

Seven Financial Perspectives (Frameworks) have been agreed since 1988. Four multiannual periods (1988 to 2013) were prepared, negotiated, agreed and implemented through soft law only. The budget of the EU, continuously increasing in volume and in importance, developed a multi-annual dimension. It successfully ensured continuity and stability to European policies: being based on cooperation and soft law, IIAs allowed for institutional progress and maturity in the spirit of loyal cooperation, as enshrined in the Treaty.

Under the Treaty of Nice regime, the Accession Treaty of Athens from 1 May 2004 reflects the outcome of the enlargement negotiations, following successive summits (Berlin, Helsinki, Laeken, Brussels) where Heads of States or Governments agreed on the terms of enlargement for ten new countries while respecting the overall ceilings of the 2000–2006 Financial Perspective. Annex XV of the Accession Treaty contains a reference to maximum supplementary amounts allocated to the new MS in accordance with the revised Financial Framework. It introduced for the first time a form of mid-term planning in primary law for the support to be provided by the EU budget to acceding countries for the main domains (CAP, structural funds and nuclear decommissioning). This resulted from the agreement reached at the intergovernmental level and adjusted by the institutions (Decision 2003/429), notably by the EP who secured additional means to adapt the needs of the new MS without jeopardising the existing support provided to the policies in place, notably those directly affecting the citizens (heading 3: Internal Policies, +€50 million for 2004; +€190 million for 2005; +€240 million for 2006).

By upgrading the Financial Perspectives into primary law, the entry into force of the Treaty of Lisbon marked a significant turn. It enhanced the visibility of the budget by regrouping the EU prerogatives relating to budget and budgetary control under Title II—Financial Provisions. Moreover, the Treaty introduced a strict hierarchical and logical order. This architecture clearly reflects the will of the legislator: the OR (article 311) determine the maximum level of resources allocated to the EU; the level of expenses authorised is framed within the period of (at least five years) with binding ceilings (the MFF, article 312) and finally, the annual budget (article 314) must be compatible with those ceilings.

3.2   Good Practice and Soft Power: Positive and Negative Effects

The part below intends to select a few examples of pragmatic changes which contributed to strengthen the role of the EP based on soft law and, on the contrary, changes imposed by primary law which are not always favourable to the EP.

3.2.1   Changes with a Positive Effect

Pragmatic calendar of the annual procedure: The Treaty provisions did not contain sufficient leeway to facilitate the negotiations with an objective of result. A pragmatic calendar, respecting the constraints of each institution in compliance with the main milestones foreseen in the Treaty, is established and agreed upon at the beginning of each year.

To influence what was the Preliminary Draft Budget before Lisbon and what is now the Draft Budget, the EP decided to present its political priorities ahead of its adoption by the Commission (usually in May). To this end, a resolution of 'guidelines' is adopted in March with a political meaning vis-à-vis the Commission, as well as the Council. The latter also started to adopt guidelines even before the EP (usually in February). A trilogue is convened by the First Semester Presidency (usually in March) to discuss both institutions' priorities.

Trilogues: These regular meetings were initially established to facilitate the decisions between the three institutions participating in the budgetary procedure while being not foreseen by the Treaties. One can even say that their success has been taken over as an example for the ordinary legislative procedure. Trilogues increasingly became key elements of the annual budgetary procedure. They have been integrated into the IIAs on budgetary discipline and in the Financial Regulation. They are now fully part of the aforementioned pragmatic calendar and exist in parallel to, and in compliance with, the Treaty provisions.

Trilogues, which the EP imposed to hold at the political level (in presence of Ministers), aim to place the two arms of the budgetary authority on an equal footing. The experience so far shows that the model has not been extended to the MFF negotiations.

Budgetary conciliation: The conciliation procedure, existing in the previous IIAs on budgetary discipline and improvement of the budgetary procedure, was enshrined in the Treaty of Lisbon (article 314.7 d), becoming the key period of 21 days where the EP and the Council should agree on a joint text. The original spirit of conciliation prevailed and the EP strived to impose its role in the decision-making process, now engraved in primary law.

3.2.2 Changes with a Mitigated or Negative Effect

Suppression of the distinction between CE and NCE: This simplification has obviously made the budget more readable. It has granted the same power to the EP and the Council on all expenses, although most of the previous CE (agriculture (first pillar) and fisheries agreements) remain in the sole Council's field of competence at the legislative level. Both legislators must now select priorities across the board rather than focus on the part of the budget over which they had the last say. This has created a new type of balance between the two arms of the budgetary authority. In the recent post-Lisbon annual procedures, one could see the Parliament defending more commitments and the Council defending less payments. As a side effect, the negotiators lose sight of commitments which are the main tools for policy setting and have always been a Parliament's core issue.

Suppression of the second reading: The single reading certainly simplifies the procedure but it has also weakened the Parliament's position in the annual budgetary procedure. Indeed, it leads to a reduced room for manoeuvre for both the Council and the Parliament, as none of them can any longer impose decisions against the will of the other. With the ability of the budgetary authority to amend the draft budget reduced, the power of the institution responsible for the draft budget and which can modify it during the procedure—the Commission—increases accordingly. Consequently, the conciliation effect makes it difficult, if not impossible, for the EP to exert its power of control via the establishment of the budget. In practice, it no longer has the possibility to enter amounts in reserve with certain political or legal conditions since each budget line requires the agreement of both institutions in the context of the joint text.

Triggering mechanisms: These mechanisms foreseen by the Treaty are more favourable to the institution supporting a lower level of expenditure (the Council). In addition, the Parliament has lost the power of overall rejection by qualified majority in the second reading. Both institutions must now agree on everything, with each a power of rejection in concilia-tion (by a blocking minority within the Council or by a simple majority within the Parliament). The 'behind closed doors' negotiations do not allow for the same transparency as a vote in plenary.[4]

3.3   The Role of the EP in Shaping EU Policies

Over the course of the budgetary procedure, both the EP and the Council modify the proposals put forward by the Commission and consequently influence political choices.

Considered as being usually more ambitious than the Council—and even than the Commission—notably for payments given the constrained nature of the multiannual ceilings, the EP has used the budget to promote and defend its political priorities (as it can be seen in the budgetary amend-ments and budgetary resolutions adopted). By stressing the added value and complementary nature of the EU budget against 28 national budgets, the EP is keen to highlight the investment character and the leverage impact of the EU budget. The MEPs might therefore either act to defend policies that the Council has under-funded (e.g., support to growth and competitiveness initiatives, youth employment and research, transports, SMEs) or act together with the Council to promote shared concerns (e.g., Northern Ireland peace process, cohesion policy, fight against terrorism, migration policy).

Apart from its rights of amendment for financing priorities, the EP has often used the budget as a tool for political dialogue to extend the scope of its prerogatives. The following section aims to illustrate, through a selected number of examples, how the EP has pushed for more interinsti-tutional cooperation and exploited the power of procedures (declarations, IIAs) to exert its political influence.

3.3.1   Agriculture Policy
It is one of the EP's major achievements to get at the doorstep of the CAP, traditionally a prerogative of the Council. A special procedure introduced in the 1993 IIA required the Commission to present an Amending Letter (AL) to the Preliminary Draft Budget at the end of October. Due to the late calendar of this adjustment, it did not allow for a double reading

---

[4] This point refers to the 'reverse point' described notably by G. Benedetto (2017).

before the final adoption by the Council (CE). To facilitate the agreement, the EP obtained that the Commission would introduce in this AL some of the EP's requests and priorities as voted in the first reading.

Through soft law, the Parliament obtained in fact a co-decision on agricultural expenditure 17 years before the Treaty of Lisbon. This procedure, still in use (2013 IIA, Annex, point 9), was confirmed by the Court of Justice (ECJ Case 41/95).

3.3.2   Common Foreign and Security Policy

Common Foreign and Security Policy (CFSP) is an intergovernmental policy and has been, in the last decades, an area of dispute between the two arms of the budgetary authority during the annual negotiations of the budget. The Council used to impose its political authority over decisions although CFSP expenses were not considered as CE. The EP therefore refused to limit its role to *paying the cheque*. In November 1997, a special IIA referred to as 'Gentleman's Agreement' was agreed between the three institutions. It contained three parts: co-decision of the Council on the amounts to be entered in the budget; ad hoc procedure to facilitate the agreement on the basis of the Council's first reading; and consultation and information procedure for the EP against the commitment to enter the appropriations in the budget. In further conflicts, the committee on budgets, supported by a large majority of the EP, voted to enter part of the appropriations dedicated to CFSP in the reserve (possible before Lisbon) and released them in the second reading to obtain more information, notably on sensitive operations. In 2002, new elements of transparency were added to the IIA (e.g., dividing CFSP in chapters and imposing a distinction between decided, foreseen, to be adopted instruments). These procedures took the form of two declarations and were later incorporated into the IIA. The 2013 IIA, notably points 23 and 24, reflect the development of this ad hoc political dialogue with the Council in the field of CFSP.

The Parliament also succeeded in establishing a structural relationship with both the EEAS and the High Representative (HR), and consequently increasing its role in the supervision of CFSP in the long run (Raube 2012). From a formal point view, the Parliament only had to be consulted about the set-up of the EEAS (article 27 TEU). However, during the negotiation process, MEPs challenged the borders of their legal role and gained significant concessions not only from the Council, but also the HR. By linking the set-up of the EEAS to the overall budgetary deal, in the legislative co-decision for the financial regulation, it achieved unexpected concessions (Jorgensen et al. 2015).

3.3.3   Fisheries Agreements

Despite the fact that the Council considered the fisheries agreements as CE, and given their important budgetary implications,[5] the Parliament has sought to get prior information about their cost, to not only passively accept the requested funding into the budget. Following a conflicting period, the EP accepted, in a joint declaration (1996), to differentiate agreements already decided (CE and last word for the Council) from those being under negotiation (NCE and last word for the EP), provided it got an increased right of information and the possibility to make recommendations on substantial aspects of the agreement.

Part C of the 2013 IIA (points 19, 20 and 22) still contains specific provisions which illustrate how the EP has obtained a *droit de regard*, imposing the participation of MEPs as observers in the bilateral and multilateral negotiations, and provide for regular exchanges of views in the form of a trilogue.

3.3.4   Environmental Policy

The EU financial assistance for the environment was first made available in the early 1980s. In 1982, the EP emphasised the importance of providing sufficient financial means for habitat protection and succeeded in introducing a small budget line for nature conservation. Despite its small scale, the impact was significant and led the initial funding to be renewed in 1983.[6]

The adoption of the Single European Act in 1986 enshrined the EU environmental policy in the Treaty. In the 1990s, the EP continued to be a precursor and created a Pilot Project in the 1991 Budget (rapporteur A. Lamassoure) under the name of LIFE whose importance grew in a spectacular manner in the following years (LIFE I programme, 1992–1995). In the context of the 1988–1993 FP revision for the German reunification, it was decided to use part of the LIFE programme funds for the Eastern Länder brownfields sites. Since 1992, there have been four complete phases of the LIFE programme, financing some 3954 projects across the EU, amounting to some €3.1 billion (European Commission 2017). In the wake of the development of LIFE, the EP launched the

---

[5] For the adoption of international fisheries agreements, Parliament's consent is required.

[6] The scope of this EU assistance was broadened by the establishment of the ACE (Action communautaire pour l'Environnement) financial instrument from 1984 to 1987 and ACE II until July 1991.

'Greening of the Budget' slogan[7] through conditional amendments applying to a number of policies.

3.3.5 Asylum and Migration Policies

The EP has played a key role in raising awareness, fighting early for an integrated EU approach for migration and asylum. Already in the 1997 budget, the EP managed to lie down the embryo of a European Refugee Fund (Resolution on guidelines for the 1997 budget procedure, 1996),[8] calling the 'rich' MS for their financial support in the care for refugees as a compensation of their workforce demand. The 1997 Budget used the instrument of a Pilot Project, which developed into a Preparatory Action, and was later converted into several legal bases whose funding increased constantly over the past decades. Since then, in a context of increasing migratory challenges, and despite the budget cuts in the 2014–2020 MFF, the Parliament endeavoured to secure more funding to face the refugee crisis[9] and to support a decent asylum policy by using all flexibility means provided for in the IIA. The huge needs for the financing of this policy were at the core of the negotiations of the 2014–2020 Mid-Term Review.

More examples of policies which participated in the empowerment of the EP, notably through soft law and IIAs, in a budgetary context, relate to the reconstruction processes in third countries where the EP, as part of the budgetary authority, conditioned its financial support to its participation to pledging international conferences (Balkans, Haiti) at the side of the Commission representing the EU. They also concern the financing of agencies and European schools (part B, point 31 of the 2013 IIA) for which prior information and specific procedures have been laid down. The case of comitology is also a good example where the budgetary authority used its power to defend the EP legislative prerogatives by entering the appropriations allocated to comitology in reserve. This 'weapon' has however been lost with the Treaty of Lisbon where the aim of conciliation implies consensus.

---

[7] 1996 budget by Rapporteur Florenz (Parliament's resolution of 5 April 1995 on the guidelines for the 1996 budget).

[8] Following the proposal of the general rapporteur for the budget, L. J. Brinkhorst.

[9] Although lower than the amount initially proposed by the Commission (€3.8 billion), the €3.1 billion available under the AMIF for 2014–2020 still represent an increase from the €2.1 billion for 2007–2013 (D'Alfonso, AMIF, 2015, 6).

The few abovementioned examples show how the interplay between both arms of the budgetary authority, and especially the Parliament's ambitious and proactive attitude, can often serve as a determinant factor in ultimately shaping the budget.

4   FUTURE PERSPECTIVES: FROM A FULLYFLEDGED LEGISLATOR TO A FULLYFLEDGED BUDGETARY AUTHORITY

The Treaty of Lisbon had the merit to update the EU primary law and to adjust the budgetary means and decisions to the needs and historical developments of the EU policies. However, how has the balance between both arms of the budgetary authority been influenced?

Indeed, the difficult annual procedures with the failed agreements on a joint text for the 2011, 2013 and 2015 budgets, the contentious climate of the 2014–2020 MFF negotiations and the recent tensions to agree on a mid-term revision show that the parliamentary branch of the budgetary authority is still not considered as an equal partner by the Council. Compared to the legislative area and the rules of soft law of the pre-Lisbon period, an institutional unbalance has been re-created.

The next part identifies four, interlinked, domains where the EP could gain (or lose) power.

4.1   *The Annual Budgetary Procedure*

Theoretically, the EP's powers have been maintained by the Lisbon Treaty and the establishment of a special legislative procedure (article 311 TFEU) based on the ordinary legislative procedure.

The effect of simplification provided by the single reading for the adoption of the budget is presented as a positive step. However, in practice, it has produced a different impact on both institutions' prerogatives. While the Council usually proceeds to linear reductions of the amounts proposed in the Commission's Draft Budget, the EP proceeds to a more analytical reading and amends the Council position with its own political priorities. Over the last years, the Council has been more successful in imposing its position on the EP and the Commission, notably on payments with the argument of national budgetary constraints. Before the entry into force of the Lisbon Treaty, the Parliament could use the 'weapon' of the qualified majority required, also in the second reading, to impose its priorities, including on the level of payments (soft power). This 'weapon' no longer exists in the context of the Conciliation Committee which is bound by the objective of result. The Treaty of Lisbon has clearly increased the power of the Commission in the annual budgetary procedure. Practically, the two branches of the budgetary authority no longer decide on the budget alone, but the three institutions do jointly.

Following the failure of three annual procedures (2011, 2013 and 2015), the Parliament could make room for a de facto second reading in advancing the pragmatic calendar and voting in September with a conciliation concluded (or not) in October. In the event of a second Draft Budget, more time would be available for meaningful negotiations. This could also lead to accepting that provisional twelfths are not an unsatisfactory alternative but a workable transitional arrangement.

In addition, the effect of binding ceilings enshrined in article 312 TFEU diminishes the scope of the annual procedure. It has somehow become an accounting exercise which consists in finding an agreement on a 'slice' of the MFF. The effect of financial envelopes to secure the financing of multiannual programmes decided by the legislative authority are predetermined amounts which the budgetary authority has the obligation to respect. Knowing that 85% of EU legislation is now adopted under co-decision, a number of fixed envelopes hamper the room for manoeuvre during the annual budgetary procedure. The specialised parliamentary committees are often looking to preserve the amount allocated in the Draft Budget according to the financial programming. A more flexible approach, notably based on implementation, could be followed.

The EP could therefore make a better use of the control powers granted by the Treaty. It has the bodies and structures to look after the qualitative and quantitative implementation of EU policies from a legislative and budgetary angle. Such monitoring would be a complementary role to the delegated and implementing acts. The EP has the right to give or to refuse discharge to the Executive (the Commission). The Council limits itself to an accountable overview of the spending which justifies its linear cuts made in the annual budgetary procedure. The Parliament could however develop a more political and responsible role through a systematic scrutiny of how and how much policies receiving funding from the EU budget are implemented. Such control would not only make its position stronger during the negotiations but also contribute to a better interinstitutional balance.

4.2   Own Resources

'A technical problem which became a political issue' (A. Lamassoure, MEP, chairman of the committee on budgets, 2009–2014). Due to the budgetary constraints on national treasuries and the sovereign debt crises, the ministers of finance have imposed rigour to the EU budget without considering its leverage effect nor its capabilities for growth and investment. Apart from the political rationale of having rigorous budgets, there is another indirect cause for the problem of payments, more of an institutional nature, which is the system of OR. A total of 75% of the revenue allocated to the EU budget by the decision on OR (Council Decision 2014/1335) are drawn from the so-called fourth resource, namely GNI. This resource, which reflects MS' wealth, has developed into *le poison du juste retour* (Le Cacheux 2005).

Revenue of the EU budget have so far remained the sole prerogative of the MS and are decided at the intergovernmental level. In its battle for balance, the EP has highly contributed to the reflexion on reforming the current system to fit the initial aim of genuine OR (Report Haug et al. 2011).

Most recently, the EP imposed, as one of the sine qua non conditions for the approval of the 2014–2020 MFF, to set up a High-Level Group (HLG) on OR. Convinced that the current distortions strongly impact the process and outcome of the MFF negotiations between MS whose main objective is a 'zero sum game', the impetus of the EP has been major. The HLG, composed of representatives of the EP, the Council and the Commission and chaired by Mario Monti, had the mandate 'to undertake a general review of the Own Resources system […] On the basis of this work, the Commission will assess if new Own Resources initiatives are appropriate' (Monti 2016 p. 36 and 76). The HLG delivered its final report in December 2016 (Monti 2016).

The EP's determination also responds to the principle of *no taxation without representation* since the parliamentary branch of the budgetary authority remains with no say on the revenue side of the budget.

There again, the Treaty opens a small door for change. Article 311 TFEU provides that the EP should give its consent to the future Council decision on implementing measures for the OR. In the context of a reformed system, the EP should find a role in influencing the Council decision, both in procedure and content. The EP could, like in other cases, take advantage of the consent procedure to rebalance its powers and contribute to a more democratic dimension of the EU budget.

4.3   Payments and RAL[10]

A shortage of payments has systematically grown up and become a contentious issue between the institutions. After the suppression of the distinction between CE and NCE in the Lisbon Treaty, the recent budgetary negotiations have shown the existence of two budgets: the Parliament is more interested in commitments to support political objectives; the Council is more vigilant about payments, while the Commission implements the budget, including the treasury shortage.

This asymmetry between the two branches of the budgetary authority concerning payments has been exacerbated, on the one hand, by the constraints of the financial crisis on national treasuries and the imposed rigour on the EU budget and, on the other hand, by the new responsibilities given to the EU by the Lisbon Treaty and supported by the EP, as well as by the recent crises and challenges. Such a new share of prerogatives is made at the detriment of EU policies and EU citizens.

Through resolutions, the EP repeatedly stated that new tasks for the EU have not been matched with sufficient resources. However, political support (and related majorities) has not been found so far to either identify 'negative priorities' and reductions of some policies to create space within the margins or convince the Council to agree on more flexibility.

The existence of a huge backlog (RAL) (around €274 billion at the end of 2017) is a side effect of both the shortage of payments and the multiannual nature of the EU budget. The definition of the UK share of RAL was part of the liabilities identified in the Brexit financial settlement agreed in December 2017.

A better re-use of the unspent appropriations and the recovery of fines in the annual balance could contribute to solving the payments and RAL problems while rebalancing the powers between the EP and the Council by giving the EP also more 'political responsibilities' over the EU budget and alleviating the image of 'Spending Parliament'.

4.4   The Multiannual Financial Framework

The negotiations of the 2014–2020 MFF from 2012 to 2013 and, more recently of the mid-term revision (September 2016 to March 2017), have

---

[10] Reste à liquider (RAL): the sum of outstanding commitments not yet translated into payments.

been arduous and lacked common goals (finance migration and stimulate growth policies). As such, they have shown the magnitude of diverging interests involved. Before the Treaty of Lisbon, and under the soft law regime, the EP was actively associated with the negotiations of the IIAs which reflected the deal achieved on a five- or seven-year Multiannual Perspective/Framework. Under the Treaty of Lisbon, primary law has dissociated the role of the Council who decides on the MFF regulation by unanimity, from the role of the EP who is invited to give its consent by qualified majority.

The first experience under the Lisbon regime has not been satisfactory from the Parliament's point of view, neither on results nor on process. The 'post mortem' initiative report adopted by the EP in April 2014 (Resolution on the 2014–2020 MFF, 2014) raised awareness about the role of the EP in this quite new procedure versus its prerogatives as one branch of the budgetary authority. The main criticisms expressed refer to political and institutional aspects.

However, the Treaty (article 312.5 TFEU) opens a door for a greater involvement of the EP into the negotiations before it is required to simply approve or reject the deal of the Council (consent procedure). In their letter of 6 June 2011 to President Buzek, the Hungarian, Polish, Danish and Cypriot Presidencies made an offer by inviting the EP negotiating delegation team to a briefing and a debriefing meeting with the representatives of the Trio Presidency before and after each General Affairs Council meeting where the MFF was discussed. The process, which was continued by subsequent Presidencies and is now considered an established practice, has nonetheless been deemed insufficient by the Parliament (Resolution on the 2014–2020 MFF, 2014, 1) certainly not replacing a real negotiation team, working on an equal footing. It could be mentioned that further progress was made with the introduction of trilateral meetings (but not trilogies) on the 2014–2020 MFF mid-term revision under Slovak Presidency.

Another element which complicated even more the negotiations (Resolution on the 2014–2020 MFF, 2014, 6) was the increasing role of the European Council in the field of the legislative authority, in contradiction with article 15.1 TEU (stating that the European Council is not involved in legislation). Such involvement clearly prevents the legislative authority from acting autonomously and indirectly increases the supremacy of the Council over the Parliament. It can be recalled that the Treaty (article 312.2 TFEU) offers the possibility for the Council to decide on the MFF by qualified majority, which could improve the chances of a satisfactory negotiation between the EP and the Council.

Strong political will and more efforts will be needed from both sides to restore the balance between the two arms of the budgetary authority, including on the duration of the MFF, which according to the Treaty could last for 'at least five years' (article 312.1 TFEU). Such a timeframe, matching the Parliament's mandate, would consequently strengthen its legitimacy when negotiating the MFF and the related legal acts.

5 CONCLUSION: STRUGGLING FOR SUPREMACY OR FOR RESTORING INSTITUTIONAL BALANCE?

The Treaties of Luxembourg (1970) and Brussels (1975) had defined the rules of the game between the two arms of the budgetary authority at a time where the European institutions were building up in search for democracy. This period culminated with the First European direct elections in 1979 which highly contributed to creating a new leeway for more legislative influence. However, this legislative vocation could not develop without the support of the budget.

The decade from 1978 to 1988 was marked by a period of intense conflicts between the EP and the Council. Four times the budget could not be adopted timely and in some cases, the conflict was brought to the Court. By advocating to maintain the institutional balance between the two arms of the budgetary authority, the Court redefined the balance between the institutions, which reinforced the negotiating capacity of the EP. With its increasing size, the budget had become a political leverage and not only a tool. The power game was progressively conducted at the institutional level, with the EP looking for supremacy over the Council, and sometimes within the institution itself, to maintain an equilibrium between legislative and budgetary prerogatives.

This chapter aimed to show how soft law has contributed to shaping EU policies and how the EP played the game and managed to gain power or to restore the balance of power through IIAs. Based on consensus and loyal cooperation, conflicts were often useful in defending the EP's budgetary powers. In general, a soft law regime allows indeed for more flexibility in annual and multiannual procedures. The Treaty of Lisbon however formalises soft law, and by doing so, it replaces pragmatism by more rigidity. This is why, as has been demonstrated, the power game continues and faces new challenges in the aftermath of Lisbon. Future negotiations will demonstrate whether the decline in the EP's power over the annual budget since Lisbon has been matched with the increase in its power over the MFF or OR. The budget and legislation are the core instruments of EU action, and the EP must preserve its position as a fullyfledged part of the budgetary authority.

References

Benedetto, G. (2017). Power, Money and Reversion Points: The European Union Annual Budgets Since 2010. *Journal of European Public Policy, 24*(5), 633–652.

Council Regulation (EU, Euratom) No 608/2014 of 26 May 2014 Laying Down Implementing Measures for the System of Own Resources of the European Union, OJ L 168, 7.6.2014, 29.

Council Regulation (EU, Euratom) No. 1311/2013 of 2 December 2013 Laying Down the Multiannual Financial Framework for the Years 2014–2020, OJ L 347, 20.12.2013, 884.

D'Alfonso, A. (2015). *Asylum, Migration and Integration Fund (AMIF)*. EPRS Briefing.

De Feo, A. (2017a). The European Budget: Motor or Brake of European Integration? A Walk Through 40 Years of Budgetary Decisions. In S. Becker, M. W. Bauer, & A. De Feo (Eds.), *The New Politics of the European Union Budget* (pp. 33–81). Nomos: Baden-Baden.

De Feo, A. (2017b). EU Budget Politics perspective Looking forward. In S. Becker, M. W. Bauer, & A. De Feo (Eds.), *The New Politics of the European Union Budget* (pp. 281–293). Nomos: Baden-Baden.

Decision 2003/429 EC of the European Parliament and of the Council of 19 May 2003 on the Adjustment of the Financial Perspective for Enlargement, OJ L 147, 14.6.2003, 25.

European Commission. (2014). *European Union Public Finance* (5th ed.). Luxembourg: Publications Office of the European Union.

European Commission, *Agenda 2000: For a Stronger and Wider Union*, 15.07.1997, COM (97) 2000 final.

European Commission, *Report from the Commission to the European Parliament and the Council on the functioning* of the Interinstitutional Agreement on budgetary discipline and sound financial management, COM/2010/0185 final.

European Commission. The LIFE Programme. Retrieved on 29 October 2017, from http://ec.europa.eu/environment/life/about/index.htm#history.

European Court of Justice. (1986). Case 34/86, Council of the European Union vs European Parliament (Budget).

European Court of Justice. (1995). Case 41/95, Council of the European Union vs European Parliament (Budget).

European Parliament. (1996). Resolution on the Guidelines for the 1997 Budget Procedure – Section III – Commission, A4-0076/1996.

European Parliament. (2014). Resolution of 15 April 2014 on Negotiations on the MFF 2014-2020: Lessons to be Learned and the Way Forward, P7_TA (2014) O378.

Haug, J., Lamassoure, A., & Verhofstadt, G. (eds.) (2011). *Europe for Growth: Towards a Radical Change in Financing the EU*. Centre For European Policy Studies & Notre Europe.

Interinstitutional Agreement of 17 May 2006 Between the European Parliament, the Council and the Commission on Budgetary Discipline and Sound Financial Management, OJ C 139, 14.6.2006, 1.

Interinstitutional Agreement of 2 December 2013 Between the European Parliament, the Council and the Commission on Budgetary Discipline, on Cooperation in Budgetary Matters and on Sound Financial Management, OJ C 373, 20.12.2013, 1.

Interinstitutional Agreement of 29 October 1993 on Budgetary Discipline and Improvement of the Budgetary Procedure, OJ C 331, 7.12.1993, 1.

Interinstitutional Agreement of 6 May 1999 Between the European Parliament, the Council and the Commission on Budgetary Discipline and Improvement of the Budgetary Procedure, OJ C 172, 18.6.1999, 1.

Interinstitutional Agreement on Budgetary Discipline and Improvement of the Budgetary Procedure, Signed by the European Parliament, the Council and the Commission on 29 June 1988, OJ L 185, 15.7.1988, 33.

Joint Declaration of the European Parliament, the Council and the Commission of 30 June 1982 on Various Measures to Improve the Budgetary Procedure, OJ C194, 28. 7. 1982, 1.

Jorgensen, E., et al. (2015). *The SAGE Handbook of European Foreign Policy*. Thousand Oaks, CA: SAGE Publications Ltd.

Le Cacheux, J. (2005). *Budget européen: le poison du juste retour*, Notre Europe, série Etudes et recherches no. 41.

Monti, M. (2016). *Future Financing of the EU*. Final report and Recommendations of the High Level Group on Own Resources.

Raube, K. (2012). The European External Action Service and EP. *The Hague Journal of Diplomacy, 7*(1), 65.

Report on negotiations on the MFF 2014-2020: lessons to be learned and the way forward (2014/2005(INI)), 2014, A7-0254/2014.

Zangl, P. (1989). The Interinstitutional Agreement on Budgetary Discipline and Improvement of the Budgetary Procedure. *Common Market Law Review, 26*(4), 675–685.

PART III

EP Politics

CHAPTER 10

The European Parliament and Civil Society

Amandine Crespy and Louisa Parks

1 INTRODUCTION

This chapter aims to shed light on the array of forms that can take the relationship between the European Parliament (EP) and organised civil society. Organised civil society groups have paid more attention to the EP as its power has grown, both with successive treaty reforms and as a result of its willingness to wield newly bestowed powers and stake its position in the European Union's (EU) core institutional triangle. Even though the European Commission remains the first port of call for such groups as the initiator of legislation, the EP is crucial for securing amendments to proposed legislation, and on the occasion of a veto point to end legislative proposals or trade deals. In addition, like the Commission, the Parliament must rely on some information from outside groups to influence its decision-making, given the size of its personnel and resources compared to the breadth and extent of its tasks as a co-legislator. The Parliament has thus been active both in reflecting on the differentiated nature of organised

A. Crespy (✉)
Université libre de Bruxelles, Brussels, Belgium
e-mail: acrespy@ulb.ac.be

L. Parks
Università degli Studi di Trento, Trento, Italy
e-mail: louisa.parks@unitn.it

© The Author(s) 2019   203
O. Costa (ed.), *The European Parliament in Times of EU Crisis,*
European Administrative Governance,
https://Doi.org/10.1007/978-3-319-97391-3_10

civil society and in developing a range of areas where its members engage with it in more or less transparent ways. These reflections and spaces for engagement are complicated by the role of the Parliament as the Union's primary representative democratic institution. Here, the Parliament seems on occasion caught in a dilemma: as the 'voice of the people', it often seeks to be more open to civil society, yet, at the same time, retains suspicion of organised civil society and lobby groups that may not represent 'the people's' opinion.

The chapter will pose a series of questions to be discussed. First, it will look at the Parliament as a whole and its role in the regulation of relations with interest groups within the EU. It will ask to what extent its practice is influential and explore how practices differ between the Parliament and the Commission. The following section will look at some of the formal spaces for relations with civil society within the Parliament: intergroups, public hearings and spaces linked to European Citizens' Initiatives. The third section will focus on the micro level and consider the relations between organised civil society and members of the European Parliament (MEPs) linked in turn to social movement campaigns and protest and 'insider-outsider' coalitions. Finally, some considerations on the role of individual Eurosceptic MEPs in the promotion of right-wing populism and nationalism within the EU will be offered, in order to illustrate how individual members of the Parliament have played a role in shaping civil society movements within the Member States in unintended ways. These discussions will underpin a concluding section which will return to the central dilemma of organised civil society in a representative democratic institution, reflecting on the types of democracy that are fostered by the EP in its diverse relationships with civil society.

2   The Role of the EP in Regulating Relations with Organised Civil Society

The Parliament's enduring interest in the question of how best to regulate relations with organised civil society is linked to the longstanding debate over the EU's democratic deficit. At its heart, the discussion about how to regulate relations with civil society flows from issues central to claims about the democratic deficit—specifically that the EU has and continues to lack transparency and accountability. The European Commission in particular has, on various occasions, pinned its hopes for increased transparency and accountability on its relations with organised civil society, suggesting it would act as a conveyor belt for information on the EU and bring citizens into decision-making. For the EP, the need to engage with organised civil society causes some friction. As a co-legislator, it needs the 'input' that the expertise and information held by organised civil society provides, yet at the same time there are qualms about engaging with organised, often particularistic groups, rather than directly with citizens. In this vein, the Parliament has been the only EU-level institution to consistently call for obligatory lobby registers. A brief history of the Parliament's attempts to create obligatory interest registers illustrates its role in pushing the EU steadily towards higher institutional transparency, as opposed to the voluntary regulatory models backed by the Commission.

The first push to regulate lobbying dates back to the 1992 Galle report and the 1996 Ford report. Although the first became bogged down in contentious discussions, it allowed a more fruitful approach in the second report, which suggested that the longstanding administrative rules applied by the Parliament's Quaestors be made official—without adhering to these rules, no access passes would be issued (Balme and Chabanet 2008). The resulting register of Accredited Lobbyists made information on who was accessing the Parliament available for the first time, though there was no obligation to apply for the pass, and temporary permits could still be issued for all types of visitors to the institution.

The Commission's 2001 White Paper on Governance, which brought issues of democratic deficit to the fore, was the next big event in EU interest group regulation. The White Paper argued that consulting civil society was key to improving EU legitimacy, since consultation would strengthen channels for the dissemination of information about the EU, contributing in turn to make the EU more transparent to its citizens. Rather than regulating a latent threat to democratic transparency, the White Paper also outlined principles considered as a non-binding code of conduct for the Commission, other EU institutions and organised civil society—openness, participation, accountability, effectiveness and coherence (Commission 2001). To achieve these principles, among other things, the Commission created the CONNECS database of civil society groups. However, the rules for inclusion in the database, particularly around formal organisation, led to a reinforced impression that business interests would find it easier than others to gain access to the Commission (Parks 2015), and the register remained voluntary.

The rejections of the Constitutional Treaty in referenda in France and the Netherlands in 2005 were considered to underline a continuing and growing sense of distrust in the EU and its institutions. The Commission made the decision to launch the European Transparency Initiative, including 'Plan D for democracy' as part of a strategy for greater openness in this context (Commission 2005). This move continued in the vein of the previous White Paper, conceiving an organised civil society as a key element for the EU's accountability and transparency. In this new iteration, however, the emphasis was placed firmly on the need for organised civil society itself to display democratic values, seen by some as shifting the blame for the EU's opacity (Friedrich 2011). Nevertheless, the Transparency Initiative was linked to the ideas of the Alter EU group, also founded in 2005 to call attention to the need for a lobby register, as well as the issue of preferential access to the Commission for industry groups. However, the Transparency Initiative resulted in another voluntary Register of Interest Representatives in 2008. This register now includes information on client bases as well as payments. In the same year, however, the EP adopted the Stubb report and called again for an obligatory register—this time arguing that it should apply across the three core institutions: Parliament, Council and Commission. Once again, the pattern of the Commission viewing organised civil society and consultation as unproblematic and helpful for increasing transparency, and thus creating voluntary registers, while the Parliament remained mindful of a need for more stringent regulation, applied to this period.

More recent developments suggest that this pattern may be broken. Following various lobbying corruption scandals, the Parliament's long-held view about the need for obligatory registers has taken precedence over the Commission's previous voluntary versions. In March 2011, the 'cash for amendments' scandal erupted. As Holman and Luneburg (2012, 93) recount, journalists from the UK's Sunday Times posed as lobbyists, offering favours in exchange for the tabling of amendments by MEPs. The fact that a number of MEPs responded favourably led to a third wave of discussions on transparency, accountability and democracy in the institution, and the Parliament's president called for a mandatory register and code of ethics (ibid.) for all institutions. The call for an inter-institutional register was then taken up by the Commission, and its Register of Interest Representatives was merged with the Parliamentary equivalent in July 2011. This register remained voluntary, but further scandals on 'revolving door' issues involving ex-Commissioners—including former Commission

President Barroso—as well as conflicts of interest coming to light, created further momentum to move to an obligatory register. The EP sought to drive the issue forward, calling for and then participating in an inter-institutional working group on an obligatory register in 2013, and issuing another decision calling for the same in 2014 (P7_TA(2014)0376). The voluntary register was revised and renamed the Joint Transparency Register in the same year. Most recently, in September 2016, a proposal for an inter-institutional agreement on a mandatory lobby register was published by the three core institutions, which 'recognise the necessity to establish a mandatory Transparency Register by making certain types of interactions with them conditional upon prior registration' (Commission 2016).

This brief history illustrates the Parliament's worries concerning lobbying and transparency, based on its identity as a representative democratic institution. Despite this, the Parliament is obliged to seek outside opinions and information in order to fulfil its role as co-legislator. At the same time, the Parliament has clearly remained concerned about the transparency of such relations. This has shaped its approach to the issue, and its successive and ultimately successful calls for obligatory registers. The Commission, on the other hand, appears more at peace with the idea of consultation. In successive communications, the Commission has portrayed its relations with organised civil society as crucial to the production of high-quality legislative proposals and central to achieving more democratic and transparent processes. This position has led the Commission to prefer voluntary registers until recently. Indeed, this overview suggests that while the Commission has been obliged to begin to question links with organised civil society more, the Parliament has gradually come to accept its need to work with these groups (while acting to ensure transparency in those relations) (Lehmann 2009). Formal spaces for relations between the Parliament and organised civil society are explored in the following section.

3   The EP as a Venue for Setting the Agenda and Shaping Deliberation

The Parliament hosts a number of formal spaces where its members interact with representatives of civil society groups. An overview and discussion of these spaces demonstrates how these spaces inform the Parliament's agenda and debates, with clear effects on decision-making in some cases.

3.1   Intergroups

The oldest formal spaces designed to host relations between the Parliament and organised civil society groups are intergroups, which have existed since direct elections of the EP began in 1979. These bodies gather MEPs across parties and political groups to discuss particular issues, for instance, bioethics or viticulture, and membership ranges from approximately 60 to 150 MEPs. Intergroups also constitute an important point of access for civil society groups to mobilise MEPs and, potentially, place new initiatives on the political agenda. Because they are not institutionalised bodies within the EP (unlike political groups or committees), they have however remained relatively informal, and their work does not have to comply with the formal rules of the assembly. Thus, as underlined by Dutoit (2003, 123), intergroups can be seen as providing MEPs with fora to discuss issues completely freely, allowing for the formation of bonds across parties and for individual MEPs to profile themselves as defending a particular cause. On the other hand, they can also be seen as the Trojan horse of lobbyists in the sense that a number of them were set up under the auspices of interest groups, seeking to expand their influence within the assembly.

For that reason, rules have been adopted over time to avoid their excessive proliferation, in line with the Parliament's concern over transparency in its relations with civil society (Earnshaw and Judge 2006, 66). In 1999, the Conference of Presidents decided to allocate a fixed total of signatures to political groups in proportion to their size. For the present legislature (eighth legislature 2014–2019), this number ranges from 7 (for the EFDD, the Greens/EFA and GUE/NGL), to 9 (ALDE and ECR), to 22 (for the EPP and S&D) for a total of 28 intergroups. Although they are sponsored by political groups, intergroups must remain open to members from all political parties. While they may receive operational or financial support from involved interest groups, the chairs are required to declare any such support. In 2015, only 5[1] of the 28 existing intergroups declared support in cash or kind provided by (mainly private) interest groups. In a number of existing bodies, secretariat functions are performed by external interest groups, while for others these tasks fall to MEPs' assistants. Few have hired a special coordinator, that is a full-time employee acting as a

---

[1] Wine, spirits and quality foodstuffs, Sky and space, Small and medium enterprises, Long-term investment and reindustrialisation, Biodiversity, hunting and countryside.

first point of access for all MEPs as well as interest groups outside the Parliament.

Alongside these official, registered intergroups, a number of unofficial bodies also exist. The total number of intergroups (both formal and informal) has varied from about 50 in 1990 increasing to 75 in 2002–2003 and then decreasing to approximately 55 in 2010 (Nedergaard and Jensen 2014, 197).

As displayed in Table 10.1, intergroups can be grouped into six thematic clusters: social and human rights, environmental issues, economic and social affairs, particular territories, culture and sports and world politics. Over time we had witnessed a decline in those focusing on world politics, while those dealing with economics and social affairs (for instance, creative industries and the digital agenda) have become more numerous. While most issues are defined broadly and can be regarded as relevant for the general interest, many are linked to the particular interests of social groups or private industries. Roughly one-third of all intergroups have existed since 1999 and can therefore be argued to exert influence through their continuous presence. This is the case, for example, for 'animal welfare, fishing and hunting'; 'ageing'; 'linguistic minorities'; 'disability'; 'wine, spirits and quality foodstuffs'; 'islands and coastal areas'; 'anti-racism'; and 'sky and space'.

Table 10.1   Number of intergroups per topic and legislature

	Fifth Legislature 1999–2004	*Sixth Legislature 2004–2009*	*Seventh Legislature 2009–2014*	*Eighth Legislature 2014–2019*
Social and human rights	4	6	7	8
Environment	4	3	5	5
Economic and social affairs	1	5	6	8
Territories	1	2	3	3
Culture and sports	1	3	3	3
World politics	6	3	1	
Others	3	2		1
Total	20	24	25	28

Source: www.europarl.europa.eu

From a social network perspective, recent research on intergroups (Nedergaard and Jensen 2014) gives an overview of their main characteristics. First, they vary greatly from an organisational point of view. While some are well established, endowed with many resources and very active, others have very limited resources and little visibility. Second, although all strengthen policy makers' networks, only a few can be conceived of as policy communities that bind their members closely. Third, 'participation in these bodies is characterized by interest, non-hierarchical negotiations, easy communication lines, and trust between MEPs from different political groups' (p. 206). Fourth, the two authors find that intergroups in the EP resemble the caucuses of the US Congress in many ways, as they allow parliamentarians to 'signal their preferences, exchange information and coordinate legislative initiatives' (p. 192). Fifth, they argue that only a limited number actually have an impact on legislative activity and policymaking.

While it remains difficult to assess the influence of intergroups on the decision-making process, their role is non-negligible, especially as far as agenda setting is concerned. They perform the role of an interface between MEPs and civil society. By organising meetings and conferences, they offer a platform for various representatives of civil society to disseminate expertise and information and to exchange best practices or opinions on topical issues. In some cases, their creation pursues the salience of political issues. In the fifth legislature, for instance, the intergroup on 'Capital taxation and globalization' was sponsored by the Socialists and Democrats (S&D), the Greens/European Free Alliance (Greens/EFA) and the Gauche Unie Européenne/Nordic Green Left (GUE/NGL). More recently, the intergroups on 'creative industries', 'the new media' and 'the digital agenda' have reflected the rise of (private) interests in these fields. In international affairs, intergroups serve to facilitate the exchange of information between MEPs (Dutoit 2016). Meetings take place in Strasbourg during the plenary sessions of the EP and host debates which may overlap with those on legislative resolutions (Costa 2001, 348–349). A recent case study (Ricetti 2017) on the Anti-Racism and Diversity Intergroup founded in 2016 finds that, while its influence remains fairly concealed, it has had a significant impact on the legislative work of the EP. From a sample of 104 amendments formulated by the intergroup across nine pieces of legislation, 69 were adopted. The 104 suggested amendments were supported by 56 MEPs across six political groups. Such an efficient legislative impact is mainly due to the work of the full-time coordinator, who can actively engage with both non-legislative work—mainly the organisation and the participation in events as well as press activities—and legislative work, including drafting parliamentary questions, amendments, resolutions, written declarations and initiative reports and organising public hearings.

Public hearings are indeed the main forums in which the EP can invite the representatives of various interest groups to provide input to its work. Most hearings take place in the framework of the drafting of a legislative report. The organisation of hearings is regulated by a set of rules adopted in 2003 (and amended in 2014 and 2016), and, because they are a prerogative of parliamentary committees, they require the authorisation of the Parliament's Bureau. Each committee is allowed to hear a maximum of 16 guests for whom expenses will be covered by the assembly. They are widely used with most committees holding one hearing every month (on average). During the election year 2014, only 63 public hearings were held, although 116 were organised in 2015 and 148 in 2016. The average number is therefore around 100 public hearings per year. A mid-term review of the current legislature (2014–2019) shows that the distribution of hearings across committees ranges from 3 for the Committee on Budgets (BUDG) to 24 for the temporary Committee on Emission Measurements in the Automotive Sector (EMIS) (Fig. 10.1).

Public hearings provide MEPs with the additional expertise to deliberate on various issues. As such, they constitute a main point of entry for all kinds of interest groups, including representatives of employers (Business Europe) and workers (European Trade Union Confederation).

Fig. 10.1 Number of hearings in the first half of the eighth parliamentary term (July 2014–December 2016). Source: European Parliament Directorate General for Internal Policies of the Union, Legislative Coordination

The question of what is seen as relevant expertise for parliamentary deliberation raises the issue of the representativeness of the 'experts' invited. Apart from the basic rules mentioned above, the organisation of hearings is not tightly regulated and left instead to the discretion of each committee. Experts are selected either by the Chair, the Bureau or the group coordinator (Corbett et al. 2007, 315). Invited experts provide written statements on the subject matter at stake, present their contribution before the committee and answer questions from MEPs. Other institutions, especially the Commission, also attend hearings and can be asked to react.

While no such study is available for the EP, a study on the German Bundestag points to the non-negligible role of interest groups' impact through public hearings. Eising and Spohr (2017) point out the key role of private interest groups in obtaining changes in legislation due to their control of production and investment. They also find that the more interest groups oppose a bill, the more likely it is to be modified during the legislative process. Again, this means that the balance in terms of the interests expressed during hearings does matter with regard to decision-making and policy outcomes.

3.2   The European Citizens' Initiative

Following its introduction in the Treaty of Lisbon, the European Citizens' Initiative (ECI) entered into force in 2012. An organising committee registers, with the commission, an idea for a petition concerning an issue falling under the EU's competence, then seeks to collect one million supporting signatures in at least seven Member States within one year, passing a minimum threshold of signatures set for each country. If the ECI is successful, the European Commission is required to respond to the claims made and to consider legislative action. Due to the organisational skills and resources needed to launch an ECI and reach out transnationally, it has de facto been used by civil society organisations to advance their claims and attempt to put specific proposals on the legislative agenda of the EU. So far, 43 ECIs have been launched, though 14 were withdrawn for not meeting the formal criteria enshrined in the regulation. Eighteen did not collect a sufficient number of signatures, while eight are still open. Only three ECIs have thus been successful: the campaign to ban animal testing, the petition to ban the use of human embryos in research and the ECI seeking to make access to water a guaranteed human right and exempt from market liberalisation. While an ECI allows an issue to gain in exposure on the political agenda, legislative consequences have proved difficult if not elusive. In none of the three cases has the Commission decided to propose new legislation as a response to citizens' claims.

The Parliament, as a representative democratic institution, has worked to reinforce the ECI as a method of direct contact with citizens in several ways. First, the EP was a strong advocate for the creation of ECIs as important tools for promoting participatory democracy and citizens' involvement at a European scale. It has also been very active in the evaluation of its procedural functioning and limitations, notably through its Constitutional Affairs Committee. MEPs have consistently advocated an amendment of the regulation to better facilitate the launch and success of ECIs. The EP in fact pioneered the creation of the ECI with a 2009 report (EP, OJ C 212 E, 5.8.2010, 99) describing the instrument eventually included in the Lisbon Treaty. During the treaty revision negotiations, MEPs argued that signatures should come from one-quarter (instead of one-third) of the EU Member States. When the assessment process of the ECI took place in 2014–2015, the EP commissioned research about the obstacles faced by ECI organisers (EP, PE 509.982). In 2015, it adopted a resolution (EP, P8_TA(2015)0382) asking for a simplification of the rules and procedures and for enhanced support for organisers. The aim of the Parliament is to make the procedure more user-friendly and to improve peoples' awareness about this possibility to participate in EU politics. The revision of the Regulation on the European citizens' initiative (No 211/2011, COM (2017) 482) is ongoing at the time of writing.[2]

Second, the EP contributes to the resonance of ECIs in various ways. Individual MEPs may play a role in controversies about particular ECIs, and—according to article 211 of the EP's Rules of Procedure—competent committees must organise a public hearing for each ECI registered by the European Commission. The extent to which the said hearings actually provide a space for genuine deliberation is, however, debatable. As Boronska and Monaghan report (2017, 54–55), the organisers of the 'One of us' campaign on the use of human embryos, for instance, did not

---

[2] In a 2016 initiative, the European Commission proposed methods for tackling the practical hurdles faced by ECI organisers, such as the high rate of rejections at the registration stage by the Commission, the requirements related to signatories' data, the period of only 12 months to collect signatures and the difficulties of the online collection of signatures.

wish to give those opposing the petition the possibility to express their views in a contentious discussion in the EP. A controversy also broke out between a group of pro-'One of us' MEPs led by the Polish EPP member Anna Záborská and Edite Estrela, a Portuguese ALDE MEP who had been very critical of the ECI in the columns of *The Parliament Magazine* and refused to take part in the public hearing. Another interesting example relates to the 'Right2Water' campaign, where one stakeholder complained that the EP did not allow him to participate in the hearing on the respective ECI. Broader discussions took place about the need to invite experts both favourable to and critical of an ECI, so as to offer balanced information on the subject matter. In some cases, ECIs can also interfere with the EP's legislative work. In the case of the Transatlantic Trade and Investment Partnership (TTIP), for instance, a proposed ECI was rejected by the Commission on formal grounds despite eventually collecting over three million signatures in 21 EU countries. Due to its competence to approve or reject the agreement, the EP organised several public hearings on the issue. Many MEPs, in particular those from the GUE/NGL and Greens/ALE groups, contributed to the opposition to both the TTIP and the CETA. However, the Parliament could not organise a hearing on this particular ECI, as it was not registered by the Commission. On 10 May 2017, the European Court of Justice ruled that the Commission was wrong not to register the 'Stop TTIP' ECI and that a public hearing should have taken place at the EP.

3.3   The EP as an Arena for Building Opposition

The following section addresses interactions between civil society and the Parliament at the micro level of individual MEPs. Aside from its more formal approach as a body to relations with civil society, it is important to consider the ways that individual MEPs and groups of MEPs work with civil society to build support for particular issues within the Parliament.

3.3.1   MEPs' Support for Social Movement Campaigns

The following section briefly describes two emblematic cases, in order to underpin reflections on the opportunities the Parliament and MEPs offer to social movement campaigns under different legislative procedures (the former co-decision, now the ordinary legislative procedure and the consent procedure). The first case is the campaign against the Directive on Services in the Internal Market. When introduced by the Commission in early 2004, this directive came as a surprise to European-level trade union groups, who argued that, as social partners, they should have been consulted prior to publication. Opposition to the proposal grew fast, as the text was seen to threaten the right to strike as well as collective agreements and its country of origin principle was more generally viewed as a catalyst for social dumping. Within the campaign, European-level trade unions held transnational protest marches and drew strategically on different sector-level members in Brussels to mount concerted lobbying campaigns within the Parliament, concentrating in particular on political groups not considered as the natural allies of trade unions (in line with the findings of Marshall 2015). National trade unions mounted numerous protests in the Member States alongside a number of social movement organisations, scaling these protests up to the European level via e-mailing campaigns and petitions. Most importantly, national trade union groups paraded the directive as an example of Europe's neoliberal character in French debates leading up to the referendum on the Constitutional Treaty (Brouard and Tiberj 2006; Crespy 2007). The European Parliament negotiated a compromise package, resulting in a watered-down directive after its vote in 2006.

The second example is more recent. In July 2012 the European Parliament withheld its consent for the signature of the Anti-Counterfeiting Trade Agreement (ACTA), thus wielding its newly acquired power over the signature of trade agreements contained in the Treaty of Lisbon. ACTA had worried a range of groups for a range of reasons; however digital rights groups concerned about draconian punishments for file sharing as well as stifling effects for innovation were the most organised in their campaigning efforts. Their European-level campaign focused on the EP given its new power, and alongside allies in the Greens/EFA group, successfully engineered a resolution against the opacity surrounding the agreement. Although the campaign was stalling by 2012, this changed in the wake of the popular protest movement against the Stop Online Piracy Act and the Protect Intellectual Property Act in the United States. With ACTA dubbed the 'European SOPA PIPA', protests began in Poland and quickly spread throughout the region and into western Member States. Digital rights campaigners targeted the Parliament, whilst their MEP allies in the Greens/EFA and, now, the S&D groups drew on this popular movement and split it causing a majority to sign against ACTA in the Council (Parks 2015; Crespy and Parks 2017).

To complement reflections on how MEPs engage with social movement campaigns, the cases are summarised in Table 10.2 according to

Table 10.2 Summary of two social movement campaigns targeting MEPs

	Services Directive	*ACTA*
Political opportunity structure	Commission closed—no prior consultation on proposal, no dialogue with trade unions after release. EP—open to dialogue, socialist and left groups initially, all groups after French 'no'. Council—some openings in national contexts, little at EU level.	Commission closed—acting on behalf of EU in secret international negotiations, incomplete sharing of documents with EP. EP—open to dialogue on transparency early in campaign, some groups and individual MEPs (Greens-EFA, GUE-NGL) campaigned against from beginning, other groups opened up from early 2012 protest wave on.
Campaign actions	EP main EU-level target—strategic lobbying, hearings, protests. Council main national level target—high-level meetings, protests, constitutional debate linkage.	EP main EU level target—strategic lobbying, hearings, meetings, e-mail campaigns etc. No engagement with Commission. Council—national governments targets of national-level protests.
Campaign outcomes	Watered down directive passed by EP in 2006	Consent for signature withheld by EP in 2012

Source: Adapted from Parks (2015) and Crespy and Parks (2017)

open and closed EU institutions, actions taken by campaigning groups and the outcomes of campaigns.

Admittedly these are just two, relatively rare, examples of widespread social movement campaigns. Nonetheless, they serve to illustrate the dynamics that can characterise relations between MEPs and social movements, as well as the circumstances that allow effective opposition at the European level. Other campaign analyses, including campaigns that have not seen outcomes, reinforce these findings.[3]

The campaigns also underline two more general points in relation to organised civil society. In contrast to the tension and suspicions that underpin the EP's position on lobby regulation, individual MEPs seem willing to fight alongside civil society when they perceive social movement campaigns as genuine representations of 'the voice of the people', and even occasionally perform U-turns on previously held positions. In the

---

[3] Including, for example, successful campaigns against the services directive and the port directives, and less successful campaigns on green and social procurement and the REACH chemicals regulation. For further discussion see Crespy and Parks (2017).

Services Directive case for example, the socialist group worked in concert with trade unions throughout, while a cross-party group of MEPs committed to engage with trade unions to hammer out a compromise after the French rejection of the Constitutional Treaty. In the ACTA case, the election of two Pirate Party MEPs provided a kernel of parliamentary support, and these MEPs considered themselves a part of the movement. After popular protests spread in 2012, many other MEPs made complete changes in their positions as a result. These relations can be termed insider-outsider coalitions, in which organised civil society becomes crucial to the construction of opposition majorities within the Parliament. Such coalitions function by providing civil society actors (when these are considered as representing the 'voice of the people') access to a powerful arena for decision-making, while protest and activism create resonance in the public sphere, allowing voting majorities to take shape (Crespy and Parks 2017).

3.3.2   A Change for the Worse?

In recent years, evidence that opportunities for civil society organisations to influence the EP's decision-making may have reduced has begun to accrue. This is due to two reasons. First, policy preferences within the EP have not matched those of recent protest movements, especially over free trade. Second, the EP has been marginalised in the macro-economic governance model that emerged in the aftermath of the financial and debt crisis of 2008–2010.

The Treaty of Lisbon granted the EP the power to approve (or reject) international agreements through the consent procedure. As the case of ACTA showed, this was seen as good news for civil society actors critical of both the policy implications and the procedural aspects of the EU's international free trade agreements. Since the failure of the Multilateral Investment Agreement in 1997, civil society has consistently criticised WTO and EU policies of liberalisation and deregulation. Moreover, because international trade agreements are conducted behind closed doors and no draft agreements are publicly available, they are often deemed undemocratic and incompatible with the extent to which such agreements affect people's everyday lives. The issue of relevant information and documents being communicated to the EP has, in this regard, repeatedly been a bone of contention.

The EP has often echoed critical voices from civil society on trade agreements, as seen, for example, in the campaign against the General Agreement on Trade in Services (Crespy 2016, Chap. 3) from 2003 to

2007. However, the EP's ability to fully echo civil society concerns over free trade cannot be taken for granted, as recent debates over the TTIP and CETA have shown. In June 2015, and against the background of intense contestation—notably via the abovementioned ECI—an EP vote for a resolution on TTIP had to be postponed, with the EP President M. Schulz using article 175 of the EP's rules of procedure for the first time in order to do so. This was due to the very high number of amendments tabled and also due to the will of the EP's president to secure a majority. On 8 July 2016, a resolution (P8_TA(2015)0252) which backed the negotiations was adopted, although it called on the Commission to exercise caution with regard to regulatory standards and for more transparency in the negotiations.

Similarly to the TTIP, CETA was highly controversial (TTIP and CETA were contested jointly in civil society campaigns). In the case of CETA, the controversy reached its climax when the Walloon Parliament in Belgium expressed its determined opposition to the agreement, and the region's minister-president, Paul Magnette, announced that Wallonia would block the ratification process in Belgium. Despite heated debates, the EP, on 15 February 2017, voted with 408 votes for, 254 against and 33 abstentions in favour of the agreement. This provided evidence that, where contentious free trade issues are concerned, the EP can no longer be seen by civil society as a reliable ally since a majority of MEPs are in favour of trade liberalisation (and less critical of its potential negative impacts) than campaigning organisations.

Another consideration that puts the role of the EP as a key ally for civil society in question is its marginalisation in post-crisis macro-economic governance. In the most active period of crisis management from 2009 to 2010, the European Central Bank (ECB) was at the forefront of the monetary policy response, while key decisions on bailouts were agreed in intergovernmental summits among heads of state and government. Arguably, some national parliaments, especially the German *Bundestag*, played a more important part in these decisions than the EP. Later, when more long-term institutional arrangements were agreed, the Council and the Commission were empowered to control and issue recommendations on each member state's budget and fiscal policy as well as on programmes of macro-economic and social reforms.

Arguably, the EP has caught up in some respects. It had a decision-making role on key regulations such as the 'Two-pack' and 'Six-pack' which tightened fiscal discipline and increased its influence outside the traditional framework of the so-called Community Method. This occurred for the most part through the institutionalisation of the 'Economic Dialogue' (or 'exchange of views') whereby the EP can be informed of, and deliver, input on the various aspects of the European Semester, by inviting all key actors from the Commission, Council, especially the Eurogroup, or the member states. In 2016, 12 meetings of this sort took place. Thus, the EP has gradually become 'the 'go-to' body for other actors concerned about their political legitimacy' and that of the European Semester (Schmidt 2016, 21).

We argue, however, that these transformations of EU governance have reduced the opportunities for civil society, and have rendered the European level less favourable to the channelling of its claims into institutional politics. The new forms of parliamentary influence are informal and limited to deliberation within confined circles of decision makers, within the EU institutions, and thus fail to reach the wider public. Civil society appears to have perceived this change in the EU opportunity structure, and civil society campaigns against austerity and the powerful influence of market actors, such as banks, have not specifically targeted the EP (Pianta and Gerbaudo 2016). With the exception of a few protest actions targeting the ECB in Frankfurt, and a few Indignados marching to Brussels in 2012, protest against austerity has remained fragmented across various local sites. This is a function, not only of the need to respond to immediate necessities at the local level by providing services such as food banks and legal assistance, but also of the dismissal of the European level as a valid interlocutor (della Porta and Parks 2018).

4   ACTIVISM OF EUROSCEPTIC MEPS IN NATIONAL POLITICS

A final type of linkage between the EP and civil society relates to the involvement of MEPs in campaigns on EU issues at the national level, especially during referendum campaigns. Paradoxically, the EP has served as a springboard for many Eurosceptic personalities to voice their criticism of the EU and its workings. This is partly due to the fact that EP elections are seen as second-order elections and follow the proportional representation system. In some countries, notably those with majoritarian systems including France and the UK, EP elections have accompanied the electoral rise of Eurosceptic movements such as the UK Independence Party (UKIP) or the Front National. MEPs from these parties seek to exert 'outsider opposition' through various strategies and roles. Most choose the 'empty chair strategy', remaining largely absent from the EP's work, or 'noisy opposition' through public orations, using the plenary meetings of the assembly as a sounding board (Brack 2015, 348).

A telling example is that of Jens-Peter Bonde, a Danish journalist who was active in the People's Movement against the EU, a cross-party association founded in 1972 to oppose Denmark's accession. Bonde was elected as an MEP for the June Movement (partly a successor to the People's Movement against the EU) in 1979. He became famous for his involvement in the campaign against the Treaty of Maastricht in Denmark. He was re-elected at every EP election until 2008 and promoted the creation of a new pan-European party: the Europeans United for Democracy—Alliance for a Europe of Democracies, which he led from 2005 to 2009. He was an important figure not only within Danish Eurosceptic circles, but also for organisations such as the European No Campaign, a cross-party network gathering NGOs campaigning against the European Constitutional Treaty in 2005. Nigel Farage is another well-known example. Elected as an MEP in 1999 for UKIP, Farage and fellow UKIP MEPs have consistently used the EP as a platform for expressing their party's central objective—leaving the EU and denouncing its practices. Thus, the Parliament has played a crucial role in providing an institutional stage for UKIP, providing a platform as well as significant funding (allegedly misspent in the campaign for Brexit).

On the other end of the political spectrum, the left-wing French leader Jean-Luc Mélenchon was also a prominent figure in the leftist No campaign against the ratification of the European Constitutional Treaty in 2005, and two MEPs from the Parti Socialiste's left wing, Vincent Peillon and Benoit Hamon, also took part in the No campaign. While Mélenchon was not an MEP at the time, the campaign against the European Constitutional Treaty boosted his popularity in French politics. He was elected to the EP in 2009 and re-elected in the subsequent legislature. While he is known for being mainly absent from the assembly and fully absorbed by national politics, he occasionally profiles himself within the EP as a critical voice of the EU and its policies.

5   Conclusion

Relations between the EP and civil society have undeniably become central to the body's identity within the European institutional architecture. While relations with civil society are also crucial to the Commission's work, there are clear differences in the nature of these relations for the two institutions. Since the White Paper on Governance from 2001, the European Commission has fostered a weakly politicised conception of democracy, rooted in the good governance principles, such as openness and transparency. In this perspective, it has valued the consultation of stakeholders as a means to above all make policy making more efficient by ensuring smoother passage through the legislative procedure or securing better implementation. While the Commission has been criticised for its proximity to large corporations in various sectors, a larger opening to citizen interests was a means for the technocratic body to enhance its own democratic profile. The EP has equally seen consultation procedures as a source of expertise which can feed into the policy-making process. However, its relations with various groups have been shaped by the more traditional model of representative democracy, which the assembly is the only one to embody in the EU institutional architecture. The Parliament often appears to be the most open among the EU institutions. It has consistently pushed for transparency to allow citizens to see with which groups it (and other institutions) engages and hosts a number of formal spaces for civil society voices. The politicisation of EU matters in the public sphere, and profiling itself as a channel for echoing 'the voice of the people' has clearly been an institutional strategy pursued by the EP. At the individual level, a number of individual MEPs have supported critical voices. Several tensions and interesting developments stem from the coexistence of these two—equally incomplete—models of democracy for the EU. Thus, while the EP has consistently pushed for more citizen involvement, for instance, through fostering and facilitating the European Citizens' Initiative, it has also had to endorse a peculiar role in controlling the modalities and effects of interest groups' involvement in the European political process, for example, through the creation of a mandatory lobby register. In a long-term perspective, the continuous strengthening of the EP has gradually shaped a political opportunity structure which has on several occasions been favourable to grassroots movements and organisations. These groups have often accused EU policies of threatening the capacity to regulate markets in the public interest, civil liberties or the democratic nature of will formation at the European scale. This potential nevertheless remains contingent and dependent on the internal balance of power among political groups and the issues at stake. Furthermore, the latest developments in the aftermath of the 2008 financial crisis seem to have put the key role of the EP in structuring public debates over crucial political decisions into question. The fact that some nationalists have been particularly vocal from within the EP, with profound ramifications at the national level as they remain a key addressee for progressive movements within civil society in times of crisis, is a challenge for the EP.

REFERENCES

Balme, R., & Chabanet, D. (2008). *European Governance and Democracy: Power and Protest in the EU.* Lanham, MD: Rowman & Littlefield.

Boronska, K., & Monaghan, E. (2017). The European Citizen Initiative as a Democratic Legitimacy-Enhancing Tool: Toward a Broader Conceptualisation. In B. Perez de las Heras (Ed.), *Democratic Legitimacy in the European Union and Global Governance* (pp. 41–64). Basingstoke: Palgrave.

Brack, N. (2015). The Roles of Eurosceptic Members of the European Parliament and Their Implications for the EU. *International Political Science Review, 36*(3), 337–350.

Brouard, S., & Tiberj, V. (2006). The French Referendum: The Not So Simple Act of Saying Nay. *Political Studies, 39*(2), 261–268.

Costa, O. (2001). *Le Parlement européen, assemblée délibérante.* Bruxelles: Editions de l'Université de Bruxelles.

Crespy, A. (2007). Dissent over the European Constitutional Treaty within the French Socialist Party: Between Response to Anti-Globalization Protest and Intra-Party Tactics. *French Politics, 6*, 23–44.

Crespy, A. (2016). *Welfare Markets in Europe: The Democratic Challenge of European Integration.* Basingstoke: Palgrave.

Crespy, A., & Parks, L. (2017). The Connection Between Parliamentary and Extra Parliamentary Opposition in the EU. From ACTA to the Financial Crisis. *Journal of European Integration.* https://doi.org/10.1080/07036337.2017.1309038.

della Porta, D., & Parks, L. (2018). Social Movements, the European Crisis, and EU Political Opportunities. *Comparative European Politics, 16*(1), 85–102.

Dutoit, L. (2003). L'influence au Parlement européen: les intergroupes. *Politique européenne, 1*(9), 123–142.

Dutoit, L. (2016). The International Role of the European Parliament's Intergroups. *Hague Journal of Diplomacy, 11*(2–3), 182–195.

Earnshaw, D., & Judge, D. (2006). No Simple Dichotomies: Lobbyists and the European Parliament. *The Journal of Legislative Studies, 8*(4), 61–79.

Eising, R., & Spohr, F. (2017). The More, the Merrier? Interest Groups and Legislative Change in the Public Hearings of the German Parliamentary Committees. *German Politics, 26*(2), 314–333.

European Commission. (2001). *European Governance: A White Paper.*

European Commission. (2002). *Towards a Reinforced Culture of Consultation and Dialogue – General Principles and Minimum Standards for Consultation of Interested Parties by the Commission.*

European Commission. (2005). *The Commission's Contribution to the Period of Reflection and Beyond – Plan-D for Democracy, Dialogue and Debate.*

European Commission. (2016). Proposal for a Interinstitutional Agreement on a Mandatory Transparency Register.

Friedrich, D. (2011). *Democratic Participation and Civil Society in the European Union.* Manchester: Manchester University Press.

Holman, C., & Luneburg, W. (2012). Lobbying and Transparency: A Comparative Analysis of Regulatory Reform. *Interest Groups and Advocacy, 1*(1), 75–104.

Lehmann, W. (2009). The European Parliament. In D. Coen & J. Richardson (Eds.), *Lobbying the European Union: Institutions, Actors and Issues* (pp. 39–69). Oxford and New York: Oxford University Press.

Marshall, D. (2015). Explaining Interest Group Interactions with Party Group Members in the European Parliament: Dominant Party Groups and Coalition Formation. *Journal of Common Market Studies, 53*(2), 311–329.

Nedergaard, P., & Jensen, M. D. (2014). The Anatomy of Intergroups – Network Governance in the Political Engine Room of the European Parliament. *Policy Studies, 35*(2), 192–209.

Parks, L. (2015). *Social Movement Campaigns on EU Policy: In the Corridors and in the Streets.* Basingstoke: Palgrave Macmillan.

Pianta, M., & Gerbaudo, P. (2016). In Search of European Alternatives: Anti-Austerity Protests in Europe. In M. Kaldor & S. Selchow (Eds.), *Subterranean Politics in Europe* (pp. 31–59). Basingstoke: Palgrave Macmillan.

Ricetti, D. (2017). *L'influence des intergroupes au Parlement européen.* MA Thesis, Université libre de Bruxelles, defended on August 31.

Schmidt, V. A. (2016). He 'New' EU Governance: 'New', Intergovernmentalism Versus 'New' Supranationalism Plus 'New' Parliamentarism. Retrieved September 5, 2018, from http://cevipol.ulb.ac.be/sites/default/files/bxl_working_paper_5_2016_issue_on_eu_economic_governance.pdf.

CHAPTER 11

Parliamentary Questions and Representation of Territorial Interests in the EP

Nathalie Brack and Olivier Costa

1   INTRODUCTION

There is a common understanding that modern democratic politics is strongly linked to political representation (Best and Cotta 2000; Sartori 1987; Schapiro et al. 2010). And although political representation has numerous meanings, it generally refers to the process by which a community is made present within an assembly (Deschouwer 2005; Pitkin 1967). Because of its central role in modern democracies, the mechanisms of parliamentary representation have been extensively discussed and analysed in different ways by various sub-disciplines of political science.

In the EU, even if several 'representative modes' remain (Lord and Pollak 2010), parliamentary representation has become central with the

N. Brack (✉)
Cevipol, Université libre de Bruxelles, Brussels, Belgium

College of Europe, Bruges, Belgium
e-mail: nathalie.brack@ulb.ac.be

O. Costa
College of Europe, Bruges, Belgium

CNRS, Bordeaux, France
e-mail: olivier.costa@coleurope.eu; o.costa@sciencespobordeaux.fr

© The Author(s) 2019   225
O. Costa (ed.), *The European Parliament in Times of EU Crisis*,
European Administrative Governance,
https://doi.org/10.1007/978-3-319-97391-3_11

empowerment of the European Parliament (EP) and the parliamentarization of the European polity. Since its direct election, the EP has indeed played a growing role in order to alleviate the democratic deficit. As noted by Kröger and Friedrich (2013, 56), 'political representation is a *sine qua non* for the legitimacy of any democratic political system'. Therefore, parliamentary representation is not only the main vehicle for citizens' participation in European politics, but it also plays a key role in the legitimization of the EU (Goetze and Rittberger 2010). This has finally been acknowledged in article 10 of the treaty on the European Union stating that '1. The functioning of the Union shall be founded on representative democracy; 2. Citizens are directly represented at Union level in the European Parliament (...)'.

It is therefore not surprising that representation in the EU has attracted a growing attention from scholars, especially in recent years. While some authors have tried to evaluate the political or social representativeness of the chamber, others focused on the way Members of European Parliament (MEPs) conceive and carry out their mandate. They have tested theories, developed in the framework of the US Congress, on the EP and its members (Marsh and Norris 1997; Hix et al. 2003; Yordanova 2011). They have examined how MEPs vote, why they defect from the party line and how coalitions are formed (Coman 2009; Faas 2003; Hix et al. 2007; Kreppel 2002; Trumm 2015). Through sophisticated analysis of roll-call votes, this literature has considerably enriched our knowledge of legislative politics in the EP.

However, the bulk of these studies has adopted a restrictive vision of the parliamentary mandate. They tend to concentrate only on one relation—the triangular relation between MEPs, their national parties and their parliamentary group—and one specific conduct: voting in plenary. Recently, with the 'representative turn in EU studies' (Kröger and Friedrich 2013; Piattoni 2013), a burgeoning literature has analysed how MEPs perform their representative function and their activities besides voting (Poyet 2018). By drawing on the insights of role theory developed in other parliamentary settings, research has showed that MEPs have various and sometimes contradictory allegiances, and that they face a potentially infinite number of possibilities for action with a finite number of time, energy and resources (Costa 2002; Farrell and Scully 2007). Despite the specialization and professionalization of MEPs, there remains a great variety of ways they select their priorities, interact with citizens and follow various models of representation at the EU level (Farrell and Scully 2010; Costa and Navarro 2003; Navarro 2009b).

This chapter aims to contribute to this reflection on parliamentary representation at the supranational level. More particularly, we will focus on the territorial dimension of the European mandate. This dimension is generally considered as a central part of the process of representation at national level, but has been neglected so far in the EP. Rather than assuming an electoral disconnection in the EP, we will therefore take an inductive approach to examine empirically to what extent territorial representation is reflected in MEPs' practices.

To do so, we rely on an analysis of their written parliamentary questions, which constitutes another understudied topic. The content of MEPs' questions is used here as indicators of MEPs' priorities and centres of interest. Through an analysis of a sample of more than 8000 questions, we show that a significant minority of these questions deal with national or subnational issues rather than pan-European concerns. And we also find that the focus of the questions can be explained by the MEP's political affiliation and nationality, as well as the electoral system. The analysis also reveals that the crisis did not lead to a stronger focus on regional or national issues, at least when it comes to parliamentary questions.

This chapter is structured around six sections. The first one provides a brief state of the art and highlights the lack of studies on territorial representation in the EP. The second section explains the choice to concentrate on written questions and explains the hypothesis while the third one describes the data. The fourth section constitutes a first examination of the database and concentrates on the territorial focus of the written questions of MEPs. The next section seeks to explain the variation in focus of MEPs' parliamentary questions. Finally, we will examine whether the crisis has had an impact on the territorial focus of questions in the recent years.

2 TERRITORIAL REPRESENTATION IN THE EUROPEAN PARLIAMENT, A 'BLIND SPOT' IN EU STUDIES

Representation is not only at the heart of modern democratic politics, it is also a central notion in which the EU realizes its democratic legitimacy. The EP has therefore served as a research laboratory for scholars to investigate political representation beyond the national level. As a multifaceted and complex phenomenon, representation has been studied from various perspectives. Most research has long tended to focus on 'descriptive' or symbolic representation (Pitkin 1967): authors have compared the social characteristics of the representatives with those of the represented, to determine to what extent this assembly could be considered a microcosm or a mirror of European societies (Beauvallet and Michon 2009; Norris 1997; Norris and Franklin 1997). Others, inspired by the theoretical model of policy congruence (Miller and Stokes 1963; for a methodological update: Golder and Stramski 2010), have analysed the similarities between citizens and their representatives by examining the opinion congruence of voters and MEPs or their (Euro) party, on the left/right and pro/anti-integration scales in EP elections (Arnold and Franklin 2012; Lefkofridi and Katsanidou 2014; Marsh and Wessels 1997; Mattila and Raunio 2012; Thomassen et al. 1999). More recently, studies have instead considered representation as a dynamic process by which it matters less to know who the representatives are than to know how they conceive and carry out their mandate. Inspired by a constructivist approach, scholars sought to understand the performative side of representation, focusing on non-electoral representation, or analysing representation in the EU from a more normative perspective (Bellamy and Castiglione 2010; Lord and Pollak 2010). Others concentrated on the representative activities of MEPs and revealed that 'there is no univocal interpretation of the European mandate' (Costa 2002, 9). Facing multiple principals, MEPs are relatively free to set their own priorities and carry out their mandate in various ways. Following the principal-agent perspective, the bulk of these studies tends to focus on the relationship between MEPs and their two main principals: the national party and the EP political group (Hix et al. 2007; Mülböck 2012). The aim of these studies is to determine whether and why MEPs choose to defect from the party or group line, and if we should refer to national or European parliamentarians (Scully et al. 2012). They have considerably improved our understanding of legislative politics in the EP, but due to their restrictive vision of the parliamentary mandate, we still know little about how MEPs perform their representative function and their activities, besides voting (Busby 2013; Priestley 2008).

Moreover, given the 'widely-held assumption that any electoral connection to the EP is weak because of the way EP elections (do not) work' (Hix et al. 2003, 194), the territorial dimension of the European parliamentary mandate remains largely overlooked by these scholars. The linkage between voters and their elected representatives is a fundamental aspect of the representative process (Pitkin 1967), and many studies on national parliaments have demonstrated that elected representatives spend much of their time and energy dealing with constituency representation

(Cain et al. 1987; Fenno 1978; Mayhew 1974; Wahlke 1962; Brack et al. 2016; Brack and Costa 2018).

However, in the case of the EP, a very limited literature addresses the issue of territorial representation (Beauvallet and Michon 2010; Scully and Farrell 2001, Farrell and Scully 2007; Brack and Costa 2018; Poyet 2018). These studies show that MEPs prioritize certain of their allegiances and attempt to communicate with citizens despite the institutional constraints. Indeed, the regionalization of the European elections and the possibility of preferential voting (or single transferable vote) in a majority of countries, combined with the empowerment of the EP, all give incentives to MEPs to engage in constituency service, or at least to develop closer relationships with their voters. A territorial dimension is thus emerging in the EP's deliberation, mostly as a way for MEPs to increase their representativeness and the EP's legitimacy. This territorial dimension is reflected in the activities of the MEPs, through their choice of committees, their belonging to an intergroup or through their parliamentary questions (Costa 2002). But their activities and relations with their voters remain very heterogeneous (Brack and Costa 2013; Farrell and Scully 2010). Katz (1997) argues that the variation in the way MEPs deal with their relations with their constituents is due to the national political culture, whereas other studies stress the impact of the electoral system as well as individual-level factors, such as previous political experiences and MEPs' attitudes towards the EU (Scully and Farrell 2001; Farrell and Scully 2007; Chiru and Dimulescu 2011). Navarro (2009a) also shows that MEPs use written questions to please constituents and that a significant proportion of them contain a territorial reference.

By building on these few studies, this chapter aims to examine the emergence of this territorial dimension in the EP's deliberation, and to analyse the variation among MEPs according to their EP group, the type of electoral list they are elected under and their nationality. To do so, we rely on a new database that focuses on MEPs' parliamentary questions.

3 PARLIAMENTARY QUESTIONS AS INDICATORS OF MEPs' PRIORITIES

Parliamentary questions are an important tool for measuring individual MPs' role, orientations and more particularly, their focus of representation (Blidook and Kerby 2011; Rozenberg and Martin 2011). This instrument is certainly not the most powerful legislative mechanism, but its use induces very low costs for legislators, and makes it easy for them to address issues of their interest. It is therefore an excellent indicator of their priorities (Chiru and Dimulescu 2011; Navarro and Brouard 2014; Raunio 1996) and the perceptions they have of their parliamentary mandate.

Questions can be used for various reasons. They perform several macro-functions such as gaining information, controlling the executive and developing a reputation regarding a specific topic. Most scholarly work has used parliamentary questions to address issues of accountability and control, or to test for policy specialization among MPs (Martin 2011; Proksch and Slapin 2011; Jensen et al. 2013). But parliamentary questions also perform micro-functions for legislators such as generating publicity, defending territorial interests and showing concern for the interests of constituents (Bailer 2011; Lazardeux 2005; Raunio 1996). MPs may thus use parliamentary questions to cultivate more personal relationships with their constituents, as well as to maintain an electoral connection (Saalfeld 2011). Russo (2011) for instance showed how parliamentary questions can serve MPs to appear as though they are constituency-oriented. More importantly, in contrast to other activities such as voting, tabling amendments and making speeches which are more controlled by party discipline or institutional constrains, questions allow MEPs a greater room for manoeuver at the individual level (Raunio 1996) which allows them to display their true preferences and interests.

In the case of the EP, one would not expect a strong electoral connection. Indeed, there is a great uncertainty about whom MEPs are supposed to represent. Additionally, formal and informal rules encourage MEPs to act not as representatives of a constituency or a particular country, but as representatives of the 'European people'. According to the treaty, the EP is composed of representatives of the European citizens and MEPs have always favoured a 'general' conception of their mandate (Costa 2002): they claim to represent collectively the EU citizens and thus have refused to exclude the MEPs from given countries when deliberating about policies for which they enjoyed opting outs. In addition to that, the nature of the EP's competence and the priority given to a technical approach of legislative work discourage MEPs to import local issues or individual constituents' cases in the chamber (Brack and Costa 2013). On an informal basis, most MEPs avoid making references to their nationality during debates and speeches, or do it only to illustrate their arguments (with the exception of some Eurosceptic and nationalist members). But even though

MEPs are supposed to represent the general interest of European citizens, MEPs are elected at the national level. Although it has been discussed for many years, there are no European-wide lists yet. If there are some common basic principles for EP elections, the rules are not harmonized and MEPs are elected in national contexts, sometimes on regional (anchored) lists and/or with preferential voting (Costa 2015). Moreover, these elections are largely second order: emphasis is more on national than European issues and voter turnout is generally low compared to general election (Reif and Schmitt 1980; Marsh 1998; Viola 2015). In addition to that, the general European interest is a quite abstract notion and since the end of the 1990s, MEPs have promoted closer relations with regional and local levels as a way to balance the abstract nature of the supranational mandate and to increase the legitimacy of the institution and its members (Costa 2002, 15).

It is therefore not that surprising that MEPs tend to refer to (sub-) national territories in their parliamentary activities, especially in their questions. The study of Navarro (2009a) shows indeed that a significant proportion of questions mention local, regional or national issues and that if questions are used in relation to MEPs' specialization, they are also used to please their constituents. Similarly, Chiru and Dimulescu (2011) demonstrated that even though most questions of Romanian MEPs are related to issues discussed in committees, confirming the specialization logic, the second most important pattern they found was related to constituency work.

On the basis on these few studies as well as on the literature on role orientations in the EP, this chapter examines the focus of representation of MEPs through an analysis of their parliamentary questions. We expect (*H1*) to find a significant proportion of questions mentioning local, regional or national issues, attesting to the (often neglected) importance of territorial representation and constituency service in the EP. We also expect (*H2*) that the priority given to territorial issues will vary according to the MEP's political affiliation, nationality and the electoral system. More precisely, MEPs from small, marginalized and Eurosceptic groups are expected to ask more questions (*H2.1*) and to focus more on local, regional and national issues given their opposition or reluctance towards European integration and European policies (*H2.2*) (Brack 2015, 2017; Proksch and Slapin 2011). Indeed, they will make more use of this mechanism to control the EU institutions as well as their national government. And these questions are likely to concentrate on the national or subnational level, which is often considered by Eurosceptics as the sole or most important level for democracy. Moreover, following Navarro's work (Navarro 2009a), we could also expect (**H2.3**) that MEPs from the periphery of Europe concentrate more on territorial issues than MEPs from founding member states. Finally, the work of Farrell and Scully (Farrell and Scully 2007; Farrell and Scully 2010; Scully and Farrell 2001) as well as of Bowler and Farrell (1993), along with a rich literature on the relation between the electoral system and legislators' attitudes and behaviour (see a.o. Carey and Shugart 1995; Deschouwer and Depauw 2013; Hetshusen et al. 2005), has shown how the electoral system influences substantially the constituency orientations of MEPs. We expect (**H2.4**) that MEPs elected under closed lists will orient their activities around the needs of the party leadership while those elected under open lists will focus more on the concerns of their constituency because they have to compete with fellow candidates from the same party.

Finally, we will analyse the evolution of MEPs' territorial focus through time. Our main database covers the period 1994–2011, but we have also collected data on the more recent period of time, with a less detailed coding (2011–2016). This allows us to determine if things have changed through time, especially as a result of the rise of Euroscepticism. Indeed, with the crisis, the visibility of EU affairs increased along with the share of populist and Eurosceptic MEPs after the 2014 EP election. We could hypothesize that it has had an impact on parliamentary questions, in the sense of a growing focus on national issues. We thus expect (**H3**) a rise in the national focus of questions in the recent years, as a consequence of the success of populism and Euroscepticism.

4   DATA

There are three main types of questions in the EP. First, *questions for oral answer with debate* may be put to the Council or to the Commission by a committee, a political group or at least 40 members; the Conference of Presidents (of groups) decides whether they should be placed on the agenda. Second, *questions during 'question time'*, inspired by the House of Commons after the enlargement to the UK, are mainly addressed to the Commission; however, specific question hours may be held with the Council, the President of the Commission, the High Representative of the Union and the President of the Eurogroup. Questions must be submitted in writing to the President of the EP, who rules on their admissibility and on the order in which they are to be taken. Given the high number of question proposals, it is not easy for an MEP to be granted the right to ask a question. Third, *questions for written answer* must be submitted in writing to the President who forwards them to the addressees (Commission, Council, President of the European Council, High Representative of the Union or the ECB). Although there are not many institutional constrains on these written questions, MEPs must respect the 'guidelines for questions for written answer'.[1]

This chapter focuses on questions for written answer, directed at the Commission, for three main reasons. First, this is the most stable procedure, which allows for comparison over time (Navarro 2009a). Second, they are the most popular form of questioning. While in 1962, 180 written questions were asked, there were 2692 written questions in 1987, 6660 in 2007 and 11,321 in 2011 (data from the EP, Directorate-General for the Presidency). The number has reached a peak in 2015 (15,329), and declined since (9313 in 2016 and 7563 in 2017) as a result of an institutional strategy to limit the use of this tool (see below). Third and most importantly, questions for written answer are the less constrained form of questioning. The other types of questions (of the Question time or for oral answer with debate) are more or less controlled by political groups and highly constrained by the agenda. For a very long period of time, there was basically no limitation to the number of written questions that could be formulated by MEPs, some members asking more than 1000 questions during a parliamentary term. Since the 2014 European elections, the European Commission has criticized the inflation of the number of written questions and the cost they induce (1.500 euros by question on average). In July 2014, MEPs where called to limit the number of their written questions to 5 per month. Since the last general revision of the rules in December 2016, an MEP can ask 'a maximum of twenty questions over a rolling period of three months' (rule 130.3).

Overall, the rules now limit the number of questions MEPs can ask, but they can still make an extensive use of that tool, with a maximum of 80 questions per year as the main author, and as many as they want as a supporter. Also, this limitation is quite new (July 2014). We consider therefore that an analysis of MEPs' written parliamentary questions is a reliable

---

[1] Annex to the Rules of Procedure which stipulates that questions must be clear regarding their target, fall within its sphere of competence, be of general interest, be concise and understandable, contain no offensive language and should not relate to strictly personal matters.

method for gaining better understanding of their preferences and, more particularly, for examining territorial representation in the EP.

In order to determine if territorial issues are mentioned in MEPs' questions, two databases have been created by 'extracting' information from the EP's website. The first one includes all the written questions from 1 September 1994 to 30 September 2011; this makes 84,169 cases, that is, an average of 5000 questions per year. The second database runs from September 2011 to June 2016. It includes 58,903 written questions, that is, an average of nearly 12,000 a year. For each question, the databases include the following information: date of the question, target, topic, author, political group, question (full text) and Internet link. Considering the huge number of questions, we have coded a sample of 6022 questions in the first database and 2522 in the second one (only for the 8th legislature, i.e. 1 July 2014—30 June 2016), by selecting a random sample for each year. For those questions, we have added three types of information that were not present on the EP's website in order to test our hypothesis. First, we added the nationality of the author. Second, following the classification of Farrell and Scully (2010), a variable mentions the type of electoral lists used in the country of the MEP for EP elections (open and STV—ordered—closed); it should allow to determine if MEPs from candidate-based systems are more focused on territorial issues. Another variable specifies whether the lists are regional (or regionally anchored) or not. Third, the territorial dimension of each question has been coded. The objective here is to indicate the lowest territorial level to which the question refers (including in arguments, explanations, examples, etc.).

To do so, the coding was done in several steps. First, the 'territorial level' of the question was coded. The code indicates for each question the lowest territory mentioned:

1. Individual Dimension: Single cases, particular demands (linked to a territory)
2. Local Dimension (town, 'home', sub-regional entity, electoral stronghold)
3. Regional Dimension
4. The MEP's Own Constituency (explicit notion)
5. National Dimension
6. EU Dimension
7. International Dimension/Foreign Country/EU's Relation to a Foreign Country

8. Global Dimension/International Organizations
9. No Indication of Any Geographical Focus
10. EU Institutional Dimension

In the analysis here below, for matters of readability, we use two simplified typologies:

- individuals (1); local (2); regional (3 and 4); national (5); EU (6); outside EU (7, 8);
- subnational (1–4); national (5); EU (6); Non-EU (7–8).

Second, we distinguished whether this level of territoriality was mentioned as the main object of the question (e.g. problem in a factory within the constituency, economic crisis in Greece, floods in a region, etc.), or if it is only mentioned as a way to illustrate a question that refers more generally to the EU, to a country or to general interest. Often, MEPs write a question that has a general purpose but is illustrated by references to the situation in a specific territory. This can be the result of the MEPs' will to better explain the question, but also of his/her interest in a specific situation that needs to be framed in a broader context to render the question acceptable.

Finally, a last code is devoted to references to a category of the population as an example. We have used a dummy that takes the value 1 when the question is referring to a specific group (students, farmers, disabled persons, etc.) and 0 when no specific group is mentioned. For instance, a question related to the Erasmus programme, mentioning the situation of the students of a specific university, will be coded '5' (Europe) regarding the main territorial level, '3' regarding the illustration (region) and '1' regarding the reference to a precise group of population (students).

5   An Exploration of the Content of MEPs' Parliamentary Questions Over Time

The question of the territorial focus of Members of Parliament is in no way specific to the EP. As demonstrated by various scholars, it is central in the theory of representation (Pitkin 1967; Wahlke 1962). In all parliaments, there is a tension between the level of public action (the nation, federation, state or whatever) and the level of attention of MPs (their constituency, their fief, their town, etc.). Various studies have demonstrated the importance of geographical representation and the necessity for elected representatives to keep in touch with their voters (Wahlke 1962; Davidson 1969; Fenno 1978; Cain et al. 1987; Nay 2002; Farrell and Scully 2010). At the same time, there is a strong tradition of prohibition of imperative mandate in Europe: MPs are not supposed to follow the instructions of their voters or constituents, but to focus on (their own perception of) the general interest—and, more concretely, the instructions of their political group.

It is thus interesting to see how those two sets of factors are combined: do MEPs nevertheless bring local, regional or national issues to the EP, as brokers of those levels, or do they follow the 'European' approach to the mandate promoted by the rules?

Globally speaking, we see in Fig. 11.1 that MEPs are following the rules: the majority (51.4%) of their questions deals with EU issues,

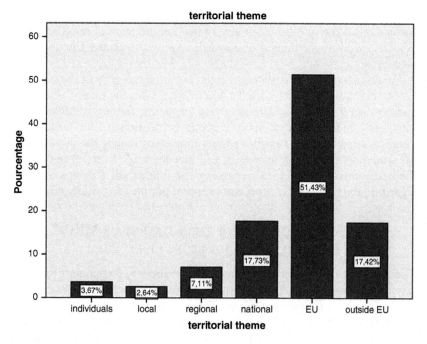

Fig. 11.1   Breakdown of questions by territories as main theme

attesting to the common approach of representation in the EP. It is rather striking to see that individual and local cases are mentioned in less than 7% of the questions. However, we can also note that national issues represent a bit less than one-fifth of the questions (17.7%) and that references to individual cases together with subnational and national issues account for a third of the questions (31.2%). As for the issues outside the EU (non-EU countries and international organizations), they represent 17.4% of the questions in our sample, which shows that the EU external action is an important topic for the EP (Stavridis and Irrera 2015). Crises in other regions of the world are at the centre of some questions asked by MEPs.

As we explained earlier, the focus on pan-European issues is largely due to institutional constraints. It is difficult for MEPs to import local issues into the chamber due to the nature of the EP's competences and the way the institution functions. The EP, like all EU institutions, does not deal with local matters or with policies that only impact certain regions. Generally speaking, MEPs are thus not likely to easily obtain resources for their constituency through their European mandate. As opposed to many national chambers, there is no specific legislative or budgetary tool that allows MEPs to practise 'pork barrel politics'. The priority given to a technical approach for the EP's legislative work is another limitation, since it discourages members from dealing with concrete or individual cases. But despite this institutional context, a significant minority of questions still deals with national, local and regional concerns. This proves that MEPs are not disconnected from their territorial basis.

If we turn to the examples mentioned in the questions, the territorial dimension of representation is even clearer: MEPs are often inspired by cases from the national, regional or local levels or even specific individuals. Indeed, more than ¼ of the questions mention a national example, 9% specific individual cases and 11% local or regional territory. 'Only' 31% of the questions refer to an EU-wide example (Fig. 11.2).

So for instance, MEPs may either frame a broad question concerning a directive but be inspired by their own national situation, or try to avoid getting their questions rejected for being outside the EU's competence or being too precise:

▶ **Subject: Payment of periodic training courses for lorry drivers**   📰 Answer(s)

Directive 2003/59/EC of the European Parliament and of the Council[1] of 15 July 2003 requires drivers undertaking carriage of goods to update every 5 years 'the knowledge which is essential for their work, with specific emphasis on road safety and the rationalisation of fuel consumption'.

A recent judgment by the Danish Labour Court ruled that employers are not obliged to pay for the periodic training required, but that the drivers themselves should bear the costs. In other words, drivers should pay for the further training needed in order to work as drivers — or else they lose their jobs.

Can the Commission confirm that employers can demand of drivers that they pay for their own further training if they wish to keep their jobs? Or does the Commission consider that this is an expense that should be met by employers?

Can the Commission say what stage the other Member States have reached in implementing this directive? Can the Commission say whether drivers in the other Member States have to pay for their own further training? In Denmark, drivers lose their right to exercise their profession if they do not follow the courses in question. Is this also the case in the other Member States?

(1)OJ L 226, 10.9.2003, p. 4.

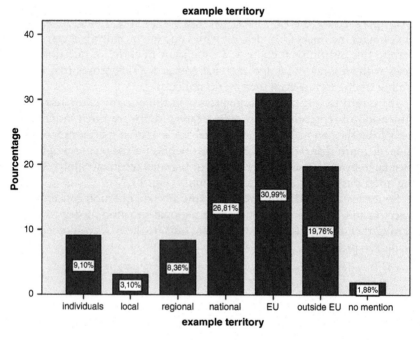

Fig. 11.2 Breakdown of questions by territories as example

5.1 Variation According to the EP Political Group

The literature about representation styles, focus and roles has underlined the impact of ideological orientations and party membership on MPs' behaviour (Davidson 1969; Wessels and Giebler 2011). We expect therefore to find an impact of the group variable on the territorial level they consider (H2). More precisely, our hypotheses are that MEPs from small and marginal groups tend to ask more questions (H2.1) and to focus more on territorial issues than MEPs from the main groups (H2.2).

First, in terms of level of activity, we can see from Table 11.1 that MEPs from Eurosceptic groups are a bit more likely to ask written questions than the average. This is also the case of non-attached members, who do not have many other tools that allow them to be active within the EP. If we focus on the 7th EP term (2009–2014), the differences among groups are clearer (Tables 11.2 and 11.3). Indeed, small groups and Eurosceptic MEPs use more often questions than members from large groups (see also Behm 2015, 2016; Morris 2013). This is due to two elements. First, they are more often excluded from the decision-making process in the EP and less likely to be in charge of a report or opinion. So they tend to be more prone to use individual means such as questions and speeches. Second, given their critical stance towards the EU, they tend to use their questions to gain information that can then be used in their campaign against the EU at home (Brack 2018).

Table 11.1 Number of questions by MEP and by group (1994–2011)

	Number of questions (coded)	Percentage	Number of MEPs 1994–2011	Number of questions by MEP
Radical left	225	9.9	152	1.5
Greens/regionalists	185	8.2	172	1.1
Socialists	494	21.8	778	0.6
Liberals	195	8.6	264	0.7
ChristianDem/ conservatives	687	30.3	967	0.7
ECR	30	1.3	75	0.4
UEN	75	3.3	72	1
Eurosceptic	100	4.4	111	0.9
Radical right group	10	0.4	18	0.6
Non-attached	240	10.6	103	2.3
UPE	28	1.2	34	0.8
Total	**2269**	**100**	**2746**	**0.8**

Table 11.2   Number of questions by MEP/group between 2009 and 2014

	Number of questions	Number of questions by MEP
Radical left (GUE/NGL)	4568	130.5
Greens/regionalists (greens/EFA)	4294	75.3
Socialists (S&D)	12,296	62.73
Liberals (ALDE)	7778	93.71
Christian Dem/conservatives (EPP)	22,890	83.85
ECR	4964	87.1
EFD	6581	212.3
Non-attached	5829	176.64
Total	**69,200**	**94.02**

Table 11.3   Territorial focus of the questions according to EP groups

EP GROUP			Territorial questions				Total
			Subnational	National	EU	Outside EU	
EP group	Far-left	N	155	178	254	111	698
		% in group	22.2%	25.5%	36.4%	15.9%	100.0%
	Greens/regionalists	N	130	106	245	106	587
		% in group	22.1%	18.1%	41.7%	18.1%	100.0%
	Social democrats	N	135	160	677	202	1174
		% in group	11.5%	13.6%	57.7%	17.2%	100.0%
	Liberals	N	47	77	315	66	505
		% in group	9.3%	15.2%	62.4%	13.1%	100.0%
	Christian democrats	N	189	303	1020	282	1794
		% in group	10.5%	16.9%	56.9%	15.7%	100.0%
	Conservatives	N	56	68	160	72	356
		% in group	15.7%	19.1%	44.9%	20.2%	100.0%
	Eurosceptics	N	26	67	141	71	305
		% in group	8.5%	22.0%	46.2%	23.3%	100.0%
	Non-attached	N	70	109	285	139	603
		% in group	11.6%	18.1%	47.3%	23.1%	100.0%
Total		N	808	1068	3097	1049	6022
		% in group	13.4%	17.7%	51.4%	17.4%	100.0%

$p < 0.001$, Cramer's $V = 0.118$

We see that there are important differences between the groups regarding the territorial focus of questions. The three main groups (Socialists, Conservatives/Christian Democrats and Liberals) focus more on the EU level, which is coherent with their global support for European integration, as well as their will to make the EP an arena where pan-European issues can be discussed. Our hypothesis (H2.2) seems thus confirmed. The percentage of EU-related questions is much lower for the Conservatives, Eurosceptics, the Radical left and non-attached members, which is once again coherent with their critical approach of European integration and their will to promote a more intergovernmental conception of Europe or to defend the nation-state. They also pay quite some attention to subnational issues (i.e. individuals, local or region concerns).

It reflects the tendency of many Eurosceptic MEPs to consider themselves as promoters of their region or district in the EP, or to use the parliamentary questions either as a way to control their own government on national, regional or local issues or as a tool to show to their voters that their interests are brought forward in the EP (Brack 2015; Proksch and Slapin 2011). For instance, these MEPs clearly used parliamentary questions in order to deal with constituency or regional issues:

Parliamentary questions

26 February 2010 E-0985/10

WRITTEN QUESTION by Martin Ehrenhauser (NI) to the Commission

▶ **Subject: Constituent's question: possible EU funding for building**   Answer(s)
intergenerational housing

This question is tabled at the request of a constituent from the State of Styria in Austria. For the care and nursing of older people, intergenerational housing projects not only present financial advantages when compared with traditional care centres for older people, they also prevent social exclusion and promote intergenerational exchanges. Owing to demographic change, new housing concepts are needed for the older members of society. Younger families can also benefit from such housing concepts, since older people can also help with child care.
1. Is the Commission aware of the concept of intergenerational housing?
2. Has it already contributed towards such projects through the regional and structural funds, a pilot project or any other provision of funds?
3. Is it aware of any projects (co-)financed by the Commission or Member States?
4. What options already exist for funding or promoting such projects with EU funds?
5. Does the Commission intend to give the funding of intergenerational projects greater attention in future?

Original language of question: **DE**

Whereas others tend to use questions in order to control the national government and its actions:

26 June 2001	E-1846/01

WRITTEN QUESTION by Esko Seppänen (GUE/NGL) to the Commission

▶ **Subject: Finnish system of tax credits on dividends**   📧 Answer(s)

It is clear that the system of tax credits on dividends applicable in Finland disproportionately favours Finnish shareholders over foreign shareholders. Has the Commission considered this unusual system, and does it intend to take any action to ensure the equal taxation of national and foreign shareholders?

Original language of question: **FI**

Table 11.4 Territorial focus of the examples mentioned in the questions according to EP group

EP group			Territorial example					Total
			Subnation	Nation	EU	Non-EU	No.	
EP	Far-left	N	215	227	120	124	7	693
group		% in group	31.0%	32.8%	17.3%	17.9%	1.0%	100.0%
	Greens/	N	169	142	144	121	8	584
	regionalists	% in group	28.9%	24.3%	24.7%	20.7%	1.4%	100.0%
	Social	N	187	297	445	228	21	1178
	democrats	% in group	15.9%	25.2%	37.8%	19.4%	1.8%	100.0%
	Liberals	N	91	126	188	80	19	504
		% in group	18.1%	25.0%	37.3%	15.9%	3.8%	100.0%
	Christian	N	316	459	629	345	36	1785
	democrats	% in group	17.7%	25.7%	35.2%	19.3%	2.0%	100.0%
	Conservatives	N	89	98	89	71	8	355
		% in group	25.1%	27.6%	25.1%	20.0%	2.3%	100.0%
	Eurosceptics	N	42	97	81	78	7	305
		% in group	13.8%	31.8%	26.6%	25.6%	2.3%	100.0%
	Non-attached	N	125	163	164	139	7	598
		% in group	20.9%	27.3%	27.4%	23.2%	1.2%	100.0%
Total		N	1234	1609	1860	1186	113	6002
		% in group	20.6%	26.8%	31.0%	19.8%	1.9%	100.0%

If we turn to the examples mentioned in the questions (Table 11.4), we can see a similar pattern: MEPs from the main groups are more likely to mention EU examples, whereas members from the radical left and radical right (non-attached) tend to refer more often to (sub)national concerns, in order to illustrate their point of view in their parliamentary questions.

5.2   Variations According to Nationality and the Electoral System

Nationality seems to interact with the focus on representation in MEPs' parliamentary questions ($p < 0.001$). As expected, MEPs from periphery countries (Southern and to some extent Eastern European countries) tend to refer more to subnational or national concerns. This is particularly the case for Spanish, Portuguese, Italian as well as Polish MEPs who mention subnational issues in one-fifth of their questions. Others, such as the Irish (21.5% of their questions), Bulgarian (23.1%), Czech (36.8%), Maltese (57%), Greek (34%), Swedish (20.5%) and Hungarian MEPs (45%), rather tend to concentrate on national concerns. But for several countries, especially from the latest enlargements, the number of questions in our database is too low to allow us to draw conclusions.

As far as the electoral system is concerned, it seems that our hypothesis is not confirmed by the data. Indeed, MEPs elected under an open list are as likely to mention subnational or national issues as those elected under a closed list. And they asked more EU-related questions than MEPs under closed-list systems (Table 11.5). In addition to that, those elected on regional (or regionally anchored) lists tend to focus more on pan-European issues, whereas MEPs elected on national lists more often mention (sub)national concerns (Table 11.6).

Table 11.5   Focus of representation according to the type of electoral list for EP elections

			Territorial questions				Total
			Subnational	National	EU	Outside EU	
Electoral lists	Open	Count	183	248	721	217	1369
		%	13.4%	18.1%	52.7%	15.9%	100%
	Ordered	Count	96	159	529	210	994
		%	9.7%	16.0%	53.2%	21.1%	100%
	Closed	Count	529	661	1847	622	3659
		%	14.5%	18.1%	50.5%	17.0%	100%
Total		Count	808	1068	3097	1049	6022
		%	13.4%	17.7%	51.4%	17.4%	100.0%

$p < 0.001$, Cramer's $V = 0.048$

Table 11.6   Focus of representation according to regional/national list for EP elections

			Territorial questions				Total
			Subnational	National	EU	Outside EU	
EP lists	National	Count	418	624	1325	521	2888
		%	14.5%	21.6%	45.9%	18.0%	100%
	Regional	Count	390	444	1772	528 ⁻	3134
		%	12.4%	14.2%	56.5%	16.8%	100%
Total		Count	808	1068	3097	1049	6022
		%	13.4%	17.7%	51.4%	17.4%	100%

$p < 0.001$, Cramer's $V = 0.119$

6   EXPLAINING THE VARIATION IN MEPs' FOCUS OF REPRESENTATION

In order to test further our hypotheses, we performed two binary logistic regressions.

For the first regression all member states are taken into account, and we want to determine the effect of political affiliation as well as the electoral system on the focus on representation of MEPs. The dependant variable is the reference to territory, more precisely the fact that a question does (or not) mention a national or subnational level of territory. The independent variables are, all things being equal, the EP political group to which the MEP belongs to (with the largest group, that is, Christian Democrats, being the reference category) and the degree of openness of the electoral lists for EP elections (the open lists are the reference category). We did not include in the model the regional or national nature of constituencies, since there is too much collinearity with the previous variable (Table 11.7).

The regression confirms our previous observations: all things equal, Far-Left MEPs are 2.6 times more likely to mention a given territory than the Christian Democrats. The ratio is 1.9 for Greens, 1.2 for non-attached and 1.4 for Conservatives. This tends to confirm our hypothesis on the territorial focus of MEPs from small, marginalized and Eurosceptic groups (H2.1) although the 'Eurosceptic' group is not the most territorially oriented (and does not reach the level of significance).

If we look at the type of electoral lists, distinguishing 'ordered' and 'closed' lists, we see that MEPs elected on ordered lists have 1.5 times less chance (1/0.65) of mentioning a national or subnational territory in their

Table 11.7 Regression 1: effect of political affiliation and electoral system (all member states)

```
Logistic regression    Number of obs  =   6022
                       LR chi2(9)  =  184.05
                       Prob > chi2  =  0.0000
Log likelihood = -3644.3022
Pseudo R2  =  0.0246
```

territoria~c	Odds Ratio	Std. Err.	z	P>|z|	[95% Conf. Interval]
EPgroup5 (ref=Christians dem.)|					
2 (far-left)	**2.566703***** .2398863		10.09	0.000	2.137084 3.082689
3 (Green/regionalists)|	1.943967*** .1965704		6.57	0.000	1.594472 2.370068
4 (Social Dem.)	.884822 N.S. .0759253		-1.43	0.154	.7478518 1.046879
5 (Liberals)	.9233923 N.S. .1081244		-0.68	0.496	.7340321 1.161602
6 (conservatives)	1.387617*** .1733493	2.62		0.009	1.086257 1.772584
7 (euroscept.)	1.151465 N.S. .156964		1.03	0.301	.8814905 1.504124
8 (Non-Attached)	1.216936* .128967		1.85	0.064	.9886901 1.497874
lists (ref=open)|					
1 (ordered)	**.6458576*****	.0630561	-4.48	0.000	.5333749 .7820615
2 (closed)	1.025893 N.S.	.0732333	0.36	0.720	.8919467 1.179954

The level of significance are: *** p<0,01 ** p<0,05 * p<0,1

question than MEPs elected under open lists. But the results for MEPs on a closed list are not in the expected direction and do not reach statistical significance. This partially confirms our hypothesis H2.4: there is less incentive for MEPs elected on ordered lists to be focused on their constituency, contrary to MEPs elected under open-list systems or STV.

In order to analyse the impact of the country of election, another logistic regression was performed, taking into account a sample of member states. Indeed, the number of questions in our sample is low for many member states, especially those that only recently entered the EU (countries of the enlargements of 2004 and 2007) or that have only a very limited number of MEPs (Luxembourg). The analysis is therefore restricted to nine countries: France, Belgium, the Netherlands, Germany, Spain, Italy, Portugal, Greece and the UK.

Table 11.8   Regression 2: 9 member states representing at least 5% of the sample (including the variable 'lists')

Regression 2: 9 member states representing at least 5% of the sample (including the variable 'lists')						
Logistic regression		Number of obs = 5005				
		LR chi2(15) = 299.19				
		Prob > chi2 = 0.0000				
Log likelihood = -2984.4118		Pseudo R2 = 0.0477				
territoria~c	Odds Ratio	Std. Err.	z	P>|z|	[95% Conf.	Interval]
nationality						
2 (Belgium)	1.245593 N.S.	.2761691	0.99	0.322	.8065852	1.923543
3 (NL)	1.380456 N.S.	.2809764	1.58	0.113	.9263396	2.057194
5 (Germany)	2.012779***	.4055346	3.47	0.001	1.356113	2.987419
6 (Spain)	2.92062***	.53564	5.84	0.000	2.038756	4.183935
7 (Italy)	2.302992***	.4259872	4.51	0.000	1.602672	3.309331
8 (Portugal)	2.767416***	.5709443	4.93	0.000	1.846986	4.146536
9 (Greece)	3.716456***	.6930934	7.04	0.000	2.578611	5.35639
10 (UK)	1.41726*	.2582709	1.91	0.056	.9915917	2.025658
2 (far-left)	2.330396***	.2560882	7.70	0.000	1.878845	2.890471
3 (Green/regionalists)	2.218627***	.2487909	7.11	0.000	1.780872	2.763985
4 (Social Dem.)	1.062216 N.S.	.1054962	0.61	0.543	.8743268	1.290481
5 (Liberals)	1.261117*	.1681631	1.74	0.082	.971074	1.637791
6 (conservatives)	1.651632***	.2334477	3.55	0.000	1.251991	2.178839
7 (euroscept.)	.9561796 N.S.	.1562189	-0.27	0.784	.6941794	1.317065
8 (Non-Attached)	1.471507***	.1836082	3.10	0.002	1.152267	1.879193
EPgroup5 (ref=Christians dem.)						
lists						
1	(omitted)					
2	(omitted)					

We could not consider in this regression the variable related to the type of lists, since it presents, for obvious reasons, a high degree of collinearity with the respective countries of MEPs.

It can be seen from Table 11.8 that the country of election of MEPs is a significant predictor of the focus on representation in parliamentary questions. Hence, a Greek MEP has 3.7 times more chance to ask a question dealing with a given level of territory than a French one. This also applies to the other Southern countries that entered the EU in the 1980s: Spain (2.9) and Portugal (2.7). The ratio is far lower for the UK, the Netherlands and Belgium. We can conclude that the hypothesis H2.3 is confirmed, at least for the countries that joined the EC in the 1980s: MEPs from the periphery of Europe concentrate more on territorial issues than MEPs from founding member states with the exception of Italy. However, it remains to be verified for the countries that entered the EU in the 2000s, for which the number of cases in our database is too low.

If we look at groups, considering only the nine 'big'/'oldest' member states, we see again that political affiliation matters: far-left, green and conservative MEPs are more likely to make a reference to a given territory than EPP or S&D MEPs.

7   The Variation in MEPs' Focus of Representation Through Time

Finally, we analyse the evolutions of the territorial focus of MEPs since the European elections of May 2014, and before the entry into force of the new rules, that have limited the use of written questions by MEPs. To do so, we used a second database and examined the territorial focus of written questions submitted between 1 July 2014 and 30 June 2016. As mentioned previously, we expect (*H3*) a rise of the focus on national issues, as a consequence of the growing number of populist and Eurosceptic MEPs in the house and, more generally, of the success of critical voices towards European integration in most EU countries. As hypothesized by Cristoforetti and Querton in this volume, we can even assume a 'contamination effect' of mainstream MEPs by the more nationalist approach of Eurosceptic members. Indeed, as populist and Eurosceptic actors claim to represent the people and denounce the gap between elites and citizens, it might lead mainstream MEPs to show their concerns for their voters or national citizens through their parliamentary questions.

The data, however, does not support this hypothesis: the figures for 2014–2016 are totally in line with those for 1994–2011, and we can even notice a slight decline in the national focus of MEPs' written questions (Table 11.9).

Table 11.9 Territorial focus of the questions—comparison 1994–2011/ 2014–2016

EP group			Territorial questions			
			Subnational	National	EU	Outside EU
EP group	Far-left	1994–2011	22.2%	25.5%	36.4%	15.9%
		2014–2016	17.5%	16.2%	36.2%	29.9%
	Greens/ regionalists	1994–2011	22.1%	18.1%	41.7%	18.1%
		2014–2016	17.3%	14.2%	49.6%	18.9%
	Social democrats	1994–2011	11.5%	13.6%	57.7%	17.2%
		2014–2016	7.0%	12.0%	62.2%	18.5%
	Liberals	1994–2011	9.3%	15.2%	62.4%	13.1%
		2014–2016	7.3%	14.1%	53.6%	25.0%
	Christian democrats	1994–2011	10.5%	16.9%	56.9%	15.7%
		2014–2016	5.9%	9.0%	68.7%	16.1%
	Conservatives	1994–2011	15.7%	19.1%	44.9%	20.2%
		2014–2016	12.2%	18.6%	44.7%	24.5%
	Eurosceptics	1994–2011	8.5%	22.0%	46.2%	23.3%
		2014–2016 EFDD	34.9%	10.0%	37.0%	18.0%
		2014–2016 ENF	8.3%	8.3%	60.0%	24.0%
	Non-attached	1994–2011	11.6%	18.1%	47.3%	23.1%
		2014–2016	10.7%	24.6%	46.7%	18.0%
Total		1994–2011	13.4%	17.7%	51.4%	17.4%
		2014–2016	11.6%	13.6%	54.7%	19.9%

8   Conclusion

This chapter shows that MEPs make different uses of written questions and have diverging foci of representation. In most cases, they refer to EU issues, with no reference to a given territory. The general focus is thus a European one, and they act quite in line with the general approach of the mandate, as it is promoted by the leaders of the institution: a non-imperative approach, oriented towards the defence of all European citizens' interests. However, in a significant minority of cases (a third), MEPs ask questions about their country, region or constituency. This confirms our first hypothesis. Our results reveal the multidimensionality of the European mandate. Since MEPs are quite free using parliamentary questions, they can use this tool to advocate for local or national issues, or to act as interest brokers for their citizens or actors in their constituency. This is another way to show (next to interview-based studies of representation focus and style and to discourse or roll-call vote analysis) that MEPs are not acting mainly along national lines and that they combine different approaches to their mandate. They adapt their behaviour to their beliefs and to the expectations of their electors or party, not only during votes and speeches, but also when they ask questions.

This first analysis also partially confirms other hypotheses. Generally speaking, the MEP's likelihood of giving priority to territorial issues varies according to their political affiliation, nationality and the electoral system. More precisely, MEPs from small, marginalized and Eurosceptic groups are asking more questions (H2.1) and tend to focus more on local, regional and national issues (H2.2). MEPs from the periphery of Europe concentrate more on territorial issues (H2.3). MEPs elected under ordered lists have a more EU approach than those elected under open lists, who are more concerned with their constituency (H2.4).

Finally, we have seen that, despite the rise of Euroscepticism within the EP and in the member states, and notwithstanding the context of doubts that surrounds European integration, the territorial focus of MEPs did not change (H3) in the recent years (2014–2016).

These results attest of the relevance of studying parliamentary questions in order to understand the linkage between MEPs and the different levels of governance. Further analysis is however needed to explain the variations among MEPs in their focus on representation, notably by adding other types of predictors such as MEPs' previous political experiences, the status of their national political party but also by refining variables related to the electoral system.

REFERENCES

Arnold, C., & Franklin, M. (2012). Introduction: Issue Congruence and Political Responsiveness. *West European Politics, 35*(6), 1217–1225.

Bailer, S. (2011). People's Voice or Information Pool? The Role Of, and Reasons For, Parliamentary Questions in the Swiss Parliament. *The Journal of Legislative Studies, 17*(3), 302–314.

Beauvallet, W., & Michon, S. (2009). Les transformations sociologiques des parlementaires européens. *Revue politique et parlementaire, 1052*, 83–89.

Beauvallet, W., & Michon, S. (2010). L'institutionnalisation inachevée du Parlement européen. Hétérogénéité nationale, spécialisation du recrutement et autonomisation. *Politix, 89*(1), 147–172.

Behm, A.-S. (2015). The Rise of the Eurosceptics – A Threat to the European Parliament? Retrieved from https://maeeurope.wordpress.com/2015/04/27/the-rise-of-the-eurosceptics-a-threat-to-the-european-parliament/.

Behm, A-S. (2016). The Rise of the Eurosceptics: Obstructionism Or Assimilation? A Comparative Analysis of the MEPs' Behaviour in the Current Legislature. Master Thesis, Freie Universität Berlin.

Bellamy, R., & Castiglione, D. (2010). Democracy by Delegation? Who Represents Whom and How in European Governance. *Government and Opposition, 46*, 101–125.

Best, H., & Cotta, M. (2000). *Parliamentary Representatives in Europe 1848–2000: Legislative Recruitment and Careers in Eleven European Countries*. Oxford: Oxford University Press.

Blidook, K., & Kerby, M. (2011). Constituency Influence on 'Constituency Members': The Adaptability of Roles to Electoral Realities in the Canadian Case. *The Journal of Legislative Studies, 17*(3), 327–339.

Brack, N. (2015). The Roles of Eurosceptic Members of the European Parliament and Their Implications for the EU. *International Political Science Review, 36*(3), 337–350.

Brack, N. (2017). Eurosceptic Members of the European Parliament: Foxes in the Henhouse? In S. Usherwood & N. Startin (Eds.), *Handbook of Euroscepticism*. London: Routledge.

Brack, N. (2018). *Opposing Europe in the European Parliament*. London: Palgrave.

Brack, N., & Costa, O. (2013). The Challenges of Territorial Representation at the Supranational Level: The Case of French MEPs. *French Politics, 11*(1), 1–23.

Brack, N., & Costa, O. (Eds.). (2018). The EP Through the Lens of Legislative Studies: Recent Debates and New Perspectives. *Journal of Legislative Studies, Special Issue, 24*(1), 72–89.

Brack, N., Costa, O., & Kerrouche, E. (2016). MPs Between Territories, Assembly and Party – Investigating Parliamentary Behaviour at the Local Level in France, Belgium and Germany. *French Politics, 14*(4), 395–405.

Busby, A. (2013). Normal Parliament': Exploring the Organisation of Everyday Political Life in an MEP's Office. *Journal of Contemporary European Research, 9*(1), 94–115.

Cain, B., Ferejohn, J., & Fiorina, M. (1987). *The Personal Vote: Constituency Service and Electoral Independence*. Cambridge: Harvard University Press.

Carey, J. M., & Shugart, M. S. (1995). Incentives to Cultivate a Personal Vote: A Rank Ordering of Electoral Formulas. *Electoral Studies, 14*(4), 417–439.

Chiru, M., & Dimulescu, V. (2011). *Tribunes Versus Experts: An Analysis of the Romanian MEPs' Questions.*

Coman, E. (2009). Reassessing the Influence of Party Groups on Individual MEPs. *West European Politics, 32*(6), 1099–1117.

Costa, O. (2002). Les députés européens entre allégeances multiples et logique d'institution. *Journal of European Integration, 24*(2), 91–112.

Costa, O. (2015). *The History of European electoral Reform and the Electoral Act 1976: Issues of Democratisation and Political Legitimacy*. Historical Archives of the European Parliament, European Parliament Research Service, European Union History Series, 44 p.

Costa, O., & Navarro, J. (2003). La représentation au PE. Qui représentent les parlementaires européens? In S. Saurugger (Ed.), *Les modes de représentation dans l'Union européenne* (pp. 123–152). Paris: L'Harmattan.

Davidson, R. H. (1969). *The Role of the Congressman.* New York: Pegasus.

Deschouwer, K. (2005). Pinball Wizards: Political Parties and Democratic Representation in the Changing institutional Architecture of European Politics. In E. Römmele, D. Farrell, & P. Ignazi (Eds.), *Political Parties and Political Systems. The Concept of Linkage Revisited* (pp. 81–99). Praeger: Westport.

Deschouwer, K., & Depauw, S. (Eds.). (2013). *Representing the People.* Oxford: Oxford University Press.

Eulau, H., Wahlke, J., Buchanan, W., & Ferguson, L. (1959). The Role of the Representative: Some Empirical Observations on the Theory of Edmund Burke. *American Political Science Review, 53,* 742–756.

Faas, T. (2003). To Defect or Not To Defect? National, Institutional and Party Group Pressures on MEPs and Their Consequences for Party Cohesion in the European Parliament. *European Journal of Political Research, 42*(6), 841–866.

Farrell, D., & Scully, R. (2007). *Representing Europe's Citizens? Electoral Institutions and the Failure of Parliamentary Representation.* Oxford: Oxford University Press.

Farrell, D., & Scully, R. (2010). The European Parliament: One Parliament, Several Modes of Political Representation on the Ground? *Journal of European Public Policy, 17*(1), 36–54.

Fenno, R. F. (1978). *Home Style: Representatives in Their Districts.* Boston: Little, Brown.

Goetze, S., & Rittberger, B. (2010). A Matter of Habit? The Sociological Foundations of Empowering the European Parliament. *Comparative European Politics, 8*(1), 37–54.

Golder, M., & Stramski, J. (2010). Ideological Congruence and Electoral Institutions. *American Journal of Political Science, 54,* 90–106.

Hetshusen, V., Young, G., & Wood, D. M. (2005). Electoral Context and MP Constituency Focus in Australia, Canada, Ireland, New Zealand and United Kingdom. *American Journal of Political Science, 49*(1), 32–45.

Hix, S., Raunio, T., & Scully, R. (2003). Fifty Years On: Research on the European Parliament. *Journal of Common Market Studies, 41*(2), 191–202.

Hix, S., Noury, A., & Roland, G. (2007). *Democratic Politics in the European Parliament.* Cambridge: Cambridge University Press.

Jensen, C. B., Proksch, S. O., & Slapin, J. B. (2013). Parliamentary Questions, Oversight, and National Opposition Status in the European P arliament. *Legislative Studies Quarterly, 38*(2), 259–282.

Katz, R. (1997). Representational Roles. *European Journal of Political Research, 32*(2), 211–226.

Kreppel, A. (2002). *The European Parliament and Supranational Party System. A Study in Institutional Development.* Cambridge: Cambridge University Press.

Kröger, S., & Friedrich, D. (2013). Introduction: The Representative Turn in EU Studies. *Journal of European Public Policy, 20*(2), 155–170.

Lazardeux, S. (2005). 'Une Question écrite, Pour Quoi Faire?' The Causes of the Production of Written Questions in the French Assemblée Nationale. *French Politics, 3*(3), 258–281.

Lefkofridi, Z., & Katsanidou, A. (2014). Multilevel Representation in the European Parliament. *European Union Politics, 15*(1), 108–131.

Lord, C., & Pollak, J. (2010). The EU's Many Representative Modes: Colliding? Cohering? *Journal of European Public Policy, 17*(1), 117–136.

Marsh, M. (1998). Testing the Second-Order Election Model After Four European Elections. *British Journal of Political Science, 28*(4), 591–607.

Marsh, M., & Norris, P. (1997). Political Representation in the European Parliament. *European Journal of Political Research, 32*(2), 153–164.

Marsh, M., & Wessels, B. (1997). Territorial Representation. *European Journal of Political Research, 32*(2), 227–241.

Martin, S. (2011). Using Parliamentary Questions to Measure Constituency Focus: An Application to the Irish Case. *Political Studies, 59*(2), 472–488.

Mattila, M., & Raunio, T. (2012). Drifting Further Apart: National Parties and Their Electorates on the EU Dimension. *West European Politics, 35*(3), 589–606.

Miller, W. E., & Stokes, D. E. (1963). Constituency Influence in Congress. *American Political Science Review, 57*(1), 45–56.

Morris, M. (2013). *Conflicted Politicians, the Populist Radical Right in the European Parliament.* London: Counterpoint.

Mülböck, M. (2012). National Versus European: Party Control Over Members of the European Parliament. *West European Politics, 35*(3), 607–631.

Navarro, J. (2009a). Parliamentary Questions in the EP: What For? Paper presented at The Second ECPR Conference on Parliamentary Accountability, Paris.

Navarro, J. (2009b). *Les députés européens et leur rôle. Sociologie interprétative des pratiques parlementaires.* Bruxelles: Editions de l'Université de Bruxelles.

Navarro, J., & Brouard, S. (2014). Who Cares About the EU? French MPs and the Europeanization of Parliamentary Questions. *Journal of Legislative Studies, 20*(1), 93–108.

Nay, O. (2002). Le jeu du compromis. Les élus régionaux entre territoire et pratiques d'assemblée. In O. Nay & A. Smith (Eds.), *Le gouvernement du compromis, courtiers et généralistes de l'action politique* (pp. 47–86). Paris: Economica.

Norris, P. (Ed.). (1997). *Passages to Power: Legislative Recruitment in Advanced Democracies.* Cambridge: Cambridge University Press.

Norris, P., & Franklin, M. (1997). Social Representation. *European Journal of Political Research, 32*(2), 185–210.

Piattoni, S. (2013). Representation as Delegation: a Basis for EU Democracy? *Journal of European Public Policy, 20*(2), 224–242.

Pitkin, H. (1967). *The Concept of Representation*. Berkeley: University of California Press.

Poyet, C. (2018). Working at Home: French MEPs' Day-to-Day Practice of Political Representation in Their District. *The Journal of Legislative Studies, 24*(1), 109–126.

Priestley, J. (2008). *Six Battles that Shaped Europe's Parliament*. London: John Harper Publishing.

Proksch, S. O., & Slapin, J. B. (2011). Parliamentary Questions and Oversight in the European Union. *European Journal of Political Research, 50*(1), 53–79.

Raunio, T. (1996). Parliamentary Questions in the European Parliament: Representation, Information and Control. *Journal of Legislative Studies, 2*(4), 362–363.

Reif, K., & Schmitt, H. (1980). Nine Second Order National Elections: A Conceptual Framework for the Analysis of European Election Results. *European Journal of Political Research, 8*(1), 3–44.

Rozenberg, O., & Martin, S. (2011). Questioning Parliamentary Questions. *Journal of Legislative Studies, 17*(3), 394–404.

Russo, F. (2011). The Constituency as a Focus of Representation: Studying the Italian Case Through the Analysis of Parliamentary Questions. *Journal of Legislative Studies, 17*(3), 290–301.

Saalfeld, T. (2011). Parliamentary Questions as Instruments of Substantive Representation: Visible Minorities in the UK House of Commons, 2005–2011. *Journal of Legislative Studies, 17*(3), 271–289.

Sartori, G. (1987). *The Theory of Democracy Revisited*. Chatham, NJ: Chatham House.

Schapiro, I., Stokes, S., Wood, E., & Kirschner, A. (2010). *Political Representation*. New York: Cambridge University Press.

Scully, R., & Farrell, D. (2001). *Understanding Constituency Representation in the European Parliament*. Paper for the ECSA Conference, Madison.

Scully, R., Hix, S., & Farrell, D. M. (2012). National or European Parliamentarians? Evidence from a New Survey of the Members of the European Parliament. *Journal of Common Market Studies, 50*(4), 670–683.

Stavridis, S., & Irrera, D. (2015). *The European Parliament and Its International Relations*. London: Routledge.

Thomassen, J. J., Schmitt, H., & Thomassen, J. (1999). *Political Representation and Legitimacy in the European Union*. Oxford: Oxford University Press on Demand.

Trumm, S. (2015). Voting Procedures and Parliamentary Representation in the European Parliament. *Journal of Common Market Studies*. Article First Published Online March 20. https://doi.org/10.1111/jcms.12237.

Viola, D. M. (Ed.). (2015). *Routledge Handbook of European Elections*. London: Routledge.

Wahlke, J. C. (1962). *The Legislative System: Explorations in Legislative Behavior.* Wiley.

Wessels, B., & Giebler, H. (2011, August). *Choosing a Style of Representation: The Role of Institutional and Organizational Incentives.* Presentation at the 6th ECPR General Conference, University of Iceland (pp. 25–27).

Yordanova, N. (2011). The European Parliament: In Need of a Theory. *European Union Politics, 12*(4), 597–617.

CHAPTER 12

The Arduous Way Towards a Uniform Electoral System for the European Parliament

Rudolf Hrbek

1 INTRODUCTION

There have been, since 1979, eight direct elections in the European Commission/European Union (EC/EU). The legal basis for these elections is the Electoral Act of fall 1976 on the election of the representatives of the EC by direct universal suffrage. The Electoral Act (Official Journal L 278, of 8 October 1976) did only give a broad legal framework, requiring Member States to formulate various details in national laws which would then govern the European elections at Member State level. There was a treaty provision (article 138, paragraph 3 EC Treaty, later article 190 EC Treaty) envisaging a uniform electoral system in all Member States. The European Parliament (EP) was authorised to take the initiative. The Council would have to decide unanimously on the draft elaborated by the EP; and it would recommend the Member States to give their approval according to the respective constitutional rules.

R. Hrbek (✉)
University of Tübingen, Tübingen, Germany

College of Europe, Bruges, Belgium
e-mail: rudolf.hrbek@uni-tuebingen.de

© The Author(s) 2019   255
O. Costa (ed.), *The European Parliament in Times of EU Crisis*,
European Administrative Governance,
https://doi.org/10.1007/978-3-319-97391-3_12

There have been, over the years, again and again moves and initiatives towards introducing a uniform electoral system (Costa 2016). The Electoral Act, however, has been amended only once, in 2002. The amendment, introduced by a Council Decision (Official Journal, L 283, of 21 October 2002), stipulated that the Member States have to conduct the elections on the basis of proportional representation using a list system or a single transferable vote system (until this amendment, it was up to each Member State to decide on the electoral system); furthermore, it did abolish the dual mandate for Members of European Parliament (MEPs).

Article 223 TFEU took up the provisions of article 190 EC Treaty. It was on the basis of this treaty article that the Committee on Constitutional Affairs (AFCO) of the EP decided in November 2014 to draw up a legislative initiative report on the 'Reform of the EU Electoral Law' with two prominent and experienced MEPs from the two biggest party groups (Danuta Hübner, EPP, and Jo Leinen, S&D), as co-rapporteurs. A draft report was submitted on 30 June 2015. AFCO adopted the final report on 28 September 2015; 14 MEPs were in favour, 5 voted against and 3 did abstain. There was a plenary debate on 27 October 2015 (European Parliament 2015a) in which the two rapporteurs did explain the reasons for and the goals guiding the initiative. The following debate showed a divided Parliament, with support for and criticism against the reform proposal, focusing on sensitive issues. The Resolution of the EP (of 11 November 2015)(European Parliament 2015b) on the reform of the electoral law (with an Annex that included the proposal for a Council Decision for the adoption of the reform provisions) was supported by 315 MEPs, but there were 234 no-votes and 55 abstentions. It was then up to the Council to consider the proposal and make the next step in the legislative process. But by spring 2018 the reform project is still pending.

This chapter intends to discuss the recent reform proposal and to reflect on the (probable) outcome; in other words: it will try to explore, whether this time 'the arduous way towards a uniform electoral system for the EP' (as formulated in this chapter's title) may arrive at a successful end. This chapter, therefore, will briefly recall in a general way the functions of parliamentary elections in democratic political systems (Sect. 2); it will, then, summarise features of European elections since 1979, which have been widely perceived as weaknesses and, as a whole, have to be understood as a challenge to which the reform proposal will give a response (Sect. 3); it will, then, explain the reform proposal, namely, its background factors, its content and goals and its added value (Sect. 4); thereafter, it will draw the attention to various constraints for the proposal's success (Sect. 5); finally, it will give an outlook, taking into account some most recent developments (Sect. 6).

2   FUNCTIONS OF PARLIAMENTARY ELECTIONS IN DEMOCRATIC POLITICAL SYSTEMS

Dealing with elections to a parliamentary assembly, to be understood as a representative body, requires to be aware of the political actors who are primarily involved in the electoral process. There are two types of actors: individual citizens and political parties.

- As concerns citizens, elections are a prominent occasion for them to participate in the political process: by casting their vote, citizens decide on who shall represent them in the respective parliamentary assembly. They decide directly on mandate-holders and indirectly on office-holders. Casting their vote means that the citizens—as electors—decide between competing candidates; this implies a decision on policies, since a candidate (in most cases representing his/her political party; 'independent' candidates being the exception) represents and offers the respective party's programme. The right of the individual citizen to vote is closely linked with the principle of electoral equality.
- As concerns political parties, they compete with each other and parliamentary elections are the occasions in which the competition is in the foreground. Parties are key actors in the electoral process; they are expected to perform the following electoral functions: selection and nomination of candidates and the formulation of programmes, both to be offered to the electorate; furthermore, they are preparing and conducting the election campaign; last not least, they have to make efforts to mobilise the citizens.

On this basis, we can list the following functions of parliamentary elections which are always related to the two major types of actors:

- Offering all citizens the opportunity for political participation and allowing them to link their preferences with political parties and with political institutions and their respective members (=office-holders).
- They give strong incentives to political parties towards recruiting political elites and they offer citizens—as electors—the opportunity

to convey trust to mandate- and office-holders and to political parties which compete with each other.

- They are a framework for the representation of interests and opinions of individual citizens, of groups of citizens and of societal organisations; and for allowing the articulation of such interests.
- Mobilisation of the citizens, as electors; this means informing the citizens on the parties' values, programme positions and political goals; furthermore, it means making them aware of political issues (the *res publica*) and of alternatives for problem-solving, offered by the parties which compete with each other.
- Offering an arena for intense political communication, especially for political competition between political parties as concerns alternatives (personalities and programmes).
- Giving the mandate for political leadership (via office-holding) and contributing to the recruitment of leadership personalities.
- Giving legitimacy not only to mandate- and office-holders but to the political system and the political process in general.

These functions apply, in general, to European elections as well, as can be seen in the arguments in favour of introducing direct elections to the EP in the 1970s: direct elections would bring about effects which are in line with the above-mentioned functions attributed to parliamentary elections. Citizens in the EC Member States would be given a very important instrument of political participation: the right to elect the MEP; national political parties would need to prepare for and develop their role related to these elections (the establishment of transnational organisations of parties belonging to the three established party-families of Socialists/Social Democrats in 1974, Christian Democrats and Liberals in 1976 has to be seen as indicator for their determination to respond to the new challenge); the political discourse on the integration project and its further development would be intensified; last but not least, the whole electoral process would contribute to generating (greater) legitimacy to the political system of the EC and the integration project in general. One specific function, which we find in the list of functions attributed to parliamentary elections, did not apply to European elections: since there was no parliamentary system of government in the EC, these elections would not be oriented towards the formation of a governmental body which can count and rely on the support of a (stable) parliamentary majority and the formation of an 'opposition' by the minority. However, in the debates around the introduction of direct European elections, there were expectations that these elections, in the medium term, could and would contribute to make the EC develop an institutional design with typical features of a parliamentary system of government.

3 FEATURES OF AND EXPERIENCES WITH EUROPEAN ELECTIONS 1979–2014

The EP Resolution of 11 November 2015 on the reform of the electoral law of the European Union (2015/2035(INL)) lists features of previous European elections which are understood as starting points for a thorough reform: aiming towards enhancing the democratic and transnational dimension of the European elections and the democratic legitimacy of the Union decision-making process; reinforcing the concept of citizenship of the Union; strengthening the principles of electoral equality and equal opportunities; enhancing the effectiveness of the system for conducting European elections; and bringing MEPs closer to their voters (*Point B of the Resolution*). These criticised features are seen as challenges and the reform proposals as the proper and necessary response.

The following features, listed below, have been identified in the Resolution as weaknesses requiring a comprehensive reform. The most crucial weakness: the elections are lacking a genuine and obvious 'European' character, which can be seen in various aspects:

- European elections have been governed by national laws; campaigning remains national; European political parties are not involved prominently so that they cannot sufficiently fulfil their treaty-based mandate ('contribute to forming European political awareness and to expressing the will of the citizens of the Union', as article 10, paragraph 4 TEU stipulates) (*Point L*).
- Lacking a stronger role (especially in the campaigns) and visibility, European parties cannot show the link between a vote for a particular national party and the impact it has on the size of a party group in the EP (*Point M*).
- The procedure for nominating candidates for elections (especially as concerns transparency and democratic standards, which are essential for generating trust in the political system) varies from Member State to Member State and from party to party (*Point N*).

- Other procedural aspects vary as well such as the deadlines for finalising the electoral lists (*Point O*) or the deadlines for finalising the electoral roll ahead of the elections (*Point P*). Furthermore, there is no common voting day (*Point U*) and there is no harmonised time for the close of polling which may result in the publication of election results at different times (*Point S*).
- Another severe weakness has to be seen in the fact that previous attempts to set up an EU-wide constituency and list (for only a limited number of seats) did fail (*Point Q*). Such an innovation would have made European parties visible for the electorate.
- There are differences in the (still national) provisions on minimum age, both for standing as a candidate and the right to vote (*Point AC*).
- EU-wide provisions concerning the right to vote from abroad outside the EU (*Point Z*) are lacking, as are provisions on postal, electronic or Internet voting (*Point AE*); and there is not yet an electoral authority for the EU as a whole, acting as a network of Member States' authorities (*Point AB*).
- Concerning thresholds (which in general are recognised as a legitimate means of enabling parliaments to function properly), national electoral laws differ greatly (*Point R*).
- The resolution draws the attention to the issue of gender balance; it mentions divergences between Member States and it refers to gender quotas or zipped lists used as a general means to contribute towards achieving greater gender balance (*Points AG and AH*).

Furthermore, the resolution takes up the issue of *Spitzenkandidaten*, which—contrary to the above-mentioned weaknesses—is understood as an innovation (introduced and experienced in the 2014 elections), with the potential to strengthening the interests of citizens in the elections (*Points V, W and X*) and, as a consequence, to having a positive impact on the electoral turnout, which has been decreasing continuously since 1979.

4   The Reform Proposal of November 2015

4.1   New Background Factors: Incentives for the Reform Initiative

In the aftermath of the European elections in 2014, members of the European Parliament decided to make a new attempt aiming at the introduction of a uniform electoral system for the EP. They were well aware of the fact that a series of previous initiatives, launched in the past decades, had failed. But since they were not only generally convinced that a comprehensive reform would be vital for strengthening the Union's legitimacy, but they also expected that new background factors would have a favourable effect, they felt encouraged to prepare a new initiative at the beginning of the EP's new election period (2014–2019).

As concerns new background factors, the following five would represent and could be used as arguments supporting the reform project:

- The strengthened position and role of the EP under provisions of the Treaty of Lisbon, especially in two fields: (1) legislation and (2) forming the Commission (its President and the College of Commissioners). The introduction of a uniform electoral system would contribute to enabling the EP to make proper and efficient use of its new powers.
- The new definition of the mandate of MEPs under the Treaty of Lisbon (article 14, paragraph 2 TEU), declaring that they are representatives of the citizens of the Union (and not any longer 'of the peoples of the States brought together in the Community'). A uniform electoral system should stipulate provisions which are in accordance with this definition of the parliamentary mandate and the definition of the voters as citizens of the Union.
- The existence and consolidation of political parties at European level, officially recognised for the first time, in 1992/1993, in article 138a of the Treaty of Maastricht (in the Treaty of Amsterdam it was article 191, in the Treaty of Lisbon article 10, paragraph 4 TEU) and attributed a special function which now reads: 'Political parties at European level contribute to forming European political awareness and to expressing the will of the citizens of the Union.' Based on this treaty provision, the European Parliament and the Council decided in November 2003 on a regulation—'on the regulations governing political parties at European level and the rules regarding their funding' (Regulation No. 2004/2003)—labelled as Party Statute, which introduced public funding from the EU budget and triggered the founding of new parties at European level. With the entering into force of the regulation, their number has doubled to 10, rising to 13 in 2014. The regulation of 2003 soon became amended in December 2007. The new regulation (Regulation No. 1524/2007)

introduced the so-called political foundations at European level, which had to be affiliated to parties at European level and whose activities should support and supplement the goals of the respective parties. Since the foundations became entitled to receive financial support from the EU budget, each formally recognised party established 'its' foundation. With the amendment of the 2007 regulation in November 2014 (Regulation No. 1141/2014), parties at European level—now labelled as 'European political parties'—were given European legal personality. Additional institutional innovations—amongst them primarily the establishment of an 'Authority', entrusted with the task of controlling and, if necessary, sanctioning both parties and foundations—are aiming towards further consolidating European political parties and contributing to the development of a genuine transnational European party system. A uniform electoral system could serve as a supplementary arrangement and framework in that it would give incentives to accelerating this development.

- The introduction of the *Spitzenkandidaten* procedure, experienced for the first time in the 2014 European elections, has proved its potential to giving the electoral process new dynamism in various respects. Provisions introduced in a uniform electoral system, related to this new procedure, could be expected to add to that dynamism.
- Last but not least, there is article 223 TFEU, authorising the European Parliament to submit draft proposals aiming towards changing the electoral law of the Union, namely, to introduce a uniform electoral system for the European Parliament.

An additional very strong argument in favour of introducing a uniform electoral system stems from the criticism continuously brought forward against major features of all previous European elections, as described above (under Sect. 3). The criticism can be summarised as follows: European elections, held under rules and procedures set by each Member State autonomously, have been lacking a genuine 'European' character; the electoral turnout has been, since 1979, steadily in decline; there is no direct link between voters (casting their votes for members of national parties which, as such, are not visible in the European Parliament[1]) and the EP

---

[1] With the exception of national delegations within the transnational political groups.

party groups as their representatives. And there is an even stronger argument, overarching the whole discourse on the current situation of the Union and the perspectives for its future development: the more and more severe and dangerous weaknesses in the democratic legitimacy of the Union and the decision-making process therein. Various measures, amongst them the introduction of a uniform electoral system, are expected to reduce these weaknesses and contribute to generating greater legitimacy.

4.2   Content, Aims and 'Added Value' of the Reform Proposal

In its resolution of 11 November 2015 on the reform of the electoral law of the European Union (2015/2035(INL)), the European Parliament—having regard to the report of its Committee on Constitutional Affairs (see above under point 3)—has submitted a list with 26 concrete points dealing with various aspects of the electoral procedure which should be reformed. The wording, however, differs: the European Parliament 'proposes', 'considers', 'encourages Member States', 'determines', 'deems it essential', 'suggests', 'calls on Member States', 'recommends to Member States (as a future step)', 'calls for', 'highlights', 'deems it to be desirable'. The addressee of these considerations, proposals and demands are the Member States, represented by their governments in the Council; in an Annex, forming part of the resolution, the European Parliament, therefore, submits a 'Proposal for a Council Decision adopting the provisions amending the Act concerning the election of the members of the European Parliament by direct universal suffrage'. The proposal says—presenting concrete formulations—how the 1976 Act should be amended: via replacing parts (articles, paragraphs) of that Act by new provisions, via inserting new articles, via deleting parts of that Act.

The proposal claims to give the proper response to what has been identified as shortcomings and weaknesses of the previous elections (see section 3 above); furthermore, it takes into account and reacts to some of the new background factors (see section 4.1. above). And the major aims of the reform initiative have to be taken as criteria for evaluating the 'added value' of each individual proposal.[2]

---

[2] The European Added Value Unit of the European Parliamentary Research Service (EPRS) has published an In-Depth Analysis (Nogaj and Poptcheva 2015). This chapter draws on and follows the authentic argumentation of the analysis.

The new Electoral Act would underline at the beginning, in article 1, paragraph 1, that members of the European Parliament 'shall be elected as representatives of the citizens of the Union' (in line with the formulation in article 14, paragraph 1 TEU), replacing the former version which spoke of MEPs as representatives of the peoples of the Member States. The new characterisation would clearly be related to Union citizenship, thus emphasising the European dimension and character of the elections. And article 6, paragraph 1 of the new Electoral Act would stipulate that MEPs, equipped with a free mandate (which means that they 'shall not be bound by any instructions'), 'shall represent all Union citizens', thus putting emphasis on a direct link between the citizens of the Union (as voters) and the deputies as members of transnational political groups in the EP.

The key innovation of the reform proposal aims at giving European political parties a very prominent role in the elections. Their visibility shall be enhanced in that their names and logos—besides those of the respective national party—shall be placed on the ballot papers (new article 3e); the voter should become aware of the affiliation of the respective national party to the European political party. Names and logos of European political parties should, as a consequence, also appear during the campaign (in broadcasts, posters and other material); the Member States 'shall encourage and facilitate the provision of those affiliations'. And, 'campaign materials shall include a reference to the manifesto of the European political party, if any, to which the national Party is affiliated' (new article 3e). The message should be: European elections are not *second-order national elections* (Reif and Schmitt 1980; Schmitt 2005),[3] with some 200 national parties competing for seats, but have a 'genuine European character'. The strategy of relying on strengthening the role of European political parties in the electoral process as a means to make the elections adopt a European character has been advocated again and again (Mittag 2006; Mittag and Steuwer 2010; Hrbek 2011). Enhancing the visibility of European political parties would contribute to achieve greater transparency for the citizens.

The focus on involving European political parties in the electoral process more intensely becomes manifest in another new and complementary

---

[3] Karlheinz Reif and Hermann Schmitt (1980) have coined this term in 1980. Hermann Schmitt, 25 years later, confirms in general the evaluation of 1980, but identifies factors which have already started to reduce the second-order character. This trend has continued in the 2009 elections (Hrbek 2011).

provision of the new Electoral Act: 'European political parties shall nominate their candidates for the position of President of the Commission at least 12 weeks before the start of the electoral period ...' (new article 3f). The institutionalisation of the *Spitzenkandidaten* procedure should make voters understand better that there is a direct link between electing MEPs and the election of the Commission President. Since each lead candidate would stand for the political programme of his/her European party, casting the vote for a person would automatically be linked with support for the candidate's political programme, dealing with European topics; this Europeanisation of the electoral campaign could, in a long-term perspective, help developing a common European public space. And, furthermore, the formal institutionalisation of a lead candidate could be linked with the more ambitious constitutional perspective of further parliamentarisation.

The European Parliament, in its resolution of 11 November 2015, comes back to a reform proposal which had been discussed frequently since a couple of years, but had not found sufficient support, by emphasising that 'the establishment of a joint constituency in which lists are headed by each political family's candidate for the post of President of the Commission would greatly strengthen European democracy and legitimise further the election of the President of the Commission' (*Point Q*). This very ambitious reform proposal, known as 'Duff Report' (a first version had been presented by liberal MEP Andrew Duff at the beginning of the seventh election period 2009–2014), although unsuccessful until the 2014 elections (Donatelli 2015),[4] appears again on the agenda in the Proposal for a Council Decision (Annex to the Resolution of the of 11 November 2015): a new article 2a stipulates: 'The Council decides by unanimity on a joint constituency in which lists are headed by each political family's candidate for the post of President of the Commission.'

The reform proposal contains another innovation: the determination of an obligatory threshold for the allocation of seats. This threshold—not lower than 3 per cent and not higher than 5 per cent of the votes cast in the constituency or the single-constituency Member State—should be set by the Member States. The new rule should apply for Member States

---

[4] Lorenzo Donatelli, on the basis of his Master Thesis, submitted in 2015 to the Department of European Political and Administrative Studies in the College of Europe, Bruges, has produced a detailed analysis.

which send more than 26 deputies in the EP, namely, France, Germany, Italy, Poland, Romania, Spain (and the UK); the Netherlands with 26 seats would not fall in this category (new article 3). The intentions of introducing an obligatory threshold are twofold: avoiding a further fragmentation of the EP and ensuring its operability. The reform proposal has to be seen against the background of two decisions of the German Federal Constitutional Court: on 9 November 2011 the Court has ruled against the 5 per cent clause in the German Act for European elections (BVerfGE 129, 130 ff)[5]; on 26 February 2014, the Court has declared the 3 per cent clause (which had been set in the reformed Act for European Elections in Germany of June 2013) unconstitutional (BVerfGE 135, 259–312).[6] The Court has, in both cases, underlined that its ruling only relates to the German Act, with—until then—no European Electoral Act existing.

With respect to the goal of enhancing the democratic quality of the European elections, the proposal for a new Act stipulates the following: 'Political parties participating in elections to the European Parliament shall observe democratic procedures and transparency in selecting their candidates for these elections' (new article 3c).

The reform proposal, furthermore, deals with some organisational aspects of the electoral process against the background of very diverse rules governing the electoral laws in the Member States. Reform proposals do not aim to harmonise organisational provisions and achieve a uniform pattern, but to introduce minimum requirements which should be binding for all Member States: (1) The 'deadline for the establishment of lists of candidates [...] shall be at least 12 weeks before the start of the electoral period' (new article 3a). This would correspond to the time frame envisaged for the nomination of lead candidates; it would give candidates more time for campaigning and voters more time for preparing their decision; it would allow to link national campaigns and, thereby, underline the European character of the elections. (2) 'The deadline for the establishment and finalisation of the electoral roll shall be eight weeks before the first election day' (new article 3b). This would allow all, who claim the right to vote, to demanding for corrections of the roll in due time.

Another reform proposal aims to determine a uniform end of voting. Member States shall fix the date or dates for holding the election which

[5] See, in addition, Hrbek (2013), 259–278.
[6] See, in addition, Haug (2014), 467–489.

'shall fall within the same period starting on a Thursday morning and ending on the following Sunday. The election shall end in all Member States by 21:00 hours CET on that Sunday' (new article 10, paragraph 1). This would underline the European character of the election, showing that there exists one common electorate composed of Union citizens casting their votes in their respective constituency and polling station. The new rule would, furthermore, allow to create an electoral evening as a pan-European event.

Complementary new rules stipulate that 'Member States shall not officially make public the results of their count until after the close of polling', that 'official projections of the results shall be communicated simultaneously in all Member States at the end of the electoral period' and that 'prior to this no exit poll-based forecasts may be published' (new article 10, paragraph 2); and, last but not least, that 'the counting of postal votes shall begin in all Member States once the polls have closed in the Member State whose voters vote last ...' (new article 10, paragraph 3). This should guarantee that no undue influence from other Member States could affect the voting behaviour of citizens who have not yet cast their votes.

There are reform proposals dealing with special aspects of exercising the right to vote of individual citizens: (1) 'Member States may introduce electronic and internet voting [...]' (new article 4a), which has already been experienced in elections at national level in some Member States, and (2) 'Member States may afford their citizens the possibility of casting their vote by post [...]' (new article 4b), as has been practised in some Member States as well. The proposals aim at offering citizens new forms of casting their votes, which can be expected to increase the turnout.

The reform initiative, furthermore, considers the situation of Union citizens living or working in a third country as concerns their right to vote and submits the following solution: 'Member States shall take the necessary measures to ensure the exercise of this right' (new article 9a). The proposal does not accept and recognise the argument that these Union citizens would be too far away—not in a geographical sense—from the Union and its political agenda and could not be expected to be well informed, a necessary condition to exercise voting rights. It insists in electoral equality and argues that information technology and new media promise easy access to reliable information.

There are two final points, relating to two different categories of citizens, which are considered in the reform initiative: (1) The new article 3d says: 'The list of candidates for election to the European Parliament shall ensure gender equality'. Here, the proposal prefers a non-binding approach and solution; it calls upon the Member States and political parties to consider the issue of gender equality and to take action, respectively. (2) The Resolution, under point 15, recommends to Member States—explicitly labelled 'as a future step'—that they should consider ways to harmonise the minimum age of voters at 16, in order to further enhance electoral equality among Union citizens, as already introduced in Austria. The point does not appear in the Proposal for a Council Decision.

The overview shows that a reformed electoral system of the EU would have to deal with a broad spectrum of issues: some of them of primarily technical character, some others very political and as such sensitive. Whereas for some new rules and provisions an agreement amongst the Member States might be achieved easily, there are, however, others where a consensus seems improbable or at least difficult to be reached.

5   Constraints for the Realisation of the Reform Proposal of November 2015

It was the goal of the initiators to reform the Electoral Act, that the new provisions could be applied in the 2019 elections. Concerning the steps necessary to introduce a new Electoral Act, article 223, paragraph 1, TFEU stipulates the following: (1) 'The European Parliament shall draw up a proposal to lay down the provisions necessary for the election of its members by direct universal suffrage in accordance with a uniform procedure in all Member States or in accordance with principles common to all Member States.' This step was done with the Resolution of the European Parliament of 11 November 2015, the content of which has been explained above. (2) It would be up to the Council to take the next step: to consider the proposal submitted by the European Parliament and decide (the Treaty article says: 'lay down the necessary provisions'); there are, however, two procedural conditions: the Council would have to act 'unanimously', and it could act only 'after obtaining the consent of the European Parliament, which shall act by the majority of its component members'. (3) The last step would then be the 'approval by the Member States in accordance with their respective constitutional requirements'.

By spring 2018 the situation is as follows: the first step has been done in November 2015; the Council, however, has not yet taken action. Observers agree that the application of these new provisions in the 2019 elections, as envisaged by the initiators of the reform, will not be possible. Various constraints are responsible for the delay.

To begin with, as already mentioned in the Introduction (Sect. 1), the European Parliament did approve the Resolution with only a very narrow majority (which was significantly smaller than the one achieved in the AFCO): 315 votes in favour, 234 against and 55 abstentions. These numbers do not represent a convincing support for the reform project, presented by the two rapporteurs; the number of no-votes and abstentions reflect widespread opposition and criticism against the reform proposal inside the European Parliament, which allows to conclude that the same attitudes can be found within national political parties at Member State level; and these numbers will rather weaken the position of the European Parliament in negotiations with the Member States in the Council.

The plenary debate in the European Parliament on 27 October 2015 (CRE 27/10/2015–16), prior to the vote on the Resolution in the session on 11 November 2015, did display some of the major arguments raised against the reform proposal. One major point was opposition against and rejection of what has been perceived as the constitutionalisation of the position of lead candidates (*Spitzenkandidaten*). A second major point was opposition against and rejection of the upgrading of European political parties with effects at the expense of national political parties. A third major point was lacking support for the introduction of an obligatory threshold, articulated explicitly by deputies from smaller party groups and smaller national parties, including some Liberals.

Beyond criticism against this or that specific detail of the reform proposal, there is a widespread general attitude hostile to all steps aiming towards deepening the integration process, including the strengthening of the European Parliament as supranational institutional actor at the expense of domestic concerns of the respective Member State.

As concerns the Council—the dominant institutional actor to accomplishing the second step in the decision-making process according to the provisions in article 223 TFEU—it seemed to be very unlikely that it would be ready and willing to give (unanimously) approval to the reform proposal. A confidential *Non-Paper*, submitted by the Dutch Presidency in April 2016, spoke—not at all surprisingly—of the more or less unanimous rejection of a constitutionalisation of the position of *Spitzenkandidaten* by the Member States governments (see Maurer 2016, 69–80). And a first debate in the General Affairs' Council on 3 June 2016 showed resistance against linking the European Election with the decision on the Commission

President. Furthermore, proposals on introducing E-Voting—obviously, although only a detail, a very sensitive issue—were rejected.

Since summer 2016, there is an additional new factor which will further delay the amendment of the Electoral Act as envisaged and initiated by the European Parliament with its November 2015 proposal: *Brexit* will have consequences for the composition of the European Parliament and the apportionment of the number of seats to the Member States. Alternative models, paying attention to their implications for equality of representation, on how a new composition could look like, have been elaborated (Kalcik and Wolff 2017). Since a re-allocation of seats—irrespective of which model would be used—is a very sensitive issue, affecting more or less all Member States, they will consider carefully the consequences of such changes and link this question with the project of reforming the Electoral Act. One could not expect that the chances for reaching an agreement would improve.

The Committee on Constitutional Affairs of the European Parliament dealt with this complex issue and elaborated in fall 2017 a Report on the composition of the EP (2017/2054(INL)—2017/0900(NLE)) with Danuta Hübner (EPP) and Pedro Silva Pereira (S&D) as co-rapporteurs. On this basis, AFCO prepared a Motion for a Resolution of the EP and, in an Annex, a Draft Proposal for a Decision of the European Council establishing the composition of the EP post-Brexit. The two key elements of the rapporteurs' proposal are: (1) to reduce the size of the Parliament down to 705 MEPs and re-allocate the seats amongst the Member States and (2) 46 seats should remain available for potential future enlargements or be partially used for a joint constituency.

AFCO on 23 January voted on the Motion (20 in favour, 4 against, 1 abstention) and on the Draft Proposal (21 in favour, 4 against, no abstention). A Minority Opinion, on behalf of the ECR Group, did focus on two points: (1) It rejected the proposal to re-distribute seats and favoured to reduce membership to 678 MEPs via using the total of 73 UK parliamentarians. (2) It rejected the perspective of having transnational lists, arguing that transnational MEPs who would be beyond traditional electoral boundaries, would only serve to make citizens feel even more distant from the EU.

The plenary dealt with the issue on 7 February 2018 and did approve the Hübner/Silva Pereira-Report on the (new) composition of the EP (400 in favour, 183 against). The AFCO proposal on transnational lists, however, was voted down by 368 to 274 votes. The EPP Group was not any longer ready and willing to support the introduction of transnational lists as an element of a Union-wide electoral system. This ambitious project seems to be, once again, postponed for long.

It was not only the EP which dealt with the issue; the governments of the Member States contributed to the debate, as well. When the heads of states and governments of the EU Member States met on 20 October 2017, they elaborated and agreed on a common working programme, with a sequence of meetings, until mid-2019, that is to say: until the next European elections. They scheduled an informal meeting of the European Council to be held on 28 February 2018. This meeting should be devoted to deliberations on a series of institutional questions; amongst them—in view of the 2019 European elections—the following three points: (1) the composition of the European Parliament following the withdrawal of the 73 UK deputies, as part of the Brexit; (2) a joint constituency with transnational lists of candidates; and (3) nominations and appointments, which would include the issue of *Spitzenkandidaten* of European political parties, first experienced in the 2014 elections, and the post of the Commission President.

Background for this agenda has been, without any doubt, the **speech of the French President Macron** on 26 September 2017 at the Sorbonne under the title 'Initiative for Europe' (Ouest France 2017). In this speech, Macron had expressed himself in favour of transnational lists, offering to European citizens the opportunity to cast their votes for a coherent and common project; 50 per cent of the MEPs should be elected via these lists. As concerns the 73 UK seats, Macron declared himself against distributing them amongst the remaining 27 Member States; instead, they should be used for seats coming from the transnational lists.

Macron's statement, not at all vague, but designating special points related to both the project of reforming the Electoral Act and the question of adjusting the composition of the European Parliament after Brexit, can be understood as a signal that both issues—obviously linked with each other—should be discussed in the near future. Putting these issues on the agenda of a meeting of the European Council, which would be, as mentioned above, only an informal reunion, was neither an indicator for consensus on these sensitive and contested questions amongst the Member States, nor did it allow to expect agreement.

The informal meeting, which took place on 23 February 2018, did not produce concrete results. In the statement of President Tusk to the press it was said: 'As regards transnational lists, leaders will come back to this issue in the future.' Obviously, the participants of the meeting did not at all deal with the project to introduce a new uniform electoral system.

6   Outlook

Initiators and supporters of the project to bring about a substantial reform of the electoral law, launched after the 2014 European elections in the EP, had the intention that the rules for a uniform electoral system would enter into force in due time before the next European elections in 2019 and that the new rules could be applied in 2019. As was shown above the decision-making process—with various actors (not only the EP) involved—did not proceed as expected by those favouring the project.

The situation, one year before the 2019 European elections, is as follows: the rules for these elections will be those set by each Member State, as before. Member States may, perhaps, take up elements of the reform proposal of November 2015 and modify national rules, respectively. And it can be expected that the *Spitzenkandidaten* procedure will be practised again—although on a non-constitutionalised basis—most probably by the same European political parties as in 2014. The reform proposal of November 2015 was much more ambitious as regards this aspect.

The whole issue seems to follow the well-known pattern of determining the integration process from the very beginning: the process develops slowly, in a pragmatic and incremental way, with only small steps which, having been practised for some time and, therefore, been widely accepted, later can and will be codified. This applies to the issue of introducing a uniform electoral system for the European Parliament as well. It remains an arduous way towards this aim.

References

Costa, O. (2016). The History of European Electoral Reform and the Electoral Act 1976: Issues of Democratisation and Political Legitimacy. *European Parliament History Series*, European Parliamentary Research Service, Brussels, October.

Donatelli, L. (2015). A Pan-European District for the European Elections? The Rise and Fall of the Duff Proposal for the Electoral Reform of the European Parliament. Published as No. 44/2015 in the Series '*Bruges Political Research Papers*'.

European Parliament. (2015a). Debate on the Reform of the Electoral Law of the EU (Debate), October 27. http://www.europarl.europa.eu/sides/getDoc.

do?type=CRE&reference=20151027&secondRef=ITEM-016&language=DE &ring=A8-2015-0286.
European Parliament. (2015b). European Parliament Resolution of 11 November 2015 on the Reform of the Electoral Law of the European Union (2015/2035(INL)).
Federal Constitutional Court (Germany). (2011). Judgement of the Second Senate of 9 November 2011–2 BvC 4/10 – Rn. (1–160).
Federal Constitutional Court (Germany). (2014). Judgment of the Second Senate of 26 February 2014 – 2 BvE 2/13 – paras. (1–30).
Haug, V. M. (2014). Muss wirklich jeder ins Europäische Parlament? Kritische Anmerkungen zur Sperrklausel-Rechtsprechung aus Karlsruhe. *Zeitschrift für Parlamentsfragen, 2,* 467–489.
Hrbek, R. (2011). Europawahlen als "Second-Order National Elections"? Ein Paradigma im Licht der Europawahlen 2004 und 2009. In J. Mittag (Ed.), *30 Jahre Direktwahlen zum Europäischen Parlament (1979–2009): Europawahlen und EP in der Analyse* (pp. 63–79). Baden-Baden: Nomos.
Hrbek, R. (2013). Deutsche Europawahlen künftig ohne Sperrklausel? Das Urteil des Bundesverfassungsgerichts vom November 2011 und seine Folgen. *Integration, 4,* 259–278.
Kalcik, R., & Wolff, G. B. (2017). Is Brexit an Opportunity to Reform the European Parliament? *Bruegel Policy Contribution,* Issue no. 2/2017.
Maurer, A. (2016). Europäisches Parlament. In W. Weidenfeld & W. Wessels (Eds.), *Jahrbuch der Europäischen Integration 2016* (pp. 69–80). Baden-Baden: Nomos.
Mittag, J. (Ed.). (2006). *Politische Parteien und europäische Integration. Perspektiven transnationaler Parteienkooperation in Europa.* Essen: Klartext.
Mittag, J., & Steuwer, J. (2010). *Politische Parteien in der EU,* Wien.
Nogaj, M., & Poptcheva, E.-M. (2015). The Reform of the Electoral Law of the European Union. European Added Value Assessment Accompanying the Legislative Own-Initiative Report (Co-Rapporteurs Hübner, D./Leinen, J.)', September 2015, European Parliamentary Research Service (PE 558.775).
Official Journal of the European Communities. (1976). Decision of the representatives of the Member States meeting in the Council relating to the Act concerning the election of the representatives of the Assembly by direct universal suffrage, 8 October 1976, L 278.
Official Journal of the European Union. (2002). Council Decision of 25 June 2002 and 23 September 2002 Amending the Act Concerning the Election of the Representatives of the European Parliament by Direct Universal Suffrage, Annexed to Decision 76/787/ECSC, EEC, Euratom, L 283, 21 October 2002.
Official Journal of the European Union. (2003). Regulation (EC) No. 2004/2003 of the European Parliament and of the Council on the Regulations Governing

Political Parties at European level and the Rules Regarding Their Funding, 4 November 2003, OJ L 297, 15.11.2003, 1.

Official Journal of the European Union. (2007). Regulation (EC) No. 1524/2007 of the European Parliament and of the Council on the Regulations Governing Political Parties at European Level and the Rules Regarding Their Funding, 18 December 2007 Amending Regulation (EC), No 2004/2003, L 343/5.

Official Journal of the European Union. (2014). Regulation (EU, EURATOM) No. 1141/2014 of the European Parliament and of the Council, 22 October 2014 on the Statute and Funding of European Political Parties and European Political Foundations, L317/1.

Ouest France. (2017). Sorbonne Speech of Emmanuel Macron, September 26. Retrieved 26 April 2018, from http://international.blogs.ouest-france.fr/archive/2017/09/29/macron-sorbonne-verbatim-europe-18583.html.

Reif, K., & Schmitt, H. (1980). Nine Second-Order National Elections. A Conceptual Framework for the Analysis of European Elections Results. *European Journal of Political Research, 1*(8), 3–44.

Report on the composition of the European Parliament (2017/2054(INL) – 2017/0900(NLE)), 26 January 2018.

Schmitt, H. (2005). The European Parliament Elections of June 2004: Still Second-Order? *WEP, 3*(2005), 650–679.

CHAPTER 13

Euroscepticism at the EP Elections in 2014: A Reflection of the Different Patterns of Opposition to the EU?

Birte Wassenberg

1 INTRODUCTION

Since the failure of the EU Constitution in 2005, the European Union (EU) has been afflicted by severe internal and external crises (Fabbrini 2015). The rejection of the constitutional Treaty after the negative referenda of the Dutch and French population abruptly stopped the assumption that euphoria would always accompany the process of European integration. The rescue bid of the so-called simplified Lisbon Treaty had barely re-launched the European zest in 2008 when the international economic and financial crisis de-stabilized the Euro zone to such an extent that Greece was threatened with exclusion from the Economic and Monetary Union (EMU). And while the EU Member States were still haggling with each other over reform packages to solve this crisis, the next one was already beginning to emerge: for years, the refugee problem had been visible at the maritime borders of Italy, Spain, and Greece as well as at the Schengen border of the Channel Tunnel between Calais and

B. Wassenberg (✉)
IEP, Université de Strasbourg, Strasbourg, France
e-mail: birte.wassenberg@unistra.fr

© The Author(s) 2019
O. Costa (ed.), *The European Parliament in Times of EU Crisis*,
European Administrative Governance,
https://doi.org/10.1007/978-3-319-97391-3_13

Dover. In summer 2015, it escalated when Hungary blocked its external border, and the Dublin agreement was suspended. In addition, after the failed attempt of an economic agreement with Ukraine and the resulting conflict between Russia and Ukraine in 2014, the EU has been struggling to defend its tediously established European Neighborhood Policy (ENP).

It does not come as a surprise that in this context, the breeding grounds of anti-European movements have been growing exponentially (Libera et al. 2016). In fact, in almost every EU Member State, Eurosceptic parties clearly increased their share of the vote at the 2014 European elections (Moreau and Wassenberg 2016a, b). One may even wonder whether there is not a special link between the manifestation of resistance to Europe and the European elections: why do absenteeism, Euroscepticism, and anti-Europeanism assert themselves with such magnitude at the time of the European elections? Does this not suggest that the European election periods are epiphenomena where opposition to Europe is particularly visible? This chapter will first question both theoretically and historically the link between Euroscepticism and European elections. It will then follow on to illustrate the rise of Eurosceptic and anti-EU political forces in the 2014 elections to the European Parliament (EP) emphasizing the need for a country-specific, differentiated analysis and thus identifying different logics working behind the general banner of anti-Europeanism. Finally, the chapter will embed the current results of the EP elections into the general framework of European integration by demonstrating that we are confronted with a deeply rooted phenomenon of Euroscepticism that has accompanied this process of integration from its start.

2   THE LINK BETWEEN EP ELECTIONS
AND EUROSCEPTICISM

Is there a special relationship between European elections and Euroscepticism? One might argue that this special relationship not only springs from the role of the EP as a mirror of existing Eurosceptic forces in Europe but also from the seemingly paradoxical connection which has existed from the start between this European democratic institution set up with the very purpose to increase public support for the European idea and the expression of Euroscepticism in EP elections. However, the right of opposition to Europe is also part of the democratic principle and it is therefore only logical that not only pro-European political parties are represented in the EP. In order to analyze the link between EP elections and Euroscepticism, it therefore first has to be clarified what is exactly meant by the terminology.

The studies of political scientists on Eurosceptic political parties have initially distinguished between two types of opposition to Europe. They have shown that a Euroscepticism 'in principle', which rejects the whole logic of the EU with its supranational European political and economic integration, should not be confounded with a more attenuated 'qualified' Euroscepticism that accepts the idea of European integration as such but challenges the principles of socioeconomic organization within the EU's actual configuration. Indeed, Szczerbiak and Taggart differentiated between 'hard' and 'soft' Euroscepticism and on these grounds elaborated a scale allowing for the classification of political parties (Taggart and Szerbiak 2008). But this typology was not accepted undisputedly by all political scientists. According to Kopecky and Mudde, for example, a 'black and white' distinction posed significant problems such as a far too large scope of definition of soft Euroscepticism as well as the impossibility to clearly distinguish between the two types of Euroscepticism. Also, they criticized that this model only used the criterion of EU membership as a way how to distinguish between hard and soft Eurosceptics. Thus, inspired by David Easton (1965, 267), they suggested a two-dimensional typology constructed on the basis of a distinction between 'diffuse' opposition to the concept of European integration on the one hand and a more 'specific' opposition to the EU on the other (Kopecky and Mudde 2002, 297–326). Other researchers emphasized instead a more gradual approach comprising several categories of Euroscepticism that could be situated on one or several continuums (Rovny 2004). Globally, two schools of thought appeared in political sciences: one school insisted on the strategic and pragmatic character of oppositions to Europe, whereas the other retained more the ideological component (Lacroix and Coman 2007).

For the analysis of the EP elections, both the distinction between 'soft' and 'hard' and between 'pragmatic' and 'ideological' might be relevant for a party-related analysis, but in order to understand the overall picture of Euroscepticism in the EP, we propose to add two supplementary criteria (Moreau and Wassenberg 2016a, 11–27): first, the 'Eurosceptic' groups of the EP have to be distinguished from those groups in which Eurosceptic tendencies might also be present but which do not label themselves as

Eurosceptic (especially mainstream political parties from the left or the right of the political spectrum). Second, in order to accentuate the difference between 'soft' and 'hard' Euroscepticism, this chapter suggests using the term of 'anti-EU' for hard Eurosceptic political parties which advocate leaving the EU and/or reject its principal ideological foundations. Knowing of course that Euroscepticism is a far larger phenomenon englobing many different anti-European movements and forces and not necessarily focused on the EU, this seems more appropriate for an analysis centered on the EP elections.

From a historical point of view, the connection between Euroscepticism and EP elections gives rise to a paradox (Bitsch 2016, 15–23). In principle, in the collective imaginary, the direct election of the EP—a democratic act by definition—was supposed to bring Europe closer to its citizens and strengthen their feeling of belonging to the EU. In the 1950s, the fathers of Europe saw in this election by universal suffrage the means of consolidating European integration. Robert Schuman, for example, who was convinced that citizens were more in support of Europe than the politicians, repeatedly said that citizens must be relied on to advance integration and, as early as 1956, he favored a Parliament elected by direct suffrage (Deloye 2005, 35). In 1960, the European Parliamentary Assembly then drew up a proposal for its election by direct universal suffrage, which had been already a provision of the Treaty of Rome but was rejected at the time by the French authorities. When the decision was finally taken in the mid-1970s, it was hailed as a qualitative leap for European integration and as a means to address the democratic deficit in the European Community (Wassenberg 2007, 263).

However, from the very first election in 1979, disillusionment reigned: the citizens did not mobilize massively, either in support of European integration or even to vote (Bernard 2013, 157). From that first experience, the abstention rate, which was quite low in countries where voting is compulsory (Belgium, Italy, Luxembourg), reached on average 38% in the Community of nine Member States. Many circumstances can explain partly these reserves. Europe was coming out of the three post-war decades' boom: unemployment, high oil prices, and the economic crisis were (again) affecting Europe. The European Community, which had expanded since 1973, was struggling to integrate the UK which, in 1979, had elected to power the as first resolutely Eurosceptic head of government in the Community. However, during the next elections in 1984, the lack of enthusiasm remained. The mistrust in Europe was also visible on other occasions. It was manifest especially with low rates of participation during the referenda on the ratification of the reform treaties (Maastricht, Nice, Lisbon) without forgetting the rejections of the Constitution in 2005 (Rambour 2010, 93–109). For some years, voice has been given to this mistrust in the media, in particular on the Internet. It is regularly evaluated by the polls, including the Eurobarometer ones, which normally rather seek to measure the degree of adherence. Even if EU institutions generally rank higher in trust than national institutions, the European elections visibly do not passionate the European people. Facts must therefore be faced: there are structural reasons for the poor turnout at elections and Euroscepticism.

This growing disinterest in European elections and the rising degree of abstention weakens the legitimacy of the EP (Costa 2001, 486). However, whether this means that Euroscepticism increases as well in the elections is less evident to proof. At first glance, abstention seems to come under indifference rather than hostility: after all, European elections are generally regarded as 'second order elections' and therefore do not mobilize as much as national elections. But it probably means a less benevolent indifference than that which has long inspired the permissive consensus. Furthermore, anti-European parties whose voters are more likely to vote than others benefit from this. The rate of abstention in the European elections has increased constantly between 1979 and 2014 to 41% in 1984 and 1989, then to 43.3% in 1994, to 50.5% in 1999 to reach 56.9% in 2009, and 57.46% in 2014 (Rambour 2016, 65). There are however considerable variations according to the Member States of the EU concerned. During the European elections in 2014, the abstention rate was situated between 10 and 87%: in Luxemburg and Belgium where the vote is obligatory it was 10–15%, whereas in Slovakia it reached the highest rate in the EU of 87%. However, its average rate is at about the same level as in some national elections of EU Member States. It is therefore not abnormally high and a blank or invalid ballot paper might thus be representative more of a rebellious attitude towards the principle of elections and the political establishment than of opposition to Europe (Bertoncini and Chopin 2014).

Nonetheless, abstention appears to be also linked to the very nature of the European elections and the way they are organized. Michel Hastings, who studied the 2004 elections, wrote: 'This is not a European poll', meaning that in fact, it was rather a juxtaposition of a series of national elections (Hastings 2005, 536–541). Several factors contribute to this national appropriation of the European elections: first, they are not held on exactly the same date in all Member States but are spread out over four consecutive days, from Thursday to Sunday, taking into account the different voting habits in the various countries; second, the voting rules are not uniform even if they are gradually becoming more similar; third, electoral lists are comprised of national candidates; and, finally, election campaigns are strongly influenced by national concerns and even the political issues are often more national oriented than European (Lefèbvre 2005, 161–167). However, the national considerations of these elections are also quite weak since they neither determine the parliamentary majority nor the composition of the national government. Thus, they are often considered to be 'low priority', 'intermediary', or 'subsidiary' elections. This weakness of the issues at stake may thus explain the voter's apathy: citizens may be tempted to abstain or to cast a protest vote against their national government (Reif and Schmitt 1980, 3–45).

Moreover, the European issues at stake during these elections also seem limited, or are perceived as such. They could be considered unimportant for two reasons: the EP is still perceived by citizens as the weak link in the institutional system of the EU, which it has indeed been for a long time. Since the Treaty of Maastricht, treaty by treaty, however, Parliament has gained in power, even if it is still not comparable to a national parliament, for it is not the sole legislator of the EU (Jauzein 2016, 47–49). New powers have been added, little by little, to the original supervisory powers and the right to censure, for example, budgetary power (to adopt or reject the annual budget). It therefore does now have major legislative power, thanks to the ordinary legislative procedure with the Council (of Ministers) for numerous texts, as well as the possibility to influence the composition of the Commission, as the Treaty of Lisbon stipulates that the EP has to approve by vote the Commission's president and members. During the 2014 European elections, the main political families in Europe had even each chosen a lead candidate (the so-called *Spitzenkandidaten* procedure) who was claiming the Commission presidency if his/her side was to win the election. Nonetheless, the average abstention rate has been at its peak during this election (Courrier International 2014). If one qualifies abstention as possibly Eurosceptic behavior, the link between European elections and Euroscepticism therefore still exists and finds itself even fortified when looking at the success of anti-EU political parties at the 2014 EP elections.

3 THE RISE OF EUROSCEPTIC POLITICAL FORCES IN THE 2014 EP ELECTIONS: A GENERALIZED BUT MULTI-FACETED TENDENCY

The results of the EP elections in 2014 clearly show an increase of what are generally called 'Eurosceptic' political forces and this in nearly all EU Member States (Moreau and Wassenberg 2016b, 15) (Fig. 13.1).

When looking at the overall results of the 2014 European elections, three anti-EU factions were immediately identifiable in the EP (Backes 2016, 47–71). On the right-wing political spectrum, two political groups can be identified: the European Conservatives and Reformists (ECR) regrouping Eurosceptic conservative parties (e.g. the Czech Civic Democratic Party, the German *Alternative für Deutschland*, the British Conservative Party, and the Finns Party) and the Europe of Free and Direct Democracy (EFDD) faction regrouping national populist and far-right parties (Danish People's Party, Italian Five Star Movement, Sweden Democrats). On the other side of the political spectrum, the European United Left-Nordic Green Left (GUE-NGL) brings together far left-wing political parties (e.g. the Cypriote Progressive Party of Working People, the German *Linke*, the Irish *Sinn Fein*, or the Spanish *Podemos*). Together, these three political factions (ECR, EFFD, and GUE-NGL) collected 22.8% of the European votes and received 170 out of 751 seats.

The increase with regard to the previous period is considerable, but not exponential: they held 124 seats during the 2009–2014 electoral period, that is, 17.6% of the votes (Veivodová 2016, 71–85). Not all anti-European

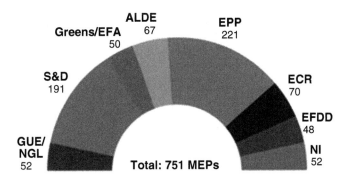

Fig. 13.1 The European elections 2014. Source: Pinterest

political parties are members of a faction, but in June 2015, Marine Le Pen and Marcel de Graaff launched the Europe of Nations and Freedom (ENF) group, mainly composed of the French *Front National* (FN) and Geert Wilders' Dutch Party of Freedom. They thus introduced a third right-wing anti-EU faction counting 40 Members of the European Parliament (MEPs). In all, a total 220 out of 751 are anti-EU MEPs in this legislative term of the EP, that is, 29%—practically one third.

A country-specific analysis of the 2014 European elections first reveals that anti-EU and Eurosceptic parties have spread to a majority of EU Member States (Libera 2016, 39–47). Whereas the UK is known for a 'traditionally' high proportion of Eurosceptic forces in the EP, mainly represented in the ECR group, it came as a surprise in 2014 that in almost all founding Member States of the European Community—with the exception of Luxemburg—a large number of anti-EU forces from the extreme right or left were elected into the EP. This surprise was especially big in Germany and Italy which are normally identified as continuous defenders of the European integration process.

But even in the UK, the 2014 EP elections resulted in a new situation which could be qualified as an increase in extreme anti-EU positions. Hard Euroscepticism has thus shifted from the British Conservative Party who gained 23.31%, that is, 19 seats to the new UK Independence Party (UKIP) which obtained the highest national party score with 26.77%, that is, 24 seats in the EP (Tournier-Sol 2016, 105). This positive outcome for the 'new' anti-EU political force in the UK also provoked the radicalization of the Conservative Party's positions on European integration, pushing it form 'softer' to 'harder' Euroscepticism (Alexandre-Collier 2016, 85–99). Even compared with the anti-EU British National Party (BNP), UKIP was the clear winner of the 2014 European elections: the BNP only achieved 1.1% of the votes and is no longer represented in the EP. Presently, UKIP is therefore the strongest anti-EU British force in the EP, even if its leader, Nigel Farage, has resigned after the Brexit referendum in 2016. UKIP's anti-European positions during the EP election campaign focused on the UK's withdrawal from the EU. Their rejection of the European project is based on the defense of British national sovereignty (Hanley 2016, 117–120). Due to its strong emphasis on national identity, the party was able to attract voters from all established parties and one of the consequences of this success was that it pushed David Cameron to organize the referendum on UK's EU membership in June 2016.

However, Euroscepticism did not only increase in the UK. The support for anti-EU movements was also strong in the EU founding Member States. For two of them, France and the Netherlands, the tendency towards 'hard' Euroscepticism has already been palpable since the mid-2000s. The rejection of the European Constitution at the referendum in France by 54, 68% of the population, and in the Netherlands by 61.54% clearly indicated a shift away from the 'permissive consensus' on the European integration process. Still, the extreme right-wing FN only obtained 6.3% of votes in France, that is, three seats in the 2009 European elections, while it became the leading national political force in France with the highest turnout in 2014, gaining 24.86% of votes and 23 seats in the EP. Being a hard Eurosceptic party, the FN flatly rejects the project of European integration and calls for France's withdrawal from the EU (Ivaldi 2016, 131–149). The same hardline anti-European position is defended by the right-wing populist Dutch Freedom Party (PVV) which obtained 13.3% of votes, that is, four seats in the 2014 European elections. However, despite the popularity of its leader Geert Wilders, the party lost one seat with regard to the previous electoral period where it had a score of 17% of the votes and five seats in the EP. This is probably due to the fact that in the Netherlands, Euroscepticism has assumed different flavors which are represented in a largely pluralist political party system (Otjes and Voerman 2016, 185–205). It is not only present at the extreme right-wing political spectrum but also exists in parties of orthodox Protestants (Christian Union and Political Reformed Party (SGP)), left-wing socialists (SP), as well as 'animal rights activists' (PvdD). All of them reject the deepening of the process of European integration. On the scale of Euroscepticism, the radical right-wing Freedom Party is nonetheless the most, and the two orthodox Protestant parties are the least, anti-EU. The PVV's decision to cofound together with the French FN a new hardliner anti-European faction in the EP clearly confirms this analysis.

As for Germany and Italy, hard Eurosceptic forces have made their entry after the 2014 European elections, respectively, from the extreme right and extreme left-wing camp. In Germany, the Eurosceptic extreme right-wing Populist Party Alternative for Germany (AfD) achieved 7.10% of the votes and obtained seven seats in the EP. When adding up the Eurosceptic left-wing party, *Die Linke*, which obtained 7.4% and also seven seats in the elections, there are now two German Eurosceptic parties represented in the EP. However, the German result was a shock mainly with regard to the success of the AfD. Indeed, *Die Linke* had already obtained nine seats in the previous elections in 2009 and it actually lost one seat in 2014. Furthermore, its anti-Europeanism is questionable, as it does not reject the EU in principle. In contrast, the AfD which had failed to pass the 5% hurdle at the German national elections in 2013 now succeeded in entering the EP (Neu 2016, 159–161). Its right-wing extremist anti-EU positions are comparable to those of the French FN or the Dutch PVV, but the historical memory of Nazi Germany confers to this election result of a German nationalist party on the European level a specific symbolism. However, compared to the FN, for example, the outcome of the AfD is still relatively low and therefore has to be relativized with regard to the weight of other extreme right-wing anti-European forces in the EP. Indeed, the AfD as an anti-EU right-wing party is still a newcomer in Germany, where the European integration process has been regarded after World War II as one major solution in order to prevent Germany to fall back into neo-nationalist tendencies. Contrarily, since 1984, the FN has established itself in the EP as a permanent force with 10–11% of the French votes at each European election with the exception of 1999 (5.9%). The AfD has also not joined the ENF group but belongs to the now 'softer' Eurosceptic ECR faction in the EP. In Italy, the surprising success of anti-European forces came from the far left-wing political side. Beppe Grillo's Five Star Movement achieved a major score finishing runner-up at the European elections (Pasquinucci 2016, 169). His party obtained the second best national result with 21.15% of votes and obtained 17 seats in the EP. This success is alarming because the party is diametrically opposed to the concept of democracy of the European institutions thus undermining the basic principles of the EU. It is therefore a just as 'hard' Eurosceptic party as the extreme right-wing populist forces in the EP.

Analyzing the 2014 EP election results in the Southern/Mediterranean Member States of the EU allows for the identification of a dominant push factor for increased Euroscepticism there: the consequences of the economic and financial crisis in Europe since 2008. Most of these states have suffered from a massive economic slump and a disastrous debt spiral and the population has been struck by growing unemployment, the rollback of social welfare system and the experience of a lack of solidarity from the richer EU Member States, especially Germany. At the European elections, it is therefore almost a logical consequence, that Eurosceptic parties were particularly successful. This development can be well observed in Spain and in Greece. For Pablo Iglesias and his radical left-wing party *Podemos*, the 2014 election to the EP was the first step to a political rise on the national scene (Elorza 2016, 38). The Spanish party obtained 7.98% of the votes and five seats in the EP and intended to use this score in order to gain domestic political power. While it defends 'traditional' left-wing anti-EU positions, for example, against ultra-liberal capitalism, its standpoint is not 'hard' Euroscepticism to the point of wanting to leave the EU. Indeed, it mainly considers Euroscepticism as the means to the end of reaching national political goals. In contrast to this, the important rise of Eurosceptic votes in Greece is a clear sign of the Greeks turning away from the EU (Konstantinidis 2016, 42–45). This 'new' hard opposition against the EU is not only proven by the electoral success of anti-EU parties at the 2014 European elections, but continued during the 2015 referendum when the Greeks rejected the agreement proposed by the European partners, thus endangering Greece remaining an EU member. The referendum outcome indeed confirms that the anti-EU discourse of the Eurosceptic parties responded to the general 'Eurosceptic' mood of the population and helps to explain the reasons why the electorate chose to vote for them. During the EP elections, on the left side of the political spectrum, the Coalition of the Radical Left reached the highest national score with 26.57% of votes and six seats, and on the extreme right side, the Independent Greeks obtained one seat with 3.46% of the votes. Both political parties defend 'hard' anti-European positions against the EU and the principle of European integration itself.

However, the election results of other Southern EU Member States show that a generalization of Southern/Mediterranean Euroscepticism cannot easily be undertaken. In Cyprus, for example, the picture of the resistance against the EU is not quite so clear (Stergiou 2016, 55–67). Besides the two anti-EU parties (the Cypriot communist party AKEL and the right-wing extremist party ELAM), there are many heterogeneous, non-partisan Eurosceptic perceptions which can be assigned neither to the classic 'hard' nor to 'soft' Euroscepticism. Also, whereas AKEL obtained the second best national score with 26.98% of votes and two seats, ELAM did not manage to obtain any seat in the EP. However, all in all, the election results globally account for a strong Eurosceptic movement in Cyprus. The best counterexample concerning Southern Euroscepticism is Portugal. Indeed, in terms of rising anti-Europeanism at the 2014 European elections, Portugal can justly be called the exception among the Southern European states (Cunha 2016, 75–76). Despite the deep economic crisis and ensuing problems like debt and unemployment, there was no rise of hard Euroscepticism in Portugal. The electoral results of right-wing and left-wing extremist anti-European parties are comparable with those of the previous European elections in 2009 and most of them are not represented in the EP apart from the communist Democratic Unity Coalition (CDU) which obtained 13.71% of votes and three seats.

When looking at Eurosceptic political forces of Member States that have joined the EU following the fourth round of enlargement in 1995, Austria presents a quite specific case (Moreau 2016, 117–147). Indeed, Austrian 'hard' Eurosceptic positions have been represented in the EP since the rise of the right-wing party *Freiheitliche Partei Österreichs* (FPÖ) which already obtained 12.71% of the votes and two seats in the previous European elections in 2009. It managed to consolidate its place in the EP in 2014 by doubling its representation (it won four seats for an increased election turnout of 19.72%). Ideologically, the FPÖ is a hard anti-EU party, but its success at the 2014 European elections is above all the result of the disappearance of all other right-wing extremist groups in Austria. This enabled the FPÖ to attract a far wider range of the Austrian electorate. Furthermore, it appears clearly that opposition against Europe has become a mainstream position in Austria, for the FPÖ is placed only shortly after the two leading political parties, the *Österreichische Volkspartei* (ÖVP) with 26.98% and five seats and the *Sozialdemokratische Partei Österreichs* (SPÖ) with 24.4% and equally five seats in the EP. This mainstream tendency of Austrian Euroscepticism has been amplified by the economic crisis, the rise of unemployment, and immigration.

As for the Scandinavian states, the 2014 European elections reveal two major tendencies. There is a 'traditional' 'soft' Nordic Euroscepticism which has accompanied the European integration process from its start. This has to be differentiated from the rise of new anti-European movements which are reflected in the results of the EP elections. Sweden and Finland are good examples to illustrate this twofold tendency. Since its accession in 1995, Eurosceptic Sweden has adopted an increasingly positive attitude towards the EU (Ersson 2016, 81–86). But anti-Europeanism enjoyed something of a renaissance due to the electoral success of the new populist Sweden Democrats (SD) in 2014: they achieved a score of 9.91% of votes and were accorded two seats in the EP. However, this party does not primarily fight the EU as a regional integration community, but more specifically its impact on immigration. It champions anti-EU views particularly with regard to this issue. In Finland, too, no party strives for the country's withdrawal from the EU. The five anti-EU extra-parliamentary parties that ran MEP candidates for the EP in 2014 only obtained 1.2% of the total vote and no seat (Arter 2016, 111–112). However, mostly due to the Finish single transferable vote, Eurosceptic candidates were able to win a quarter of the votes at the 2014 European elections. Especially the more 'soft' Eurosceptic parties, that is, the True Finns, Christian Democrats, and Left Alliance, together managed to attract 27.4% of the electorate (with three seats in the EP) and some notable Eurosceptic candidates in other parties got also elected.

In Central and Eastern Europe, the situation is again very specific. Much success of Eurosceptic parties in the European elections 2014 can be traced back to a growing disappointment with the Union and a disillusioning process after the initial enthusiasm of having joined the EU. When looking at the individual Members States, they experience in fact very different forms of Euroscepticism. Czech 'hard' Eurosceptic movements are, for example, still very weak. At the 2014 European elections, anti-EU party positions had little importance (Kaniok 2016, 157–158). Still, there were Eurosceptic candidates, mainly from the Communists (KSČM), the Civic Democrats (ODS), and the Party of Free Citizens (SSO), but they did not achieve their expected outcome: the Communists ended fourth with 10.98% of the votes and lost one seat with regard to the previous period (three instead of four) and the ODS only attracted 7.67% of votes dropping from seven to two seats. The only Eurosceptic winner was the SSO which obtained one seat with a turnout of 5.24%. Compared to the Czech Republic, the Slovak situation, however, shows a major increase of 'hard' Euroscepticism. Whereas at the end of the 1990s, all political parties had responded positively to European integration due to the prospect of EU membership, by the end of the 2000s, Euroscepticism within the party system had substantially grown (Spáč 2016, 163–166). Due to the disenchantment with the EU, four Eurosceptic parties ranging from the liberal to the right-wing extremist spectrum thus competed successfully at the 2014 European elections: the liberal Sloboda a Solidarita (SaS) (6.7% of votes), the populist Obyčajni Ludia a nezávislé osobnosti (OLaNO) (7.5% of votes, one seat), the nationalist Slovenská národná strana (SNS) (3.6% of votes), and the extreme right Ludová strana Naše Slovensko (LSNS) (1.7% of votes). However, whereas the SaS and OLaNO, respectively, obtained one seat in the EP, the latter two forces are finally not represented in the EP. Therefore, the established political parties which maintain their positive stance on the EU still weigh within the EP. In contrast to this, in Hungary, anti-Europeanism is much more pronounced. There are profound changes of the Hungarian party system since the accession to the EU in 2004. Being faced with the downside of European integration, that is, the political and social consequences of long-term economic austerity policies in order to comply with the economic criteria for EU membership, national pride has grown to the extent that Euroscepticism is prevailing in almost every political party (Csingár 2016, 185–190). At the 2014 European elections, predominantly 'hard' Eurosceptic positions were advocated, even though their form and intensity differed. The main anti-EU force remains the right-wing extremist *Jobbik* party which reached a similar score compared to the 2009 election (14.67% of votes and three seats in the EP).

An interesting insight into the multifaceted picture of Eurosceptic political parties in the EP can be drawn from the analysis of the 2014 European elections in the Baltic States. Euroscepticism has very different origins there as the cases of Estonia and Latvia show. In Estonia, the rejection of the EU mirrors the distrust of the Estonian political elite rather than 'true' anti-EU attitudes (Alatalu 2016, 197–202). The Estonian people indeed turned away from the three established pro-EU political parties—the Reform Party, the Pro Patria and Res Publica Union (PRU), and the Social Democrats—which together collected only 36.2% of the votes. They preferred to give their votes to individual candidates and this explains the electoral success of some independent Eurosceptic politicians who entered the EP as protest candidates. However, the EU-critical Centre party obtained a share of 22.4% of votes (one seat). In contrast to this general trend of growing Euroscepticism in Estonia, the Latvian population—including the Russian speakers—is generally (still) pro-EU. Euroscepticism is more likely fueled by the Russian language media controlled by Russia. Here, the roots of Euroscepticism are rather domestic and connected with the treatment of the Russian-speaking minority in Latvia (Rozenvalds 2016, 213–216). However, in the EP elections 2014, the National Coalition (Col. Na) which is part of the Eurosceptic ECR faction was ranked second in the country with 14.25% of votes (but only one seat in the EP).

This selective and comparative state by state analysis of the 2014 European elections leads to two major conclusions concerning Euroscepticism. First, there has been a progressive and substantial increase in the representation of both 'hard' and 'soft' Eurosceptic political parties in the EP after 2014 and this is the case for most of the 28 Member States of the EU including those who founded the European Community in 1957. Second, the election results in each country reveal a non-homogeneous picture of Eurosceptic and anti-European parties ranging from the far left-wing spectrum to far right-wing populist parties. The character of these political parties is multi-facetted and the motives for opposition to Europe of their electorate are variable. There seems to be no coherent thread neither for a standard Eurosceptic political party type nor a standard anti-European voter in Europe.

Furthermore, this country-specific analysis of the 2014 European elections must be placed into a larger political and historical context in order to grasp the deeper roots of Euroscepticism.

4   EUROSCEPTICISM IN THE EP: A DEEPLY ROOTED PHENOMENON?

Going beyond this comparative state by state analysis of rising Eurosceptic political forces in the 2014 EP elections, three supplementary factors ought to be considered.

First, the examination of this phenomenon should not over-emphasize the current situation. Previous research of political scientists and recent findings of contemporary historians have indicated that Euroscepticism and anti-Europeanism have been widely known phenomena well before the 2014 European elections (Wassenberg et al. 2010; Gainar and Libera 2013; Libera et al. 2016). It is widely known that from the 1980s, political scientists have started to identify Euroscepticism entering the British political arena with Margaret Thatcher's rejection of the European Community (Spiering 2004, 127–150; Usherwood 2013, 75–87). Historically, Euroscepticism can be even traced back much further: opposition to Europe is in fact as old as the idea of European integration itself. Numerous European projects that existed in the interwar period of the 1920s and 1930s, for example, failed due to the generally anti-integrationist attitude of this period (Bitsch 2010, 19–27). Contemporary historians also point out that Euro-pessimism existed during the early crises of the process of European integration, for example, during de Gaulle's policy of the empty chair in 1965 or during the period of Euro-sclerosis in the 1970s (Crespy and Verschueren 2010, 121–141).

Second, it is important for the analysis of Eurosceptic and anti-EU movements in the EP to study this political phenomenon within its global sociopolitical and societal context. Since the early 1990s at the latest, opposition against the EU has become a generalized European problem concerning large parts of the population within the EU. Since the Danish rejection of the Maastricht Treaty in 1992 and the very narrow French majority for this further step towards European integration, Euroscepticism has been on a steady rise and has in fact become a major problem for the EU (Wassenberg 2016, 27–39). The negative reactions at various referenda on European Treaties—the European Treaty of Nice in 2001, the European Constitution in 2004, or the Lisbon Treaty in 2007—demonstrate the end of the so-called permissive consensus on European integration, that is, the end of the passive acceptance of this process by the European citizens (Lindberg and Scheingold 1970). Reasons persistently named for the loss of this 'permissive consensus' are 'the lack of political legitimacy' of the EU institutions, the remoteness of the Brussels bureaucracy, and the failure to explain the elitist construction of the European institutions to the citizens. Thus, a part of the growing success of anti-EU political parties may also result from the rise of 'public' Euroscepticism (Bernard 2016, 39).

Third, when identifying anti-European and Eurosceptic movements, we have to take into consideration, that since the 1990s, within the political spectrum, the 'classic' marginal parties from the left- or right-wing extreme camp (neo-communist, post-communist, national populist, and right-wing extremist groups) are no longer the exclusive advocators of Euroscepticism (Müller-Härlin 2010, 141–153). In addition, new anti-EU parties have entered the scene (e.g. the Five Star Movement in Italy, *Podemos* in Spain, or the AfD in Germany) while some mainstream parties (the British Conservatives or French neo-Gaullists) also continue to champion 'soft' or 'hard' Eurosceptic positions. For this reason, Euroscepticism and anti-Europeanism prove to be a particularly complex phenomenon which is neither homogeneous in its political expression nor evenly distributed, uniform, or equally strong in all European countries.

As a consequence, while analyzing the successes of Eurosceptic and anti-EU political forces at European elections certainly helps to deliver a first key for the understanding of resistance to Europe, in order to give them a true meaning, it is necessary to integrate 'historical' elements into the analysis, namely, to confront them systematically with the respective chronological and national contexts. Indeed, political scientists have already studied how opposition to Europe is rooted and constructed within certain national political spaces—a methodology similar to a historical approach (Harmsen and Spiering 2004; Neumayer and Zalewski 2008). They focus their research on cultural and historical variables, for example, by analyzing national discourses on European integration. However, these studies have also resulted in an ever-growing differentiation of the phenomenon of opposition to the EU and make it very difficult to attempt comparative analyses (Hamman 2010, 39–61). This differentiation has also led to the introduction of a new terminology on Euroscepticism proposing a whole series of options in order to examine certain aspects of the subject: Euro-indifference, Euro-phobia, Euro-realism, critical Europeanists, and Euro-cynic (Abst and Krouwel 2007). Until today, the different scientific approaches to Euroscepticism and anti-Europeanism have not managed to provide for neither a unique definition of the concept nor for a homogeneous analysis of origins, actors, and forms of appearance.

The analysis of Eurosceptic forces in European elections also focusses on only one specific actor of Euroscepticism, that is, the political party. But there are many others (Blanc 2010, 449–461): indeed, one must consider the sociocultural origins and motivations of Eurosceptic movements in general, be it political parties or other groupings and their supporters (or electorate). The analysis is not necessarily unanimous: some identify the process of European integration as an affair reserved for political elites and 'superior societal classes' thus pointing to the lower classes of the population as the most probable clients for anti-European movements (Trefás 2010, 249–269). Others allocate Eurosceptic positions mainly to the political spectrum of left-wing or right-wing extremist parties (Lang 2010, 61–93). Still others speak of argumentative models of opposition to European integration to be potentially found in every political party (Müller-Härlin 2010, 142–143). Thus, mainstream political parties might also become anti-EU or Eurosceptic and this is not necessarily visible at first sight when looking at the seat distribution, factions, and group affiliations within the EP. Whether focusing on socioeconomic groups of the population or on political parties, the study of actors opposing Europe finally shows a wide range of possibilities for analysis: there is no such thing as a typical Eurosceptic actor or political party, but any actor might potentially partake in the process of resistance to Europe (Wassenberg 2011, 95). The anti-European labeled political forces in the EP can thus be interpreted as the top of the iceberg under which many other Eurosceptic tendencies might be hidden.

For historians, the question of chronology also remains a guiding principle for understanding the process of opposition to European integration. Some dates emerge already as key moments or turning points for the rise of Euroscepticism: the year 1979 marked both a step forward in the democratization of the EU's institutional system and in the emergence of a Euro-pessimistic current in conjunction with the economic crisis (Bitsch 2016, 13–14). Citizens grasped the opportunity presented by the first EP elections by universal suffrage not only to express their satisfaction with finally being involved in European integration but also to express their disinterest or criticism for an organization that had failed to solve the problems of the economic crisis. 1986 could be considered a period low in Euroscepticism thanks to the dynamism of the Commission chaired by Jacques Delors, the Single European Act which opened up new perspectives, the accession of Spain and Portugal who had recently returned to democracy, and to the adoption of the European symbols of the flag and anthem. But this hypothesis remains to be confirmed: in 1992, the year in which the Single European Market was accomplished, the Maastricht Treaty was rejected at first by the Danes and ratified in France only after a narrowly won referendum. Was there finally not so much support for a Europe without borders? Maastricht seems to have opened the floodgates to Euroscepticism that was gaining ground in more or less all of the Member States. 2004–2005 represented another highlight with the great enlargement to the East which was sometimes poorly accepted in the West; the no vote from the French and the Dutch for the European Constitution which was indeed abandoned before even the most hostile of countries to this project were able to express their opinion. The Lisbon Treaty in 2009 never received the support that would have been necessary to protect the EU from growing Euroscepticism (Berrod 2010, 109–121). The weakening of the Euro zone, which was exposed in 2010, gave also way to a multifaceted crisis (economic, political, institutional, identity) which were the background to the success of anti-European forces at the 2014 elections (Clavert 2010, 195–207). Finally, in 2015, the Brexit seems to indicate the peak of anti-Europeanism and its disastrous consequences for the EU.

The chronology shows that the European elections and their outcome since 1979 are only screenshots of a general development of growing discontent of the people with the European integration process. And the EP elections are not the only measure scale for this discontent: the frequently organized referenda in EU Member States on the successive European Treaty reforms indicate just as well whether part of the European population is 'for' or 'against' the EU (Rambour 2010, 93). Thus, the Maastricht Treaty of 1992 was only adopted by a small majority of 51% in France and rejected by 51.7% of the Danish population. In Ireland, European referenda were two occasions to express public opposition to the EU: the Irish rejected the Treaty of Nice in 2001 with a 53.9% majority and the Treaty of Lisbon in 2008 with a 53.2% majority. And most significantly, the European Constitution failed in 2005 when two founding member states of the EU organized a referendum on the issue: it was in fact rejected by 55% of French voters and by 61.5% of Dutch voters. This unattended outcome posed the question of whether Euroscepticism was indeed becoming a more and more generalized trend among the European people.

5   CONCLUSION

The 2014 European elections have undoubtedly led to an increase of Eurosceptic and anti-EU political forces in the EP: the three main European factions in the EP—ECR, GUE-NGL, and EFDD—have strengthened their electorate in comparison to 2009. At the right-wing side of the spectrum, the ECR won 70 against 57 seats in the previous period and the EFDD won 48 against 31, whereas at the left-wing side, the GUE-NGL almost doubled its seats with 67 against 35. Furthermore, by 2015 a new hard Eurosceptic faction had been created in the EP, the ENF, which is composed of right-wing extreme populist parties. This is without counting the numerous Eurosceptic voices of candidates who belong to the other European factions in the EP which are normally labeled as being pro-European.

Euroscepticism has therefore become, it seems, a kind of generic expression for opposition to Europe that is gaining ground in many parties, including the governing ones (e.g. Mark Rutte's People's Party for Freedom and Democracy (VVD) in the Netherlands or Viktor Orbán's Hungarian Civic Alliance Fidesz in Hungary), many of which are divided on European issues. The 'soft' and 'hard' versions of Euroscepticism certainly deserve to be explored in all their finer aspects. Whereas the anti-EU factions in the EP are more radical, generally defending sovereignism over European integration and going as far as to push for the exit of their respective national states from the EU, the soft Eurosceptics adopt a more constructive attitude wanting a different Europe, a 'better' Europe, or even more European cooperation, but still more or less demonstrating a systematic hostility to the EU. The 2014 EP results thus reveal a paradoxical link between European elections and Euroscepticism: on the one hand, the hard Eurosceptic political forces oppose the ideological foundations of the EU including the institution for which they apply as members—the European Parliament. On the other hand, within the EP, the presence of 'hard' Eurosceptic political forces might also be interpreted as a proof for the correct functioning of the very principle of democracy.

Overall, the alarming results of growing Eurosceptic political forces in the EP in 2014 have to be analyzed beyond the current crises of the EU—be it economic, financial, the migration crisis, or the terrorist threats. They are the expression of a deeply rooted phenomenon of opposition to Europe which has existed since the very beginning of the process of European integration in the 1950s and which has been amplified since then. It concerns not only political parties, but all sorts of public and private actors—economic, social, political—and ultimately the European people who are the ones casting their votes to Eurosceptic parties at the EP elections. There is thus evidence in the history of European integration of a moving away from the European idea, specifically from the EU.

There are many words to use when talking about this opposition or waning interest in the EU—disinterest, disaffection, disenchantment, disappointment, disillusionment, hopelessness—and the list of grievances, too, is very long. The EU has been criticized for its institutional complexity, its opacity, its bureaucratic functioning, its liberal or indeed 'ultraliberal' orientation, or rather its excessive or even 'pernickety' interference, especially its inability to protect citizens from the harmful effects of globalization, unemployment, immigration, the high cost of living and also its inability to guarantee peace at the gates of Europe: yesterday in the Balkans, now in Ukraine, or even in Syria or Africa. As for whether Europe is responsible for all evils, sometimes it does not take much: the EU—'Brussels'—easily becomes a scapegoat. In order to stop the progress of anti-EU political forces in the EP, one has to therefore think about a new approach to the European public debate which gives room not only for criticism against but also for support of the EU.

References

Abst, K., & Krouwel, A. (2007). Varieties of Euroscepticism and Populist Mobilization: Transforming Attitudes from Mild Euroscepticism to Harsh Eurocynicism. *Acta Politica, 42*(2–3), 252–270.

Alatalu, T. (2016). Estonia: Party-Based EU Loyalty, Our-Guy-In-The-EP-Based Euroscepticism and the Russian's Attitude still Unclear. In: Moreau and Wassenberg, pp. 197–219.

Alexandre-Collier, A. (2016). The British Conservative Party and the 2014 European Elections: Towards Harder Euroscepticism? In: Moreau and Wassenberg, pp. 85–99.

Arter, D. (2016). The Case of the Eurosceptic Tail Wagging the Dog? The 2014 European Parliament Election in Finland. In: Moreau and Wassenberg, pp. 103–117.

Backes, U. (2016). Varianten des antieuropäischen Extremismus und die Europawahlen 2014. In: Moreau and Wassenberg, pp. 47–71.

Bernard, E. (2013). Déficit démocratique et Parlement européen. In M. Gainar & M. Libera (Eds.), *Contre l'Europe? Anti-européisme, euroscepticisme et alter-européisme dans la construction européenne de 1945 à nos jours (Volume 2): Acteurs institutionnels, milieux politiques et société civile* (pp. 157–175). Stuttgart: Steiner-Verlag.

Bernard, E. (2016). L'élection européenne de 2014: Vers une Union plus démocratique? In M. Libera, S. Schirmann, & B. Wassenberg (Eds.), *Abstentionnisme, euroscepticisme et anti-européisme dans les élections européennes de 1979 à nos jours* (pp. 31–45). Stuttgart: Steiner Verlag.

Berrod, F. (2010). La persistance des résistances à l'Europe: quelles solutions juridiques? In: Wassenberg, Clavert, Hamman and Philippe, pp. 109–121.

Bertoncini, Y., & Chopin, T. (2014). *Des visages sur des clivages. Les élections européennes de mai 2014.* Paris: Notre Europe, Etudes et rapports.

Bitsch, M.-T. (2010). Préface. In: Wassenberg, Clavert and Hamman, pp. 19–27.

Bitsch, M.-T. (2016). Introduction. In: Libera, Schirmann and Wassenberg, pp. 15–31.

Blanc, M. (2010). Postface: rêves d'Europe. In: Wassenberg, Clavert and Hamman, pp. 449–489.

Clavert, F. (2010). Les concepts et fondements théoriques de l'opposition à l'euro. In: Wassenberg, Clavert and Hamman, pp. 195–207.

Costa, O. (2001). *Le Parlement européen, assemblée délibérante.* Brussels: Editions de l'Université de Bruxelles.

Courrier International. (2014, May 26). Européennes 2014. La grande victoire de l'abstention, Paris.

Crespy, A., & Verschueren, N. (2010). Les résistances à l'Europe: une approche interdisciplinaire des conflits sur l'intégration européenne. In: Wassenberg, Clavert and Hamman, pp. 121–141.

Csingár, P. (2016). Der parteipolitische Euroskeptizismus der Gegenwart und der letzten Jahre in Ungarn. In: Moreau and Wassenberg, pp. 181–197.

Cunha, A. (2016). The 2014 European Parliament Elections in Portugal and the Lost Cause of Anti-Europeanism. In: Moreau and Wassenberg, pp. 67–81.

Deloye, Y. (Ed.). (2005). *Dictionnaire des élections européennes.* Paris: Economica.

Easton, D. (1965). *A Systems Analysis of Political Life.* New York: John Wiley.

Elorza, A. (2016). Podemos: The Road to Power. In: Moreau and Wassenberg, pp. 27–41.

Ersson, S. (2016). The 2014 European Election in Sweden and Euroscepticism. In: Moreau and Wassenberg, pp. 81–103.

Fabbrini, S. (2015). *Which European Union? Europe After the Euro Crisis.* Cambridge: Cambridge University Press.

Gainar, M., & Libera, M. (Eds.). (2013). *Contre l'Europe? Ani-européisme, euroscepticisme et alter-européisme dans la construction européenne de 1945 à nos jours (Volume 2): Acteurs institutionnels, milieux politiques et société civile.* Stuttgart: Steiner Verlag.

Hamman, P. (2010). Un regard sociologique: penser les résistances à la construction européenne, des concepts aux territoires. In: Wassenberg, Clavert and Hamman, pp. 39–61.

Hanley, D. (2016). The UK Independence Party: Gathering Up the Periphery? In Moreau and Wassenberg, pp. 113–131.

Harmsen, R., & Spiering, M. (Eds.). (2004). *Euroscepticism: Party Politics, National Identity and European Integration.* Amsterdam: Rodopi.

Hastings, M. (2005). Les élections européennes de juin 2004. In: Deloye, pp. 536–554.

Ivaldi, G. (2016). Le Front National and the Politics of Euroscepticism in France. In: Moreau and Wassenberg, pp. 131–149.

Jauzein, M. (2016). Evolutions institutionnelles et élections européennes: une analyse à la lumière du processus d'adoption du traité de Lisbonne. In: Libera, Schirmann and Wassenberg, pp. 45–63.

Kaniok, P. (2016). Eurosceptics we Remain? Czech Republic, Euroscepticism and the 2014 EP Election. In: Moreau, Wassenberg, pp. 147–163.

Konstantinidis, I. (2016). Anti-Europeanism on the Rise: The Case of Greece. In: Moreau and Wassenberg, pp. 41–55.

Kopecky, P., & Mudde, C. (2002). The Two Sides of Euroscepticism: Party Positions on European Integration in East Central Europe. *European Union Politics, 3*(3), 297–326.

Lacroix, J., & Coman, R. (Eds.). (2007). *Les résistances à l'Europe. Cultures nationales, idéologies et stratégies d'acteurs.* Brussels: Université de Bruxelles.

Lang, S. (2010). Kein Integrationsfortschritt ohne Kritik. Die Funktion Europakritischer Positionen für die Weiterentwicklung der europäischen Integration. In: Wassenberg, Clavert and Hamman, pp. 61–93.

Lefèbvre, J.-B. (2005). Le Parlement européen: expression d'une démocratie européenen? In E. Du Réau, C. Manigand, & T. Sandu (Eds.), *Dynamiques et résistances politiques dans le nouvel espace européen* (pp. 161–167). Paris: Harmattan.

Libera, M. (2016). Le succès des anti-Européens aux élections européennes de 2014: le poids de l'Histoire, la responsabilité des politiques européennes et le concours de la conjoncture. In Moreau and Wassenberg, pp. 39–47.

Libera, M., Schirmann, S., & Wassenberg, B. (Eds.). (2016). *Abstentionnisme, euroscepticisme et anti-européisme dans les élections européennes de 1979 à nos jours*. Stutgart: Steiner-Verlag.

Lindberg, L., & Scheingold, S. (1970). *Europe's Would-Be Polity: Patterns of Change in the European Community*. New Jersey: Prentice Hall.

Moreau, P. (2016). The FPÖ: A Winner Party? The 2014 Elections to the European Parliament Compared with the 2013 Legislative Elections. In: Moreau and Wassenberg, pp. 117–147.

Moreau, P., & Wassenberg, B. (Eds.). (2016a). *European Integration and new Anti-Europeanism I, The 2014 European Election and the Rise of Euroscepticism in Western Europe*. Stuttgart: Steiner Verlag.

Moreau, P., & Wassenberg, B. (Eds.). (2016b). *European Integration and new Anti-Europeanism II, The 2014 European Election and New Anti-European Forces in southern, Northern and Eastern Europe*. Stuttgart: Steiner Verlag.

Müller-Härlin, M. (2010). Die Gegner Europas: Argumentationsmuster im politischen Diskurs. In: Wassenberg, Clavert and Hamman, pp. 141–155.

Neu, V. (2016). Die AFD in Deutschland. In: Moreau and Wassenberg, pp. 149–169.

Neumayer, R. A., & Zalewski, F. (Eds.). (2008). *L'Europe contestée. Espaces et enjeux des positionnements contre l'intégration européenne*. Paris: Lignes de Repères.

Otjes, S., & Voerman, G. (2016). Four flavours of Euroscepticism in the Netherlands. In: Moreau and Wassenberg, pp. 185–205.

Pasquinucci, D. (2016). 'Second Generation' Euroscepticism: The Five Star Movement and the European Union. In: Moreau and Wassenberg, pp. 169–185.

Rambour, M. (2010). Les oppositions à l'Europe sont-elles structurées politiquement ? In: Wassenberg, Clavert and Hamman, pp. 93–109.

Rambour, M. (2016). Des élections européennes sans électeurs? De quelques caractéristiques électorales (1979–2009). In M. Libera, S. Schirmann, & B. Wassenberg (Eds.), (pp. 63–79).

Reif, K., & Schmitt, H. (1980). Nine Second-Order National Elections: A Conceptual Framework for the Analysis of European Elections. *European Journal of Political Research, 8*(1), 3–45.

Rovny, J. (2004). *Conceptualising Party-Based Euroscepticism: Magnitude and Motivations*. Bruges: College of Europe.

Rozenvalds, J. (2016). Russian-speakers in Latvia: Between Brussels, Riga and Moscow. In: Moreau and Wassenberg, pp. 219–235.

Spáč, P. (2016). Anti-Europeanism and Euroscepticism in Slovakia. In: Moreau and Wassenberg, pp. 163–181.

Spiering, M. (2004). British Euroscepticism. In R. Harmsen & M. Spiering (Eds.), *Euroscepticism: Party Politics, National Identity and European Integration* (pp. 127–150). Amsterdam: Rodopi.

Stergiou, A. (2016). Euroscepticism in Cyprus. In: Moreau and Wassenberg, pp. 55–67.

Taggart, P., & Szerbiak, A. (Eds.). (2008). *Opposing Europe? The Comparative Party Politics of Euroscepticism*. Oxford: Oxford University Press.

Tournier-Sol, K. (2016). The 2014 Elections to the European Parliament in the UK; The United Kingdom Independence Party (UKIP) and the British National Party (BNP). In: Moreau and Wassenberg, pp. 99–113.

Trefás, D. (2010). Die Vielfalt des Euroskeptizismen in der öffentlichen Kommunikation: eine Analyse der Debatte um die europäische Verfassung 2005 in der deutschen und britischen Kommunikationsarena. In: Wassenberg, Clavert and Hamman, pp. 249–269.

Usherwood, S. (2013). Margaret Thatcher and British Opposition to European Integration: Saint or Sinner? In: Gainar, Libera, pp. 75–87.

Veivodová, P. (2016). The Anti-EU Groups in the European Parliament. In: Moreau and Wassenberg, pp. 71–85.

Wassenberg, B. (2007). Les campagnes pour les élections européennes de 1979, en France et en Allemagne. In B. Marie-Thérèse, W. Loth, & C. Barthel (Eds.), *Cultures politiques, opinions publiques et intégration européenne* (pp. 263–284). Bruylant: Brussels.

Wassenberg, B. (2011). Regards croisés sur la construction européenne. Diversité des coopérations et des résistances à l'Europe. Habilitation Thesis, vol. 1, Strasbourg.

Wassenberg, B. (2016). European Integration and New Anti-Europeanism. In: Moreau and Wassenberg, pp. 27–39.

Wassenberg, B., Clavert, F., & Hamman, P. (Eds.). (2010). *Contre l'Europe ?, Anti-européisme, euroscepticisme et alter-européisme dans la construction européenne de 1945 à nos jours (Volume I) : les concepts*. Stuttgart: Steiner Verlag.

CHAPTER 14

Migration Policies Debates in the European Parliament: Does the Mainstream Right Stand Its Ground?

Brice Cristoforetti and Lara Querton

1   INTRODUCTION

The last decade has seen two major crises severely hitting the European Union (EU) and its member states. Since 2008, EU countries have been struggling to recover their economic health after the explosion of the debt crisis and its economic follow-up. Over the same years, EU countries have had to cope with unprecedented waves of migration especially in the aftermath of the Arab Spring and as a result of the war in Syria. EU member states were faced with different levels of pressures and contributed differently to responding to these two challenges. Yet in all cases, economic and migration policies have experienced heavily debated evolutions.

In this crisis context, the party competition in Europe was shattered by new or challenger parties defying traditional political actors (Hobolt 2015). Turning their back on the latter, voters shaped their preferences on issues directly linked to these European crises affecting their daily lives: the austerity measures, the migration phenomenon and the level of European

B. Cristoforetti (✉) • L. Querton
College of Europe, Bruges, Belgium
e-mail: brice.cristoforetti@sciencespo-lyon.fr; lara.querton@ulb.ac.be

© The Author(s) 2019   299
O. Costa (ed.), *The European Parliament in Times of EU Crisis*,
European Administrative Governance,
https://doi.org/10.1007/978-3-319-97391-3_14

integration. In Greece, the socialist PASOK reached unprecedented electoral lows, mirroring a similar situation, albeit to a lesser extent, in France or in the UK. Simultaneously, peripheral parties such as *Syriza* in Greece, the *Five Star Movement* in Italy, the *Front National* in France or *Alternative für Deutschland* in Germany gained momentum and increased their electoral shares.

In the wake of the 2014 European elections, the erosion of mainstream parties could also be witnessed within the European Parliament (EP), where both the conservative (*European People's Party* or EPP) and the liberal (*Alliance of Liberals and Democrats for Europe* or ALDE) groups lost prominence (going from 35.8% and 10.8% of the votes to 29.4% and 8.9%, respectively). The *Socialists and Democrats* (S&D) conversely managed to remain stable (from 25.6% to 25.4%). The radical left and the Eurosceptic conservatives conversely won new seats. On the right side of the political spectrum, the *European Conservatives and Reformists* group (ECR) became the third most important group and *Europe of Freedom and Democracy* (EFD) also reinforced its presence due to the UK Independence Party (UKIP) electoral results and the decision of the Italian *Five Star Movement* to join the group. Furthermore, the *Europe of Nations and Freedom* group's (ENF) establishment in June 2015 added 39 members to the far right and Eurosceptic institutionally organized fringe.

In the light of this institutional development, it is of particular interest to determine whether this consolidated peripheral right-wing political force could affect the 'diminished' mainstream policy position, as expressed in its public discourses, or if the mainstream is 'too big to change'. At the European partisan level, this phenomenon remains unexplored so far, yet this is of importance.

As a powerful democratic actor, the EP is co-legislator for most of the European laws. Any significant alteration in the assembly's composition could reconfigure its inter-groups dynamics, impact the policy outcome of some pieces of legislation voted within the EP and eventually affect policies negotiated at the European level.

Tackling this specific political context, the objective of this chapter is to analyse the policy position changes of the mainstream right group (EPP) which is the oldest and biggest political group of the European parliamentary arena. An eight-year period (2009–2017), covering two overlapping crises (i.e. the economic and the migratory crises), has been selected.

This chapter aims at giving an answer to the following question: to what extent does the electoral success of peripheral right groups in the EP inspire changes in the mainstream right group discourses about migration policies? We expect that, following the 2014 European elections, the EPP adapts its migration discourses reflecting a more restrictive position in response to the rise and electoral breakthrough of peripheral right groups.

Including visa policy, the management of temporary and permanent migration as well as refugees, migration policies can be defined as a set of 'informal and formal measures designed to govern the entry, stay and return of migrants' (Hansen 2007, 330). Concentrating on these policies is consistent with our ambition to highlight potential alterations of discourses and positions since the literature shows that, in several cases, European mainstream parties started considering stricter, more nationalist and restrictionist positions on the migration debate in response to the electoral success of populist/radical right parties (Bale et al. 2009; Camia 2013; Harmel and Svasand 1997; Odmalm and Bale 2014; Van Spanje 2010; Camia 2013). Yet, the literature reveals mixed results, which makes a comparison with a study on this topic at the European level enlightening.

The EP as a 'laboratory' gives the researchers the advantage of gathering various ideological groups expressing their beliefs and stances on the same topic at the very same time. By exploiting this fertile ground, we carry out a systematic comparison between the EPP group and three peripheral right groups' (ECR, EFD(D) and ENF) discourses so as to observe two facets of the issue in question. As a first step, we determine whether the EPP discourses over the migration policies have changed over time, and particularly in between the seventh and eighth legislatures. Second, we examine if these potential discursive alterations could be induced by a 'contagion effect' coming from peripheral right groups, which have significantly strengthened after the last European elections. In this perspective, we rely on the literature positing that radical right electoral results do have an influence on mainstream positions with regard to the migration issues. This second aspect is of importance as the mainstream group could also modify its position without automatically accommodating it to the one of its peripheral colleagues, making the contagion effect hypothesis non-evident at the European level.

2   Interactions Between Mainstream and Peripheral Parties

This chapter mainly deals with the interactions between peripheral and mainstream parties, with a double focus: migration policies and the right side of the political spectrum.

Migration policies are topical, very divisive and have often been subject to studies focusing on the impact of the emergence and/or the electoral success of populist and radical parties on their mainstream counterparts. Besides this explanatory factor, parties may also react to other immigration 'shocks' (Odmalm and Bale 2014) as 'multiple factors exist independently of each other and will often create a feedback loop in the political discourse' (Odmalm and Bale 2014, 5). Real-world problems (increase in migration flows), the electorate (the public attention to the migration issue), the media (the media attention to the question of migration) and the party leader (whether after a change of leader, or after a leader's change of opinion) can also have an effect on mainstream parties' responses, positions and strategies (Bale and Partos 2014; Odmalm and Bale 2014).

Our second emphasis—the mainstream and peripheral right-wing groups—stems from the fact that most of the literature on this subject has focused on far-right parties' influence on mainstream parties (on both the right-wing and the left-wing). Green and far-left parties' effects on their mainstream counterparts are understudied (Meijers 2015; Williams and Ishiyama 2018). The same trend holds true when we speak about migration policies. Scholars working on parties have primarily tackled the migration issue in two limited contexts: (1) far-right parties and (2) party competition and positioning (Bale 2008).

One should also note that most of the literature on the influence of peripheral parties on their mainstream colleagues focuses on the national partisan spheres, and hardly ever on the European level. A few studies do examine groups' positions in the EP, but either they don't concretely adopt a longitudinal approach or they don't tackle this particular phenomenon (McElroy & Benoit 2007; Proksch & Slapin 2010; Gianfreda 2018).

Based on these observations, our choice to concentrate on right-wing groups in the EP enables us to first continue exploring this field and second to compare the results with studies having already observed these phenomena in the national political arenas.

Depending on the case under scrutiny (countries, parties, policies, etc.), these studies reveal different results. *On the one hand,* several scholars proved that the electoral score of peripheral parties explains mainstream's change of positions or programmes (see e.g. Harmel and Svasand 1997; Van Spanje 2010; Davis 2012; Camia 2013; Meijers 2015; Abou-Chadi 2016). Some of them used and mobilized the concept of *contagion* to depict alterations of political programmes or shifting of positions in response to peripheral parties' emergence and/or electoral success.

In this first case, however, scholars do not come to the same conclusions with regard to which (mainstream) party is influenced the most. When speaking of policy agenda, right-wing parties would be more prone—rather than left-wing parties—to adjust it in response to radical right success (Abou-Chadi 2016). When speaking about policy position more broadly, some scholars affirm that anti-immigration parties can touch and hit the entire party system and that mainstream right parties are not the ones affected the most (Van Spanje 2010). In the case of Eurosceptic parties' influence, centre-left parties might even be more affected than right-wing parties as they are impacted by both the radical right and radical left successes (Meijers 2015).

On the other hand, some studies do not demonstrate such correlations (see e.g. Rooduijn et al. 2014; Van Heerden et al. 2014) and rather show that contagion effects are weak, inexistent or too difficult to identify. Rooduijn and his colleagues conclude that populism is not contagious, in a sense that mainstream parties' manifestos of five Western European countries have not become more populist or more radical in response to the rise of populist parties over the last two decades (Rooduijn et al. 2014). In the same vein, authors demonstrate that most of the discursive and programmatic changes made by Dutch mainstream parties did not mostly and directly arise from the electoral breakthrough of anti-immigration parties (Van Heerden et al. 2014). In the framework of other studies, some authors suppose that this limited or conditional contagion effect comes from the fact that mainstream parties lack the flexibility to change their position. Being larger than challengers, mainstream parties could be subject to an 'innate conservatism' (Harmel and Svasand 1997), and therefore they might not be prone to make any substantial changes to their programmes in response to the rise and/or electoral success of peripheral parties.

In a nutshell, the literature shows various and heterogeneous results when tackling the influence of the periphery on mainstream's positions. Depending on the case examined, the former may exert a certain influence on the latter.

In this framework, the main objectives of this chapter are precisely to determine (1) if the mainstream right group at the European level has changed its position over time when migration policies have been debated, (2) if any discursive influence coming from peripheral right discourses can be identified and (3) if the post-May 2014 period was a turning point for potential discursive changes, since the eighth legislature has seen a major change in the European right fringe composition with a significant consolidation of the peripheral forces.

3   Methodological Framework

3.1   *The Narrative Policy Framework*

Our discourse analysis consists of the observation and the comparison of discursive elements within the plenary speeches of four political groups. Adopting a constructivist approach, we focus on the elucidation of the groups' policy discursive reality, which is rooted in their policy beliefs and eventually reflects the groups' principles and values. We opted for an analysis at the meso-level, which aims at observing 'the strategic construction and communication of policy narratives to achieve a desired policy goal' (Jones et al. 2014, 15). We indeed state that political groups constitute a type of 'advocacy coalition' that do wish to achieve a policy objective, which we expect to be reflected within their plenary discourses.

For this purpose, we chose the Narrative Policy Framework (NPF) which is a systematic approach to narrative policy analysis in order to qualitatively dissect and examine the policy narratives presented by the Members of the European Parliament (MEPs). According to NPF seminal work, the minimal qualities a narrative must possess to be considered as a narrative are (1) the setting, (2) the plot, (3) the character(s) and (4) the moral of the story (Jones & McBeth 2010).

Applying the NPF, we do believe that stories are paramount for individuals as well as groups, and for the actions they undertake. We thus expect plenary speeches to contain these narrative elements.

The NPF is a recent research framework that emerged in response to a descriptive and interpretative study of narratives in public policy. It arose as 'an effort to apply objective methodological approaches (i.e. science) to a subjective social reality (i.e. policy narratives)' (Jones et al. 2014, 3). While the majority of NPF applications have henceforth made use of quantitative methods, an additional interpretative and inductive NPF has recently materialized for the purposes of processing small sample sizes and of conducting qualitative studies (Gray and Jones 2016). Best reflecting our methodology and operationalization, we also opted for an inductive and more descriptive approach.

This way we expect the NPF to efficiently capture the belief systems of the groups' speakers as elected members from different partisan groups are likely to use distinct narrative content within their narrative structural elements. Considering these narratives as the dependent variable, we aim at examining what influences their construction, positing that the electoral results of the peripheral right-wing groups can play a role.

3.2   Data Collection, Filtering and Sorting

First and foremost, four out of seven groups currently sitting in the EP constitute our case study. One group is considered as 'mainstream' (EPP), while three groups are categorized as peripheral (the ECR group, the *Europe of Freedom and Direct Democracy* [EFDD] group and the ENF group).

We define 'mainstream group' as the largest and oldest political group, which mainly includes national political parties in government. We define 'peripheral groups' as the political groups at the right side of the mainstream formation, which are smaller and more recent than the latter.

Considering these four groups, we applied four selection criteria to collect our data and compose our corpus of analysis. In total, our initial corpus comprised 71 debates, spread over a period of eight years (September 2009 to April 2017).

First, we selected the debates of the seventh and part of the eighth legislatures. This timeframe covers two crises during which European member states have notably experienced a consolidation of peripheral right and left forces, or what could be called a 'fleeing the centre' movement (Hobolt 2015). The latter constitutes our core explanatory variable and thus makes this timeframe particularly relevant for our contagion effect analysis. *Second*, we picked plenary debates tackling migration policies with the help of selected keywords[1] that we identified in the debate titles. *Third*, we privileged plenary speeches over debates in committees, as the former are much more ideological and therefore less technical in comparison to the

---

[1] Asylum; Borders; Expulsion; Frontex; Immigration; Lampedusa; Migrant; Migration; Refugee; Relocation; Resettlement; Schengen; Stockholm Programme; Visa.

Table 14.1   Breakdown of debates per sub-topics

	Border management	*Humanitarian emergencies*	*Asylum and refugees*	*Visa policy*
Number of debates	13	10	16	11
Timeframe	Sept. 2011– Feb. 2017	April 2012–Jan. 2017	April 2010–Dec. 2016	Sept. 2009–April 2017
Number of debates pre- and post-May 2014	9 4	4 6	10 6	7 4

latter. *Fourth*, only the oral intervention of the first speaker of each group has been selected as this first speech is supposed to be the most representative of the overall group policy position on the discussed topic (the groups themselves choose the order in which their MEPs take the floor). This last criterion allows us to work on an aggregated and median position of the groups on each debate, even when several speakers (not inevitably defending similar positions) from the same group take the floor during the same debate.

After grouping the 71 selected debates in sub-topics, four themes stood out from the selected data: (1) border management, (2) humanitarian emergencies, (3) asylum and refugees and (4) visas. Out of the 71 debates, 21 were categorized as unclassifiable, and were removed from the definitive corpus.[2] These four selected categories turned out to be well suited and solid as they highlight complementary facets of migration policies (Table 14.1).[3]

3.3   Coding Process: Dissecting the Groups' Discourses

The main objective of the coding process is to identify the patterns of discursive convergence between the three peripheral groups and the mainstream one. By methodologically dissecting the MEPs' discourses

---

[2] Twenty-one debates were categorized as unclassifiable and were removed from the final corpus. Two other categories, focusing on irregular and regular migration respectively, were not sufficiently substantiated to constitute a relevant cluster. Moreover, a significant number of debates appeared either too horizontal or too specific to be allocated to any of the categories.

[3] Specific descriptions of the clusters can be provided by the authors upon request.

according to the narrative elements, we were also able to see whether the speakers do structure their speeches as a story, with a definable plotline and moral, as well as with several characters (however, assessing the 'narrativity degree' of their plenary speeches was not the focus of the research). From the four minimal narratives' structural elements, we constructed a more detailed and tailor-made codebook (see Appendix), which we further fine-tuned following a preliminary exploration of the two first years of our timeframe (2009–2010).

First, we included five types of characters based on the NPF literature (mostly Shanahan et al. 2013) and specified six types of plots following Deborah Stone's typology of plotlines (Stone 2012; McBeth et al. 2012). *Second,* we detailed the moral category by sub-dividing it into two sub-categories. On the one hand, we included the policy solution envisioned in terms of visa, border management, asylum and humanitarian emergencies. On the other hand, we added the type of actors (or combination of actors) presented in the discourses by the speakers and involved in the aforementioned policy solution as leader(s) or manager(s). *Third,* we added a last category tackling the global speech tone and reflecting the group's general position in order to further examine its sets of values and beliefs with regard to the topic debated.

With the outcome of the coding process, we were able to determine (1) whether and when a discourse's alteration was visible, (2) which group it involved and (3) what type of change was manifest. Knowing exactly when the changes occurred (year/month; sub-theme debated) allowed us to draw parallels between the discourses and the consolidation of peripheral groups, in the sense that, if systematic and significant changes appear after May 2014, we could see a potential correlation between the two.

4 Results

4.1 Border Management

When discussing this topic, the EPP does not mimic the discursive style of any of the three peripheral groups, neither before 2014, nor after. We however observe a slight change in its speeches after 2014, potentially due to the distinct type of debates (from 2013 onwards, the debates have focused more on the external dimension of European borders) put on the agenda. This trend remains yet to be confirmed.

First, the EPP group builds most of its narratives around a positive plot of control. By way of example, the group claims the situation to be under control thanks to the creation of the EUROSUR Agency, or in the case of Romania and Bulgaria joining the Schengen area. Post-May 2014, the group still predominantly states that the current situation is under control thanks to the establishment of Smart Borders and the European Border and Coast Guard Agency. The same trend goes for the ECR, but not for the two remaining peripheral groups, which mostly tell negative stories (in a mix of pessimistic plotlines) before and after the 2014 elections.

Second, the mainstream group is the only one to predominantly support policy recommendations on opening the borders in order to facilitate the free movement of persons, especially inside the Schengen area. In view of this, the reintroduction of (internal) border controls is assimilated with 'a concession to populism and a threat to the common heritage'.[4] However, there might be a tonality alteration in the EPP discourse for this particular category, as the group strongly supports the reinforcement of checks at the external borders with the creation and intervention of additional and new controlling and surveillance agencies. In its post-May 2014 discourses, the group seems to put an emphasis on the principle that reinforced external EU borders are a necessity to the internal freedom of movement. The group clearly re-emphasizes the physical existence of these external borders. In a comparative perspective, the ECR appears to be torn between the different types of policy solutions. Predictably, the EFDD and ENF groups are continuously in favour of restricting the free movement of persons, both inside the EU (e.g. by suspending the entry process to the Schengen scheme for Bulgaria and Romania), as well as from outside the EU (by strongly reinforcing the controls in order to be able to determine who arrives within the member states).

Third, and with regard to the subsidiarity question, the EPP appears divided between an explicit European lead and a clear coordination of both levels of power. Although the group is never favouring a national lead in this matter, it no longer encourages a European management after May 2014 and is more inclined towards a coordinated action. As for the

[4]COELHO (EPP), July 6, 2011.

last narrative element, the ECR group appears to be divided. Conversely, the EFDD and the ENF groups almost always promote a national lead.

Ultimately, half of the EPP group's interventions are explicitly demonstrating a positive tone: Schengen is praised as 'one of the Union's major pillars', as 'freedom in place of borders, cooperation in place of egoism and working together instead of working against one another'.[5] Yet, as time advances, the EPP speakers deliver what we could call 'non-belief-oriented interventions' by focusing on technical aspects of the file or of the procedure. Especially after May 2014, the tone of EPP speeches becomes more and more indefinable, devoid of any clear policy convictions. Once more, the ECR appears as the most heterogeneous group as no trend in its intervention is discernible. The EFDD and ENF provide for either negative or undefined tonalities in their speeches.

In conclusion, and contrary to our expectations, no significant shift in the EPP discursive style and content is observable during this time period. Yet, a sign of alteration seems to appear in three out of the four aforementioned narrative elements, especially in the aftermath of the 2014 elections.

4.2   Humanitarian Emergencies

Looking at the evolution of the narrative patterns over time, the EPP keeps to rather similar narrative designs before and after May 2014 also when debating humanitarian emergencies.

First of all, the period before May 2014 shows the use of rather negative plots by EPP MEPs, which to some extent unsurprisingly reflects the inherently negative aspect of the topic debated. However, the post-May 2014 election period witnessed the appearance of several positive plots inexistent in the previous period. Initially, the EPP built most of its narratives around two antagonistic plot poles: *control* and *helplessness.* If policy solutions are presented and supported (*control*), MEPs present situations without any ready-made solutions at hand (*helplessness*). Mostly, they tackle the overburdening of Lampedusa, deaths in the Mediterranean, and precarious and dangerous living conditions of the migrants arriving in the EU. Unsurprisingly, speeches are especially distressful when Greek EPP

---

[5] WEBER (EPP), July 4, 2017.

MEPs take the floor: 'with Greece bearing 90% of the burden of illegal immigration, things are becoming difficult', 'extremely difficult to manage'[6] and so on.

If we compare with the three other groups, one first notes that the ECR shows very similar narrative patterns to the EPP, all over the time period under consideration. Both the EPP and the ECR alternatively use negative 'illusion'/'helpless' plots and more positive 'control' plots, and both start using the 'control' plots after May 2014. Tackling the worsening situation in Lampedusa in October 2013, when an EPP MEP considers that 'efforts are genuine',[7] he follows by highlighting what the real policy instruments should be, most notably advocating an EU-wide resettlement mechanism. His ECR counterpart highlights the EU's 'inability to manage immigration'.[8] In October 2015, however, both EPP and ECR MEPs are confident about the capacity of the EU to welcome refugees in decent conditions.

Quite clearly, EPP MEPs could not have imitated any other right-wing group on this as the pre-election period showed very negative plots being used by the three other groups under analysis. They all offer rather dramatic accounts of the situation on the ground, especially in terms of refugees' deaths on the road and the incapacity of EU member states to welcome them in a decent way.

Looking at the adequate management of maritime and terrestrial migration roads, the EPP and the ECR share the same tone of ambiguity. Both groups avoid tackling the refugee issue as a matter of 'opening or closing the door', but focus on how to better implement the current rules in the interest of all, while keeping a balance between solidarity and security (including socioeconomic security). EPP MEPs typically emphasize the need 'to keep economic migrants clearly distinguished from refugees who have the right to asylum'.[9]

Another key narrative item is the policy solution that the MEPs offer regarding who should be in charge of dealing with this humanitarian situation. For the EPP, the solution is definitely to be found at the EU level. They therefore request EU instruments to deal with the situation: 'The

---

[6] GIANNAKOU (EPP), April 19, 2012.
[7] IACOLINO (EPP), October 9, 2013.
[8] MUSCARDINI (ECR), October 9, 2013.
[9] IACOLINO (EPP), October 9, 2013.

solution must be at the European level'.[10] After 2014, they propose solutions which give more space to the member states and in which the EU lead is much less dominant. They seem to acknowledge the fact that, even in light of the seriousness of the situation, policy solutions which would need to transfer part of sovereign competencies to the EU were unrealistic or ineffective (e.g. the allocation of refugees towards all EU countries on a systematic basis). On this matter, the EPP could not have imitated any of the three other groups, as both the ECR and the EFDD similarly express policy solutions favouring the EU level before the 2014 elections, and switch to a more coordinated approach with the member states after May 2014.

After 2014, both the EPP's and the ECR's general policy belief on migration is often undefined, probably as they are careful not to judge too quickly, considering the high sensitivity of the topic ('to solve this crisis there is no easy answer'[11]). Their narratives focus on pragmatic discourses dealing with the policy tools at hand. On the contrary, the EFD(D) and the ENF are much less cautious: 'common sense would like us to think first of ours before thinking of others'.[12]

As a conclusion, and when considering this cluster of debates, the EPP narratives are too specific and too antagonistic to those of the EFD(D) and ENF groups to let us spot any kind of discursive contagion following the 2014 European elections. As for a potential contagion from the ECR, the fact that they share very similar narrative patterns with the EPP both before and after the 2014 elections makes it very unlikely.

4.3   Asylum and Refugee Policy

Over the whole period under consideration, the EPP builds most of its stories around a positive plot of *control*, which indicates that things are within the control of actors and policymakers. An exemple for this *control* plot is: 'There are grounds for a Neighbourhood policy finally worthy of the name, for a European Mediterranean Strategy finally worthy of the name'.[13] EPP MEPs often emphasize the positive role played by

---

[10] WOZEMBERG-VRIONIDI (EPP), October 2015.
[11] KAMALL (ECR), April 29, 2015.
[12] AGEA (EFDD), November 25, 2014.
[13] MAURO (EPP), April 4, 2011.

institutional *heroes* and *allies* such as various Commissioners, the Council or other fellow MEPs: 'The Commission's idea for a corrective fairness mechanism is a good step in the right direction'.[14]

Comparing the results before and after the 2014 elections, one can notice that EPP MEPs after 2014 are even more prone to use cues of positive plotlines, showing confidence in the issues being properly tackled. Regarding the peripheral groups, their plots overall evolve on the contrary around stories of decline and self-illusion, both before and after 2014. This refutes any possible contagion from the three other groups, whose typical plot before 2014 was negative. ECR and EFD(D) MEPs are targeting the EU reallocation scheme in particular, which would automatically allocate a certain number of refugees to every member state.

In similar proportion before and after 2014, the *moral* of the EPP narratives predominantly is to open the borders, even if they sometimes present more ambiguous solutions: 'we must distinguish between people who are really persecuted and people who enter illegally'.[15] The three radical right-wing groups have a much more restrictive approach towards borders, and view migration flows much more negatively, expressed in metaphors like 'the asylum tsunami also floods my country'.[16] If there is a breaking point in 2014, it is for the ECR, which moves from statements favouring openness and ambiguity towards tough restrictive statements.

EPP MEPs also want to put EU decision-makers in charge in order to adopt policies at the EU level; a position that doesn't seem at all to have been impacted by the results of the 2014 elections. One can interestingly notice that both the ECR and the EFD(D) are heavily split between the promotion of EU-level action and instruments to deal with migration issues, and their idea that the member states should keep control of migration policies. After 2014, their speeches tend to favour EU-led policy solutions, something the EPP advocated for since 2010. Therefore, if there is contagion, it is certainly not from the periphery towards the mainstream.

In terms of its overall tonality, the EPP group largely tends to have a positive view of refugee migration flows and war migrants. One can note a clear difference between the EPP on one side, and the ENF and EFD(D) on the other side, during the entire period analysed. The EPP seems

---

[14] METSOLA (EPP), May 11, 2016.
[15] WEBER (EPP), October 9, 2013.
[16] MAEIJER (ENF), December 16, 2015.

careful not to use judgmental wording, probably thanks to the sensitivity of the issue, whereas the ENF seems much more confident about adopting a strong judgmental tone. What is more interesting is the fact that the ECR starts out with positive policy statements in the pre-2014 legislature, and rather abruptly changes to negative statements in the next legislature. This results in a blunt 'desynchronization' from the EPP, especially when considering the similarity between these two groups in other narrative aspects.

As a conclusion, dramatic differences between the plots lead us to eliminate the possibility of a real influence of the 2014 election results on the EPP moving closer to the peripheral right groups. The EPP seems simply too independent.

4.4   Visa Policy

When compared to the former clusters of debates, it is even more explicit that there is neither a discursive change nor an adaptation from the EPP that would be significant after the 2014 European elections.

First, and as for the three former sub-topics, the EPP favours positive stories in the form of control plotlines. A clear division appears between two duos: EPP & ECR and EFD(D) & ENF, respectively, developing similar discursive pattern. Without interruption from 2009 until 2017, the EPP and ECR state the situation to be under control by facilitating the visa procedures with the Western Balkans, or, more particularly, by granting visa waivers to Ukrainian and Georgian citizens. On the contrary, the EFD(D) and ENF mostly tell negative stories before and after the 2014 elections.

Second, the same separation applies to the types of policy solutions recommended by the political groups. The EPP and the ECR largely favour extending the list of countries whose citizens are exempt from a visa requirement and promote visa facilitation agreements with non-EU countries such as Ukraine, Moldova or Georgia. Both groups' discourses evolve in a similar manner: before 2014 as much as after, they favour a positive and open development of the European visa policy, by welcoming new members and granting new visa waivers. Contrariwise, the majority of policy solutions of the two remaining peripheral groups envision restrictive measures regarding visa policy.

Third, the duos' dynamics fade when it comes to the subsidiarity issue. The EPP is noticeably encouraging an EU lead on this matter, by notably congratulating the Commission for its initiative or showing strong confidence in its evaluation and role. From September 2009 to April 2017, the EPP persistently presents European actors as the most convenient to be involved in their policy solution. This is much less evident for the ECR group, which again appears divided. As can be expected, the EFD(D) and ENF groups either favour national action or do not specify the actor(s) who should command and manage the policy recommendations envisaged. In the former situation, the groups argue that individual member states must decide who does and who does not enter their country, with the help of 'very well-guarded borders'.[17]

Finally, a clear division between the two pairs is again significant when observing their policy beliefs. All except one EPP speech demonstrate a positive tone, and almost the same trend is observable for the ECR group. From 2009 to 2017, the EPP tone is encouraging, optimistic and positive: promoting stability in the Balkans, notably through 'breaking the sense of isolation',[18] appears as a top priority for the group. Visa waiver is viewed as a 'remarkable tool that allows to connect people and build bridges among populations'.[19] In a completely different view, EFD(D) and ENF speeches' tones are either negative or indefinable. Yet, most of the time, visa exemptions and facilitation agreements are assimilated with illegal immigration or the increase of asylum applications and terrorism.

In conclusion, no imitation or contagion effect is discernible when the four groups debate the European visa policy. The EPP does not develop or adopt the peripheral discursive style and does not demonstrate any sign of accommodation to these discourses over time.

4.5   Aggregated Results

By aggregating and ordering the results in a longitudinal table,[20] we brought out the most frequent types of narrative elements mobilized by the group speakers (a clear distinction is made before and after May 2014 in order to observe the temporal evolution of the respective groups' narratives).

---

[17] KIRKHOPE (ECR), October 9, 2013.
[18] CORAZZA BILDT (EPP), October 6, 2010.
[19] BONI (EPP), April 5, 2017.
[20] The table of aggregated results can be provided by the authors upon request.

Arranged this way, the results confirm that EPP discursive patterns have largely stayed similar over time for the first three narrative components. Two additional results must however be highlighted. *First*, and most significantly, the speech tonality of the group shifts from being mostly positive to being predominantly indefinable. *Second*, we also notice that the group appears less and less firm and determined with regard to the type of policy recommendation to offer. After May 2014, the mainstream group seems more cautious about delivering a policy solution aiming towards opening the borders.

It looks like EPP MEPs integrated the fact that the migratory issue became even more salient within a growingly sceptical public opinion, and that pronouncing an explicitly positive and welcoming speech about the arrival and management of newcomers might simply have become more sensitive and harder.

Without being similar, the EPP 'discursive equation' after May 2014 is the most comparable to the ECR discursive cocktail. The policy solution offered is the only discursive element distinguishing the EPP and the ECR speeches after May 2014. Yet, the similarities observed do not allow for drawing parallels with a discursive contagion effect coming from the peripheral group and affecting the mainstream one. The EPP policy solution after the last European elections does not completely mimic the direction of its peripheral counterpart, which is clearly announcing restrictive recommendations.

In any case, neither the EFD(D) nor the newly established ENF group could pretend being discursive influencers of their mainstream counterpart.

5   Concluding Remarks

Focusing on migration policies, the current chapter aimed at determining the extent to which the electoral success of peripheral right-wing groups within the EP (ECR, EFD(D) and ENF) led to a change in mainstream right-wing group (EPP) discourses. Relying on the strand of the literature positing that peripheral right parties' electoral results can affect mainstream positions on migration issues (Abou-Chadi 2016; Bale and Partos 2014; Harmel and Svasand 1997; Van Spanje 2010), we assumed that the EPP group accommodates its discourses towards a more restrictive position in the aftermath of the 2014 European elections. We expected to spot 'discursive contagion effects' coming from the peripheral groups and affecting mainstream discourses.

However, this initial assumption could not be verified. Contrary to our expectations, the EPP group showed a high level of discursive independence towards the three peripheral right groups as if the altered political composition of the European parliamentary assembly had no effect on its position and discourses. With few and minor exceptions, the EPP narrative patterns have kept a distinct content and have stayed similar over time. A change in discourse is yet somewhat apparent in some clusters of debates, but should be further corroborated with the analysis of the remaining debates of the 8th legislature. Furthermore, no significant difference could be perceived in the EPP's discursive evolution over the four topics of debates.

In this perspective, the EPP group might be 'too big to change', and this interpretation would be in line with the strand of the literature not demonstrating strong correlations in between mainstream parties' change of positions, discourses or programmes and the electoral success of their peripheral counterparts. With this in mind, we can probably state that, being *the* policymaker group in the EP, the biggest and oldest group, the EPP, appears to be immune to a peripheral contagion coming from the right of the mainstream right.

We could also modestly connect our results with the extensive study of the political contestation at the supranational level as this research also sheds some light on how the partisan cleavage determines or structures plenary speeches of right-wing MEPs regarding the migration issue.

We would have expected the structuration around the left-right axis at the EP to be more significant. In other words, we anticipated to see more convergent elements between the four groups, as altogether they form the right fringe in the assembly. However, this did not turn out to be the case, as each group tends to develop its own discursive style on the migration issue. Yet, if a group analogy were to be made, two pairs (namely EPP/ECR and EFD(D)/ENF) would be the most accurate ones. This division often emerged as an internal cleavage to the right side of the European political spectrum, especially when visa policy is debated.

Focusing on an extremely topical policy, our study's findings can be summarized as follows. First, substantial alterations in the political composition of the parliamentary assembly do not significantly affect mainstream group positions and discourses on this particular topic, as no significant discursive changes could be observed in the aftermath of the 2014 European elections on the analysed policies. Second, to the positioning on the European political spectrum corresponds a distinct discursive content. No significant discursive contagion effect could be identified when MEPs discussed migration policies between 2009 and 2017. It remains clear however that further study should be carried out to extend the timeframe under scrutiny—the results of the forthcoming European elections might be decisive—and to incorporate new topics to allow for comparison between different policies. Interviews with MEPs, parliamentary assistants and groups' staff would prove very helpful. Additional explanatory factors, such as national pressures on individual MEPs and delegations, migration pressures and their media coverage, or public opinion with regard to the migration issue, could be controlled for as well.

Appendix

Table 14.2 Codebook of narrative elements

Narrative elements	Codes	Description
Policy setting		Specific context of the policy narrative; basic assumptions of the policy controversy
Characters	Ally	Entity identified as holding a policy position with which the author of the discourse agrees
	Hero	Entity praised for potentially correcting the situation
	Opponent	Entity identified as holding a policy position with which the author of the discourse disagrees
	Victim	Entity portrayed as mistreated and/or harmed
	Villain	Entity blamed for some wrongdoing and/or perpetuating the harm
Plot	Stymied progress Decline Change is only an illusion Helplessness Control Conspiracy Blame the victim *Undefined*	The plot connects the setting to the characters and the characters to one another; different types identified: Stymied progress: prior progress is threatened or impeded Decline: things will get worse if the opposing solution is enacted Change is an illusion: perceived improvement/decline is the opposite of reality Helplessness: bad situation is out of control Control: bad situation is within control Conspiracy: fated bad situation is in fact controlled by a selected few Blame the victim: victims control/perpetuate the situation

(continued)

Table 14.2   (continued)

Narrative elements	Codes	Description
Moral	**(1) Borders:** RESTRICTED/ OPEN/STATUS QUO/ AMB/*Undefined*	Policy preference or policy solution (*what should be done*) regarding the management of (EU) borders.[a]
	(2) Policy lead: EU LEAD/ COORD/MS LEAD/ AMB/*Undefined*	Actors or group of actors who are referred to in the group speeches as managing/leading the policy recommendation. _EU LEAD:_ speaker expresses policy solutions in favour of a unique (or principal) supranational policy lead. _COORD:_ speaker offers policy solutions in favour of a coordination/cooperation between EU institutions and member states. _MS LEAD:_ speaker expresses policy solutions in favour of a unique (or principal) national policy lead. _AMB:_ speaker expresses uncertainty or indecision regarding the level of authority that should be primarily involved in the policy problem-solving.
Policy Belief	POS MIG/NEG MIG/AMB MIG/*Undefined*	Set of values and beliefs reflecting the main policy position/ideological tenets of the group regarding migration. _POS MIG:_ speaker expresses constructive and favourable feelings, emphasizes positive aspects of migration. _NEG MIG:_ speaker expresses unconstructive and unfavourable feelings, emphasizes negative aspects of migration. _AMB:_ speaker expresses uncertainty or indecision regarding migration.

[a]The coding methodology of this particular item can be provided by the authors upon request

References

Abou-Chadi, T. (2016). Niche Party Success and Mainstream Party Policy Shifts: How Green and Far-Right Parties Differ in Their Impact. *British Journal of Political Science, 46*(02), 417–436.

Bale, T. (2008). Turning Round the Telescope. Centre-Right Parties and Immigration and Integration Policy in Europe. *Journal of European Public Policy, 15*(3), 315–330.

Bale, T., Green-Pedersen, C., Krouwel, A. A., Luther, K. R., & Sitter, N. (2009). If You Can't Beat Them, Join Them? Explaining Social Democratic Responses to the Challenge from the Populist Radical Right in Western Europe. *Political Studies, 58*(3), 410–426.

Bale, T., & Partos, R. (2014). Why Mainstream Parties Change Policy on Migration: A UK Case Study – The Conservative Party, Immigration and Asylum, 1960–2010. *Comparative European Politics, 12*(6), 603–619.

Camia, V. (2013). Mainstream Parties and their Conceptions of Europe: The Populist Contagion, Working Paper No. 60, *National Centre of Competence in Research* (NCCR).

Davis, A. J. (2012). *The Impact of Anti-Immigration Parties on Mainstream Parties' Immigration Positions in the Netherlands, Flanders and the UK 1987–2010: Divided Electorates, Left-Right Politics and the Pull Towards Restrictionism.* Doctoral dissertation, European University Institute, Florence, Italy.

Gianfreda, S. (2018). Politicization of the Refugee Crisis?: A Content Analysis of Parliamentary Debates in Italy, the UK, and the EU. *Italian Political Science Review/Rivista Italiana di Scienza Politica, 48*(01), 85–108.

Gray, G., & Jones, M. (2016). A Qualitative Narrative Policy Framework? Examining the Policy Narratives of US Campaign Finance Regulatory Reform. *Public Policy and Administration, 31*(3), 193–220.

Hansen, R. (2007). Migration Policy. In C. Hay & A. Menon (Eds.), *European Politics*. Oxford: Oxford University Press.

Harmel, R., & Svasand, L. (1997). The Influence of New Parties on Old Parties' Platforms. The Case of the Progress Parties and Conservative Parties of Denmark and Norway. *Party Politics, 3*(3), 315–340.

Hobolt, S., & Tilley, J. (2015). *Fleeing the Centre: The Rise of Challenger Parties in the Aftermath of the Euro Crisis.* Paper prepared for presentation at the EES 2014 Conference, November 6–8, 2015, MZES, University of Mannheim.

Jones, M. D., & McBeth, M. K. (2010). A Narrative Policy Framework: Clear Enough to Be Wrong? *Policy Studies Journal, 38*(2), 329–353.

Jones, M. D., Shanahan, E. A., & McBeth, M. K. (2014). Introducing the Narrative Policy Framework. In M. D. Jones, E. A. Shanahan, & M. K. McBeth (Eds.), *The Science of Stories: Applications of the Narrative Policy Framework in Public Policy Analysis* (pp. 1–26). New York: Palgrave Macmillan.

McBeth, M. K., Shanahan, E. A., Arrendale Anderson, M. C., & Rose, B. (2012). Policy Story or Gory Story? : Narrative Policy Framework, YouTube, and Indirect Lobbying in Greater Yellowstone. *Policy & Internet, 4*(3–4), 159–183.

McElroy, G., & Benoit, K. (2007). Party Groups and Policy Positions in the European Parliament. *Party Politics, 13*(1), 5–28.

Meijers, M. (2015). Contagious Euroscepticism: The Impact of Eurosceptic Support on Mainstream Party Positions on European Integration. *Party Politics, 23*, 1–11.

Odmalm, P., & Bale, T. (2014). Immigration into the Mainstream: Conflicting Ideological Streams, Strategic Reasoning and Party Competition. *Acta Politica*, 50(4), 365–378.

Proksch, S., & Slapin, J. (2010). Position Taking in European Parliament Speeches. *British Journal of Political Science, 40*(3), 587–611.

Rooduijn, M., de Lange, S. L., & van der Brug, W. (2014). A Populist Zeitgeist? Programmatic Contagion by Populist Parties in Western Europe. *Party Politics, 20*(4), 563–575.

Shanahan, E. A., Jones, M. D., McBeth, M. K., & Lane, R. R. (2013). An Angel on the Wind: How Heroic Policy Narratives Shape Policy Realities. *Policy Studies Journal, 41*(3), 453–483.

Stone, D. (2012). *Policy Paradox: The Art of Political Decision Making*. New York: WW. Norton.

Van Heerden, S., de Lange, S. L., van der Brug, W., & Fennema, M. (2014). The Immigration and Integration Debate in the Netherlands: Discursive and Programmatic Reactions to the Rise of Anti-Immigration Parties. *Journal of Ethnic and Migration Studies, 40*(1), 119–136.

Van Spanje, J. (2010). Contagious Parties. Anti-Immigration Parties and Their Impact on Other Parties' Immigration Stances in Contemporary Western Europe. *Party Politics, 16*(5), 563–586.

Williams, C., & Ishiyama, J. (2018). Responding to the Left: The Effect of Far-Left Parties on Mainstream Party Euroskepticism. *Journal of Elections, Public Opinion and Parties, 32*, 1–24.

CHAPTER 15

Possible Future European Union Party-Political Systems

Martin Westlake

The views expressed in this paper are entirely personal and do not commit any other person, institution or organisation.

A first version of this chapter was presented at a 29–30 May 2017 Joint Conference of the College of Europe Department of European Political and Governance Studies and the European Parliamentary Research Service (EPRS), Brussels. I would like to thank Eva-Maria Poptcheva of the EPRS for her constructive comments as discussant on that occasion. I would like also to thank the following for having read and commented on a subsequent draft: Jim Cloos, Richard Corbett, MEP, Sir Ivor Crewe, Paul Culley, Alfredo De Feo, Andrew Duff, David Earnshaw, Adrian Ellis, James Hanning, Geoffrey Harris, Simon Hix, Francis Jacobs, Anand Menon, Pierpaolo Settembri, David Spence, Luuk van Middelaar, Philippe van Parijs, Sir Graham Watson, Klaus Welle and John Williams. Their criticisms and corrections have immeasurably improved this Chapter, though length restrictions precluded me from exploring some of their many excellent suggestions for further analysis and consideration. A much fuller version of this chapter has been published as Bruges Political Research Paper No. 60, 'Possible Future European Union Party-Political Systems,' available here: https://www.coleurope.eu/news/ bruges-political-research-paper-no-60-martin-westlake.

M. Westlake (✉)
College of Europe, Bruges, Belgium

European Institute, London School of Economics, London, UK

321

1   INTRODUCTION: 'A SYSTEM APPROPRIATE TO A CONTINENT'

In 1979, the British political philosopher and commentator David Marquand wrote a forward-looking analysis of the European Parliament (EP) on the eve of the first direct elections. Towards the end of his analysis, Marquand speculated about a 'Party Europe' and predicted that, ultimately, a nationalist-supra-nationalist system would evolve. This evolution would not be quick or tidy and would probably overlap 'in a puzzling and superficially illogical way' with the existing left-right system. However, what was under discussion was 'the possible emergence of *a system appropriate to a continent*' (Marquand 1979, 125, the author's emphasis). The aim of this chapter is to engage in a 'thought experiment' by considering the possible ways in which the European Union's (EU's) emerging party-political system might, in the longer term, evolve and the possible ramifications of such developments. What might a system appropriate for the European continent look like? The 'experiment' is based on three assumptions. The first is that the EU is irreversibly set on being a parliamentary Union. The second is that the EU is irreversibly set on being a party-political Union. The third, perhaps more debatable, is that the *Spitzenkandidaten*/lead candidate procedure is here to stay.[1]

2   'KNOWN UNKNOWNS'

This chapter engages in some speculation about possible developments in the evolution of EU political parties and party systems, but to keep the 'experiment' relatively simple, no attempt is made to take into account six probable or possible future developments. As such, these developments are 'known unknowns,' flagged up here, but not considered further, because they would add too much complexity to an already complex exercise but worth bearing in mind all the same.

The first 'known unknown' concerns the future geographical dimensions of the EU. Even if the current Juncker Commission has frozen the possibility of accession during its mandate (and ruled out the possibility of

---

[1] To see these assumptions and the developments behind them, see Westlake, Martin, 'Possible Future European Union Party-Political Systems,' https://www.coleurope.eu/news/bruges-political-research-paper-no-60-martin-westlake.

Turkey acceding), the longer-term perspective taken by this chapter implies strongly that further accessions to the EU will have taken place, particularly from among the current candidate countries (Albania, the former Yugoslav Republic of Macedonia, Montenegro, Serbia, Turkey) and those waiting in the wings (Bosnia and Herzegovina, Kosovo…). In the case of each of those countries, political parties and party-political systems have evolved, and will continue to evolve, in distinctive and idiosyncratic fashion, and they would bring their own specific identities into the Union. It is impossible to speculate about the effects such parties and systems might have, though the prevalence of nationalisms and regional concerns suggests that such accessions would have some, if not considerable, impact.

The second concerns the structure and institutional arrangements of the EU in general. An Intergovernmental Conference (IGC) might seem highly unlikely in the immediately foreseeable future, but what about in 20 or 30 years' time?[2] For the time being, the Union may probably prefer to find alternative ways of reordering its affairs—perhaps through hybrid extra-treaty arrangements in some cases (e.g., defence)—but in the longer run amendments to the Treaties will surely be necessary (some Treaty amendments may well already be necessary to deal with Brexit). Again, it is difficult to speculate about exactly what those might be and how they might impact on the evolution of a future Union parliamentary party-political system.

The third 'known unknown' more specifically concerns governance of the eurozone. Consolidation of the eurozone, whether along the lines initially set out in the October 2015 'Five Presidents' Report' (Juncker et al. 2015) or the European Commission's 31 May 2017 follow-up *Reflection Paper on the Deepening of the Economic and Monetary Union* (European Commission 2017b) or according to the visions set out in President Emanuel Macron's 26 September 2017 Sorbonne speech (and for which he has a specific electoral mandate—Münchau 2017) or possibly in some other way, is a political and economic imperative that all have recognized (including, it should be noted, the 2015–2017 British govern-

---

[2] Though Angela Merkel did not rule out such a possibility in her 15 May 2017 summit meeting with new French President Emmanuel Macron, Andrew Duff believes that 'the next IGC, and hopefully Convention, will take place before 2024—not least to tackle eurozone governance, adjust post-Brexit, tackle immigration competence and electoral reform and seat apportionment' (10 August 2017 correspondence with the author). See also Duff (2015c).

ment and its predecessor). The draft February 2016 *Settlement for the United Kingdom within the European Union* (European Council 2016) would, if it had been implemented, have enabled such consolidation to go ahead. Through its March 2017 *White Paper on the Future of Europe*, the European Commission has effectively launched a reflection process about whether other means can be found to achieve the same aims, particularly for scenarios 4—doing less more efficiently—and 5—doing much more together (European Commission 2017a). In its follow-up *Reflection Paper*, the European Commission considers how a strengthened EMU architecture can be anchored in terms of democratic accountability. It considers equipping the European and national parliaments with 'sufficient powers' of oversight (p. 27), but rightly ventures no further in considering whether a specific configuration of the EP might be appropriate. Chang and Hudson (2017), on the other hand, suggest that a dedicated Sub-Committee of the EP with appropriate membership might be the best structural response. With or without such reforms, calls for democratization of the eurozone have been increasing (see, e.g., Piketty 2017; Hennette et al. 2017; Magnette 2017).

It is simply too early to be able to know how such consolidation and democratization will take place and in what way although, clearly, the creation of some sort of 'core' eurozone with some sort of parliamentary arrangement would have consequences for the way in which EU political parties evolve—in terms of both substance and structure. The point could be made more broadly with regard to any differentiated architecture, which is surely one of the reasons why, in his 13 September 2017 State of the EU address to the EP, Jean-Claude Juncker robustly rejected the idea in declaring; 'The Parliament of the euro area is the European Parliament' (Juncker 2017, 16).[3]

A fourth 'known unknown' concerns the evolution of the European Council and of the Council of the EU. Space precludes a substantive treatment of this issue, but questions would include the consequences of a consolidated *Spitzenkandidaten* procedure for the competences of the

---

[3] On the other hand, as Sir Graham Watson has pointed out, 'Political parties can deal with differentiated architecture. For example, the ALDE Party had a debate (at a Council meeting in 2013) about whether congress delegates from non-EU member states should have the right to vote in elections to choose the ALDE *Spitzenkandidat*. We decided they should, for 2014, but I can see this question being posed again in the future' (7 June 2017 correspondence with the author).

Commission and the European Council; would it force 'purity' on them both? Would the Commission have to shed its 'neutral' functions (competition, anti-fraud,[4] and so on) and become 'only' an executive? Would the European Council/Council have to shed its executive functions? What sort of relationship might evolve with the Council and the European Council, and how might those two bodies evolve in the same context? And what if, as Jean-Claude Juncker proposed in his 2017 State of the EU address, the two presidencies should somehow be combined? (Juncker 2017, 18) And how, in any case, would an emerging party-political system cope with the unsynchronized electoral systems of the member states?

The fifth 'known unknown' concerns the specific case of the future of the 73 seats in the EP that will, if the UK exits the EU as foreseen, be freed up as of 2019. More particularly, a number of actors have called for the seats to be reallocated to create a pan-EU constituency (De La Baume 2017; Kalcik and Wolff 2017) echoing, notably, the recommendations set out in then Member of the European Parliament (MEP) Andrew Duff's 2011 report to the EP's Constitutional Affairs Committee (see Duff 2015b).[5] Again, the new French President, Emmanuel Macron, incorporated such an idea in his presidential programme (Macron 2017). Duff's basic idea, though it would require Treaty change, would create a 'joint constituency' to elect the European Commission president, with lists headed by each political party's candidate. Macron's more simple idea (though it would still require Treaty change), shared by many, including former MEP Daniel Cohn-Bendit, for example, is simply to create a transnational, trans-European list of 73 seats, a possibility endorsed by Jean-Claude Juncker in his 13 September 2017 State of the EU address.[6] But just recently (7 February) rejected by the Parliament itself (Hübner and Pereira 2018)—see below. There were practical reasons for rejecting the possibility so close to the May 2019 elections and the idea might yet resurface during the 2019–2024 mandate.

---

[4] The creation of the European Public Prosecutor's Office will to some extent achieve this already.

[5] Although the concept of some sort of European political constituency is as old as the directly elected European Parliament itself, if not older. I am grateful to Francis Jacobs for pointing this out.

[6] Although, as Geoffrey Harris points out, in the longer run, 'the assumption that a special EU-wide list for the 73 ex-UK seats would mostly go to federalists is a risky one' (4 July 2017 correspondence with the author).

The sixth, related, 'known unknown' concerns whether, and how, the EP might finally react to the German Constitutional Court's June 2009 ruling regarding the legality of the Lisbon Treaty and, in particular, the criticisms made about the legitimacy of the Parliament, given that its members are not elected by a uniform system, and given also that the number of MEPs per member state is apportioned through the principle of degressive proportionality (*Bundesverfassungsgericht* 2009)—a principle enshrined in TEU Article 14.2. As Duff describes: 'If each MEP does not have an equal vote, is each citizen equally represented at the European Union level, as the Treaty requires? The Court points out that the change made by the Lisbon Treaty to the mandate of MEPs—becoming 'representatives of the Union's citizens' rather than, as previously, 'representatives of the peoples of the States'—is flatly contradicted by the fact that seats are still apportioned entirely per member state. Moreover, the *Bundesverfassungsgericht* does not believe that the vague federalist concept of degressive proportionality amounts to a serious method of distributing seats. In the Court's view, in spite of the Union's pretensions to European citizenship, the European Parliament is in fact made up of national contingents' (Duff 2015b, see also Westlake 2016, 41–42).[7]

Decisions about the composition of the EP and about the allocation of seats between member states are notoriously difficult. According to Article 14.2 of the Treaty on the EU, the composition of the Parliament is adopted through a special legislative procedure, where a European Council decision is taken upon an initiative of the EP and requires its consent (by simple majority). Andrew Duff has cogently argued that the only 'intelligent approach' in the longer run would be the so-called CamCom method of apportionment (see Duff 2015a, 105–107, for a succinct presentation of this methodology).

At the time of going to press (April 2018), the EP has just adopted (7 February) its resolution and proposal for the composition of the EP in the 2019–2024 mandate (the co-rapporteurs were Danuta Hübner [EPP] and Pedro Silva Pereira [S&D]), Parliament's work having been badly delayed by the Brexit process. (The Committee was authorized to begin work on the substance of the file only after the UK lodged its notification under Article 50 TEU.) The report adopts a pragmatic approach in pro-

---

[7] On the other hand, if the *Spitzenkandidaten* procedure is consolidated in 2019, then the Court's argument about the non-justification for a threshold will surely be weakened because of the consolidated linkage to the executive.

posing a reduction of Parliament's membership to 705 and a redistribution to ensure greater proportionality. The European Council will now begin its work.

3   SOME BASIC QUESTIONS

The European integration process opted, by default, and almost from the very beginning, to adopt a parliamentary model. The parliamentary system of government, increasingly wedded to universal suffrage, had only really come into its own after the First World War but would have seemed the obvious choice in the immediate post-1939–1945 war period. It is generally compared favourably with presidential systems of government. In it, the absence of the purist separation of powers in presidential systems is counterbalanced by a diffusion of powers and easier and more rapid passing of legislation. But will the parliamentary system of government still be considered favourably 20 or 30 years hence? In many countries parliaments are currently regarded critically. Various corruption cases involving individual parliamentarians have added to the critical mix. Is the parliamentary model an enduring one, and will it still seem appropriate by, say, 2059?

And what, in the same context, of political parties? Funding scandals in various Western systems have undermined the legitimacy of many mainstream, well-established political parties. But beyond the peccadilloes of individual parties and their office holders, there would also appear to be more systemic problems concerning the way in which modern political parties, no longer benefitting from mass membership and reliant on public funding, leading to dependent bureaucratic structures (see Mair 2013, for a trenchant, and sustained, critique of the 'hollowing out' of democracy), have somehow smothered the very political dialogue that they are supposed to foster and facilitate (see Nothomb 2017, for a recent outburst).

What, moreover, of party government as a system? Already, in the 1980s—soon after the first direct elections to the EP had been held—scholars were beginning to question the merits and the potential of party government, especially given the decline of some of the phenomena on which it had been predicated, such as mass party membership, strong party loyalty, low volatility in voting patterns, and strong class identification (Castles and Wildenmann 1986; Wildenmann 1986). Are parties truly fulfilling an aggregation function, and are they still able to provide a stable basis for government whilst also ensuring democratic legitimacy? The sudden rise of non-parties and movements and the collapse of support for traditional parties, as occurred most recently in the 2017 French presidential election and the 2018 Italian general election, suggest that they may not—or not automatically, in any case.

And what of the particular mainstream party families that currently exist at the Union level? In 1967, Lipset and Rokkan, grandfathers of post-war political science, observed that 'the party systems of the 1960s reflect, with few but significant exceptions, the cleavage structures of the 1920s' (Lipset and Rokkan 1967a, 50, 1967b). Their conclusion was that 'the dominant electoral alternatives then prevalent in Western Europe were the outcome of a complex interaction between historically defined social cleavages and particular patterns of institutional development ... European political parties acquired a virtually independent momentum, consolidating a set of political terms of reference which seems almost as immutable as the very languages in which they were expressed' (Mair 1983, 405).

This 'freezing' phenomenon meant—and still means to a considerable extent—that Western European party-political systems were dominated by an oligopoly—Christian Democrats, Socialists, Social Democrats, Liberals, Communists—that was of declining relevance to the real cleavages, to the extent that they existed, in Western European countries' societies. Of course, there have been plenty of new arrivals—the Greens and various Eurosceptical and further right parties in particular—but it is perhaps surprising how much the Union's party politics, at the EU level, is still dominated by an oligopoly that, at member state level, corresponded to the classic cleavages of the 1920s.[8] The last section of this chapter will briefly consider other possible future cleavages.

What, also, of alternation? Most democratic systems are based on the logic that the electorate should, at some stage, be able to 'throw the rascals out,' although there doesn't need to be an intention of reproach or of

---

[8] Writing in 1979, Marquand flatly declared: 'The Community's embryonic party system is an artificial construct, which reflects national rather than Community realities' (Marquand 1979, 124). However, Hix points out that 'the historical evidence is that political parties mainly form INSIDE rather than OUTSIDE parliaments – by elites breaking away from other parties, rather than by voters spontaneously starting a new movement. This is relevant for the European party system, as it suggests that at some point in the future "new" parties/ party formulations could form if a "European party system" was truly independent from national parties. For example, could a "European progressive alliance" of MEPs, EP Groups, and national party leaders, emerge to agree a common candidate for the Commission President. Now that really would be a truly European party system' (11 July 2017 correspondence with the author).

punishment for an electorate to opt for change. Some European party systems (e.g., Belgium, the Netherlands, Denmark) are used to the permanence of coalition governments, but there is an understanding that the composition of the coalitions may change—the 'rascals' may not be out altogether, in other words, but there will be change, alternation, of a sort. Other systems—Germany, Austria—seem comfortable with rule by 'grand coalitions,' but such arrangements are regarded as being time-bound and may collapse (Austria currently being a good case in point) so that, once again, change—alternation—is possible. National systems may throw up centrist movements or parties or coalitions of parties. Tony Blair's 'New Labour' was a good example of a party that had captured the electoral centre ground. Emmanuel Macron's *En Marche!* movement, now converted into a party of sorts, provides a more recent example. But where centrist governance is structural, then there can be no real alternation.[9] Thus, whilst the reasoning in the quotation below makes sense from a punctual, transitional point of view (the word 'unique' is important), such an arrangement would be democratically unhealthy[10] in the longer run if it were to deny the European electorate the possibility to insist on change:

...the newly elected President of the European Commission represents the political centre: the political centre which exists in the current European Parliament and the political centre which exists in the European Council as well. I would not go as far as to say that Juncker is situated left of the EPP and right of the social-democrats, because if you try finding such a territory you might not succeed. But it may be fair to say that Juncker might be on the left of the EPP or on the right of the social-democrats. To me, he is exactly occupying this kind of political space which allows him to bring the different political forces of the Parliament together... This means that he is well placed at the centre of the system and has a **unique** chance to work as a unifier. And this would not have been the case had he just come from one winning party and thus been the representative of only one political wing of the European political spectrum. (Welle 2014, author's emphasis)

[9] However, whilst space precludes a proper treatment here, it should be pointed out, at least in passing, that some authors argue that the Swiss model of non-alternation (so nobody can be thrown out) might be more relevant to the EU (see, e.g., Van Parijs 2015, 2017). Richard Corbett has argued that 'The Commission would appear to be edging towards a hybrid of Swiss-style collegiality in its overall composition, but with a more majoritarian approach to designating its President' (in Kenealy et al. 2015).

[10] Sartori, among others, pointed a warning finger to the unhappy fates of the French Fourth Republic and Weimar Germany (see Hanning 1984, 437 for a consideration of this).

Lastly, and linked to the importance of alternation, the existence of viable opposition within the system is as important as the possibility for viable governance. Peter Mair has written persuasively on this subject (Mair 2007, 2013). As Albert Hirschman had pointed out in the 1970s, in the absence of any possibility for 'voice,' the only alternative is 'exit' from the system altogether (Hirschman 1970). Luuk Van Middelaar has been a more recent proponent of the same argument (Van Middelaar 2017). If Euroscepticism as a viable force is somehow not permitted within the system, then it risks being transformed into anti-Europeanism (or anti-EUism, at least).

These 'basic questions,' as they have here been termed, require careful reflection and deliberation as the embryonic European parliamentary party-political system starts to emerge. In short, we cannot be certain that parliamentary party-political democracy is the most enduring of systems nor necessarily the most appropriate system for the future EU (what can we know about future political developments, particularly as technology is evolving so rapidly?). But it is what the Union has, cumulatively, opted for. The challenge will be to ensure that it functions sufficiently well to ensure not only good governance but also good opposition, not only stability but also alternation, not only aggregation but also relevance. Rising to that challenge requires, in turn, careful reflection on the implications and consequences of each step on the way. In particular, the strategic long-term objective of good and viable governance and opposition should not be inadvertently prejudiced by short-term tactical considerations. As Sartori recalled, electoral reform is as much about the effects of parties on electoral systems as the other way around (Sartori 1983) or, as Hanning more baldly put it, 'it would be fruitless to estimate the effects of the new electoral system without reference to *the reasons for its introduction*' (Hanning 1984, 434).

4   Party-Political Systems and Some of Their Discontents

Giovanni Sartori was one of a number of Italian political scientists who could see plainly, from the way Italy's democracy functioned in the 1960s and 1970s, that party-political systems of themselves did not guarantee effective governance or legitimacy. Some of the discontents that he and his contemporaries identified are potentially of relevance to a future EU party-political system and are here considered briefly.

A first concerns the phenomenon of *bipartitismo imperfetto*, a term coined by Giorgio Galli (1967). Galli's theory was later dismissed for being nostalgic about a system (a two-party system with regular alternation) which, with the exception of the US and the UK, didn't really exist— at least, not at that time. However, part of Galli's analysis concerned the situation in which a large party, the Communist Party (PCI), was excluded from governance, and the effects this had on the balance of the overall system and its legitimacy and governability. Could a future Union party-political system contain a large party that, for one reason or another, might be considered beyond the pale? What would happen if such a party were to win a majority in European elections?

A second, related, phenomenon is that of a so-called dominant party system (Sartori 1976). This could best be defined as a system in which one political party predominates, has won successive elections and seems unlikely to lose any elections for the foreseeable future. The phenomenon, and its risks, had already been identified by Maurice Duverger in the 1950s, with Sartori later considering the Italian case in particular (Duverger 1954; Sartori 1976). Contemporary examples of dominant party systems would include Sweden until recently (the Social Democrats), Japan (the Liberal Democrats) and India (the India National Congress). In the sophisticated case of the Italian Christian Democratic Party, the pseudo roles of government and opposition came to be carried out by factions (the so-called *correnti*) within the party (Jacobs 1989, 178) and these, to a considerable extent, gave centre voters at least the illusion of alternation. A critical case concerns South Africa and the African National Congress Party (ANC) which has never scored less than 62 per cent in the five national assembly elections to date and where there seems little probability that it will be out of power in the near future (see Suttner 2006, and particularly his dismissal of the party dominance theory). Could a future Union party-political system contain a predominant party or coalition of like-minded parties that would deny the perception of alternation?

A third, and again related, phenomenon is that of polarized pluralism, a term coined by Sartori. This can perhaps best be understood as a bimodal distribution of support where a relatively empty centre ground is flanked by two 'peaks' of support for relative extremes. Pre-1933 Germany provided a good example of this phenomenon, with strong support for the Communists on the left and the national socialists on the right. In the case of Italy in the 1960s and 1970s, the situation was further complicated by the fact that the Communist Party (PCI) could not accede to power and even after the 1973 *compromesso storico* was limited to state positions, but not political power. In Italy, the central vacuum was gradually filled in by the Socialist (PSI), Liberal (PLI) and Radical (PRI) Parties, but the existence of such polarized pluralism created severe governance challenges, leaving the country never far from an existential challenge. Also of potential relevance in Sartori's various analyses are the presence of anti-system parties (how does a system cope with its potential nemesis?), bilateral oppositions (a dominant party astride the centre ground condemned to remain dominant because of extreme parties to its left and right)[11] and irresponsible oppositions—parties that were not interested in governing, but only in bringing about change. Again, could a future Union system throw up a similar situation and similar challenges (some would argue that it already has done)?

5   A Possible Precedent and a Pointer

Can other countries and continents tell us anything about how the EU's parliamentary party-political system might evolve? The most obvious historical examples (and perhaps the only directly comparable ones) are those of the American First and Second Party Systems. These were the systems Marquand had in mind, both descriptively and also normatively, when he considered the consequences of the first direct elections in 1979. Facile comparisons should of course be avoided, but the object of the exercise is simply to look for possible pointers. Marquand argued that analogies with existing state systems in EU member states were misleading. Rather, the right analogy was with United States party politics in the 1830s and 1840s. Then, the American Whigs and Democrats were 'loose coalitions of state parties, which usually operated at the state level, but which came together once every four years to contest presidential elections. They were held together, to the extent that they held together at all, by their views on federal questions. Their views on state questions were often not merely different, but opposed' (Marquand 1979, 125).

---

[11] *A propos*, as Pierpaolo Settembri has pointed out, 'A possible long-term scenario is one where 'opposition parties' command, if not a single majority, at least several blocking minorities in the European Parliament, thus preventing the formation and the operation of a grand coalition' (5 June 2017 correspondence with the author).

Though Marquand acknowledged that the American analogy could not be pushed too far, he insisted that it was a useful backdrop. Seen against it, 'the divisions within the nationalist and supra-nationalist camps in present-day Europe are neither particularly surprising nor particularly deep: 'If they come into being they will be coalitions of national parties. They will be divided at the national level though united at the Community level: so were their American counterparts in the days of Andrew Jackson and Martin Van Buren. The Members returned under their banners, if and when they contest elections in their own right, will not always vote on party lines: nor did American Whig and Democratic Congressmen in the 1830s and 1840s. Sometimes, they will vote on national lines instead: in exactly the same way, American Whig and Democratic Congressmen often voted on state lines' (Marquand 1979, 126).

What the early American experience seems to indicate is that federal parties and party systems evolve out of loose coalitions between parties that may compete at state level and that those parties tend to coalesce around the twin binary issues of more-or-less central government and more-or-less central budget. What Europeans would consider as traditional ideologies, on the left-right scale, are less salient at federal level than at state level in the US. The big difference is that state-based parties in the US did not evolve along left-right lines and didn't evolve out of socioeconomic adjustments to industrialization and class, and in Europe there was no general division over slavery and no civil war. Notwithstanding these differences, Fabbrini's seminal study has demonstrated how EU-level politics '[h]as become constantly characterized by sectional rather than class or religious cleavages. Certainly, within the EP, traditional divisions are apparent, such as the division between the left ... and the right ... However, the structural division in the EP, as well as within the ... Council of Ministers, is not between left and right' (Fabbrini 2007, 137). In becoming more sectoral, and in becoming increasingly about whether there should be 'more' or 'less' Europe, EU-level politics is becoming more like American politics, despite those very different beginnings.

There may be other pointers closer to today including, perhaps, elements from the 2016 UK referendum debate. During the referendum campaign, voice was also given to what might be termed enlightened left-wing critiques of the EU and arguments therefore in favour of leaving the Union. Such arguments strongly echoed left-wing critiques of the European integration process voiced in the early 1950s and 1960s. For example, 'We voted Leave because we believe it is essential to preserve the two things we value most: a democratic political system and a social-democratic society. We fear that the European Union's authoritarian project of neoliberal integration is a breeding ground for the far right. By sealing off so much policy, including the imposition of long-term austerity measures and mass immigration, from the democratic process, the union has broken the contract between mainstream national politicians and their voters. This has opened the door to right-wing populists who claim to represent "the people," already angry at austerity, against the immigrant' (Johnson 2017).

This enlightened left-wing case frequently refers back to Friedrich Hayek's argument in favour of 'inter-state federalism' as a way of weakening nation-states' interference in the workings of the free market. To favour federalism (meaning European integration) is therefore to fall into the Hayekian trap. This critique goes on to argue that the only defence against the sort of 'neo-liberal integration' referred to above is by maintaining strong nation-states, which is where the true *demos* is to be found (on this point, as Philippe van Parijs has illustrated, this brand of the left and Margaret Thatcher would make common cause—Van Parijs 2016). Thus, 'Democracy needs a *demos*, a people for whom government is of, by and for. Without one, all you have is inter-elite management, treaty law and money grubbing. But how will "the people" be constructed? Politics will decide. A left populism will not seek to define the people as the far right does, in opposition to the immigrant other, but in opposition to those powerful neoliberal elites that are no longer able, as Professor Streeck says, "to build a social framework around the hot core of capitalist profit making" ' (Ibid.).

Leaving aside the recent work on 'demoicracy' (i.e., the writings of those who argue that there is no need for a single *demos*), there would appear to be two logical weak points in such argumentation. The first is that the existence of strong nation-states does not by itself guarantee left-wing government nor defend against neo-liberalism at the nation-state level. The second, of more relevance to this analysis, is that a cooperative inter-relationship between nation-states involving inter-governmental, confederal and federal elements need not necessarily result in a dominantly neo-liberal policy mix. Indeed, there is a strong prescriptive left-wing case arguing precisely the opposite. To take Van Parijs again, 'But if the utopian project we need is to have any chance of being realized, it will have to protect itself against the pressure of globalization... Above all, it will need to strengthen its federal institutions and develop the EU-wide demos required to make them work' (Van Parijs 2016, 7). In other words, Van Parijs argues, the answer is not less integration, but more.

At the least, proponents of both the left-wing and the right-wing cases are to be found on both sides of the European integration process. Put another way, cogent cases can be made both for and against European integration on both the left and the right. Hayekian capitalists might argue in favour of integration because it weakens the interfering state. The reformist Labour Party of the late 1980s came to accept European integration as the best defence against the policies of a Hayek-inspired Conservative government *within* a member state. If there were only nation-states, Labour and Conservative supporters would happily exist on opposing sides of the political divide. But pro-European Labour and pro-European Conservatives find themselves together, no matter how uncomfortably, on the same side of the political divide at pan-EU level (a divide that will surely continue even after Brexit has occurred). The process is even more evident when anti-integration parties arise outside the mainstream parties, whether on the left or the right, since they push the pro-European parties (Social Democrats and Christian Democrats, Socialists and Republicans) into political space where they broadly agree. It is surely one of the reasons why it so hard for the mainstream parties to find distinctive political stances on EU issues in the European elections and also the reason why in such contests they tend to fall back on domestic politics, where the distinctions between them are clearer and more legible to the electorate. *Pace* Reif (1984, 1985), that is *also* the reason why European elections tend to be second-order national elections.

If we look, as it were, through the other end of the telescope, at the emerging consequences of globalization, then other trends would also appear to be increasingly salient. Marchetti (2016, especially 154–158), for example, considers the possibility of a new political cleavage, more appropriate to a globalized world, of globalism versus localism. Beyond the arguably stale notions of left and right, this new division would 'take us into the framing debates of neo-liberalism (is free trade a good thing? are international markets?), cosmopolitanism (aren't we all globe-trotters now, even if we never leave our sitting rooms and computer screens?), localism (the world of 'traditional values' and the menace of 'the other'); and—ugly term—civilizationism (are we all advancing with the onward progress of civilization together, or are there rather 'clashes' between different civilizations?)' (Westlake 2017b).

It is perhaps to this emerging alternative political cleavage that Welle looks when he argues:

'that there is also a conflict between a more national and a more internation-alist viewpoint. Based on this traditional conflict in the political arena, I think that what we are seeing for the moment is that this quarter of the political matrix, which is defined by a combination of social and national viewpoints, this quarter is for the moment the growth market for political parties. We have a surge of political parties which can be described as '**social nationalist**'. We have in France Mme. Le Pen. We have Mr. Wilders in the Netherlands. We have a major party in Denmark. We have the AfD party in Germany. And we have Mr. Trump in the United States. For me, all of them build on a strong need for protection. They are 'social' in the sense that these parties put a very strong stress on protection. Protection is also inter-preted by them in the nationalist sense of the word as a protection against international or internationalist influence. So this is a movement which is directed against liberalisation, against Europeanisation and against globali-sation. At the same time 'identity politics' is back.' (Welle 2016)

So far, the traditional state-based systems have reproduced themselves at EU and European level, where they exercise oligopolistic powers. But some similarities with the US experience would nevertheless seem to be emerging, including the emergence of loose coalitions of parties for and against greater central government and greater central budgets. Indeed, perhaps the most obvious precedent is the Union itself. For what, it might be asked, was the so-called technical agreement in the EP, and what is the current European People's Party-Socialists & Democrats pro-Juncker Commission coalition now, if not a 'loose coalition'—at times, even an electoral coalition? Are we not witnessing Marquand's prediction gradually becoming a reality? It is nei-ther quick nor tidy, but maybe, just maybe, Europe's pro-integration par-ties—whatever their ideological divides in the domestic political context—are increasingly engaging in loose political coalitions at the EU level.[12] The ques-tions then arise (if we believe in the democratic healthiness of alternation of

---

[12] Note that already 'There is growing evidence of a shift in the critical political cleavage at national level in Europe, from left-right to pro-globalisation vs anti-globalisation. This has been accompanied by a shift in the socio-demographic basis of party choice from social class to age and education. I would expect this to be gradually replicated at EU parliamentary level, although it will not always align itself with the further integration vs no further integra-tion division' (18 June 2017 correspondence with Sir Ivor Crewe).

parties in power and of strong opposition as well as government); what faces them, or what *should* face them?

6 CONCLUSION: A PARLIAMENTARY PARTY-BASED DEMOCRACY—BUT WHAT SORT?

The citizens of today's EU surely want their children, and their children's children, to live in a democratic Union. But as the Union continues to evolve, and as the integration process seems likely to continue, it is surely increasingly important also to go beyond that simple (and perhaps simplistic) assertion and ask, 'what sort of a parliamentary party-based democracy?' As I have argued elsewhere, commentators and analysts of the EU tend to oversee the long-term 'wood' (in terms of trends and their consequences) in favour of the 'trees' (punctual events, such as Treaty change and the European elections themselves) (Westlake 2017a, 37). The Union will always remain a *sui generis* organization, as much a process as a fixed end state, but by opting for the *Spitzenkandidaten*/lead candidate procedure in May–July 2014 (and assuming the procedure occurs again in 2019), the EU has taken a decisive step in a particular direction—namely, towards a parliamentary, party-based democracy. Towards exactly what *sort* of parliamentary, party-based democracy, though, is still not yet clear, but it surely does no harm to start wondering. It is in any case as well to be aware that the existence of a parliament and of political parties and, now, of an executive-legislature electoral link guarantees neither a functioning democracy nor an effective party-political parliamentary system.

REFERENCES

Bundesverfassungsgericht. (2009) Federal Constitutional Court Judgment, BVerfG, 2 BvE 2/08. 13 Article 9 TEU. 6, 30 June.

Castles, F., & Wildenmann, R. (Eds.). (1986). *Visions and Realities of Party Government*. Berlin: Walter De Gruyter.

Chang, M., & Dermot, H. (2017). *The EP and the Oversight of EMU Before and After the Euro Crisis.* Paper delivered at the 29–30 May 2017 Joint College of Europe and European Parliamentary Research Service conference on 'The European Parliament in Times of Crisis: Dynamics and Transformations.'

De La Baume, M. (2017, May 15). MEPs Debate Who Inherits British Seats. *Politico.*

Duff, A. (2015a). *Pandora, Penelope, Polity; How to Change the European Union.* London: John Harper Publishing.

Duff, A. (2015b). Democratic Legitimacy in the European Union: Taking a New Look at the Composition and Electoral Procedure of the European Parliament. In *The Electoral Reform of the European Parliament: Composition, Procedure and Legitimacy, In-Depth Analysis for the AFCO Committee*, European Parliament, Directorate General for Internal Policies, PE 510.002.

Duff, A. (2015c). *The Protocol of Frankfurt: A New Treaty for the Eurozone.* Brussels: European Policy Centre.

Duverger, M. (1954). *Political Parties. Their Organisation and Activity in the Modern State.* London: Methuen and Co.

European Commission. (2017a, March 1). *White Paper on the Future of Europe: Reflections and Scenarios for the EU 27 by 2025*, Brussels.

European Commission. (2017b, May 31). *Reflection Paper on the Deepening of the Economic and Monetary Union*, Brussels.

European Council. (2016, February 23). A New Settlement for the United Kingdom Within the European Union. *Official Journal of the European Union, 59*(C69I), 1–16.

Fabbrini, S. (2007). *Compound Democracies: Why the United States and Europe Are Becoming Similar.* Oxford: Oxford University Press.

Galli, G. (1967). *Il Bipartitismo Imperfetto: Comunisti e democristiani in Italia.* Bologna: Il Mulino.

Hanning, J. (1984). Twenty Years of Polarized Pluralism. *European Journal of Political Research, 12*, 433–443.

Hennette, S., Piketty, T., Sacriste, G., & Vauchez, A. (2017, May 14). For a Treaty Democratizing Euro Area Governance – (T-Dem). *Social Europe* (blog). Retrieved from https://www.socialeurope.eu/2017/04/treaty-democratizing-euro-area-governance-t-dem/.

Hirschman, A. O. (1970). *Exit, Voice, and Loyalty: Responses to Decline in Firms, Organizations and States.* Cambridge, MA: Harvard University Press.

Hübner, D. M., & Pereira, P. S. (2018). European Parliament Resolution of 7 February 2018 on the Composition of the European Parliament (2017/2054(INL) – 2017/0900(NLE)). http://www.europarl.europa.eu/sides/getDoc.do?type=TA&reference=P8-TA-2018-0029&language=EN&ring=A8-2018-0007.

Jacobs, F. (1989). *Western European Political Parties: A Comprehensive Guide.* Harlow: Longman.

Johnson, A. (2017, March 28). Why Brexit Is Best for Britain: The Left-Wing Case. *New York Times.*

Juncker, J.-C. (2017, September 13). The State of the Union: Catching the Wind in Our Sails. Retrieved from http://europa.eu/rapid/press-release_IP-17-3164_en.htm.

Juncker, J.-C., Donald, T., Jeroen, D., Mario, D., & Martin, S. (2015, October 21). *Completing Europe's Economic and Monetary Union*, Brussels.

Kalcik, Robert, & Wolff, Guntram B. (2017). *Is Brexit an Opportunity to Reform the European Parliament?* Policy Contribution, Issue No. 2, Breugel.

Kenealy, D., Peterson, J., & Corbett, R. (Eds.). (2015). *The European Union: How Does It Work?* Oxford and New York: Oxford University Press.

Lipset, S. M., & Rokkan, S. (1967a). *Party Systems and Voter Alignments: Cross-National Perspectives.* New York: Free Press.

Lipset, S. M., & Rokkan, S. (1967b). Cleavage Structures, Party Systems and Voter Alignments: An Introduction. In S. M. Lipset & S. Rokkan (Eds.), *Party Systems and Voter Alignments: Cross-National Perspectives.* New York: Free Press.

Macron, E. (2017). *Le Programme de Emmanuel Macron, Le Monde.* Retrieved from http://www.lemonde.fr/personnalite/emmanuel-macron/programme/.

Magnette, P. (2017). Ten Thoughts On the Treaty Democratizing the Euro Area (T-DEM). *Social Europe.* Retrieved from https://www.socialeurope.eu/2017/06/ten-thoughts-treaty-democratizing-euro-area-t-dem/.

Mair, P. (1983). Adaptation and Control: Towards an Understanding of Party and Party System Change. In H. Daalder & P. Mair (Eds.), *Western European Party Systems: Continuity and Change.* London: Sage.

Mair, P. (2007). Political Opposition and the European Union. *Government and Opposition, 42*(1), 1–17.

Mair, P. (2013). *Ruling the Void: The Hollowing of Western Democracy.* London: Verso.

Marchetti, R. (2016). *Global Strategic Engagement.* London: Lexington Books.

Marquand, D. (1979). *Parliament for Europe.* London: Jonathan Cape.

Münchau, W. (2017, May 8). Emmanuel Macron Sets His Sights on Economic and Eurozone Reforms. *Financial Times.*

Nothomb, C.-F. (2017, May 15). La particratie actuelle tue la démocratie. *La Libre Belgique.*

Piketty, T. (2017, March 22). What Would a Democratic Euro Zone Assembly Look Like? Le blog de Thomas Piketty. *Le Monde.* http://piketty.blog.lemonde.fr/2017/03/22/what-would-a-euro-zone-assembly-look-like/.

Reif, K. (Ed.) (1984). *European Elections 1979/81 and 1984.* European Electoral Studies. Berlin: Quorum.

Reif, K. (Ed.). (1985). *Ten European Elections.* Aldershot: Gower.

Sartori, G. (1976). *Parties and Party Systems: A Framework for Analysis.* Essex: European Consortium of Political Research.

Sartori, G. (1983). *Teoria dei partiti e caso Italiano.* Milan: Sugar Co Edizione.

Suttner, R. (2006). Party Dominance 'Theory': Of What Value? *Politikon South African Journal of Political Studies, 33*(3), 277–297.

Van Parijs, P. (2015). Justifying Europe. In P. Van Parijs & L. van Middelaar (Eds.), *After the Storm. How to Save Democracy in Europe* (pp. 247–261). Tielt: Lannoo.

Van Parijs, P. (2016). Thatcher's Plot – And How to Defeat It. *Social Europe: Politics, Economy & Labour* (blog). Retrieved from https://www.socialeurope. eu/2016/11/thatchers-plot-defeat.

Van Parijs, P. (2017). Demos-cracy for the European Union: Why and How. In L. Cabrera (Ed.), *Institutional Cosmopolitanism*. New York: Oxford University Press.

Welle, K. (2014, September 9). Why This Time Is Different?' – Presentation at Martens Centre for European Studies. Retrieved from http://www.europarl. europa.eu/the-secretary-general/en/activities-multimedia/why-this-time-is-different-presentation-at-martens-ces.

Welle, K. (2016, May 5). Are the EU and the US Becoming Similar?' Talk delivered at the LUISS University, Rome. Retrieved from http://www.europarl. europa.eu/the-secretary-general/en/activities-multimedia/%E2%80%98are-the-eu-and-the-us-becoming-similar-%E2%80%99-%E2%80%93-klaus-welle-at-the-luiss-university.

Westlake, M. (2016, January). Chronicle of an Election Foretold: The Longer-Term Trends Leading to the *'Spitzenkandidaten'* Procedure and the Election of Jean-Claude Juncker as European Commission President. LSE Europe in Question Discussion Paper Series, No. 102.

Westlake, M. (2017a). *The Inevitability of Gradualness: the Longer-term Origins of the 23 June 2016 'Brexit' Referendum*. Bruges Political Research Papers, College of Europe, Bruges, No. 56.

Westlake, M. (2017b). Globalisation, Civil Society and New World Orders. *European Political Science, 16*, 1–5.

Wildenmann, R. (1986). The Problematic of Party Government. In F. Castles & R. Wildenmann (Eds.), *Visions and Realities of Party Government*. Berlin: De Gruyter.

Van Middelaar, L. (2017, March 25). Three Things the EU Must Do to Survive. *The Guardian*.

PART IV

The EP and EU Policies

CHAPTER 16

Reforming the European Parliament's Monetary and Economic Dialogues: Creating Accountability Through a Euro Area Oversight Subcommittee

Michele Chang and Dermot Hodson

1   INTRODUCTION

Parliamentary oversight—which McCubbins and Schwartz (1984, 165) define as the attempt to detect and remedy the failure of executives to comply with legislative goals—is an essential characteristic of democracies.[1]

[1] An earlier version of this chapter was presented at a workshop organized by the College of Europe and the European Parliament Research Service in May 2017. Thanks to the work-

M. Chang (✉)
College of Europe, Bruges, Belgium
e-mail: michele.chang@coleurope.eu

D. Hodson
College of Europe, Bruges, Belgium

University of London, London, UK
e-mail: d.hodson@bbk.ac.uk

© The Author(s) 2019   343
O. Costa (ed.), *The European Parliament in Times of EU Crisis*,
European Administrative Governance,
https://doi.org/10.1007/978-3-319-97391-3_16

Oversight is especially important in relation to economic policy, an area where executive slippage can have profound implications for people's standards of living and society more generally. Although there are arguments for freeing elements of economic decision-making from day-to-day control by politicians, these do not negate the need for democratic checks and balances. Indeed, the turn towards independence in economic decision-making since the 1980s strengthens the case for robust parliamentary oversight in this domain (Berman and McNamara 1999). While some would argue that the European Parliament's (EP's) powers are more limited than those of national parliaments, the influence of the latter should not be overstated. The United States' Congress is sometimes viewed as a pedigree economic watchdog (Waller 2011), but Cheryl Schonhardt-Bailey's research casts doubt on whether the House and Senate banking committees truly hold the US Federal Reserve to account (Schonhardt-Bailey 2013, 318–320). Some legislatures are intimately involved in economic decision-making, but the turn towards independent central banks and fiscal rules in advanced industrial democracies over the last two decades has depoliticized economic policy in ways that do not always favour democratic accountability (Buller and Flinders 2005). European integration has reinforced this trend, leading some scholars to speak of the deparliamentarization of policy-making in the economic sphere as well as others (O'Brennan and Raunio 2007).

The global financial crisis of 2007–2008 was testament to parliamentarians' collective failure to hold economic policymakers' feet to the flames. The European Union (EU) paid a higher price for this shortcoming than most, given the sovereign debt crisis that followed. National parliaments are the chief culprits for failing to spot the catalogue of policy errors that led to these twin crises, underlining the need for more robust parliamentary oversight at the national level. The EP, for its part, should have done more to hold EU and national policymakers to account and to address systemic problems and spillovers in the EU and euro area. Increased oversight is a common response to crises, and a series of reforms to euro area governance enacted in the light of the global financial crisis have gone in this direction. Member states' agreement under the Fiscal Compact[2] to

shop's participants and a number of European Parliament officials for extensive feedback. The views presented in this chapter and any errors that remain are the authors' alone.

[2] Also known as the Treaty on Stability, Coordination, and Governance.

establish independent fiscal councils to oversee compliance with EU fiscal rules is one manifestation of this trend. So, too, are the so-called public hearings between the EP's Economic and Monetary Affairs Committee (ECON)[3] and heads of the institutions involved in European Banking Union.[4] Moreover, the EP has engaged in ad hoc hearings with the heads of the European Stability Mechanism, Eurostat, and the European Investment Bank, and it conducts meetings with national parliaments under the European Semester.

The euro area's economic governance reforms (specifically the regulations in the Six-Pack and Two-Pack) have given the EP additional opportunities to engage with EU- and national-level actors. Can we equate this with enhanced accountability? Grant and Keohane (2005, 29) defined accountability as a situation in which 'some actors have the right to hold other actors to a set of standards, to judge whether they have fulfilled their responsibilities in light of these standards, and to impose sanctions if they determine that these responsibilities have not been met'. How can the EP provide effective parliamentary oversight for the EU, given that its legal and political arsenal is limited compared to its national counterparts? A concern among new intergovernmental scholars is that the EP trades off influence for accountability, that is, it provides for a seat at the negotiating table without ensuring that the results of this negotiation carry democratic checks and balances in line with the Community method. The creation of the Economic Dialogue under the Six-Pack and Two-Pack poses an interesting challenge in this regard (e.g. Pollak and Slominski 2015).

This chapter contrasts the EP's Monetary Dialogue with the European Central Bank (ECB), which has run since 1998, with the Economic Dialogue, a forum launched in 2011 to hold EU institutions and member states involved in EU economic governance to account.[5] It charts the creation of these dialogues and evaluates their implementation. The Monetary Dialogue, it argues, has helped to promote greater transparency over euro area monetary policy, although it would benefit from focusing on a narrower range of policy issues and closer cooperation between Members of

---

[3] This committee has been known by various names and acronyms, including EMAC, but we stick to ECON for simplicity's sake.

[4] That is the Single Supervisory Mechanism, the Single Resolution Board, the European Supervisory Agencies, and the European Systemic Risk Board.

[5] Article 2a, Regulation (EU) No. 1177/2011.

the European Parliament (MEPs). The Economic Dialogue is a welcome addition to the EU's economic governance architecture, it concludes, but its effectiveness has been constrained by a lack of resources and institutional constraints. The chapter calls for the Monetary and Economic Dialogues to be delegated to a new euro rea oversight subcommittee (EAOS) to enhance the democratic oversight of Economic and Monetary Union (EMU).

2   The Origins of ECON and the Monetary Dialogue

The EP is the EU's competence maximizer par excellence. Rarely has it missed an opportunity to increase its oversight of EMU even if the treaties provided limited scope for doing so. Once the European Council agreed to move forward with plans for EMU, the members of the Economic and Monetary Affairs (ECON) Committee opened informal channels of dialogue with the Committee of Central Bank Governors on monetary matters, the Commission and the Council on economic matters (Jacobs 1991). This was a continuation of efforts by this committee and its antecedents to gain a foothold in EMU. ECON was not among the original EP committees established by the Treaty of Rome, but an Economic and Financial Committee was established shortly afterwards. By the early 1970s, it had changed its name to ECON and was, on its own initiative, keeping a watching brief on the implementation of the Werner Report (see Bousch 1974). Calls for greater EP oversight of economic policy to be strengthened date from this period. In 1974, a high-level study group led by the British economist Alexander Cairncross called for the creation of a committee of economic advisors to the EP to strengthen democratic oversight of the embryonic EMU (Cairncross 1974). ECON's inclusion among the standing committees established by the EP in 1979 enhanced its status, as did the appointment of Jacques Delors as its chair. Delors played an active role in monitoring the European Monetary System, even though this system operated at one remove from the treaties, before he left to become French finance minister and, later, Commission president.

The 1989 Delors Report, which revived and reworked plans for EMU, saw no great need for increased oversight in relation to the project's economic dimension. A new monetary institution should be put within the EP's 'constellation', the report accepted, but the tasks assigned to the EP in the economic domain by the Treaty of Rome would otherwise suffice (Committee for the Study of EMU 1989). Council decisions concerning economic policy coordination in EMU's third stage should be done with the cooperation of the EP, it was suggested. The Maastricht Treaty diluted this provision by stipulating that the EP should be kept informed of the Council's surveillance efforts. The EP was also authorized to invite the president of the Council to appear before its competent committee in the event that a member state was sanctioned for breaching the Broad Economic Policy Guidelines[6] (BEPGs) or for failing to correct excessive budget deficits.[7] These provisions were a deep disappointment for the EP, which had proposed the extensive use of co-decision on the adopting of conjunctural measures and guidelines relating to economic and social policies in its proposals to the intergovernmental conference on EMU (Jacobs 1991, 378).

During the Maastricht Treaty negotiations, the EP unsuccessfully sought the insertion of a legal obligation for the ECB president's appearance before the EP akin to the obligations of the US Federal Reserve System. In the end, the Maastricht Treaty's provisions on EP oversight of the ECB were quite limited. The ECB was required to report annually on its activities to the EP, which was given the authority to hold a general debate on that basis.[8] The Treaty also allowed ECB Executive Board members to be heard before 'the competent Committees' of the EP at the instigation of either party.[9] Despite the lack of a firm legal basis, the EP 'could be seen defining its role keeping the ECB accountable in a proactive way' (Amtenbrink and van Duin 2009, 569) by including in its rules of procedure an invitation to the ECB president to visit ECON on a quarterly basis to make a statement and answer questions. Similarly, the stipulation that any MEP could demand a written answer to a question also finds its roots in rules of procedure.

The ECB accepted the EP's proposal and the first exchange of views took place in September 1998, building on the European Parliament's ongoing exchange of views with the European Monetary Institute since 1994. The modalities of this new forum, which came to be known as the Monetary Dialogue, were set out in an inter-institutional agreement between the EP and ECB (Collignon and Diessner 2016, 1302). Few

---

[6] Article 121(5) TFEU.
[7] Article 126 TFEU.
[8] Article 109b, TEC.
[9] Article 109b, TEC.

commentators expected the Monetary Dialogue to amount to much, but it has proved to be a mutually beneficial forum. For the ECB, the Monetary Dialogue offers further evidence of the Bank's commitment to transparency and a public platform from which to expound on policy issues in a less technical way. For the EP, the Monetary Dialogue offers a chance for MEPs to (be seen to) hold the ECB to account, as well as a foothold in an area of EU policy-making in which the legislature has limited competences.[10] Although it is difficult to measure the precise impact of the Monetary Dialogue, Amtenbrink and Van Duin (2009) argue that the EP has achieved a level of oversight for euro area monetary policy beyond that envisaged in the Treaty, even if doubts remain about whether the ECB is being held sufficiently to account. The ECB president appears with greater frequency before the EP than do the heads of the Federal Reserve and Bank of England before their respective legislatures (Eijffinger and Mujagic 2004). This lends credence to the ECB's claims of accountability in response to criticisms over its independence (Buiter 1999).

3   THE MONETARY DIALOGUE IN ACTION

The Monetary Dialogue occurs four times a year and typically lasts two hours. The ECB president begins with an introductory statement, which is followed by questions from the ECON members. A monetary expert panel supports ECON by providing briefing papers on a range of issues related to monetary policy. Since 2006, for each hearing, two topics are identified for which the experts write papers, and the ECB president is expected to comment on them during his introductory statement. Neither the ECB president nor the ECON members have been bound by the identified topics; the former frequently fails to mention the topics in the opening statement, and the latter do not limit themselves to asking questions about them (Amtenbrink and Van Duin 2009).

The Monetary Dialogue is similar in structure to the hearings that the US Federal Reserve and the Bank of England have with their respective

---

[10] It could be argued that MEPs rather than the EP are holding the ECB to account through the Monetary Dialogue. Committees have the authority to decide on draft resolutions but resolutions can only be adopted in plenary sessions. This procedural point, though it is correct, overlooks the significant legitimacy exercised by EP committees. When the ECB attends ECON, the former is widely seen as appearing not *at* but *before* the EP (see e.g. Amtenbrink and Van Duin 2009).

legislatures, with the key difference being that the EP lacks the possibility to sanction the ECB. For some scholars, this makes the euro area monetary authority 'less accountable or transparent than the Bank of England or the Fed' (Claeys et al. 2014, 2). What is clear is that the ECB faces no direct consequences as a result of its dialogue with ECON. The dialogue is, moreover, conducted between the ECB and individual MEPs. Although MEPs speak on behalf of their constituents and, perhaps, their political group, they do not speak for the EP. The EP's own-initiative report in response to the ECB's annual report is more representative of the institution in this regard, since it is voted on in plenary prior to the annual debate with the ECB president.

The Monetary Dialogue evolved during its first decade as the ECB operated not only according to the limited accountability constraints of the Maastricht Treaty but the political dynamics of the time; the ECB arguably took refuge behind its expertise, portraying itself as a technocratic institution that provided a public good while the EP fought its monopoly on the monetary policy discourse by discussing their political ramifications (Jabko 2000). During this period, the ECB was 'highly responsive to the ECON' (Eijffinger and Mujagic 2004, 190) and the dialogue seemingly had an impact on the ECB's procedures, such as the May 2003 reform that removed M3 from the policy analysis and refined the definition of price stability (Sibert 2005). The Parliament's approach also evolved, moving away from the focus on price stability to include topics like the ECB's general mission and level of transparency (Amtenbrink and Van Duin 2009).

The Monetary Dialogue, the Bank concluded in its report on ten years of EMU, 'allows the ECB to be effectively held accountable to the EU's elected representatives and the public' (European Central Bank 2008). An EP resolution at this time declared the Monetary Dialogue 'a success' (European Parliament 2008). In spite of these assessments, the Monetary Dialogue has been viewed as inadequate by some. Charles Wyplosz (2007) referred to it as a 'gentlemanly discussion' in which accountability is neither mentioned nor achieved. Moreover, the expansion of the ECB's activities during the sovereign debt crisis could merit additional accountability measures (Braun 2017). Given that its forays into unconventional monetary policy (including the Securities Market Programme, Long-Term Refinancing Operations, as well as its Emergency Liquidity Assistance) and its participation in the troika, the ECB has expanded its responsibilities de facto if not de jure. These policies, however, have clear fiscal and distributive consequences and have raised the spectre of fiscal domination. The ECB may have played a critical role in saving the euro (Chang and Leblond 2015), but this creeping competence should not be overlooked (Chang 2018). The methods of accountability remain the same, focusing on transparency and the Monetary Dialogue.

How has the Monetary Dialogue changed since the euro crisis? For one thing, it has exposed the ECB to a broader range of questions from MEPs. During the first decade of EMU, MEPs focused on growth and employment, while the ECB tended to restrict remarks to issues concerning price stability. From 2013 to 2016, however, about half of the MEPs' questions related to financial supervision, country surveillance, and euro area governance reforms, and the number of questions posed to the ECB increased significantly. While the Monetary Dialogues do not seem to have influenced financial market expectations, they have contributed to greater transparency and therefore legitimacy (Collignon and Diessner 2016).

And yet, the Monetary Dialogue has been driven to a large extent by the ECB itself. The treaty obligations of the ECB towards the EP are quite slim, and the ECB entered into the exchange of views with ECON voluntarily to bolster its own claims for legitimacy by engaging in the Monetary Dialogue helped the ECB address criticisms regarding its high degree of independence, making the exchange mutually beneficial (Jabko 2000). The ECB's responsiveness to ECON demands is also voluntary, as the EP holds no formal sanctioning mechanism against the ECB. In contrast to the US Federal Reserve's hearings before the US Congress, the ECB can reject the EP's suggestions with little cost, except perhaps for reputational damage. In this respect, the Monetary Dialogue serves more as ex-post scrutiny by the EP that also provides an opportunity for the ECB to enhance its transparency than as a mechanism for democratic accountability.

Since the sovereign debt crisis, the EP's 'competence has only been marginally strengthened and thus remains rather limited' (Jančić 2017, 145). Considering the fiscal implications of ECB actions during the sovereign debt crisis, there is an argument for strengthening the Monetary Dialogue to ensure even greater accountability (Belke 2014). Karl Whelan (2014) suggests that the dialogue improves its focus and in particular makes more use of the analyses provided by experts. Indeed, MEPs could work more closely together in ECON, focusing on fewer topics and working more in unison to commit itself to at least enhancing the ECB's transparency, if not holding the ECB to account.

4   THE ORIGINS OF THE ECONOMIC DIALOGUE

The need for—and paucity of—parliamentary oversight of economic policy is a recurring theme in the history of EMU. The 1970 Werner Report, an early ill-fated proposal for EMU, called for the creation of a Centre of Decision for Economic Policy that would be accountable to the EP (Werner 1970, 13), although it offered limited detail on what powers the former would possess and how the latter would hold it to account. The report did argue, however, that the budgetary powers of the EP would need to be increased as a result of EMU and it dropped a heavy hint about the need for direct elections. The EP, it concluded, 'will have to be furnished with a status corresponding to the extension of the Community missions, not only from its powers, but also having regard to the point of views of method of election of its members' (Werner 1970, 13).

After EMU was finally realized in 1999, the success of the Monetary Dialogue led to calls for the creation of an Economic Dialogue to focus on economic surveillance (see Hallerberg et al. 2012, 36–37). Deroose et al. (2008) were early advocates for such a dialogue, which they argued could help the EP to play a more effective role in relation to the BEPGs, as well as to strengthen the democratic accountability of economic governance more generally. To this end, they called for the Commissioner for Economic and Monetary Affairs and the president of the Economic and Financial Affairs (ECOFIN) Council to appear before the EP at regular intervals. Finance ministers of member states facing Council recommendations should also be invited to extraordinary sessions of the Economic Dialogue, they added, to discuss their country's economic situation.

The EP continued to press for greater oversight of euro area economic policy during EMU's first decade. In 2006, an ECON report on the European Commission's annual report on the euro area called for a joint dialogue between the Eurogroup, the Commission, and Parliament to take place at least annually (García-Margallo y Marfil 2006). A joint appearance by the Eurogroup president and Commissioner for Economic and Monetary Affairs in July 2007 to discuss the Commission's annual report on the euro area constituted a step forward in this regard.

The idea of an Economic Dialogue was formally taken up in the Six-Pack, Two-Pack, and the Fiscal Compact (although the Fiscal Compact does not form a legal basis for dialogues in EP). Under the Six-Pack, a set of six laws adopted by ECOFIN and the EP in 2011, an Economic

Dialogue may be created for the Commission to make its analysis public, to promote discussion with the Commission, the presidents of the Council, European Council, Eurogroup, and member states. Specifically, this legislation allows the competent committee of the EP to invite the Commission and the presidents of the Council, European Council, and Eurogroup to discuss matters relating to the Stability and Growth Pact's corrective[11] and preventive[12] arms, the corrective arm of the Macroeconomic Imbalance Procedure,[13] the BEPGs, economic and multilateral surveillance, and the European Semester.[14] The EP may also invite member states for an exchange of views, specifically those:

- facing recommendations for corrective action for failing to respect the BEPGs or otherwise jeopardizing the smooth functioning of EMU by breaching medium-term budgetary objectives[15];
- facing disciplinary action under the Stability and Growth Pact's corrective[16] or preventive arms[17];
- subject to sanctioning under the Macroeconomic Imbalance Procedure's corrective arm.[18]

Under the Two-Pack, which entered into force in May 2014, euro area members that are party to an economic adjustment programme and subject to fines under the excessive deficit procedure may be invited to an exchange of views with the EP.[19] In addition, the EP may invite the Commission and the presidents of the Council, European Council, and Eurogroup to discuss the following:

- Commission's assessment of budgetary situation and prospects for the euro area as a whole;
- economic partnership programmes;

[11] Article 2a, Regulation (EU) No. 1177/2011.
[12] Article 3, Regulation (EU) No. 1173/2011.
[13] Article 6, Regulation (EU) 1174/2011.
[14] Article 14, Regulation (EU) 1176/2011.
[15] Article 2-ab, Regulation (EU) No. 1175/2011.
[16] Article 2a, Regulation (EU) No. 1177/2011.
[17] Article 3, Regulation (EU) No. 1173/2011.
[18] Article 14, Regulation (EU) 1176/2011.
[19] Article 15, Regulation (EU) No. 473/2013.

- the corrective arm of the Stability and Growth Pact[20]; or
- the economic and budgetary surveillance of euro area member states experiencing or threatened with serious difficulties with respect to their financial stability.[21]

The Fiscal Compact, a treaty between a subset of EU member states that entered into force in December 2012, stated that the president of the Euro Summit shall present a report to the EP after each Euro Summit meeting.[22]

5 THE ECONOMIC DIALOGUE IN ACTION

Assessing the effectiveness of parliamentary oversight is complicated because executives' compliance with legislative goals depends on a combination of factors that are within and beyond their control as well as difficult to disentangle. It can also be challenging to identify non-compliance by an executive until well after the fact, if at all. Possible remedies to non-compliance vary, and it is not always clear whether naming and shaming, the most common form of oversight, is a judicious policy instrument or merely parliamentary grandstanding.

One way of evaluating the effectiveness of parliamentary oversight is to consider the resources devoted to its preparation. The EP's Economic Governance Support Unit assigns three full-time officials to the preparation of briefings for the Economic Dialogues with the other EU institutions and member states.[23] Inputs provided cover both internally prepared factual notes and, in some cases, externally prepared studies or in-depth analyses. This compares favourably to the Monetary Dialogue, which has just one dedicated official, and it is on a par with the House of Lords Economic Affairs Committee, which has one clerk, one policy analyst, and one assistant. But it falls well short of the US Senate Committee on Banking, Housing, and Urban Affairs, which has 44 full-time staffers, and

---

[20] Article 15, Regulation (EU) No. 473/2013.
[21] Article 18, Regulation (EU) No. 472/2013.
[22] Article 13, Fiscal Compact.
[23] This figure does not include those EP staff in, for example, the Directorate-General for Internal Policies of the Union or the European Parliamentary Research Service that occasionally produce analysis for the Economic Dialogue.

the House of Commons Treasury Committee, which has 1 clerk, 2 senior economists, 3 committee specialists, 2 assistants, and 1 media officer.[24]

The Monetary Dialogue has a reputation for being 'thoroughly prepared' (Gros 2004). Before each meeting, ECON's coordinators commission briefings, notes, or in-depth studies by monetary experts (typically academic economists or think tank staff) on two or three specific topics. Receiving multiple papers on each topic, the MEPs who sit on the Monetary Dialogue are informed about key issues relating to monetary policy. ECON has commissioned briefings only for Economic Dialogues with the Eurogroup president and not, it would appear, with interlocutors from other EU institutions. When analysis is commissioned, between three and five contributions are provided on just one topic depending on the length of the document. In consequence, the Economic Dialogue is more heavily reliant on short notes prepared by the Economic Governance Support Unit. These notes typically offer a general overview of the economic situation and compliance with EU procedures and objectives.

The success of the Monetary Dialogue partly lies in its transparency. Minutes of meetings are published on ECON's website, as are the briefings of its outside experts. In contrast, no minutes are published for the Economic Dialogue, though ECON publishes preparatory notes and expert briefings (where available). The availability of video recordings of Economic Dialogues on the EP's website helps to redress this deficit to some degree but they are not quite as useful for journalists and academic researchers seeking to track discussions between MEPs and the invitees to Economic Dialogues.

A weakness of the Economic Dialogue is that there is limited follow-up to its deliberations. The ECB has agreed to answer written questions from MEPs, which are published along with answers in the EU's *Official Journal*. The Monetary Dialogue also encourages follow-up by pressing particular policy recommendations in recurring meetings with the ECB president. The ECB's willingness to give ground on one of these points—the publication of ECB staff projections—provided an early win for the Monetary Dialogue. No such points have been pressed in the Economic Dialogue, which at the time of writing has yet to secure a discernable policy concession from its participants. MEPs may address written questions to the European Commission but not the Eurogroup or the member states.

---

[24] Source: http://congressional-staff.insidegov.com/d/a/Senate.

The Monetary Dialogue, as noted earlier, relies on the willingness of the ECB to hold itself to account in ways that go beyond Treaty requirements. The Economic Dialogue is underpinned by secondary law, which creates an expectation (although not a legal requirement) that invitees will attend. But the Economic Dialogue remains reliant on the goodwill of its invitees; they come to the EP to engage in dialogue, not to give a deposition. Among the parties to the Economic Dialogue, the European Commission has the strongest incentive to engage in a full and frank exchange of views with MEPs. This is not only because the European Commission is (increasingly) beholden to the EP because of the rules concerning the hiring and firing of the College of Commissioners. It is also because the Economic Dialogue provides a public forum for an institution that sometimes struggles to make its message heard. This explains why the Commission is the most frequent participant in the Economic Dialogue, attending five times in 2016, for instance, compared to four for the ECOFIN president and two for the Eurogroup president. As with the Monetary Dialogue and the ECB, the Economic Dialogue provides the Commission with a useful platform to explain its views and demonstrate its transparency and accountability. The European Parliament may invite the presidents of the Council, Commission, Eurogroup and European Council[25] as well as representatives from the Commission, the ECB, and the International Monetary Fund (IMF)[26] to take part in an Economic Dialogue, though neither regulation compels participation.

The Eurogroup president has been a somewhat reticent participant in the Economic Dialogue. Jeroen Dijsselbloem limited his appearances at the Economic Dialogue to two times per year. These meetings took place in the spring and autumn, sometimes at short notice. Often, the topics under discussion were long since decided by the Eurogroup; for example, the dialogue on the third Greek bailout programme took place four months after the Eurogroup and Greek government had found an agreement (De la Parra 2016). Ideally for the EP, the Eurogroup president would attend the Economic Dialogue at regular and predictable intervals. This would help with the preparation of the Economic Dialogue, particularly regarding the commissioning of expert briefings. Chairing the Eurogroup at a time of crisis was an arduous task, even before Dijsselbloem's responsibilities as finance minister of the Netherlands were taken into

[25] Article 15, Regulation (EU) No 473/2013.
[26] Article 3, Regulation (EU) No 472/2013.

account. But the current situation undermines the EP's oversight of the Eurogroup's decisive role in the governance of EMU.

A conspicuous absentee from the Economic Dialogues is the president of the European Council. The fact that Euro Summits have not taken place regularly has also reduced the scope for dialogue envisaged under the Fiscal Compact. Herman Van Rompuy, the first full-time president of the European Council, furthermore, declined the opportunity to participate in the Economic Dialogue in favour of periodic appearances before the EP plenary. Van Rompuy's successor, Donald Tusk, continued this tradition. This situation is less than satisfactory, we contend, as speaking time available to MEPs in plenary sessions is more curtailed than is the case in committees. According to Miller (2009), the speaking time in EP plenaries ranges from five to six minutes for a party or group spokesperson and around two minutes for others. There are no such constraints in committee meetings.

ECON's ability to invite member states to an Economic Dialogue is constrained by legislation underpinning this forum. Whereas this legislation assumes that the Eurogroup president, for example, will attend discussions 'where appropriate',[27] the obligations placed on member states to attend are weaker. First, the legislation recognizes that EU institutions (rather than member states) are 'the counterparts' of the European Parliament.[28] Second, it requires only that member states be offered 'an opportunity to participate in an exchange of views' and makes clear that such participation is voluntary.[29] Third, this exchange of views is contingent on the triggering of certain disciplinary actions in relation to EU economic governance. Member states facing a recommendation in the event of significant deviations from medium-term budgetary objectives,[30] sanctions in relation to the preventive or corrective arm of the Stability and Growth Pact,[31] disciplinary measures under the excessive deficit procedure[32] or the macroeconomic imbalance procedure,[33] and enhanced

---

[27] Article 12, Regulation (EU) No 1173/2011.
[28] Article 12, Regulation (EU) No 1173/2011.
[29] Article 12, Regulation (EU) No 1173/2011.
[30] Article 2(a-b), (EU) Regulation 1175/2011.
[31] Under Article 3, (EU) Regulation 1173/2011.
[32] Article 2a, (EU) Regulation 1177/2011.
[33] Article 14(2), (EU) Regulation 1176/2011 and Article 6, (EU) Regulation 1174/2011.

monitoring of national budgetary plans[34] and macroeconomic adjustment programmes may all be invited to appear before the Economic Dialogue.[35] These constraints have proved even tighter in practice than they are in design. This is due to the European Commission's preference for using the preventive rather than the corrective arm of the Macroeconomic Imbalance Procedure. Under Regulation (EU) 1176/2011, the Commission is required to conduct an in-depth review for all member states facing excessive imbalances or the risk thereof, and it did so on 74 occasions between 2012 and 2016. Where it decides that a member state failed to take corrective action to correct an excessive imbalance, the Council can decide, on the basis of a recommendation from the Commission, that the member state is non-compliant, a procedural step that paves the way for the levying of financial penalties and fines against the member state in question. Between 2012 and 2016, the Council found no member state to be non-compliant. As a result, the corrective arm of the Macroeconomic Imbalance Procedure remained dormant. An unintended consequence of this is that the Economic Dialogue was not in a position to invite member states for the express reason of discussing the Macroeconomic Imbalance Procedure.

ECON showed itself willing to go beyond the legislation underpinning the Economic Dialogue by inviting member states for an informal exchange of views. Such invitations were used sparingly, however. In the case of Portugal and Spain, an exchange of views followed Economic Dialogues linked to non-compliance with the Stability and Growth Pact. Germany, the euro's largest economy, was invited on one occasion only. Latvia and Lithuania were the only other member states to receive such an invitation. Bulgaria, the Czech Republic, Denmark, Estonia, Luxembourg, the Netherlands, Austria, Poland, Romania, Slovakia, Slovenia, Finland, Sweden, and the United Kingdom were invited to neither an Economic Dialogue nor an exchange of views.

Bowler and Farrell (1995, 221) argue that EP committees, whatever their powers, will be effective only if 'members take such committee work seriously' (Bowler and Farrell 1995, 221). Drawing on the literature on US congressional committees, these authors suggest that MEP's involvement in and commitment to EP committees reflect collective, individual,

---

[34] Article 15(2), (EU) Regulation 473/2013.
[35] Article 3(8), 7(10), and 14(3), (EU) Regulation 472/2013.

and party interests. Members have a collective interest in creating committees so as to pool expertise and information in specific areas in order to enhance executive oversight. Individual interests concern the extent to which committee membership serves the concerns of key constituents and maximizes the influence and visibility of members within the EP. Party interests concern the desire of EP party groups to ensure that they are represented in key policy committees and have an opportunity to lead committees. Seen in these terms, MEPs have a collective interest in the work of the Economic Dialogue, which allows a subset of members to track a substantively and procedurally complex area of EU policy. Political groups also have a strong incentive to ensure that their members are present when a high-profile dossier such as EU economic surveillance is discussed. That said, individual interests are probably weaker in the case of the Economic Dialogue than for other EP committees. Whereas MEPs representing constituents with a strong agricultural sector have an incentive to join the Agricultural Committee (Bowler and Farrell 1995, 227), the Economic Dialogue deals with an issue of general concern to constituents and one that attracts limited interest from interest groups.

MEPs with close connections to trade unions and business are more likely to join the Economic and Monetary Affairs Committee (Bowler and Farrell 1995), although their influence will be diluted to some degree by the desire of party groups to ensure a seat at the table for their members. The Monetary Dialogue provides a clear-cut opportunity to hold euro area authorities to account in a way that is typically not available at the member state level. The same is true for Economic Dialogues with the European Commission and Eurogroup, although these officeholders lack policy-making instruments that are on a par with those wielded by the ECB.

Participation in the Economic Dialogue conforms to these expectations, especially in relation to member state dialogues, with MEPs showing more interest in questioning ministers from their own member state. The Economic Dialogue with Croatia in March 2017 saw only eight speakers (apart from the chair), and two of those were from Croatia. MEPs who were willing to interrogate ministers from across the EU are scarce. Pervenche Berès (a former ECON chair) is a noticeable exception in this regard. Those MEPs who do speak, as Sergio De la Parra (2016) observes, too often make long and unwieldy points that leave limited time for meaningful discussion with invitees.

6   Reforming the Economic and Monetary Dialogues

The Economic and Monetary Dialogues do not need to be strengthened, it could be argued, because the EP's oversight of the ECB is working well and economic policy in the EU—and euro area—is decentralized. While it makes sense to hold an EU institution with a centralized policy instrument, such as the ECB, to account, neither the Commission nor the ECOFIN Council nor the European Council possesses similar powers. Member state governments, meanwhile, are accountable to their own electorates in accordance with national constitutional traditions. While we see merits in this argument in relation to EU economic policy, we take a different view in relation to euro area governance. Economic policies are no less important for EMU because they are decentralized. The euro crisis plainly illustrated the potential for cross-border economic spillovers from large and small member states alike. The diffusion of executive power across multiple institutions and levels of government, likewise, makes EP oversight all the more essential (Bovens and Curtin 2016).

Responsibility for the Monetary and Economic Dialogues should be delegated to a new ECON euro area oversight subcommittee (EAOS). This division would help to separate ECON's legislative and non-legislative functions from its oversight responsibilities in relation to the EU. The EAOS would require a dedicated staff with expertise in economics and a standing committee of external experts drawn from academia and think tanks to advise on the preparation of the Monetary and Economic Dialogues. Membership of the subcommittee would be drawn from the senior ranks of the ECON Committee with the party groupings agreeing to put forward members with high-level experience and expertise in economic and monetary affairs. Closer cooperation between subcommittee members would be required to ensure that the EAOS focuses on key policy issues. The duration of Economic Dialogues will vary according to the subject matter, but they should be arranged so as to allow for a significant amount of speaking time for subcommittee members and answers from invitees. This is not always possible at present, with the Economic Dialogue with Croatia in March 2017 lasting just 45 minutes.

As things stand, the trigger for Economic Dialogues is too constraining. Rather than waiting for member states to face disciplinary measures under the Macroeconomic Imbalance Procedure (MIP), all member states that are at risk of non-compliance should be routinely invited for either an

Economic Dialogue or an exchange of views. The current frequency of dialogues with the Commission seems appropriate but there is a case for the Eurogroup president to attend at least four times per year at predetermined intervals. We would also argue that the European Council president should attend the EAOS twice per year.

To ensure the transparency of the EAOS, full transcripts of the Economic and Monetary Dialogues should be published, encompassing preparatory briefings form EP officials and external experts, the opening statements from invitees and the subsequent question and answer session. Members should be allowed to put written questions to the Eurogroup president rather than the Commission alone and an annual report of the subcommittee's activities should be published on its website.

The proposed committee would not, of course, come without costs, challenges, and limitations. The distinction between euro area and non-euro area members is a valid one in relation to monetary policy but it is more blurred in relation to economic governance. The Stability and Growth Pact, for example, has a special importance for the euro area but it also applies to other EU member states. For this reason, there is a danger that the EAOS would duplicate discussions happening elsewhere in the EP. Excluding non-euro area MEPs would also be contentious and very much at odds with current practices inside the EP. Finally, the term subcommittee denotes standing as well as specialization. There is a risk that a subcommittee would carry less weight than an EP committee and so struggle to achieve the level of oversight it desired. Indeed, ECON established a subcommittee on monetary affairs in 1992 and it was this forum that hosted the first meetings of the Monetary Dialogue before the EP decided in 1999 to 'upgrade' such discussions to full committee level.

Such points warrant careful consideration but they do not negate the potential of the EAOS. Careful coordination between the EAOS and other EP committees could minimize the scope for duplication. Allowing MEPs from non-euro area members to participate in the EAOS from time to time if they so wish could also help to address concerns over the exclusivity of this body as well as mirroring practices in the Euro Summit.[36] A subcommittee need not carry less weight, meanwhile, if its members, as suggested above, are drawn from ECON's most experienced members.

---

[36] Article 12(3) of the Fiscal Compact allows the heads of state or government of non-euro area members to attend the Euro Summit when certain agenda items are discussed.

A subcommittee would also be preferable to the creation of a euro area parliament, an idea that has been interrogated by scholars (see Maurer 2013) and politicians, including François Hollande, Jacques Delors (Chazan 2015), and Emmanuel Macron (2017a). Whereas a subcommittee would deepen the EP's existing role in relation to EMU, a euro area parliament has the potential to undermine not just this role but the democratic standing of the EP more generally. At best, the EP and the euro area parliament would have rival democratic mandates. At worst, a second electoral cycle could depress turnout in EP elections yet further. For this reason, perhaps, proposals for a euro area parliament often leave some ambiguity about whether they are proposing a separate institution or, like us, new structures within the existing EP. Having proposed a euro area parliament in his presidential election manifesto, Emmanuel Macron subsequently argued that the European Parliament should be a 'crucible' for deeper integration in the euro area and EU (Macron 2017b).

7   CONCLUSION

This chapter has explored the origins and early experiences of the Monetary and Economic Dialogues, forums created for enhancing democratic oversight of EMU. The Monetary Dialogue gave the ECB and the EP a mutually beneficial arrangement that increased the transparency and legitimacy of the former and enhanced the profile of the latter. While it has exceeded expectations, the quality of the discussion between the ECB and EP could be improved through more internal coordination on the part of the EP. Inspired by the EP's Monetary Dialogue with the ECB, the Economic Dialogue provides MEPs with an opportunity to hold various EU and member state actors to account for their role in EU and euro area economic governance. The effectiveness of the Economic Dialogue, it was argued, has been limited in several ways. First, the preparation of the Economic Dialogue has lagged behind that of the Monetary Dialogue and instances of oversight in other political systems. Second, the Eurogroup president has been somewhat reticent about attending the Economic Dialogue and the president of the European Council has yet to attend. Third, the Economic Dialogue has been more constrained than anticipated, with EU policymakers' reluctance to trigger the corrective arm of the macroeconomic imbalance procedure reducing the scope for Economic Dialogues on this all-important issue. Finally, MEPs have been somewhat reticent in their engagement with the Economic Dialogue, with parliamentarians tending to engage with dialogues that concern their own member state. To address these shortcomings, this chapter proposed the creation of an ECON Euro Area Oversight Committee with greater resources and a more expansive approach to holding those who govern the euro to account. This committee would not be a panacea but it would be useful step towards greater accountability in this crucial policy domain.

REFERENCES

Amtenbrink, F., & Van Duin, K. (2009). The European Central Bank Before the European Parliament: Theory and Practice After 10 Years of Monetary Dialogue. *European Law Review, 34*(4), 561–583.

Belke, A. (2014). *Monetary Dialogue 2009–2014: Looking Backward, Looking Forward*. Ruhr Economic Papers 477.

Berman, S., & McNamara, K. R. (1999). Bank on Democracy – Why Central Banks Need Public Oversight. *Foreign Affairs, 78*(2), 2–8.

Bousch, J.-E. (1974). Report Drawn up on Behalf of the Committee on Economic and Monetary Affairs on the Proposal from the Commission of the European Communities to the Council (Doc. 280/74) Concerning the Annual Report on the Economic Situation in the Community. Working Documents 1974–1975, Document 286/74.

Bovens, M., & Curtin, D. (2016). An Unholy Trinity of EU Presidents? The Political Accountability of Post-Crisis EU Executive Power. In D. Chalmers, M. Jachtenfuchs, & C. Joerges (Eds.), *The End of the Eurocrats' Dream: Adjusting to European Diversity* (pp. 190–217). Cambridge: Cambridge University Press.

Bowler, S., & Farrell, D. M. (1995). The Organizing of the European Parliament: Committees, Specialization and Coordination. *British Journal of Political Science, 25*(2), 219–243.

Braun, B. (2017). *Two Sides of the Same Coin? Transparency and Accountability of the European Central Bank*. Brussels: Transparency International EU.

Buiter, W. H. (1999). Alice in Euroland. *Journal of Common Market Studies, 37*(2), 181–209.

Buller, J., & Flinders, M. (2005). The Domestic Origins of Depoliticisation in the Area of British Economic Policy. *The British Journal of Politics and International Relations, 7*(4), 526–543.

Cairncross, A. (1974). *Economic Policy for the European Community: The Way Forward*. Berlin: Springer.

Chang, M. (2018). The Creeping Competence of the European Central Bank During the Euro Crisis. *Credit and Capital, 51*(1), 41–53.

Chang, M., & Leblond, P. (2015). All In: Market Expectations of Eurozone Integrity in the Sovereign Debt Crisis. *Review of International Political Economy, 22*(3), 626–655.

Chazan, D. (2015, July 19). Francois Hollande Calls for Eurozone Government. *The Telegraph.*

Claeys, G. et al. (2014, March 3). European Central Bank Accountability: How the Monetary Dialogue Could Be Improved. *Bruegel Policy Contribution.*

Collignon, S., & Diessner, S. (2016). The ECB's Monetary Dialogue with the European Parliament: Efficiency and Accountability During the Euro Crisis?'. *JCMS: Journal of Common Market Studies, 54*(6), 1296–1312.

Committee for the Study of Economic Monetary Union. (1989). *Report on Economic and Monetary Union in the European Community.* Brussels: European Commission.

De la Parra, S. (2016). The Economic Dialogue: An Effective Accountability Mechanism? In L. Daniele (Ed.), *The Democratic Principle and the Economic and Monetary Union* (pp. 101–120). Berlin: Springer.

Deroose, S., Hodson, D., & Kuhlmann, J. (2008). The Broad Economic Policy Guidelines: Before and After the Re-Launch of the Lisbon Strategy. *Journal of Common Market Studies, 46*(4), 827–848.

Eijffinger, S. C., & Mujagic, E. (2004). An Assessment of the Effectiveness of the Monetary Dialogue on the ECB's Accountability and Transparency: A Qualitative Approach. *Intereconomics, 39*(4), 190–203.

European Central Bank. (2008). *Monthly Bulletin: 10th Anniversary of the ECB.* Frankfurt AM: ECB.

European Parliament. (2008). European Parliament Resolution of 18 November 2008 on the EMU@10: The First Ten Years of Economic and Monetary Union and future Challenges, 2008/2156(INI).

García-Margallo y Marfil, J. (2006). *Report on the 2006 Annual Report on the Euro Area.* ECON Committee PE 378.814v02-00, A6-0381/2006.

Grant, R. W., & Keohane, R. O. (2005). Accountability and Abuses of Power in World Politics. *American Political Science Review, 99*(1), 29–43.

Gros, D. (2004). *Five Years of Monetary Dialogue.* Brussels: ECON Committee, European Parliament.

Hallerberg, M., Marzinotto, B., & Wolff, G. B. (2012). An Assessment of the European Semester. In *Study for the Directorate-General for Internal Policies, Economic and Scientific Policy, PE* (Vol. 475). Brussels: European Parliament.

Jabko, N. (2000). Expertise et politique a l'age de l'euro: La Banque Centrale Europeenne sur le terrain de la democratie. *Revue Francaise de Science Politique, 51*(6), 903–931.

Jacobs, F. B. (1991). European Parliament and Economic and Monetary Union. *The Common Market Law Review, 28*, 361–382.

Jančić, D. (2017). Accountability of the European Central Bank in a Deepening Economic Monetary Union. In D. Jančić (Ed.), *National Parliaments After the Lisbon Treaty and the Euro Crisis* (pp. 141–158). Oxford: Oxford University Press.

Macron, E. (2017a). *Emmanuel Macron President: Programme*. Paris: En Marche.

Macron, E. (2017b, September 26). Sorbonne Speech of Emmanuel Macron. Full Text. Retrieved from http://international.blogs.ouest-france.fr/archive/2017/09/29/macron-sorbonne-verbatim-europe-18583.html.

Maurer, A. (2013). From EMU to DEMU: The Democratic Legitimacy of the EU and the European Parliament. Istituto Affari Internazionali Working Paper IAI 13/11.

McCubbins, M. D., & Schwartz, T. (1984). Congressional Oversight Overlooked: Police Patrols Versus Fire Alarms. *American Journal of Political Science, 28*(1), 165–179.

Miller, V. (2009). European Parliament Political Groups. *House of Commons Briefing Paper*, Vol. SN/IA/5031.

O'Brennan, J., & Raunio, T. (2007). Introduction: Deparliamentarization Through European Integration? In J. O'Brennan & T. Raunio (Eds.), *National Parliaments Within the Enlarged European Union: From 'Victims' of Integration to Competitive Actors?* (pp. 1–19). Abingdon: Routledge Advances in European Politics.

Pollak, J., & Slominski, P. (2015). The European Parliament: Adversary or Accomplice of the New Intergovernmentalism? In C. J. Bickerton & D. Hodson (Eds.), *The New Intergovernmentalism: States and Supranational Actors in the Post-Maastricht Era* (pp. 245–262). Oxford: Oxford University Press.

Schonhardt-Bailey, C. (2013). *Deliberating American Monetary Policy: A Textual Analysis*. Cambridge, MA: MIT Press.

Sibert, A. (2005). *The European Parliament's Monetary Dialogue with the ECB and Its Panel of Experts*. Paper prepared for the European Parliament's Committee on Economic and Monetary Affairs. ECON Committee, European Parliament, Brussels.

Waller, C. J. (2011). Independence + Accountability: Why the Fed Is a Well-Designed Central Bank. *Federal Reserve Bank of St. Louis Review, 93*(September/October), 293–302.

Werner, P. (1970). *Report to the Council and the Commission on the Realization by Stages of Economic and Monetary Union in the Community*. Brussels: European Commission.

Whelan, K. (2014). The Monetary Dialogue and Accountability for the ECB. Paper prepared for the European Parliament's Committee on Economic and Monetary Affairs, IP/A/ECON/NT/2014-01. Brussels: ECON Committee, European Parliament.

Wyplosz, C. (2007, May 12). Wake-Up Call for the ECB. *VOXEU*.

CHAPTER 17

The European Parliament and Energy Poverty: *Such a Long Way to Develop a Distinctive Voice in the Energy Union*

Frédérique Berrod, Louis Navé, and Samuel Verschraegen

1 INTRODUCTION

Energy policy at European Union (EU) level has traditionally been driven by the European Commission (EC), while member states managed to keep important prerogatives in this strategic sector. The contribution of the European Parliament (EP) to the development of an EU energy policy has mainly been characterised by a growing support of the majority of

F. Berrod (✉)
Institut d'Etudes Politiques de Strasbourg, Strasbourg, France

College of Europe, Bruges, Belgium
e-mail: f.berrod@unistra.fr

L. Navé
Centre d'Études Internationales et Européennes, Université de Strasbourg, Strasbourg, France
e-mail: louis.nave@coleurope.eu

S. Verschraegen
College of Europe, Bruges, Belgium
e-mail: samuel.verschraegen@coleurope.eu

© The Author(s) 2019   365
O. Costa (ed.), *The European Parliament in Times of EU Crisis*,
European Administrative Governance,
https://doi.org/10.1007/978-3-319-97391-3_17

Members of the European Parliament (MEPs) to the integration of the internal energy market, most of the time in line with the Commission's priorities (Eikland 2011). Thus, it may be argued at first glance that this institution has had a limited influence on the policy agenda setting and is not much of a policy-maker in the field of energy policy.

However, the development of alternative priorities than the liberalisation of energy markets at EU level has emerged, alongside the issues arising from energy transition. These have allowed the EP to reinforce its position and legitimacy in the decision-making process (Birchfield 2011). This is particularly noticeable with the issue of energy poverty. This question has steadily gained salience at EU level, as well as in academic literature. Numerous contributions have studied the characteristics and causes of energy poverty, and brought significant input to the debate on energy policy in the EU (Thompson et al. 2017; Bouzarovski and Tirado Herrero 2017; Derdevet 2013). However, few—if any—authors specifically treated the issue of energy poverty from the specific angle of the EP. This may come as a surprise considering the active role this institution played in the recognition of energy poverty in the third energy package in 2009, alongside the notion of vulnerable customer. Some MEPs have been—and still are—active supporters of an enhanced action of the EU on energy poverty. However, the extent to which the EP's contribution has translated into legislative texts remains unclear. The following analysis tries to identify the influence the EP had bringing the issue of energy poverty to the political agenda.

This chapter has two enshrined objectives. First, it examines if the EP actually brought a significant contribution to the fight against energy poverty at EU level. To this end, a review of legal constraints is conducted, specifically concerning the ability of the EP to weigh in the legislative process in relation to energy poverty. Second, the chapter analyses the ability of the EP to act as a policy-maker in the field of energy, drawing on the observations made on the specific issue of energy poverty.

It may be argued that the EP used different means, including resolutions and dialogue with the civil society, to influence the debate on energy poverty at EU level. The emphasis on consumers and energy efficiency in the proposals formulated by the Commission in the Clean Energy for All Europeans package of November 2016 confirms this influence of the EP on the issue of energy poverty. Most of the analysis of this chapter draws on a legal methodology, as it is assumed that the influence of the EP in this policy may have been diminished by legal principles, that is, the division of competences and the principle of subsidiarity. These specific constraints partly explain that the influence of the EP in the definition of European means to fight against energy poverty is limited. Another constraint is the political division of the EP along similar lines that the ones dividing the Council of the EU on the issue. Indeed, it has been considered that energy poverty can be solved either by a proper functioning of the energy markets free from public intervention or that it should remain a domain of action of member states, based on their preferences in terms of social policy.

In the first section, we will explore the reasons that led the EU to address energy poverty, although the issue falls primarily under the responsibility of the member states as part of their competence in the definition of social policy. The second section will explain that despite the growing impetus for a European approach to energy poverty, some important legal obstacles stand in the way of a fully-fledged EU policy on the matter. It explains the difficulties encountered by the EP when trying to find a political consensus in order to influence the Energy Union in this respect. The EP is therefore trying to defend the Europeanisation of the fight against energy poverty as a constitutive part of the Clean Energy for All Europeans package discussed since November 2016. It was not able to find a political majority to develop specific EU means to fight against energy poverty. Its influence as a policy-maker is diluted in this respect, as the third section of this chapter will demonstrate.

2   THE MAJOR ROLE OF THE EP IN THE EMERGENCE OF ENERGY POVERTY AS A EUROPEAN POLITICAL ISSUE

On the one hand, we will see that the European energy policy, despite having been primarily characterised by the liberalisation of the energy markets, has always included a social component that was progressively translated into EU law. From this perspective, the protection of the (vulnerable) consumers can be seen as the corollary of the internal energy market's deepening, or a way to offset its negative consequences (Sect. 2.1).

On the other hand, we argue that the EU decision-makers had to acknowledge and tackle the issue because of its increasing saliency (Sect. 2.2). Addressing the issue appears even more crucial as it will condition the success of the energy transition (Sect. 2.3).

2.1   The Liberalisation of Energy Markets Has Always Gone Hand in Hand with the Reinforcement of Social Objectives

National energy sectors, like other network industries, have historically been characterised by a strong involvement of the state and it is only since the last two decades that the creation of a genuine internal energy market has been part of the EU's legislative agenda. Through the means of directives, the process of opening up the national electricity and gas markets was initiated, but quickly raised concerns as to its potential social impact. It was therefore deemed imperative that the liberalisation process featured the necessary safeguards to make sure it would at no point be detrimental to consumers' interest (Nowak 2006; Houben 2008; Bartl 2010).

Such concerns were included in the liberalisation directives on gas and electricity markets, which were adopted in 1996 and 1998 respectively as part of the first energy package. Those clearly focused on market opening, but included the concept of Public Service Obligations (PSOs) (Henry 1993). PSOs enable member states to impose obligations on undertakings operating in the electricity or gas sectors, relating, for instance, to quality and price of supplies or even environmental protection.

With the adoption of the second- and third-energy packages in 2003 and 2009, the member states had to guarantee high public service standards, provide universal service[1] and take appropriate measures to protect vulnerable customers.[2] Although these social requirements were reinforced, the member states, in line with the subsidiary principle, retained a large margin of appreciation in these areas. For instance, disconnection of gas or electricity supply to vulnerable customers is prohibited in critical times. But the definition of such customers is left for member states to decide (Deruytter et al. 2011).

Despite the objective of decreasing energy prices through market liberalisation, while safeguarding the protection of the most vulnerable customers under the responsibility of member states, numerous experts have

---

[1] Public service obligations provide the right of consumers to be connected to the grid and to be supplied with electricity at an affordable cost, which is termed universal service in the Directive 2009/72/EC 2009 concerning common rules for the internal market in electricity.

[2] Following articles 3 of both gas and electricity 2009 directives, 'Member States shall take appropriate measures to protect final customers, and shall, in particular, ensure that there are adequate safeguards to protect vulnerable customers'.

pointed out the considerable amount of European citizens still exposed to energy poverty (Bouzarovski 2018). This is why several actors are advocating for a revision of the current gas and electricity directive, in order to address more explicitly and efficiently the issue of energy poverty.

2.2   The Progressive Recognition of Energy Poverty Throughout the EU

According to the widely commented studies of the EU Survey on Income and Living Conditions (EU SILC), a growing number of citizens, close to 10% of the EU population, are unable to keep their home adequately warm (Pye et al. 2015). These numbers translate into a growing discontent in European public opinions, as well as a flourishing scientific literature on the issue of energy poverty. National policy-makers also began to pay greater attention to the problem, resulting, for instance, in new definitions of energy poverty in some member states (Pye et al. 2015).

A first obstacle for defining energy poverty at EU level lies in the difficulty to quantify this complex and multifaceted issue, as data from one country to the other is often not comparable (Eurelectric 2017). The concept of energy poverty is inconsistently recognised in different member states, and very few of them formally define it (Thompson and Snell 2016). Broadly speaking, energy poverty occurs when a household experiences inadequate levels of essential energy services such as heating, cooling, lighting and the use of appliances at affordable costs (Bouzarovski and Petrova 2015). Definitions among authors slightly differ. Some of them stress the threshold of incomes spent on energy (e.g., the 10% threshold applied in the United Kingdom [European Parliament 2017]), while others stress the absence of savings and the poorly equipped accommodation, resulting in an overall reduction in living standards, sometimes affecting, in turn, the people's health and mental well-being (Thompson et al. 2017).

The risk for a household to be exposed to energy poverty depends on five factors (Preston et al. 2014): (1) the rate of energy prices versus income growth, (2) the ability to access cheaper energy prices, (3) the households' energy needs, (4) the efficiency or energy use and (5) policy interventions. This set of five factors gives us an idea of the plurality of policy responses that can either be privileged or combined in order to address this issue.

Yet, even if the current debates on energy poverty have allowed a basic understanding of its main causes to emerge, agreeing on a common EU-wide definition remains a difficult task. This difficulty stems from different causes, but the absence of a common definition may very well result in a practical impossibility to improve the fight against energy poverty at EU level. This would indeed require to adopt consistent standards and indicators of energy poverty across the EU, as a prerequisite to any form of coordinated action on the issue.

Therefore, the issue has been identified as a key European policy priority (Bouzarovski et al. 2012). Consequently, strong policy mandates for harmonised statistics and estimates of energy poverty have been issued by several EU institutions, especially the EP, the European Economic and Social Committee, and the Committee of the Regions. Without imposing a common definition, the EC has already suggested that energy poverty could be measured using consensual indicators from existing pan-EU surveys (Thompson et al. 2017).

However, even if a large majority of the actors agree on the prevalence of the problem, there is still a division concerning EU's further action or on the most adequate governance framework. The purpose of the chapter is not to take a stance on the relevance of the EU action. But we believe that the debate gained saliency, and that the decision-makers, including the EP, realised that the energy transition will not be carried out successfully if the Energy Union does not address the issue of energy poverty.

2.3   *The Relationship Between Energy Transition and Energy Poverty*

The main ambition of the European energy policy since the 1990s was to guarantee EU citizens secure, competitive and affordable energy through the liberalisation of national energy markets. Yet, the benefits in terms of price decreases have not lived up to expectations as electricity and gas retail prices have increased over the last decade. As a result, a rising number of households are unable to pay their energy bills (Preston et al. 2014).

During the last decades, Europe faced several challenges that led to fundamental changes in national energy systems. Namely, the fight against climate change, the digitalisation of economies, the fierce international economic competition and the unstable relations with Europe's neighbours forced the EU to rethink and reshape the way we produce, transport and consume energy. These challenges have led Europe to embark on the path towards energy transition, and the ambition of the Commission is to accompany this transition with the Energy Union project (European Commission 2015).

For now, this energy transition comes at a certain price. The cost of sustainable policies and the difficulty to integrate renewable energy sources into the power systems led to higher prices for consumers (Thompson 2016). This also diminishes the purchasing power of certain households for which the situation already worsened in the aftermath of the 2008 economic and financial crisis (Hiteva 2013; Bouzarovski and Tirado Herrero 2017). The energy transition towards low-carbon economy is now seen by the majority of decision-makers as a necessity. But the public acceptance of this project would be compromised if the poorest and most vulnerable consumers feel they lose out on this transition. The fight against energy poverty can thus be seen a *sine qua non* condition for the Energy Union to deliver.

The EP has spearheaded some measures relating the energy poverty in the current legislative framework, especially in the 2009 third energy package. Moreover, the issue seems to be gaining momentum as multiple references to energy poverty have been introduced in the Commission's Clean Energy for All Europeans package proposals. For instance, energy efficiency, which appears as the priority of this new legislative package, is not only considered as a means to address energy security and create growth, but predominantly relates to the protection of vulnerable consumers and the fight against energy poverty (European Commission 2016a). It is very likely, considering the constant cooperation between the EP and the Commission, that the drafting of the 2016 package proposals took into account some of the recommendations included in the 2016 EP Initiative Report on the anti-poverty target, in the light of increasing household costs, especially concerning energy efficiency (European Parliament 2016a).

Therefore, the use of resolutions, as well as other non-legislative actions of the EP, may be seen as a way to shape the debate on energy poverty at EU level. This is particularly interesting considering the limited competence of the EU to address the issue, which can mostly act in areas related to internal market and energy policies. Following the strong emphasis set by the EP on the social component of energy policy, the proposal for a recast of the energy efficiency directive by the Commission clearly indicates in its impact assessment that the 'social aspects of energy efficiency' should be reinforced through obligations imposed on member states to specifically tackle energy poverty. The social impact of the proposed directive goes on highlighting that it would result in direct jobs, and that the reduction in bills paid for energy would result in less energy poverty and would solve the problems linked to inequality and social exclusion (European Commission 2016b). This may be seen as the result of an attempt by the EP to shape the debate on energy poverty and influence the drafting of new pieces of legislation.

Moreover, with this activism in favour of energy poverty, the EP emerges as a distinctive voice in the debate on energy policy, so as to take into account social consequences of the energy transition. The position endorsed by many Socialists and Democrats (S&D) and Greens MEPs, considering energy poverty as a core social element of the EU energy policy, echoes the claims that energy transition should also reflect a 're-balancing of the global energy system' that includes 'fairness and equity at the heart of energy solutions' (McCauley 2018). This was concretely promoted by the EP in the revision of the directive to enhance cost-effective emission reductions and low carbon investments, relating to the EU emission trading system (EU ETS) (European Commission 2015b). The EP voted to introduce a 'Just Transition Fund' to support regions with a high share of workers in carbon-dependent sectors and a GDP per capita well below the Union average. Although it did not feature a fund specifically dedicated to social purpose, the final version of the directive recognises that the Modernisation Fund established shall 'support the redeployment, re-skilling and up-skilling of workers, education, job-seeking initiatives and start-ups, in dialogue with the social partner' (EP and Council of the EU 2018).

Since 1996 and the first electricity market directive, the orientations of the energy policy were mainly the prerogative of the EC, as energy policy was mainly driven by the liberalisation of the electricity and gas markets (EP and Council of the EU 1996). The outcome of the Clean Energy for All Europeans package, and especially the measures relating to energy poverty, may also indicate if member states endorse this renewed emphasis brought by the EP on the legislative agenda.

3   THE LEGAL OBSTACLES ON THE WAY TO A EUROPEAN ENERGY POVERTY POLICY: A DIFFICULT POLITICAL POSITIONING FOR THE EP

The first legal obstacle to develop a European policy against energy poverty is constituted by the difficulty to come up with a European definition of energy poverty, even though it constitutes a necessary prerequisite to any coordinated action at EU level, which goes hand in hand with the important variety of situations and experiences of energy poverty throughout the EU. This may clearly collide with the subsidiarity principle and represent an argument against a uniform response to this multifaceted phenomenon, which will be analysed thereafter (Sect. 3.1). Then, the choice of a legal basis for an EU action is considered, as it widely determines the implication of the EP in the drafting of an EU policy targeting energy poverty (Sect. 3.2).

3.1 Compliance with the Subsidiarity Principle

The main arguments raised against an EU action on energy poverty is that it would entail an EU-wide and uniform solution. Therefore, it would not sufficiently take into account local specificities, and thus, would likely render such response inadequate and ineffective. Indeed, energy poverty is experienced very differently across the EU. It often arises from national or even regional specificities, as the varying manifestations of energy poverty also stem from different climatic conditions and the socio-economic context. For instance, it has been noted that this social 'energy divide' has a higher incidence in Southern and Eastern European countries, with the acute impact of rapid price rises, inadequate social protection and low residential energy efficiency in post-communist countries (Bouzarovski and Tirado Herrero 2017).

The varying acuity and nature of energy poverty across member states logically result in diverse responses to the issue throughout the EU. The variety of indicators on energy poverty, such as the varying prices of energy or cost of living, as well as the subsequently diverging policies undertaken by member states contribute to a very fragmented picture. (Thompson et al. 2017). This situation clearly highlights the difficulty for an EU action to comply with the requirements of subsidiarity in this area, thus questioning the relevance of such an action in general.

According to article 5(3) of the Treaty on the EU, the subsidiarity principle requires that the 'Union shall act only if and in so far as the objectives of the proposed action cannot be sufficiently achieved by the member states (…)'. This principle has been widely respected in the current legislative framework, as member states may refer to energy poverty when defining the concept of vulnerable customer in the 2009 electricity directive for instance.

However, the current framework has shown limited success to effectively address energy poverty. Barely half of member states actually defined the concept of vulnerable consumer and most of them have a diverging understanding of the issue (Pye et al. 2015). Also, rural areas and small owners are often excluded or 'forgotten' by social policies of member states (Le Roux 2015). Therefore, a rigorous application of the subsidiarity principle may result in a greater role for the EU to tackle energy poverty. Indeed, the EU could introduce better coordination of member states' policies and bring consistency to all components of energy poverty, especially regarding the relationship between social and market-based measures (Derdevet 2013).

3.2   The Choice of the Policy and Legal Basis to Address Energy Poverty

Energy poverty has been subject to an enhanced focus in the recent years, as well as to the need to address it at EU level (Thompson et al. 2017). However, the inherently social nature of the issue may cast doubts on the ability of the EU to act on the matter.

Many voices in the European institutions and among member states have called for a social approach of the energy poverty issue, which is to rely on the important competence of member state in this area. For instance, the EC indicated in its 2015 Energy Union Communication that it should be tackled (EC 2015). This approach may be in contradiction with the views of some political groups within the EP that have clearly expressed their will of an EU action in this area to be developed (Socialists and Democrats Group 2016).

The current legislation adopted by the EU to fight energy poverty is based on the energy-related legal basis of the treaty. EU measures are scattered among different instruments, of which efficiency has not clearly been proven (Derdevet 2013). The most significant EU measures may be found, for example, in the obligation for member states to define the concept of a vulnerable customer and to adopt protective measures (Electricity Directive 2009), or in the improvement of energy efficiency, which tends to enhance households' living standard, via specific obligations for the member states. This is especially relevant to energy poverty regarding the energy performance of buildings (EPB Directive 2010). Any action of the EU in this area is constrained by the division of competences enshrined in the Treaties. As a result, most of these measures were adopted on legal basis relating to the energy policy.

Alternative legal basis in EU treaties has been advanced, such as public health policy at article 168 of the treaty on the functioning of the European Union (TFEU). However, in this area, the competence conferred to the EU is limited and can only lead to measures supporting national policies. It is impossible to harmonise the different national approaches on this basis. Articles 36 and 38 of the Charter of Fundamental Rights of the EU have also been mentioned in relation to the fight against energy poverty (Derdevet 2013). These articles relate to the access to public services and consumers' protection, but they are unlikely to allow specific EU measure to be adopted on energy poverty.

Moreover, the opinion that energy poverty should be tackled through social measures is widely shared among member states and in some institutions. This clearly rules out any measure reinforcing a social approach to energy poverty at EU level, as the competence to adopt social measures largely belongs to member states. The Council of the EU, the Commission and a substantial proportion of MEPs tend to privilege solutions at member states level, such as PSOs, which are foreseen by the existing rules on the internal energy market. The refusal to endorse the creation of the Just Transition Fund is a good example of this reluctance. The Commission presented in December 2017 a 'Platform for Coal Regions in Transition' at the One Planet Summit in Paris. This mechanism is financed at EU level to avoid energy poverty to be created by energy transition. The social challenges induced by such a transition are tackled by 'stakeholders' such as member states, regions or private actors. The EU is playing a collateral role, only to promote cooperation and the exchange of good practices. The example of this financial mechanism highlights that, in this area, no harmonisation is allowed at EU level, as the social dimension of energy transition is mainly decided at national level.

Therefore, energy policy-related measures may seem sufficient to effectively address energy poverty at EU level. The priority given to energy efficiency in the Clean Energy for All Europeans package of November 2016 is a clear sign in this direction (EC 2016a). The EP underestimated this legal aspect in its strategy to develop specific EU means to fight energy poverty. As energy poverty is part of energy policy, the question is to assess to what extent has the EP managed to amend the proposals from the Commission to develop a specific EU response to energy poverty. The same analysis may apply to the Clean Energy for All Europeans package, for which the EP struggled to be a decisive policy-maker on the issue of energy poverty.

4   THE EFFORTS OF THE EP TO BRING ENERGY POVERTY POLICY AT THE EU LEVEL

As a preliminary remark, it is not the purpose of this section to propose a conceptualisation of the legislative power of the EP or to assess how powerful the EP has been in the institutional game. Rather, we will stress the fact that the EP or some of its members are able to promote and/or enforce their agenda on energy poverty by being active on multiple fronts. Those fronts have been opened up in correlation with the rising powers of the EP, but also alongside several trends in the way the institution is working, both internally and in relation with the other institutions.

We will see that the institution has pushed for a greater protection of the vulnerable consumers during the negotiation of the third energy package and is now determining its position concerning the recently tabled Clean Energy for All European Package (Sect. 4.1). This will shed light on the political division within the EP and on how this impacts its legislation-shaping ability. We will then see how some political groups and MEPs attempt to overcome this division by using resolutions and cooperation with civil society to enhance the saliency of energy poverty on the EU's agenda (Sect. 4.2).

4.1   The EP's Influence in the Legislation-Making

Less than a month after the EC tabled its proposals, the socialist MEP Eluned Morgan was appointed rapporteur for the directive on the internal market in electricity. While energy poverty was not mentioned in the proceedings of the Council, she drafted a report setting a strong emphasis on the protection of vulnerable consumers. Most of her amendments were revolving around the idea that each member state would have to adopt a national definition of energy poverty on the basis of indicators provided by the EC. They would also have an obligation to report their progress through National Energy Action Plans. In this respect, the explanatory statement of the aforementioned draft report is rather eloquent and already pinpoints at the main issues that we have identified:

> Although energy poverty and the protection of vulnerable customers is an area of national competence, there is clearly a link with EU policy. The EU must set out a clear definition of energy poverty, and insist that Member State energy poverty plans are submitted and monitored by the Commission. However, the tools used to protect vulnerable customers must work with,

and support, the pre-requisites of open, competitive markets. We need to guarantee that customers, particularly pensioners, who are unable to pay will not be cut off and there is no discrimination in terms of pricing models against poor consumers. Combating fuel poverty can be done best through promoting energy efficiency and energy saving measures and we should explore how to strengthen the link between this directive and energy efficiency requirements.

After committee debates that highlighted a cross-party concern to critically address the issue of the energy poverty, the Parliament came up with a first reading text that foresaw several obligations for the member states and kept most of the rapporteur's amendments regarding vulnerable consumers (European Parliament 2007).

Despite a seemingly favourable response of the Commission,[3] a much less constraining wording has been finally adopted in which the member states have to define vulnerable consumers but without mandatorily mentioning the concept of energy poverty. According to article 3 of the final directive, member states shall take appropriate measures to address energy poverty where identified, including in the broader context of poverty. In addition, those measures 'shall not impede the effective opening of the market [...]' (Directive 2009).

This final wording did not allow for any kind of formal supranational control and largely resulted in a lack of compliance of the member states (interview 1). But more than the wording of the final directives, it is interesting to see how intransigent Parliament was on the matter:

There cannot be anyone within the European Union who has not noticed the massive increase in energy prices in recent months. All over the European Union there are people struggling to pay their energy bills so we believe that the issue of 'energy poverty' should be placed firmly on the EU agenda. After all, the ETS system and the renewables targets are European and they impact on energy prices.

We have respected subsidiarity, Commissioner, in our request that Member States should come up with their own definitions of energy poverty and an action plan for dealing with the problem. So, if the Council wants a deal on this package, they need to understand that this is a central requirement of Parliament. (Morgan 2008)

---

[3] See the reaction of Commissioner Piebalgs during the plenary debates on 17 June 2008—Strasbourg.

If there was an overall consensus between MEPs that member states should not be allowed to run away from their responsibility, the party spectrum could not agree on the legislative means to address the issue. The European People's Party (EPP) was already stressing the fact that any kind of energy poverty policy should remain in the remit of member states' competences. Likewise, the mere suggestion that member states use social tariffs as a means to address energy poverty was deemed too controversial as it would increase the overall costs of electricity.

Despite this internal dissent within the EP, the recognition of energy poverty in EU law was seen at the time as a victory for Parliament (Euractiv 2009).

Energy poverty recently came back on the legislative agenda when, in November 2016, the EC presented the Clean Energy for All European package which includes eight legislative proposals among which four contain provisions targeting explicitly the issue of energy poverty.

It stands out from the study of these proposals and the accompanying documents that the Commission has taken into account the call for mainstreaming the energy poverty issue and even uses it to assert the necessity and pertinence of its proposals (Bouzarovski and Tirado Herrero 2017).

The directives on energy efficiency and on energy performance of buildings are clearly presented as relevant tools to tackle energy poverty[4] and further impose on member states to take the issue into consideration (European Commission 2016a).

The electricity directive proposal further acknowledges the problem in its article 29 dedicated to energy poverty.[5] Last but not least, the proposal on the governance of the Energy Union provides that the national objectives on energy poverty and the number of households in energy poverty shall be included in the integrated report on internal energy market.

---

[4] Interestingly the proposal even proposes a quantification of the energy poverty in Europe: 'This proposal could contribute to taking out from energy poverty between 515,000 and 3.2 million households in the EU (from a total of 23.3 million households living in energy poverty—Eurostat)'.

[5] According to which, 'Member States shall define a set of criteria for the purposes of measuring energy poverty. Member States shall continuously monitor the number of households in energy poverty and shall report on the evolution of energy poverty and measures taken to prevent it to the Commission every two years as part of their Integrated National Energy and Climate Progress Reports in accordance with article 21 of [Governance Regulation as proposed by COM(2016)759]'.

What has been the response from the EP so far? At the time of writing this chapter, the four proposals are still awaiting committee decision or the first reading. But more than a year after their publication, the main political lines have emerged and the political relevance of this package was partly reflected by the allocation of rapporteur and shadow-rapporteurships to prominent MEPs, including the Chair, three Vice-Chairs and six Coordinators who all have a substantial experience in European energy policy. It is also noteworthy that rapporteur positions are dominated by the main political groups.[6] The political sensitivity of these files has also been exemplified by the late decision of the S&D group to replace Adam Gierek (Rapporteur on the Energy Efficiency Directive) who was taking too much liberty from his group's political line (Euractiv 2017).

Although each proposal raises discussions that are specific to the topic at hand, we can notice two overall trends drawing a dividing line between MEPs on how to address energy poverty. On the one hand, those considering that a well-functioning energy market is the most adequate way to guarantee affordable prices for all consumers. This approach is notably supported by Krisjanis Karins—rapporteur for the electricity directive and EPP group coordinator. He advocates for a 'market first' approach according to which public intervention such as regulated tariffs—targeting or not vulnerable consumers—should be restricted to its minimum (Kariņš 2017, 67).

On the other hand, socialists MEPs rather consider that energy poverty should be addressed via public intervention and therefore requires stronger obligations laid upon the member states, notably through the introduction of common measurement tools provided by the Commission (Belet 2017).

4.2   Overview of the Non-Legislative Initiatives

Being formally unable to initiate legislation, EP has used own-initiative resolutions to enhance the prominence of energy poverty on the EU's agenda. Already during the negotiation of the third energy package, the EP voted a resolution encouraging the Commission to propose a European Charter on the Rights of Energy Consumers (European Parliament 2008).

---

[6] EPP group allocated three rapporteurships; S&D group allocated three rapporteurships; ALDE group allocated one rapporteurship; Greens/EFA group allocated one rapporteurship.

This resolution was drafted by Mia De Vits, a Belgian socialist Rapporteur who, like Eluned Morgan (S&D), was campaigning for the recognition of energy poverty at the EU level.

Another notable resolution on delivering a new deal for energy consumers was drafted and upheld by the socialist MEP Theresa Griffin before being voted in May 2016. This own-initiative report was purposely adopted a few months before the publication of the Clean Energy Package (interview 1) and it notably called 'for enhanced coordination at EU level to combat energy poverty through the sharing of best practices among Member States and the development of a broad, common but non-quantitative definition of energy poverty, focusing on the idea that access to affordable energy is a basic social right; urged the Commission to prioritise measures to alleviate energy poverty in upcoming legislative proposals and to present a dedicated action plan by mid-2017' (European Parliament 2016b).

If the adoption of the resolution was seen as a success for the socialists, Theresa Griffin had to lower her ambitions and water down the content to gain the support of the majority (interviews 1 and 2). This further exemplifies the recurrent division within the EP on the issue of energy poverty. Overall, the left-wing parties—and especially the S&D—are, however, keen to ensure a stronger protection of vulnerable consumers. Their legislative agenda faces some reluctance from the other political groups and the governments who generally doubt the pertinence of imposing stricter obligations to the member states (interviews 1 and 3)

Faced with this resistance, Socialist and Greens MEPs have displayed an ever-increasing activism that translated into several initiatives and projects aiming to move their agenda forward (Bouzarovski 2018). For instance, the aforementioned resolution on delivering a new deal for energy consumers was mainly inspired from an S&D Manifesto on energy poverty published in March 2016 which is part of a wider campaign called 'END energy poverty'.

In the same vein and as a follow-up to the EP's Initiative Report on the anti-poverty target in the light of increasing household costs (European Commission 2016a), MEP Tamas Meszerics (Greens, Hungary) acted as editor of a Handbook on Energy Poverty gathering the contributions of experts and academics on the topic (Meszerics et al. 2016). This kind of collaboration between civil society and MEPs has been prolonged with numerous workshops held in the EP or several European cities in order to provide a better understanding of the problem and consequently raise public awareness on the topic.

5 Conclusions: The Difficulty of the EP to Be a Distinctive Voice in the European Energy Policy

The EP had to face its own divisions when deciding what type of EU policy it should defend. MEPs with a more ambitious stance on energy poverty went around this inner obstacle by spreading their views using alternative means. It is thus noticeable that some MEPs from Greens and S&D groups did not only confine their activity to the traditional instruments of the EP, but also tried to stir the debate with civil society. This contributed to widen the audience of their position on energy poverty, with increased considerations among academics and possibly within the EC.

But this political opposition continues to divide the MEPs and limits the possibility of the EP to actively weigh in the legislative process. The position defended by the S&D MEPs is that the fight against energy poverty is part of a more decisive social EU policy. On the contrary, a conservative majority in the Parliament supports the idea that an effectively functioning energy market should bring sufficient responses to the energy poverty issue. The division within the EP along political lines clearly points at the fundamental dichotomy characterising the debate on energy poverty within the EU.

Different approaches to energy poverty may be distinguished between the 'social' or 'energy' policy-led actions and measures. Member states' policies are also differentiated along those different perspectives (Pye et al. 2015). For some member states, the social approach to energy poverty is privileged, and therefore makes it a component of poverty (Pye et al. 2015). In this view, responses to energy poverty mainly rely on public intervention and solidarity mechanisms. For other member states and policy actors, the issue is related to energy policy and can be tackled through specific measures, such as energy efficiency, and could be addressed by energy market prices. Such a distinction also exists among and within EU institutions, as the Commission, for instance, considers that additional regulation and taxes increase the energy retail prices for consumers, instead of lowering them (EC 2016c). In this regard, market principles should be able to bring down energy prices for the benefit of consumers.

These opposing views further affect the room for manoeuvre of the EP, especially considering the division of competences between the EU and member states. The promotion of energy poverty as a component of a social policy should lead to limited realisations at EU level. Moreover, the solution to energy poverty formulated through EU measures should essentially rely on energy-related responses, such as the reinforcement of energy efficiency. Insofar as the energy policy is concerned, the EU can introduce very limited social considerations, that cannot exceed the imposition of public service obligations to member states which are compatible with the functioning of the internal energy market.

Nevertheless, it should be noted that those MEPs who favoured an ambitious and socially oriented action on energy poverty actively contributed to the evolution of the debate at EU level, despite the institutional and political constraints at stake. The EU integration process is more and more often criticised by national public opinions because the EU legislation has been developed for mobile citizens but does not provide for any benefits for non-mobile citizens. If we consider energy transition, we may conclude that it has been conceived for rich, mobile and green citizens more than for poor ones concentrated on their own economic conservation. The EP may have a special responsibility in the protection of all the citizens, most particularly those who are perceived as the 'losers' of the energy transition.

REFERENCES AND INTERVIEWS

Bartl, M. (2010). The Affordability of Energy: How Much Protection for the Vulnerable Consumers? *Journal of Consumer Policy, 33*(3), 225–245.

Belet, I. (2017, December). Opinion on the Proposal for a Regulation of the European Parliament and of the Council on the Internal Market for Electricity (Recast). Committee on the Environment, Public Health and Food Safety, EP.

Birchfield, V. (2011). The Role of EU Institutions in Energy Policy Formation. In V. Birchfield & J. Duffield (Eds.), *Towards a Common European Union Energy Policy: Problems, Progress and Prospects* (pp. 235–262). Palgrave Macmillan: Basingstoke.

Bouzarovski, S. (2018). *Energy poverty: (Dis)Assembling Europe Infrastructural Divide* (p. 41). Cham: Palgrave Macmillan.

Bouzarovski, S., & Petrova, S. (2015). The EU Energy Poverty and Vulnerability Agenda: An Emergent Domain of Transnational Action. In J. Tosun, S. Biesenbender, & K. Schulze (Eds.), *Energy Policy Marking in the EU: Building the Agenda* (pp. 129–144). Berlin: Springer.

Bouzarovski, S., & Tirado Herrero, S. (2017). The Energy Divide: Integrating Energy Transitions, Regional Inequalities and Poverty Trends in the European Union. *European Urban and Regional Studies, 24*(1), 69–86.

Derdevet, M. (2013). La pauvreté énergétique, un chantier européen prioritaire. *Géoéconomie*, *3*(66), 37–50.

Deruytter, T., Geldhof, W., & Vandendriessche, F. (2011). Public Service Obligations in the Electricity and Gas Markets. In B. Delvaux, M. Hunt, & K. Talus (Eds.), *EU Energy Law and Policy Issues* (pp. 63–95). Cambridge: Intersentia.

Directive (EU) 2018/410 of the European Parliament and of the Council of 14 March 2018 to Enhance Cost-Effective Emission Reductions and Low-Carbon Investments, OJ L 76/3 of 19 March 2018.

Directive 2009/72/CE of the European Parliament and of the Council of 13 July 2009 Concerning Common Rules for the Internal Market in Electricity, OJ L 211/55 of 14 August 2009.

Directive 2010/31/EU of the European Parliament and of the Council of 19 May 2010 on the Energy Performance of Buildings, OJ L 153/13 of 18 October 2010.

Directive 96/92/EC of the European Parliament and of the Council of 19 December 1996 Concerning Common Rules for the Internal Market in Electricity, OJ L 27/20 of 30 January 1997.

Directive 98/30/EC of the European Parliament and of the Council of 22 June 1998 Concerning Common Rules for the Internal Market in Natural Gas, OJ L 204/1 of 21 July 1998.

Eikland, O. (2011). EU Internal Energy Market Policy: Achievements and Hurdles. In V. Birchfield & J. Duffield (Eds.), *Towards a Common European Union Energy Policy: Problems, Progress and Prospects* (pp. 13–40). Basingstoke: Palgrave Macmillan.

Euractiv. (2009). EU Strikes Deal on Energy Market Liberalisation. Retrieved August 20, 2017, from https://www.euractiv.com/section/energy/news/eu-strikes-deal-on-energy-market-liberalisation/.

Euractiv. (2017). Le député chargé de la directive sur l'efficacité énergétique écarté, décembre 6. https://www.euractiv.fr/section/energie/news/controversial-mep-replaced-as-lead-on-energy-savings-file/.

Eurelectric. (2017, April). Energy Poverty: A Eurelectric Position Paper. Retrieved April 6, 2018, from https://www3.eurelectric.org/media/325597/energy-poverty-final-2017-2500-0003-01-e.pdf.

European Commission. (2015a, February 25). Communication from the Commission to the European Parliament, the Council, the European Economic and Social Committee, the Committee of the Regions and the European Investment Bank, A Framework Strategy for a Resilient Energy Union with a Forward-Looking Climate Change Policy, COM(2015) 80 Final, Brussels.

European Commission. (2015b, July 15). Proposal for a Directive of the European Parliament and of the Council Amending Directive 2003/87/EC to Enhance Cost-Effective Emission Reductions and Low Carbon Investments, COM(2015) 337 Final, Brussels.

European Commission. (2016a, November 30). Communication 'Clean Energy for All Europeans', COM(2016) 860 Final, Brussels.

European Commission. (2016b, November 30). Proposal for a Directive of the European Parliament and of the Council Amending Directive 2012/27/EU on Energy Efficiency, COM(2016) 761 Final, Brussels.

European Commission. (2016c, November 30). Report on Energy Prices and Costs in Europe, COM(2016) 769 Final, Brussels.

European Parliament. (2007). Resolution of 10 July 2007 on Prospects for the Internal Gaz and Electricity Market, 2007/2089 (INI).

European Parliament. (2016a). Resolution of 14 April 2016 on Meeting the Antipoverty Target in the Light of Increasing Household Costs (2015/2223(INI)).

European Parliament. (2016b). Resolution of 26 May 2016 on Delivering a New Deal for Energy Consumers (2015/2323(INI)).

European Parliament. (2017). Energy Poverty Workshop. Study for the ITRE Committee. Retrieved from http://www.europarl.europa.eu/RegData/etudes/STUD/2017/607350/IPOL_STU(2017)607350_EN.pdf.

Henry, C. (1993). Public Service and Competition in the European Community Approach to Communications Networks. *Oxford Review of Economic Policy, 9*(1), 45–66.

Hiteva, R. (2013). Fuel Poverty and Vulnerability in the EU Low-Carbon Transition: The Case of Renewable Electricity. *Local Environment: The International Journal of Justice and Sustainability, 18*(4), 487–505.

Houben, I. (2008). Public Service Obligations: Moral Counterbalance of Technical Liberalization Legislation? *European Review of Private Law, 16*(1), 7–27.

Interview with an MEP Assistant on 17 July 2017, Strasbourg.

Interview with an MEP Assistant on 6 June 2017, Brussels.

Interview with an Official from DG Ener on 1 September 2017, Brussels.

Kariņš, K. (2017, June 16), Draft Report on the Proposal for a Regulation of the European Parliament and of the Council on the Internal Market for Electricity (Recast). Committee on Industry, Research and Energy, EP.

Le Roux, D. (2015). Précarité énergétique et milieu rural en France : le rôle des structures de médiation. *L'Europe en Formation, 4*(378), 90–104.

McCauley, D. (2018). *Energy Justice: Re-Balancing the Trilemma of Security, Poverty and Climate Change.* London: Palgrave Macmillan.

Meszerics, T., Csiba, K., Bajomi, A., & Gosztonyi, A. (Eds.). (2016). *Energy Poverty Handbook.* Brussels: European Union.

Morgan, E. (2008, June 17). Intervention During Plenary Debate on the Internal Market in Electricity, Strasbourg.

Nowak, B. (2006). The Electricity and Gas Sector in the EU: The Dilemmas of Public Service Obligations in the Context of State Aid. *Yearbook of Polish European Studies, 10*, 151–167.

Preston, I., White, V., Blacklaws, K., & Hirsch, D. (2014, June). Fuel and poverty: A Rapid Evidence Assessment for the Joseph Rowntree Foundation. Centre for Sustainable Energy (CSE).

Pye, S., Dobbins, A., Baffert, C., Brajkovic, J., Deane, P., & De Miglio, R. (2015). Addressing Energy Poverty and Vulnerable Consumers in the Energy Sector Across the EU. *L'Europe en Formation, 4*(378), 64–89.

Socialists and Democrats. (2016, March). Fighting Energy Poverty – S&D Manifesto: An EU Framework to Fight Energy Poverty. Industry, Research & Energy.

Thompson, A. (2016). Protecting Low-Income Ratepayers as the Electricity System Evolves. *Energy Law Journal, 37*(2), 265–306.

Thompson, H., Bouzarovski, S., & Snell, C. (2017). Rethinking the Measurement of Energy Poverty in Europe: A Critical Analysis of Indicators and Data. *Indoor and Built Environment, 26*(7), 879–901.

Thompson, H., & Snell, C. (2016). Definitions and Indicators of Energy Poverty Across the EU. In T. Meszerics, K. Csiba, A. Bajomi, & A. Gosztonyi (Eds.), *Energy Poverty Handbook.* Brussels: European Union.

CHAPTER 18

The European Parliament's Role in Monitoring the Implementation of EU Trade Policy

Laura Puccio and Roderick Harte

1 Introduction

Scrutiny is normally associated with two different functions: the first relates to the power to hold other institutions accountable, and the second is not a stand-alone function and relates to the last phase of the policy-making cycle and the evaluation and monitoring of policies' implementation

---

Dr. Laura Puccio (Bsc, MA, LLM, PhD law) is Policy Analyst for trade law at the European Parliamentary Research Service (EPRS) and teaches at the Institut d'Etudes Européennes of the Université Libre de Bruxelles.
Roderick Harte (BA, LLB, LLM, MA) is Policy Analyst for international trade at the EPRS.
Responsibility for the information and views set out in this article lies entirely with the authors.

L. Puccio (✉) • R. Harte
European Parliament, European Parliamentary Research Service,
Brussels, Belgium
e-mail: laura.puccio@europarl.europa.eu; roderick.harte@europarl.europa.eu

© The Author(s) 2019   387
O. Costa (ed.), *The European Parliament in Times of EU Crisis*,
European Administrative Governance,
https://doi.org/10.1007/978-3-319-97391-3_18

(Maurer 2008). This chapter focusses entirely on the latter function of monitoring policies' implementation,[1] in particular its application by the European Parliament (EP) to the European Union's (EU's) trade policy.[2] The EP has itself on various occasions indicated that it takes its monitoring role seriously. Recently, the chair of the EP's Committee on International Trade (INTA), Bernd Lange, stated that 'after the agreements has [*sic*.] entered into force, as for instance has been the case for the EU-South Korea agreement, my committee is also keen to play its role in monitoring its implementation, in order to verify if these agreements are actually delivering on their promises' (Lange 2017).

This concern to engage more in monitoring of the implementation of free trade agreements (FTAs) also derives from the increased debate surrounding the legitimacy and impact of these agreements, as shown by the recent civil society movements during the negotiations on the Transatlantic Trade and Investment Partnership (TTIP) and before the signing of the EU-Canada Comprehensive Economic and Trade Agreement (CETA). The EP's monitoring of FTA implementation therefore becomes a tool to ensure that EU objectives and citizens' expectations are met. It also follows on from the EP's prior engagement in the FTA negotiation process, which has been analysed extensively in the context of TTIP and CETA in a rich literature (e.g. Van den Putte et al. 2014; Roederer-Rynning 2017; Wessel and Takács 2017).

The EP's monitoring of (trade) policies, however, has so far received limited attention in the literature as the focus has mainly been on the EP's rising legislative power. The literature has primarily looked into the co-legislator power and the introduction of the consent procedure for trade treaties (Dimopoulos 2008; Kohler 2013; Krajewski 2013; Hix and Hoyland 2013; Finke 2016; Da Conceição-Heldt 2017; Finke 2017; Frennhoff Larsen 2017). The legal literature has also explored the Lisbon Treaty's innovations and the EP's use of the Court of Justice of the EU to assert its new powers (Hoffmeister 2011; Leal-Arcas 2012). Some scholars have provided a comprehensive overview of the EP's legal and political role and influence in the negotiation and conclusion of FTAs post-Lisbon

---

[1] The chapter by Poptcheva (2017) in this book tackles the issue of accountability.

[2] This contribution does not cover the power of appointment and motion of censure, nor the committees of inquiry or the right of petitions, which are intrinsically linked to the power to hold the executive accountable. It will also not refer to control of the budget via the EP which is particularly important for monitoring development policy but is not a substantial instrument for the monitoring of trade policy as such.

(Devuyst 2014; Van den Putte et al. 2014; Sicurelli 2015; Meissner 2016). However, this literature did not comprehensively explore the EP's monitoring of the implementation of concluded FTAs; Devuyst (2014) looked at the issue very briefly and Weiss (2017) focusses on the scrutiny of trade treaties' implementing bodies (which happens to be an area where the EP has very little monitoring instruments). While there has been an increasing focus on the EP's scrutiny of delegated and implementing acts (Christiansen and Dobbels 2013; Mendes 2013; Brandsma and Blom-Hansen 2016) and on some aspects of the EP's monitoring functions in external relations (Kleizen 2016; Wessel and Takács 2017), these do not specifically involve EU trade policy.

To our knowledge, this is therefore the first attempt at presenting an overview of the EP's instruments for the monitoring of EU trade policy implementation. To that end, this chapter will first analyse the rationale behind EP monitoring and how this has evolved post-Lisbon. Next, we will discuss the EP's main monitoring instruments in trade policy. The chapter concludes with case studies of the EP's monitoring of three distinct areas of EU trade policy, namely FTAs, trade defence instruments (TDIs) adopted via European Commission (Commission) implementing acts and the Generalized System of Preferences (GSP) involving Commission delegated acts.

The chapter follows a mixed methodology relying on legal analysis, on the one hand, and empirical analysis of the results of a survey sent to members of INTA and the Committees on Development (DEVE) and Agriculture (AGRI), on the other hand. There were 13 replies to our survey, of which 11 came from either Members of the EP (MEPs) or their assistants, while the last two came from political groups' advisors. Only one respondent mentioned that he did not monitor trade policy.[3] All positive answers came from INTA members' offices; no replies were received from AGRI members. Ten answers came from members of the two biggest political groups (European People's Party (EPP) and Progressive Alliance of Socialists and Democrats (S&D)), one answer came respectively from the European Conservatives and Reformists (ECR), European United Left - Nordic Green Left (GUE/ NGL) and Alliance of Liberals and Democrats for Europe (ALDE).

---

[3] We are aware of the fact that there is a double selection bias: (1) we contacted MEPs that participate in committees with an active role in EU trade policy, and (2) it is likely that only those MEPs participating in monitoring would reply. However, these selection biases do not affect our analysis as we are interested in how monitoring is carried out and not on whether monitoring is done by all MEPs.

2   The Rationale for the European Parliament's Monitoring of Trade Policy Implementation

2.1   Rationale for Monitoring by the Legislature: A Principal-Agent and Normative Perspective

Monitoring the implementation phase of policies is a fundamental part of decision-making whereby the decision-maker assesses the implementation progress in achieving the objectives and effectively addressing the problems at hand (Cerna 2013). Inherently, monitoring of policy implementation is part of an effort to ensure that legislation achieved its policy objectives and provides the basis for better future law-making. Accordingly, monitoring of policy implementation is one of the main tasks of the Commission as the 'executive power' in charge of the implementation of policies and in charge of legislative initiative in the EU.[4]

However, monitoring is also a specific task of legislatures. Their monitoring function derives from the *agent-principal relationship existing between legislature and executive*, whereby the legislature (the 'principal') delegates power to implement legislation to the executive (the 'agent') (Brandsma and Adriaensen 2017; Gailmard 2014). The literature presents two main reasons for the delegation of implementing powers to the executive: efficiency and trust (Brandsma and Blom-Hansen 2017; Franchino 2002). The need for efficiency entails the need for day-to-day operation of technical tasks, which often require a certain expertise. The higher the technical complexity, the higher the incentive to delegate implementing powers and relinquish political control over implementation. The need to achieve a trustworthy commitment can also lead to delegation; institutions, which are 'independent', perform certain tasks better.

The interest of the 'principal' delegating the power and the interest of the 'agent' are not necessarily the same, thus creating agency costs. There will therefore be a trade-off between incentives to delegate and the desire to control, which will result in a compromise between the relative agency costs and costs of exercising control (Gailmard 2014). While delegating implementation, the principal will thus maintain some instruments to

---

[4] This role is embedded in the implementation, executive and management function enshrined in article 17 of the Treaty on European Union (TEU).

ensure scrutiny. Legislatures have a double rationale to maintain scrutiny powers: ensuring input- and output-legitimacy. Scharpf (2003) regards *input legitimacy* as derived from institutional arrangements ensuring that the government operates in a responsive way to citizens' preferences (*government by the people*). The legislature will specifically want to verify that the executive follows the democratic procedures. *Output legitimacy* corresponds to the legitimacy derived from effectively reaching the policy outcomes that are beneficial for the citizens (*government for the people*). Scrutiny as regards output legitimacy is linked to the differences in preferences of the executive (agent) and the legislature (principal).

Scrutiny of implementation by the legislature will also come from a second principal-agent relationship between *the legislature, as the 'agent', and the electorate, as the 'principal'* (Gailmard 2014; Persson and Tabellini 2000). In this framework, the rationale for scrutiny of the implementation is verifying that policies achieve the objectives that maximize the preference of the electorate in order to ensure re-election in the subsequent legislative term. In this context, the legislature can inter alia use scrutiny to assess the need for reforms if the outcomes achieved do not correspond to the desired objectives (scrutiny for better law-making). Scrutiny implies a certain cost for the legislature's administration and is subject to constraint both institutionally and capacity related (time, staff, finances). Therefore, scrutiny will be subject to some prioritization. Stronger politicization of a topic will increase the incentive of the legislature to monitor its implementation and scrutinize the executive as it will increase the pressure on the legislature to deliver within the principal-agent framework existing between the electorate and the legislature. Hence, the two principal-agent relationships described will interact in creating incentives for the legislature to monitor policies' implementation, in line with the idea that a chain of delegation exists between electorate, representatives in the legislature, and executive government (Strøm 2000).

2.2   Monitoring of Trade Policy by the European Parliament

While control is one of the first powers that were attributed to the consultative Assembly under the Treaty of Rome (article 137), such control power was not given much clout beyond the capacity to collectively dismiss the Commission (article 144). The main instruments at that time were the parliamentary written and oral questions and the capacity to ask the Commission to issue reports (articles 122 and 140 Treaty of Rome).

Since then, the role of the EP in decision-making increased extensively, first via the assent and co-operation procedure under the Single European Act and then through the co-decision procedure in the Maastricht Treaty. The latter's coverage would subsequently be expanded by the Lisbon Treaty under the name of ordinary legislative procedure. 'Lisbon' increased the EP's powers in EU trade policy in particular by introducing the ordinary legislative procedure and the EP consent to adopt trade agreements (articles 207 and 218 of the Treaty on the Functioning of the European Union (TFEU)). The EP is now co-legislator for EU trade regulations and effectively has a veto over any EU FTA.

The EP's power and capacity to monitor EU trade policy have evolved with its legislative powers. The increase in legislative powers allowed the EP to become a 'principal' in the context of the first aforementioned principal-agent relationship between legislature and executive. Moreover, the increase in powers as a legislature also meant that, as suggested by some of the respondents to our survey, the EP itself became responsible and accountable with respect to the proper implementation of EU trade policy. It has, therefore, become an 'agent' for the purpose of the second principal-agent framework between electorate and legislature.

The main changes for EP monitoring concern the scrutiny over measures taken by the Commission to implement policies. The Lisbon Treaty replaced the comitology procedure to issue derivative acts with delegated and implementing acts. While the EP had no control over non-legislative acts in the field of trade prior to Lisbon, it now has some control over them. Article 290 TFEU specifically gives the power to the EP as a co-legislator to revoke delegation or object to a specific delegated act. Delegated acts are widely used in trade and allow the Commission to modify non-essential parts of a regulation, such as technical annexes (i.e. the GSP regulation). The EP's rationale for scrutinizing delegated acts covers both input and output legitimacy. Implementing acts are used in the day-to-day application of a regulation, for example, in the context of TDIs. In this area, the rationale for delegation to the executive is the need for technical knowledge and independence (similar to the need for independent competition authorities). Nevertheless, some EP control mechanisms were still included (Brandsma and Blom-Hansen 2012): a right of information and a right to indicate if an act is 'ultra vires' (Regulation (EU) No. 182/2011). Such powers were limited to verifying that actions of the Commission do not go beyond the scope of the implementing power given (input legitimacy). Scrutiny power over output could have been seen as endangering the independence needed to enact these acts.

Table 18.1   The EP's monitoring objectives

Monitoring objectives	Average grade (out of 5)	Number of respondents
Meeting the objectives of EU policies	4.6	12
Meeting EP demands	4.8	12
Checking Commission's delegated and implementing powers	4	12
Addressing new developments	4.6	12
Others	5	1

Source: Authors' survey data

Still, the EP insisted on a basic right of information that would allow MEPs to be aware of acts taken and assess the impacts of such measures on their constituencies (in line with the principal-agent relationship between electorate and MEPs). As shown in Sect. 4, this appears to be the main reason for some MEPs to monitor TDI implementation, which though technical can remain politically sensitive for certain constituencies.

The introduction of the consent procedure for the adoption of international trade agreements has given the EP the possibility to be involved in FTA negotiations from the very start (Corbett et al. 2011). Though the EP is not formally involved in the definition of the negotiating mandate and the negotiations, it is starting to assert some power to influence the outcome of those negotiations.[5] With the introduction of consent, monitoring of FTA implementation takes a very different value, as the EP can also verify that the agreement is applied in line with the guidelines that it had set during the negotiations prior to giving consent. Moreover, rising political interest by civil society and citizens over FTAs' impact on domestic regulation and local employment increased the incentive for more EP monitoring. While there is a rationale for the EP to monitor implementation of FTAs, the EP has limited formal instruments to do so and had to complement those with informally established monitoring groups (see Sect. 3).

The survey responses on the rationale for monitoring (Table 18.1) show that MEPs' focus on monitoring corresponds to output legitimacy: meeting the EP demands that were raised during the legislative or negotiating process, meeting the objectives of EU policies and addressing new

[5] TTIP and the change from Investor-State Dispute Settlement to an Investment Court System are a good example of this rising influence; see L. Puccio and R. Harte, From ISDS to ICS: The evolution of the CETA model, EPRS, June 2017.

Table 18.2   Evolution of perceived monitoring workload since Lisbon

Change in workload	During the current mandate (number of respondents)[a]	Compared to previous mandate (number of respondents)
Decreased	1	0
The same	2	1
Increased	9	5
Not answered	1	7

Source: Authors' survey data

[a]Nota bene: When asked how many mandates they had been in the EP, only five respondents indicated having been in the EP for more than one mandate. Seven respondents answered that they were in their first mandate and one did not reply

developments (including citizens' evolving expectations). Checking the Commission's delegated and implementing powers, which hints more at input legitimacy, appears to be a lesser concern though it still scores high. The survey replies also reflected the increase in the monitoring workload since Lisbon (Table 18.2). This is on the one hand connected to the EP's increased powers but on the other hand also connected to the increased political attention given to FTAs (such as TTIP and CETA) as their reach and scope have expanded in this parliamentary term leading to political controversies.

3   The European Parliament's Instruments for Monitoring

According to Brandsma (2015), control will have three major components: information (the agent provides information/documents to the principal), discussion (interaction between agent and principal) and consequences (sanctions).[6] On a general note, when asked which monitoring instruments were most and which were least effective, four survey respondents replied that it was difficult to say which instruments were 'least effective'. One of them specified that all instruments can contribute to the understanding of the 'big picture' and another stated that each of them had its own role and might come into play at different moments. This respondent further added that the use of different instruments would depend on time, degree of responsibility and accessibility/proximity.

---

[6]In this chapter, we also explore softer actions as opposed to the definition of consequences given by Brandsma (2015).

Indeed, scrutiny instruments will often be subject to constraints, both institutional (legal deadlines, voting) and capacity-related (financial, staff) that will play a role in their effective use.

3.1 Access to Information and Discussion

3.1.1 Access to Information from the European Commission
Information is key as there is an asymmetry of information between the 'agent' and the 'principal'.[7] The EP therefore needed a solid *right to information from the Commission* and *equality of treatment with the Council of Ministers* (Council). The TFEU establishes *specific rights of the EP to be informed* in the field of trade, which focus on progress of negotiations and conclusion of FTAs.[8] Further rights are established in interinstitutional agreements such as the Framework Agreement on relations between the EP and the Commission. The Framework Agreement formulates a principle of equality between Council and EP as regards access to information and specifies the need for regular and direct flow of information between the Member of the Commission and the Chair of the EP Committee responsible.

With respect to delegated acts, *equal access to documents* is ensured in the Inter-institutional Agreement on Better Law-Making. The Inter-institutional Agreement allows the *participation of an EP expert to Commission expert groups* preparing the delegated act. For trade-related matters, the INTA secretariat will send an administrator, who will report back to the INTA coordinators. The latter are MEPs selected by each political group at the start of each legislative term and to whom the Committees can delegate a series of actions. Capacity constraints can determine the choice of reporting, making the entire EP Committee intervene only if there is a need to. Under the Inter-institutional Agreement, the institutions also committed to set up a joint functional register of delegated acts 'to enhance transparency, facilitate planning and enable traceability of all the different stages in the lifecycle of a delegated act'. This register[9] was launched on 12 December 2017 and there have been several sessions for EP staff to present and encourage its use.

---

[7] The 'agent' has information that the 'principal' does not possess and needs in order to make a decision.

[8] See articles 207(3) and 218 TFEU.

[9] It can be found at https://webgate.ec.europa.eu/regdel/#/home.

As opposed to delegated acts, there is no legal rule for EP staff to follow comitology committees on implementing acts. The relevant legislation (Regulation (EU) 182/2011) merely specifies that the EP receives meetings' agendas, the draft implementing act submitted for consideration to the comitology committee and the final implementing act. The EP can also ask the summary records, the voting results, information concerning adoption and statistical data on the work of the comitology committee. The difference in access of information between delegated and implementing acts matches the difference in power explained earlier. It has become established practice to include in the basic legislative act the requirement for the Commission to issue a report and submit it to the EP on the implementation of a certain legislation especially (but not only) where implementing acts are taken. This is the case for antidumping, and according to our survey results, these Commission evaluations were considered one of the most important instruments for TDI monitoring.

In relation to FTAs, the Framework Agreement specifies that the EP shall receive *access to information regarding the implementation of multilateral international agreements* from treaties' implementing bodies under the same conditions as during the negotiations of treaties. The *access as observers to the meetings of these treaties' implementing bodies* by MEPs should also be facilitated (e.g. in Ministerial Conferences of the World Trade Organization). As mentioned by Weiss (2017), this right is limited to multilateral trade agreements whenever EP consent or legislation via the ordinary legislative procedure is required for implementing decisions of these bodies in EU law. This means, that the Framework Agreement does not cover treaties' implementing bodies under FTAs. Weiß (2017) and Weiß (2018) highlights that this is a limitation for the EP's scrutiny capacity. Still, such a limitation could be dictated by some capacity constraints, also considering the number of FTAs. The EP therefore had to find alternative ways to scrutinize FTA implementation and for that reason *monitoring groups*, created during the last legislature to scrutinize negotiations, were maintained also to obtain information on the agreements' subsequent implementation.

Finally, individual MEPs can ask *written or oral questions* to the Commission (or to the Council), including on trade policy implementation. The number of questions is limited to ensure the capacity of the other institutions to reply; each MEP can put a maximum of 20 questions for written answer over a period of two months. Written question can take up to six weeks to be answered, unless it is a priority question. However, MEPs can only ask one priority question per month.

3.1.2   Access to Information: Diversification of Sources of Information
Monitoring incentives can come from the principal-agent relations existing between the electorate and the elected EP. In that context, MEPs will often maintain *contacts with civil society*, including non-governmental organizations (NGOs), trade and labour associations, businesses, consumer groups, academia and think tanks and constituency members. In our survey, these contacts were always considered as one of the more important tools for obtaining information (see Table 18.3).

According to our survey results, EP *relations with the European Economic and Social Committee* (EESC) *and the Committee of the Regions* (CoR) have been less prominent as a source of information. We also received low results with respect to *contacts with domestic advisory groups* (DAGs), for which the EESC provides a secretariat. One of the reasons for this could be that DAGs currently only help monitor implementation of trade and sustainable development chapters and don't deal with FTAs' overall implementation. Therefore, DAGs' importance for the EP might be limited to the monitoring of specific environmental and labour issues connected to FTAs. An institutional factor causing this result could be that consultation between the EP and the EESC and the CoR is not compulsory in the field of trade.

Relations with third countries' representatives are also considered important for MEPs to assess the implementation of FTAs. Some agreements, such as the Cotonou Agreement, institute a Joint Parliamentary Assembly. The purpose of such an assembly is to discuss matters related to democracy and development, but this can obviously also involve trade and devel-

Table 18.3 The importance of other actors for the EP in terms of receiving information about the implementation of EU trade policy

Actors	Average grade	Count replies
European Commission	4.9	12
European Council/Council of Ministers	4.3	11
European Parliament	3.7	11
Civil society	3.7	11
European External Action Service (EEAS)	3.4	11
National constituencies	2.5	11
European Economic and Social Committee	2.1	11
Committee of the Regions	1.8	11

Source: Authors' survey data

opment issues. Beyond interparliamentary relations that were established on the basis of treaties (Joint Parliamentary Assemblies), the EP has set up interregional parliamentary assemblies such as the Euro-Latin American Parliamentary Assembly. The EP may also establish *standing interparliamentary delegations with countries or groups of countries*. Ordinary meetings of standing delegations are limited to one a year (unless otherwise specified in international agreements). *Missions* are also limited and cannot exceed five days, or seven days if the mission covers more than one country. After the mission, the delegations' chairs will send reports to the chairs of the different committees that collaborated, report orally to those committees and may make proposals for follow-up actions. If the Conference of Presidents so decides, delegations' chairs may be invited to make a statement to the plenary. Furthermore, *ad-hoc delegations* can be authorized by the EP's Conference of Presidents to discuss specific topics related to the EP's legislative or scrutiny priorities with foreign officials and foreign civil society. A recent example is the visit in February 2018 of an INTA delegation to Colombia and Peru to assess the implementation of the EU's FTA with those countries.[10] Such meetings and missions are limited in number for financial reasons. Political groups can also organize their own missions abroad whenever needed.

In order to further improve quality of its information, the EP has equipped itself with *in-house research units*. EP committees can refer to the *Policy Department for External Relations (EXPO)* for in-house written expertise or for external studies on INTA-related files. Due to financial constraint, decisions on studies to be outsourced are taken collectively by coordinators. The EP recently also created a new Directorate-General dedicated to research, namely the *European Parliamentary Research Service* (EPRS). Its *Directorate for Impact Assessment and European Added Value* (Directorate C) provides services related to the analysis of impact assessments and added value for all EU policies. It provides initial appraisals of impact assessments made by the Commission and can also provide deeper studies called European Implementation Assessments that can be used as background documents for an EP Implementation Report (see Sect. 3.3). Like EXPO, Directorate C can externalize studies within a limited budget. Figure 18.1 shows the number of studies published in the

---

[10] European Parliament, 9 February 2018, MEPs assess implementation of trade agreement with Colombia and Peru, Press Release.

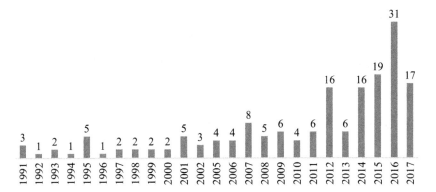

Fig. 18.1 Number of studies published by the EP under the topic 'international trade'. Source: European Parliament, Public Register of Documents, downloaded in December 2017

Table 18.4 Number of requests to the EPRS Members' Research Service on trade matters

EMS requests	Bibliographic and data questions	In person briefing	Tailored analysis
2013	48	0	0
2014	71	0	1
2015	120	1	17
2016	135	10	33
2017 (Provisional)	134	5	34

Source: EPRS data

field of international trade by both services. Although the EP's public register does not distinguish between studies that were written for legislative or monitoring purposes, this figure shows a substantial increase in the number of studies published on trade-related issues.

Finally, individual MEPs can ask Directorate A, the *Members' Research Service (MRS) of the EPRS,* for information on trade-related topics, including implementation. Most answers from the MRS give bibliographical research on a topic; fewer answers entail a deeper analysis called a tailored analysis (see Table 18.4). The MRS does not have the capacity to externalize studies, so the answers will be limited to what the internal capacity allows within the time allocated per request.

In general, financial constraints restrict the EP's ability to commission econometric studies analysing the impact of trade (such as computable general equilibrium). The EP's research units will instead engage in a literature review of econometric studies conducted for the Commission or by academia.

3.2   Frameworks for Discussion

Discussion between actors is important to assess issues from different angles and exchange information. EP committees can organize *hearings and workshops* on trade policy implementation. Workshops are organized by EXPO after a decision by the coordinators. They are normally more academic in nature and bring together established researchers and practitioners. Hearings are organized on the basis of a proposal from the rapporteur or from the coordinators. They aim to have speakers representing all perspectives on the issue, including officials, industry and association members, NGOs and academia. Hearings and workshops rely on a limited budget. Political groups can also organize other events with their own budget.

Another forum for discussing technical issues on implementation are *monitoring groups*. According to our survey replies, monitoring groups exist for all areas of EU trade policy, including FTAs, TDIs and the GSP. Almost all respondents (11 out of 13) indicated that they were part of one or more monitoring groups that track the status of a particular aspect of EU trade policy. Twelve respondents considered monitoring groups to be one of the most important instruments in monitoring EU trade policy. Most respondents were members of monitoring groups that covered EU FTAs or trade negotiations (mostly ongoing negotiations but also several concluded ones), examples being the EU-South Korea FTA, the Economic Partnership Agreement with Eastern Africa and the Trade in Services Agreement (TiSA). One respondent indicated participation in a monitoring group on TDIs and GSP. The exact composition of monitoring groups differs on a case-by-case basis, but they typically consist of at least several INTA members (and their assistants), EP staff and Commission staff. Monitoring groups can also invite EEAS staff, Council staff, representatives of NGOs and civil society, and diplomats from partner countries. Monitoring groups discuss in camera in order to relay any restricted or confidential information. The monitoring group's standing rapporteurs will then report to the relevant EP Committee to relay the information received. The frequency with which monitoring groups meet differs and is decided by the monitoring group's standing rapporteur, who will also take into account suggestions from the INTA Secretariat, shadow rapporteurs and group advisors. In the case of concluded FTA negotiations, it appears that monitoring groups meet less frequently than for FTAs under negotiations, sometimes just once a year or even less. Monitoring groups on the GSP also appear to meet less frequently. One respondent also mentioned that there can be logistical problems connected to monitoring groups: timing of meetings (which should not coincide with official meetings) and limited possibility to obtain interpretation services.

Lastly, whenever a basic legislation act foresees the writing of a report on the implementation by the Commission, it also provides the possibility for the EP to *invite the Commission to present such a report* and discuss it during an ad-hoc meeting of its responsible Committee (see e.g. article 23 of Regulation (EU) 2016/1036 on antidumping or article 40 of Regulation (EU) No. 978/2012 on GSP). Those discussions allow MEPs to raise issues on the implementation, and on methodology to assess effective implementation. An example is the exchange of views between INTA members and the Commission on the implementation of the GSP 2016–2017, following the latter's report of 19 January 2018.[11] Trade agreements do not usually have such a reporting requirement. However, in the framework of the Regulation (EU) No. 19/2013 implementing the bilateral safeguard clause and the stabilization mechanism for bananas of the EU Trade Agreement with Colombia and Peru, the EP managed to introduce a requirement for an annual report on the implementation of both the agreement and the regulation. The EP can invite the Commission to discuss general reports issued on implementation of a policy (e.g. the debate on the report on the implementation of FTAs).[12] Questions asked to the Commission or the Council can include *a debate*. Oral questions always allow for the formulation of a supplementary question on the issue being debated. Questions for written answers with the possibility for debate are called *major interpellations*. Written and oral questions were mentioned in the survey responses as a frequently used instrument for monitoring, albeit also one of the least important ones. The main reason for this could be that the resulting answers are generally concise and maintain an institution's official position on the topic. Oral and written question can nevertheless be used by MEPs to signal a concern.

[11] INTA meeting of 20 February 2018.
[12] INTA meeting of 28 November 2017.

3.3   Frameworks for Action

In the context of delegated acts, the EP has a treaty-based right of objection to a delegated act and a right of revocation of delegated 'powers'. *The right of objection* allows the EP or the Council (or both) to object to a delegated act on any ground. However, such a right can only be exercised within the deadline foreseen in the legislative act, which cannot be less than and is usually only two months. A motion to object must be approved by a majority of the component MEPs.[13] Objection signifies that the delegated act cannot be adopted (or if the act has been taken following the urgency procedure, it must be repealed). In that sense, the right of objection constitutes a clear sanction. Moreover, the EP and the Council can *revoke delegated powers*. Decisions to revoke in full or in part delegation powers by the EP also require the majority of its component members. Whether used or not in practice, the right to revoke those powers serves as a deterrent instrument.

In the context of implementing acts, the EP's action consists of a *right of objection* if the Commission's course of action is 'ultra vires'. The EP can do that by issuing a resolution which asks the Commission to withdraw, amend or submit a new legislative proposal. Here, the Commission only has a duty to inform the EP and the Council on its subsequent course of action. The Commission can accordingly decide to ignore the EP's request and maintain its original implementing act.

The EP also has a series of softer powers whereby it can signal its concerns or new demands on a file. For example, *implementation reports* are a type of own-initiative report analysing the state of implementation of Union legislation or of international agreements and give recommendations on potential actions. Implementation reports were subject in the past to a quota that included other own-initiative reports. Recently, however, they were taken out of that quota.[14] That change in procedure allowed the Committees to use this instrument more frequently. Recently, the EP used

---

[13] Recently, a group of MEPs submitted a motion to object to a delegated act on GSP+ treatment for Sri Lanka, which was rejected by the EP. European Parliament resolution on the Commission delegated regulation of 11 January 2017 amending Annex III to Regulation (EU) No 978/2012 of the European Parliament and of the Council applying a scheme of generalized tariff preferences (C(2016)8996 – 2017/2511(DEA)).

[14] Decision of the Conference of Presidents on the procedure for granting authorisation to draw up own-initiative reports of 12 December 2012 as amended in 2016.

it to report on the implementation of the EU-South Korea FTA[15] and it plans to issue two more on the implementation of the Common Commercial Policy and on the implementation of FTAs in general. *Legislative own-initiative reports* could also be used to signal the interest of the EP to reform or to introduce a new measure after analysis of an implementation issue. Finally, *resolutions* are often used by EP to present its positions with respect to the relations between the EU and a third country. The EP can in this context also make reference to key rules that it wants to see (e.g. the criteria to obtain GSP+).[16] When writing implementation and own-initiative reports, rapporteurs will frequently use a combination of the aforementioned instruments to gather information (such as analytical support from Directorate C or fact-finding missions to third countries). Respondents to our survey viewed own-initiative reports and resolutions as among the most important and the most frequently used instruments for monitoring after the monitoring groups.

4 THE EUROPEAN PARLIAMENT'S MONITORING OF THE IMPLEMENTATION OF THE EU'S FREE TRADE AGREEMENTS, TRADE DEFENCE INSTRUMENTS AND GENERALIZED SYSTEM OF PREFERENCES

This section will present the main results of the survey on EP monitoring of implementation of FTAs, TDIs and the GSP.

4.1 Involvement in Monitoring

Our survey included various questions to determine respondents' involvement in EP monitoring activities. At the outset, it is interesting to note that nearly all respondents indicated that they monitor the implementation of FTAs, TDIs and the GSP in one way or another. Although slightly more respondents monitor the implementation of FTAs (85 per cent)

---

[15] Report on the implementation of the Free Trade Agreement between the European Union and the Republic of Korea (2015/2059(INI), 10 April 2017). European Parliament resolution of 18 May 2017 on the implementation of the Free Trade Agreement between the European Union and the Republic of Korea (2015/2059(INI)).

[16] See, as an example, the European Parliament Resolution of 15 June 2017 on Pakistan, notably the situation of human rights defenders and the death penalty (2017/2723(RSP)).

than TDIs (69 per cent) or the GSP (77 per cent), the differences between these different areas are relatively small. This demonstrates a clear commitment among the respondents to monitor the implementation of EU trade policy in a comprehensive way. The differences between the three policy areas in levels of attention could probably be explained by levels of politicization. For example, one respondent, who focused on monitoring FTA, considered TDIs and the GSP to be far too technical, not easy to communicate and limited in terms of political visibility.

In contrast, the type of monitoring activities conducted by the respondents differs somewhat between the three selected areas of EU trade policy. In the respective cases of FTAs and the GSP, 69 per cent and 62 per cent of the respondents indicated that they monitor implementation primarily in either a systematic way or both a systematic and an ad-hoc manner. This is different for TDIs, where the majority of respondents indicated that they monitor TDIs' implementation mostly on an ad-hoc basis (46 per cent), as opposed to 23 per cent who monitor it systematically. The reason for this could be that TDIs are technical and politicization will depend on highly localized economic impacts. MEPs are therefore more likely to select specific cases to monitor. Indeed, most of the respondents also indicated that ad-hoc monitoring of TDIs' implementation is triggered primarily by Commission investigations that are politically sensitive in the EP.[17] One of the respondents even specified that ad-hoc monitoring involved specific investigations, namely those affecting sensitive sectors, in particular when there was a potential economic or labour impact on the constituency and important cases parallel to new negotiations.

Respondents nevertheless indicated that they sometimes also monitor the implementation of FTAs and the GSP on an ad-hoc basis. In the context of FTAs' implementation, ad-hoc monitoring seems to be triggered in more or less the same degree by three types of issues[18]: trade issues or economic aspects, human rights developments and issues on standards (technical, environmental and labour). Ad-hoc monitoring of FTAs' implementation in the EP is thus influenced by a wide range of issues, relating both to the EU's own interests and to those of partner countries. As regards the GSP, respondents answered that ad-hoc monitoring is trig-

---

[17] The issue was mentioned five times while other factors were mentioned only by one respondent.

[18] All issues were mentioned either seven or eight times.

gered primarily by political developments in the beneficiary countries (mentioned six times) and to a lesser degree by Commission decisions to add or remove beneficiary countries (mentioned three times). This result is in accordance with the fact that the EP is often perceived as a vocal monitor of developments in third countries and the conditionality of GSP.

Differences across trade policies also appear with respect to the frequency of typical monitoring activities. Respondents indicated that they typically monitor FTA implementation more than once a year (46 per cent),[19] although this can also depend on the FTA (38 per cent). In the case of TDI monitoring, respondents replied that the frequency of monitoring primarily depends on the investigation or review at issue (38 per cent), while a few replied that they typically monitor TDIs' implementation either more than once a year (15 per cent) or once a year (15 per cent). For the GSP, respondents mostly frequently answered that typical monitoring activities occur either more than once a year (31 per cent) or only when there is a new application or graduation for GSP+ (31 per cent), where human rights conditionality is particularly important.

For none of these areas of EU trade policy did respondents indicate that typical monitoring activities occur less than once a year. This again shows a clear interest in the EP to actively monitor trade policy implementation, although the frequency of monitoring differs depending on the issue.

4.2   *Priorities of Monitoring*

Our survey contained a number of questions on the priorities of monitoring. With respect to FTAs, respondents were specifically asked which type of agreement they monitored most intensely (Table 18.5). A majority of respondents answered 'new' FTAs (concluded <u>after</u> Lisbon), closely followed by both 'new' FTAs and 'old' FTAs (concluded <u>before</u> Lisbon), while none of the respondents answered 'old FTAs'. There could be several reasons for this result. The first one is institutional: monitoring groups were originally created after Lisbon to follow negotiations of the then new FTAs and were, after conclusion of those agreements, maintained to mon-

---

[19] All the percentages refer to positive replies to the question as a percentage of the total respondents to the survey (i.e. 13). Nota bene: some respondents sometimes gave more than one answer. For example, a respondent could have mentioned both that they monitored more than once a year but that it also depended on the FTA.

Table 18.5 Of which EU FTAs do you monitor the implementation most intensely?

Type of FTA	Score
Old FTA	0%
New FTA	46%
Both	38%
No answer	15%

Source: Authors' survey data

Table 18.6 Issues important for monitoring EU trade policy

Issue	Average score (out of 5)		
	FTAs	TDIs	GSP
Impact on whole EU economy (jobs, industries, imports, exports)	**4.7**	**5.0**	3.0
Impact on EU standards (health, environmental, labour, human rights)	**4.7**	**4.8**	3.8
Impact on national constituency	**4.5**	**4.8**	3.1
Impact on foreign partner's economy	3.6	3.1	**4.6**
Impact on foreign partner's standards (health, environmental, labour, human rights)	3.9	4.0	**4.8**

Source: Authors' survey data

itor their implementation. Monitoring groups to monitor pre-Lisbon agreements were not, however, created directly after Lisbon but came later. The second reason can be found in the greater politicization of the 'new' FTAs because of their scope and reach. Last but not least, the EP, having given consent to the post-Lisbon agreements, also feels responsible for their monitoring as evidenced by INTA Chairman Lange's quote in the introduction of this chapter. The last two explanations are also in line with both principal-agent frameworks explained in Sect. 2.

Our survey also revealed different priorities with respect to the different trade policies being monitored. Table 18.6 provides a comparison of the importance of various issues when comparing the EP's monitoring of the implementation of FTAs, TDIs and the GSP.

When it comes to monitoring FTAs' and TDIs' implementation, respondents indicated that they consider EU issues to be the most important ones, namely the respective impacts on the EU economy, EU standards and national constituencies. These topics correspond to typical concerns of EU civil society in these areas. Moreover, for both policy areas, respondents considered issues in the partner country (impact on its economy and standards) less important than the aforementioned EU issues. These 'foreign issues' (standards in particular) nevertheless received relatively high scores. This strengthens the general impression that foreign standards, in particular in the area of sustainable development, play an important role in the EP's monitoring of FTA and TDI implementation. With respect to TDI monitoring, it is striking that all EU issues (impact on the EU economy, EU standards and national constituencies) received nearly maximum scores, which underlines TDIs' objective of protecting the EU against unfair foreign trade practices. A second noteworthy finding is the relative difference between the scores assigned to the impact on a foreign partner's economy (3.1) and the impact on its standards (4.0). This suggests that in the area of TDIs, the EP is more concerned about the impact of a foreign partner's standards than its economy. As regards monitoring of GSP implementation, respondents' answers show exactly the opposite of what was observed for FTAs and TDIs: partner country issues are generally considered much more important than EU issues. This result is in line with what would be expected of the monitoring of GSP implementation, which is more about the foreign partner than the EU and the EP's focus on conditionality in this area.[20]

4.3 Instruments for Monitoring: Most and Least Important

Respondents were also asked in our survey which three instruments they considered most and least important for monitoring the implementation of EU trade policy. As expected, their answers differed somewhat depending on the area of EU trade policy at issue, although some wider trends could also be observed.

Starting with the latter, respondents considered contacts with civil society one of the most important monitoring instruments for all areas of EU trade policy (although somewhat surprisingly, they simultaneously regarded it as one of the least important ones for TDIs). This suggests that contacts with civil society have a real added-value for the EP when it comes

---

[20] See footnote 17 for an example involving Pakistan, or see the discussion surrounding the GSP+ treatment of Sri Lanka in footnote 14.

to monitoring the implementation of EU trade policy. It is unclear who respondents had in mind when they referred to 'civil society', which could include many different entities ranging from NGOs to businesses. Given the importance of this instrument for the EP (and its resulting impact on monitoring of trade policy), this could be an interesting topic for future research.

Monitoring groups were also mentioned as one of the most important instruments for monitoring (this was the case for FTA and GSP implementation). As set out in Sect. 3, monitoring groups seem to be one of (if not) the main discussion fora for FTA implementation. This is reflected in the difference in the score between monitoring groups (mentioned nine times) and the other most important instruments for monitoring FTAs (mentioned at most five times). As regards the topics most frequently discussed in monitoring groups, respondents generally seem to refer to issues in ongoing FTA negotiations, which are less relevant in the context of this chapter. However, implementation of FTAs is mentioned more than once as a topic that frequently comes up in monitoring groups, which again confirms the relevance of this instrument for the EP's monitoring activities. In relation to the concluded EU-South Korea FTA, for example, one respondent answered that the monitoring group frequently discusses the evolving trade balance between the two parties, correction of mistakes in the annexes to the FTA-text, and labour and environmental standards in South Korea.

Unfortunately, very little data was received on what is typically discussed in monitoring groups on TDIs and the GSP. One respondent did, however, indicate that TDI monitoring groups focus primarily on the effects on employment (presumably in the EU itself), which is in line with the findings in Sect. 4.2. GSP monitoring groups, on the other hand, usually focus on the implementation of international conventions on the environment (such as the Paris Agreement), social rights (specifically the International Labour Organization conventions) and human rights (presumably primarily in the partner country). That is also consistent with results presented in the previous sub-section.

An interesting finding is that respondents consider the instrument of asking written or oral questions to the Commission one of the least important monitoring instruments for all three areas of EU trade policy (which was also alluded to earlier in Sect. 3.1). At the same time, questions to the Commission are also viewed as one of the most important instruments for monitoring the implementation of TDIs, which is somewhat contradictory, hinting that further research would be needed to analyse that result.

Research units within the EP also appeared as one of the least important monitoring instruments, in particular in relation to the implementation of the GSP (both the EXPO and EPRS) and FTAs (only the EPRS). A possible explanation is that these internal units generally rely on publicly available information without necessarily having access to information on the ground in foreign countries, while the impact on those countries is considered an important (if not the most important) monitoring issue in these areas of EU trade policy (see Sect. 4.2).

5   Conclusion

Legislatures have a double interest in monitoring the implementation of policies: on the one hand, ensuring that the executive does not exceed its powers when enacting non-legislative acts (input legitimacy) and, on the other hand, assessing that policies achieve the objectives that benefit the people (output legitimacy). From these perspectives, the EP's incentive to monitor implementation of EU trade policy has certainly increased with the responsibility as a co-legislator and the consent-giver for the conclusion of trade agreements. The EP has a vast and growing variety of instruments at its disposal to exercise control. However, the most comprehensive instruments are found with regard to gathering information, while in the area of discussion and action, its formal instruments remain more limited and are generally of a softer nature (such as implementation reports). Stronger powers have been given in the framework of delegated acts, where the EP can both object on grounds of procedure but also content, as well as revoke delegation powers. Instruments are often subject to either institutional or capacity constraints, which we have detailed as much as possible in this chapter. Our survey's results with respect to three case-studies (FTAs, TDIs and the GSP) show almost equal interest of the respondents in monitoring all these areas, but the modalities and objectives of their monitoring differ depending on the issue.

References

Brandsma, G. J. (2015). Holding the European Commission to Account: The Promise of Delegated Acts. *International Review of Administrative Sciences, 86*(4), 656–673.

Brandsma, G. J., & Adriaensen, J. (2017). The Principal–Agent Model, Accountability and Democratic Legitimacy. In T. Delreux & J. Adriaensen

(Eds.), *The Principal Agent Model and the European Union* (pp. 35–53). Cham: Palgrave Macmillan.

Brandsma, G. J., & Blom-Hansen, J. (2012). Negotiating the Post-Lisbon Comitology System: Institutional Battles Over Delegated Decision-Making. *Journal of Common Market Studies, 50*(6), 939–957.

Brandsma, G. J., & Blom-Hansen, J. (2016). Controlling Delegated Powers in the Post-Lisbon European Union. *Journal of European Public Policy, 23*(4), 531–549.

Brandsma, G. J., & Blom-Hansen, J. (2017). *Controlling the EU Executive? The Politics of Delegation in the European Union.* Oxford: Oxford University Press.

Cerna, L. (2013). *The Nature of Policy Change and Implementation: A Review of Different Theoretical Approaches.* OECD, pp. 1–31.

Christiansen, T., & Dobbels, M. (2013). Delegated Powers and Inter-Institutional Relations in the EU After Lisbon: A Normative Assessment. *West European Politics, 36*(6), 1159–1177.

Corbett, J., Jacobs, F., & Shackleton, M. (2011). *The European Parliament.* New York: John Harper Publishing.

Da Conceição-Heldt, E. (2017). 'Multiple Principals Preferences, Types of Control Mechanism and Agent's Discretion in Trade Negotiations. In T. Delreux & J. Adriaensen (Eds.), *The Principal Agent Model and the European Union* (pp. 223–225). Cham: Palgrave Macmillan.

Delreux, T., & Adriaensen, J. (Eds.). (2017). *The Principal Agent Model and the European Union.* Cham: Palgrave Macmillan.

Devuyst, Y. (2014). The European Parliament and International Trade Agreements: Practice after the Lisbon Treaty. In I. Govaere, E. Lannon, P. Elsuwege, & S. Adam (Eds.), *The European Union in the World: Essays in Honour of Marc Maresceau* (pp. 171–189). Leiden/Boston: Martinus Nijhoff.

Dimopoulos, A. (2008). The Common Commercial Policy After Lisbon: Establishing Parallelism Between Internal and External Economic Relations? *Croatian Yearbook of European Law and Policy, 4*(4), 101–129.

European Parliament. (2016). Decision of the Conference of Presidents of 12 December 2002 on the Procedure for Granting Authorisation to Draw-up Own-Initiative Reports, as Last Amended by Corrigendum of 15 July 2016.

European Parliament. (2017, January). Rules of Procedure, 8th Parliamentary Term.

Finke, D. (2016). The Burden of Authorship: How Agenda-Setting and Electoral Rules Shape Legislative Behaviour. *Journal of European Public Policy, 23*(4), 604–623.

Finke, D. (2017). Bicameralism in the European Union: Parliamentary Scrutiny as a Tool for Reinforcing Party Unity. *West European Politics, 40*(2), 275–294.

Framework Agreement on the relations between the European Parliament and the European Commission, OJ L 304, 20.11.2010.

Franchino, F. (2002). Efficiency or Credibility? Testing the Two Logics of Delegation to the European Commission. *Journal of European Public Policy, 9*(5), 677–694.

Frennhoff Larsen, M. (2017). The Increasing Power of the European Parliament: Negotiating the EU-India Free Trade Agreement. *International Negotiation, 22*(3), 473–498.

Gailmard, S. (2014). Accountability and Principal-Agent Models. In M. Bovens, R. E. Goodin, & T. Schillemans (Eds.), *Oxford Handbook of Public Accountability*. Oxford: Oxford University Press.

Hix, S., & Hoyland, B. (2013). Empowerment of the European Parliament. *Annual Review of Political Science, 16*(1), 171–189.

Hoffmeister, F. (2011). The European Union's Common Commercial Policy a Year After Lisbon – Sea Change or Business As Usual. In P. Koutrakos (Ed.), *The European Union's External Relations a Year After Lisbon* (pp. 83–96). The Hague: Centre for the Law of EU External Relations Working Papers 2011/3.

Interinstitutional Agreement between the European Parliament, the Council of the European Union and the European Commission on Better Law-Making, OJ L 123, 12.05.2016.

Kleizen, B. (2016). Mapping the Involvement of the European Parliament in EU External Relations – A Legal and Empirical Analysis. *Centre for the Law of EU External Relations Working Papers* 2016/4.

Kohler, M. (2013). European Governance and the European Parliament: From Talking Shop to Legislative Powerhouse. *Journal of Common Market Studies, 52*(3), 600–615.

Krajewski, M. (2013). New Functions and New Powers for the European Parliament: Assessing the Changes of the Common Commercial Policy from a Perspective of Democratic Legitimacy. In M. Bungenberg & C. Herrmann (Eds.), *Common Commercial Policy After Lisbon* (pp. 67–85). Berlin: European Yearbook of International Economic Law, Springer.

Lange, B. (2017, April 10). Committee Guide: INTA Committee Working Hard to Hold the COMMISSION to Account on Trade Deals. *The Parliament Magazine*, Opinion.

Leal-Arcas, R. (2012). The European Union's New Common Commercial Policy After Lisbon. In M. Trybus & L. Rubini (Eds.), *The Treaty of Lisbon and the Future of European Law and Policy* (pp. 262–284). Cheltenham: Edward Elgar.

Maurer, A. (2008). *The European Parliament After Lisbon: Policy-Making and Control.* Paper presented at the Federal Trust Workshop 'The European Parliament in an enlarged European Union: Beyond the Lisbon Treaty', London.

Meissner, K. (2016). Democratising EU External Relations: The European Parliament's Informal Role in SWIFT, ACTA and TTIP. *European Foreign Affairs Review, 21*(2), 269–288.

Mendes, J. (2013). Delegated and Implementing Rulemaking: Proceduralisation and Constitutional Design. *European Law Journal, 19*(1), 22–41.

Persson, T., & Tabellini, G. (2000). *Political Economics – Explaining Economic Policy*. Cambridge: MIT Press.

Pollack, M. (2005). *The Engines of European Integration: Delegation, Agency, and Agenda Setting in the EU*. Oxford: Oxford University Press.

Regulation (EU) 2016/1036 of the European Parliament and of the Council of 8 June 2016 on protection against dumped imports from countries not members of the European Union, OJ L 176, 30.6.2016.

Regulation (EU) No. 182/2011 of the European Parliament and of the Council of 16 February 2011 laying down the rules and general principles concerning mechanisms for control by Member States of the Commission's exercise of implementing powers, OJ L 55, 28.02.2011.

Regulation (EU) No. 19/2013 of the European Parliament and of the Council of 15 January 2013 implementing the bilateral safeguard clause and the stabilisation mechanism for bananas of the Trade Agreement between the European Union and its Member States, of the one part, and Colombia and Peru, of the other part, OJ L 17, 19.1.2013.

Roederer-Rynning, C. (2017). Parliamentary Assertion and Deep Integration: The European Parliament in the CETA and TTIP Negotiations. *Cambridge Review of International Affairs, 30*(5–6), 507–526.

Scharpf, F. (2003). Problem-Solving Effectiveness and Democratic Accountability in the EU. Max Planck Institute for the Study of Societies, Working Paper 03/1.

Shackelton, M. (2017). Transforming Democracy in the EU? The Role of the European Parliament. *Journal of European Integration, 39*(2), 191–205.

Sicurelli, D. (2015). The EU as a Promoter of Human Rights in Bilateral Trade Agreements: The Case of the Negotiations with Vietnam. *Journal of Contemporary European Research, 11*(2), 230–245.

Strøm, K. (2000). Delegation and Accountability in Parliamentary Democracies. *European Journal for Political Research, 37*(3), 261–289.

Van den Putte, L., De Ville, F., & Orbie, J. (2014). The European EP's New Role in Trade Policy: Turning Power Into Impact. CEPS Special Report 8, Centre for European Policy Studies.

Wessel, R. A., & Takács, T. (2017). Constitutional Aspects of the EU's Global Actorness: Increased Exclusivity in Trade and Investment and the Role of the European Parliament. *European Business Law Review, 28*(2), 103–118.

Weiß, W. (2017). The European Parliament's Role in the Operation of Trade Agreements: Non-Delegation and Parliamentary Control in External Action. Paper presented to the Conference *Recalibrating Executive-Legislative Relations in the European Union* Organised by Maastricht University, 18 and 19 January.

Weiß, W. (2018, forthcoming). Delegation to Treaty Bodies in EU Agreements: Constitutional Constraints and Proposals for Strengthening the European Parliament. *European Constitutional Law Review*, 1–35.

CHAPTER 19

Parliamentary Diplomacy: Democracy Support at the European Parliament

Beatrix Immenkamp and Naja Bentzen

1   INTRODUCTION

Since the mid-1990s, the European Parliament (EP) has aimed to boost its impact on the European Union's (EU's) foreign policy and become a diplomatic actor in its own right (Nitoiu and Sus 2017, 71). The Lisbon Treaty granted the EP extensive new powers as 'co-legislator' in many areas of EU competence. However, in the area of foreign policy and external action, an area traditionally dominated by member state governments, the EP's formal influence remains somewhat limited. Consultation and information rights have been extended, legal procedures of consent and co-decision have been made the norm, and budgetary control has been reinforced. However, formal (hard) powers have not been extended to all domains of European external action, and exclude certain key areas, including the Common Foreign and Security Policy (CFSP) and the Common Security and Defence Policy (CSDP) (Moussis 2016, 220ff).

This creates a certain paradox. National parliaments of individual member states exert democratic control over their government's foreign poli-

B. Immenkamp (✉) • N. Bentzen
European Parliament, European Parliamentary Research Service,
Brussels, Belgium
e-mail: beatrix.immenkamp@europarl.europa.eu; naja.bentzen@europarl.europa.eu

© The Author(s) 2019   413
O. Costa (ed.), *The European Parliament in Times of EU Crisis*,
European Administrative Governance,
https://doi.org/10.1007/978-3-319-97391-3_19

cies. At the same time, the EP exerts control over the external relations of EU member states in areas in which the EU has exclusive competence and in which the EP has been granted formal powers, such as trade in goods under the common commercial policy. By contrast, when member states act together—through the Council—to define the EU's foreign policy in the area of sanctions or international negotiations (such as with Iran), their actions are not controlled either by national parliaments or by the EP.

Since the creation of the CFSP by the Treaty of Maastricht in 1993, Members of the European Parliament (MEPs) have striven to maximise the role of the EP in the Union's foreign policy (Barbe and Herranz 2006, 1). This is an area where parliamentary bodies—such as standing committees, subcommittees, inter-parliamentary delegations, working groups—and individual members, including the President, have sought informal ways of shaping policies and exerting influence, beyond the normative parliamentary powers granted by the treaties (Thym 2009, 309). These include an impact on the positions of other EU institutions and member states, as well as an impact on policies and actions of third parties, including foreign actors. An area in which the influence of the EP in external relations is arguably growing and where activity has expanded significantly in recent years is that of parliamentary diplomacy (Bajtay 2015, 8).

Parliamentary diplomacy refers to a wide range of activities undertaken by MEPs, or parliament as an institution, to 'increase mutual understanding between countries', 'to improve scrutiny of government' (or the EU executive branch) and to 'increase the democratic legitimacy of intergovernmental institutions' (Weisglas and de Boer 2007, 93–94). Parliamentary diplomacy is understood to comprise (regular) consultations with foreign actors, such as representatives of non-EU countries, international organisations, non-state actors and civil society. At times of conflict, parliamentary diplomacy can extend to mediation activities between the parties to the conflict.

The EP's diplomatic activities take place within the overall framework of the official foreign policy positions of the EU—as defined by the Council, the High Representative of the Union for Foreign Affairs/Vice-President of the Commission High Representative of the Union for Foreign Affairs and Security Policy / Vice-President of the Commission (HR/VP) and the Commission—and/or its member states. As a result, the effectiveness or the concrete results of the EP's 'independent' diplomatic efforts have, at times, been questioned. However, it has also been argued (Gianniou 2015, 248) that an active EP in the diplomatic field is very much in the EU's interest. The Parliament's official declarations and the actions of its members have the potential to move forward the EU position on a particular issue, with the Parliament often in a position to 'present more resolute positions transcending EU official red lines' (Gianniou 2015, 248). This has in the past led to a dialogue on issues that would be considered anathema to the EU's official foreign policy stance, but has also on several occasions put the EP in direct opposition to the Council (Zanon 2006, 107).

The EP has increasingly served as a vehicle for consultation with representatives of non-EU countries, international organisations, non-state actors and civil society. It is more and more used by external actors as an open forum for pursuing foreign policy interests and trying to make an impact on international or national developments. At the same time, the EP also plays a proactive role through the activities of its many inter-parliamentary delegations as well as pre-planned and ad hoc missions to third countries by individual members and various parliamentary bodies. The EP has become a respected and influential international actor over the years. The institution is perceived by partners to be capable of exerting influence on developments and decisions both externally and internally (Bajtay 2015, 16).

By way of an example, the Parliament's handling of the Yugoslav crisis in 1991–1992 has been cited as a parliamentary involvement that was useful in publicising issues, mobilising public opinion and strengthening internal parliamentary cohesion on a sensitive foreign policy matter (even if it could not stop armed conflict) (Viola 2000, 176). MEPs were also credited with contributing to a peaceful and democratic transition of power in Albania after the 2013 elections, and with providing crucial input to resolve a domestic political crisis in the Former Yugoslav Republic of Macedonia (FYROM) in 2015–2017 (Fonck forthcoming). The most intense involvement by MEPs, including the President, in any crisis to date has been in Ukraine, focus of the second part of this chapter.

The EP is 'perceived on the international scene as a capable moral force with strong focus on strengthening human rights, supporting democracy and enhancing the rule of law worldwide' (Bajtay 2015, 17). Consequently, those who believe parliamentary democracy to be a stabilising factor domestically, and in international relations overall, increasingly ask the Parliament to be involved in the building of parliamentary democracy (Bajtay 2015, 16).

The following chapter sets out the political and administrative framework that the EP has developed to respond to the growing demand for a stronger role for its members in supporting parliamentary democracies worldwide. The second part of this chapter focuses on the specific role that MEPs have played in supporting the nascent democracy in post-Maidan Ukraine. This chapter traces the EP's post-Lisbon evolution as a 'policy entrepreneur' (Redei and Romanyshyn 2015, 2), from invisible go-between to agenda-setter in Kyiv, thereby also increasing its visibility and credibility in Brussels. The EP's expanding toolbox includes the development and implementation of its multi-faceted 'Comprehensive Approach to Democracy Support' (CDSA), including monitoring and follow-up of elections, mediation efforts of MEPs in Ukraine, as well as training of staff and members of the Ukrainian parliament.

The findings of this chapter are largely based on interviews with MEPs and EP officials who have been or still are directly involved in democracy support and mediation activities.

2   Democracy Support in EU External Relations

2.1   Council Conclusion on Democracy Support in EU External Relations

One of the objectives of EU external action is 'to develop and consolidate democracy and the rule of law, and respect for human rights and fundamental freedoms' (Council conclusions, 17 November 2009). In 2009, the Council adopted conclusions on Democracy Support in EU External Relations, together with an EU Agenda for Action, which outlined a new strategy for supporting democracy by means of a country-specific approach involving various stakeholders.

3   Democracy Support at the European Parliament

As the only directly elected EU institution, the EP is particularly committed to supporting sustainable democracies throughout the world (Lerch 2017, 2). This commitment is regularly highlighted in the EP's resolutions. At the EP, democracy support activities focus on a small number of priority countries and are closely associated with the Parliament's role in election monitoring in these priority countries and other non-EU countries. The EP almost always organises democracy support activities around the electoral cycle. The aim is to establish a better link between election observation and complementary activities such as mediation, follow-up to elections, parliamentary support activities and human rights actions (Democracy Support Work Programme 2018).

3.1   The Democracy Support and Election Coordination Group

In 2014, the EP set up a Democracy Support and Election Coordination Group (DEG), which provides political guidance for all activities supporting democracy (Decision of Conference of Presidents of 13 September 2012). It consists of 15 MEPs and is co-chaired by the chairs of the Parliament's Committee on Foreign Affairs and Committee on Development. The Vice-President responsible for Human Rights and Democracy and the Sakharov Network and the Chair of the Subcommittee on Human Rights are *ex officio* permanent members. The DEG grew out of a parliamentary body initially set up in 2001, the European Parliament Election Coordination Group.

The DEG provides political guidance for the monitoring of elections, election follow-up, support for parliamentary democracy through training of staff and members of parliaments, assistance with elaborating legislation, activities in connection with the Sakharov Network and human rights-related actions, as well as mediation. All activities are geared towards underpinning longer-term efforts to strengthen newly emerging democracies.

In 2012, the Parliament decided to create the Directorate for Democracy Support. In setting up this Directorate as part of the Directorate-General for External Policies of the Union, four units were created, namely the Democracy and Election Actions Unit, the European Parliament Mediation and Dialogue Support Unit, the Human Rights Action Unit and the Pre-Accession Unit. The Directorate provides the administrative support for the EP's democracy support activities in general, and the members of the DEG in particular.

4   A Comprehensive Approach to Democracy Support

To ensure that the EP's democracy support activities are well coordinated and complementary, they are organised around the electoral cycle. It was recognised that a sustainable democracy-building process requires more than support for democratic elections through election monitoring. In response, the EP developed an approach which goes beyond election monitoring and its focus on the period around the actual elections, to supporting parliaments throughout the entire electoral cycle. The so-called CDSA encourages pre-election dialogue and puts more emphasis on the follow-up to election observation, including following up on recommendations of the election observation mission (EOM) (Internal note 2014, 1–2). With a view to strengthening the institutional capacity of parliaments in third countries, the EP organises training programmes and study visits for members and officials of third-country parliaments. The EP has also built up a mentoring system involving MEPs and newly elected parliamentarians from priority countries. Providing support for mediation and dialogue was added as new types of interventions, with a view to preventing election-related conflicts and violence.

Key elements of the CDSA approach, which was established by the DEG at beginning of the 2014–2019 parliamentary term, include the definition of a limited number of priority countries, where the EP's democracy support activities take place (DG EXPO Internal Note 2014, Annex 1). Moreover, one MEP is chosen as the 'Lead Member' for each priority country. In 2018, the priority countries and regions and their respective Lead Members are Ukraine (Elmar Brok, European People's Party - EPP), Moldova (Petras Auštrevičius, Alliance of Liberals and Democrats for Europe - ALDE), Georgia (Ana Gomes, Group of the Progressive Alliance of Socialists and Democrats in the European Parliament - S&D), Tunisia (Michael Gahler, EPP), Morocco (Antonio Panzeri, S&D), Peru (Renate Weber, ALDE), Nigeria (Santiago Fisas Ayxeia, EPP) and the Pan-African Parliament (Michael Gahler, EPP). In two priority countries, Myanmar (Judith Sargentini, The Greens / European Free Alliance in the European Parliament - GREENS/EFA) and Tanzania (David Martin, S&D), activities are on standby (Democracy Support Work Programme 2018). The EP's democracy support activities fall into three broad thematic areas, namely capacity building, mediation and dialogue support, and support for human right actions.

The following sections describe certain constituent elements of the CDSA in greater detail.

4.1   The European Parliament's Role in Election Monitoring

MEPs have been involved in election observation activities since 1984—most recently in, Lebanon, Pakistan and Zimbabwe[1]—with the aim of strengthening the legitimacy of national electoral processes and increasing public confidence in elections. EOMs assess events on election day, as well as the entire electoral process, to gauge the state of democratic develop-

---

[1] NB: This needs to be updated just before the publication date, to take account of missions in the second half of 2018.

ment in a given country at a particular time. Long-term observers usually begin operating two months before the elections and follow the entire electoral process through to the announcement of the official results and the appeals procedure. Short-term observers monitor polling day and the tallying of votes. Parliament delegations always form part of existing EU EOM or EOMs of the Office for Democratic Institutions and Human Rights (ODIHR) of the Organisation for Security and Cooperation in Europe (OSCE). The EP is consulted on the identification and planning of EU EOMs and on the subsequent follow-up. The Chief Observer of an EU EOM is always an MEP. The EP has started to brief MEPs who act as Chief Observers in mediation awareness techniques, through e-learning course available on the EP's website.

4.2 'Capacity-Building' Activities in Priority Countries

The EP is particularly interested in helping parliaments beyond the EU's borders strengthen their institutional capacity, both before and after the electoral period. Activities include joint training programmes and study visits for members and officials of third-country parliaments. In addition, the Democracy Fellowship Programme (DFP) provides staff of non-EU parliaments with the opportunity to spend several weeks at the EP, working with their counterparts within the EP's Secretariat. The programme, which was created in 2008, has hosted nearly 60 fellows to date.

Joint activities with priority countries have focused on various aspects of parliamentary work, including:

- functioning of a modern multi-national parliament, including planning, budgetary oversight and general oversight of the executive, managing diversity and the role of committees;
- cooperation between the executive and the legislature;
- role of political groups in a parliament;
- consensus-building;
- Parliament's role in the trade negotiations and in fighting money laundering;
- Parliament's relations with civil society;
- gender equality and women's participation in parliamentary life;
- rnsuring checks and balances between different branches of power and the democratic roles of the parliamentary majority and the opposition;

- parliamentary oversight of the European integration process; and
- legislative role of trans-border parliaments.

Moreover, the Parliament has organised multilateral training seminars, bringing together representatives of parliaments from the priority countries and regions. A 2017 seminar on the Legislative Cycle brought together over 60 committee chairs from the parliaments of the Western Balkans: Bosnia and Herzegovina, FYROM, Montenegro, Serbia as well as Turkey; Moldova, Georgia, Tunisia, Morocco, Myanmar, Peru, Nigeria and Tanzania; and—as part of the Pan-African Parliament delegation—Burkina Faso, Burundi, Cameroon, Congo, Djibouti, the Ivory Coast, Rwanda, Senegal and Togo. The event provided an opportunity for an extremely lively exchange of views and best practices between MEPs and the external participants.

4.3   Mediation and Dialogue Support

The EP's support for mediation and dialogue takes place within wider EU efforts to address conflict situations. The EU is a global actor that is committed to supporting peace, democracy, human rights and sustainable development. It is generally seen as a credible and ethical actor in situations of instability and conflict and is, as such, well placed to mediate, facilitate or support mediation and dialogue processes. The EU's priorities focus on acting early to prevent conflict, responding when necessary to stop crises escalating and supporting the post-conflict restoration of peace and democracy. One of the main European actions in this field aims to strengthen third countries' capacities in conflict prevention and mediation.

The EU's activities have shown that diplomacy and mediation can deliver results even in the most challenging international situations, such as in the ongoing facilitated dialogue between Serbia and Kosovo, or in the difficult negotiations with Iran over its nuclear ambitions (de los Garcés 2018, 7–9). This has led to calls for further development of the EU's conflict prevention and mediation capacities (Quille 2014).

In 2014, the EP set up a dedicated service to allow it to better respond to the growing demands upon MEPs to get involved in mediation efforts beyond the EU's borders. The European Parliament Mediation Support (EPMS) Service, which became the European Parliament Mediation and Dialogue Support Unit in July 2017, provides expert policy advice and practical operational support to MEPs in the areas of conflict prevention, mediation, and facilitation and dialogue initiatives. Services available to individual members engaged in mediation activities include providing policy advice and conflict analysis, organising events and accompanying delegations engaged in conflict prevention, mediation and dialogue. The EPMS is also the Parliament's 'mediation interface' vis-à-vis the European External Action Service, external mediation experts and civil society organisations.

Mediation activities mainly take place within the framework of two specific programmes—the Jean Monnet Dialogue for peace and democracy, and the Young Political Leaders (YPL) programme—as well as on an ad hoc or country-specific basis, focusing on but not limited to the priority countries.

4.3.1 Jean Monnet Dialogue for Peace and Democracy
The EP prides itself on having a 'culture of dialogue', a set of norms and rules that requires political opponents to engage in dialogue to bring about a compromise. Efforts have been made to 'export' this culture of dialogue to non-EU parliaments, through a mediation and consensus-building process known as the 'Jean Monnet Dialogue for peace and democracy'. Named after one of the founding fathers of the EU (Perchoc 2017), Jean Monnet dialogues take place at the historical Jean Monnet House. Located in rural France, far away from the media spotlight of either Brussels or national capitals, it has proven to be an ideal location for constructive dialogue among opposing political factions. Three series of dialogues with representatives of the Verkhovna Rada of Ukraine (VRU) have taken place so far, and there are plans to start a Jean Monnet Dialogue to enhance political dialogue in FYROM.

4.3.2 Young Political Leaders Programme
The EP is committed to building strong and lasting relations with future leaders outside of the EU. A programme targeting young political leaders was set up in 2015. The YPL programme, led by MEP Fabio Massimo Castaldo, expands on existing activities organised by the EP, such as the Annual Fora for Young Leaders from the European Neighbourhood (Maghreb, Middle East, Eastern Partnership), and the YPL initiative for the Sudan. The programme cooperates with young political activists, including political party representatives, civil society actors and young business leaders in the European Neighbourhood countries, priority coun-

tries agreed under the CDSA, and ad hoc countries requiring assistance in the area of parliamentary conflict prevention and democracy support. Recent YPL activities targeted young leaders from Israel and Palestine, the Maghreb, the Middle East and North Africa (MENA) region, the Western Balkans, Armenia and Azerbaijan.

5   From Back-Door Monitor to Agenda-Setter in Ukraine: Expanding the European Parliament's Diplomatic Role Before and After the Revolution of Dignity

The notion of the EP's post-Lisbon development as a 'policy entrepreneur, constantly expanding its role and influence' (Redei and Romanyshyn 2015, 2), materialises particularly visibly in the context of Ukraine, which signifies an ideological battlefield between not only Western and European values on the one side and post-Soviet authoritarianism on the other side, but more specifically the struggle for the respect for international law, which Russia violated when it illegally annexed the Crimean peninsula in March 2014 and launched a hybrid war against Ukraine.

This case study focuses on the EP's evolution as an actor in the field of democracy support after the Euromaidan revolution. The case of Ukraine is a pivotal example of the EP's evolving diplomatic visibility in times of external crises, from invisible back-door diplomacy to evident agenda-setting actions, thus effectively influencing EU foreign policy (Fonck 2018, 15).

Although recent studies still neglect the EP as a diplomatic actor (Baltag 2018), its role in the lead-up to the Revolution of Dignity has been dealt with in a number of publications (Nitoiu and Sus 2017; Fonck 2018; Moskalenko 2016; Redei and Romanyshyn 2015). In this context, we will therefore only briefly touch upon this mission in order to set the scene for the post-Maidan developments. The EP's role after Euromaidan has been scrutinised to a far lesser extent, as the post-2014 parliamentary cycle and the EP's actions in Ukraine's parliament (Verkhovna Rada) are still ongoing. We explore how the EP, as an evolving diplomatic EU actor in Ukraine, has contributed to projecting the EU's external power. We demonstrate how the EP has increased and solidified its agenda-setting power since the beginning of the Euromaidan crisis—not only externally in Ukraine, but also within the EU diplomatic puzzle—in particular through democracy support and mediation.

5.1   Pre-Maidan: From Back-Door Monitoring Mission to Officially Recognised Mediation Tool

Nitoiu and Sus (2017, 72) argue that the EP played a key role in developing the EU's engagement with Ukraine before the Euromaidan revolution, and that the Cox-Kwasniewski mission to Ukraine in 2012–2013 provides a 'good testing ground for the way the EP's parliamentary diplomacy shapes and constitutes EU power in times of crisis'. Martin Schulz, then President of the EP, launched the monitoring mission in June 2012 to observe the appeals process and court proceedings involving former Ukrainian Prime Minister Yulia Tymoshenko. Schulz appointed former Polish President Aleksander Kwasniewski as well as former EP President Pat Cox to lead the mission.[2] What began as a low-profile, 'back-door' (Moskalenko 2016, 39) diplomatic tool aiming to resolve the issue of 'selective persecution' (EP resolution of 9 June 2011 (2011/2714(RSP))) and contribute to 'restoring mutual confidence in EU-Ukraine relations'[3] gradually expanded its scope and was recognised by member states and the European Commission as a key EU diplomatic tool, aiming to prepare the ground for signing the EU-Ukraine Association Agreement (AA) at the Eastern Partnership Summit in Vilnius in November 2013. The mission visited Ukraine some 27 times, but had limited practical success and is therefore seen by some analysts as a 'failure' (Kudelia 2013). Although three political prisoners were released, Tymoshenko was not, and then-President Viktor Yanukovich used the Tymoshenko case as an opportunity to back away from signing the EU-Ukraine AA on the eve of the Eastern Partnership summit.[4] His decision sparked the Euromaidan revolution (the four-month unrest in Ukraine resulting in at least 100 casualties), ultimately paving the way for Yanukovich's ousting in February 2014, following the Agreement on settlement of political crisis in Ukraine.[5] The long-term political impact of the 18-month-long mission was manifold, albeit not all foreseeable in 2013. As regards the diplomatic role of the EP,

[2] 'Ex-Presidents of EP and Poland to monitor Yulia Tymoshenko's appeal', Unian 7 June 2012.

[3] PR Newswire, 'Kwasniewski and Cox to monitor Tymoshenko appeal in a bid to repair EU-Ukraine relations', PRNewswire, 7 June 2012.

[4] 'Ukraine freezes talks on bilateral trade pact with EU', Financial Times, 21 November 2013.

[5] Interview, Elmar Brok, Strasbourg, 4 October 2017.

the mission significantly boosted the Parliament's visibility and agenda-setting abilities both externally in Ukraine and inter-institutionally:

- While initially limited to monitoring the Tymoshenko legal proceedings, the EP-initiated mission later expanded its function, which arguably gave momentum to the promotion of the EU's approach vis-à-vis Ukraine and acted as an official EU diplomatic tool in the country. Cox and Kwasniewski mediated between the governing elites and the opposition in Ukraine as well as between the Commission and Ukraine in the negotiation of the AA (Nitoiu and Sus 2017, 72–73).
- Furthermore, the mission's reputation of impartiality and independence—not least due to the negotiation skills and personal networks of former EP President Pat Cox and Elmar Brok, the Chair of the ommittee on Foreign Affairs (AFET)[6]—facilitated the later work of the post-Euromaidan Needs Assessment Mission (NAM), further boosting the EP's diplomatic reputation and role in Kyiv and, consequently, its visibility in Brussels.

5.2   Post-Maidan: The European Parliament Increases Its Impact Through Election Observation, Democracy Support and Mediation

In the wake of the Euromaidan revolution, the EP significantly stepped up its support for Ukraine's democratisation process. The EP sent an election observation delegation to observe the presidential election on 25 May 2014, with Petro Poroshenko as the winner (see report, election observation delegation to the presidential elections in Ukraine).

The beginning of the eighth EP legislature in July 2014 and the subsequent launch of the CDSA coincided with a number of key political developments in Ukraine, which held its first post-Maidan parliamentary elections on 26 October 2014, resulting in a clear pro-EU majority.

---

[6]On 20 April 2017, Ukrainian President Petro Poroshenko presented the Order of Yaroslav the Wise of the V grade to Brok, thanking him for supporting Ukraine in his former position as Chair of the Committee on Foreign Affairs of the EP, particularly noting his role in the context of the Revolution of Dignity, the ratification of the Ukraine-EU Association Agreement, the provision of visa-free regime for Ukrainians by the EU and democratic support to Ukraine.

Following the EP's EOM, the EP election observation delegation, chaired by Andrej Plenković, in its report recommended to the DEG, in cooperation with the AFET Committee and the EP delegation to the EU-Ukraine Parliamentary Association Committee, to:

- include Ukraine as a priority country under the CDSA[7];
- closely follow up the conclusions and recommendations of the final OSCE/ODIHR report;
- develop specific democratic support and parliamentary capacity-building activities with the Verkhovna Rada (such as study visits of parliamentarians, staff trainings and measures encouraging the development of a competent, independent, non-partisan parliamentary secretariat); to assist the new Verkhovna Rada in elaborating and implementing the EU-oriented legislative reform agenda;
- facilitate dialogue between the new Verkhovna Rada and civil society organisations by organising thematic roundtables with the leaders of major political parties and civil society actors;
- inform the High Representative of the Union for Foreign Affairs and Security Policy (HRVP) and the Commissioner for European Neighbourhood and Enlargement Negotiations of the intended democracy support activities and explore how to include such complementary parliamentary activities in the EU's work to help consolidate democracy in Ukraine as well as provide additional parliamentary mediation and facilitation capacity.

Following the simultaneous ratification of the EU-Ukraine AA by the EP and the Verkhovna Rada on 16 September 2014—in itself a historical demonstration of the commitment of both parties to develop solid inter-parliamentary ties—the EU-Ukraine Parliamentary Association Committee met for the first time in Brussels on 24–25 February 2015 and reconfirmed the mutual intention to support Ukraine's pro-EU reforms. At their meeting on 24 February 2015, EP President Martin Schulz and then

---

[7] In 2015, the DEG began to select 'priority countries', on which democracy support activities would focus. For 2018, the priority countries include Georgia, Moldova, Morocco, Myanmar, Nigeria, Peru, Tanzania, Tunisia and Ukraine. Ukraine has been a priority country since 2015.

Chairman of the Verkhovna Rada, Volodymyr Groysman, agreed to launch a broad parliamentary support programme for Ukraine.

In line with these recommendations, the EP's DEG decided to make Ukraine a priority country for parliamentary capacity-building and dialogue-facilitation activities. The EP and the Verkhovna Rada signed a memorandum of understanding (MoU) in Kyiv on 3 July 2015 with the stated purpose of establishing a joint framework for parliamentary support and capacity-building of the Verkhovna Rada, specifying the following goals and objectives:

- Ensuring efficient implementation of the constitutional roles of law-making, oversight and representation by the Verkhovna Rada
- Increasing the quality of Ukrainian parliamentarism
- Increasing the transparency, predictability, efficiency and openness of the proceedings of the Verkhovna Rada
- Implementation of the EU-Ukraine AA

As regards the implementation of the capacity-building partnership, the MoU prioritised strengthening the constitutional roles of law-making, oversight and representation of the Verkhovna Rada as well as improving the quality of legislation and of the legislative process in Ukraine (Report and Roadmap on Internal Reform and Capacity-Building for the Verkhovna Rada of Ukraine (RRIRCB), February 2016, iv).

With the goals and objectives thus agreed, the scope and activities were still to be defined. To this end, a NAM led by Pat Cox was conducted in Ukraine. Between September 2015 and February 2016, the NAM conducted six expert fact-finding missions to the Verkhovna Rada and held over 100 meetings with the Verkhovna Rada leadership, political faction leaders, committee chairs, individual MPs, the Verkhovna Rada Secretariat, the Government of Ukraine, Ukrainian and international civil society organisations as well as other representatives of the international community. The NAM also visited Brussels and Strasbourg to conduct high-level meetings, including with the President of the EP (RRIRCB 2016, v).

As a result of these activities, the mission prepared a Report and Roadmap on Internal Reform and Capacity-Building for the Verkhovna Rada of Ukraine, presented in Brussels on 29 February 2016 during the high-level Ukraine Week. The report and roadmap contained 52 recommendations on a programme of parliamentary support and capacity-building of the VRU with implementation beginning in 2016.

In line with the MoU's reference to 'improving and facilitating interaction between the majority and the opposition, between the political factions as well as between the committees of the Verkhovna Rada' as a focus of work for the parties, the report underlined that strengthening inter-party dialogue as a long-term agenda should accompany the process of implementation of the comprehensive reform agenda of the Verkhovna Rada. To this end, the idea of the EP playing a supporting role by offering to host regular dialogues at its Jean Monnet House was introduced (RRIRCB 2016, 31).

The Verkhovna Rada adopted Resolution 1035-VIII, recognising all 52 proposed recommendations for reform, and the 'Rada za Evropu' ('Rada for Europe') project was developed as an outcome of the NAM. 'Rada for Europe' was launched in June 2016 (Rada za Evropu: Capacity-Building in Support of the Verkhovna Rada of Ukraine, EEAS, 1 June 2016) and is implemented by the United Nations Development Programme (UNDP) and the Verkhovna Rada, in partnership with the EP. With €1.3 million financial support from the delegation of the EU to Ukraine, the project runs until 31 December 2018, facilitating the implementation of the AA with the EU, by 'helping Ukraine raise up to European standards and adopt viable and efficient legislative procedures on the long-term' (UNDP, project summary, Rada for Europe: driving reforms across Ukraine).

With the ultimate goal of the Verkhovna Rada becoming a more transparent and open institution, the project focuses on three priority areas:

- Support the streamlining of legislative processes to enable Ukraine's democratic reforms to be implemented in a timely and transparent manner
- Strengthen the Verkhovna Rada Secretariat and Committee staff to enable them to provide effective, non-partisan services and drive the transformation of the institution into a modern, democratic parliament from within
- Support greater transparency and openness of the Verkhovna Rada and more consistent communication and dialogue with the citizens

5.3   The Jean Monnet Dialogue with the Verkhovna Rada

The 'Jean Monnet Dialogue for Peace and Democracy' was developed as a parliamentary mediation support initiative by the EPMS unit in the context of the democracy support for Ukraine. As mentioned above, the idea of conducting regular mediation sessions with the Verkhovna Rada was introduced in the 2016 Report and Roadmap on Internal Reform and Capacity-Building for the Verkhovna Rada, which was presented at the context of the high-level 'Ukraine Week' in February–March 2016. During this high-level event, EP Secretary-General Klaus Welle and Acting Secretary-General of the Verkhovna Rada, Volodymyr Slyshynskyi, signed an Administrative Cooperation Agreement (ACA—the 'administrative pillar' of the MoU between the two institutions) between the Secretariat of the VRU and the General Secretariat of the EP to support the implementation of the reform process (Signature of an Administrative Cooperation Agreement between the General Secretariat of the EP and the Secretariat of VRU, 2 March 2016). According to this agreement, and in line with the recommendations in the Cox report on inter-party dialogue and mediation, the EP expressed its willingness to 'facilitate a series of dialogues to be held under its auspices on the premises of the Jean Monnet House' (Directorate for Democracy Support, EP Mediation Support, Background Information on Jean Monnet Dialogue for Peace and Democracy—CDSA Ukraine, July 2017).

The MoU and the ACA broadly reflect the EP's two overall pillars of support for the Verkhovna Rada: support for the members on the one side (through the Mediation and Dialogue Support Unit), and support for the political staff on the other side (through other EP DGs and Services, including DG PERS, DG EPRS, DG COMM, DG ITEC).

Support for political groups/factions—aiming to strengthen a culture of inter-party dialogue—is an innovation for the EP. This aspect of parliamentary support is set to be applied in other countries in the future.

The need for mediation support and increased dialogue within the Verkhovna Rada was identified in the Cox report, which stated that 'The atmosphere in the VRU parliament in the current challenging geopolitical and domestic climate is characterised by mistrust and a lack of political confidence that is pervasive in the VRU and among the political parties (including within the governing coalition). While the VRU is not short of rules and procedures, there is a political culture of circumventing rules to pass legislation under extreme conditions and at the last minute' (RRIRCB 2016, 31). Thus, the report asserted that 'It is therefore imperative that these obstacles are addressed if the VRU is to achieve its reform objectives and to develop a democratic parliamentary culture of dialogue, compromise and consensus building. Inter-party dialogue can help parties move beyond short-term electoral or personal interests and build consensus on areas of national importance' (RRIRCB 2016, 31).

Against this backdrop, the first ever Jean Monnet Dialogue was organised for the Verkhovna Rada in October 2016 at the historical Jean Monnet House in Bazoches, France, which was used as a 'discreet and inspiring' location.[8] The process was launched by Pat Cox and Lead Member Andrej Plenković (who has since been succeeded by Elmar Brok, MEP, EPP/DE). The Dialogue is seen as a process which includes a 'cycle of preparatory activities', leading to meetings and follow-ups that enable the factions to build consensus and implement concrete issues. Each activity cycle is focused on a specific topic selected in advance and agreed by consensus with the faction leaders. In addition to the faction leaders, the factions are represented by another MP from the faction as well as a senior member of the faction staff. The speaker and the leadership of the Verkhovna Rada also participate.

Ahead of the first Jean Monnet Dialogue, all factions agreed on the following rules of engagement (Background Information Jean Monnet Dialogue for Peace and Democracy—CDSA Ukraine, July 2017):

- Mediation principles will apply if needed (including facilitated breakout sessions).
- Every political faction engages on equal terms.
- Zero is not an option (i.e. doing nothing or not having an outcome).
- Nothing is ruled in or ruled out in advance.
- Nothing is agreed until everything is agreed.
- No media communication until there is a concrete outcome.
- Pre-existing proposals, motions or draft laws should not be submitted.
- If there is a political agreement on a topic, a drafting methodology will apply.
- Any agreed common draft can then be submitted jointly by factions.

---

[8] As noted in the Background Information Jean Monnet Dialogue for Peace and Democracy—CDSA Ukraine, the use of 'discreet and inspiring locations has long been an important tool for mediation processes (e.g. in Rambouillet during the Balkan Wars or Camp David for the Middle East) and the Jean Monnet House offers important capacity for the EP as it increases its activities in this field.

5.4   The Outcome of the First Three Verkhovna Rada Jean Monnet Dialogues

The first Jean Monnet Dialogue, led by Pat Cox, was held on 27–29 October 2016. The high-level participants included Prime Minister Volodymyr Groysman, Andriy Parubiy, Speaker of the VRU, as well as seven leaders of political factions or groups of the Verkhovna Rada, in addition to the Secretary-General of the EP, Klaus Welle (EP—VRU: 'Jean Monnet Dialogue' for Peace and Democracy, Programme, 29–29 October 2016). The objective was to build consensus on two of the first four selected priority topics. However, all four topics were addressed and an implementation mechanism for the agreement reached in Paris was discussed. The outcome included a decision to implement a 'white paper consultation', according to which a discussion 'white paper' on substantial pieces of legislation should be submitted to the relevant parliamentary committee for discussion and be the subject of an Opinion by the Verkhovna Rada. The parties agreed to establish a working group, chaired by Andriy Parubiy and composed of representatives of the leaders of the factions and groups, to put into practice the consensus-building methodology.[9] In addition, a discussion on the role of the parliamentary opposition was launched (Background Information Jean Monnet Dialogue for Peace and Democracy—CDSA Ukraine). The conclusions, signed by the speaker of the Verkhovna Rada and all participating leaders of political factions and groups, were handed over to the director of the Jean Monnet Association and deposited at the Jean Monnet House.

The second Jean Monnet Dialogue took place in Irpin, Ukraine, on 19 April 2017. Building upon the outcome of the first Jean Monnet Dialogue, a key focus of the Irpin dialogue was the regulation and status of the parliamentary opposition. A number of steps for ensuring the rights of the opposition were agreed, including the equitable distribution of parliamentary positions, a new Law on Committees and/or amendments to the Rules of Procedure, boosting the role of all factions. The factions also agreed on how to implement some of the decisions taken in the first Jean Monnet Dialogue; for example, the need for a draft law on proportional representation in Verkhovna Rada committees and delegation as well as an update on the Rules of Procedure to introduce white papers and annual

---

[9] Between its establishment and the second Jean Monnet Dialogue, this working group held five meetings, according to the Conclusions from the second Jean Monnet Dialogue, Irpin, Ukraine, 19 April 2017.

minister reports into the legislative process. The main achievement of the second Jean Monnet Dialogue was the consensus on the need for reducing the number of committees, as well as the decision to draft a regulation to provide a specific legal basis for the operation of faction secretariats and amending the Rules of Procedure of the Verkhovna Rada to bring it into compliance with the constitution of Ukraine (Conclusions from the second Jean Monnet Dialogue, April 2017).

The extension of the MoU between the EP and the Verkhovna Rada, as well as the renewal of the Administrative Cooperation Agreement between the two parliaments, was announced in the context of the second Jean Monnet Dialogue by Andriy Parubiy and Elmar Brok, on behalf of EP President Antonio Tajani by the end of this mandate (press release, European Parliament, 20 April 2017).

The third Jean Monnet Dialogue took place at the Jean Monnet House, Bazoches, on 22–24 November 2017. The parties confirmed the commitment to moving from dialogue and consensus-building to effective and immediate implementation on the following issues:

- Reform of the Committee structure for the next convocation of the Verkhovna Rada: 'emerging consensus' on the need to reduce the number of committees to a maximum of 20 in the next convocation of the Verkhovna Rada was identified;
- Amendments to the Rules of Procedure of the VRU to bring it into compliance with the constitution of Ukraine (registered draft Law no. 5522 and the responsive opinion of the Venice Commission). There was an 'emerging consensus' that the Rules of Procedure should not be enshrined in Law;
- As a follow-up to the second Jean Monnet Dialogue, it was proposed to align salaries with the provisions of the Law on the Status of the People's Deputy of Ukraine;
- The speaker proposed that factions should share their positions on draft laws in advance to make more efficient use of plenary time;
- Regulation and Status of the Parliamentary Opposition (recommendation No. 44) and allocation of committee seats (recommendation No. 18): building upon the results of the second Jean Monnet Dialogue, a consensus was reached to consider a draft law on the application of the d'Hondt method to ensure an equitable distribution of parliamentary positions for committee chairs and the allocation of ordinary sears on committees for the next convocation.

5.5   *From Back Door to Centre Stage: Key Successes of the European Parliament's Post-Maidan Parliamentary Diplomacy*

Summarising the EP's increasing visibility in the context of democracy support for Ukraine in the post-Maidan era, the evolution from backdoor diplomatic actor to agenda-setter in Ukraine is exemplified by the following key developments:

- The simultaneous ratification of the EU-Ukraine AA by the EP and the Verkhovna Rada on 16 September 2014 was a historical demonstration of the commitment of both parties to develop solid inter-parliamentary ties, laying the ground for the continued mutual commitment to democracy support activities.
- The EP's NAM prepared the ground for the EU/UNDP project 'Rada for Europe: driving reforms across Ukraine', with 52 recommendations recognised in the March 2016 Verkhovna Rada resolution 1035-VIII.
- Launched within the framework of the EP's democracy support activities for Ukraine in 2016, the 'Jean Monnet Dialogue'—the concept of using the Jean Monnet House in Bazoches (France) for mediation and dialogue activities—expanded in 2017. This concept is set to further evolve and expand, as the EP is gaining experience and 'demonstrating the added value of parliamentary mediation as a soft power tool to complement overall EU approaches' (Objectives of the EPMS Service for 2017; Background Information Jean Monnet Dialogue for Peace and Democracy—CDSA Ukraine). A concrete step was taken in August 2017 in the context of the mediation activities of the three MEPs (Eduard Kukan, Knut Fleckenstein and Ivo Vajgl) in FYROM, who started working with political leaders in Skopje towards the Jean Monnet Dialogue process (programme of visit, August 2017).

6   Conclusions

Recent literature on parliamentary diplomacy has identified peace-building and conflict management activities as 'key real and potential roles for parliamentary institutions' (Irrera 2015). The EP's recent interventions in

Ukraine and FYROM have shown that structured, systematic and pro-longed involvement can produce important immediate results. However, sustainable, broad returns of these diplomatic investments will only mate-rialise over the longer-term, the efforts being a contribution to 'the inter-national communities' strategic objectives for the stability and democratic future' of the countries involved (Background Information Jean Monnet Dialogue for Peace and Democracy—CDSA Ukraine, 3). The case of Ukraine is a pivotal example of the EP's evolving diplomatic role in times of external crises, from invisible 'back-door' diplomacy to agenda-setting actions.

It is particularly encouraging that there is a growing interest in the EP's mediation and dialogue support activities in the context of elections that are tense and have the potential to lead to violence. In their capacity as chief election observers, MEPs have found themselves to be acting as mediators engaged in efforts to prevent election violence.[10] In response, the DEG has developed a new 'pre-election instrument'. First used in the run up to the 2017 Kenyan general elections, it is a tool to facilitate dia-logue with parliamentarians and political parties about concerns over election-related violence and how to mitigate or prevent violent conflict prior to elections. In 2018, the DEG will continue to focus on prevention of election-related violence with policy dialogues (seminars/conferences) as well as specific pre-election activities in Cambodia, Zimbabwe, Lebanon and the Democratic Republic of Congo.

The CDSA developed by the EP has only been applied for a few years. Still, there are encouraging signs that this approach, implemented in close collaboration with the European Commission and the European External Action Service as well as other concerned institutions and organisations, is resonating with the EP's foreign partners and producing the first concrete results. Although a relatively new actor in the field of democracy support, with particular focus on conflict prevention, mediation and dialogue, the EP is fast gaining experience and demonstrating the added value of 'par-liamentary mediation' as a soft power tool to complement overall EU approaches.

---

[10] Interview with Gerrard Quille, Head of Unit, European Parliament Mediation Support Unit, 13 July 2017.

ANNEX I

Timeline: Key EP diplomatic activities regarding Ukraine
2012–2013: Cox-Kwasniewski mission
November 2013–February 2014: Euromaidan protests
23–26 February 2014: V. Yanukovich is ousted and flees Ukraine, A. Yatsenyuk is nominated PM.
25 May 2014: EP election observation delegation mission, presidential election
11–12 September 2014: EP President Schulz conducts official visit to Ukraine
16 September 2014: EP and the Verkhovna Rada simultaneously ratify the EU-Ukraine AA
26 October 2014: EP election observation delegation mission, parliamentary election
24 February 2015: Verkhovna Rada Chair Volodymyr Groysman visits EP
24–25 February 2015: First meeting of the EU-Ukraine Parliamentary Association Committee in Brussels
3 July 2015: MoU, the EP and the Verkhovna Rada
September 2015–February 2016: EP NAM to the Verkhovna Rada
October 2015: EP election observation delegation mission, local elections
February–March 2016: Ukraine Week, EP Brussels: NAM report is presented, Administrative Cooperation Agreement is signed
October 2016: First Jean Monnet Dialogue for peace and democracy, Bazoches, France
19 April 2017: Second Jean Monnet Dialogue, Irpin, Ukraine
20 April 2017: MoU extended until 2019 (subsequently, Administrative Cooperation Agreement is also extended)
22–24 November 2017: Third Jean Monnet Dialogue, Bazoches, France.
6 March 2018: NAM+2 conference (taking stock of developments two years after the presentation of the NAM report), EP Brussels
25–27 March: Fourth Jean Monnet Dialogue (place tbc)

REFERENCES

Bajtay, P. (2015). *Democratic and Efficient Foreign Policy? Parliamentary Diplomacy and Oversight in the 21st Century and the Post-Lisbon Role of the European Parliament in Shaping and Controlling EU Foreign Policy.* Working Papers, Robert Schuman Centre for Advanced Studies, European University Institute.

Baltag, D. (2018). *EU External Representation Post-Lisbon: The Performance of EU Diplomacy in Belarus, Moldova and Ukraine. The Hague Journal of Diplomacy, 13*(1), 75–96.

Barbe, E., & Herranz, A. (Eds.) (2006). Introduction. In *The Role of Parliaments in European Foreign Policy: Debating on Accountability and Legitimacy* (pp. 1–14). Barcelona: Publication of the EU Information Office in Spain

Fonck, D. (2018). Servants or Rivals? Uncovering the Drivers and Logics of the European Parliament's Diplomacy during the Ukrainian Crisis. In K. Raube, M. Müftüler-Bac, & J. Wouters (Eds.), *Parliamentary Cooperation and Diplomacy in EU External Relations*. Cheltenham: Edward Elgar.

Fonck, Daan (2018) 'Parliamentary Diplomacy and Legislative-Executive Relations in EU Foreign Policy: Studying the European Parliament's Mediation of the Macedonian Political Crisis (2015–2017)'. JCMS: *Journal of Common Market Studies* Vol. 56, No.6, pp. 1305–1322.

Gianniou, M. (2015). The European Parliament and the Israeli-Palestinian Conflict. In S. Stavridis & D. Irrera (Eds.), *The European Parliament and Its International Relations* (pp. 237–249). London: Routledge.

Kudelia, S. (2013, November 22). The Failure of the Cox-Kwasniewski Mission and Its Implications for Ukraine, Ponars Eurasia.

Lerch, M. (2017). *Promoting Democracy and Observing Elections*. Fact Sheets on the European Union.

Garcés de los Fayos, F. (2018). *Iran: The Joint Comprehensive Plan of Action in Danger*. DG EXPO, European Parliament.

Moskalenko, O. (2016). The European Parliament in the Ukrainian Association Puzzle. *East European Quarterly, 44*(1–2), 39.

Moussis, N. (2016). *Access to the European Union* (22nd ed.). Cambridge: Intersentia.

Nitoiu, C., & Sus, M. (2017). The European Parliament's Diplomacy – a Tool for Projecting EU Power in Times of Crisis? The Case of the Cox-Kwasniewski Mission. *Journal of Common Markets Studies, 55*(1), 71–86.

Perchoc, P. (2017). *Jean Monnet, l'inspirateur – Un père de l'Europe*. European Parliamentary Research Service.

Quille, G. (2014). *The EU and Conflict Prevention and Mediation*. European Parliamentary Mediation Support Unit.

Redei, L., & Romanyshyn, I. (2015). *The EU's Invisible Diplomacy: The European Parliament's External Action in the Lead-Up to the Ukraine Crisis*. Paper for the European Union Studies Association Biennial Conference, March.

Thym, D. (2009). Foreign Affairs. In A. Von Bogdandy & J. Bast (Eds.), *Principles of Constitutional Law* (pp. 309–345). Oxford: Hart Publishing Ltd.

Viola, D. (2000). *European Foreign Policy and the European Parliament in the 1990s: An Investigation into the Role and Voting Behaviour of the European Parliament's Political groups*. Aldershot: Ashgate.

Weisglas, F., & de Boer, C. (2007). Parliamentary Diplomacy. *The Hague Journal of Diplomacy, 2*, 92–99.

Zanon, F. (2006). The European Parliament: An Autonomous Foreign Policy Identity. In E. Barbe & A. Herranz (Eds.), *The Role of Parliaments in European Foreign Policy: Debating on Accountability and Legitimacy* (pp. 107–119). Barcelona: Publication of the EU Information Office in Spain.

OFFICIAL EU DOCUMENTS

COUNCIL

Council Decision of 26 July 2010 Concerning Restrictive Measures Against Iran and Repealing Common Position 2007/140/CFSP.

Council of the European Union, Council Conclusions on Democracy Support in the EU's External Relations, 17 November 2009.

FACTSHEET

EUROPEAN EXTERNAL ACTION SERVICE

Rada za Evropu: Capacity-Building in Support of the Verkhovna Rada of Ukraine, EEAS, 1 June 2016.

EUROPEAN PARLIAMENT

Conclusions from the second Jean Monnet Dialogue, Irpin, Ukraine, 19 April 2017.

Decision of Conference of Presidents of 13 September 2012 on Mandate and Composition of DEG, 13 September 2012.

Democracy Support and Election Coordination Group, *Democracy Support Work Programme in 2018.*

Democracy Support and Election Coordination Group: Developing a Comprehensive Democracy Support Approach (CDSA), Internal Note of the Directorate-General for External Policies of the Union (DG EXPO), Directorate for Democracy Support, October 2014.

Directorate for Democracy Support, EP Mediation Support (EPMS), Objectives of the EPMS Service for 2017, 14 December 2016.

Directorate for Democracy Support, EP Mediation Support, Background Information on Jean Monnet Dialogue for Peace and Democracy – CDSA Ukraine, Internal Note of the Directorate-General for External Policies of the Union (DG EXPO), Directorate for Democracy Support, July 2017.

European Parliament – Verkhovna Rada of Ukraine: 'Jean Monnet Dialogue' for Peace and Democracy, Programme, 29–29 October 2016.

European Parliament, Press Release, European Parliament and Verkhovna Rada Extend Their Partnership, 20 April 2017.

European Parliament, Programme of Visit of MEPs Mr Kukan, Mr Vajgl And Mr Fleckenstein to Skopje, Former Yugoslav Republic Of Macedonia, Version 29 August 2017.

Memorandum of Understanding between the European Parliament and the Verkhovna Rada of Ukraine on a Joint Framework for Parliamentary Support and Capacity Building, Kyiv, 3 July 2015.

Report and Roadmap on Internal Reform and Capacity-Building for the Verkhovna Rada of Ukraine, February 2016.

Report, Election Observation Delegation to the Parliamentary Elections in Ukraine (26 October 2014).

Report, Election Observation Delegation to the Presidential Elections in Ukraine (25 May 2014).

Resolution of 9 June 2011, 'Ukraine: The Cases of Yulia Tymoshenko and Other Members of the Former Government' (2011/2714(RSP)).

Ukraine Week at the European Parliament – High-Level Conference EP – Verkhovna RADA of Ukraine on Capacity Building for Reform. Signature of an Administrative Cooperation Agreement Between the General Secretariat of the European Parliament and the Secretariat of Verkhovna Rada of Ukraine, 2 March 2016.

OTHER OFFICIAL DOCUMENTS

Resolution of the Verkhovna Rada of Ukraine: On Action to Be Taken to Implement the Recommendations Concerning Internal Reform and Capacity-Building for the Verkhovna Rada of Ukraine, Bulletin of the Verkhovna Rada, 2016, No. 14, p. 149.

UNDP, 'Rada za Evropu: Capacity-Building in Support of the Verkhovna Rada of Ukraine', Project Annual Report June 2016–May 2017.

UNDP, Project Summary, Rada for Europe: Driving Reforms Across Ukraine, June 2016.

CHAPTER 20

The European Parliament in Security and Defence: The Parliamentary Contribution to the European Defence Union

Elena Lazarou

1 INTRODUCTION

In 2014, an analysis by the Italian Institute for International Political Studies (ISPI) observed that the drive of the European Parliament (EP) with regard to security and defence issues had been waning over the previous parliamentary term in conjunction with a general sense of 'CSDP fatigue' in the European Union (EU). The author attributed this phenomenon to the reallocation of financial resources away from the area of security and defence as a consequence of the financial crisis, to the frustration deriving from the lack of implementation of the Lisbon Treaty in this area, but also to the pronounced failure of the EU to coordinate an EU level reaction to the crises in Libya and Mali (Herranz-Surrales 2014, 6). As a result, she observed a significant reduction in the quantity and substance of debates on security and defence,

E. Lazarou (✉)
European Parliament, European Parliamentary Research Service,
Brussels, Belgium
e-mail: eleni.lazarou@europarl.europa.eu

© The Author(s) 2019
O. Costa (ed.), *The European Parliament in Times of EU Crisis*,
European Administrative Governance,
https://doi.org/10.1007/978-3-319-97391-3_20

and Common Security and Defence Policy (CSDP) in particular, in plenary.

Three years later, at the time of writing of this chapter, the situation has changed significantly. Indeed, 2016 and 2017 have marked an unprecedented amount of activism on security and defence issues across EU institutions, including in the EP. The changing geopolitical and security environment in the periphery of the EU, and the direct effects of these shifts in the EU—among other things, through the severe deterioration of security within the EU—led to a pointed prioritisation of security on the EU agenda. The launching of the EU Global Strategy in June 2016 (Council of the European Union 2016) was an important milestone in this direction and one that has shaped action and initiatives in the security and defence area for all institutions.

The Global Strategy and its implementation in the area of security and defence, also known as the 'Winter Package on Defence', form the backdrop of this chapter, along with the marked external changes which precipitated the necessity for EU action in assuming more responsibility for its security and defence. These issues are covered in the next section which aims to examine the main positions of the EP in the progressive framing of the European Defence Union (EDU). The chapter then moves on to analyse the EP's role in the inception and realisation of policy in this area during the conception, presentation and implementation of the Global Strategy in security and defence. To facilitate the reader's understanding, it also briefly covers the competences of the EP as those have developed following the Treaty of Lisbon (2009) and the organisational aspects of the Parliament's functions in this policy area.

2   A New Geopolitical Reality

The past decade has been marked by undisputable and challenging shifts in the EU's security environment. Evolving security challenges, such as the rise of global terrorism, Russian aggression in the east, war in eastern Ukraine, the implications of civil war in Syria, the proliferation of cyber-attacks and of weapons of mass destruction and the emergence of hybrid warfare, grow not only in number but also in complexity. Emerging global actors, such as Russia, China and India, have increasingly boosted their defence spending and upgraded their military capabilities (Lazarou 2017a). Military defence has been steadily rising on the global and regional security agenda, increasingly also for the EU as the necessity of hard power has become more pronounced.

At the same time and largely due to the effects of the economic and financial crisis, defence spending in the EU-28 experienced a significant fall for almost a decade and only rose for the first time by 2.3% in 2014, according to the European Defence Agency's (EDA's) Defence Data (2015). The reconciliation of the need for a stronger and more capable EU in defence on the one hand, with the constraints imposed upon national budgets, on the other, has been an issue of concern in recent years. Numerous studies have pointed to duplication, lack of interoperability and insufficient collaboration in EU level defence research and acquisition as sources of relative inefficiency in European defence (EPRS 2017).

Against this backdrop, calls for deeper cooperation and integration in the field of security and defence—both from the expert community and from national capitals—increased in number. According to Eurobarometer polls in 2014, almost two-thirds of EU citizens were in favour of 'more Europe' in security and defence, in spite of the fact that decisions on security and defence policy are, most of the time, taken by the EU-28's national governments and usually without public scrutiny (Dobreva, Grosek and Pawlak 2016). In a survey by the Pew Research Centre, 74% of EU citizens polled responded that they thought the EU should play a more active role in world affairs than it does today (Stokes, 2016).

3 European Defence After the Global Strategy

The debate on the state of defence in Europe was initially reignited by the European Council in 2013, which mandated a series of actions to deepen defence cooperation. The Council requested the High Representative of the Union for Foreign Affairs and Security Policy and Vice-President of the European Commission (HR/VP), Federica Mogherini, in cooperation with the Commission, to assess the impact that changes in the global environment have had on security (European Council 2013). In June 2015, the European Council acknowledged the dramatic change in Europe's security environment and committed to the continuation of work 'on a more effective, visible and result-oriented CSDP, the further development of both civilian and military capabilities, and the strengthening of Europe's defence industry, including Small and medium-sized enterprises (SMEs)'. It also tasked the HR/

VP with continuing 'the process of strategic reflection with a view to preparing an EU global strategy on foreign and security policy in close cooperation with Member States' (European Council 2015). This gave birth to the EU's Global Strategy, presented by the HR/VP in 2016 and subsequently implemented—in the area of security and defence—through a series of actions known as the 'Winter Package'. The package included actions and plans that, among other things, set the basis for the progressive establishment of the EDU, most notably among them the European Defence Fund (EDF), the Coordinated Annual Review on Defence (CARD) and the Permanent Structured Cooperation (PESCO), as well as EU- North Atlantic Treaty Organization (NATO) relations. These initiatives aim—to a larger or lesser degree—to tackle inherent weaknesses of the European defence market and the EU defence industry, as well as to enhance and optimise EU defence capabilities (Lazarou 2017a).

Significant progress on all fronts was made during 2017 with the cooperation of all EU institutions. In November 2016, the Commission unveiled the European Defence Action Plan which would involve setting up the EDF to support collaborative research in innovative defence technologies and the development of defence products jointly agreed by the Member States. The Fund was launched in June 2017, consisting of two legally distinct but complementary windows: (a) the research window[1] and (b) the capability window, supporting joint development and joint acquisition of key defence capabilities.

In June 2017, the Commission published a Proposal for a regulation on a European Defence Industrial Development Programme (EDIDP) as part of the EDF (European Commission, 2017). The aim of the proposal is to improve the competitiveness and innovative capacity of the EU defence industry, including cyber defence, by supporting the cooperation between undertakings in the development phase of defence products and technologies. The programme would fund projects such as defining common technical specifications, prototyping, testing, qualification and certification of new and updated defence products, as well as feasibility studies and other support activities. It would offer financial assistance via grants, financial instruments and public procurements to projects implemented by at least three undertakings established in at least two Member States with a proportion of the budget going to SMEs.

---

[1] Which is already delivering, in the form of the Preparatory Action on Defence Research (launched on 11 April 2017).

PESCO, which is enshrined as a possibility in the Treaty of Lisbon, was launched in December 2017 with the participation of 25 EU Member States (Lazarou 2017b). It operates on the basis of concrete projects and commitments, several of which are geared towards a strengthening of the EU defence sector. For example, PESCO members commit to increasing national defence budgets in real terms, increasing defence investment expenditure (towards 20% of total defence spending) and investing more in defence research and technology (towards 2% of total defence spending). In addition, they pledge to develop and provide 'strategically relevant' defence capabilities in accordance with the Capability Development Plan (CDP), the CARD and the EDA and to act jointly and make use of the financial and practical support provided by the EDF. Moreover, they assume the obligation to contribute to projects that boost the European defence industry and the European Defence Technological and Industrial Base (EDTIB). Finally, a trial run of the CARD began in autumn 2017. Essentially, CARD is a process of monitoring the defence plans of EU Member States to help coordinate spending and identify possible collaborative projects (EDA 2017).

The challenges faced by the EU in the process of implementation of these initiatives are manifold. The European arms industry is very fragmented and linked to national procurement priorities and markets. Consequently, opening up defence procurement is one of the main challenges for the EU. The European defence sector is characterised by persistent fragmentation (80% of national contracts are awarded nationally) with unnecessary duplication of capabilities (the EU has 19 types of armoured infantry fighting vehicles while the USA has one), organisations and expenditure. This problem was further aggravated by the shrinkage in national defence budgets and a major reduction in defence research and development (R&D) investment (around 20% up to 2015) on which the future competitiveness of the industry as well as its autonomy depends. There is also a growing blurring of the dividing line between defence and security, as the defence sector increasingly relies on civil technologies and products, while at EU level, there are many challenges on the way to a more comprehensive approach towards developing more joined-up policy-making for both sectors. In this context, a strong, competitive and innovative EDTIB needs more defence cooperation, a more efficient internal market, more robust security of supply guarantees, competitive and integrated supply chains supported by efficient defence and dual-use export controls, and support to research and innovation. Lack of interoperability and insufficient collaboration in EU level defence research have also been significant hurdles to efficiency in EU defence. According to the European Political Strategy Centre (EPSC), these, among other reasons, explain why, in spite of being the world's second-largest military spender, the EU is far from being the second-largest military power (EPSC 2015).

At the same time, there is a considerable divergence concerning defence capabilities and budgets within the EU. Further, no common strategy exists on how to make use of them. While the UK (GBP35.998 billion), France (€50.408 billion), Germany (€37.135 billion) and Italy (€25.259 billion) belong to the 'Top 15 defence budgets 2016'[2] worldwide, other EU Member States spend only a fractional amount of the above-mentioned figures on defence. For instance, the military expenditures of the Baltic States amounted to respectively €368 million (Latvia), €454 million (Estonia) and €575 million (Lithuania) in 2016. After the Russian annexation of Crimea in early 2014, the Baltic republics announced a rapid increase in their defence budgets. Taken together, their expenditures are expected to reach more than €2 billion in 2020. All Baltic republics are on the road to reach NATO's 2% defence spending target soon. Currently, only five EU Member States comply with the latter: The UK, Greece, Poland, France and Estonia spend at least 2 % of their gross domestic product (GDP) on defence. The EU Member State with the lowest defence budget in absolute terms is Malta; it spends 0.6% of its GDP on defence which amounted to €52 million in 2016.[3]

The prospect of Brexit has aggravated concerns regarding the volume and capacity of the EU defence apparatus and of the EU defence industry. The UK is the largest EU defence spender, leading to Brexit being synonymous with a 20% reduction in the EU's overall capabilities. It is also a United Nations Security Council (UNSC) member and a nuclear power, with high-level expertise in the field of defence. Brexit will also have serious implications for the EU's overall budget, creating a financial gap in the next Multiannual Financial Framework (MFF) from which the EDF should be financed. However, the UK government has indicated that it is

---

[2] The respective figures are extracted from the SIPRI military expenditure database (2017) while the ranking of the 'Top Defence Budgets 2016' was published as part of the IISS Military Balance 2017. https://www.sipri.org/databases/milex https://www.iiss.org/-/media//images/publications/the%20military%20balance/milbal%202017/final%20free%20graphics/mb2017-top-15-defence-budgets.jpg?la=en.

[3] Military expenditure by country, in local currency, 2007–2016 SIPRI 2017 https://www.sipri.org/databases/milex.

willing to consider options for participation in the EDF and the EDIDP (Bakker et al. 2017).

All of these challenges, and the concerns regarding how to pave the way towards more European defence while overcoming them, have been subjects of ample debate in the EP, as illustrated by the following sections.

4 THE EP'S ROLE IN SECURITY AND DEFENCE POLICY AFTER THE LISBON TREATY

While foreign and security policy remains in the intergovernmental sphere, to a much larger extent than other policy areas, the Lisbon Treaty has, by all accounts, contributed to a considerable increase in the EU's supranational institutions' contribution in this area. With respect to Parliament, the most relevant provisions relate to consultation, oversight, accountability and budgetary functions.

The Lisbon Treaty, in article 36 TEU, obliges the High Representative to regularly consult Parliament on the principal aspects and choices of the Common Foreign and Security Policy (CFSP) and CSDP and to inform Parliament on the evolution of policies, requiring that its views be taken 'duly into consideration'. Therefore, the European Parliament holds debates on the state of play of the CFSP and of the CSDP twice a year, on the basis of annual progress reports on the implementation of these policies. In response to the annual reports, the EP also votes on two annual own initiative reports (INI) on the implementation of the CFSP and CSDP respectively. It also asks questions to the High Representative and makes recommendation to her and to the Council on related matters. Indicatively, in the years 2016–2017 the HR/VP was asked to make 62 plenary statements, out of which approximately 10 were on defence initiatives.

Parliament also exercises authority in security and defence matters through its function as budgetary authority. Budgetary power is perceived by some scholars as the most notable indirect power that the EP holds in order to exert a role in CFSP and CSDP (Riddervold and Rosen 2016, 692). However, in defence, this is only the case when expenditures are financed by the EU (such as, for example, parts of the foreseen EDF) and not by Member States, which is the case of the operational expenditures of CSDP military operations. Nevertheless, the EP oversees the civilian aspects of CSDP which are financed by the EU budget (article 41 TEU).

The 'Declaration on Political Accountability' (DPA) (Council of the European Union 2010), agreed to by the HR/VP during the negotiations on the creation of the European External Action Service (EEAS), contains additional commitments by the HR/VP towards the EP. With the declaration, the HR/VP pledges to respect article 36 TEU; to keep the EP fully and immediately informed at all stages of negotiating international agreements in the CFSP field; to enhance the practice of Joint Consultation Meetings on CFSP missions financed out of the EU budget (taking place at least five times a year) between selected Members of the EP (MEPs) and the Council, the EEAS and the Commission; to comply with the provisions of the 2002 Inter-institutional Agreement (IIA) on access by the EP to sensitive information in CSDP, and to provide access to other documents in the CFSP area on a need-to-know basis to other MEPs; to allow exchanges of views between MEPs and diplomats nominated for high-level EEAS positions, Heads of Delegations and EU Special Representatives (EUSRs), before they take up their posts; and to establish a system to ensure that the HR/VPs replaced when unable to appear before Parliament in person (Cirlig 2016).

Several scholars have argued that through the subsequent relationship established between the EP and the EEAS during the latter's creation (including through the DPA), the former's role in the oversight of CFSP and CSDP has been significantly empowered, despite its official limited role in those areas. Raube (2012) argues that the EP's attempt to hold the EEAS accountable needs to be seen in the context of increasing CFSP and CSDP oversight over time. The EP's empowerment, here, is perceived in legislative, budgetary control and supervisory elements such as scrutinising the HR/VP and the EEAS, acquiring more access to classified information on CFSP/CSDP, holding the HR/VP and other EEAS staff accountable and by controlling the budget of the EEAS. Henokl (2015) maintains that the establishment of the EEAS and the new control and accountability relations it created between the EEAS and the EP were unique in that they allowed parliamentary scrutiny in a 'domaine réservé' of the executive.

In spite of the Lisbon Treaty's innovations, the CFSP and consequently the CSDP remain policy areas where decisions are essentially made by Member State consensus, which in essence translates into a pronounced and primary role for the Council. However, the role of the EP in these areas should be examined, not only through the strict prism of the treaties but also through other facets of influence. With this assumption,

Riddervold and Rosen (2016) argue that the influence of the EP can be assessed through a closer examination of functions such as bargaining, framing of a policy issue and normative argumentation. The latter is particularly relevant, as it refers to the EP's profile of 'defending and promoting a principled foreign policy', including with a focus on human rights (Riddervold and Rosen 2016, 694). Based on a case study method, the authors concluded that, in CFSP/CSDP, the EU's influence is strongest in the post-decision phase—namely in scrutiny and control—as there is limited space for legislation in these areas.

5   The SEDE Subcommittee

The role of the EP in Security and Defence cannot be discussed without special reference to the Security and Defence Subcommittee (SEDE). SEDE was established in 2004 as a subcommittee of the Foreign Affairs Committee (AFET). Initially, its main task was to monitor civilian and military operations under CSDP. The Chair of SEDE is part of the special EP committee with right of access to confidential documents relating to CFSP/CSDP held by the Council. The 2002 IIA with the Council on access by the EP to sensitive information in the field of CSDP establishes an arrangement whereby a special committee of five designated MEPs is allowed access, usually on the premises of the Council, to classified information (Top Secret, Secret or Confidential) at the request of the Chair of the Foreign Affairs Committee or Parliament's President. Additionally, the HR/VP regularly briefs the special committee and answers questions from its Members (Cirlig 2016). While the role of the SEDE committee is relatively under-researched in scholarly work, McDonagh (2016) carries out an enlightening comparison of SEDE with the role of national parliaments in scrutinizing and overseeing military missions—in this case CSDP missions. Based on interviews with members of the committee and on documentary analysis, the author concludes that, while there is desire in the EP to strengthen its role in the CSDP area (possibly by elevating SEDE to full committee status), there is a lack of political will and reluctance by other EU institutions to do so. One consequence of this is that amendments and votes of the SEDE draft resolutions are done in the Foreign Affairs Committee (AFET) before reaching plenary. [4]

[4] For example, in the proposed regulation of the EDIDP the main committee is the Committee on Industry, Research and Energy (ITRE), with the Committee on Foreign Affairs (AFET) as Associated Committee.

6   THE EP AND THE EDU: AN AGENDA SETTER?

An overview of the EP's resolutions on security in defence in the years following the 2013 European Council and particularly following the presentation of the Global Strategy suggests an increasing activism—within the limitations set by their institutional competences—of MEPs in promoting the implementation of the Lisbon Treaty provisions on defence and in urging for the efficient and timely implementation of the component of the defence union.

6.1   Calling for Stronger and More Efficient EU Defence

Parliament has been a long-standing supporter of the development of a strong CSDP and defence cooperation among Member States and has been active in pushing in that direction in past years. In May 2015, it adopted a resolution on implementing the CSDP, which stressed 'as a matter of the utmost urgency' the need for the EU and its Member States to 'adapt to the new security challenges, in particular by making effective use of the existing CSDP tools, including by linking these better to the EU's foreign affairs tools, humanitarian assistance, and development policy' (European Parliament, 2015b). In its resolution on financing the CSDP, Parliament called on the HR/VP and the Member States 'to unleash the full potential of the Lisbon Treaty [...] with regard to a faster and more flexible use of the CSDP missions and operations'. In the resolution on the mutual defence clause following the Paris attacks, Parliament referred to the activation of the clause as 'a unique opportunity to establish the grounds for a strong and sustainable European Defence Union' and suggested setting up an EU civil-military headquarters to prepare contingency plans, inter alia for collective defence (European Parliament, 2015a). In a May 2015 resolution on the impact of developments in European defence markets on the security and defence capabilities in Europe, MEPs emphasised that the cutting of defence budgets was weakening the defence potential of Member States and the EU and stressed the need for further cooperation in defence (European Parliament, 2015c). They also asked Member States to remove national rules that did not comply with Directives 2009/43/EC and 2009/81/EC (Lazarou 2017a).

Parliament was also vocal in emphasising the necessity to step up defence efforts in the Global Strategy. In fact, the HR/VP first expressed her intention to engage in a process of strategic reflection—the process which culminated in the Global Strategy—at her hearing at the EP in 2014 (Tocci 2016).

In April 2016, in anticipation of the release of the Global Strategy, Parliament voted on a resolution on the EU in a changing global environment, in which it called on the EU and the Member States to step up their defence capabilities, in order to be prepared to respond to the broad spectrum of civilian, military and hybrid threats and risks, in synergy with NATO, and to make full use of the Lisbon Treaty provisions on CSDP. It urged the EU to enhance its cooperation on defence research, on the industrial base and on cyber defence through pooling and sharing, and to launch an EU-funded defence research and capability development programme (European Parliament 2016c).

Following the launch of the Global Strategy and the various aforementioned ensuing proposals and action plans by the Commission and the EEAS, the EP has continued to maintain the same line, advocating for the implementation of the Lisbon Treaty Provisions on CSDP and for progress towards the progressive framing of a common defence policy as enshrined in article 42 of the TEU.

The Resolutions on the Annual Reports on the Implementation of the CSDP of 2016 and 2017, as well as the 2016 Resolution on the EDU, illustrate the coherence and continuity of this position. According to MEP David McAllister, Chair of the AFET Committee, 'with this annual report on the common security and defence policy, we try to identify the major issues our Union faces and outline a possible way forward'.[5]

The 2016 resolution on the Implementation of the CSDP calls for an overhaul of CSDP to allow the EU to act autonomously for collective security and defence. It supports the creation of a permanent headquarters for the EU to command peacekeeping and crisis management operations under the CSDP. This resolution also emphasises transatlantic cooperation and complementarity with NATO, but notes that the EU should be able, using its own means, to protect EU non-NATO Member States. It underlines the fact that 'NATO is best equipped for deterrence and defence, and is ready to implement collective defence (article 5) in the case of aggression against one of its members, while the CSDP currently focuses on peace-keeping, conflict prevention and strengthening international security' (European Parliament 2016b).

---

[5] MEP statements derived from the Plenary Debate of 12 December 2017, available at: http://www.europarl.europa.eu/sides/getDoc.do?pubRef=-//EP//TEXT+CRE+2017 1212+ITEM-012+DOC+XML+V0//EN&language=EN.

The resolution on the EDU calls for more spending (2% of GDP) on defence, and a fairer and more transparent defence industry. It highlights compatibility and cooperation with NATO, particularly in the east and the south, to counter hybrid and cyber threats, improve maritime security and develop defence capabilities, and welcomes the 2016 EU-NATO Joint Declaration. However, it also states that 'the EU should aspire to be truly able to defend itself and act autonomously if necessary, taking greater responsibility' in cases where NATO is not willing to take the lead, a statement that is in line with the idea of 'strategic autonomy' as embodied in the global strategy (European Parliament 2016a).

On 16 March 2017, the EP voted on a resolution on the constitutional, legal and institutional implications of a common security and defence policy: possibilities offered by the Lisbon Treaty, in which it urges the Council to move towards the harmonisation and standardisation of the European armed forces, to facilitate the cooperation of armed forces personnel under the umbrella of a new EDU. Parliament also called on the Council and the HR/VP to elaborate a white book on security and defence and a roadmap with clear phases and a calendar towards the establishment of a defence union and a more effective common defence policy (European Parliament 2017c).

The 2017 Resolution on the implementation of the CSDP welcomed PESCO and highlighted the facts that the Commission and an increasing number of Member States have committed themselves to launching EDU and that there is a strong support for this among European citizens but stressed that the launch of a real EDU requires continued political will and determination. It urged the Member States to commit themselves to a common and autonomous European defence, and to aim to ensure that their national defence budgets amount to at least 2% of their respective GDPs within a decade. It added that a common cyber defence policy should be one of the first building blocks of EDU, within the PESCO framework, and called for the establishment of a Directorate General (DG) Defence within the Commission. The EP stressed the need for close coordination of all CSDP-related activities, in particular CARD, PESCO and the EDF (European Parliament 2017b).

In the plenary debate with HR/VP Mogherini which preceded the vote on the resolution, MEP Gahler, member of SEDE and rapporteur of the resolution, stated that the EP had, in fact, been working on activating PESCO longer than the HR/VP and the Member States as early as the CSDP report of 2010. He also highlighted the role of the EP in calling for more support for defence research and for its financing, having already introduced an EU defence and defence research budget as a pilot project (PP) for the annual budgets 2015 and 2016. In the same debate, MEPs McAllister and Gomes reiterated the role of the EP as representative of the people. The former, recalled the surveys showing that 75% of Europeans are in favour of a common security and defence policy, while the latter maintained that the Parliament should take on the responsibility of democratic control in order to guarantee 'trust, efficiency and respect for the international legitimacy of the CFSP and the CSDP'.[6]

6.2   *The EDIDP: The EP as Co-Legislator in Defence*

As mentioned previously, a significant aspect of the defence union is the development of the EDTIB. Actions in this area, such as the European Defence Action Plan and the linked Defence Fund, fall under the competence of the Commission (DG Grow).

The area of defence research and industrial development constitutes an aspect of the framing of EDU in which there has been strong EP activism. In a 2013 resolution on the EDTIB, the EP put forth its own assessment that the previous strategies of the Commission to boost the European defence industry had been 'insufficiently implemented because of the lack of a common understanding of EDTIB resulting from differing national and industrial interests, and the persistence of established national habits in the armaments sectors' given that there were huge discrepancies between Member States, including some with no national defence industry of their own. The resolution illustrated the EP's conviction that the added value of the EU supported defence research and development should be pursued both by the EU institutions and the Member States.

On the initiative of the EP, a PP on defence research was successfully included in the 2015 (and 2016) EU budget with the aim to test the conditions for Defence research in the EU framework. The PP is an instrument envisaged under article 54 of the 2014–2020 MFF; its duration is set at a maximum of two years and funding is limited to around €2 million. For the first time, this inclusion allowed EU funds to be transferred to the EDA in support of research into military requirements (EDA 2016). The PP paved the way for the Preparatory Action on Defence Research (PADR) which was subsequently launched by the Commission with a view to

[6] Ibid.

developing a future European Defence Research Programme (now incorporated in the proposal for the EDIDP).

In June 2017, the Commission presented a proposal for a regulation establishing the EDIDP to finance the Fund, which was submitted to the Council and to the EP through the Ordinary Legislative Procedure (OLP). In this instance, beyond the oversight, scrutiny and accountability functions mentioned above, the EP's role is that of full co-legislator. In February 2018, the Committee on Industry, Research and Energy (ITRE), with AFET acting as associated committee, adopted its report. The EP's starting position focuses on protecting the Union's—and their industries—interests by avoiding support to firms controlled by foreign enterprises or countries, and by earmarking a part of the funding for SMEs. Other key concerns of the EP include strengthening EU independence in the area of defence (the objective of EU strategic autonomy), strengthening the role of the EP itself in this area, making sure that the financing of the programme should be drawn exclusively from unallocated margins of the MFF or through the mobilisation of special instruments and making sure the programme is conditional upon cooperation between Member States, that is, undertakings established in at least three Member States (European Parliament 2017a) The EP also placed emphasis on the exclusion of certain categories, such as weapons of mass destruction, from eligibility to be funded by the EDIDP.

7   Concluding Remarks

This chapter illustrated the main positions held by the EP in the progressive framing of the EDU, understood as a series of initiatives deriving from the Lisbon Treaty and from the implementation of the EU Global Strategy. It has briefly presented the main developments in EU defence policy following the launching of the EU Global Strategy and outlined the main possibilities for the EP to act within the framework of security and defence policy. It has then focused on the initiatives related to the EDU and gone over the main positions of the EP, as these are presented in resolutions and opinions. Through the academic literature and the EP documentation, it appears that as defence policy progresses and more initiatives become subject to co-decision, such as the EDIDP, as well as subject to the EU budget, Parliament becomes more decisive for security and defence policy. Yet, the powers of consultation, oversight and accountability should not be overlooked, as they have played an important role on framing the issues. Overall, the EP has maintained its position throughout the ongoing process of development of EU defence. This position includes more institutionalisation of defence, a focus on the implementation of the Treaty of Lisbon, a call for effectiveness and efficiency and a human dimension, including a focus on military staff and on SMEs.

REFERENCES

Bakker, A., Drent, M., & Zandee, D. (2017). The Implications of Brexit for European Defence Cooperation? *Clingendael Spectator.* Online.

Cirlig, C. (2016). Parliament and High Representative: A New Partnership? Plenary At a Glance, European Parliamentary Research Service.

Council of the European Union. (2010). Declaration by the High Representative on Political Accountability (Annexed to Council. Decision 427/2010, establishing the EEAS).

Council of the European Union. (2016). Shared Vision, Common Action: A Stronger Europe. A Global Strategy for the EU's Foreign and Security Policy. Retrieved from https://europa.eu/globalstrategy/sites/globalstrategy/files/eugs_review_web.pdf.

Dobreva, A., Grosek, K., & Pawlak, P. (2016). Public Expectations and EU Policies – Security and Defence Policy. Briefing, European Parliamentary Research Service.

European Commission. (2017). Proposal for a Regulation of the European Parliament and of the Council Establishing the European Defence Industrial Development Programme Aiming at Supporting the Competitiveness and Innovative Capacity of the EU Defence Industry, 2017/0125 (COD).

European Council. (2013). Conclusions 19/20 December, EUCO 217/13.

European Council. (2015). Conclusions 25/26 June, EUCO 22/15.

European Defence Agency. (2015). *Defence Data.*

European Defence Agency (2016, May 13). Call for Proposals for the Pilot Programme on Defence Research.

European Defence Agency. (2017). Coordinated Annual Review on Defence (CARD). Retrieved January 20, 2018, from https://www.eda.europa.eu/what-we-do/our-current-priorities/coordinated-annual-review-on-defence-%28card%29.

European Parliament. (2015a). Resolution of 23 November 2016 on the Implementation of the Common Security and Defence Policy (Based on the Annual Report from the Council to the European Parliament on the Common Foreign and Security Policy) (2016/2067(INI)).

European Parliament. (2015b). Resolution of 21 May 2015 on Financing the Common Security and Defence Policy (2014/2258(INI)).

European Parliament. (2015c). Resolution of 21 May 2015 on the Impact of Developments in European Defence Markets on the Security and Defence Capabilities in Europe (2015/2037(INI)).

European Parliament. (2016a). European Parliament Resolution of 22 November 2016 on the European Defence Union (2016/2052(INI)).

European Parliament. (2016b). Resolution of 23 November 2016 on the implementation of the Common Security and Defence Policy (based on the Annual Report from the Council to the European Parliament on the Common Foreign and Security Policy) (2016/2067(INI)).

European Parliament. (2016c). Resolution on the EU in a Changing Global Environment—A More Connected, Contested and Complex World (2015/2272(INI)).

European Parliament. (2017a). Draft Report on the Proposal for a Regulation of the European Parliament and of the Council Establishing the European Defence Industrial Development Programme Aiming at Supporting the Competitiveness and Innovative Capacity of the EU Defence Industry, 2017/0125 (COD).

European Parliament. (2017b). European Parliament resolution of 13 December 2017 on the Annual Report on the Implementation of the Common Security and Defence Policy (2017/2023 (INI)).

European Parliament. (2017c). European Parliament Resolution on the Constitutional, Legal and Institutional Implications of a Common Security and Defence Policy: Possibilities Offered by the Lisbon Treaty (2015/2343(INI)).

European Parliamentary Research Service. (2017). *Mapping the Cost of Non-Europe, 2014–19 – Fourth Edition.*

European Political Strategy Centre. (2015). In Defence of Europe, EPSC Strategic Notes. Issue 4, June 15.

European Union, Treaty of Lisbon Amending the Treaty on European Union and the Treaty Establishing the European Community, 13 December 2007, 2007/C 306/01.

Henokl, T. (2015). *Political Accountability in the EU's Foreign and Security Policy.* Paper presented at the Fourteenth Biennial EUSA Conference, March 4–7, Boston (MA), USA.

Herranz-Surrales, A. (2014). Parliamentary Oversight of EU Foreign and Security Policy: Moving Beyond the Patchwork?' Milan: Istituto per gli studi di politica internazionale (ISPI), Analysis No. 230.

Lazarou, E. (2017a). European Defence – A Year on from the Global Strategy. Briefing, European Parliamentary Research Service.

Lazarou, E. (2017b). Permanent Structured Cooperation: From Notification to Establishment, at a Glance, European Parliamentary Research Service.

McDonagh, K. (2016). CSDP Missions and the security and Defence Committee of the European Parliament. *Irish Studies in International Affairs, 27,* 223–233.

Raube, K. (2012). The European External Action Service and the European Parliament. *The Hague Journal of Diplomacy, 7*, 65–80.

Riddervold, M., & Rosen, G. (2016). Trick and Treat: How the Commission and the European Parliament Exert Influence in EU Foreign and Security Policies. *Journal of European Integration, 38*(6), 687–702.

Stokes, B., et al. (2016, June 13). Europeans Face the World Divided. *Pew Research Center.*

Tocci, N. (2016). The Making of the EU Global Strategy. *Contemporary Security Policy, 37*(3), 461–472.

Index[1]

---

[1] Note: Page numbers followed by 'n' refer to notes.

Printed by Printforce, the Netherlands